Science and Football V

The Proceedings of the Fifth World Congress on Science and Football

Edited by

Thomas Reilly

Jan Cabri

and

Duarte Araújo

Routledge
Taylor & Francis Group

LONDON AND NEW YORK

First published 2005 by Routledge
2 Park Square, Milton Park, Abingdon, Oxon, OX14 4RN

Simultaneously published in the USA and Canada
by Routledge
270 Madison Ave, New York NY 10016

Routledge is an imprint of the Taylor & Francis Group

Transferred to Digital Printing 2008

Publisher's Note
This book has been produced from camera-ready copy supplied
by the authors

Every effort has been made to ensure that the advice and information
in this book is true and accurate at the time of going to press. However,
neither the publisher nor the authors can accept any legal responsibility
or liability for any errors or omissions that may be made. In the case of
drug administration, any medical procedure or the use of technical
equipment mentioned within this book, you are strongly advised to
consult the manufacturer's guidelines.

British Library Cataloguing in Publication Data
A catalogue record for this book is available from the British Library

Library of Congress Cataloging in Publication Data
A catalog record for this book has been requested

ISBN10: 0–415–33337–7 (hbk)
ISBN10: 0–415–48480–4 (pbk)

ISBN13: 978–0–415–33337–5 (hbk)
ISBN13: 978–0–415–48480–0 (pbk)

Contents

Preface

The current volume represents the proceedings of the Fifth World Congress of Science and Football. The event was held in Lisbon, Portugal from April 11th to 15th, 2003, hosted at the Faculty of Human Kinetics (Faculdade de Motricidade Humana) of the Technical University of Lisbon (Universidade Tecnica de Lisboa) and organised on behalf of the University by Jan Cabri. The Congress continued the line of previous conferences held under the aegis of the International Steering Group on Science and Football. The series of conferences was initiated at Liverpool in 1987, later followed by meetings at Eindhoven (1991), Cardiff (1995) and Sydney (1999). The Proceedings providing a scientific record of these events have been published by E. and F. N. Spon or by the publishers of this volume – Routledge.

The Steering Group on Science and Football is one of a number affiliated to the World Commission of Science and Sports. This body is charged by the International Council for Sports Science and Physical Education (ICSSPE) with building bridges between theory and practice in specific sports. It does so by orchestrating regular conferences and a major World Congress on a 4–yearly basis, co-ordinated by the relevant Steering Group and publishing the Proceedings. This publication therefore is a compendium of research activities and findings which are both up to date and relevant to practice. Its usefulness is reflected in the large number of citations evident in peer-reviewed publications within mainstream journals.

The International Steering Group on Science and Football operates not just to effect links between research and its applications but also to identify common threads between the various football codes. The Congress therefore provides a unique opportunity for cross-fertilization between the football games and the transfer of ideas across them. The end result is a strengthening of sport science support work by extending the knowledge base from which personnel working in an applied setting can draw.

The Fifth World Congress benefited from the administrative help at the Technical University of Lisbon and from its links with Sporting Lisbon Football Club. Jan Cabri shouldered the bulk of the organisational work, ably supported by his academic colleagues, among whom Pedro Mil-Homens acted in liaison with the football club. Jan was ably assisted by Duarte Araújo in conducting the work of the Scientific Programme Committee and its chairperson José Gomes-Pereira, along with many other colleagues from within the University and some from universities abroad. Without the support of Francisco Alves, Dean of the Faculty, and the highly efficient secretarial help from Isabel Morais, the Congress administration would have buckled under the massive workload.

The Congress programme included keynote addresses, oral communications, posters, demonstrations, symposia and workshops. A special thanks goes to David Wilson for organising the demonstration of amputee football at the training grounds of Sporting Lisbon and to Pedro Mil-Homens for setting up the workshop on 'Football Academies'. Technical support at the formal sessions was co-ordinated by Jose Carvalho, and ably implemented by the students of the Faculty of Human Kinetics of the Technical University.

An innovation at the Closing Ceremony of the Congress was the passing of an Australian Rules football on to the organisers of the 6th World Congress of Science and Football. The literal pass from podium to platform symbolised the inclusion of the different football codes at this gathering as well as the forward progression of the 'science and football' movement. The location of the next Congress was decided after formal presentations by candidates for host. The outcome was that Turkey was selected as the site of the 6th World Congress in 2007. The intervening years are likely to witness further burgeoning in research programmes to reach fruition for communication at this attractive forum for scientific exchanges.

Thomas Reilly, June 2004
Chair, International Steering Group on Science and Football
of the World Commission of Science and Sports.
(A service group of the International Council for Sports Science
and Physical Education)

Introduction

This volume represents the Proceedings of the Fifth World Congress on Science and Football held at Lisbon in April 2003. It is the fifth volume in the Science and Football series, and reflects the sustained research output of those conducting investigations related to different aspects of football. All the football codes are represented among the studies that range broadly in topic investigated and in scientific discipline employed.

The proceedings provide a formal record of contemporary research in the various football codes. Some of the reports are outcomes of laboratory-based investigations, others are firmly mounted in an applied field context. Irrespective of the scientific approach, what is evident is the applied nature of all the work being communicated. Whatever the setting, the reports were required to pass the quality control procedures implemented by the editorial team.

It was not possible to reproduce all of the manuscripts from the Congress submitted for publication. Those accepted provide a good flavour of the work communicated at the Congress and the questions that researchers in football science set themselves.

The book is divided into nine parts. These are roughly in correspondence with the specialisations in earlier volumes in the series. The reports in each part are related by theme or by scientific discipline. Sometimes the categories overlap, for example studies of fitness assessment in young players could fit into either 'Paediatric exercise science' or 'Fitness assessment'. The choice of location within the book was made to provide a balance of contributions in each part, although the decision was in part arbitrary.

The Editors are grateful to the contributors for their careful preparation of manuscripts and for their responses to editorial queries and requests. We owe a debt of gratitude also to those members of the sports science community who helped in refereeing manuscripts. In particular, thanks go to Rita Oliveira at the Vrije Universiteit, Amsterdam for her invaluable assistance.

The painstaking work of coping with electronic submissions was assisted by the office staff at the Technical University of Lisbon (notably Isabel Morais) and at Liverpool John Moores University (especially Rachel Martyn). A sincere 'thanks' goes to them for the invaluable help in preparing the text for camera-ready reproduction.

Thomas Reilly
Jan Cabri
Duarte Araújo

Part I
Introductory Keynote Address

1   Science and Football: A History and an Update

Thomas Reilly

Research Institute for Sport and Exercise Sciences, Liverpool John Moores University, Henry Cotton Campus, 15–21 Webster Street, Liverpool, L3 2ET

1. INTRODUCTION

The football games have common origins and appear to have a role in many different cultures. In contemporary sport there are many links between the different football codes which range from social factors among the audiences to physical preparation for competition. It is therefore timely to consider historical aspects of football games before focusing on the more recent approaches towards excellence in performance.

This review at first provides an outline of the history of football games that helps to place their current global appeal in perspective. There are common threads between the football codes, each has a central role in the local and national culture and all nowadays at top level utilise sports science support systems. The main features of sports science support for performance are considered in the second part of this review which culminates in identifying some remaining issues to be addressed.

2. THE ORIGINS OF FOOTBALL

The origins of football games can be traced through different cultures across the globe. In this review the material is selective and excludes the traditional ball games of Mayan and Inca's culture where the ball was played primarily with the hand. Similarly, the games of North American Native Indians and native Eskimos are not considered. Instead the search starts in the Far East in China and moves westwards to culminate in the formalisation of rules of play in England in the 19th century.

Approximately 3,000 years ago the game of tsu chu was played in China. Its name derives from tsu (kick the ball with feet) and chu (a ball made of leather and stuffed).

Later there was evidence of a different form of play in Japan. Balls were made of animal bladders pumped with air. In the original tsu chu, goals were comprised of gaps in a net placed between bamboo poles reaching up to 10 m in height. The games were used to celebrate the Emperor's birthday. The games in Japan were a gentler form of exercise, aimed at keeping the ball in the air when played between pairs. The first indication of international participation was between Chinese and Japanese players in Kyoto, 681 AD.

This international dispersion of the game is supported by theories of cultural diffusion whereby different societies interact. There were specific features of these crude football games that fulfilled their local cultural roles. These included celebration of significant events (Far East), religious ceremonies (west East), *fertility rites* (Egypt) and preparation of warriors for battle (Greece and Rome).

The form of the game in the Roman Empire was known as harpastum. It is likely that Roman soldiers introduced this game into Britain during the Roman invasion. Activity lasted for >50 minutes, and consisted of about 25-a-side. The games, like in other cultures, were violent and cruel contests involving killings and serious injuries (Peiser and Minten, 2003). Later the game of calcio emerged during the renaissance period. Rules were introduced in 1580 with contestants numbering 27-a-side. The objective was to kick, carry or pass the ball over a line.

During the Roman occupation of Britain, there is evidence of harpastum being implemented in various ways. By 217 AD, locals kicked skulls of defeated Roman soldiers from liberated villages. By the 11th century similar treatments were afforded to conquered Vikings.

3. RECENT HISTORY IN BRITAIN

By the 14th century, football had become unacceptable to the authorities. In 1314 King Harold II ordered citizens to stop playing. The declaration was as follows:

For as much as there is a great noise in the city caused by hustling over large balls, from which many evils may arrive, what God forbid, we can command and forbid on behalf of the King, on pain of imprisonment, such games to be used in the city in future.

Nevertheless football games continued in popularity and were timed with religious dates, for example what became known as "mob football" played on Shrove Tuesday. These events pitted villages or parishes against each other. Goals were up to 5–10 km apart. Participants amounted to 500-a-side and balls varied in weight. Fouls included murder or manslaughter but otherwise kicking opponents was permitted and serious injuries were commonplace.

In the early 1800s the public schools developed their own rules. Nevertheless, William Webb Ellis is attributed to have run with the ball out of impatience rather than kick it along, an event associated with the birth of Rugby Football (Macklin, 1962). In 1846, the headmaster of Rugby School, Thomas Arnold, developed rules of play for the generic game. Handling the ball was allowed and kicking the legs below the knees was permitted. In 1862 the so-called Cambridge rules regulated the throw-in (Cox et al., 2002).

In 1863 the Football Association was formed, restricting play to the feet and separating the game from Rugby Football. In the universities the games were colloquialised as "soccer" and "rugger". The Scottish FA was established in 1873, the FA of Wales in 1875 and the Irish FA in 1880. Very soon, associations were established elsewhere in Europe and the formalisation of rules of play spread . world-wide. This development culminated in the establishment of FIFA in 1904.

The Rugby Football Union was set up in 1871, 8 years after the formation of its soccer counterpart. The first international match between Scotland and England was played in Edinburgh in the same year. This decade represented the "shoving age of Rugby Football" with forward packs consisting of 13 men (Bowker, 1976). In 1892 the rules restricted teams to 15-a-side. By 1895 the Northern Union had split to form a breakaway professional Rugby League, a divide which existed until Rugby Union adopted professionalism in 1995. In 1996 there was a historic reunion when the national champions in Rugby League and Rugby Union (Wigan and Bath) exchanged matches in their respective codes (see Reilly, 1997).

National identities were expressed when the Gaelic Athletic Association was formed in Ireland in 1884. Further reference to the game of Gaelic Football is contained in the statutes of Galway which allowed the playing of football but banned hurling (de Burca, 1980). The latter is a ball-and-stick game which has ancient links in China and Egypt and is attributed to be the ancestor of field – hockey (Reilly and Borrie, 1992).

The development of Gaelic games was linked with the movement for national independence. Gaelic football incorporates use of the hands and feet and generates a unique style. Foreign games – including soccer, Rugby, hockey and cricket – were banned for members, encompassing spectating as well as participating. The ban was rescinded in 1971 but the sport is regulated by a 32-county (i.e. all Ireland) association. Meanwhile, emigrants to Australia were instrumental in developing Australian Rules football. Similarly, American Football emerged as suited to its national culture without attaining universal popularity.

Historical aspects of football are not restricted to male participants. There is evidence of women's football being played in Scotland in the 17th Century. Married women played their unmarried counterparts in Inveresk. Spectators were largely prospective husbands for the latter group.

Women's participation in football did not have the support of medical practitioners. An article in the British Medical Journal represented the attitude of physicians of the time:

We can in no way sanction the reckless exposure to violence of organs where the common experience of women had led them in every way to protect.

British Medical Journal, 1884

The participation of women was built round the organisation of exhibition matches. The fabled Betty Honeybell played at Crouch End Athletic in 1895. After the First World War there was a resurgence in women's participation. The majority of matches were organised to support charities but nevertheless drew large crowds. Spectators at Goodison Park for a match between teams from Preston and St Helens in 1920 numbered 53,000 (Cox et al., 2002). As the professional clubs refused access to the female players for competitive games, women's football declined in popularity until its revival at World Championship level in 1991.

Many of the top association football clubs are now into their second century. For example, Everton FC last year celebrated its centenary in the top flight whilst

Real Madrid did likewise in 2003. The world's ruling body marks its centenary in 2004 whilst the European Cup is also now almost 50 years old. In the other codes, Rugby Union had its 5th World Cup championship finals in Australia 2003, attracting record viewing figures on satellite television. Despite the crude commercialisation of the games, spectator interest is unprecedented.

4. THE SCIENCE AND FOOTBALL AGENDA

The application of science to football is relatively recent, marked by the First World Congress on Science and Football in 1987. This event was auspicious in that it was the first occasion when American Football, Australian Rules, Association Football, Rugby League, Rugby Union and Gaelic Football were formally represented at the same forum.

Table 1. Content of communications to the first four Science and Football Congresses.

Science and Football: Proceedings	
Soccer	131
Rugby Union	28
Australian Rules	12
American Football	8
Gaelic Football	8
Rugby League	7
≥2 Codes	6
Germaine to all	6
Touch Football	2

The science and football congresses held every four years demonstrate that the majority of research is directed towards soccer, followed by Rugby Union and Australian Rules (see Table 1). There is a particular focus on performance and the intention here is to illustrate some of the contributions of researchers in selected areas. These include player characteristics, fitness levels, match demands, computer-aided analysis, and aspects of learning.

In the first instance the physiques of Rugby Union international players provide an example of how the shape of competitors at top level has changed. Both backs and forwards have become much more muscular and less endomorphic. The change has become more pronounced with the professionalisation of the game and with movement of players from Rugby League to Rugby Union. The trends are reflected in the migration of average somatotypes for both forwards and backs to the north-west border of the conventional somatochart.

Estimates of muscle mass can be compared across three of the football codes. These include measurements of international players in a Rugby Sevens Tournament in Punta del Este in Uruguay (Rienzi et al., 1999), soccer teams competing in Copa America in Uruguay (Rienzi et al., 2000) and similar measures on the Mayo Gaelic Football county team (Reilly and Doran, 2001). The data show that all groups are highly muscular in make-up and supranormal in terms of proportionate muscle mass. This trend was reflected also in a comparison of the respective somatotypes (Table 2).

Table 2. Somatotype of top players in three football codes.

	Rugby Sevens **(n = 30)**	**Gaelic Football** **(n = 33)**	**Soccer** **(n = 110)**
Endomorphy	2.3 ± 0.6	2.7 ± 0.7	2.0 ± 0.5
Mesomorphy	5.9 ± 0.9	5.7 ± 1.0	5.3 ± 0.8
Ectomorphy	1.5 ± 0.6	1.9 ± 0.8	2.2 ± 0.6

Whilst the physiques of players have changed, is this reflected in physiological measurements such as maximal oxygen uptake? Apor (1988) showed the importance of aerobic fitness in players in the Hungarian leagues with overall average values for $\dot{V}O_{2\,max}$ being correlated with finishing position in the league. Nevertheless average values have not increased much since then, at least in $\dot{V}O_{2\,max}$. There are fewer players with lower values, endurance capabilities are improved, players are faster and have reduced adiposity. Nevertheless values are not homogenous across teams, varying according to positional roles (Bangsbo, 1994; Reilly et al., 2000).

The next question to address is whether the demands of the games have changed. Here consistent data are available only for soccer. The approach favoured has been to record work-rate in terms of actions, intensity, duration and frequency, alongside recovery periods between bouts. There is evidence that work-rate has increased systematically over the last two decades (see Reilly and Williams, 2003). The characteristics of international strikers indicate that less than 2% of the total distance is covered in possession of the ball. So the message for all codes is that probably the major contribution of fitness is to facilitate support of the player on the ball. As with the aerobic fitness data, the earliest observations identified position-specific work-rate requirements (Reilly and Thomas, 1976).

One of the classical studies of football was that of Saltin (1973) which opened up the application of nutrition to the football context. It was shown that players starting with reduced muscle glycogen stores performed poorly towards the end of a game compared with those who had rested the day before. The importance of boosting glycogen stores in preparation for matches was highlighted and the role of sports nutrition emphasised. Later developments included the facility for simulating the work-rate of football in the laboratory (Drust et al., 2000) or in gymnasium conditions (Nicholas et al., 2000) in which dietary manipulations can be investigated.

Reilly and Ball (1984) showed how discrete aspects of the game can be studied. They compared the energy cost of dribbling a ball with that of running normally. The oxygen consumption was increased by a constant amount at each of the four speeds examined whilst the inflection point in blood lactate accumulation occurred at a lower speed when dribbling. The interpretation was that training drills with the ball could be encouraged to provide a good stimulus for physiological adaptation.

The fuel for exercise during soccer is largely from glycogen stores. Nevertheless fat utilisation comes into play during the second half, more or less paralleling the responses to endurance exercise. The main determinant of the game may still be anaerobic, so that speed off the mark and the timing of sprints are important in all codes.

A comparison of work-rates during games between seasons before and after the Premier League was introduced in England demonstrates how the pace of the game has increased (Williams et al., 1999). The increased work-rate is manifest in all outfield positions. Not only has the distance covered increased but also players have less time for making critical decisions, including the timing and execution of tackles. There is a question of whether players are now exercising close to capacity and whether any further increases in pace of play (e.g. if substitutes are freely allowed) would compromise safety.

There are some excellent studies of the epidemiology of injuries in both soccer (Ekstrand, 1982; Inklaar, 1994) and Rugby Union. Intervention programmes are monitored to improve injury prevention. Additional detailed analysis incorporates critical incident analysis in which precursors of injuries are identified (Rahnama et al., 2002). The identification of injury predispositions would enable preventive strategies to be implemented.

The investigation of the myriad of events occurring in a game was made possible by computer-aided match analysis. The pioneering work of Hughes (1988) illustrated how recording event, location in the field of play, player involved, outcome of action could be synthesised into a pattern of play. The first example of use of notation analysis alongside anthropometry and work-rate analysis was in Copa America, 1995. Observation showed how the winning team Uruguay displayed a more direct style than the other semi-finalists. In contrast, Colombia and Brazil demonstrated a more intricate passing pattern with more passes, more players involved in each move and less distance covered per move (Rienzi et al., 2000).

A comparison of the work-rates of Copa America players with those exhibited in Premier League matches indicates the faster pace in the latter (Rienzi et al., 2000). The English League players covered an average of 1 km more than their South American international counterparts.

A further example of an integrated approach to studying elite footballers was reported by Rienzi et al. (1999). They provided an anthropometric profile of players (see Table 2) and an analysis of activity during an international Rugby Sevens tournament. It was shown that:-

- Forwards were taller than backs, had greater body mass, muscle mass and adipose mass.
- Fatigue was evident in a lowered activity in the second half.
- Muscle mass and mesomorphy were negatively correlated with high intensity activity.
- Work-rate and anthropometric profiles could not distinguish between winning and losing players.

5. THE TRAINING CONTEXT

There is clearly a need to focus on training, appropriate to the game, the player's role in it and the age of players involved. The applied sports scientist is now assisted by evidence based texts (e.g. Elliott, 1998; Reilly and Williams, 2003) and contemporary technology. The latter includes short range radio telemetry for studying heart rate and oxygen uptake.

Having established the physiological responses to playing football matches, the next step is to use heart rate to regulate the training intensity. In a "recovery day", heart rate may be maintained at about 125 beats.min^{-1} (e.g. use of "head tennis"), aerobic training can be regulated at about 160 beat.min^{-1} (e.g. 7 vs 7 drill) whilst high intensity exercise (2 vs 2; 1 min on, 1 min active recovery) may entail an average heart-rate of 175 beats min^{-1}.

Conventional "interval-training" can also be considered in small-group work with the ball, such as in 5-a-side (6×4 min; 3 min rest) (see Reilly and White, 2003). The heart-rate response can be as high as that reached by runners carrying out an interval-training session.

Monitoring heart-rate responses may sometimes require additional information about the players concerned. Reilly and Doran (2001) showed how players reacted differently to matches depending on their motivation. In this respect the heart rate indicates not the demands imposed by the game but the physiological demands which players are prepared to impose on themselves.

For young players the opportunity for skills practice is a major consideration alongside any physiological issues. Platt et al. (2001) compared 3 vs 3 and 5 vs 5 in young players. The smaller group games provided more high-intensity activity, less low-intensity activity and the higher mean heart rate throughout 15 minutes of play (see Figure 1). Besides, those playing 3-a-side executed more tackles, dribbles, short passes and medium passes than in the 5-a-side games. These findings highlighted the values of small-group games for young players.

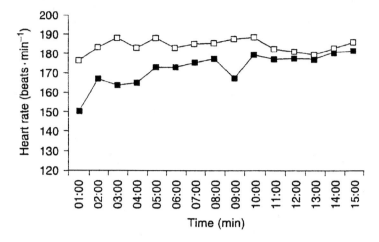

Figure 1. Mean heart rate data in three-a-side (□) and five-a-side (■) games (redrawn from Platt et al., 2001).

In summary, the following are factors in football specific training which have applications across the football codes. They are presented as recommendations to coaches and trainers:-

- Construct small-sided games.
- Determine conditions of play.
- Manipulate exercise to rest ratios.
- Utilise and modify existing coaching drills.
- Identify non-specific requirements which may need to be isolated for training without the ball.

There is a need to mature and develop young players, especially those who display outstanding talent. There is nowadays a serious quest for optimal talent detection, identification and development systems. In this respect science can play a role alongside coaching experts, although there is no prescriptive formula for talent identification. The multidisciplinary aspects of talent identification and its development have been reviewed by Williams and Reilly (2000).

6. OVERVIEW

The applied sports scientist working in football is faced with a dynamic environment in which solutions must match the impending circumstances. The most prominent considerations are to:-

- Regulate the training intensity as required.
- Consider the day of the week and the days between matches.

- Implement recovery and tapering strategies.
- Fit cycles of training into an overall annual periodisation.
- Avoid overuse and "burn-out".

It is evident that there are many threads within the football codes, notwithstanding that a majority of work is reported on soccer players. On the practical side there is a focus on optimising preparation for games, designing the best training programmes and adapting them to fit changing circumstances. There is special attention given to accelerating recovery processes post-game, to the needs of young players and helping them achieve their potential.

In a historical context, the systematisation of sport science support for football teams is a relatively recent development which all of the football codes have followed to varying degrees. The role of football in local cultures, alongside its current global appeal, is recognised. In light of developments over recent decades who can predict what football will be like in 100 years time, let alone over the next 3 millennia.

REFERENCES

Apor, P., 1988, Successful formulae for fitness training. In Science and Football, edited by Reilly, T., Lees, A., Davids, K. and Murphy, W.J. (London: E and F N Spon), pp. 95–107.

Bangsbo, J., 1994, The physiology of soccer – with special reference to intense intermittent exercise. Acta Physiologica Scandinavica, **15**, Suppl. **619**, 1–156.

Bowker, B., 1976, England Rugby. (London: Cassell).

Cox, R., Russell, D. and Vamplew, W., 2002, Encyclopaedia of British Football. (London: Frank Cass).

De Burca, M., 1980, The GAA: A History of the Association. (Dublin: Cumann Luithchleas Gael).

Drust, B., Reilly, T. and Cable N.T., 2000, Physiological responses to laboratory-based soccer specific intermittent and continuous exercise. Journal of Sports Sciences, **18**, 885–892.

Ekstrand, J., 1982, Soccer injuries and their prevention. Medical Dissertation No 130, Linköping University.

Elliott, B., 1998, Training in Sport: Applying Sport Science. (Chichester: Wiley).

Hughes, M., 1988, Computerized notation analysis in field games. Ergonomics, **31**, 1585–1592.

Inklaar, H., 1994, Soccer injuries. Sports Medicine, **18**, 55–73.

Macklin, K., 1962, The History of Rugby League Football. (London: Stanley Paul).

Nicholas, G.W., Nuttall, F.E. and Williams C., 2000, The Loughborough intermittent shuttle tests: a field test that simulates the activity pattern of soccer. Journal of Sports Sciences, **18**, 97–104.

Peiser, B. and Minten, J., 2003, Soccer violence. In Science and Soccer (2nd Edition), edited by Reilly, T. and Williams, A. M. (London: Routledge), pp. 230–241.

Platt, D., Maxwell, A., Horn, R., Williams, M. and Reilly T., 2001, Physiological and technical analysis of 3 v 3 and 5 v 5 youth football matches. Insight: The FA Coaches Association Journal, **4** (4), 23–24.

Rahnama, N., Reilly, T. and Lees, A., 2002, Injury risk associated with playing actions during competitive soccer. British Journal of Sports Medicine, **36**, 354–359.

Reilly, T., 1997, The physiology of Rugby Union football. Biology of Sport, **14**, 83–101.

Reilly, T. and Ball, D., 1984, The net physiological cost of dribbling a soccer ball. Research Quarterly for Exercise Science and Sport, **55**, 267–271.

Reilly T. and Borrie, A., 1992, Physiology applied to field hockey. Sports Medicine, **14**, 10–26.

Reilly T. and Doran, D., 2001, Science and Gaelic Football: a review. Journal of Sports Sciences, **19**, 181–193.

Reilly, T. and Thomas, V., 1976, A motion analysis of work-rate in different potential roles in professional football match-play. Journal of Human Movement Studies, **2**, 87–97.

Reilly, T. and White, C., 2003, Small-sided games as an alternative to interval training for soccer players. In Book of Abstracts: Science and Football 5th World Congress. (Lisbon: Gymnos), p. 134.

Reilly, T. and Williams, A.M., 2003, Science and Soccer. (London: Routledge).

Reilly, T., Bangsbo, J. and Franks, A., 2000, Anthropometric and physiological predispositions for elite soccer. Journal of Sports Sciences, **18**, 669–683.

Rienzi, E., Reilly, T. and Malkin, C., 1999, Investigation of anthropometric and work-rate profiles of Rugby Sevens players. Journal of Sports Medicine and Physical Fitness, **39**, 160–164.

Rienzi, E., Drust, B., Reilly, T., Carter, J.E.L. and Martin, A. 2000, Investigation of anthropometric and work-rate profiles of elite South American international soccer players. Journal of Sports Medicine and Physical Fitness, **40**, 162–169.

Saltin, B., 1973, Metabolic fundamentals in exercise. Medicine and Science in Sports, **5**, 137–146.

Williams, A.M. and Reilly, T., 2000, Talent identification and development in soccer. Journal of Sports Sciences, **18**, 657–667.

Williams, A.M., Lee, D. and Reilly, T., 1999, A Quantitative Analysis of Matches played in the 1991–1992 and 1997–1998 seasons. (London: The Football Association).

Part II
Biomechanics and Mechanics

2 Measurement of Out of Balance Forces in Soccer Balls

D.S. Price, P.J. Neilson, A.R. Harland and R. Jones
Sports Technology Research Group,
Wolfson School of Mechanical and Manufacturing Engineering,
Loughborough University, UK

1. INTRODUCTION

The fundamental equipment requirement for the game of soccer is the ball. With over 200 million active players worldwide (Stamm and Lamprecht, 2001), it is understandable that sales of balls are estimated at 40 million annually. These balls vary in their design and construction to suit the entire spectrum of customer requirements. At the top of the range, contemporary soccer balls used in professional match play are constructed from a range of modern rubber and polymer materials using a variety of innovative manufacturing processes. The aim of such technological advances is to produce balls that are more consistent in their physical dimensions and properties as well as in their behaviour during play.

The need to maintain consistency in soccer ball characteristics and performance was recognised by Fédération Internationale de Football Association (FIFA), the world governing body for soccer in 1996, with the introduction of the FIFA Quality Concept (ISL Marketing, 1999). As part of this concept, FIFA established a series of laboratory tests designed to assess a variety of ball parameters. These parameters include weight (mass), circumference, sphericity, water absorption, pressure loss, and rebound. An acceptable range is stated for each of the parameters, and once a sample of manufactured balls has been demonstrated to conform to the requirements, the manufacturer is permitted to enter into a licensing agreement whereby the FIFA logo may be displayed on the ball. For size 5 soccer balls for outdoor usage, two levels of certification are available:- Inspected and Approved. The more rigorous of these, which is generally required for a ball to be considered for use in competitive matches, is Approved. Whilst only one additional criterion is introduced, that of shape retention of a ball subject to 2000 repeated impacts, the acceptable ranges for the remaining criteria are reduced.

The assessment of weight, circumference, sphericity and pressure loss both as specific tests and as part of the shape retention test following the impacts represent entirely static measurements. Indeed, in all of the prescribed tests, the ball is stationary when the measurement is made. Given that soccer is a dynamic game where the ball spends the majority of its time in motion or involved in impacts, it might be argued that there is a need for more dynamic testing to be carried out which replicates practical play conditions more closely.

Two of the most significant features of ball performance during play are flight through the air and rebound characteristics after impact with such surfaces as the ground or players' heads or feet. Many factors can contribute to inconsistent dynamic behaviour of a ball, including poor sphericity, inconsistent aerodynamic flow across the ball surface and uneven mass distribution within the ball. An uneven mass distribution has the effect of displacing the centre of mass from the centre of geometry of the ball, which is a major cause of 'wobble' during flight and inconsistent bounce and roll during interaction with the ground. Given the complex construction of modern soccer balls, it is unlikely that any ball may be considered to be perfectly balanced.

In recognition of this, FIFA has adopted a 'balance' test, although this is currently included only as part of the indoor soccer ball test criteria. This assessment involves plotting the deviation from a central axis of a ball allowed to roll down a chute. Whilst undoubtedly the mass distribution within the ball will be an important determinant of the direction of its roll, a number of additional factors, such as sphericity and surface material properties will also be influential.

There is, therefore, a need for a test where mass distribution or out-of-balance can be quantified in isolation. The work reported here describes a suitable method, which has been assessed for its repeatability and random uncertainty.

2. THEORETICAL BACKGROUND

Rotating components such as shafts, rotors and wheels have found widespread application throughout science and engineering. The integration of the material density throughout the volume occupied by the component enables a centre of mass to be established. The product of the perpendicular distance of the centre of mass from the axis of rotation with the total mass yields the moment caused by the out of balance within the system. It is this moment that must be eliminated or minimised in order to prevent unwanted vibrations or inconsistencies in the rotational velocity of the component. Consequently, in many circumstances, the successful, safe and reliable operation of such parts is reliant on an even mass distribution within the rotating structure.

Considering out of balance within a freely rotating sphere, such as a soccer ball, is an inherently more complex problem than that of a shaft or wheel since the rotation is not restricted around a single axis. Therefore, the effect caused by a given centre of mass position will be dependent on the position of the axis of rotation. Consequently, it is not possible to minimise the distance of the centre of mass from a particular axis of rotation, rather, the distance from the geometric centre must be considered, to account for rotation about any arbitrary axis.

The construction of contemporary soccer balls includes a number of layers of different materials. Typically, a rubber bladder is inflated which expands to fill the cavity created by a continuous hollow structure of stitched composite panels. The composite panels generally consist of several fabric layers bonded together with a durable polyurethane (PU) outer layer. Several geometric arrangements of panels are employed in soccer ball design, the two most common being based on a truncated icosahedral structure, consisting of 20 hexagons and 12 pentagons or a cubic structure, consisting of 18 rectangular panels. Given the presence of each of these components, together with the stitching itself, it is understandable that some variation exists in both the position of the centre of mass and the sphericity of the ball.

The overall effect of a discrepancy between the centre of mass and the geometric centre of the sphere may also be considered as a single mass positioned at the circumference of the ball. For much of the work reported here, this approach is taken to simplify understanding of the problem. The equivalent single mass, M, acting at the centre of mass was split into two smaller masses, m_1 and m_2, positioned at the centre of geometry and at the surface of the ball respectively, as depicted in Figure 1. The sum of the masses m_1 and m_2 is equal to the total mass of the ball, M.

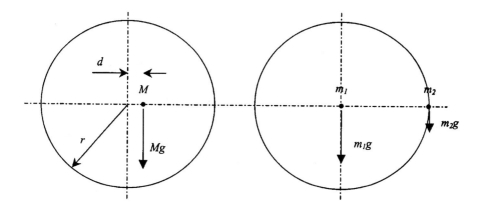

Figure 1. Equivalent point masses representing uneven mass distribution within a soccer ball.

One of the major benefits of utilising the approach described in Figure 1 is that it enables well established balancing techniques and equipment to be applied. The prevalence of rotating components within engineering has both required and facilitated the development of a range of balancing machines designed to measure out of balance. One such machine designed to measure the magnitude and position of out of balance within a variety of components is the 777/10 vertical balance machine, developed and sold by BTD Ltd., Birmingham, UK. This was adapted to cater for soccer balls and used throughout the work reported here. The principle of operation by which the machine is able to quantify out of balance is based around the measurement of the lateral acceleration experienced at the bearings of a vertical rotating shaft upon which the component under examination is mounted. From the measurements of acceleration recorded by accelerometers positioned at the shaft bearings, a measure of the amplitude of the lateral force caused by imbalance within the component can be established. The angular position of the component with time is recorded using a rotary encoder, which provides a reference by which the location of the out of balance can be located from the relative phase of the acceleration signal.

In the case of a soccer ball where the centre of mass and the centre of geometry do not closely coincide, inconsistency, or wobble, is apparent during the ball's flight and passage across the ground.

3. METHODOLOGY

The experimental work was divided into two sections designed to develop and assess the proposed measurement technique. Firstly, the fidelity of the experimental set-up was assessed using a ball pre-loaded with a range of known masses and secondly, a series of commercially available soccer balls were assessed using the technique to establish a measure of the consistency of mass distribution within each ball.

Each ball was considered to have a total mass, M, consisting of two components positioned at the centre, m_1, and the perimeter of the ball, m_2, respectively, as depicted in Figure 1. In order to enable measurements to be made by the vertical balancing machine, each ball was required to be positioned with the out of balance mass positioned within the equatorial plane of the ball in the test fixture. This required a method of establishing the location of the equivalent mass, m_2. This was achieved by floating the ball on the surface of a water bath and allowing the combination of the pendulum-like oscillation induced by the eccentric mass and the motion damping caused by the friction to stabilise the ball with the out of balance mass positioned at its nadir. This point was identified and marked on each ball and represented the position where additional masses were added as required.

Each ball was inflated to 1.0 bar and rotated at 400 rev.min^{-1}, a figure deemed representative of typical spin-rates experienced during match-play. The software accompanying the vertical balancing machine required the radius of the ball, r, to be provided and a nominal value of 110 mm was used. The acceleration measured at the bearings, together with the diameter and rotational velocity of the ball, enabled the software to provide a measure of the equivalent mass, m_2, for each measured ball. The measured values of m_2 were compared directly to the known masses added to the ball to enable a measure of the reliability of the system to be made.

Using the principle of moments (Meriam and Kraige, 2002), the displacement of the centre of mass from the centre of geometry, d, was calculated for each measured value of m_2:

$$d = \frac{rm_2}{M} \tag{1}$$

Measurements were subsequently made on a series of commercially available balls to assess the natural imbalance present within their respective constructions.

4. RESULTS

During the first phase of testing, a single ball was measured using the vertical balancing machine and its equivalent inherent out of balance mass, m_2, was derived to be 7.77 g. A known mass of 5.5 g was then added at the location of the equivalent mass m_2, which caused the out of balance mass derived from the machine measurements to increase to 13.27 g. A further 5.5 g caused the measurement to increase to 18.40 g. Agreement between the derived and known masses was within 3.8% and 1.6% respectively.

A series of 20 measurements were then recorded from the commercially available balls, which enabled an equivalent out of balance mass, m_2, to be established for each ball. The mean equivalent mass and standard deviation thereof are presented for each ball type in Table 1.

Table 1. Mean equivalent out of balance mass and displacement of centres of mass and geometry for five commercially available soccer balls.

Manufacturer	A	B	C	D	E
Mean Equivalent Mass, m_2, (g)	9.34	9.46	7.76	7.76	9.06
Standard Deviation (g)	0.46	0.26	0.54	0.41	0.26
Displacement, d, (mm)	2.33	2.37	1.94	1.94	2.27
Standard Deviation (mm)	0.18	0.07	0.13	0.10	0.07

Type A (random) uncertainty was accounted for using the assumption that the distribution of the measured values of equivalent mass, m_2, and consequently displacement, d, followed a normal model. Therefore, twice the standard deviation of each quantity was used to represent a confidence interval of 95%. The respective displacements, d, expressed for a 95% confidence level were therefore derived to be 2.33 ±0.23 mm, 2.37 ±0.13 mm, 1.94 ±0.27 mm, 1.94 ±0.21 mm, 2.27 ±0.13 mm. The overall mean of the series of ball samples was calculated to be 2.17 ±0.21 mm.

5. DISCUSSION AND CONCLUSIONS

The results demonstrate the suitability of the BTD 777/10 vertical balancing machine for measuring out of balance in soccer balls. Agreement between the known additional masses and those derived from experimental measurement was within 3.8% and 1.6% for the two mass increments. A number of benefits in using the machine was evident, such as the speed and reliability with which measurements could be recorded.

The measurements made on commercially available soccer balls demonstrate the presence of out of balance masses within their construction. Whilst certain ball types such as balls B and E demonstrated good consistency (low standard deviation), the equivalent mass present in each was above the overall average. By contrast, balls C and D exhibited equivalent masses below the mean, although their respective standard deviations were greater than the mean.

In deriving quantities such as the equivalent mass m_2, and the displacement of the centres of mass and geometry, the ball was assumed to be a perfect, continuous sphere. It is recognised that this is unlikely to be the case and further refinement of the technique would require such inconsistencies to be taken into consideration.

Whilst the effects of uneven mass distribution within soccer balls are not well understood, it is likely that it is a significant cause of unpredictable and irregular motion during flight and surface rebound. The reliable measurement method reported in this work offers the opportunity for further quantitative studies of mass distribution within soccer balls to be undertaken. It is envisaged that future standards for soccer balls will take into account mass distribution in order to improve their dynamic performance.

Acknowledgements

The authors would like to acknowledge BTD Ltd, Birmingham, UK, for their assistance and use of facilities in this work.

REFERENCES

ISL Marketing AG, 1999, FIFA Quality Concept for Footballs, Switzerland, October.

Meriam, J. L. and Kraige, L.G., 2002, Engineering Mechanics, Volume 1, Statics, 5th edition. (Chichester: John Wiley and Sons, Inc).

Stamm, H. and Lamprecht, M., 2001, Big count, Football 2000 worldwide – Official Survey", L and S Social Research und Consultation. AG Zurich, February.

3 Dynamic Soccer Ball Performance Measurement

P.J. Neilson and R. Jones

Sports Technology Research Group, Wolfson School of Mechanical and Manufacturing Engineering, Loughborough University, UK

1. INTRODUCTION

The FIFA Denominations programme was devised in 1994 to regulate and assess the performance and quality of top match soccer balls. As with most ball sports the tests tend to be quasi-static and the specification does not provide for the assessment of dynamic ball performance. In order to develop dynamic ball performance tests and standards, it is necessary to appreciate ball launch values obtained from professional players. These data could then be used to enable realistic parameters to be established for dynamic ball tests. The first part of this study has endeavoured to obtain ball launch data based on three different kick types using professional players from English League clubs. The second part of the study examined the effect of valve location at impact. It is apparent that many professional soccer players believe that valve position at impact can affect the ball launch characteristics, yet no published data exist to support this theory.

A number of investigators have reported initial ball velocity after kicking to be in the range of 18–34 m.s^{-1}, typically as part of a biomechanics investigation into the kicking action. Asai and Akatsuka (1998) used three amateur players as subjects, and measured average ball velocities in the range 22–27 m.s^{-1} with an average of 23.38 m.s^{-1} for an instep swerve kick. A high-speed camera running at 4,500 frames per second was used to measure ball spin rates in the range of 7–10 rev.s^{-1}. Plagenhoef (1972) filmed one ex-professional test subject and measured ball velocities in the range 24–28 m.s^{-1}. Roberts and Metcalfe (1968) used a combination of professional and amateur subjects and recorded ball velocity values in the range of 23–31 m.s^{-1}. The test subjects were filmed using a camera set at 64 frames per second with a shutter speed of 1/400. Isokawa and Lees (1988) recorded ball velocities in the range of 18–22 m.s^{-1} for an instep kick with varying approach angles. The test utilised amateur subjects filmed using a camera set at 150 frames per second.

Asami and Nolte (1983) measured a maximum ball velocity of 34.0 m.s^{-1} for a power kick, from six subjects including four professional players and two amateurs. The average velocity was 29.9 m.s^{-1}. Two high-speed cameras operating at 500 and 100 frames per second were used to film the kicks, one from the side and one from behind the kicker, respectively. Tsaousidis and Zatsiorsky (1996) used two amateur test subjects to perform a toe kick, reporting ball velocities in the range 24–26 m.s^{-1}. A high-speed camera operating at 4000 frames per second was used in the testing.

This study aims to produce a comprehensive set of test data regarding ball launch conditions achievable from elite players. These data may then be used as a benchmark for further soccer ball developments and specifications.

2. METHODS

2.1. Player testing

Player testing was carried out at five senior professional English football clubs using a total of 25 test players including two full internationals and five Under-21 internationals. The clubs consisted of three FA Premiership clubs, one first division club and one third division club. Testing at all clubs was carried out on Astroturf surfaces, three of which were indoors and two outdoors. A range of seven unbranded 'FIFA Approved' soccer balls inflated to 0.9 bar was utilised during the testing. The use of unmarked balls negated any player brand bias and also enabled the addition of circumferential markings to the balls. These markings enabled the accurate determination of ball spin during the digitising process.

The subjects were requested to perform three different types of kick on a stationary ball in a fixed position 20 m from goal. The first kick was a full power kick, the second an instep swerve kick and the third an outstep swerve kick. The subjects were each required to take five kicks of each type. The 25 test subjects consisted of 14 right-footed and 11 left-footed players. The test players all wore their own boots, consisting of designs from five different major boot manufacturers. The test players' details are shown in Table 1.

Table 1. Mean (± SD) test subject data (n=25).

Age (years)	19.68 ± 2.17
Body mass (kg)	76.04 ± 7.78
Body height (m)	1.81 ± 0.06
Foot size	8.02 ± 1.04

A high-speed camera operating at 500 frames per second with a shutter speed set at 1/1000 s was used to capture the initial ball trajectory after impact. The video footage was digitised and the ball velocity and trajectory numerically calculated using Flightpath software. The software requires the user to identify manually the individual ball images. The software then calculates ball velocity and launch elevation for each kick. The accuracy of measurement for velocity was ± 0.4 m.s^{-1} and for launch elevation ±1 degree.

For convenience ball spin has traditionally been specified in three components: - backspin, sidespin and rifle spin. In some games such as golf the spin component is primarily backspin, but in dynamic games an oblique spin axis is generally created. In this instance the spin measurement has been estimated by evaluating the number of frames for a quarter ball rotation. The values quoted are spin around the oblique axis.

2.2. Effect of valve position

Testing was carried out using a pneumatically driven 'pendulum' type kicking leg. The leg was fitted with a cylindrical shaped end-effector (diameter 92 mm, length 168 mm, mass 1.343 kg). Two light gates 0.7 m apart measured ball exit velocity after impact. A high-speed camera operating at 500 frames per second with a shutter speed set at 1/1000 s was used to capture the initial ball trajectory after impact. The video footage was digitised and Flightpath software used to calculate ball elevation. A 'FIFA Approved' test ball was positioned in three different orientations on an adjustable teeing mechanism. Firstly the valve location at impact was set at the top of the ball, secondly the valve position was set at the point of impact and thirdly the valve position was set at the bottom of the ball. Tests were carried out at three different ball pressures (0.6, 0.9, 1.2 bar) simulating the range of the FIFA pressure stipulation for balls in top class soccer games. Tests were repeated 10 times at each setting, giving a total of 90 impacts.

3. RESULTS AND DISCUSSION

3.1. Player testing

The test results are summarised in Table 2. These results are shown in graphical form in Figures 1 and 2.

Table 2. Mean ($\pm$ SD) test results for ball launch velocity and spin data.

Kick Type	Velocity (m.s^{-1})	Ball Spin (rev.s^{-1})
Full Power	27.05 $\pm$ 2.23	
Instep Swerve	23.52 $\pm$ 2.31	7.91 $\pm$ 2.27
Outstep Swerve	20.85 $\pm$ 3.08	7.87 $\pm$ 2.46

The measured ball velocity data showed significant differences between kick types. The full power kick produced a mean velocity of 27.05 m.s^{-1}, with a maximum-recorded velocity of 33.10 m.s^{-1}. This maximum-recorded velocity compares well with the maximum value of 34.0 m.s^{-1} recorded by Asami and Nolte (1983) for a power kick. The range of values recorded is supported by the data taken by Roberts and Metcalfe (1968), who recorded ball velocity values in the range of 23–31 m.s^{-1}. However, the maximum-recorded velocity of 31 m.s^{-1} recorded by Roberts and Metcalfe is slightly less than the maximum velocities recorded in this study and by Asami and Nolte (1983). This could be due to the use of professional players; however, the significant developments in sports turf, ball and boot manufacture since 1968 should also be taken into account. Furthermore, as with all sports, player development has been significant, particularly with the advent of television exposure and the associated rewards for success.

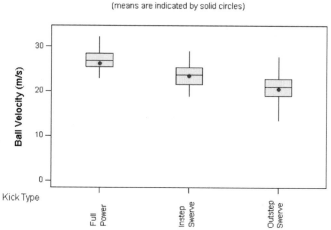

Figure 1. Box plot of ball velocity data.

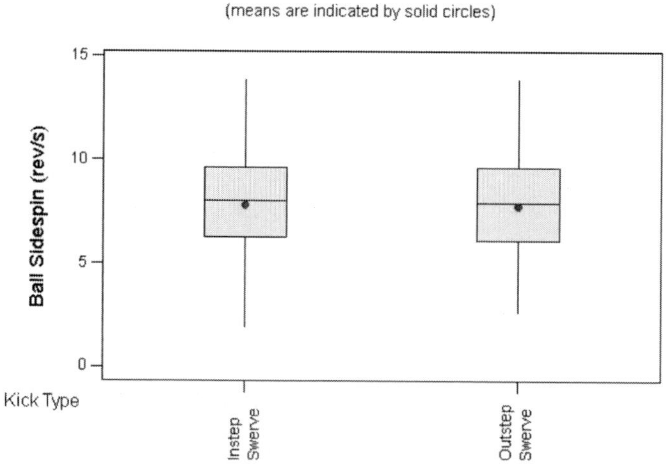

Figure 2. Box plot of ball spin data.

As might be expected the instep and outstep swerve kick types produced lower mean velocities of 23.52 and 20.85 m.s^{-1} respectively. The mean value of 23.52 m.s^{-1} recorded for the instep swerve kick compares favourably with Asai and Akatsuka (1998) who measured an average ball velocity for an instep kick of 23.28 m.s^{-1}. The range of velocity values observed was higher than those of 18 to 22 m.s^{-1} recorded by Isokawa and Lees (1988), which may have been due to the use of professional players rather than amateurs. When comparing the measured ball velocity data with those of earlier studies using amateur players, it is evident that professional players achieve higher ball velocities.

The mean spin rate values calculated for the instep and outstep swerve kicks were similar, 7.91 rev.s^{-1} for the instep swerve kick and 7.87 rev.s^{-1} for the outstep swerve kick. However, there was a considerable range of spin values recorded, from 13.89 rev.s^{-1} down to 2.60 rev.s^{-1}, indicating that consistency of performance for spin kicks is difficult to achieve. Asai and Akatsuka (1998) reported ball spin rates for an instep swerve kick to be in the range of 7–10 rev.s^{-1}, although this was using amateur players. The maximum spin rate values recorded for both the instep and outstep swerve kicks was the same, 13.89 rev.s^{-1}.

3.2. Effect of valve position

The test results are summarised in Table 3, which gives details of the average ball launch elevations and velocities measured for the three different ball orientations. The light gates were set up to measure the horizontal component of velocity. Therefore a correction was applied in order to calculate the actual ball velocity, taking into account the effect of the launch angles. These results are shown in graphical form in Figures 3 and 4.

Table 3. Ball velocity and elevation for different valve locations.

Valve Location	Ball Pressure (bar)	Mean Ball Exit Velocity (m.s^{-1})	Mean Ball Launch Elevation (deg)
Top	0.6	17.95	19.34
	0.9	18.10	18.50
	1.2	17.97	17.44
Strike Point	0.6	18.10	18.09
	0.9	18.00	16.03
	1.2	18.04	15.57
Bottom	0.6	18.07	16.86
	0.9	18.04	15.08
	1.2	18.11	14.86

The results show that valve location at impact does not have a significant effect on ball velocity. However, the results suggest that ball launch elevation is lower with the valve positioned at the bottom of the ball and with higher pressure balls. The difference in ball launch elevation between valve locations at the top and bottom of the ball is significant (P=0.03). It should be noted that the same ball was used throughout the tests.

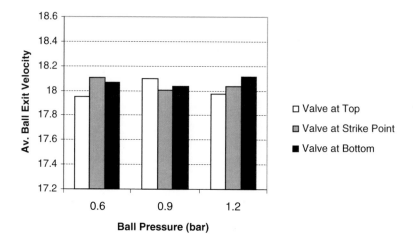

Figure 3. Graph of ball pressure against ball launch velocity.

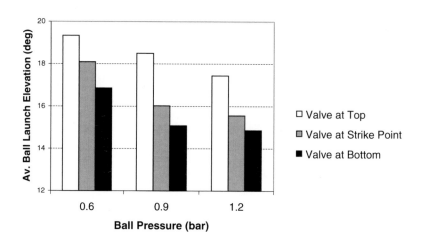

Figure 4. Graph of ball pressure against ball launch elevation.

4. CONCLUSIONS

The tests undertaken in this study present comprehensive data for the launch characteristics of three major kicking techniques. The data extend the work of previous investigators, and indicate that initial ball velocity for a range of typical kicks is in the range 18–33 m.s^{-1}, dependent on kick type. Spin rates obtained by professional players using the instep and outstep are similar but more inconsistent, with maximum values of 13.89 rev.s^{-1}, and a range of 3–14 rev.s^{-1}. The study has shown that professional players are capable of imparting initial velocities of up to 33 m.s^{-1} and spin rates of up to 14 rev.s^{-1} to a soccer ball. However, ball velocity for the outstep swerve kick is generally lower than for the instep kick.

The use of elite professional players is essential when determining the range of launch values achievable from kicking a soccer ball. They give credibility to the tests and ensure that the results obtained are close to the maximum values achievable. The data obtained from this study could be used to set appropriate dynamic standards for soccer balls to ensure ball performance consistency and limiting conditions.

It has been known for some time that professional players consider valve position to affect ball impact performance and the tests undertaken here confirm a significant effect on ball elevation. Further work is required using player tests to determine practical variations achievable. These results could be used as a basis for consideration of tests to regulate dynamic anisotropy in balls.

Acknowledgments

The authors would like to thank the Engineering Physical Science and Research Council and the Wolfson School of Mechanical and Manufacturing Engineering for providing the resources to enable this research programme to proceed. Also thanks to Adidas for providing access to its robotic kicking leg and to the football clubs who agreed to participate.

REFERENCES

Asai, T. and Akatsuka, T., 1998, Computer simulation of curve ball kicking in soccer. In The Engineering of Sport, edited by Haake, S. J. (London: Blackwell Ltd), pp. 433–440.

Asami, T. and Nolte, V., 1983, Analysis of powerful ball kicking. *Biomechanics VIII-B*, 695–700.

Isokawa, M. and Lees, A., 1988, A biomechanical analysis of the instep kick motion in soccer. *In Science and Football*, edited by Reilly, T., Lees, A., Davids, K. and Murphy, W.J. (London: E & FN Spon), pp. 449–455.

Plagenhoef, S., 1972, Patterns of Human Motion - a Cinematographic Analysis, (N.J.: Prentice Hall), pp. 89–116.

Roberts, E.M. and Metcalfe, A., 1968, Mechanical analysis of kicking. *Biomechanics I*, 315–319.

Tsaousidis, N. and Zatsiorsky, V., 1996, Two types of ball-effector interaction and their relative contribution to soccer kicking. *Human Movement Science*, **15**, 861–876.

4   The Behaviour of a Football During a Free Kick

M.J. Carré[1], S.R. Goodwill[1], T. Asai[2] and S.J. Haake[1]
[1] Department of Mechanical Engineering, University of
Sheffield, Mappin Street, Sheffield, S1 3JD, UK
[2] Faculty of Education, Yamagata University, Yamagata, Japan

1. INTRODUCTION

Previous studies of ball kick technique have focused on the kicking leg (Roberts and Metcalfe, 1968). Most of these studies have been concerned with instep kicks, and even though the technique of curve kicking is frequently used to spin the ball and bend the trajectory, there have been relatively few studies on the curve kick in football (Wang and Griffin, 1997 and Asai et al., 1998). The first part of this study, therefore, examines the curve kick using computer simulations of the interaction between the foot and the ball, focusing on the generation of spin.

The second part of the study examines what effect the generation of spin has on the flight of a ball. The aerodynamics of many sports balls (golf, cricket, tennis, baseball, volleyball) have been studied previously (Bearman and Harvey, 1976; Mehta, 1985; Watts and Ferrer, 1987; Haake et al., 2000 and Mehta and Pallis, 2001) and these studies have measured the effect of velocity and spin on the drag and Magnus forces experienced by a sports ball during flight. However, little work has been published on footballs, but this understanding is necessary to predict their behaviour during flight. Therefore, measurements in a wind tunnel were taken from stationary and spinning scaled down footballs, in order to calculate drag and Magnus coefficients. These data could then be used to simulate the flight of a football for various launch conditions.

The aim of this study was to describe the behaviour of a football (soccer) during various stages of a free kick (contact with the foot, launch and flight through the air).

2. STUDY OF THE KICK

2.1. Computer simulation

In order to obtain fundamental data of the interaction between foot and ball, six university football players were observed by means of a high-speed VTR camera, whilst performing in-step kicks (Asai et al., 2002). A basic leg shape, determined by Asai et al. (1998) was meshed using MSC/PATRAN (MSC Inc) through an IGES file. The kicking leg and the surface of the ball were described by the Lagrangian frame of reference and discretized by the finite element method. The air inside the ball was described with a Eulerian frame of reference

(Lenselink, 1991) and defined by the Gamma Law equation of State. Hexahedron solid elements were used for the leg while shell elements were used for the ball. It was assumed that the lower leg and foot could be represented by two kinds of material properties. Figure 1 shows pressure contours of the simulation model, 4 ms after impact. The model was judged to match the experimental data sufficiently to warrant use for further study (Asai *et al.*, 2002).

Figure 1. Pressure contours, 4 ms after impact.

2.2. Effect of impact location

The relationship between the foot impact location and the imparted velocity and spin of the ball was examined. Simulations for 17 different impact locations were carried out with a chosen coefficient of friction of 0.4. Results can be seen in Figure 2 (off-set distance refers to the distance of the point of impact from the centre-line of the football).

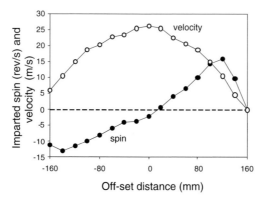

Figure 2. Effect of impact location on imparted spin and velocity.

The ball velocity decreases with an increase in the off-set distance, with maximum velocity being found when the off-set distance is zero (the ball being struck in the centre). However, although the spin generally increases with off-set distance, it rapidly decreases at large off-set distances This suggests that when the off-set distance approaches the radius of the ball, the contact area and duration rapidly decrease and the energy of the impact is only slightly transferred. Hence, it is suggested that there is a trade-off between ball velocity and spin for different amounts of off-set distance, within the range of the radius of the ball.

2.3. Effect of friction and spin

Figure 3 shows the variation of spin with coefficient of friction for impacts at 40 mm and 80 mm from the axis of the ball. It can be seen that the spin increases as the coefficient of friction increases and that doubling the off-set distance roughly doubles the spin. It is interesting to note that, even at zero coefficient of friction, spin can still be imparted to the ball. This is due to local deformation of the ball during impact, around the foot, allowing forces to be transmitted to the ball about its axis. Clearly, the off-set distance of the impact location from the ball's axis has a larger effect on spin than a variation in the coefficient of friction.

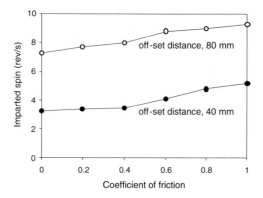

Figure 3. Effect of friction on imparted spin.

3. STUDY OF THE AERODYNAMICS

3.1. Approaches

There are two main approaches to measuring forces on sports balls during flight. The first approach is to take measurements from controlled football trajectories using high-speed video footage (Carré *et al.*, 2002). Although this is a well-recognised method that undoubtedly examines what actually happens as a ball travels through the air, it is susceptible to errors. The trajectory must be measured very accurately, as the effect of drag and Magnus force is determined by analyzing the subtle changes in the shape of the trajectory. Monitoring the change in drag due to velocity is further complicated by the fact that the velocity changes during flight. Other effects such as turbulence, camera misalignment and inaccurate velocity measurement can all lead to further inaccuracies.

The second approach is to use a wind tunnel, where the sports ball is held in place and air is blown around the ball at controlled speeds. This method has the advantage that the speed of the air can be accurately controlled and kept constant and the forces acting on the ball can be measured by attaching the ball to a force balance arrangement.

3.2. The effect of velocity on drag

The effect of velocity on drag coefficient was examined using controlled experiments in an open circuit wind tunnel (provided by the International Tennis Federation, Roehampton, UK). Due to the limiting size of the working section, a scale plastic model of a football was created (66 mm in diameter compared to 218 mm for a full size football). The model had a generic seam pattern, commonly used by many football manufacturers (consisting of 20 hexagonal and 12 pentagonal patches). This was mounted on an 'L'-shaped sting that was attached to a two-way force balance. The effect of increased drag on the body of the sting was reduced by mounting a separate shroud in front of the sting, allowing air to flow around it. The ball model, sting and shroud can be seen in Figure 4.

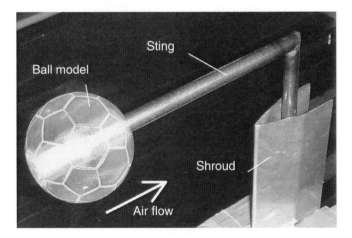

Figure 4. Scale football model (66 mm in diameter), mounted on a sting that is protected from the air flow by a shroud.

The air speed in the working section of the wind tunnel was varied from 20 m.s^{-1} (the minimum consistent speed achievable) up to 70 m.s^{-1} and back down again. The drag and lift forces experienced by the ball model were measured using the force balance at regular intervals. Three runs of tests were carried out, with the ball model mounted in three different orientations (the ball being rotated 90° about the sting between each run of tests).

When this testing was complete, the drag acting solely on the sting, the 'tare' drag, was measured. This was done by mounting a sphere 66 mm in diameter with a hole larger than the diameter of the sting, in the same place as the football model had been, using supports from the side. It was mounted so that no contact was made between the sphere and the sting and the tests were run again to measure the tare drag experienced by the sting alone. The measured drag force for the ball model and sting combined and the tare drag for the sting alone can be seen in Figure 5a, for different air flow speeds. The tare drag was found to be quite high, accounting for almost half the total drag measured on the ball-sting arrangement.

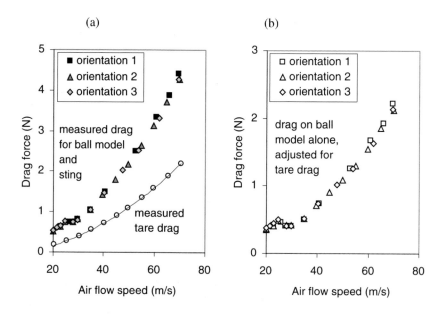

Figure 5. Drag force plotted against air flow speed: (a) measured on ball model and sting and on sting alone; and (b) adjusted for tare drag.

The measured drag forces were adjusted for tare drag and can be seen in Figure 5b. Generally, the drag force increases with air flow speed, as one would expect (for simple situations drag varies with the square of wind speed). However, there is a small fluctuation in the drag force at low speeds. There was found to be no major effect on the drag due to ball orientation as each run of tests gave very similar results.

A small football was also mounted in the wind tunnel and tests repeated in three orientations. The football used was a smaller version of the Adidas Fernova and was 140 mm in diameter (compared to 218 mm for a full size ball). The data were again adjusted for tare drag and the resulting drag force on the ball was found to vary with the square of the air flow speed. No major effect was observed due to the orientation of the ball.

To predict the drag forces that a full size football would experience during flight, the drag data from the scale model and the mini football were converted to drag coefficient data and plotted against Reynolds number. Drag coefficients, C_d, and Reynolds numbers, Re, were calculated using the following equations:-

$$F_d = \frac{1}{2} C_d \rho A v^2 \qquad (1)$$

$$Re = \frac{\rho v D}{\mu} \qquad (2)$$

(where, F_d is the drag force, ρ is density of the air, A is projected area of the ball, C_d is the drag coefficient, v is the velocity of the air, Re is the Reynolds number, D is the diameter of the ball and μ is the dynamic viscosity of the air).

In a real match situation a football has a velocity range of around 16 km.h[-1] (4.6 m.s[-1]) to 112 km.h[-1] (32 m.s[-1]). In normal atmospheric conditions, this equates to a range in Reynolds number of approximately 70,000 to 500,000. The drag coefficient data were plotted against Reynolds number and can be seen in Figure 6.

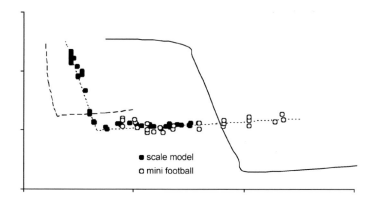

Figure 6. Wind tunnel drag coefficient data plotted against Reynolds number, compared with data for other spheres.

The data show a sharp drop in drag coefficient from about 0.5 to 0.2 over a range in Reynolds number from about 90,000 to 130,000 and then a slight increase over the rest of the range. This is due to a transition in the behaviour of the air in the boundary layer, surrounding the ball. At low Reynolds number (and therefore, low speeds) the boundary layer contains *laminar* flow, an ordered type of flow where the air can be thought of as travelling in stream tubes, which do not mix with the surrounding flow. An example of this type of flow can be seen in Figure 7a, which shows a jet of smoke travelling around the ball model, viewed from above, when the Reynolds number is 90,000 (equivalent to 6.1 m.s^{-1} for a full size football). The boundary layer separates quite early and there is a large wake behind the ball and consequently, a large drag force acting on the ball. As the speed of the air is increased, the flow in the boundary layer becomes *turbulent* and mixing occurs with the surrounding air. This gives the boundary layer sufficient energy to travel further round the ball and separate later. This effect can be seen in Figure 7b, which shows a jet of smoke travelling around the ball model for a Reynolds number of 130,000 (equivalent to 9.1 m.s^{-1} for a full size football). There is less wake behind the ball and the drag coefficient is reduced.

(a)   (b)

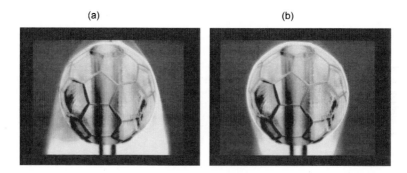

Figure 7. Smoke flow around the scale football model showing: (a) laminar flow at Re = 90,000; and (b) turbulent flow at Re = 130,000.

Also shown on Figure 6 are the results of other aerodynamic studies on spheres. Achenbach (1974) found that an increase in surface roughness had the effect of moving the transition from laminar to turbulent behaviour to a lower Reynolds number. A similar effect has been found for sports balls that have surface roughness (Mehta and Pallis, 2001). It is well known that dimples on golf balls help to reduce drag by moving the transition point to lower Reynolds number so that the flow around a golf ball is turbulent for more of its flight. Judging by Figure 6, the seam pattern on a football, seems to have a similar effect, but not to such a great extent. If a football were completely smooth, according to Achenbach's (1972) data, it would have a higher drag coefficient for most of the range of Reynolds numbers, seen in play.

3.3. Magnus force measurements

It is well recognised that spinning spheres experience a force perpendicular to both the spin axis and the velocity of the ball, that is due to the Magnus effect. This is why tennis balls with top spin generally dip and golf balls with back spin, stay in the air longer and lead to a more efficient drive.

In order to measure this effect for footballs, the scale model was mounted in the wind tunnel, by two thin-axle supports from both sides. These supports allowed the ball to be spun up to 3,000 rev.min^{-1} in both directions (top spin and back spin), the axles being driven by an electric motor, some way out of the airflow. Force transducers in the supports were used to measure the drag force acting on the ball-axle arrangement and the lift force generated by the Magnus effect. Tests were carried out at a range of wind speeds from 20 m.s^{-1} to 60 m.s^{-1}. The measured Magnus forces, F_m were then converted to Magnus coefficients, C_m, in a similar way to that used previously for the drag coefficients (see equation 1). Hence, the following equation was used:-

$$F_m = \frac{1}{2} C_m \rho A v^2 \tag{3}$$

Past studies of the Magnus effect of sports balls (Watts and Ferrer, 1987) have found it convenient to plot Magnus coefficient against a spin parameter, v_{eq}/v, where v_{eq} is the equatorial velocity of the ball surface, relative to its centre (equal to $r\omega$, the radius multiplied by the spin) and v is the ball velocity relative to the air. These data are shown in Figure 8. It can be seen that for high values of Reynolds number ($Re = 210,000$, $Re = 170,000$), the Magnus coefficient generally increased with the spin parameter and the maximum value measured was around 0.22. This was a similar relationship to that found by Watts and Ferrer (1987) for baseballs (see Figure 8) and can be explained by the conventional Magnus effect. Here the separation of the boundary layer is enhanced on the advancing side of the ball, but delayed on the retreating side of the ball causing an asymmetric pressure distribution (Mehta, 1985). This asymmetry causes a resultant force acting in the direction of the advancing side. Put simply, a ball with top spin would dip. The faster the ball spins (relative to its speed), the greater the force and the Magnus coefficient increases. This effect happens at post-critical Reynolds numbers when the boundary layer on both sides of the ball is turbulent.

However, a phenomenon known as *Reverse* Magnus effect can also be seen in Figure 8 for the football tests at lower Reynolds number ($Re = 90,000$). For low values of spin parameter, a negative Magnus coefficient was measured suggesting that a football travelling at low speed with a small amount of top spin would actually experience a slight upwards force. Reverse Magnus occurs when there is a difference in the type of boundary layer on either side of the ball. On the advancing side, the effective Reynolds number (relative to the ball surface) is high enough for turbulent behaviour and separation occurs relatively late. However, on the retreating side, the effective Reynolds number is somewhat lower allowing stable, laminar behaviour in the boundary layer. This separates early and the asymmetric pressure distribution now causes a resultant force to act in the direction of the retreating side (Mehta and Pallis, 2001). The minimum value of Magnus coefficient was measured to be around −0.3. This effect is found with smooth spheres, as shown by the data of Maccoll (1928) in Figure 8.

Mathematical fits were applied to the data to allow a Magnus coefficient to be predicted for any Reynolds number and spin parameter. The equation used for this purpose was

$$C_m = a\left(1 - e^{-bS_P}\right) - cS_p\left(1 - e^{-dS_P}\right)$$ (4)

(where S_p is the spin parameter v_{eq}/v and a, b, c and d are all coefficients that vary with Reynolds number). The calculated fits for these data are shown using dotted lines in Figure 8.

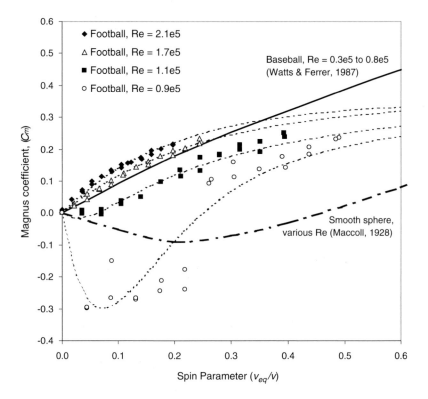

Figure 8. Smoke flow around the scale football model showing: (a) laminar flow at Re = 90,000; and (b) turbulent flow at Re = 130,000.

3.4. Effect of spin on drag

The drag forces measured during the spinning ball tests were used to examine the effect of spin on drag. The problem with these data was that the side supports were found to have a significant effect on the drag measured on the complete ball-support arrangement. The measurements of drag force with zero spin were compared with data from the experiments that used a rear mounted sting (see earlier section) to calculate the effect of the tare drag, due to the side supports. When all the data were adjusted for tare, there was found to be very little effect on the drag coefficient due to spin and the relationship was found to be very similar to that shown in Figure 6, for all values of spin parameter.

4. KICK SIMULATIONS

Now that a complete set of relationships had been found for the effect of velocity and spin on drag and Magnus force, a number of kicking situations could be simulated. This was achieved by using a three-dimensional trajectory simulation model that calculated the forces experienced by the ball at discrete time intervals during its flight using the equations 1 and 3 (a time step of 2.5 ms was used). The coefficients C_d and C_m were calculated at each time interval based on the mathematical fits of the wind tunnel data, as the velocity of the ball changed and consequently so did the Reynolds number and the spin parameter. The spin was assumed to remain in the horizontal plane throughout the flight with no significant degradation.

The first part of this study found that if a ball is struck in its centre, with a foot velocity of 25 m.s^{-1} and a coefficient of friction of 0.4, it will have an effective launch velocity of 26 m.s^{-1} and no spin (see Figure 2). According to the aerodynamic study this would lead to an initial drag coefficient of 0.22 (for a Reynolds number of 390,000) and a Magnus coefficient of 0.0. The three-dimensional trajectory model was used to simulate this kick if it was taken 18 m away from the goal, 6 m off-set to the right of the centre of the goal, with a goal being scored in the top left-hand corner ("Kick a", Figure 9). The simulation showed that the flow around the ball was turbulent throughout so the drag coefficient remained relatively constant.

If the foot impact location was off-set by 80 mm to the right, this would give a ball velocity of 18.5 m.s^{-1} and a spin of 10.2 rev.s^{-1} (64 rad.s^{-1}) (see Figure 2). The initial drag and Magnus coefficients were calculated to be 0.22 and 0.32 respectively for a Reynolds number of 270,000 and a spin parameter of 0.43. This kick, "Kick b", was simulated to score a goal in the top left-hand corner, from the same position as Kick a. The drag coefficient was again found to remain the same throughout and the Magnus coefficient also remained fairly constant due to the combined effect of reducing Reynolds number and increasing spin parameter.

In order for both free kicks to be successful, the launch angle had to be altered in the same way that a player would do instinctively for a choice of kick. The trajectory plots in Figure 9 show how Kick b curves to a much greater extent than Kick a, due to the sideways Magnus force. However, because the ball is travelling more slowly for Kick b (by approximately 30%), it must be launched higher into the air to reach the same point as Kick a. The total time required to score is 0.9 s for Kick a and 1.4 s for Kick b.

This demonstrates the choice of strategy available to a player when taking such a kick. The ball can be struck centrally to gain as much velocity as possible or it can be struck off-set from the centre to put spin on the ball. This allows the ball to be bent round a defensive wall of players. It is thought that in an actual game situation, an experienced player would be able to strike the ball with sufficient force to gain high velocity *and* spin.

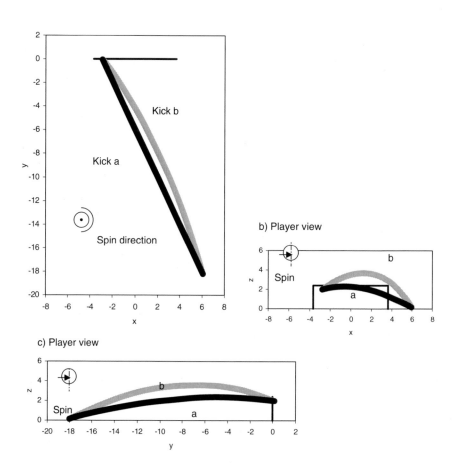

Figure 9. Prediction for flight of two free kicks based on varying foot impact location.

5. CONCLUSIONS

Ball spin was found to increase with both the off-set distance
ball axis and the kinetic coefficient of friction. For the same
a trade-off was found between ball speed and spin, for differ
   Wind tunnel measurements showed the effect of a tra
turbulent behaviour in the boundary layer, causing a low drag
Reynolds numbers. For spinning balls, the Magnus effect was observed and it was
found that reverse Magnus effects were possible at low Reynolds numbers.
   Trajectory simulations demonstrated that a ball that is struck in the centre
will follow a near straight trajectory, dipping slightly before reaching the goal. A
ball that is struck off-centre will bend before reaching the goal, but will have a
significantly longer flight time.

REFERENCES

Achenbach, E., 1972, Experiments on the flow past spheres at very high Reynolds
   numbers. *Journal of Fluid Mechanics,* **54**, 565–575.

Achenbach, E., 1974, The effects of surface roughness and tunnel blockage on the flow
   past spheres. *Journal of Fluid Mechanics,* **65**, 113–125.

Asai, T., Akatsuka, T., Nasako, M. and Murakami, O., 1998, Computer simulation
   of curve- ball kicking in soccer, In *The Engineering of Sport,* edited by Haake
   S.J., (Oxford, U. K., Blackwell Science), pp. 433–440.

Asai, T., Carré, M. J., Akatsuka, T. and Haake, S. J., 2002, The curve kick of a
   football I: Impact with the foot. *Sports Engineering,* **5**, 183–192.

Bearman, P. W. and Harvey, J. K., 1976, Golf ball aerodynamics. *Aeronautical
   Quarterly,* **27**, 112–122.

Carré, M. J., Asai, T., Akatsuka, T. and Haake, S. J., 2002, The curve kick of a
   football II: Flight through the air. *Sports Engineering,* **5**, 183–192.

Haake, S. J., Chadwick, S. G., Dignall, R. J., Goodwill, S. and Rose, P., 2000,
   Engineering tennis – slowing the game down. *Sports Engineering,* **3**, 131–144.

Lenselink, H., 1991, *Oblique penetration in ductile plates,* The MacNeal-Schwendler
   Corporation, paper 91–03, (The Mac-Neal Schwendler Corporation).

Maccoll, 1928, *Royal Aeronautical Society,* **32**, 777–791.

Mehta, R. D., 1985, Aerodynamics of sports balls. *Annual Review of Fluid
   Mechanics,* **17**, 151–189.

Mehta, R. D. and Pallis, J.M., 2001, Sports ball aerodynamics: Effects of velocity,
   spin and surface roughness, In *Materials and Science in Sports, Proceedings of
   Symposium sponsored byTMS (The Minerals, Metals and Minerals Society) ,
   San Diego,* edited by Froes F.H. and Haake S.J., (TMS Press), pp. 185–197.

Roberts, E. M. and Metcalfe, A., 1968, In *Biomechanics I,* edited by Wartenweiler,
   J., Jokl, E. and Hebbelinck, M. (Baltimore, University Park Press), pp. 315–319.

Wang, J. S. and Griffin, M., 1997, Kinematic analysis of the soccer curve ball shot.
   Strength and Conditioning, Feb, pp. 54–57.

Watts, R. G., and Ferrer, R., 1987, The lateral force on a spinning sphere:
   Aerodynamics of a curveball. *American Journal of Physics,* **55**, 40–44.

5 Simplified Flight Equations for a Spinning Soccer Ball

K. Bray and D.G. Kerwin
Department of Sport and Exercise Science
University of Bath, United Kingdom

1. INTRODUCTION

The direct free kick is an increasingly important component of the modern game, second only to the penalty in players' and spectators' expectations of a goal. This follows from a combination of the technology of the modern ball, and elite players' ability to swerve it accurately when kicked with spin. There have been numerous theoretical and practical studies of the flight of a spinning ball (Tait, 1896; Mehta, 1985; Watts and Ferrer, 1987; Alaways and Hubbard, 2001; Bray and Kerwin, 2003). In Bray and Kerwin (2003), aerodynamic properties of a soccer ball (lift and drag coefficients) were obtained by comparing a mathematical model of the flight with experimentally determined trajectories. The results were used in conjunction with a model of the defensive wall to examine attackers' and defenders' options in this important 'set play'.

One of the most important aspects of a swerving free kick is the extent to which the ball can be moved laterally, beyond the goalkeeper's reach. Lateral deflections can be obtained from the models described in Bray and Kerwin (2003), but the flight equations for a spinning ball are complex, involving coupled, three-dimensional second order differential equations. Whilst these can be solved using standard numerical routines, unfamiliarity with the techniques or lack of access to the software may deter some practitioners. In this report we show that the full differential equations for the flight can be reduced, in certain limits, to simpler forms, capable of exact solution, and more amenable to straightforward calculation.

The purpose of this report is to present simplified expressions for the lateral deflection of a spinning soccer ball in direct free kicks. Comparisons are made between the complex and simplified modelling solutions and some experimentally determined ball trajectories.

2. METHODS AND MATERIALS

2.1. 3-D flight equations

In Bray and Kerwin (2003) the equations of motion were formulated by including lift, drag and gravitational forces. Taking y as the initial direction of the kick, x as the lateral deflection and z as the vertical, and assuming pure sidespin operates throughout the flight the following differential equations are obtained:

$$\frac{d^2x}{dt^2} = -v\{k_d \frac{dx}{dt} - k_l \frac{dy}{dt}\} \tag{1}$$

$$\frac{d^2y}{dt^2} = -v\{k_d \frac{dy}{dt} + k_l \frac{dx}{dt}\} \tag{2}$$

$$\frac{d^2z}{dt^2} = -g - vk_d \frac{dz}{dt} \tag{3}$$

In these, $k_d = \rho A C_d/2m$ and $k_l = \rho A C_l/2m$, ρ is the density of air, A the cross-sectional area of the ball, m its mass and C_d and C_l the drag and lift coefficients respectively. The velocity of the ball is given by $v = \sqrt{(v_x^2 + v_y^2 + v_z^2)}$, where $v_x = dx/dt$, etc. These equations have no closed-form solutions and must be solved numerically. A further problem occurs in choosing values for the constants, especially C_d and C_l as there have been few experimental determinations of these parameters for soccer balls. Details of the approach used for determining these quantities are given in the following section.

2.2. Experimental methods: determination of C_d and C_l

The trials were undertaken in the controlled environment of a sports hall, using an experienced subject to perform the kicks (Bray and Kerwin, 2003).

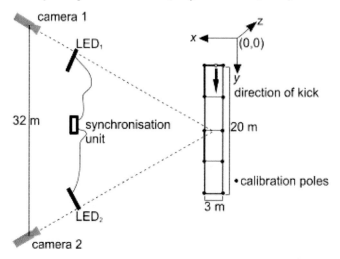

Figure 1. Camera calibration and data capture layout.

These were executed with as near perfect sidespin as our subject could attain, although the resulting spin axis of the ball in the various kicks was found to vary between 61° and 96° to the horizontal, 90° representing perfect sidespin. The subsequent flight of the ball in a previously calibrated volume was captured using two digital video camcorders (see Figure 1) and the resulting data analysed using the 'Target' system of Kerwin (1995). The full differential equations given above were solved numerically using the contributed Runge-Kutta solver within the Mathcad™ Technical Calculation Package. The lift and drag coefficients C_d and C_l were obtained by comparing measured and predicted trajectories. C_d varied from 0.25 to 0.30 and C_l from 0.23 to 0.29.

2.3. Simplified 2D flight equations

Whilst all the essential features of the flight can be determined from Equations (1) to (3), it would be useful to obtain simplified solutions which model the problem with acceptable accuracy. This can be achieved if the lateral deflection of the ball is the main parameter of interest. If it is assumed that the ball is kicked with perfect sidespin, lateral forces are maximised. Provided also that the trajectory remains flat (velocity vector very nearly parallel to the ground), vertical motion can be ignored and the resulting motion is confined to the horizontal plane as shown in Figure 2.

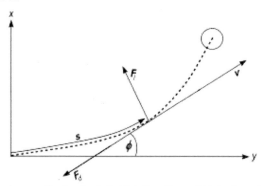

Figure 2. Intrinsic coordinates (s,ϕ). Initial direction of kick along the y axis.

The equations of motion are greatly simplified under these assumptions and using intrinsic coordinates (s,ϕ) as defined in Figure 2, the differential equations for the flight become:

$$\frac{d^2s}{dt^2} = -k_d \left(\frac{ds}{dt} \right)^2 \tag{4}$$

$$\frac{ds}{d\phi} = \frac{1}{k_l} \tag{5}$$

These can be integrated exactly, and using the transformations $dx/dt = \sin\phi \, ds/dt$, $dy/dt = \cos\phi \, ds/dt$, we find that:

$$x = \frac{1}{k_l} \{ 1 - \cos(\frac{k_l}{k_d} \ln(1 + k_d V_0 t)) \} \tag{6}$$

$$y = \frac{1}{k_l}\sin(\frac{k_l}{k_d}\ln(1 + k_d V_0 t)) \tag{7}$$

These expressions give the positional coordinates as explicit functions of t and can be used in to compute the ball's position at any instant, without recourse to complex numerical technique. Lateral deflections are given by Equation (6) for any time step. Deflections can be evaluated as functions of distance (for example at the distance from the goal line to the free kick) by determining the corresponding y value from Equation (7). It should be noted that V_0 in Equations (6) and (7) is the initial launch speed of the ball and not the general velocity v in Equations (1) to (3).

3. RESULTS AND DISCUSSION

3.1. Comparison of 2D and 3D models

The following diagrams compare the 2D and 3D models, first in terms of the predicted coordinates (Figure 3a) and then in terms of the RMS agreement between the models for various launch angles of the kick (Figure 3b).

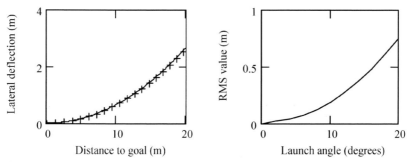

Figure 3. (a) Positional coordinates (_____ 3D ++++ 2D); and (b) RMS agreement.

Effectively, the path of the ball is represented in 'plan view', i.e. in the horizontal plane of the pitch. The same values of C_d and C_l have been used in each case ($C_d = C_l = 0.25$) and an initial kicking speed of 25 m·s^{-1} has been assumed. A launch angle of 16° has been chosen for the 3D model in Figure 3a as representative of the elevation needed to clear the defensive wall (Bray and Kerwin, 2003). For these values of the parameters the agreement between the models is seen to be good. This agreement can be demonstrated quantitatively by determining the RMS deviation between the coordinates obtained from each method, as a function of the launch angles assumed in the 3D model. This is shown in Figure 3b. In practice, sidespin free kicks from 20 m with kicking speeds of 25 m·s^{-1} would rarely be successful for launch angles much above 16°. At this value the models agree to 0.48 m RMS, equivalent to two ball diameters for a 20-m flight.

3.2. Comparison of 2D model with experimental trajectories

Similar comparisons can be made between the 2-D model and the 3-D trajectories for the trial kicks measured in Bray and Kerwin (2003). Two contrasting examples are shown in Figures 3 and 3. The C_d values are comparable: (Figure 4a = 0.29, Fig. 4b = 0.28), but the C_l value for Figure 4a (0.29) exceeded that for Figure 4b (0.24), implying that our subject imparted more spin to the ball in the former case. This is reflected in the differing curvatures of the trajectories. The launch angles of 11.5° for Figure 4a and 17.2° for Figure 4b also differ appreciably, yet the simplified 2-D model for the trajectories fits both extremes well.

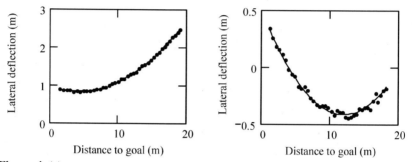

Figure 4. (a) The 2-D model and real data; and (b) The 2-D model and real data.

None of the trial kicks recorded in Bray and Kerwin (2003) exceeded launch angles much above 16°, so it was not possible to carry out a systematic examination of 'goodness of fit' between the 2-D model and the experimental data, as a function of launch angle, as in Figure 3b. This could be done if the ball could be launched controllably, and work is underway to achieve this.

4. CONCLUSIONS

The main objective of this study was to derive simplified equations for the flight of a spinning soccer ball, where the parameter of greatest interest is the degree of lateral deflection of the ball. Further objectives were to compare the results of the simplified 2-D model with those obtained from the full 3-D differential equations, and also with selected experimentally determined trajectories. It has been shown that for perfect sidespin, and launch angles restricted to those typical of actual free kicks (less than about 16°) agreement is good, so that the simplified equations can be used with confidence. These results may assist researchers and sports manufacturers who wish to apply the results in practical cases without resorting to complex numerical procedures.

It is important to note that the findings are restricted to conditions representing 'typical' sidespin free kicks. Whilst the assumed velocity of 25 m·s^{-1}, and spin and drag coefficients of 0.25 are representative of actual kicks, the envelope should not be stretched too far. More work would be needed to compare the 2-D and 3-D models in cases where the parameters differed

appreciably from these limits, although this exercise is certai
simple form of the 2-D expressions which have been derived.

Acknowledgements

We gratefully acknowledge the assistance of Mitre Spor
providing research materials and thank Andreas Wallb
Officer University of Bath, for assistance with the data collection.

REFERENCES

Alaways, L. W. and Hubbard, M., 2001, Experimental determination of baseball spin and lift. *Journal of Sports Sciences,* **19**, 349–358.

Bray, K. and Kerwin, D.G., 2003, Modelling the flight of a soccer ball in a direct free kick. *Journal of Sports Sciences,* **21**, 75–85.

Kerwin, D.G., 1995, Apex/Target high resolution video digitising system. In *Proceedings of the Biomechanics Section of the British Association of Sports and Exercise Science,* edited by Watkins, J. (Glasgow: BASES), pp 1–4.

Mehta, R.D., 1985, Aerodynamics of sports balls. *Annual Review of Fluid Mechanics,* **17**, 151–189.

Tait, P.G., 1896, On the path of a rotating spherical projectile. *Transactions of the Royal Society, Edinburgh*, Part 2 (16), 491–506.

Watts, R. G. and Ferrer, R., 1987, The lateral force on a spinning sphere. *American Journal of Physics*, **55**, 40–45.

6   Stability in Soccer Shoes: The Relationship between Perception of Stability and Biomechanical Parameters

Thorsten Sterzing and Ewald Hennig
University of Essen, Germany

1. INTRODUCTION

A comprehensive evaluation of athletic footwear in general should consist of a combination of sensory/perceptual, biomechanical and mechanical testing procedures (Lafortune, 2001). Each of these testing procedures provides by itself important insight with regard to the properties of athletic shoes. Nevertheless, it is justified to assume that there is an interdependent relationship between the different ways of testing as well as between the data gathered from it. Therefore, when data that are collected by these different sources are interpreted concurrently, the knowledge benefit should be increased.

The design of athletic shoes should follow three main criteria in order to provide an ergonomic function in their specific sport: these are performance, protection and comfort.

Soccer shoes in particular have to fulfill multiple game related demands. Footwear in soccer plays a more fundamental role in influencing the athlete's performance than it does in other sports (Rodano et al., 1988). Among other features there is primarily the need of comfort, traction and stability according to a survey asking for desirable soccer shoe properties that was carried out by the Biomechanics Laboratory of the University of Essen in 1998 (n = 249 soccer players). In addition, soccer shoes should also protect the foot against injuries (Lees, 1996). Multi-directional movements and grass surface conditions as well as cleated outsole constructions of soccer shoes require a distinguished approach towards stability in soccer in comparison to running or court sports.

The aim of this study was to identify potential correlations between (I) stability perception of soccer players in the field and (II) biomechanical parameters measured in a laboratory experiment when performing soccer movements in different soccer shoe models. For this purpose, suitable field test situations were to be identified in order to perceive soccer specific stability and a reasonable biomechanical test design for detecting stability related shoe features in the laboratory. The findings are supposed to lead to a systematic approach combining sensory/perceptual and biomechanical testing in order to increase stability in soccer shoes and thus the performance and protective properties of soccer shoes.

2. METHODS

Twenty experienced soccer players participated in this study. Seven commercially available high quality soccer shoes were included in this study. These were:- Adidas Predator Accelerator (A), Adidas Copa Mundial (B), Nike Rio (C), Nike Tiempo Premier non-elliptic (D), Nike Tiempo Premier elliptic (E), Nike Mercurial (F) and Nike Match Mercurial (G). All of these shoes had an outsole construction designed for playing on firm ground. Three of them showed elliptic outsole designs (B, C, E) whereas the other four showed non-elliptic outsole designs (A, D, F, G).

Field Test (I)
In the field test, subjects had to rate the perceived stability of each soccer shoe model on a seven-point perception scale (1 worst – 7 best). The shoes were tested in randomized order. Testing was done in four different soccer specific situations on natural grass surface:

1. Slalom parcourse
2. Sudden movement parcourse
3. Power kick
4. Game-like situation.

The slalom parcourse (1) had a total length of 80 m containing 11 turns. Subjects were asked to run through the parcource at a relatively low basic speed in order not to get fatigued but performing the turns at maximum speed. Subjects had to go through the parcourse once in each shoe condition.

The sudden movement parcourse (2) had a total length of 50 m where the subjects had to perform 4 different highly dynamic movements. These were a maximum acceleration, a complete stop and two cutting movement to the left hand and the right hand side. The basic speed for this parcourse was also relatively low. Subjects had to go through the parcourse once in each shoe condition.

The power kick situation (3) required the subjects to perform 3 maximum shots on the goal from a distance of 16 m.

The game-like situation (4) was a common practice game that is often used during warm-up having 5 players playing versus 2 on a field of 11 × 11 m. Subjects had to play 7 min in each shoe condition.

The stability rating for each shoe was done directly after having done the testing condition in the specific shoe. Ratings were required for two different kinds of stability: (a) stability referring to foot-to-shoe interaction and (b) stability referring to shoe-to-ground interaction. From these ratings an overall stability result for the different soccer shoe models was received which includes the ratings of all four soccer specific situations with regard to both different kinds of stability. Furthermore, the ratings were evaluated with respect to solely foot-to-shoe stability as well as to solely shoe-to-ground stability.

The soccer specific field test situations were analyzed for their suitability to discriminate between different soccer shoe models with respect to stability.

Laboratory Test (II)

The biomechanical test required subjects to perform a cutting movement provoking a rapid change in direction as fast as possible. Five repetitive trials in each shoe condition had to be performed from which mean values of the biomechanical parameters were calculated. The testing took place on artificial turf (DD - Soccer Grass HPF CROWN/ DIN 18035 T 7 120 µ, 8800 dtex, density 30000/ m2) in a laboratory environment. The assignment of the shoes was randomized for different subjects.

During the movement, ground reaction force data were collected by means of a Kistler force plate 9281 (size: 40 x 120 cm), angular motion data by an electrogoniometer (Milani et al., 1995) and foot pressure distribution data by 8 discrete piezoelectric pressure transducers (Halm PD-16) (Hennig et al., 1994). The pressure transducers were attached plantar to the heel, lateral midfoot and metatarsal heads I, III and V; lateral to the rear foot/ calcaneus and forefoot/ metatarsal bone V; medial to the forefoot/ metatarsal bone I. Data collection was done in a pre-trigger mode for 500 ms by a frequency of 1 kHz/ channel and a 12-bit resolution of the a/ d converter card.

The following biomechanical parameters were calculated:- vertical force, resultant shear force, force rates, median power frequency and ground contact time (ground reaction force data); supination and supination velocity (angular motion data); peak pressures and pressure rates of plantar, medial and lateral foot-to-shoe contact areas.

3. RESULTS

The perception field test (I) proved to be suitable for detecting stability differences among different soccer shoe models. Subjects were able to perceive soccer specific stability differences between different soccer shoe models. Furthermore, they were capable of differentiating between (a) stability that refers to the interaction of foot to shoe and (b) stability that refers to the interaction of shoe to ground.

All of the soccer shoe models tested were rated by the subjects to have at least good stability properties. Figure 1 shows the overall result of stability perception representing the means of the ratings of all four test situations for both (a) and (b) kinds of stability.

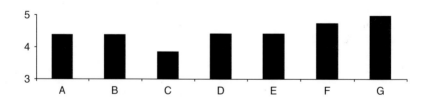

Figure 1. Stability perception – overall result (ANOVA: P < 0.01).

Figures 2 and 3 show stability perceptions with regard to solely foot-to-shoe interaction and solely shoe-to-ground interaction based on the means of all four test situations.

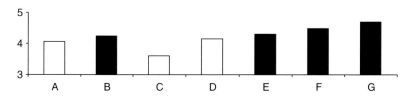

Figure 2. Stability perception – foot to shoe (ANOVA: P < 0.05).

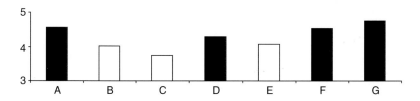

Figure 3. Stability perception – shoe to ground (ANOVA: P < 0.01).

The stability perception rating of shoe to ground places all four non-elliptic outsole construction shoes higher than all three elliptic outsole construction shoes.

The four field test situations revealed different discriminatory power with regard to statistical significance of their corresponding ANOVA. The most discriminatory results were received by the power kick situation followed by the sudden movement parcourse. Less discriminatory were the game-like situation and the slalom parcourse.

The biomechanical laboratory test (II) revealed positive correlations between peak pressure at the lateral forefoot and supination velocity versus stability perception in the field as shown in Figures 4 and 5.

Furthermore, positive correlations were found for peak pressure at the medial forefoot (r = +0.65, n.s.), peak pressure rates at the medial forefoot (r = +0.67, n.s.) and the lateral forefoot (r = +0.80, P < 0.05), maximum supination (r = +0.71, n.s.) and the ratio of shear force/ vertical ground reaction force (r = +0.72, n.s.) versus stability perception in the field.

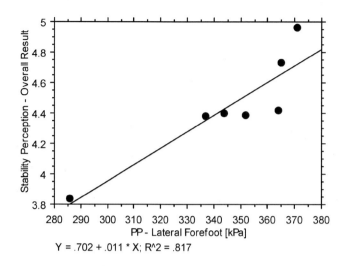

$Y = .702 + .011 * X; R^2 = .817$

Figure 4. Regression for peak pressure – lateral forefoot and stability perception – overall result (ANOVA: $P < 0.01$).

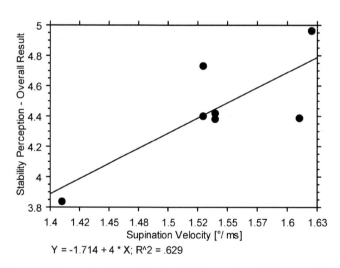

$Y = -1.714 + 4 * X; R^2 = .629$

Figure 5. Regression for supination velocity and stability perception – overall result (ANOVA: $P < 0.05$).

4. DISCUSSION

Field test situations that ask for standardized and more isolated movements like the power kick and the sudden movement parcourse are more suitable for recognizing stability properties of soccer shoes. In more complex situations the perceptual ability of subjects may be diminished by the multitude of impressions and motor task demands.

Soccer shoes showing non-elliptic outsole constructions achieve better stability properties especially with regard to stability referring to shoe-to-ground interaction. A tight, well shaped forefoot upper of the soccer shoe that prevents the foot from foot gliding inside the shoe was identified as a crucial factor for stability perception of soccer players. Thus higher medial and lateral forefoot peak pressures and pressure rates during soccer specific movements are evoked. Higher maximum supination excursion and higher supination velocities as well as higher ratios of shear force/ vertical force indicate a more dynamic performance of the cutting movement in shoes that are perceived to have better stability properties.

In conclusion, this means that biomechanical laboratory experiments help in predicting stability perception of soccer players in the field. The combined approach of perceptual and biomechanical tests provides a more systematic picture of the interaction of athlete and equipment than separate testing procedures. It allows a more strategic approach for increasing stability in soccer shoes.

An even more comprehensive understanding of stability in soccer shoe could be gained by additional appliance of mechanical testing and performance measurements, e.g. time measurements of players' performance.

Acknowledgement

This study was supported by Nike Inc., USA.

REFERENCES

Hennig, E. and Milani, T., 1994, Druckverteilungsanalysen in Sportschuhen. Medizinisch Orthopädische Technik, **114**(1), 22–25.

Lafortune, M., 2001, Measurement and interpretation of biomechanical, perceptual and mechanical variables. In Proceedings I Simpósio Brasilero de Biomecânica do Calçado, edited by Deyse Borges Machado. Gramado: pp. 17–19.

Lees, A., 1996, The biomechanics of soccer surfaces and equipment. In Science and Soccer, edited by Reilly,T. (London: E & FN Spon), pp.137–150.

Milani, T., Schnabel, G., and Hennig, E., 1995, Rear foot motion and pressure distribution patterns during running in shoes with varus and valgus wedges. *Journal of Applied Biomechanics,* **11,** 177–187.

Rodano, R., Cova, P. and Vigano, R., 1988, Designing a football boot: A theoretical and experimental approach. In Science and Football, edited by Reilly, T., Lees, A., Davids, K. and Murphy, W.J. (London: E & FN Spon), pp. 416–425.

7 A Study of Gender Difference in Football

H. Kanno and T. Asai
Faculty of Education, Yamagata Univ., Yamagata, 990-8560, Japan

1. INTRODUCTION

The number of female soccer players in the world has gradually increased. In women's football (soccer), the technique of heading the ball is one of the most basic and important techniques. Ordinarily, the body weight and muscle strength of a female are lower than that of a male. However, the ball weight used in women's football is the same as that of men's football. Some investigators have reported studies of ball heading (Burslem and Lees, 1988; Schneider and Zernicke, 1988; Reed et al., 2002), but the stress distribution at ball impact and the influence of low body weight on women and young players are still not clear. The purposes of this study are to discuss the gender (sex) difference based on physical properties and biomechanical characteristics, and to analyze the risk of the ball heading technique in women's soccer using a biomechanical approach.

2. METHODS

As a theoretical study, the peak force and the impulse during contact with the ball and the head of a player were estimated using the impulse equation (eq.1) and the triangular impulse model (eq.2): -

$$Ft = mv0 - mv1 \tag{1}$$
$$Ft = SH / 2 \tag{2}$$

where, Ft is the impulse at impact, m is mass of the soccer ball, $v0$ is the ball velocity before impact, $v1$ is the ball velocity after impact, S is the contact time at impact and H is the peak force. In this study, the ball weight, the weight of the head, contact time and the ball velocity were assumed to be 0.45 kg, 4.8 kg, 0.01 s and 15 m.s^{-1}, respectively.

The basic head and neck skeletal shape was determined using human model data (Total Human Model for Safety; Toyota Central Research and Development Lab., Inc.) and modified using MSC/PATRAN (MSC.Software Corp.). The skull, neck, brain and surface of the ball model were described by the Lagrangian frame of reference, and discretized by the finite element method (Fig. 1). The skin, muscle, ligament, fat, meninges (dura mater, arachnoid, pia mater) and cerebrospinal fluid (CSF) were not defined in this study.

The air inside the ball was described by a Eulerian frame of reference and discretized by the finite volume method: -

$$P = (\gamma-1) \rho E \tag{3}$$

where E is the specific internal energy, P is the pressure, ρ is the overall material density and γ is the ideal gas ratio of the specific heats.

Hexahedron solid elements were used for the skull and neck while shell elements were used for the surface of the ball. The air inside the ball was defined by the gamma law equation of state (eq. 3). The diameter of the ball model was 0.23 m, and the mass of the ball was 4.5 kg.

The number of elements for the skull and neck model was 7229 elements and there were 255 elements for the surface of the ball. The material properties of the heading model of this study are shown in Table 1 (Aomura et al., 2002).

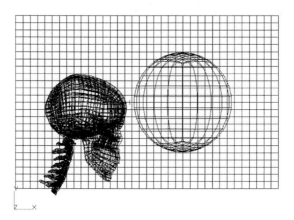

Figure 1. The finite element ball heading model.

The head and neck joint of the human body has a very complex structure, which consists of bones, muscles, ligaments and so on. The material properties of the hard tissue and soft tissue also have complex characteristics and a high non-linearity. In this study, however, a simplified material properties model was used which was represented by the isotropic, linear, elastic material as a first order analysis.

Table 1. The material properties of the heading model.

	Young's modulus	Poisson's ratio	Density (dummy) $(kg.m^{-3})$
Cervical vertebra	11 GPa	0.3	2986.2
Intervertebral disc	11 GPa	0.3	1493.1
Skull	8350 MPa	0.4	2174.0
Brain	1300 MPa	0.4	2174.0
Ball shell	70 MPa	0.3	549.44

The total mass of the base head and neck model in this study was 4.8 kg (base mass model). As an initial condition of impact, the horizontal velocity of the head and neck was 0 m.s^{-1} and that of the ball was −6.65 m.s^{-1} for the validity check. For the general parameter analysis, the velocity of the head and neck was 5 m.s^{-1} and that of the ball was −10 m.s^{-1}. The simulation was carried out for the mass of the head and neck between 100% to 50% at intervals of 10%. In this study, MSC/Dytran (MSC Software Corp.), an explicit integral solver, was used as the solver in each simulation. The MSC/Patran Software (MSC Software Corp.) was used for the pre- and post data processing. The calculation time of each simulation was about 16 hours using a PC (NEC Express 5800).

3. RESULTS AND DISCUSSION

A previous study reported that the mean of the isokinetic strength (quadriceps) of female athletes was 76.7% (BW) and that of male athletes was 82.3% (Huston and Wojtys, 1996). It was estimated that the muscle strength around the neck of women soccer players is lower than that of male counterparts.

Based on eqs. 1 and 2, it is assumed that the peak force is about 1350 N when the impact ball speed is 15 m.s^{-1} during heading in soccer. It is also estimated that the head weight of an adult woman is about 4.8 kg based on 8 percent (Ae and Hujii, 2002) of the body weight (60 kg). Therefore, it is assumed that the maximum acceleration in this case is about 281.3 m.s^{-2} (28.7 g). It seems that the real reduced mass during heading indicates a much higher value than 4.8 kg because the head is connected to the body by the neck. It is then estimated that the real acceleration at impact is less than 28.7 g (Schneider and Zernicke, 1988). The head injury criteria (HIC) value of this result was about 4.2, thus this result is not in the danger zone based on HIC (>1000; threshold for concussion). However, this HIC is concerned with only a single impact, therefore it is considered that further study regarding a repeatable stress head injury is necessary (Mertz et al., 1996). An example of the stress contours on the deformed shape of the skull and the ball (base mass model) during impact at intervals of 4 ms is shown in Figure 2. A high intensity stress is observed on the contact face (frontal skull) and the neck (1st and 2nd cervical vertebra). The stress on the contact face was about 2.0 MPa at 3 ms after impact.

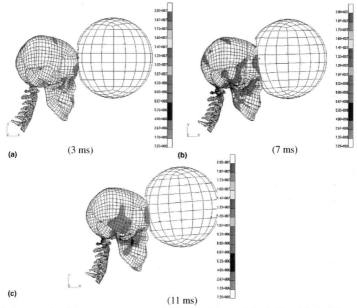

(a) (3 ms) (b) (7 ms)

(c) (11 ms)

Figure 2. An example of the stress contours on the deformed shape of the skull and the ball (base mass model) during impact at intervals of 4 ms.

The peak horizontal acceleration of the frontal node on the skull in this study was 35 g (gravity) at the ball velocity before impact of 6.65 m.s[1], that of the parietal node was 54 g and that of occipital node was 37 g (Fig. 3).

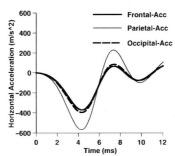

Figure 3. The peak horizontal acceleration of the frontal node on the skull at the ball velocity before impact of 6.65 m.s[1].

In a prior experimental study using a size 4 soccer ball for an adolescent football player, the mean peak linear, horizontal cranial acceleration subsequent to ball impact (6.7 m.s[1]) was 3.7 ±1.3 g (range, 1.7 8.8 g) (Reed et al., 2002). Based on the impact duration and greatest peak linear acceleration observed, this would result in a head injury criteria (HIC) score of 61. Schneider and Zernicker (1988) reported that the peak linear head acceleration registered for a soccer player during a real heading action was about 20 g for a ball velocity before impact of 6.65 m.s[1].

The peak horizontal acceleration of the frontal node on the skull in this study indicated 35 g, and it was about 1.75 times greater than that of the prior experiment

(20 g). This result may have been caused by at least two factors. First, the head and neck model in this study has no soft tissue of skin, fat, and muscle, etc., on the skull. Secondary, the damping factor of the material properties in this analysis model was only slight. It is considered that these factors increase the peak horizontal acceleration of the skull during impact. Therefore, the peak horizontal acceleration in this study requires a correction of a 57% decrease for the data matching the experimental data.

The peak horizontal accelerations of the frontal node on the skull in this study from the case of 100% (base model) to the case of 50% model are shown in Figure 4. The peak horizontal accelerations of the frontal node increased as the mass of the head and neck system decreased.

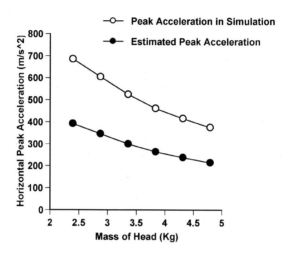

Figure 4. The peak horizontal accelerations of the frontal node on the skull in this study from the case of 100% (base model) to the case of 50% model.

Generally, the mass of the head and neck of a female is less than that of a male, thus the risk of head injury during ball heading by a female player is greater than that of a male player. However, the head injury criteria (HIC) value in the case of 100% (base model) was 8.2, and that in the case of 50% was 66.3.

These results suggest that there is a low head injury risk during ball heading (single impact) for a female player and a male player on the boundary conditions in this study. This HIC is concerned only with a head injury from a single impact; therefore, it is necessary to investigate neck injuries such as cranial whiplashes.

In the case of a single impact, it seems that both female and male players should prevent retinal haemorrhage and retinal detachment by direct grove (eye) impact. Furthermore, it is considered that the tolerance to repeated impacts may be quite different from that of a single impact. The effect of repeated stress injuries to the head in football players is one of the most important subjects for a future study.

4. CONCLUSION

In conclusion, generally the mass of the head and neck of a fe
of a male, thus the risk of head injury during ball heading b
greater than that of a male player. It is suggested that there is
injury during ball heading (single impact) for a female player an
the boundary conditions in this study. This HIC is concerned
injury from a single impact; therefore, it is necessary to investig
such as cranial whiplashes. Furthermore, it is considered that ...erance to
repeated impacts may be quite different from that of a single impact. The effect of
repeated stress injuries to the head in football players is one of the most important
subjects for a future study.

Acknowledgement

We would like to thank the Toyota Central Research and Development Lab., Inc., and Wayne State Univ. for providing the digital human dummy.

REFERENCES

Ae, M. and Hujii N., 2002, Sports biomechanics 20 lectures, Asakura syoten, pp. 40–43.

Aomura, S., Ida, T., Ikoma, T. and Fujiwara S., 2002, 3D finite element analysis of mechanism of cerebral contusion caused by external impact. *The 13th JSME Autumn Bioengineering Conference and Seminar*, JSME, pp. 133–134.

Burslem, I. and Lees, A., 1988, Quantification of impact accelerations of the head during the heading of a football. In *Science and Football*, edited by Reilly T., Lees, A., Davids, K. and Murphy, W.J. (London: E and FN Spon), pp. 243–248.

Huston, L. J. and Wojtys E. M., 1996, Neuromuscular performance characteristics in elite female athletes. *American Journal of Sports Medicine*, **24**, 427–436.

Mertz, H. J., Prasad, P. and Nusholtz G., 1996, Head injury risk assessment based on 15 ms HIC and peak head acceleration criteria. *AGARD Conference Proceedings*, **597**, pp. 1–9.

Reed, F., Feldman, K. W., Weiss A. H. and Tencer A. F., 2002, Does soccer ball heading cause retinal bleeding? *Archives of Pediatric and Adolescent Medicine,* **156**, 337–340.

Schneider, K. and Zernicke, R. F., 1988, Computer simulation of head impact: estimation of head injury risk during soccer heading. *International Journal of Sports Biomechanics*, **4**, 358–371.

An Integrated Analytical Model for the Qualitative Assessment of Kicking Effectiveness in Football

Pascual Marques-Bruna[1], Adrian Lees[2] and Mark Scott[2]
[1]School of Sciences and Sport, Edge Hill College, Ormskirk, UK
[2]Research Institute for Sport and Exercise Sciences, Liverpool John Moores University, Liverpool, UK

1. INTRODUCTION

A number of methods exist for the qualitative analysis of movement in sport (e.g. Hay and Reid, 1982; McPherson, 1990; Lees, 1999), which ultimately aim to help identify the effectiveness of performance of a sports skill. Some methods involve movement simplification by using phase analysis and others the identification of the mechanical factors affecting performance. Most methods encourage the search for critical features. A critical feature can be defined as an observable component of the movement that is essential for optimal or maximal performance (McPherson, 1990). However, very few studies have provided any sort of guidance as to how to select the critical features that are directly related to performance.

In football, effective kicking requires the player to approach the stationary ball with submaximal speed, and produce a long last step that allows opening out of the hip, flexion of the kicking knee and planting the support foot by the ball. These actions can be identified as critical features since they reflect underlying mechanical principles of movement and can therefore be used to judge the effectiveness of the kicking skill qualitatively (Bunn, 1972; Lees, 1999). No previous attempt has been made to integrate phase analysis and mechanical models to select important variables that may be used to establish the effectiveness of a skill.

Therefore, the objective of this study was to develop a systematic qualitative model that may be used for the analysis of mechanical effectiveness of a fundamental sports movement in children, namely the football kick for maximum distance.

2. DEVELOPMENT OF THE MODEL

The model was developed by integration of existing models and strategies for the analysis of movement in sport, and consisted of the eight stages described below. The model is based on observation of the maximum distance of a football kick recorded on video (side view) using a playback rate of 50 Hz. A simplified version of the complete model, showing the stage-by-stage analytical process from criterion measure identification to final score of kicking effectiveness, is presented in Figure 1. The eight stages were as follows:-

1. **Identification of the performance criterion**; that is, the range of the projected ball.

2. **a - Simplification of the kicking movement using the phase approach.** The four phases into which the kicking movement was divided were:- approach, back swing, swing and follow through. In addition, the instants of foot plant and ball contact were identified as critical instants.
   b - Parallel construction of a deterministic mechanical model specific for the football kick for maximum distance. The deterministic model was based on a generalised deterministic mechanical model developed by Hay and Reid (1982) and modified by McPherson (1990) to include technique variables.

3. **a - Identification of critical features.** Such identification was carried out using a combination of review of literature and notational video analysis of the kicking movement of professional football players.
   b - Parallel identification of important technique and performance variables. This was carried out using the deductive process of the deterministic model.

4. **Association between critical features and the mechanical (technique and performance) variables utilizing, where appropriate, mechanical principles of movement.** This process was guided by inductive reasoning in order to link a critical feature, and the associated mechanical variables, to explicit mechanical principles. This association provides the rationale for the variables chosen for inclusion in the analysis.

5. **Assessment of the contribution of critical features to kicking effectiveness.** Mechanical effectiveness of variables was classified simply as either 'negligible' or 'significant'. This process terminated with the selection of 15 technique variables (those used to describe either body posture or the direction and range of movement in a spatial framework) and 4 performance variables (consisting of magnitudes for velocity and force in a spatio-temporal framework) (see Table 1).

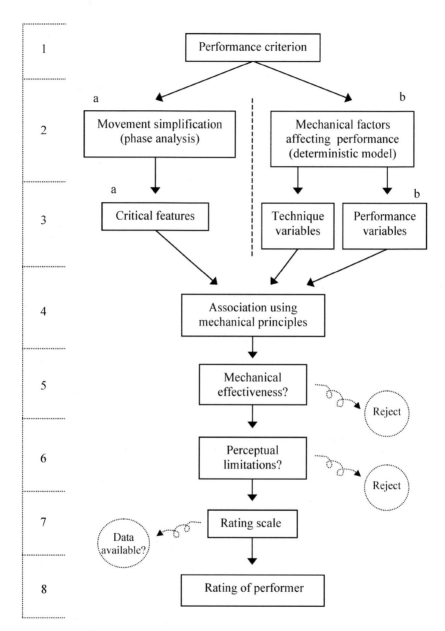

Figure 1. Simplified analytical model for the analysis of mechanical effectiveness of the maximum distance of a football kick in children.

6. **Evaluation of observer limitations regarding visual perception and the measurement of variables using video.** This involved assessing the accuracy and reliability of visually estimated kinematic quantities. The visual cues that help estimate kinetic quantities were identified (based on McPherson, 1990). Further, some variables were easily measured using standard SI units, such as degrees or metres. In contrast, other variables (e.g. velocities and force application) were best measured using categorical descriptors, such as 'slow', 'fast' or 'very fast'.

7. **Development of a scoring reference for the subjective analysis of kicking effectiveness in football.** The scoring reference consisted of rating scales for each of the 19 technique and performance variables selected for the analysis. An extract from the scoring reference appears in Table 2. The rating scales use carefully selected inter-score intervals of measures based on expected visual accuracy to discriminate between five levels of mechanical effectiveness (0–4).

8. **Rating of the child's kicking effectiveness.** The scoring reference allows scores to be obtained both per variable and by phase of the movement for a detailed analysis of the child's kicking action. A total score can be finally obtained which represents the kicking effectiveness of the child.

Table 1. The 19 kinematic and kinetic variables selected for the analysis.

Phase or instant	Variable	Type of variable	Phase or instant	Variable	Type of variable
Approach phase	Approach speed	performance	Swing phase	Shoulder adduction	technique
	Approach angle	technique		Shoulder adduction velocity	performance
Back swing phase	Last step length	technique		Forward trunk flexion	technique
	Shoulder abduction	technique		Applied forces	performance
	Knee flexion	technique	Ball contact instant	Kicking knee angle	technique
	Hip retraction	technique		Contact time	technique
Foot plant instant	Foot placement	technique	Follow through phase	Ball speed	performance
	Back trunk inclination	technique		Takeoff angle	technique
	Lateral body inclination	technique		Knee flexion & elevation	technique
			General	Coordination & rhythm	technique

Table 2. Extract from the scoring reference for the analysis of the football kick.

Movement phase	Technique / performance variable	Scores				
		0	1	2	3	4
Back swing	Angle of knee flexion (180^0 = full extension)	$>130^0$	$130–110^0$	$110–90^0$	$90–70^0$	$<70^0$
Follow through	Ball speed		very low	low	high	very high

3. IMPLEMENTATION OF THE MODEL

The kicking effectiveness of a group of 187 physically active children (106 males and 81 females), and of 31 adults who were used as controls, is shown in Figure 2. The Spearman's rho coefficients between scores of mechanical effectiveness and age of the children were -0.020 and 0.426* for knee flexion and 0.317* and 0.340* for ball speed, for males and females, respectively (* = significant; $P<0.05$).

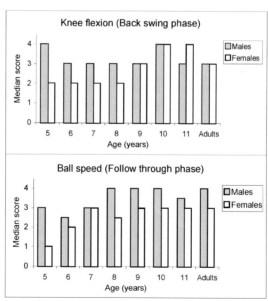

Figure 2. Median score for kicking effectiveness for selected variables.

4. DISCUSSION

The main feature of the model is the fact that it is an integrated tool that includes selected aspects from other well-established analytical models (e.g. Hay and Reid, 1982; McPherson, 1990). Further, it added other features such as association between critical features and mechanical variables using appropriate mechanical principles of movement, assessment of the accuracy and reliability of estimated kinematic quantities from video, and qualitative descriptors for the rating of relatively complex biomechanical parameters. Despite the complexity of the process involved in its development, the model allowed for the creation of a 'user-friendly' scoring reference specific for the football kick that included rating scales and diagrams to guide the analyst (see Table 2).

However, a number of limitations were identified when developing and using the model. The most important drawback was the fact that the model is limited to subjective quantification. Further, at the time of presentation of the model, no conclusive findings as to the accuracy of visually estimated measures were obtained and no real assessment of objectivity or inter-rater agreement was carried out. The scoring reference presented is limited to a specific population, that is children aged between 5–11 years, and the analysis can only detect 'gross' within-subject change and between-subject differences in mechanical effectiveness. Finally, the model can be adapted for the analysis of other football skills such as the short pass, heading the ball and the ball throw in.

5. CONCLUSION

A model for the qualitative analysis of the maximum distance football kick in children has been developed that integrates existing models of movement analysis and allows assessment of mechanical effectiveness, patterns of motor development, and gender differences in the maximum distance football kick.

REFERENCES

Bunn, J.W., 1972, Scientific Principles of Coaching, 2nd edition. (Englewood Cliffs, New Jersey: Prentice Hall).

Hay, J.G. and Reid, J.G., 1982, The Anatomical and Mechanical Bases of Human Motion. (Englewood Cliffs, New Jersey: Prentice Hall).

Lees, A., 1999, Technique analysis: Performance measurement. (Leeds, UK: *The National Coaching Foundation)*.

McPherson, M.N. 1990, A systematic approach to skill analysis. *Sports Science Periodical on Research and Technology in Sport,* **11**(1), 1–10.

9 The Three-Dimensional Nature of the Maximal Instep Kick in Soccer

Adrian Lees[1], Liam Kershaw[1] and Felipe Moura[2]
[1]Research Institute for Sport and Exercise Sciences, Liverpool John Moores University, Liverpool, L3 2ET, UK
[2]Department of Physical Education, UNESP, Rio Claro, Brazil

1. INTRODUCTION

The maximal instep soccer kick has received much attention in the literature (Lees and Nolan, 1998) and still is the most widely studied skill in soccer. Most information available from this skill is from two-dimensional (2D) studies, but over the past decade an increasing number of 3D studies have been undertaken. It is apparent from these that the motion of the kicking leg is influenced by the rotations of the pelvis, trunk and upper body. Very few of these studies have attempted to investigate the characteristics of pelvis, trunk and shoulder motions which influence the motion of the kicking leg. Where they have, they have been limited by a small number of subjects and trials used. This is not surprising given that 3D analysis is extremely time consuming. Consequently there is need for a more extensive study on the variables representing the 3D characteristics of kicking.

Recent advances in motion analysis have enabled 3D data to be collected automatically when performing a skill like a soccer kick. This has meant that data from more subjects and trials can be collected and more detailed 3D information obtained. However, there are some limitations to this method particularly in relation to marker placement and the ecological validity of a skill performed in an artificial (indoor) environment. Nevertheless, the prospect of rapidly collecting and processing large numbers of trials means that these methods are likely to become more commonplace in the future. Consequently there is a need investigate how suitable automatic motion analysis systems are for the analysis of kicking skill technique.

Therefore, the purpose of this investigation was (a) to quantify the 3D kinematic characteristics of the kicking leg, trunk and upper body during the maximal instep soccer kick using an opto-electronic motion analysis system; (b) to investigate the relationship between measured variables within the context of a model of kicking; and (c) to evaluate the suitability of automatic motion analysis for the collection of data on this skill.

2. METHODS

Eight experienced male soccer players (mean age=20.6 years; height=1.799 m; mass=72.8 kg) were each asked to perform 5 maximal instep kicks of a stationary soccer ball into a netted goalmouth using a self determined approach distance and angle, so as to represent a typical penalty kick.

The 3D locations of 16 reflective markers placed on the player's joints that defined a 12-segment biomechanical model were obtained using a six-camera Pro Reflex automatic motion analysis system (Qualysis, Savedalen, Sweden) located in an indoor laboratory. The 3D co-ordinates were sampled at 240 Hz for 6 s and digitally filtered with a Butterworth 4th order zero lag low pass filter (cut-off frequency 15 Hz, selected on the basis of a residual analysis and visual inspection of the data). From these data, lower limb and trunk kinematic variables were quantified using specially written software. Ball speed was measured by a JUGS radar gun (model PSK-DSP, Decatur Electronics Inc, Illinois, USA).

The variables chosen for the analysis were those typically reported in previous studies but with the addition of angular variables representing the orientation of the pelvis, shoulders and trunk. The 3D coordinates of the three markers defining the ankle joint were used to calculate the joint angle in the plane of the three markers. The same procedure was used for the angles at the knee and hip joints. The hip and shoulder lines were defined by the markers placed on the hip and shoulder joints respectively, while the trunk was defined as the line joining the mid point between the two hip markers and the C7 marker. The joint reference systems used were as follows:- at full extension, the hip, knee and ankle joint angles were at 180°; extension angular velocities were positive; trunk angles were measured to the vertical and were positive in the sagittal plane (front-back tilt) when leaning backwards and positive in the frontal plane (left-right tilt) when leaning away from the kicking foot and towards the support foot; the hip and shoulder lines were zero in the transverse plane (rotation) when facing forward in the direction of the kick (i.e. the line is perpendicular to the direction of the kick) and negative when retracted rearwards on the kicking leg side; in the frontal plane (left-right tilt) they were zero when horizontal and negative when below the horizontal on the kicking side. The hip-shoulder (H-S) separation angle was negative when the hips were rotated further backwards than the shoulders, and the hip-shoulder inclination was positive when the hips were angled upwards more than the shoulders. Ranges of motion (ROM) were measured from the peak value produced during the initiation of the kick to the value at impact.

For each variable, the mean for each participant was used to calculate the group mean and group standard deviation, while the standard deviation for each player was used to calculate the mean individual standard deviation. The latter value represents the expected degree of variability of repeated trials for an individual. Variables were further investigated with regard to their inter-relationships in relation to a model of kicking using correlation analysis. Statistical analyses were conducted using a software package (SPSS for Windows, Chicago, USA) and a level of $P<0.05$ was used to indicate significance.

3. RESULTS

All joints showed temporal patterning of velocity peaks in a classical proximal-to-distal sequencing except for the toes, which peaked slightly before the ankle. This was due to the plantar flexion of the foot in preparation for impact. Group mean data are given in Table 1 for selected linear kinematic variables. The data in Table 2 represent the values of selected angular kinematic variables. The data in Table 3 represent the ranges of motion of selected variables from their initiation, minimum or maximum value (as appropriate) until impact.

Correlations between relevant variables were obtained. Correlation values were significant if greater than 0.4 which included a Bonferonni adjustment for multiple use of data sets. Ball speed correlated best with approach speed (0.659), peak hip (0.652) and knee (0.703) speeds, hip ROM (0.518) and the length of last stride (0.419) but less well with peak toe speed (0.352). It did not correlate with the impact speed of the toes and ankle, nor with the angular ROM at the ankle, knee and H-S separation. The hip ROM correlated with the peak speeds of the knee (0.710) and toes (0.506) and less well with the hip (0.357) and ankle (0.386). However, the H-S separation angular ROM and knee ROM did not correlate with the peak speeds of the hip, knee, ankle and toes. These data provide some evidence that there is a link between the approach, motion around the hip, and knee speed. These are also sufficiently important determinants of kick performance to have a direct relationship with ball speed. However, there appears to be some complex actions occurring at the knee and ankle which means that further expected relationships with ankle, toe and ball velocity are absent.

Table 1. Mean (±SD) linear kinematic descriptors of the maximal instep kick.

	Group mean	Group SD	Individual SD
Approach speed (m.s^{-1})	3.7	0.58	0.23
Ball speed (m.s^{-1})	24.7	2.47	1.27
Ball/toe speed ratio	1.57	0.18	0.16
Maximum joint speed (m.s^{-1})			
Hip	4.9	0.63	0.25
Knee	9.8	1.16	0.44
Ankle	16.3	1.27	1.27
Toe (5th metatarsal)	19.5	1.91	1.50
Joint speed at impact (m.s^{-1})			
Hip	2.6	0.37	0.27
Knee	3.3	0.73	0.52
Ankle	14.3	1.63	1.84
Toe (5th metatarsal)	16.1	2.01	2.16

Table 2. Mean (±SD) angular kinematic descriptors of the maximal instep kick at impact.

	Group mean	Group SD	Individual SD
Angle at impact (deg)			
Knee	136.0	12.6	4.6
Hip (thigh-trunk)	146.8	16.6	6.2
Trunk front-back tilt	3.5	12.1	5.1
Trunk left-right tilt	−2.8	4.7	4.0
Pelvic rotation	−5.9	8.9	3.4
Shoulder rotation	−21.9	11.8	5.0
Pelvic left-right tilt	−5.5	4.3	4.4
Shoulder left-right tilt	−9.1	8.7	4.1
Maximum joint angular velocity (rad.s^{-1})			
Ankle plantar flexion	−20.1	9.5	14.7
Knee extension	28.8	3.7	4.1
Hip extension	−11.7	7.8	1.1
Angular velocity at impact (rad.s^{-1})			
Ankle plantar flexion	1.2	4.1	12.0
Knee extension	23.7	5.1	5.4
Hip extension	−1.2	1.9	1.4

Table 3. Mean (±SD) ranges of motion (ROM) for the maximal instep. Units are degrees unless otherwise stated.

	Group mean	Group SD	Individual SD
Length of last stride (m)	1.73	0.15	0.05
Ankle ROM	33.8	12.9	20.2
Knee ROM	62.8	14.2	7.0
Hip(thigh-trunk) ROM	55.6	13.9	4.3
Pelvis rotation ROM	35.5	10.8	8.9
Shoulder rotation ROM	−15.2	3.6	3.6
H-S separation at peak	−27.9	11.8	6.9
at impact	15.1	8.6	6.2
ROM	43.0	9.5	9.1
H-S inclination at peak	26.8	7.7	5.2
at impact	16.1	8.7	5.8
ROM	10.7	6.7	5.2

4. DISCUSSION

The first purpose of this study was to define selected 3D characteristics of the maximal instep kick. The kicks recorded were typical examples of a maximal instep kick as evidenced by the ball speed and appeared similar to that reported by Levanon and Dapena, (1998) and Lees and Nolan (2002). The joint speed increased proximally to distally from the hip to toes as expected, as did the timing of peak joint speed before impact which occurred earlier in the hip (0.16 s) and knee (0.079 s) and later in the toes (0.024 s) and ankle (0.021 s). The occurrence of peak ankle and toe speed before contact is generally considered to be the result of the smoothing routines used; the slightly earlier peak velocity of the toes compared to the ankle was thought to be due to plantar flexion of the ankle and/or external rotation of the foot just prior to impact. The knee and hip speed were higher in this study than for the professional players reported by Lees and Nolan (2002), suggesting that there may be some difference in technique between these two groups of players. The players in this study used a slightly higher approach speed with lower knee extension but achieved similar foot velocities to the professional players reported by Lees and Nolan (2002). The strategy used by the professionals would be beneficial in a real penalty situation as it would give less time for the goalkeeper to 'read' the kick.

These data illustrate that there are marked movements of the body in the 3rd dimension. It is commonly thought that the trunk has a backward and sideward (towards the support foot) tilt at impact and Lees and Nolan have reported this observation for the professional players. However, in this study the trunk on average was close to upright. Players were required to kick the ball towards a target placed at ground level while in the study of Lees and Nolan (2002) the target was elevated in the top right corner of the goal. If the backward and sideward lean of the trunk is related to the angle of projection of the ball, this would be another visual cue for goalkeepers to attend to when defending against a penalty kick.

The players in this study had an almost identical retraction of the pelvis (−41.4 ± 13.1 deg) to that reported by Levanon and Dapena (1998) on similar subjects, but was greater than that reported for the professionals (30.4 and 33.8 deg) in the study of Lees and Nolan. This in turn appears to lead to hip and knee speeds which are greater than shown by the professionals. However, the greater knee speed did not lead to greater foot speed, probably because of complex muscle actions at the knee joint. The variability in performance is much greater in the players of this study compared to the professionals reported by Lees and Nolan. For some players there was marked variability in some of the biomechanical variables between kicks.

A second purpose was to use the variables recorded to investigate a model of kicking which incorporated approach and upper body motion. The relationships between the variables described above relate to a model of the kick and the correlation analysis attempts to explore the validity of this. It appears that there are significant relationships between approach and the actions (ROM and speeds) around the hip and knee. The significant correlations which relate to the ball speed may be interpreted as key determinants of performance. There is no clear evidence that H-S separation or pelvic retraction is related to performance, expectations. The failure to obtain significant relationships with foot variables suggests that there is an important influence of act and ankle. The actions at the ankle are difficult to establish becal of marker drop-out for the toe marker of the kicking foot around some cases this compromised the data. Some subjects had a very ankle joint angle leading up to impact and a closer inspection revealed that on some kicks some players were dorsi-flexing their foot so as to perform a mixed style kick (somewhere between a full instep kick and a side foot kick). This type of contact has not been reported in the literature before and certainly the detailed nature of ball foot contact would be worthy of further study. This may also explain the rather high and variable ball-to-toe speed ratio.

A third purpose of the study was to establish whether opto-electronic methods are suitable for detailed investigations of the kicking skill. The system of data collection does appear to be robust and the general data seem to compare well with that reported in 3D studies which have used cine film. The variability of kinematic data obtained from the opto-electronic system has been established both for individuals repeating trials and also for a reasonably homogeneous group of skilled amateur players.

5. CONCLUSION

This study has provided normative data for the three-dimensional characteristics of the lower limb and trunk when performing a maximal instep soccer kick by skilled players. The general model of kicking is partially supported although the influence of upper body motion has not been established. The opto-electronic method appears to be robust and suitable for this type of investigation, with the exception of information around the kicking foot. This study has provided variability data which may help the planning of future studies which attempt to investigate more detailed aspects of the kicking skill.

REFERENCES

Lees, A. and Nolan, L., 1998, Biomechanics of soccer - a review. Journal of Sports Sciences, **16**, 211–234.

Lees, A. and Nolan, L., 2002, Three dimensional kinematic analysis of the instep kick under speed and accuracy conditions. In Science and Football IV, edited by Spinks, W., Reilly, T. and Murphy, A. (London: Routledge), pp. 16–21.

Levanon, J. and Dapena, J., 1998, Comparison of the kinematics of the full instep kick and pass kicks in soccer. Medicine and Science in Sports and Exercise, **30**, 917–927.

10 Comparison of Precision in the Toe and Instep Kick in Soccer at High Kicking Velocities

L.B. Kristensen, T. Bull Andersen and H. Sørensen
Department of Sport Science, University of Aarhus, Denmark

1. INTRODUCTION

Most skills required for success in soccer can be developed and learned by the player through practice, but the one technical action that could determine the outcome of a soccer match can often not be trained. These actions are performed by players who come up with a superb solution to the problem at hand: i.e. score a goal! It is therefore rarely possible to investigate these solutions during the game, because the technical skill used is a unique solution to a unique problem. Sometimes this can be done. The decisive skill of one of the semi-finals in the 2002 World Cup in the Brazil vs. Turkey match is such a solution. Here the Brazilian international Ronaldo secured Brazil's semi-final victory over Turkey with a toe kick.

Figure 1. Ronaldo scores against Turkey, FIFA World Cup 2002 (reproduced with permission of Scanpix, Copenhagen).

From a close distance between two defenders he surprised the Turkish keeper Rustu by placing the ball to his left and in the goal with the toe. This action surprised soccer-experts because the toe kick is categorized as a beginner's error and as not being very useful in soccer overall (Papagno, 2003). Likewise, a look through the soccer-coach literature apparently shows no training tips regarding this skill. So the question arises: "Is the toe kick an overlooked useful technical factor in modern soccer?"

To answer this question one must be especially aware of the biomechanical aspects of kicking. It is known that with no limitations on the run-up the instep kick is the optimal kick in terms of ball velocity (Lees, 1998) and it is also fairly precise (Peitersen, 1998). The first is due to the fact that the instep kick is an open kinetic link movement that has biomechanical advantages with pre-tension in the swing phase partly created by the run-up. While the instep has a large area the instep kick is much more precise than the toe kick in an unstressed movement (Huddleston and Huddleston, 2003). It is not obvious what happens with the precision of the two kicking types when the run-up movement is restricted – as in Ronaldo's case by the defenders – leaving the player with a shorter leg swing-phase.

This study was designed to investigate the precision of the toe kick compared to the instep kick at similar kicking velocities with movement restrictions.

2. METHODS

Eleven sub-elite soccer players served as subjects (18–28 years, 1.73–1.87 m, 63–87 kg, practice 4 times per week). The subjects were instructed to perform toe and instep kicks with the preferred kicking leg using a one step run-up at a grass turf. The ball velocities were measured with a set of ALGE double-beam photocells (ALGE-timing Ballspeed System, ALGE-timing GmBH, Lustenau, Austria). All subjects initially performed three maximal velocity kicks with instep and toe kick. After this each subject, in random order, twice performed 10 precision kicks at least 90% of the fastest velocity of the maximal kicks. Only trials with ball velocities at minimum 90% were accepted for further analysis. The subjects were instructed to hit a target 1.5 m wide, located 16 m in front of the subject (the penalty zone). On each side of this target two other 1.5 m wide zones were marked, and each trial was given a score according to which zone the ball hit. The ideal target gave the score 0, nearest zone a 1 and so forth. It was also noted to which side off-target hits were located.

No time limitations were applied and, besides the one-step run-up, there were no further technical demands for the kicks. For statisical analysis, paired Student T-tests were used.

Figure 2. A picture sequence of a toe-kick recorded during the experiment.

3. RESULTS

The results across the subjects are presented in Table 1. The statistical analysis showed that the maximal velocities of the two kicks were alike for each subject (P = 0.47). The kicking velocities for the toe and instep kicks at the 90% trials were also alike for each subject (P = 0.92). At 90% of the maximal velocity the instep kick was found significantly more precise than the toe kick (P = 0.01). As an additional result the trials also showed that the subject's shots off-target placed the ball to the outside of the kicking foot in the toe kick (P = 0.01) while there was no significant effect of side in the instep kick (P = 0.08).

Table 1. Results from the experiments.

	Maximal Velocity (m.s^{-1})	Velocity at 90% of max (m.s^{-1})	Precision Score at 90% of max Instep kick
Instep kick	23.38 [± 1.45]	21.11 [± 1.69]	0.91 [± 0.09]
Toe kick	22.99 [± 1.16]	21.13 [± 1.20]	1.24 [± 0.13]

4. DISCUSSION

It was expected that the trials would point out some advantages for the toe kick. We speculate that the precision of the instep kick would fall and the toe kick would catch up because the instep kick is naturally performed with, and possibly demands, a large swing-phase to have success. Since the lever arm is shorter in the toe kick, it could be speculated that the toe kick has no such demands. This study could not support these suggestions, perhaps due to the fact that no time limitations were introduced on the kicking. The swing phase of the instep kick may demand not only space but also time to have success. This time factor could be expected to have smaller influence on the toe kick.

5. CONCLUSION

It was found that the toe kick in soccer has no precision advantages compared to the instep kick with a one step run-up at a kicking distance of 16 m. On the contrary, at kicking velocities larger than 90% of maximum the instep kick was significantly more precise than the toe kick. Therefore, this study could find no advantages in using the toe kick when the kick is performed at the same kicking velocities with a one step run-up and no time limitations on completion of the kick.

REFERENCES

Huddleston, D. and Huddleston, K., 2003, www.soccerhelp.com.

Lees A. and Nolan, L., 1998, The biomechanics of soccer, A review. *Journal of Sports Sciences*, **16**, 211–233.

Papagno, B., 2003, www.eastonsoccer.com.

Peitersen, B., 1998, *Fodboldteknik – ungdomstræningens ABC*. (Systime: Herning, Denmark).

11 Coefficient of Restitution (COR) in Toe and Instep Soccer Kicks

T. Bull Andersen, L.B. Kristensen and H. Sørensen
Department of Sport Science, University of Aarhus, Denmark

1. INTRODUCTION

In all soccer kicks, the velocity of the ball after impact is determined by the velocity of the foot before impact, the effective striking mass of the foot and the coefficient of restitution (COR) of the impact (Plagenhoef, 1971, Bull Andersen et al., 1999). The COR in soccer kicking describes the transfer of velocity from the foot to the ball during the impact phase and is the ratio between the relative velocity (V_{ball}–V_{foot}) after impact and the relative velocity before impact. The factors determining the COR are the mechanical properties of the foot and ball, i.e. stiffness, contact area and contact point. Furthermore, the COR in two-dimensional analyses is affected by the direction of the path of the foot before impact and the path of the ball after impact.

The aim of the present study was to investigate the mechanical differences of the impact in soccer kicks with the toe and the instep in (a) a laboratory experiment designed to investigate the influence of different impact areas on the COR and (b) a kicking experiment where subjects performed toe and instep kicks at different velocities.

2. METHODS

2.1. Laboratory study (a)

A series of drop experiments (10 at each height, at each area) was performed in which, a soccer ball bounced off two different sized areas; these were a rod with a diameter of 0.03 m and a large plate attached at one end of the rod (Figure 1). The impact area was changed by turning the equipment (rod) upside down. The equipment was placed on top of a force plate, sampling the vertical force at 2000 Hz (AMTI OR5-6, AMTI, Watertown, MA, USA). Only trials where the ball bounced vertically were selected for further analysis.

The velocity before impact was calculated from the drop height and the velocity after impact was calculated by integration of the force signal divided by the weight of the ball. The COR was calculated as the ratio between the ball velocity before impact and the velocity after impact ($0 <$ COR < 1). The experiment was performed with drop heights of 0.36 m, 2.00 m and 3.60 m. The height of the bounce was verified by a video recording of the experiments. The COR in the two experiments was compared using a t-test with a 5% significance level (P<0.05). Figure 2 shows data from the force plate at drop heights of 0.36 m.

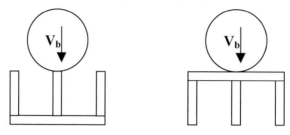

Figure 1. Model of the experimental setup in experiment (a).

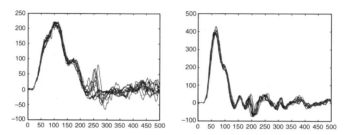

Figure 2. Data from the force plate, force versus time. Impact on small area (left) and large area (right). Note that the maximal force is approximately twice as large for impacts on the large area, and that the duration is only half as long.

2.2. Kicking experiment (b)

Six sub-elite soccer players (23-29 years, 1.73-1.87 m, 63-87 kg, practice 4 times per week) kicked 20 toe kicks and 20 instep kicks with no run-up in an indoor gymnasium. The subjects were instructed to change the execution time of the kicks ensuring a range of ball velocities after impact from 11.5 m·s^{-1} to 22.2 m·s^{-1} The kicks were high-speed filmed at 240 Hz (JVC DV 9700, JVC, USA) and the positions of the ankle joint, the head of the fifth metatarsal and the ball were digitized using APAS (Ariel Performance Analysis System, Ariel Dynamics Inc, CA, USA).

To determine the foot velocity before impact, a third order polynomial was fitted to the positions of the ankle and metatarsal during the last 15 frames before impact. The velocity of the foot just prior to impact was calculated as the average of the differentiated polynomials at the time of impact (the centre of mass of the foot (Winter, 1990)). The velocity of the ball was calculated as the average of the velocity during six frames after impact. The COR was calculated based on a standard formula adapted to soccer kicking experiments (Bull Andersen et al., 1999). The CORs were grouped (4 groups) according to the foot velocity before impact and the groups were compared using a two-way Analysis of Variance

(ANOVA) with a 5% significance level (P<0.05). A Tukey post-hoc test was used to isolate the groups that differed.

3. RESULTS

When the ball was bouncing off a small area, the COR was found to be significantly larger than bounces off a larger area (P<0.001). At drops from 0.36 m the COR was 0.91 (small area, SD=0.003) and 0.85 (large area, SD=0.004). At drops from 2 m the COR was 0.88 (small area, SD=0.006) and 0.83 (large area, SD=0.006) and at 3.6 m it was 0.86 (small area, SD=0.006) and 0.78 (large area, SD=0.008).

In the kicking experiments the COR was larger for the toe kicks when the kicks where performed with a foot velocity below 15 m·s^{-1} (corresponding ball velocity approximately 18 m·s^{-1}) (P<0.001) (Figure 3). For the instep kicks no influence of foot velocity was found but for the toe kick the COR was found to be larger for the kicks with the lowest foot velocity (11.9 m·s^{-1}) compared to the highest foot velocity (15.1 m·s^{-1}) (P=0.003).

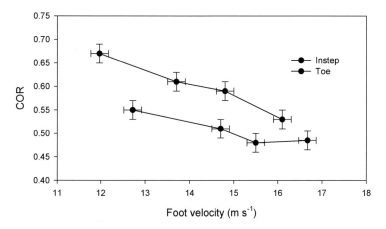

Figure 3. Coefficient of restitution at different foot velocities corresponding to the grouping into four groups. The error bars indicate the standard error of the mean (SEM).

4. DISCUSSION

The results showed that at lower impact velocities, the COR was larger when kicking with the toe. Based on the drop experiments, this phenomenon can (partly) be explained by the difference in contact area of the foot between the two kicks. However, the stiffness of the foot is not likely to be equal in the two kicks. Hence, we speculate that the reason that the impact area at larger velocities does not solely determine a difference in the COR is that the stiffness of the foot and ankle joint in the toe kicks is not large enough to keep the foot aligned during the toe-ball impact.

Based on the results from the present study it can be concluded that when kicking at low foot velocities, the ball velocity is higher when kicking with the toe. Correspondingly, if aiming at producing the highest possible ball velocity at a certain (low) foot velocity, it is advantageous to perform a toe kick.

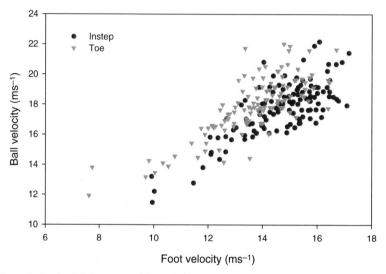

Figure 4. Graph of all the measured foot velocities and the corresponding ball velocities. It can be observed that at the lower foot velocities more velocity is transferred to the ball in the toe kicks.

5. CONCLUSION

It can be concluded that the impact area plays a significant role in determining the size of the coefficient of restitution. However, at foot velocities above approximately 15 m·s^{-1} this phenomenon is excluded, probably by the smaller stiffness of the foot when kicking with the toe. At low velocities more velocity is transferred to the ball when kicking with the toe rather than with the instep.

REFERENCES

Bull Andersen, T., Dörge, H.C. and Thomsen, F.I., 1999, Collisions in soccer kicking. *Sports Engineering*, **2**, 121–125.

Plagenhoef, S. 1971, *The Patterns of Human Motion*. (Englewood Cliffs NJ, USA: Prentice Hall).

Winter, DA. 1990, *Biomechanics and Motor Control of Human Movement, 2nd edn.* (New York, NY, USA: John Wiley & Sons).

12 Computer Simulation of Ball Kicking Using the Finite Element Skeletal Foot Model

T. Asai[1], H. Nunome[2], A. Maeda[3],
S. Matsubara[3] and M. Lake[4]
[1]Yamagata University, Yamagata, Japan
[2]Nagoya University, Nagoya, Japan
[3]Tohoku Gakuin University, Miyagi, Japan
[4]Liverpool John Moores University, Liverpool, UK

1. INTRODUCTION

Several investigators have studied the motion analysis of kicking in football (Plagenhoef, 1971; Cabri et al., 1988; Lees, 1996). However, there are only few studies of the interaction between the kicking foot and ball at impact (Asami and Nolte, 1983). The control of the initial conditions and the boundary conditions of the foot and ball at impact by an experimental approach is more difficult than that by a computational approach (Asai et al., 2002).

The purpose of this study is to clarify the relation between the stress distribution, the deformation and the impact point on the foot using a high-speed camera system and a finite element method.

2. METHODS

The impact process of kicking the ball was analyzed to obtain fundamental data for computer simulation using a high-speed video camera running at 4500 frames per second. The players kicked a ball with the instep towards a mini-football goal 4 m away. The high-speed video camera was set up 1.5 m away from the impact perpendicular to the motion of the ball.

The basic leg shape was constructed using a 3-D digitiser. The 3-D construction was meshed using MSC/PATRAN (MSC.Software Corporation) through an IGES file (Fig. 1-a). Young's modulus for the foot was 30 MPa (Asai *et al.*, 1996), Young's modulus of calf was 300 MPa and Poisson's ratio was 0.3 (Beaugonin and Haug, 1996).

The basic shape of the finite element skeletal foot-joint model was also described using a commercial foot skeletal model for computer graphics and anatomical data, and the solid model was defined after simplifying that model (Fig. 1-b). The hard tissue parts of this foot model consisted of 23 bone models such as the calcaneus, metatarsal, and so on, and the soft tissue parts that were modelled consisted of 15 joint models such as the talocalcaneal (subtalar) joint, calcaneocuboid joint, etc. (Fig. 2). Young's modulus of hard tissue parts was 15

GPa and Poisson's ratio was 0.3 (Furusu et al., 1999). Young's modulus of soft tissue parts was 1500 MPa and Poisson's ratio was 0.3 (Jacob et al., 1996).

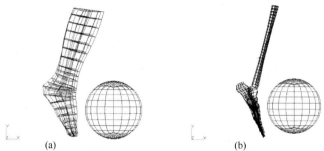

(a)   (b)

Figure 1. The finite element leg shape model (a) and the finite element skeletal foot joint model (b).

Foot skeletal model

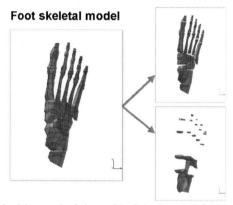

Figure 2. The hard tissue and soft tissue of the finite element skeletal foot joint model.

The ligaments and retinacula were not geometrically represented. Consequently, the stiffness of the soft tissue parts was estimated including the function of the ligaments and retinacula. The tibia was simplified and the fibula was omitted in this skeletal foot-joint model.

The kicking leg and the surface of the ball model were described by the Lagrangian frame of reference, and discretized by the finite element method. The air inside the ball was described with a Eulerian frame of reference and discretized by the finite volume method. During the analysis of the impact force, the initial speed in the horizontal direction (25 m.s^{-1}) was assumed for the entire part of the kicking leg in both models. The generation of spin depended upon the impact point of the foot on the ball in relation to the axis of the ball. This impact distance was set at 40 and 80 mm from the ball's axis and the simulation was carried out for coefficient of friction values between 0 and 1.0 at intervals of 0.2. Further simulations were carried out with a fixed coefficient of friction of 0.4 with impact distances from the axis of the ball −150 to +150 mm at intervals of 20 mm.

In the analysis of the ratio of restitution on the foot complex at impact using the finite element skeletal foot model, the impact point was defined from the axis of the ball −80 to +60 mm at intervals of 20 mm in the vertical direction. The ball velocity and the direction of the ball trajectory after impact were compared by each vertical offset distance.

3. RESULTS AND DISCUSSION

The horizontal velocities of the head of the metatarsal joint during impact for the finite element leg model and the experiment are shown in Fig. 3-a, and the base of the metatarsal for the finite element skeletal foot model and the experiment (barefoot) are shown in Fig. 3-b. The finite element leg model and the finite element skeletal foot model showed reasonable agreement with the experimental data. The ball deformed to 85% of its original diameter in the model compared to 86% experimentally. It was considered that the model matched the experimental data sufficiently enough to warrant use for further study.

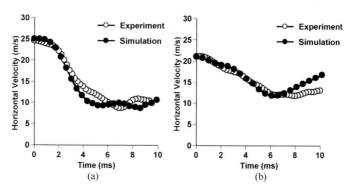

Figure 3. Comparison of the experimental data with calculated data.

The experimental results from the high-speed video camera showed that the mean of the contact distances was 0.147 m and the contact of the ball and instep was finished before the instep moved the same distance as the ball diameter (about 0.223 m). From the computer simulations using the finite element leg model, it was noted that even if the kinetic coefficient of friction is equal or nearly equal to 0, rotation of the ball occurs, though it is axiomatic that the spin of the ball increases with the increase in the kinetic coefficient of friction in both simulations. It seems that a large deformation appeared during the impact of the ball and that causes the rotation due to the impact force (Fig. 4-a). Overall, it is considered that the offset distance affects ball spin more than a coefficient of friction. It was suggested that the optimum offset distance is related to a trade-off between ball rotation and ball speed (Fig. 4-b).

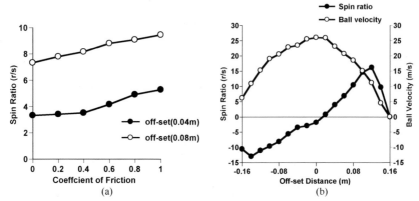

Figure 4. Relation between coefficient of friction and spin ratio (a) and relation between offset distance (horizontal), spin ratio and ball velocity (b).

Asami and Nolte (1983) reported the deformation at both the ankle and the metatarsal-phalangeal joint and found that the change in the angle at the metatarsal-phalangeal joint was significantly correlated with the ball velocity. This study concluded that the deformability of the foot should be reduced for powerful ball kicking and that this deformability was related to the deformation at the front of the foot. However, this study did not control the initial foot velocity before impact. Therefore, these results remained in the statistical analysis. It was considered that the control of the boundary condition for the computer simulation is easier than that for the experiment.

In the computer simulation using the "finite element skeletal foot" model, high intensity stress (about 50 MPa) was seen in the metatarsal, cuneiform, navicular and tibial bones at impact (Fig. 5). The ball velocity after impact with an offset distance of –20 mm was 33.4 m.s^{-1}, and that for the offset distance of +20 mm was 32.2 m.s^{-1} (Fig. 6). The maximum ball velocity after impact in this simulation was for the offset distance of –20 mm and –40 mm, while the minimum ball velocity was for the offset distance of +60 mm and –80 mm (Fig. 7-a). There was a tendency that the deformation of the foot joint in the lower impact case was greater than that of the higher impact case. It is suggested that the energy dispersion of the foot for the lower impact case is greater than that for the higher impact case.

The direction of the ball trajectory after impact (shot angle) in each case indicated a non-linear trend (Fig. 7-b). The maximum shot angle was 16 degrees for the offset distance of –20 mm. It seemed that the shot angle was influenced by the location and the deformation of the foot complex and the ball.

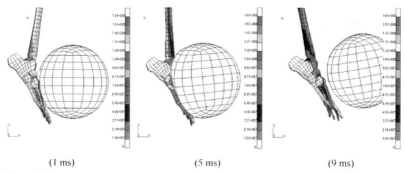

(1 ms)　　　　　　　　　　　(5 ms)　　　　　　　　　　　(9 ms)

Figure 5. The stress contours on the deformed shape during impact using the finite element skeletal foot model.

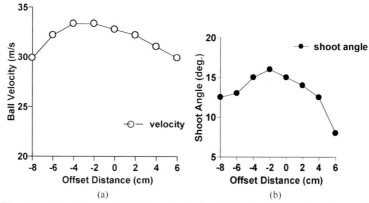

(−6 cm)　　　　　　　　　　(0 cm)　　　　　　　　　　(+6 cm)

Figure 6. The examples of deformed shape after impact in each offset distance (vertical).

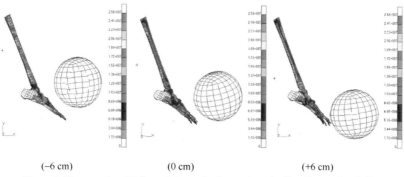

(a)　　　　　　　　　　　　　　　　(b)

Figure 7. Relation between offset distance (vertical) and ball velocity (a), relation between offset distance (vertical) and shot angle (b).

4. CONCLUSION

The purpose of this study was to clarify the relation between the stress distribution, the deformation and the impact point on the foot using a high-speed camera system and a finite element method. In the computer simulation using the finite element leg model, it was found that the offset distance affects ball spin more than the coefficient of friction. It is suggested that the optimum offset distance is related to a trade-off between ball rotation and ball speed. In the computer simulation using the finite element skeletal foot model, energy dispersion of the foot for the lower impact case is greater than that for the higher impact case. The maximum shot angle was 16 degrees for the offset distance of -20 mm. It seems that the shooting angle was influenced by the location and the deformation of the foot complex and the ball.

REFERENCES

Asai, T., Akatsuka, T. and Kamata, Y., 1996, Impact simulation of kicking using fluid and structure interaction analysis. In *Proceedings, XIV International Symposium on Biomechanics in Sports*, pp. 588–591.

Asai T., Carré M. J., Akatsuka, T. and Haake S. J., 2002, The curve kick of a football, I: impact with the ball. *Sports Engineering*, **5**, 183–192.

Asami, T. and Nolte, V., 1983, Analysis of powerful ball kicking. In *Biomechanics VIII-B,* edited by Matsui, H. and Kobayashi, K. (Champaign: Human Kinetics Publishers), pp. 695–700.

Beaugonin, M. and Haug, E., 1996, A numerical model of the human ankle/foot under impact loading in inversion and eversion. *Society of Automotive Engineers*, 962428, 239–249.

Cabri, J., De Proft, E., Dufour, W. and Clarys, J. P., 1988, The relation between muscle strength and kick performance. In *Science and Football* (edited by Reilly, T., Lees, A., Davids, K. and Murphy, W.J. (New York: E and FN Spon), pp. 186–193.

Furusu, K., Iwamoto, M., Miki, K., Kato, C. and Hasegawa, J., 1999, Development and validation of the finite element model of the human lower extremity for accidental injury. Proceedings of Japan Society of Automotive Engineers (JSAE), pp. 5–8.

Jacob, S., Patil, K. M., Braak, L. H. and Huson, A., 1996, Stresses in a 3D arch model of a normal human foot. Mechanics Research Communications, 23, 387–393.

Lees, A., 1996, Biomechanics applied to soccer skills. In *Science and Soccer,* edited by Reilly, T. (New York; E and FN Spon), pp. 123–133.

Plagenhoef, S., 1971, *Patterns of Human Motion.* (Englewood Cliffs, New Jersey: Prentice Hall), pp. 98–116.

13 A Characterisation of Technique in the Soccer Kick Using a Kohonen Neural Network Analysis

Adrian Lees and Gabor Barton
Research Institute for Sport and Exercise Sciences, Liverpool John
Moores University, Henry Cotton Campus, Webster Street,
Liverpool L3 2ET, UK

1. INTRODUCTION

Soccer skills are qualitatively assessed normally by viewing them in a holistic way and making judgements about the success or otherwise of the performance. The skilled observer is remarkably effective in being able to distinguish between levels of technical proficiency and to identify aspects of the skill which may benefit from improvement.

On the other hand, quantitative assessments are generally performed using biomechanical methods which provide data on a range of biomechanical variables but in contrast, the skilled biomechanist has great difficulty in using this information to make decisions about technical proficiency. Perhaps the main reason for this is that there are no defined criteria which link the numerous variables that can be quantified to performance *per se* for any given skill. Some models have been proposed to aid the biomechanist (see Lees, 2002 for a critical review) but each have their own shortcomings.

There is a need, then, to explore different ways in which quantitative biomechanical analysis can be used to comment on the technical proficiency of a skill. Alternative approaches may well embrace the holistic approach that seems to work so well for qualitative analysis. One such alternative approach is that which uses a neural network (NN) and represents a novel approach to the non-linear analysis of data sets. Neural networks have the ability to use all of the quantitative data presented to it and to 'organise' it in an appropriate way. Neural networks have been used for some time as methods for classifying objects (including movement types) based on a range of input data (which could be biomechanical data) and output categories (Barton and Lees, 1996). They draw relationships between input variables and output categories based on a system of non-linear weightings between input variable and output categories. Progress in applying these techniques to sport has been slow probably due to the conceptual complexity associated with the method and also the difficulty in obtaining sufficient data to enable a reasonable classification of movement.

In particular, the Kohonen NN is a specific form of NN which maps the multi-dimensional data space onto a two-dimensional (2D) plane thus reducing the data set but preserving certain characteristics of the skill. The NN can be used as a non-linear data reduction method which can be viewed in a planar graphical form. The resulting 2D 'picture' (Figure 1) is a representation of the underlying data. Locations on the planar surface are thought to be associated with characteristics of the movement (i.e. technique).

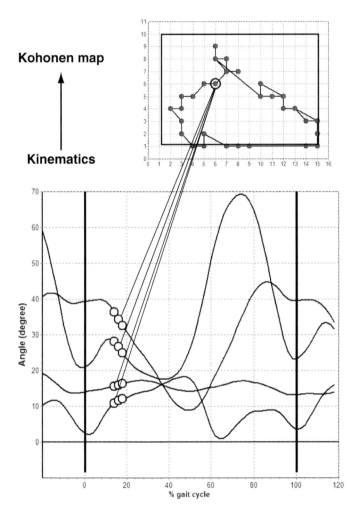

Figure 1. The Kohonen neural network which reduces input kinematic data to a planar topological map. All of the data at one instant in time reduces down to a point on the planar surface.

For any given technique the challenge is to identify areas on the surface with a particular characteristic of the movement. This has been applied with some success in the analysis of a soccer kick (Lees, 2002) where an individual performed a soccer kick with speed and accuracy as performance criteria. The two-dimensional pictures produced for each kick condition were distinctive and the modification of the kick to reflect the speed of movement was also apparent.

The purpose of this report was to extend the use of the Kohonen NN to a different and more detailed data set representing the soccer kick.

2. METHODS

Six experienced adult male soccer players were asked to perform several instep soccer kicks of a stationary soccer ball into a netted goalmouth using a self determined approach distance and angle and to hit a target with maximum speed.

The three-dimensional (3D) motion of reflective markers placed on the participant during each kick was obtained using a Pro Reflex automatic motion analysis system (Qualysis, Gothenburg, Sweden) located in an indoor laboratory. Six infrared cameras were used to obtain the 3D location of 16 spherical reflective markers which defined a 12-segment biomechanical model. The markers were placed on the side of the 5th metatarso-phalangeal joint, lateral malleoli, knee, hip, acromion process, elbow, and wrist on each side of the body and also one on the 7th cervical vertebra and one on a hat, which was placed on the participant's head. The data were sampled at 240 Hz for 6 s. The 3D co-ordinates were filtered digitally with a Butterworth 4th order zero lag low-pass filter (cut-off frequency 7 Hz) and joint angles were calculated in the plane of the three markers defining the appropriate joint angle. The joint angles entered into the analysis were left and right ankle, knee, hip (thigh-trunk), elbow and shoulder angles, together with the angles defining the orientation of the pelvis and shoulder in the transverse plane, and pelvis and shoulder tilt away from the transverse plane. These variables were chosen because they were thought to represent a reasonable definition of the general posture of the body during the kick. There is no restriction on the variables used for submission to the NN, and other variables including time related variables could equally well have been included. The joint angles from a total of 80 frames from take-off last stride to the end of the follow through of the kick (centred on the instant of ball contact) were used as input to the Kohonen NN. Various groups of data were presented to the NNs. The number of nodes and the shape of the NNs were determined by the dimensions and distribution of the data. First a NN was trained using all available data. Subsequently two NNs were trained by presenting data sets of right footed kicks and left footed kicks respectively.

3. RESULTS AND DISCUSSION

As the output was of a graphical nature, the 3 kicks from the 3 subjects who kicked with their right foot are presented below in Figure 2a while the kicks for the 3 subjects who kicked with their left foot are presented in Figure 2b.

The non-trivial problem of separating a right leg kick from a left leg kick on the basis of 3D joint kinematics was solved by the NN. The right leg kicks were mapped to the lower half and the left leg kicks to the upper half of the topological map. The two-dimensional curves were remarkably similar for repeated kicks for a specific subject and there are some clear differences among subjects too. The major difference among movement patterns was the sidedness and so this had the strongest influence on determining the shape of the resultant curves. In order to eliminate the effect of sidedness and to focus on the smaller details of the curves two separate NNs were trained with right legged and left legged kicks respectively. Figure 3 shows the resultant planar trajectories.

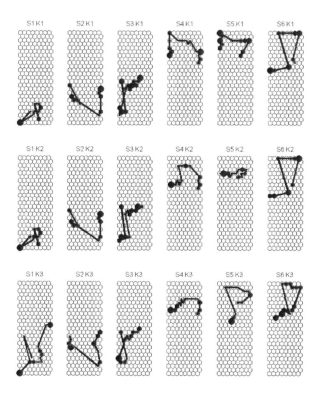

Figure 2. Two-dimensional reduction of kicks. The first three columns show right legged kicks (a) and the second group of three columns show left legged kicks (b).

The graphical output showed a characteristic shape that was assumed to be representative of the kicking skill. The projections were again remarkably similar for repeated kicks for a specific subject. In addition there were clear differences between individuals. As a result of learning, an experienced observer is able to judge the skill element of visually perceived movement patterns which the unskilled observer is unable to do. The trained NN is able to reduce the complex quantitative data into a simple curve through repeated exposure to the data. The learning process of a human expert and that of a NN are quite similar. The quality of the movement emerges from the quantitative data by processing the movement pattern through an intelligent algorithm (the human expert or an artificial neural network). It appears that neural networks may be suitable for the analysis of technique by visualising the movement in a way which puts emphasis on the skill. The method would enable unskilled observers to see the 'skill' element of movement patterns.

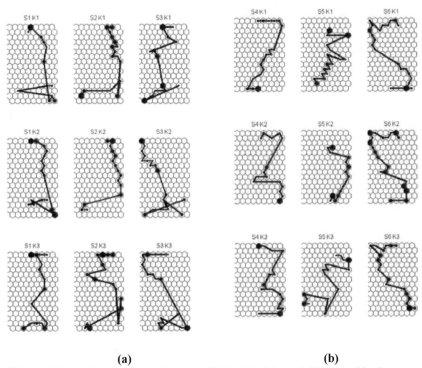

(a)   (b)

Figure 3. Two-dimensional reduction of kicks (3 trials each illustrated in the columns) for (a) subjects 1–3 (right footed) and (b) subjects 4–6 (left footed).

The regions on the each graph need to be associated with individual characteristics of performance and it is the shape of the graph in these general regions which will allow future qualitative assessments to be made. Detailed work defining these characteristics remains a challenge for the future.

4. CONCLUSION

It is concluded that the Kohonen NN is repeatable and sensitive to individual differences in performance and may provide an alternative method for characterising technique from quantitative data.

., 1996, An application of neural networks for
tterns on the basis of hip-knee angle diagrams. Gait and

que analysis in sports: A critical review. Journal of Sports
28.

14   A Biomechanical Analysis of the Soccer Throw-in with a Particular Focus on the Upper Limb Motion

Adrian Lees[1], Michael Kemp[1] and Felipe Moura[2]
[1]Research Institute for Sport and Exercise Sciences, Liverpool John Moores University, Liverpool, L3 2ET, UK
[2]Department of Physical Education, UNESP, Rio Claro, Brazil

1. INTRODUCTION

The throw-in is a method for restarting the game in soccer but can also be used tactically in attacking moves. Consequently throwing-in to achieve a high range is an important soccer skill. There has been little biomechanical investigation of this skill and the few studies (Chang, 1979; Levendusky et al., 1985; Messier and Brody, 1986; Kollath and Schwirtz, 1988) that have reported data on the throw-in have mainly reported ball release variables but none on upper body characteristics.

Chang (1979) investigated one player performing four types of throw-in (standing square i.e. with feet side by side, standing staggered i.e. with one foot in front of the other, run-up and handspring). A number of whole-body variables (height of centre of gravity, moment of inertia, angular momentum and vertical, horizontal and angular velocities) were reported but of most relevance was the data on ball release. Disregarding the handspring throw-in, which is not commonly used in contemporary soccer, the release velocities ranged from 14.63 to 15.21 m.s^{-1} and release angles from 21 to 45 degrees to the ground, with the best throw being the run-up throw-in. Levendusky et al. (1985) used 12 players to investigate the square and staggered standing throw-ins, but only reported data for the staggered throw-in. They reported a mean ball release speed of 18.3 m.s^{-1} and release angle of 29 degrees. They also identified that the throw-in followed a proximal-to-distal sequence of segment rotations from the trunk to the lower arm, and also reported data on arm motion with peak upper and lower arm angular velocities of 5.8 and 24.4 rad.s^{-1} respectively. Messier and Brody (1986) used 13 players to conduct a more detailed comparison of two types of throw-in (standing staggered and handspring). Again disregarding the handspring throw-in, the staggered throw-in produced a ball release velocity of 18.1 m.s^{-1} and release angle of 28 degrees to the ground. They also reported a proximal-to-distal motion of the upper body segments with mean angular velocity of the shoulder and elbow at release of –5.4 (i.e. slowing down) and 18.1 rad.s^{-1} respectively. These data cannot be directly compared to those reported by Levendusky et al. (1985) which were peak values for segments rather than the joints. Finally, Kollath and Schwirtz (1988) reported data from 26 trials of the square standing throw-in and 32 trials of the run-up throw-in (numbers of subjects not reported). The mean ball release velocities were

14.2 and 15.3 m.s^{-1} and release angles were 33 and 32 degrees, respectively. No angular kinematics were reported for the upper limb motion.

It can be seen from the above review of the relevant literature that it is generally agreed that the run-up throw-in is the better form of technique for players to use. While release data are well reported for the different throw-in techniques commonly used, there is great variation between studies and in particular little data on the kinematics of upper limb motion. Specifically, there are no data on the joint torques used at the shoulder and elbow which are prime muscle groups responsible for throw-in performance. Therefore the purpose of this investigation was to quantify the kinematic and kinetic characteristics of the upper body segments during two common types of the soccer throw-in.

2. METHODS

Ten male soccer players with experience of throwing-in (mean ± SD; age 22 ± 1.78 years; height 1.779 ± 0.059 m; mass 75.2 ± 6.1 kg) were each asked to perform maximal distance throw-ins using a single step into a staggered foot placement (5 repetitions) and a run-up (5 repetitions). The throws were conducted indoors in order to utilise an automatic motion capture system. Reflective markers were placed over the subject's joint centres which were used to define a 12-segment biomechanical model. The three-dimensional position of these markers were recorded by an opto-electronic motion analysis system (Qualysis, Savedalen, Sweden) at 240 Hz located in an indoor laboratory. The 3D co-ordinates were filtered digitally with a Butterworth 4th order zero lag low-pass filter (cut-off frequency 15 Hz, selected on the basis of a residual analysis and visual inspection of the data). From these data, upper limb joint kinematic and kinetic characteristics in the sagittal plane were calculated. Because no finger marker was used the wrist joint was assumed to be fixed throughout the throw. Mean data for each variable were compared using a paired t–test, unless the data were not normally distributed, in which case the Wilcoxen test (statistic W) was used. The level of significance set at P<0.05.

3. RESULTS

In both types of throw-in a proximal-to distal sequence of body segment rotations were observed. Data for the variables quantified are reported in Table 1.

The mean ball release velocity was similar to that reported by Chang (1979) and Kollath and Schwirtz, (1988) but lower than reported by the other studies. The angle of release was noticeably lower than that reported in other studies which was due to the fact that the throw-in was conducted indoors and the presence of the ceiling influenced release angle. Consequently the estimated range (computed from the release variables) was shorter than previously reported in the literature.

Table 1. Kinematic and kinetic data (mean ± SD) for the standing staggered and run-up throw. Data are mean of left and right limbs unless otherwise stated.

Variable statistic	Staggered	Run-up
Release velocity (m.s^{-1})	13.7 ± 0.83 t=6.88*	14.9 ± 0.81
Release angle (deg)	14.3 ± 3.12 t=1.34	12.6 ± 3.12
Release height (m)	1.71 ± 0.06 t=2.57*	1.68 ± 0.08
Estimated ball range (m)	13.6 ± 1.78 W=14.0	14.4 ± 1.51
Peak hip velocity (m.s^{-1})	1.57 ± 0.37 t=12.54*	2.85 ± 0.52
Peak shoulder velocity (m.s^{-1})	2.28 ± 0.20 t=7.44*	3.13 ± 0.46
Peak elbow velocity (m.s^{-1})	4.66 ± 0.66 t=3.36*	5.33 ± 0.39
Peak wrist velocity (m.s^{-1})	8.25 ± 0.78 t=6.21*	9.25 ± 0.84
Peak trunk angular velocity (rad.s^{-1})	4.90 ± 1.85 W=15.0	5.92 ± 3.11
Peak upper arm angular velocity (rad.s^{-1})	11.5 ± 1.7 t=6.27*	12.7 ± 1.2
Peak lower arm angular velocity (rad.s^{-1})	24.3 ± 2.3 t=6.33*	26.3 ± 2.43
Peak elbow angular velocity (rad.s^{-1})	17.7 ± 2.1 t=2.84*	18.5 ± 2.2
Peak shoulder retraction torque[#] (Nm)	−8.1 ± 6.9 t=3.49*	−13.6 ± 11.8
Peak shoulder propulsion torque[#] (Nm)	88.8 ± 21.1 t=4.61*	102.7 ± 21.2
Peak elbow retraction torque[#] (Nm)	−2.5 ± 3.6 t=2.76*	−4.6 ± 6.2
Peak elbow propulsion torque[#] (Nm)	37.7 ± 11.4 t=1.81	40.1 ± 11.1

* denotes P<0.05); [#] left and right limbs combined.

Nevertheless, because of release velocities similar to at least two other studies, the skill of the throw-in was judged similar to that which would be conducted in a game situation and this meant that the upper and lower arm segment kinematic and kinetic characteristics could be reported as typical values for this skill. In general, values were all greater for the run-up throw compared to the staggered throw, supporting the preferred use of this variant of the skill.

The joint torque profiles (for left and right limbs combined) are given in Figures 1A and 1B. These show that the accelerating torque about the shoulders dominates with a small proximal-to-distal sequence evident for the shoulder and elbow joints. A significant relationship was found between the shoulder retraction torque and propulsion torque for the run-up throw ($r = -0.539$, $P<0.001$, see Figure 2) but not for the staggered throw ($r = 0.235$, NS).

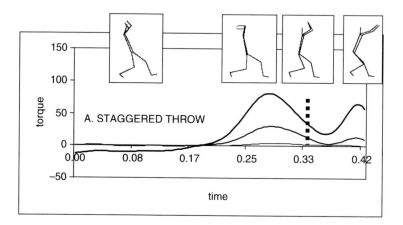

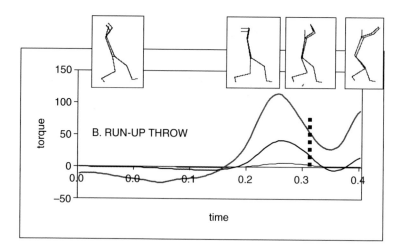

Figure 1. Joint torque at the shoulder (thick line), elbow (medium line) and wrist (thin line) for (A) the staggered throw-in and (B) the run-up throw-in. Note the greater (negative) retraction torque during the earlier stages of the run-up throw. The dashed line indicates release.

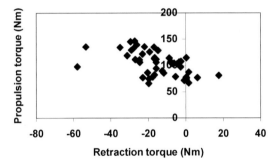

Figure 2. Scattergram of shoulder retraction torque vs. propulsion torque for the run-up throw illustrating the strong relationship ($r=-0.539$, $P<0.05$) between these two variables.

4. DISCUSSION

The velocities of release were similar to that found in other studies so it was assumed that these throws were typical of what players might perform outdoors. The sequence of segment rotations followed the proximal–to–distal sequence with ball release occurring before peak wrist velocity and just before the lower arm reached the vertical.

The velocity of ball release was 1.2 $m.s^{-1}$ greater in the run-up compared to the standing throw-in. This was similar to the speed difference of the hips, shoulder, elbow and wrist joints between the two types of throw. The angular velocities of the upper arm and the lower arm and elbow joint were greater in the run-up than the staggered throw as would be expected from the greater joint velocities, and were similar to those reported in the very little published literature available.

Joint torques for the upper limb during the throw-in have not been reported in the literature to date. The joint torques are greatest at the shoulder and lowest at the wrist. The values at the wrist are underestimates as it was assumed that the wrist was fixed as no distal hand segment marker was used. There will be some additional torque applied to accelerate the ball but this is thought to be small in comparison to the torques exerted at the shoulders and elbow. The torque at the shoulder and elbows will also be similarly underestimated. Some movement of the elbows occurs out of the sagittal plane and so there may be small contributions to actual muscle torque from these out of plane motions also leading to underestimates of actual joint torque. Nevertheless, the values calculated compare reasonably favourably to values reported for baseball pitching and American football passing of around 40 Nm at the elbow and 100 Nm at the shoulder (Fleisig et al., 1996).

It might be assumed that the superior performance in the run-up throw was due simply to the greater approach velocity as indicated by the speed of the hips, and the continuation of this speed to benefit the speed of the other joints. However, the proximal-to-distal sequence means that during the forward motion of one segment there is a backward motion of the other and so a greater velocity of one joint will lead to a greater *difference* in velocity between the two joints and thus a greater torque between them. This explains the enhanced performance of the run-up throw. The significantly greater retraction torque at the shoulder is strongly correlated with the following propulsive torque. It is likely that a 'stretch-shorten' cycle is occurring, where the muscles of the shoulders are forcibly stretched (due to the greater velocity difference between segments in the run-up throw) and then allowed to shorten rapidly. This action leads to an increase in the pre-loading of muscle and as a result, more work is done. The data presented here support the suggestion that such a mechanism is acting at the shoulder, although this does not appear to be acting at the elbow joint.

5. CONCLUSION

This study has provided normative data for the biomechanical characteristics of the upper limb when performing two types of throw-in skill. The run-up throw yields the better performance and confirms previous findings in the literature. It is concluded that the superior performance of the run-up throw is due to a more effective pre-loading of the shoulder muscles during the retraction phase and is evidenced by the significant correlation between retraction and propulsion torques at the shoulder.

REFERENCES

Chang, J., 1979, The biomechanical analysis of selected soccer throw-in techniques. *Asian Journal of Physical Education*, **2**(4), 254–260.

Fleisig, G.S., Escamilla, R. F., Andrews, J., Matsuo,T., Satterwhite, Y. and Barrentine, S. W., 1996, Kinematic and kinetic comparison between baseball pitching and football passing. *Journal of Applied Biomechanics*, **12**, 207–224.

Kollath, E. and Schwirtz, A., 1988, Biomechanical analysis of the soccer throw-in. In Science and Football edited by Reilly, T., Lees, A., Davids, K. and Murphy, W.J. (London: E. & F.N Spon), pp. 460–467.

Levendusky, T.A., Clinger, C.D., Miller, R.E. and Armstrong, C. W., 1985, Soccer throw-in kinematics, in Biomechanics in Sports II, edited by Terauds, J. and Barham, J.N. (California: Del Mar), pp. 258–268.

Messier, S. P. and Brody, M. A., 1986, Mechanics of translation and rotation during conventional and handspring soccer throw-ins. *International Journal of Sport Biomechanics*, **2**, 301–315.

15   A Three-Dimensional Analysis of Lineout Throwing in Rugby Union

M. Sayers

Centre for Sports Studies, University of Canberra, Australia

1. INTRODUCTION

Lineout possession is a critical aspect of modern Rugby Union. Prior to rule changes that allowed lifting, the lineout represented a competitive mechanism for returning the ball into play and turnovers in possession were frequent. In the years following the advent of lifting in the lineout, the team throwing the ball in won nearly all lineout possessions. The resultant possession "certainty" meant that many rugby commentators began to question the competitive role of the lineout in the game. However, rule changes and advances in the tactical and technical understanding of lineout play have reduced the advantages of the throwing team noticeably over the past four years. In order to increase uncertainty in the defensive side, teams now employ an unprecedented number of lineout alternatives, varying throw length, type and lifting options considerably both between and within matches. Accordingly, there is now increased pressure on the thrower (hooker) to deliver the ball accurately, as even small errors result in a loss of possession and/or team momentum.

Throws to the front of a rugby lineout travel typically 5–7 m, while throws to the back of the lineout travel approximately 15–18 m. The majority of lineout throws are caught around 3–3.5 m above the ground although this height varies according to the height of the jumper, and the stature and ability of the lifters. As a result, hookers must utilise a throwing technique that enables them to vary the length of throw without concurrent reductions in accuracy. The complex interactions between speed and accuracy (Etnyre, 1998) raise the possibility that a speed-accuracy paradigm exists in lineout throwing.

Despite the importance of the lineout in Rugby Union, biomechanical analyses of lineout throwing are reported infrequently. Indeed, despite numerous "coaching" articles being published by national rugby coaching bodies (for an example see Gregg, 2000), three-dimensional analyses of lineout throwing have not been presented in the scientific literature. Biomechanical analyses of the throwing actions from other football codes may provide some insights into lineout throwing technique, but such comparisons are limited. For example, a biomechanical analysis of the soccer throw-in has been reported by Kollath and Schwirtz (1988), but this research focussed on throws for maximum distance with no consideration to accuracy. Similarly, research on American football quarterback passing (Fleisig et al., 1996; Rash and Shapiro, 1996) will have limited application for lineout throwing, as the passing demands placed on a quarterback differ dramatically from those in rugby.

Therefore, the objectives of this study were (1) to quantify the three-dimensional kinematic lineout throwing characteristics of high performance hookers in Rugby Union and (2) to identify the changes in three-dimensional kinematic lineout throwing characteristics that occur as a result of throwing to the front, middle and back of the lineout.

2. METHODS

2.1. Subjects and procedures

Six international level hookers served as subjects. Each subject completed six throws over three marked distances (6 m – **short**, 10 m – **middle**, 15 m – **long**) to a "jumper" being held by two lifters. Subjects were given a traditional warm-up and several minutes of practice drills prior to data acquisition commencing. A throw was deemed successful if it was received by the "jumper" at the peak of the lift with his arms at full extension. The throw distances were randomised within and between all trials. Eighteen body, and two ball landmarks were marked with reflective tape prior to videoing. Data were collected using two Sony digital camcorders (DCR-TRV10E) operating at 50 Hz. Data were digitised and three-dimensional kinematic variables developed using APAS (Ariel Dynamics) video based motion analysis software incorporating standard DLT procedures.

2.2. Linear and joint kinematics

Absolute joint angular displacement data were calculated for the ankle, knee, hip, shoulder and elbow angles ($180°$ in full extension). Hip and shoulder orientation in the transverse plane was recorded so that $0°$ represented the segment perpendicular to the sagittal plane and facing forward (Lees and Nolan, 2002). Trunk angles were calculated with respect to the vertical. The standard convention of labelling joint extension as a positive angular velocity (recorded as $deg.s^{-1}$) was used throughout analyses of angular kinematic data. Linear displacement and velocity data for the centre of gravity (CofG) were calculated although only movements in the horizontal and vertical directions were used in this project. All maximum and minimum angular / linear displacement and velocity data were recorded from the point of throw initiation to ball release. Data post-release were not analysed in this project.

2.3. Statistics

One-way ANOVA (repeated measures) were used to compare each individual subject across each throw distance. Statistical comparisons between subjects have not been included in this project. All statistical analyses were performed using Statistica for Windows (version 5.1 – StatSoft, Tulsa, Okla., USA) software package. A significance level of $P < 0.05$ was used for all analyses. All data are presented as means ± SD unless stated otherwise.

3. RESULTS

Considerable visual differences existed in the throwing techniques of each subject and as such it was deemed that statistical comparisons would therefore add little value to a project of this nature (i.e. subjects may be achieving similar joint positions and/or velocities at different times during the throw). For example, Subject 1, a player who initiates the throw with a step forward will obviously achieve different lower limb angular kinematic data than Subject 4, a player who does not move the front of his foot throughout the throwing action (see Figure 1). The degree of inter-subject variability is also demonstrated by Figure 2, which presents the angular displacement of the shoulder at the end of the backswing for Subjects 3 and 5. Despite these two subjects achieving similar shoulder angles at release and peak shoulder flexion velocities during the propulsive phase of the movement, Subject 5 utilises a more extended backswing.

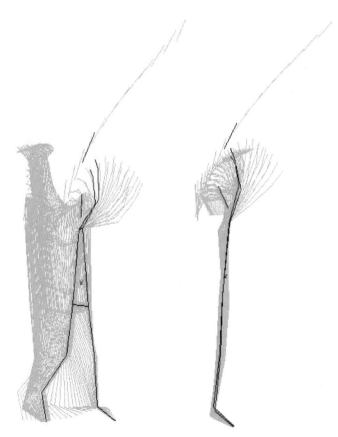

Figure 1. Sagittal plane representations of Subjects 1 and 4.

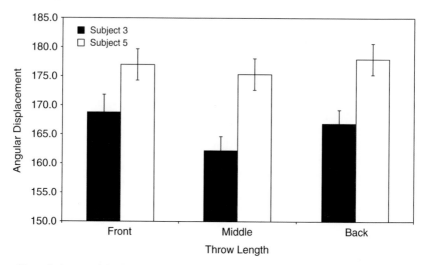

Figure 2. Amount of shoulder extension present at the end of the backswing for Subjects 3 and 5.

Table 1 indicates that ball release velocities were similar between subjects across each distance with release velocity for the throw to the back of the lineout being significantly greater than the release velocities for the throws to the middle and front. Release velocities for throws to the middle and front of the lineout were not significantly different for any subjects. Table 2 represents the peak linear resultant velocities of the centre of gravity in the horizontal and vertical planes. Data show a similar trend to that reported in Table 1, with greater linear velocities present for throws to the back of the lineout. Tables 3 and 4 show the peak angular velocity data for selected angular kinematic variables for Subjects 1 and 4, respectively. Results show a clear trend towards an increased lower limb involvement for increased throw distance (front compared to back), despite minimal changes in upper body kinematics. The trends for the remaining subjects were similar to those reported by these two subjects.

Table 1. Ball release velocities ($m \cdot s^{-1}$) for each subject across each distance (mean ±SD).

Subject	Front	Middle	Back
1	8.98 (0.57)	9.47 (0.18)	11.11 (0.27)[α]
2	9.06 (0.47)	9.56 (0.20)	10.90 (0.25)[α]
3	9.01 (0.50)	9.46 (0.22)	10.93 (0.23)[α]
4	8.63 (0.61)	9.00 (0.32)	10.59 (0.29)[α]
5	8.94 (0.58)	9.63 (0.27)	11.31 (0.28)[α]
6	8.85 (0.55)	9.45 (0.21)	10.91 (0.26)[α]

[α] indicates sample significantly different from the other two samples (P<0.001).

Table 2. Peak resultant linear velocities (m·s^{-1}) of the CofG (expressed as the vector resolution in the horizontal and vertical planes) for each subject across each distance (mean ±SD).

Subject	Front	Middle	Back
1	0.86 (0.09)	1.10 (0.05)	1.27 (0.26)$^{\alpha}$
2	0.94 (0.07)	1.05 (0.07)	1.29 (0.25)$^{\alpha}$
3	0.88 (0.09)	0.93 (0.09)	1.93 (0.23)$^{\alpha}$
4	0.31 (0.09)	0.46 (0.08)	0.79 (0.13)$^{\alpha}$
5	0.99 (0.06)	1.09 (0.10)	1.31 (0.28)$^{\alpha}$
6	0.34 (0.08)	0.41 (0.10)	0.81 (0.26)$^{\alpha}$

$^{\alpha}$ indicates sample significantly different from the other two samples (P<0.05).

Table 3. Mean (±SD) angular kinematic descriptors for Subject 1 across each distance.

Variable	Front	Middle	Back
Plantar Flexion*	83 (28)	188 (17)$^{\alpha}$	234 (17)$^{\alpha,\beta}$
Knee Extension*	34 (12)	33 (17)$^{+}$	88 (7)$^{\alpha,\beta}$
Hip Extension*	108 (31)	112 (24)	162 (30)
Shoulder Flexion	90 (46)	68 (41)	69 (25)
Elbow Extension	739 (54)	766 (67)	788 (54)

* indicates an effect for throw distance for that variable (P<0.05);
$^{+}$ indicates Middle significantly different from Front (P<0.05);
$^{\alpha}$ indicates Back significantly different from Front (P<0.05);
$^{\beta}$ indicates Back significantly different from Front (P<0.05).

Table 4. Mean (±SD) angular kinematic descriptors for Subject 4 across each distance.

Variable	Front	Middle	Back
Plantar Flexion *	91 (33)	120 (17)	330 (34) $^{\alpha,\beta}$
Knee Extension *	43 (10)	64 (16)	100 (11) $^{\alpha,\beta}$
Hip Extension	86 (31)	105 (24)	132 (30)
Shoulder Flexion	144 (38)	152 (34)	158 (27)
Elbow Extension	804 (64)	832 (77)	902 (79)

* indicates an effect for throw distance for that variable (P<0.05);
$^{+}$ indicates Middle significantly different from Front (P<0.05);
$^{\alpha}$ indicates Back significantly different from Front (P<0.05);
$^{\beta}$ indicates Back significantly different from Front (P<0.05).

Regardless of the throwing technique adopted by each subject, each hooker tended to exhibit a classical lower limb to upper limb force summation. However, the timing of the individual segmental contributions of the lower limb tended to vary with increasing throw distances (see Figure 3).

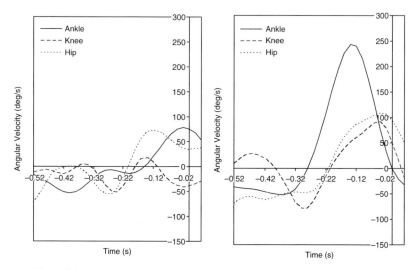

Figure 3. Lower limb angular velocity versus time graphs for Subject 1 throwing to the front (left) and back (right) of the lineout.

4. DISCUSSION

Mean maximum ball release velocities in this study are lower than those reported for a soccer throw for distance by Kollath and Schwirtz (1988), and considerably slower than those reported for American football quarterback passing (Fleisig et al., 1996; Rash and Shapiro, 1996). It is reasonable to assume that throwing to the back of the lineout did not require the subjects used in this project to throw at maximum velocity. Therefore, these data can not be compared to research where throwing range and/or velocity were the primary focus for the subjects. Rather than treating the lineout throwing as a maximum power event where the focus is on optimal proximal to distal sequencing, the primary concern of the lineout throw is accuracy. The latter is especially relevant when throwing to the front of the lineout where throw distance is short.

It is interesting to note that the release velocities present for throws to the front of the lineout in this study are more indicative of those present in accuracy based sports such as basketball (Miller and Bartlett, 1996). For example, Miller and Bartlett (1996) have presented release velocities for basketball jump shots from a distance similar to that used when throwing to the front of the lineout in rugby as ranging from 7.36 (±1.28) m·s^{-1} to 8.39 (±0.49) m·s^{-1}. Accordingly, a lineout throwing model should be based more on reliability/reproducibility of movement patterns than on absolute force production.

The differences in the throwing techniques adopted by the elite subjects used in this study, while confounding the presentation of results, provide an interesting example of the individualisation of sporting technique. A common flaw in the "coaching" literature concerns the over-emphasis of conformity to a specific lineout throwing model. While certain aspects of the throw appear important for performance, it is essential that hookers adopt a technique that is reproducible regardless of distance thrown. It is also worth noting that many of the factors suggested in the "coaching" literature as being important for throwing proficiency (Gregg, 2000) do not appear to be linked to effective performance by the subjects used in this project.

It is interesting to note that in most cases the relative magnitude of the SD of the individual subject data tended to be greater in throws to the front of the lineout than to the back. The speed-accuracy paradigm suggests that lower velocity movements (throws to the front of the lineout) would be more repeatable than the higher velocity movements present in longer throws. Such a phenomenon is difficult to explain, but may occur as a result of players using a variety of techniques for throws to the front of the lineout due to the "easy" nature of throws over this short distance. Certainly, a practice such as this would need to be monitored as intra-throw variability would not be expected to be related to consistent throwing performance (Etnyre, 1998).

Of great interest in this research are the methods adopted by the players to increase release velocity for throws to the middle and back of the lineout. In research on basketball (Miller and Bartlett, 1996) it has been suggested that players increase ball release velocity by increasing the angular velocities of both shoulder flexion and elbow extension. This phenomenon was not observed in the elite rugby hookers studied in this project. Without exception each player tended to increase throwing distance (in particular when comparing throws to the front with those to the back of the lineout) by increasing the involvement of the lower limb considerably. Increased lower limb involvement with throw distance is then linked to an increased translational velocity of the centre of gravity for throws to the back of the lineout. The latter finding is in agreement with that reported by Millar and Bartlett (1996) who showed an increase in the velocity of the centre of mass at release for basketball shots of increasing distance.

There are several advantages in utilising the lineout throwing techniques adopted by the hookers in this project. First, by increasing the involvement of the lower limb for throws of increasing velocity, hookers can minimise the changes in upper limb kinematics across all throws. The advantages of such a system are obvious, as the reproducibility of the vital upper limb kinematics appears to be enhanced. It is also prudent to note that the importance of the classic lower limb to upper limb force summation appears to diminish in throws of short distance. Finally, the adoption of a throwing technique that allows throws to the back of the lineout to be delivered at submaximal release velocities has the advantage of shifting the speed-accuracy paradigm to the right. Such a change has positive effects in enhancing lineout throwing proficiency.

5. CONCLUSION

While certain kinematic characteristics appear to be linked to lineout throwing proficiency, findings indicate that elite rugby hookers should be allowed to develop individual nuances in their throwing techniques that enable them to reproduce the action reliably. A "one technique" approach is inappropriate. The key to throwing for greater distances (i.e. to the back of the lineout) appears to be linked to the greater involvement of the lower limb, while the segmental contribution of the upper limb tends to remain relatively constant across all distances. Lineout throws of short distance are determined primarily by throwing accuracy; as a result the importance of the classic lower limb to upper limb force summation needs to be addressed with reference to sports where the accuracy component of the speed-accuracy paradigm predominates.

REFERENCES

Etnyre, B.R., 1998, Accuracy characteristics of throwing as a result of maximum force effort. *Perceptual and Motor Skills*, **86**, 1211–1217.

Fleisig, G.S., Escamilla, R.F., Andrews, J.R., Matsuo, T., Satterwhite, Y. and Barrentine, S.W., 1996, Kinematic and kinetic comparison between baseball pitching and football passing. *Journal of Applied Biomechanics*, **12**, 207–224.

Gregg, M., 2000, A biomechanical analysis of the line-out throw. *RFU Journal*, Spring, 20–22.

Kollath, E. and Schwirtz, A., 1988, Biomechanics of the soccer throw-in. In *Science and Football*, edited by Reilly, T., Lees, A., Davids, K. and Murphy, W.J. (London: E & FN Spon), pp. 460–467.

Lees, A. and Nolan, L., 2002, Three-dimensional kinematic analysis of the instep kick under speed and accuracy conditions. In *Science and Football IV*, edited by Spinks, W., Reilly, T. and Murphy, A. (London: Routledge), pp. 16–21.

Miller, S. and Bartlett, R., 1996, The relationship between basketball shooting kinematics, distance and playing position. *Journal of Sports Sciences*, **14**, 243–253.

Rash, G.S. and Shapiro, R., 1996, A three-dimensional dynamic analysis of the quarterback's throwing motion in American football. *Journal of Applied Biomechanics*, **11**, 443–459.

Part III

Fitness Test Profiles of Footballers

16 Validity of a Submaximal Running Test to Evaluate Aerobic Fitness Changes in Soccer Players

F.M. Impellizzeri[1], P. Mognoni[2], A. Sassi[1] and E. Rampinini[1]
[1]Physiology Lab, SSMAPEI, Italy
[2]Istituto Bioimmagini e Fisiologia Molecolare, Consiglio Nazionale Ricerca, Milano, Italy

1. INTRODUCTION

Aerobic fitness seems to be important for soccer players. Some studies have shown a relationship between aerobic capacity and ranking, team level and distance covered during the match (Smaros, 1980; Apor, 1988; Wisløff et al., 1998). Recently, Helgerud et al. (2001) have also shown that aerobic training can improve some soccer performance characteristics such as distance covered during a match, high intensity phases, number of sprints and involvements with the ball. For these reasons, training programmes commonly include aerobic conditioning. To control the effectiveness of training stimuli in improving aerobic capacity, several classical laboratory tests ($VO_{2\,max}$ test with determination of ventilatory or lactate anaerobic thresholds) and/or field measures like shuttle run tests (Yo-Yo test, Leger test, etc.) can be used. However, all these assessments require maximal effort and, consequently, motivation can strongly influence tests results and they are sometimes not well accepted by soccer players especially during the season or close to important matches.

A group of Italian researchers (Sirtori et al., 1993) proposed a submaximal field test to evaluate the aerobic capacity of soccer players. This field test, commonly called Mognoni's test from one of the co-authors' names, has been used by several Italian soccer teams at all levels (from professional to amateur teams) for the last 10 years. This test was based on the study of Jacobs et al. (1983) in which a significant correlation between lactate threshold and [La⁻] at the end of a single step of 6-min cycling at 200 W was found. Following a similar procedure, Sirtori et al. (1993) determined a regression equation from the correlation between [La⁻] at the end of a single 6-min run and OBLA (4 mmol·l⁻¹) (r = -0.94). Therefore, they suggested using the OBLA velocity estimation to evaluate aerobic fitness changes. Apart from the original study of Sirtori et al. (1993), there are no other data about the validity or reliability of this test. Its adoption was probably mainly due to the submaximal nature of the test, quick execution (40 min for 20 players) and, thus, good acceptance by athletes and coaches. In our view, the estimation of OBLA is not necessary but the use of [La-] at the end of the 6-min run ([La⁻]$_{FIELD}$) could itself be a useful index of aerobic changes. Furthermore, it seems that there is an increasing interest in submaximal testing, probably due to the actual difficulties in proposing maximal evaluations to soccer players. For example, Krustrup et al. (2003) have recently proposed a submaximal version of the Yo-Yo intermittent recovery test using heart rate (HR) and [La⁻] measured at the sixth minute of the test.

Thus, the aim of this study was to verify the validity of this widespread (in Italy) submaximal field test determining (a) the relationship between laboratory lactate thresholds and $[La^-]_{FIELD}$; and (b) the relationship between training induced changes in lactate thresholds and training induced changes of $[La^-]_{FIELD}$. Moreover, seasonal variations in this test for a group of professional soccer players and preliminary reliability data were determined.

2. METHODS

2.1. Validity study

Sixteen junior soccer players were involved in the study [mean and standard deviation: age 17.5 (0.6) years, body mass 70 (5.0) kg, height 1.79 (0.048) m, $\dot{V}O_{2 max}$ (best of two tests) 57.0 (3.5) ml·kg⁻¹·min⁻¹]. They were tested before (T1) and after (T2) 8 weeks of training both in the laboratory and in the field (within one week).

Laboratory test

The protocol used during the laboratory incremental treadmill test was that suggested and used by Helgerud et al. (2001): 1 km·h⁻¹ increment every 5 min, using a treadmill inclination of 3%. The $\dot{V}O_{2 max}$, OBLA (4 mmol·l⁻¹ fixed lactate threshold) and Tlac (1.5 mmol·l⁻¹ above baseline) were determined. Respiratory gases were analyzed breath by breath using a VMAX29 system (Sensormedics, Yorba Linda, CA), while lactate measurements were done using electroenzymatic technique (YSI® 1500 Sport, Yellow Springs Instruments, OH).

Field test

Submaximal running tests were performed on a track (400 m). Athletes ran for 6 min at a constant speed of 13.5 km·h⁻¹. Velocity was controlled by players using a sound signal. When these signals were emitted they had to be close to the cones placed on the track every 50 m. At the end of the 6-min run blood samples were collected and immediately analyzed by the same lactate analyzer used in the laboratory.

2.2. Seasonal variations

Seasonal changes of $[La^-]_{FIELD}$ were determined in a group of 21 professional soccer players [mean and standard deviation: age 26.3 (5.1) years, body mass 77 (7.8) kg, height 1.81 (0.07) m]. They were tested 4 times: July (before pre-competition training period), September (beginning of the season), December and March (during the season). Lactate measurements were done using a portable lactate analyzer system (Lactate Pro, Arkray, Japan). Heart rate (HR) during the field test was recorded using telemetric HR monitors (VantageNV, Polar, Finland).

2.3. Reliability

Thirteen semi-professional soccer players were recruited to determine the reliability of this test [mean and standard deviation: age 23.3 (3.4) years, body mass 73 (4.9) kg, height 1.78 (0.048) m]. They performed the field test twice within a week.

2.4. Statistical analysis

Pearson' s product moment correlation coefficients were used to determine (a) the relationship between laboratory lactate thresholds and $[La^-]_{FIELD}$, and (b) the relationship between training induced changes of lactate thresholds and training induced changes of $[La^-]_{FIELD}$. Seasonal variations were analyzed using ANOVA for repeated measures and Tukey's post hoc test. Reliability was determined using the Bland and Altman plot (Bland and Altman, 1986). Furthermore, typical error was determined as CV and ICC (Hopkins, 2000a; 2000b).

3. RESULTS

No difference was found between average laboratory results ($\dot{V}O_{2max}$, Tlac, OBLA) before and after training. Similarly, average team $[La^-]_{FIELD}$ before and after training was not different. Significant correlations were found between lactate thresholds and $[La^-]_{FIELD}$ both during the first and the second test sessions (Table 1). Significant correlations were also found between training induced changes of velocity at lactate thresholds and training induced changes of $[La-]_{FIELD}$ (Table 2). Correlations between training induced changes of $\dot{V}O_2$ at lactate thresholds and training induced changes of $[La-]_{FIELD}$ did not reach statistical significance ($0.05 < P < 0.1$).

Table 1. Correlations (r) between lactate threshold lab and $[La^-]_{FIELD}$ in T1 and T2.

	Velocity at OBLA	$\dot{V}O_2$ at OBLA	Velocity at LT	$\dot{V}O_2$ at LT
T1 - $[La-]_{FIELD}$	– 0.62 *	– 0.68 **	– 0.64 **	– 0.68 **
T2 - $[La-]_{FIELD}$	– 0.74 **	– 0.83 ***	– 0.76 **	– 0.83 ***

* P < 0.05; ** P < 0.01; *** P < 0.001.

Table 2. Correlations (r) between training induced changes of lactate thresholds and of $[La-]_{FIELD}$.

	% changes of $[La-]_{FIELD}$
% changes of OBLA velocity	– 0.54 *
% changes LT velocity	– 0.60 *

* P < 0.05.

During the season $[La^-]_{FIELD}$ results were significantly lower than the pre-season values. No differences were found in season (Figure 1).

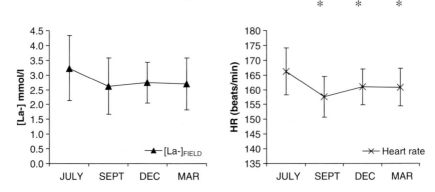

Figure 1. Seasonal variations of $[La^-]_{FIELD}$ and HR at the end of submax field test.
* P < 0.05, statistically different from JULY.

Bland and Altman scatterplots (Figure 2) showed no bias (0.01 mmol·l⁻¹) and a total error within ± 0.75 mmol·l⁻¹ (95% confidence interval). Reliability expressed as typical error as CV was 9.6%. From CV values the individual minimal detectable change (MDC) was calculated multiplying CV by 1.5 Z-score (Hopkins, 2000a) (MDC = 14.4%). The intraclass correlation coefficient, even if high (0.94), was not considered indicative of the reliability of the test due to the heterogeneity of the $[La^-]_{FIELD}$ (range from about 2 mmol·l⁻¹ to 7 mmol·l⁻¹).

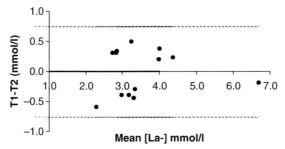

Figure 2. Bland and Altman plot.

4. DISCUSSION

The results of this study confirm the validity of this field submaximal running test in evaluating aerobic fitness changes in soccer players.

The correlations found in this investigation are in agreement with the results of Sirtori et al. (1993) and of two other similar studies (Jacobs et al., 1983; Duggan and Tebbutt, 1990). Jacobs et al. (1983) found a significant relationship (r =−0. between [La⁻] at the end of a single submaximal cycling workload at 200 W and OBLA. A similar correlation (r = −0.95) was reported by Duggan and Tebbott (1990) between OBLA velocity and [La⁻] measured during submaximal running at 12 km·h⁻¹. However, in our study correlations were lower (from r = 0.62 to r= −0.76) than those reported in these studies. The reason is not clear but could be related to different laboratory protocols, environmental variables during field tests or simply due to peculiar characteristics of our group of soccer players. Despite being significant, the correlation coefficients found do not seem to support the use of OBLA velocity estimation as suggested by Sirtori et al. (1993). In fact, the moderate correlations of this study can be sufficient to validate the use of $[La^-]_{FIELD}$ in evaluating aerobic changes but they are not sufficiently high to allow the prediction of laboratory lactate thresholds with acceptable accuracy (SEE from 7.1% to 10.2%). Even using the regression equation proposed by Sirtori et al. (1993), correlations between lactate thresholds determined under laboratory conditions and estimated OBLA velocity from $[La^-]_{FIELD}$ were moderate (from r = −0.65 to r = −0.78).

If on one hand the moderate correlations between laboratory parameters and $[La^-]_{FIELD}$ indicate a limited usefulness of this field test for inter-subject comparisons, on the other hand the significant relationships between training induced changes of lactate thresholds and training induced changes of $[La^-]_{FIELD}$ suggest a more appropriateness for longitudinal monitoring. These correlations could be explained by influences on both field and laboratory submaximal parameters of similar physiological adaptations such as changes in lactate production and/or changes in muscle clearance capacity (Stallknecht et al., 1998). As these muscle characteristics were not measured, this suggestion is still only a speculation.

Seasonal variations showed a significantly lower $[La^-]_{FIELD}$ (20%) response during the season compared to the pre-season period. During the season we found no changes in the average team $[La^-]_{FIELD}$. This is typical of various physiological assessments that sometimes could not discriminate group changes during the competitive season (Krustrup et al., 2003). However, from a practical point of view the interest of coaches and athletic trainers focuses mainly on the single athlete and so, a more individual approach during the season could be useful. Reliability expressed as typical error as CV was 9.6 % which could be considered moderate. As suggested by Hopkins (2000a), it is possible to determine statistically an acceptable individual minimal detectable change multiplying CV by 1.5 Z-score. Following this procedure, soccer players with $[La^-]_{FIELD}$ higher than 14.4% could have an acceptable probability that changes in field test results were due to an actual physiological change and not determined by measurement variability. Analyzing test results from this perspective, we found several soccer players with values higher than the minimal detectable change (Figure 3). Also HR was significantly lower during the season compared to pre-season suggesting that HR could be useful in addition to $[La^-]_{FIELD}$ to monitor aerobic fitness changes. This is in agreement with Krustrup et al. (2003) who suggested, in their submaximal version of the Yo-Yo test, to use the 6th min HR as this measure was found to be lower during the season compared to pre-season.

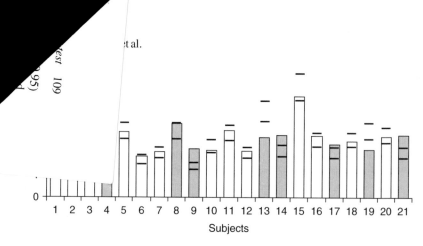

Figure 3. Individual [La⁻]$_{FIELD}$ test session in December. Players with a variation higher than the MDC (black line) determined from the previous test performed in September, are presented in grey.

Lactate concentration could be influenced by previous hard training or an over-reaching state. To overcome this problem, we suggest using the [La⁻]: RPE ratio as it has been found to decrease in an over-reaching state (Garcin et al., 2002).

In conclusion, our study suggests that this simple submaximal running test, despite some limitations, could be used to monitor aerobic capacity of soccer players as an alternative or in addition to maximal tests. Due to its submaximal nature, this test could be more accepted by athletes and, consequently, it could allow testing of soccer players more frequently and with results that are not influenced by motivation.

We hope that further studies will investigate the possibility to use submaximal tests for evaluating soccer players.

REFERENCES

Apor, P., 1988, Successful formulae for fitness training. In *Science and Football*, edited by Reilly, T., Lees A., Davids, K. and Murphy, W.J. (London: E&F.N.Spon), pp. 95–107.

Bland, J.P. and Altman, D.G., 1986, Statistical methods for assessing agreement between two methods of clinical measurement. *Lancet*, **1**, 307–310.

Duggan, A. and Tebbutt, S.D., 1990, Blood lactate at 12 km/h and vOBLA as predictors of run performance in non-endurance athletes. *International Journal of Sports Medicine,* **11**, 111–115.

Garcin, M., Fleury, A. and Billat, V., 2002. The ratio HLa:RPE as a tool to appreciate overreaching in young high-level middle-distance runners. *International Journal of Sports Medicine*, **23**, 16–21.

Helgerud, J., Engen, L.C., Wisloff, U. and Hoff, J., 2001, Aerobic endurance training improves soccer performance. *Medicine and Science in Sports and Exercise*, **33**, 1925–1931.

Hopkins, W.G., 2000a, Measures of reliability in sports medicine and science. *Sports Medicine*, **30**, 1–15.

Hopkins, W.G., 2000b, Sportscience: A new view of statistics. *http://www. sportsci. org/ resource/stats/index.html.*

Jacobs, I., Sjodin, B. and Schéle, R., 1983, A single blood determination as an indicator of cycle ergometer endurance capacity. *European Journal of Applied Physiology,* **50**, 355–364.

Krustrup, P., Mohr, M., Amstrup, T., Rysgaard, T., Johansen, J., Steensberg, A., Pedersen, P.K. and Bangsbo, J., 2003, The Yo-Yo intermittent recovery test: physiological response, reliability, and validity. *Medicine and Science in Sports and Exercise*, **35**, 697–705.

Sirtori, M.D., Lorenzelli, F., Peroni-Ranchet, F., Colombini, A. and Mognoni, P., 1983, A single blood lactate measure of OBLA running velocity in soccer players. *Medicina dello Sport*, **43**, 281–286 .

Smaros, G., 1980, Energy usage during a football match. In *Proceedings of the First International Congress on Sports Medicine Applied to Football.* Rome, edited by Vecchiet, L. (Rome: Guanilo, D), pp. 795–801.

Stallknecht, B., Vissing, J. and Galbo, H., 1998, Lactate production and clearance in exercise. Effects of training. A mini-review. *Scandinavian Journal of Medicine and Science in Sports*, **8**, 127–131.

Wisløff, U., Helgerud, J. and Hoff, J., 1998, Strength and endurance of elite soccer players. *Medicine and Science in Sports and Exercise*, **30**, 462–467.

17 Reliability and Validity of the Intermittent Anaerobic Running Test (IAnRT)

Rudolf Psotta and Václav Bunc
Charles University Prague, Faculty of Physical Education and Sport, Czech Republic

1. INTRODUCTION

A movement pattern in many invasive and net or wall based sports is represented by very high intensity intermittent exercise. In these intermittent sports the ability to perform very high intensity exercise repeatedly seems to be a more specific requirement for players' performances than is the ability to produce a single effort in a short or prolonged exercise.

To study physiological and performance responses to maximal intensity intermittent exercise, Balsom *et al.* (1992a, b) used repeated running sprints on a running track. However, there has been no systematically verified and widely used field test method incorporating an appropriate intermittent very high intensity exercise pattern with short duration work intervals. Only Fitzsimons *et al.* (1993) and Wraag *et al.* (2000) reported the reliability and/or the validity of the field repeated sprint test. However, these studies were performed with a smaller number of subjects and also factor validity was not studied.

To develop a more specific test for assessment of short term intermittent performance in soccer players, it is necessary to consider the very short duration of sprints observed during a match and the physiological demands of game performance. Bangsbo (1994) reported the mean distance of sprints to be 15–17 m. Several studies showed blood lactate concentration (BLa) during a match usually ranged from 6–10 mmol.l^{-1}, exceptionally reaching 16 mmol.l^{-1}. Ekblom (1986) found a close relation of BLa and the competitive level of football players. These findings suggest that high intensity exercise throughout a match is associated with anaerobic energy turnover and is often performed under conditions of incomplete recovery. Then the ability to produce very high intensity exercise repeatedly with short recovery periods can be very important for maintaining physical activity and the required standard of cognitive and movement skill performance during a match.

The new "Intermittent Anaerobic Running Test" (IAnRT) was proposed to evaluate the ability to repeat maximal sprints, i.e. intermittent short term performance in subjects participating in football. The purpose of this study was to establish the reliability and factor validity of the performance variables in the IAnRT.

2. METHODS

2.1. Subjects

Twenty nine young soccer players were recruited from Czech elite football clubs to participate in this study. These adolescent players underwent six to nine years of football training. Their age, height and body mass were 14.8 ± 0.3 years, 1.721 ± 0.07 m and 57.4 ± 8.7 kg, respectively. They all performed the IAnRT twice on two sessions separated by one rest day. In addition, the rest day preceded the day of the first session.

2.2. Protocol for the IAnRT

Before the test the subjects performed a standardized 10-min warm-up which included running and stretching exercises. Two 20-m submaximal sprints separated by a 20-s rest interval on an indoor tartan running track, were completed at the end of this warm-up to familiarize them with the IAnRT. Then after a 3-min rest period, the subjects performed two 20-m sprints separated by a 2-min rest interval to evaluate the maximal sprint performance. The tests were always done in a random order.

The intermittent exercise protocol consisted of ten 20-m sprints with a 20-s rest interval between each sprint. The instruction was given to complete each sprint in the shortest possible time. The sprint direction alternated for each sprint, i.e. the finishing position of one sprint became the start of the next. The lines for each standing start were placed 30 cm behind the starting photocells. The duration of each 20-s rest interval was measured by means of a digital stopwatch just from the moment that the previous sprint time showed on the electronic timer display. During the 20-s period each subject was kept informed of the time course of this rest interval, instructed to take up the standing start position in time and prepared for the next sprint in the opposite direction immediately the 20-s rest period was up. Strong verbal encouragement was given during performance of the IAnRT. The test was always completed by three subjects at the same time whereby the second and third subjects started in the same direction immediately after each discrete sprint was finished by the previous subject.

Sprint times were measured for each sprint using electronic photocells connected to a Alpha Vegasport timer (Vegasport, Czech Rep.). In an attempt to give consistent results, the photocells were placed at shoulder level of the participants. The sprint times were recorded to an accuracy of 0.001 s.

2.3. Performance measurement

The intermittent anaerobic running capacity was evaluted by the total running time T (s) or the mean running speed V_M (m.s^{-1}) respectively achieved through the ten sprints. Based on information about the mechanical power output and running speed during the intermittent running exercise (see Hamilton *et al.*, 1991; Fitzimons *et al.*, 1993) the mean running speed in the first two sprints (V_{1+2}; m.s^{-1}) should reflect the maximal sprint performance.

The ability to maintain the maximal running performance was evaluated by the following indices:

1. The absolute decline in running speed throughout the IAnRT δV (m.s^{-1}) calculated as the difference between the average running speed in the first two (V_{1+2}) and last two sprints (V_{9+10}).

2. The fatigue index FI (%) associated with running speed and calculated by the formula FI= (δV. $V_{1+2}^{-1)}$ 100.

3. The ratio of the mean running speed to the sprint speed at the beginning of this test – V_{MR} (%); $V_{MR}= V_m$ .V_{1+2}^{-1}. This variable is analogous to mean power/peak power ratio used in the Wingate anaerobic test to evaluate subjects' physiological specialization in terms of anaerobic or aerobic preconditions.

To ensure valid results for the IAnRT, a maximal effort of subjects was checked by comparing the mean running speed in the first two sprints of this intermittent test with the mean running speed achieved in two single 20-m sprints – V_S (m.s^{-1}) – performed before the series of ten sprints.

2.4. Physiological measurement

Heart rate (HR) was monitored during the IAnRT continuously and stored in 5-s intervals using short range radio telemetry (Polar 4000 Sport Tester, Polar Elektro Oy, Finland) to find the value of HR at the end of the tenth sprint (HR$_E$). Blood lactate was measured enzymatically using Boehringer sets (Boehringer, Mannheim, Germany). Capillary samples were withdrawn from a finger tip 2, 4 and 6 min after the tenth sprint, when subjects were sitting after completing the tenth sprint.

2.5. Statistical analysis

Besides the basic statistical characteristics as means, standard deviations and paired t-test, two-way ANOVA (2 by 10 design) with repetitions was applied to the times achieved by the subjects on the first and second occasions (Solo 4.0 software). The Fisher post hoc test was used to evaluate differences between subsequent time scores in the IAnRT. The probability level of 0.05 was chosen for significance. Reliability via the test-retest correlation as well as the standard error of the test procedure (SEM) was estimated. In addition, the coefficient of variation (CV) by Bland and Altman's formula (Atkinson, 1995) was calculated for an assessment of the intra-individual stability of test results.

With respect to the validity of the IanRT, the main goal of the statistical analysis was to evaluate the hypothesised two-factor structure implied by the serially repeated running tests. In theory, muscle performance during very high intensity exercise of short duration is determined by two anaerobic performance components: (i) by the ability of the neuromuscular system to generate maximal anaerobic power and (ii) the anaerobic capacity including buffering capacity of muscle and blood which is important for sustaining muscle power output. However, the ability to sustain power output in intermittent exercise can also be influenced by the recovery processes derived exclusively from aerobic pathways during the rest periods.

For this purpose, ordinary exploratory factor analysis (principal axes with varimax rotation) with two common factors was applied, using the Solo 4.0 software at first. Then confirmatory factor analysis was used incorporating a GEFA structural model with the programme created by Blahus (1992) to test different versions of the two-factor hypothesis and to establish factor validity coefficients of the consequently repeated tests with respect to the two conceptual factors of intermittent performance. Bentler's delta, probability level (P) and root mean square residual (RMSR) were used as fit indices.

3. RESULTS

The total running time in the IAnRT ranged from 32.6 s to 38.1 s. The two-way analysis of variance showed that sprint times in the first trial of the IAnRT were not significantly different from those in the second trial (P=0.76), but significant declines of sprint times occurred through the IAnRT (P<0.0001). The significantly longer sprint time occurred first in the fifth and the third sprint in test and retest respectively (P<0.05) compared with the mean running time for the first two sprints. The interaction of both factors on sprint times, i.e. the factor of test-retest repeatability and the time factor through the IAnRT, was not significant (P=0.32).

Results and the reliability values of the performance and physiological indices are shown in Table 1 and Table 2. The test-retest reliability values of the performance indices with absolute scores were significant (r = 0.79-0.87; P <0.001). On the other hand variables reflecting the decline of sprint speed through the IAnRT showed non-significant correlation coefficients (P>0.05). In the second trial of the IAnRT a significantly higher running speed at the beginning of this test (V_{1+2}) and an absolute decline in sprint speed (δV) occurred in comparison with the first trial (P<0.05).

Highest values of BLa in the test and retest (9.91 ± 1.60, 9.52 ± 2.05 mmol.l^{-1} respectively) were found for nearly all subjects 2 min after the tenth sprint. The correlation of peak BLa in the first and the second trial was not significant (P>0.05) in contrast to the high reliability of the HR_E (P<0.001). Both physiological variables were not different between the first and the second trials of the IAnRT (P>0.05).

In the exploratory factor analysis all sprint times throughout the IAnRT had very high loadings on factor I (0.83–0.94). Loadings on factor II were the highest from the seventh to the ninth sprint, although these values were not high (0.23-0.47). The coefficients of factor validity following the rotation of two factors are presented in Table 3.

The confirmatory factor analysis (Table 4) showed that sprint times through the IAnRT were best explained by one general factor and one subfactor. The latter was centred on sprint times from the sixth sprint when the sprint times from the second to the ninth sprint were included (P=0.03, Bentler's delta 0.99 and RMSR= 0.03).

Table 1. Results of the 'intermittent anaerobic running test' (IAnRT) in the test and retest.

	Test		Retest	
	Mean	SD	Mean	SD
V_S (m.s^{-1})	6.33	0.24	6.37	0.22
T (s)	33.7	1.2	33.6	1.2
V_M (m.s^{-1})	5.94	0.22	5.95	0.20
V_{1+2} (m.s^{-1})	6.04	0.20	6.11	0.23
V_{9+10} (m.s^{-1})	5.87	0.24	5.88	0.22
δV (m.s^{-1})	0.18	0.10	0.24	0.13
FI (%)	3.1	1.6	4.0	2.0
V_{MR} (%)	98.0	1.1	97.5	1.5
PBLa (mmol.l^{-1})	9.91	1.60	9.52	2.05
BLa2 (mmol.l^{-1})	9.86	1.71	9.45	1.97
BLa4 (mmol.l^{-1})	8.75	1.53	8.22	1.58
BLa6 (mmol.l^{-1})	7.72	1.59	7.17	1.53
HR_E (beats.min^{-1})	181	7.5	179	6.8

Abbreviation: SD - standard deviation, V_S = mean running speed in two separate 20-m sprints, T - total time, V_M = mean speed throughout IAnRT, V_{1+2} = mean running speed in the first two sprints, V_{9+10} = mean runnig speed in the last two sprints, δV = absolute decline of running speed, FI = fatigue index, V_{MR} = relative mean speed in ten sprints, pBLa = peak blood lactate concentration, BLa_2, BLa_4, BLa_6 = blood lactate concentration 2, 4 and 6 min after the 10th sprint, HR_E = heart rate at the end of the 10th sprint.

Table 2. Reliability values of the intermittent anaerobic running test (IAnRT).

	V_{1+2} (m.s^{-1})	V_M (m.s^{-1})	V_{9+10} (m.s^{-1})	δV (%)	FI (%)	V_{MR} (%)	BLa2 (mmol.l^{-1})	HR_E (beats.min^{-1})
r	0.83**	0.87**	0.79**	0.03	0.15	0.27	0.29	0.79**
P (t test)	0.01*	0.38	0.84	0.03*	0.09	0.12	0.39	0.13
SEM	0.09	0.08	0.11	-	1.84	1.16	1.5	3.3
CV	1.29	2.13	1.58	-	52.08	1.29	14.96	1.72

P - level of probability, ** P<0.001, *P<0.05, SEM - standard error of measurement, CV - coefficient of variation.

Table 3. Exploratory factor analysis of sprint times in consequent sprints in the IAnRT - rotated factor loadings.

Variable	Factor I	Factor II	Communality
T1	0.86	0.36	0.87
T2	0.91	0.32	0.93
T3	0.72	0.60	0.89
T4	0.68	0.58	0.80
T5	0.65	0.60	0.78
T6	0.73	0.56	0.84
T7	0.51	0.79	0.88
T8	0.29	0.92	0.92
T9	0.47	0.75	0.79
T10	0.69	0.59	0.82

85.3% accounted variance

T1-T10 – time in consequent sprints from first sprints to tenth sprint.

Table 4. Confirmatory factor analysis of sprint times in consequent sprints in the IAnRT - factor loadings and their uniqueness.

Variable	Factor I	Factor II	Uniqueness
T2	0.85	0	0.27
T3	0.99	0	0.03
T4	0.89	0	0.20
T5	0.92	0	0.16
T6	0.84	0.28	0.22
T7	0.85	0.39	0.13
T8	0.77	0.35	0.28
T9	0.70	0.64	0.10

Bentler's delta 0.99, probability level 0.03, root mean square residual 0.03.

4. DISCUSSION

4.1. Reliability of the IanRT

Correlations between the first and the second IAnRT and the other reliability indicators, i.e. the CV and the SEM, suggested good reliability in absolute scores of running performance.

The significantly higher mean running speed of first two sprints of the IAnRT (V_{1+2}) in the second trial in comparison to the first could be due to the fact that subjects had no experience of any intermittent anaerobic test. Then a strategy in outlay of effort in the first IAnRT could influence running speed in this test. However, the mean running speed achieved through this test proved to be a very reliable index. Even the CV of the V_{1+2} 2.13% suggested very high agreement of individual test-retest values in the sprints at the beginning of this intermittent test.

The CV used as a reliable indicator in this study was calculated by Bland and Altman's formula which differs from the method based on the standard deviation of each subject's repeated measurements. The application of Bland and Altman's method to the present data would have meant a standard deviation being calculated from just two observations per subject.

On the other hand the relative scores for running speed reflecting the rate of decline in running performance did not show acceptable reliability although ANOVA suggested a similar course of decline in running speed throughout the IAnRT. Lower reliability of the fatigue index ($r = 0.75$) was reported by Fitzimons et al. (1993) also for running speed in repeated 40-m sprints and by Vandewalle et al. (1987) for the power output in the continuous anaerobic Wingate test ($0.43 < r < 0.74$). In part, the reason for this is the method of calculation by which relative variables are calculated from a number of directly measured variables. The index of relative running performance capacity (V_{MR}; %) tended to be more favourable when the coefficient of variation 1.29% suggested very good intra-individual repeatibility for this index.

The highest post-exercise BLa value was found 2 min after the tenth sprint in 27 and 26 of all 29 subjects in test and retest of the IAnRT (9.86 ± 1.71 and 9.45 ± 1.97 mmol.l^{-1} respectively). For these values the test-retest correlation was not significant. Individual variation in blood lactate could be influenced by motivation, but also type of training and nutrition. However, a high degree of agreement of the mean running speed in the test and retest of the IAnRT suggested that motivation was not a reason for the lower reliability of BLa responses. According to the review by Vandewalle et al. (1987), in all-out anaerobic tests with a continuous exercise pattern, good reliability of post-exercise BLa was usually found - from $r = 0.87$ to $r = 0.98$ - but the CV ranged from 11% to 21%. Nummela et al. (1996a, b) found lower test-retest reliability for this variable in an anaerobic test with stepwise increased 20-s runs and 100-s recovery between runs ($r = 0.60$). The reliability indicators ($r = 0.29$ and CV = 14.96%) found in the present study could suggest lower repeatability of BLa measurements in anaerobic intermittent exercise. Variability of BLa in the IAnRT can be attributed to the intermittent feature of this exercise. Biological variability in the production and transport of lactate across the membranes, space of lactate diffusion and oxidation of lactate (Åstrand and Rodahl, 1986) could be affected by alternating the work and recovery periods.

Good reliability of HR at the end of the IAnRT would support its use in the assessment of physiological loading during high intensity intermittent exercise.

4.2. Validity of the IanRT

The aim of the IAnRT is to evaluate the ability to repeat maximal sprints within a phase of moderately high level of metabolic acidosis indicated by BLa. The number of sprints in the test was critical when the distance of sprint and work/rest ratio were established as the first step. The construct validity of the IAnRT was supported by the peak BLa 9.91 ± 1.60 and 9.52 ± 2.05 mmol.l^{-1}, when blood lactate responses during match-play in soccer usually oscillate from 5 to 10, and extremely to 16 mmol.l^{-1} (Bangsbo, 1994).

The hypothesis of this study was that the IAnRT measures two different components of running sprint performance in intermittent exercise. Firstly, the individual highest sprint speed was achieved in the first or second sprint except for three and four subjects in the test and retest reaching the highest speed in later sprints. Hamilton *et al.* (1991) and Fitzimons *et al.* (1993) observed the highest speed in the first or second bout. Our findings support the view that the mean speed in the first two sprints could be a valid performance index of maximal sprint performance. In addition, the validity of this performance index was supported by a high correlation to running speed achieved in a 20-m single sprint performed before IAnRT (r=0.86, 0.89; P<0.01).

The mean speed in the first two sprints of the IAnRT was lower on average by 0.29 and 0.22 m.s^{-1} (P<0.01) compared with the speed in the separate sprint performed before the IAnRT. These differences could be affected by personal tactics and a lower degree of experience with intermittent exercise testing.

Further, a recent study assumed the IAnRT could help to evaluate the ability to maintain maximal running speed. Performances in IAnRT showed a progressive decline of running speed over ten sprints, being significant from fifth and third sprint in test and retest respectively. This trend in performance decline was similar to those reported by Balsom *et al.* (1992a, b) and Fitzimons *et al.* (1993) for running speed and by Brooks *et al.* (1990) for mechanical power output through repeated sprints.

The fatigue index as an indicator of the ability to maintain maximal running performance, demonstrated average values of 3.1± 1.6% and 4 ± 2.0%, similar to observations by Hamilton *et al.* (1991) and Fitzimons *et al.* (1993) in ten repeated 6-s sprints with similar work/rest ratios. The individual fatigue index in the IAnRT ranged from 1.7% to 10.8%. The inter-individual differencies in the ability to maintain the intermittent maximal intensity running could be determined when the standard error of measument for the fatigue index was 1.82%. However, discussion about validity of the fatigue index in the IAnRT must be limited because its reliability was lower and therefore other studies are needed.

The results of the factor analysis confirm the hypothesis that the performance in the IAnRT can be determined by two performance components. Factor I, extracted as the first, was interpreted as a general factor because there were high factor loadings for running times of all sprints throughout the IAnRT (0.84-0.94). Then the confirmatory factor analysis sustained the general factor for the subsequent sprint times.

The running speed in sprints 1 and 2 had the highest loading on this general factor among all the sprints. The running speed in these sprints achieved the highest values and at the same time correlated with the speed in separately performed single 20-m sprints (r = 0.86 and 0.89; P<0.01). During the acceleration phase of sprinting the highest level of maximal power output is generated in the first to third second of sprinting, as found by Brooks *et al.* (1993). Then the definition of the general factor could be related to the maximal anaerobic power involved in the 20-m running sprint. However, the maximal sprint speed is determined also by neuromuscular and mechanical factors, including running skill.

Using the explorative factor analysis following rotation of two uncorrelated factors, the loadings of the seventh, the eighth and the ninth sprint time on factor II were higher than those on factor I (general factor). Thus, running performance in the second part of the IAnRT was also partly determined by the other performance components. The final best fit was found with the general factor and one subfactor (factor II) which represented performances from the sixth sprint.

Theoretically, the subfactor could be identified as the ability to maintain maximal sprint speed. This is probably due to physiological factors. Gaitanos *et al.* (1993) suggested that subjects with the higher maximal anaerobic power, rate of glycolytic metabolism and percentage FT fibres achieved the higher power output in the first exercise bouts but also a higher decrease of power output through intermittent anaerobic exercise compared to subjects with higher aerobic characteristics. The intramuscular buffering capacity and the ability to recover after very high intensity anaerobic exercise associated with oxidative metabolism, could influence the maintenance of performance in this type of intermittent exercise. The influence of the mechanical efficiency of running and a modification of the running technique during intermittent running exercise could be also suggested.

5. CONCLUSIONS

This study has shown that the IAnRT can yield reliable data about the ability to perform repeated maximal intensity bouts of running exercise. From all verified relative indices, the mean running performance throughout the test related to maximal sprint speed seems to be a reliable indicator for assessment of the ability to maintain running performance during intermittent exercise. The post-exercise blood lactate concentration was unable to reflect the physical loading during high intensity intermittent exercise with the accuracy required, in contrast to measurement of heart rate. According to contemporary trends these findings are favourable for sport training practice and diagnostics when the measurement of heart rate is noninvasive, practical and low cost.

The factor analysis suggested that the running performance in the IAnRT was mainly determined by the ability to generate maximal running sprint speed and partly by a different factor related to the ability to maintain maximal speed in the second part of this intermittent test.

Acknowledgements

This study was founded by the Grant of Czech Ministry of Education MSM 115100001.

REFERENCES

Åstrand, P. O. and Rodahl, K., 1986, Textbook of Work Physiology. (New York: McGraw Hill).

Atkinson, G., 1995, A comparison of statistical methods for assessing measurement repeatability in ergonomics research. In Sport, Leisure and Ergonomics, edited by Atkinson, G. and Reilly, T. (London: E & F N Spon), pp. 218–227.

Balsom, P.D., Seger J.Y., Sjodin, B. and Ekblom, B. 1992, Maximal-intensity intermittent exercise: effect of recovery duration. *International Journal of Sports Medicine,* **13**, 528–533.

Balsom, P. D., Seger, J. Y., Sjodin, B. and Ekblom, B., 1992, Physiological responses to maximal intensity intermittent exercise. *Euopean Journal of Applied Physiology* 1992, **65**, 144–149.

Bangsbo, J., 1994, The physiology of soccer: with special reference to intense intermittent exercise. *Acta Physiologica Scandinavica,* **151**, 151–155.

Blahus, P., 1992, A simple model for generalized confirmatory factor analysis with application to educational research. *Acta Universitatis Carolinae Gymnica,* **28**, 37–53.

Brooks, S., Nevill, M. E., Meleagros, L., Lakomy, H.K.A., Hall, G.M., Bloom, S.R. and Williams, C., 1990, The hormonal responses to repetitive brief maximal exercise in humans. *Euopean Journal of Applied Physiology,* **60**, 144–148.

Brooks, S., Nevill, M.E., Gaitanos, G. and Williams, C., 1993, Metabolic responses to sprint training. In *Intermittent High Intensity Exercise: Preparation, Stresses and Damage Limitation,* edited by MacLeod, D.A.D., Maughan, R. J., Williams, C., Madeley, C. R., Sharp, J. C. M. and Nutton, R. W. (London: E&FN Spon), pp. 33–48.

Ekblom, B., 1986, Applied physiology of soccer. *Sport Medicine,* **3**, 50–60.

Fitzimons, M., Dawson, B. Ward, D and Wilkinson, A., 1993, Cycling and running tests of repeated sprint ability. *Australian Journal of Science and Medicine in Sport,* **25**, 82–87.

Gaitanos, G.C., Williams, C., Boobis, L.H. and Brooks, S., 1993, Human muscle metabolism during intermittent maximal exercise. *Journal of Applied Physiology,* **75**, 712–719.

Hamilton, A.L., Nevill, M.E., Brooks, S. and Williams, C., 1991, Physiological responses to maximal intermittent exercise: Differences between endurance-trained runners and games players. *Journal of Sports Sciences,* **9**, 371–382.

Nummela, A., Albert, M., Rijntjes, R.P., Luhtanen, P. and Rusko, H., 1996a, Reliability and validity of the maximal anaerobic running test. *International Journal of Sports Medicine,* **17**, 97–102.

Nummela, A., Mero, A. and Rusko, H. 1996b, Effects of sprint training on anaerobic performance characteristics determined by the MART. *Interntional Journal of Sports Medicine,* **17**, Suppl. 2, S114–S119.

Vandewalle, H., Peres, G. and Monod, H. 1987, Standard anaerobic exercise tests. *Sports Medicine,* **4**, 268–289.

Wraag, C., Maxwell, N. and Doust, J., 2000, Development of a multidirectional soccer-specific field test of repeated sprint ability: validity and reliability. In *Proceedings of the 5th Annual Congress of the European College of Sport Science,* Jyväskylä , edited by Avela, J., Komi, P.V. and Komulainen, J. (Jyväskylä: ECSS and LIKES Research Center), p. 799.

18 Differences between Football Players' Sprint Test Performance across Different Levels of Competition

Jaime Sampaio and Victor Maçãs, Sports Sciences Department, University of Trás-os-Montes e Alto Douro, Portugal

1. INTRODUCTION

The work-rate profile of a football player ranges between low-level activities like walking, jogging, and those of high intensity like sprinting. The final outcome of a match may be dependent upon a player's ability to perform a sprint faster than an opponent. Despite the fact that sprinting in a game represents less than 10% of total distance covered (Bangsbo et al., 1991), this performance is considered as one of the most critical. Available research has shown that professional players are faster than non-professional players over distances ranging from 5 to 40 m (Davis et al., 1992; Kollath and Quade, 1993). Additionally, in top class players the inter-player performance variation with these distances is very small, raising difficulties for the measurement and evaluation of this fitness component. For example, Balsom (1994) recorded sprint times from the Swedish National team performed on grass and measured with photoelectric cells over a course of 15 m and results ranged from 2.32–2.38 s.

The need of performing a sprint during a game varies and players must be ready to perform, recover and perform it again at the highest possible level. Thus, research should be focused to the measurement and evaluation of the ability to perform quality sprints consecutively. One sprint test (Bangsbo, 1994) consists of seven 34-m sprints interspersed with 25-s active recovery periods and is often used by coaches as a field tool for measuring this ability. At the moment, methodological information regarding this test is limited to the study of Wragg et al. (2000) in which the authors have demonstrated the validity and reliability of the test.

A very important topic of research that has not been adequately investigated is the ability of the sprint test in discriminating player performance across different levels of competition. In fact, these data can be turned into very valuable information for the development of specific physiological profiling, talent detection and player selection. Additionally, they can guide coaches more effectively through conditioning and training programmes across a season and also can help coaches to understand differences between players.

Therefore, the purpose of this study was to compare sprint test performances achieved by players of different levels of competition.

2. METHODS

2.1. Subjects

One hundred and forty six Portuguese football players from different teams volunteered to participate in this study (Table 1). Before taking part, participants provided written informed consent and were told that they were free to withdraw at any time.

Table 1. Characteristics of the football players by competition level.

Group	Competition Level	Age (years)	Mass (kg)	Height (m)	Training sessions/week
$G_1(n=19)$	1st national	26±3	72.7±5.5	1.77±5.6	7
G_2 (n=17)	2nd national	24±2	70.4±6.1	1.76±4.4	7
G_3 (n=30)	1st regional	29±5	76.5±8.2	1.73±4.3	3
G_4 (n=24)	Under 16 yrs	-	60.7±4.4	1.70±3.9	5
G_5 (n=32)	Under 14 yrs	-	55.1±5.3	1.66±5.9	4
G_6 (n=24)	Under 12 yrs	-	46.8±5.7	1.50±6.0	3

2.2. Procedures

At the time of test execution, all teams were approximately in the middle of the competition period. On the morning of the test, subjects were advised to consume two small snacks approximately 2–3 h before exercise. Each snack was designed to have an energy content of 100–150 kcal (420–630 kJ) and containing 60–65% carbohydrate. To ensure proper euhydration and 2 h prior to the test, subjects were instructed to consume approximately 1 l of water. Additionally and during the 24 h before the test, subjects were advised to avoid drinking alcohol and fluids containing caffeine and also refrain from any type of exercise. Subjects had all these instructions in writing; however, verbal confirmation of compliance was given prior to test execution. All groups were tested between 10.00 and 13.00 h to avoid any circadian variability. The test was performed outdoors on a grass surface. All subjects wore shorts and studded boots.

Before the test, subjects completed a 20-min oriented warm up of jogging, sprinting and stretching, followed by a 5-min rest. In the sprinting period, each subject was allowed to perform one sprint along the test course for familiarization purposes. These pre-test procedures were the same for all groups.

The protocol consisted of seven maximal sprints (7×32.4 m) along the portions A–B of the course (Figure 1). Photoelectric cells (Digitest 1000, Digitest Oy, Finland) were used to measure the subjects' performance and to increase test reliability. Following each sprint was a period of active recovery (25 s to cover a distance of 40 m), that consisted of jogging the B–A part of the course. Immediately after passing point B, the timing of the subject's recovery began. The recovery run had to be timed (stop-watch) in order to ensure that subjects returned to point A between the 23th and 24th second. Additionally, verbal feedback was given at 5, 10, 15, and 20 s of the recovery.

Performance was measured as the mean sprint time in seconds.

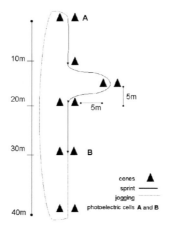

Figure 1. Diagram of sprint test protocol.

2.3. Data analysis

A two-factor repeated measures ANOVA was carried for the statistical analysis with level of competition and sprint trial as factors (between and within factors, respectively). A Tukey post-hoc test was carried where appropriate. All data undergoing ANOVA were tested for assumptions of normality, homogeneity of variance and covariance matrices and sphericity. Neither assumption was violated. Statistical significance was set at 5%.

3. RESULTS

A 6 (level of competition: 1st div vs. 2nd div vs. 1st reg div vs. sub 16 vs. sub 14 vs. sub 12) × 7 (sprint trial: sprint 1 vs. sprint 2 vs. sprint 3 vs. sprint 4 vs. sprint 5 vs. sprint 6 vs. sprint 7) repeated measures ANOVA was carried out on subjects sprint times. The main effects of level of competition was reliable ($F_{5,140}$ = 106.28; $P < 0.001$). Tukey tests revealed that all pairwise comparisons between levels of competition were significant (all P values <0.05) with the exception of G_3 vs. G_4 and G_3 vs. G_5.

Subjects from G_1 were significantly faster than subjects from G_2. Subjects from G_3 obtained similar performances when compared to G_4 and G_5 levels. Subjects from G_6 level were the slowest (Figure 2).

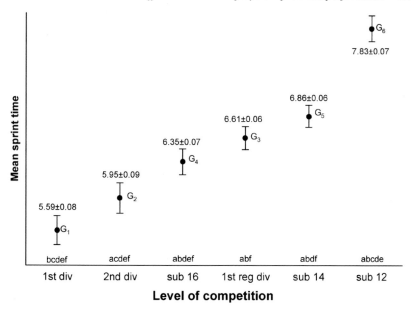

Figure 2. Mean sprint time across levels of competition. Legend: a → significant different from G_1; b → from G_2; c → from G_3; d → from G_4; e → from G_5; f → from G_6.

The main effect of sprint trial was also reliable ($F_{6,840} = 7.37$, $P < 0.001$). Mean sprint times from the first trial were significantly slower than mean sprint times from the second, third and fourth trials. Results from the fifth, sixth and seventh trials were slower (Figure 3).

The two main effects were qualified by a significant level of competition × sprint trial interaction ($F_{30,840} = 9.47$, $P < 0.001$), identifying markedly different performance profiles (Figure 4).

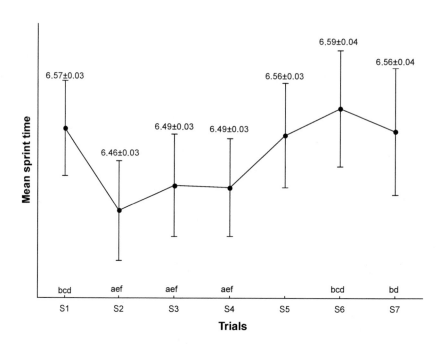

Figure 3. Mean sprint time across the seven trials. Legend: a → significantly different from S_1; b → from S_2; c → from S_3; d → from S_4; e → from S_6; f → from S_7.

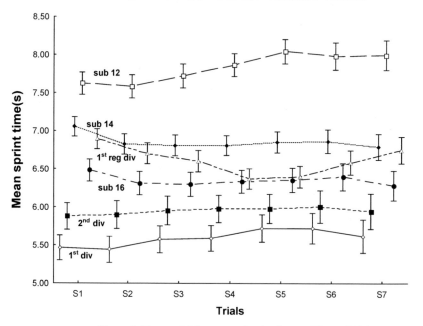

Figure 4. Mean sprint time across levels of competition and trials.

4. DISCUSSION

The main purpose of this study was to compare sprint test performance between six different groups of football players. We reasoned that these data can be turned into very valuable information for talent detection, fitness evaluation and planning. Despite its utility for coaches, published research focused on sprint tests is limited to the study of Wragg *et al.* (2000). The sample studied (seven national level student players from the United Kingdom) averaged 7.66±0.29 s to complete a sprint, which is a result substantially different from those obtained in the senior groups of our study (G_1, G_2 and G_3). These differences can be explained by a modification done by the authors in the original protocol that involved adding a random right or left turn (using two light-emitting diodes, LED) in order to improve game specificity and also to place a load upon both legs. Therefore, players were not aware if they had to make a right or left turn until the corresponding LED illuminates. This reaction might have slowed them down.

Results from the main effects of level of competition revealed different performance profiles between the groups. On the other hand and based on previous research (Wragg *et al.*, 2000), we believe that results from the main effects and pairwise differences of sprint trials seem to have identified the first sprint as a familiarization bout. Thus, it might be advisable to increase familiarization bouts in pre-test procedures or withdraw the first sprint results from the subsequent analysis.

Interestingly, the two main effects were qualified by a significant interaction, identifying markedly different performance profiles. These findings might help to support the general hypothesis that an athlete's ability to maintain power over time is associated with age and fitness level. However, there is no doubt that considerable human variation exists in the ability to perform maximally over a short period of time. According to Van Praagh and Doré (2002), differences between children and young adults' performances can be attributable to size dependent factors (e.g., muscle size) and size independent factors (e.g., genetics, hormonal factors). Anaerobic performance is mainly determined by fibre type proportion and glycolytic enzyme capacity of skeletal muscle which are highly influenced by genetic factors, although there is always a training potential to be considered (Simoneau and Bouchard, 1998).

Anaerobic trainability increases with age (from childhood to adulthood with greater increases during puberty, Bar-Or, 1997) and also with the increase in glycolytic enzyme activity (particularly phosphofructokinase) triggered by training (Eriksson et al., 1973; Fournier et al., 1982). The findings of our study seem to provide some additional field test support to these differences because groups of different ages (G_4, G_5 and G_6) and groups of different training quality (G_1, G_2 and G3) were clearly discriminated by sprint test performances.

Therefore, considering that during childhood and adolescence direct measurements of the rate or capacity of anaerobic pathways for energy turnover present several ethical and methodological difficulties (Van Praagh and Doré, 2002), sprint tests appear to offer a good alternative field tool. Coaches should be aware that normative data regarding this test could play a very important role if used frequently and consistently during the whole season.

REFERENCES

Balsom, P., 1994, Evaluation of physical performance. In *Football (Soccer)*, edited by Ekblom, B. (London: Blackwell Scientific Publishers), pp. 102–123.

Bangsbo, J., 1994, Fitness Training for Football: A Scientific Approach. (Copenhagen: HO + Storm).

Bangsbo, J., Nørregaard, L. and Thorssøe, F., 1991, Activity profile of competition soccer. *Canadian Journal of Sports Science*, **16**, 110–116.

Bar-Or, O., 1997, Anaerobic performance. In *Measurement in Pediatric Exercise Science*, edited by Docherty, D. (Champaign, IL: Human Kinetics), pp. 161–182.

Davis, J., Brewer, J. and Atkin, D., 1992, Pre-season physiological characteristics of English First and Second Division football players. *Journal of Sports Sciences*, **10**, 541–547.

Eriksson, B., Gollnick, P. and Saltin, B., 1973, Muscle metabolism and enzyme activities after training in boys 11–13 years old. *Acta Physiologica Scandinavica*, **87**, 485–497.

Fournier, M., Ricci, J., Taylor, A., Ferguson, R., Monpetit, R. and Chaitman, B., 1982, Skeletal muscle adaptation in adolescent boys: sprint and endurance training and detraining. *Medicine and Science in Sports and Exercise*, **14**, 453–456.

Kollath, E. and Quade, K., 1993, Measurement of the sprinting speed of professional and amateur soccer players. In *Science and Football II*, edited by Reilly, T., Clarys, J. and Stibbe, A. (London: E & F.N. Spon), pp. 31–36.

Simoneau, J. and Bouchard, C., 1998, The effects of genetic variation of anaerobic performance. In *Paediatric Anaerobic Performance*, edited by Van Praagh, E. (Champaign, IL: Human Kinetics), pp. 5–21.

Van Praagh, E. and Doré, E., 2002, Short-term muscle power during growth and maturation. *Sports Medicine*, **32**, 701–728.

Wragg, C., Maxwell, N. and Doust, J., 2000, Evaluation of the reliability and validity of a soccer-specific field test of repeated sprint ability. *European Journal of Applied Physiology*, **83**, 77–83.

19 Differences in Fitness and Psychological Markers as a Function of Playing Level and Position in Two English Premier League Football Clubs

K.T.D. Power[1], G.M. Joe Dunbar[2] and D.C.Treasure[3]
[1]Performance Edge Associates Ltd, Park House, Ducks Hill Road, Northwood, Middlesex, HA6 2NP
[2] Joe Dunbar Sport, Orchard Thatch, Teynham, ME9 9QW, United Kingdom
[3] Arizona State University, Department of Kinesiology, Tempe, AZ 85287–0404, United States of America

1. INTRODUCTION

Over the past five years, an increasing number of English Premiership soccer clubs have utilized sport science services as a means to evaluate and enhance playing performance. However, in trying to understand which factors differentiate playing level, researchers and practioners have focused on a mono-disciplinary approach to explain these differences. This reliance on using only one discipline of sport science to measure differences in playing level in soccer provides only a limited understanding of performance. It is therefore proposed that using an inter-disciplinary approach to measure and monitor performance in soccer provides a greater range of sport science information from which to understand performance.

More specifically, mono-disciplinary support focuses on one sub-discipline of sport science supporting a performance programme. For example, this could be psychological support or physiological support. Multi-disciplinary sports science support would involve a group of people from different sub-disciplines working on a common topic in parallel (Burwitz *et al.*, 1994). Inter-disciplinary support would involve a much stronger relationship in that it would be an integration of information from more than one sub-discipline of sports science (Burwitz *et al.*, 1994).

There is a lack of both research and applied work with regard to multi-disciplinary or inter- disciplinary approaches to understanding differences in performance level of soccer players. This study sought to begin addressing this gap in theory and practice by using fitness and psychological markers, i.e., the integration of two sub-disciplines of sport science, to understand differences in playing level and position of players at two English Premier League football clubs. Whilst only two sub-disciplines of sport science have been utilized for the purpose of this study, it should be noted that a systematic process-driven counseling approach (Schein, 1992) underpinned by an entire spectrum of inter-disciplinary sport science is used to measure, monitor and manage soccer performance.

2. METHODS

Participants were 42 first team (M age = 25.38 years, SD = 4.97 years, range 18–35 years; M mass = 80.57 kg, SD 6.21 kg, range 70–98 kg) and 18 reserve team players (M age = 20.89 years, SD = 3.69 years, range 19–32 years; M mass = 75.17 kg, SD 7.04 kg, range 65–87 kg) whose playing position was classified as goalkeeper, defender, midfielder, or forward from two English Premier League Football teams.

The participants completed a battery of fitness and psychological tests during the early season period (August-September) in the year testing took place. Fitness testing included electronically timed sprints over 10 m and 20 m, a vertical jump test as a crude index of leg power and an Illinois agility run. An intermittent sprint test using the mean time of eight 40-m runs (including two changes of direction) separated by a 20-s recovery period, gave an index of speed endurance (Dunbar and Woledge, 1995).

Players completed an adapted version of the Sport-related Psychological Skills Questionnaire (Nelson and Hardy, 1990) that assesses seven psychological skills hypothesized to underlie sport performance, namely imagery skill, mental preparation, self-efficacy skills, cognitive anxiety (i.e., the ability to control cognitive anxiety), concentration skills, relaxation skills, and motivation. Based on Personal Construct Theory, the players also completed a performance profile (Butler and Hardy, 1992) to determine their current rating of the constructs they believed an elite level football player possesses. For the purposes of the present study the individual constructs identified were classified as mental, tactical, technical, or physical by a FIFA "A" licensed equivalent qualified coach and collapsed to form scales reflecting a rating of 1 (poor) to 10 (excellent) on the general construct.

3. RESULTS

Three 2 X 4 (playing level X position) multivariate analysis of variance procedures were conducted with the participants' fitness markers, psychological skills and performance profile data serving as the dependent variables in the respective analyses. In regard to the fitness data, although approaching significance (P=0.06), no significant Playing level by Position interaction effect emerged. A significant main effect did emerge for playing level. The mean fitness profile scores as a function of playing level are illustrated in Table 1.

Table 1. Mean (±SD) fitness profile results as a function of playing level.

Playing Level	10 m	20 m	Power	Agility	Anaerobic Endurance
First Team (n = 42)	1.74 (0.07)	3.01 (0.10)	60.9 (6.8)	14.60* (0.39)	8.17* (0.19)
Reserves (n = 18)	1.73 (0.06)	2.98 (0.09)	59.9 (4.5)	14.99 (0.45)	8.27 (0.18)

* significantly different from reserves (P<0.05).

Follow up univariate analyses for playing level revealed that first team players performed better than the reserve team players in the agility and anaerobic tests. No significant differences emerged in terms of the psychological skills assessed by the Sport-related Psychological Skills Questionnaire for playing level or position. A significant main effect for playing level emerged for the performance profile data. Follow up univariate analyses revealed that the first team players rated themselves higher than the reserve team players on their current level of mental (first team $\underline{M}$ = 8.00, $\underline{SD}$ = 0.82; reserve team $\underline{M}$ = 7.10, $\underline{SD}$ = 0.76: P<0.001), tactical (first team $\underline{M}$ =7.43, $\underline{SD}$ = 0.84; reserve team $\underline{M}$ = 6.82, $\underline{SD}$ = 0.68: P<0.01), technical (first team $\underline{M}$ = 7.46, $\underline{SD}$ = 0.81; reserve team $\underline{M}$ = 6.93, $\underline{SD}$ = 0.76: P<0.05), and physical skills (first team $\underline{M}$ = 7.88, $\underline{SD}$ = 0.87; reserve team $\underline{M}$ = 7.11; $\underline{SD}$ = 0.69: P<0.01).

4. DISCUSSION

The results of the present study suggest that select fitness tests and performance profile ratings discriminate professional soccer players of different playing levels during the early part of the competitive season. In regard to the physiological markers assessed, the findings reveal that straight line sprinting speed over distances of 10 and 20 metres and leg power, as indicated by a vertical jump, do not discriminate between playing level. With many soccer managers regularly quoting the importance of speed and power in the modern game, particularly the English Premier League, this seemed a little surprising. However, the significant differences were observed between first team and reserve team players in the running tests that involve change of direction.

In both the agility and anaerobic endurance tests, rapid acceleration and deceleration are required. In our experience, it is the deceleration factor that is often underestimated in terms of importance to fitness for soccer. Detailed match-analysis investigations of the 2 teams studied have also shown that straight line sprinting over 10 and 20 metres is indeed rare. Runs in match play tend to be curved or multi-directional in nature and it may be that first team players are better conditioned at these, where there is also a skill element.

The superior anaerobic endurance of the first team players is likely to be a function of better specific conditioning, given that the basic speed of the two playing levels is similar. In light of the significantly different age of the two groups (the first team players being older), this conditioning effect may have been acquired over successive seasons, rather than in the pre-season and early season period of the current year in question.

Whilst the fitness profile used here is not fully match specific, it must be remembered that the profile is used as one tool in the overall interdisciplinary package. The main use is to form a guide for individual training prescription, rather than to predict match fitness. Specific match fitness is accurately measured and monitored using the Prozone (Leeds) system to provide team and individual feedback with regards to fitness, tactics and other soccer related activity, on a match-by-match basis.

That no significant differences emerged in terms of the psychological skills assessed by the Sport-related Psychological Skills Questionnaire for playing level is somewhat surprising in view of the research that suggests that at the elite level of sport psychological factors often differentiate between successful and unsuccessful performers (e.g., Mahoney *et al.*, 1987). In working with Premiership and Football League clubs, the use of mental skills questionnaires may be culturally inappropriate.

Previous research with elite level performers in a number of sports has shown performance profiling to be an effective means to quantify and understand athletes' perceptions concerning ability and performance (Butler and Hardy, 1992). From an applied perspective, performance profiling has an advantage over more standardized assessments of mental skills as the athlete is an active agent in describing and evaluating his or her unique sport experience. As such, the approach offers coaches and sport scientists insight into the athlete's version of reality and view of the world; this insight should enhance interactions between members of the coach and sport science support staff and the players.

The correlational nature of the present study, however, does not enable us to make any comments about the causal nature of the relationship between playing level and the performance profile results. Specifically, do first team players, or those that expect to be first team players, have higher perceived ability in the four soccer performance areas assessed compared to reserve team players as a function of their perceived playing level or do differences in performance profiles predict playing level? Although a more rigorous prospective research design would be required to address the issue of causality, from an applied perspective, the results of the present study provide support for the use of performance profiling in an integrated approach to understanding soccer performance.

5. CONCLUSIONS

In conclusion, whilst in this study it was not possible to compare directly the merit of a mono-disciplinary approach against multi-disciplinary and interdisciplinary approaches to understanding soccer performance, the results do illustrate that the interdisciplinary combination of psychological and fitness markers do discriminate different soccer playing levels. Given the complex nature of elite level soccer performance, it would seem logical that using several sub-disciplines of sport science in co-ordination is a more effective approach to measure and monitor performance in soccer than using a singular sport science approach. More research and applied work in this area are therefore encouraged.

REFERENCES

Burwitz, L., Moore, P.M. and Wilkinson, D.M., 1994, Future directions for performance-related sports science research: An interdisciplinary   approach. *Journal of Sports Sciences,* **12**, 93–109.

Butler, R.J. and Hardy, L., 1992, The performance profile: Theory and application. *The Sport Psychologist,* **6**, 253–264.

Dunbar, G.M.J. and Woledge, J., 1995, An investigation into the order of tests performed by games players in a battery of field tests. *Journal of Sports Sciences,* **14**, 77–78.

Mahoney, M.J., Gabriel, T.J. and Perkins, T.S., 1987, Psychological skills and exceptional athletic performance. *The Sport Psychologist,* **1**, 181–199.

Nelson, D. and Hardy, L., 1990, The development of an empirically validated tool for measuring psychological skills in sport. *Journal of Sports Sciences,* **8,** 71.

Schein, E., 1992, *Organizational Culture and Leadership (second edition).* (San Fransisco: Jossey Bass).

20 Variation in Selected Fitness Attributes of Professional Soccer Players during a League Season

A.R. Aziz, F. Tan and K.C. Teh
Sports Medicine & Research Centre,
Singapore Sports Council

1. INTRODUCTION

While other athletes can peak at critical times of the season based on their sports' competitive season, soccer players need to be at their best or close to their optimal performance throughout the entire playing season. Published literature on soccer players' physiological attributes throughout a competitive season is scarce. This is partly due to the problems with scheduling as a result of their extensive training and match involvement and at times, injuries.

The present study aims to describe the seasonal variation of physiological attributes of a relatively large sample of players playing in a Southeast Asian professional soccer league.

2. MATERIALS AND METHODS

Forty-one professional outfield position players (25.7 ± 3.9 years; 1.74 ± 0.083 m, 70.6 ± 10.3 kg) from the twelve clubs involved in Singapore's top soccer competition, the S-League, completed all the tests requirements.

The S-League season is typically nine months long spreading from January to October. The S-League clubs generally follow the English club system of preparation. The local clubs begin their pre-season training phase in January when the players generally train 6–7 times a week for 90–120 min per session. During the competitive season, they are training 4–5 times a week and play one or two matches a week. During the 2001–2002 season when the tests were conducted, each club would have played 33 league matches and 3–6 cup matches. The players were tested on four occasions: (1) in early January on return from the off-season phase (OFF); (2) in late February after completion of the pre-season training phase (PRE); (3) in June in the middle of the league season (MID); and (4) in October near the end of the league season (END).

The measurements taken were:- height, body mass, percentage body fat, aerobic endurance, sprinting ability and jumping performance. All performance tests were done in the outdoors on the running track. Percentage body fat was assessed with a leg-to-leg bioelectrical impedance analyzer (*model TBF-105, Tanita Corporation, Tokyo, Japan*). This method is fast, non-invasive and the analyser used has a high correlation with dual-energy X-ray absorptiometry

(r = 0.93 and 0.73; $P < 0.05$ for fat mass and fat-free mass, respectively) [Andreoli et al., 2002] and is shown to be valid when compared with the skinfold method in athletes (Utter et al., 2001). Aerobic endurance was assessed via estimated maximal aerobic power (or $\dot{V}O_2$ max) using the 20-m multi-stage shuttle run or "Beep" test (*CD Australian Sports Commission*). Sprinting times were from a standing start 40 cm behind the starting gates; the player was required to sprint all-out for 20 m. Timing was taken with automatic light-cell gates (*Speed Light Sports Timing, Swift Performance Equipment, Lismore, NSW, Australia*) placed at the 0, 5 and 20-m marks. Each player was allowed three sprints and the best 5-m and 20- m times were noted. Jumping performance was assessed via the Sargeant jump test. Players jumped from a stationary standing double-leg take-off with a counter-movement arm swing and jump height was recorded using a device *(Yardstick II, Swift Performance Equipment, Lismore, NSW, Australia)*.

For statistical analysis, SPSS 10.0 was used. One-way analysis of variance was used to determine significant differences in the fitness variables across the different phases of training (or time). Tukey post-hoc tests were used to detect the location of differences. Pearson product correlation (r) analysis was also performed on the magnitude of changes (in %) made between the different test occasions on selected variables. Significance was set at $P < 0.05$.

3. RESULTS

The S-League players' physical characteristics and performances are generally within the range of mean values reported for professional soccer players (Table 1).

Although there was a decreasing trend, there were no significant differences in the players' body mass and percentage body fat across the entire season. A post-hoc test showed that players' aerobic endurance was significantly higher at PRE compared to the OFF phase, only. No other significant differences were observed between the other time points. Players' sprinting times showed a trend for faster times across the four test points, but only the performance between the OFF and END phase was statistically significant. Players' vertical jumping showed significant improvements across the three time points, from OFF to PRE, and from PRE to MID training phases.

Correlation analysis showed a significant association between body fat and 5 m *(r = 0.35, $P < 0.05$)* and 20-m *(r = 0.43, $P < 0.01$)* sprint times for the time points between PRE to MID training phase. No significant correlation was observed at other time points.

Table 1. Professional S-League players' ($N = (41)$) physical characteristics and exercise performance tests results on return from the off-season (OFF); after completion of the pre-season training phase (PRE); in the middle of competitive league season (MID), and at the end of league season (END).

	OFF	PRE	MID	END	P
Body mass (kg)	70.6 ± 10.3	69.7 ± 10.1	69.4 ± 9.8	69.7 ± 10.1	*0.952*
Body fat (%)	11.0 ± 2.7	10.6 ± 2.3	10.3 ± 2.3	10.4 ± 2.3	*0.564*
5-m sprint time (s)	$1.04 \pm 0.06^\dagger$	1.03 ± 0.06	1.02 ± 0.07	1.00 ± 0.05	*0.014*
20-m sprint time (s)	$3.04 \pm 0.16^\dagger$	3.01 ± 0.10	3.00 ± 0.11	2.95 ± 0.09	*0.005*
Vertical jump (cm)	$55 \pm 5^*$	59 ± 5	$62 \pm 6^\ddagger$	62 ± 6	*0.0001*
Est. $\dot{V}O_{2\,max}$ (ml·kg^{-1}·min^{-1})	$52.7 \pm 3.4^*$	55.7 ± 3.1	55.5 ± 3.0	56.0 ± 3.0	*0.0001*

Est. $\dot{V}O_{2\,max}$ = estimated maximal aerobic power;
*significant differences between OFF and the other three time points, $P < 0.01$;
†significant difference between OFF and END, $P < 0.001$;
‡significant difference between PRE and MID, $P < 0.01$.

4. DISCUSSION

As observed previously in others studies (Reilly and Thomas, 1977; Thomas and Reilly, 1979; Heller et al., 1992), the soccer players did not show any significant reduction in body fat over the entire season, in particular for the period between OFF and PRE training phase. A plausible reason for this could be that the present players already possessed very low levels of body fat (~11%) at the initial OFF phase, which is on the lower end of the range of 9–16%, previously observed in other professional league players.

The significant improvement of 5.7% in estimated $\dot{V}O_{2\,max}$ from OFF to PRE phase is largely due to both the players' relatively low level of fitness at the start of PRE phase as well as the traditional focus on aerobic conditioning training methods during this period (Reilly and Thomas, 1977; White et al., 1988). The maintenance of aerobic endurance fitness during the rest of the league season is supported by some studies (Thomas and Reilly, 1979; Heller et al., 1992; Casajus, 2001; Dunbar, 2002). Interestingly however, some investigators have found that players significantly reduced their aerobic fitness towards the end of the season (Mohr et al., 2002) while in contrast, others have reported that players were able to improve their aerobic endurance continuously throughout the league season (Brewer, 1990; Rebello and Soares, 1997; Edwards et al., 2003). The latter is obviously favourable for the teams concerned and was due mainly to the optimal training stimulus (i.e., intensity and frequency) and recovery from the weekly games imposed on the players throughout the season (Heller et al., 1992; Bangsbo, 1994). It must also be pointed out that in the studies cited above, the investigators have used various criteria as indicators of aerobic endurance fitness. Both maximal exertion tests like the intermittent field run, incremental treadmill running with gas measurements and progressively faster shuttle runs to exhaustion as well as sub-maximal type tests like lactate profile curve, lactate response at specific running speeds, speed or gas values at lactate and ventilatory thresholds, and the Harvard step test, have been utilized. The non-soccer specific protocol and consequently, the lack of sensitivity of these tests to detect the subtle changes in aerobic training status of soccer players throughout the season could be possible reasons for the contrasting findings among the studies (Edwards et al., 2003).

The present study's finding of a low but significant correlation between the changes in sprinting times with changes in body fat or body mass between PRE to MID training phases partly supports previous assertions that improvements in sprint times were associated with reduction in percentage body fat (Ostojic and Zivanic, 2001). However, it is more likely that much of the improvement in sprinting times was due to the clubs' emphasis on repeated short bursts of high-intensity sprints during the competitive in-season training sessions (A.R. Aziz, unpublished observations) rather than the reduced body fat *per se*.

The significant changes in the vertical jump test throughout the season appear to indicate that this test may be a sensitive indicator of players' training status. Further research is required to confirm this recommendation.

There are several limitations to this study. Although the sample size was relatively large, the players were taken from several different clubs and thus we were not able to document in detail the type, frequency and intensity of the training sessions that the players undertook throughout the period of the study. The number of tests conducted was limited due to time and clubs' commitments.

5. CONCLUSION

The present study indicated that S-League players improved significantly in all the fitness variables measured from OFF to PRE phase of training. This is expected since players generally do not train during the 8–10 weeks of off-season and thus arrived at pre-season training in a relatively poor state of fitness (personal communications, Jan Poulsen, Technical Director, Football Association of Singapore). Nevertheless, the S-League players were able to maintain the level of fitness acquired during the pre-season training phase throughout the rest of the competitive league season, although opportunities for specific fitness training are much reduced during the latter period.

REFERENCES

Andreoli, A., Melchiorri, G., De Lorenzo, A., Caruso, I., Salimei, P.S. and Guerrisi, M., 2002, Bioelectrical impedance measures in different position and vs dual-energy X-ray absorptiometry. *Journal of Sports Medicine and Physical Fitness*, **42**, 186–189.

Bangsbo, J., 1994, *Fitness Training in Football – a Scientific Approach.* (Copenhagen: HO & Storm).

Brewer, J., 1990, Changes in selected physiological characteristics of an English first division soccer squad during a league season. *Journal of Sports Sciences,* **8,** 716–717.

Casajus, J.A., 2001, Seasonal variation in fitness variable in professional soccer players. *Journal of Sports Medicine and Physical Fitness,* **41**, 463–469.

Dunbar, D.M.J., 2002, An examination of longitudinal change in aerobic capacity through the playing year in English professional soccer players, as determined by lactate profiles. In *Science and Football IV,* edited by Spinks, W., Reilly, T. and Murphy, A. (London: E & FN Spon), pp. 72–75.

Edwards, A.M., Clark, N. and Macfadyen, A.M., 2003, Lactate and ventilatory thresholds reflect the training status of professional soccer players where maximum aerobic power is unchanged. *Journal of Sports Science and Medicine,* **2**, 23–29.

Heller, J., Prochazka, L., Bunc, V., Dlouha, R. and Novotny, J., 1992, Functional capacity in top league football players during the competitive season. *Journal of Sports Sciences,* **10**, 150.

Mohr, M., Krustrup, P. and Bangsbo, J., 2002, Performance and physiological characteristics of elite soccer players during a season. *Medicine and Science in Sports and Exercise,* **34** (Suppl.), 24.

Ostojic, S.M. and Zivanic, S., 2001, Effects of training on anthropometrics and physiological characteristics of elite Serbian soccer players. *Acta Biologiae et Medicinae Experimentalis,* **27**, 48 (Abstract in English).

Rebelo, A.N. and Soares, J.M.C., 1997, Endurance capacity of soccer players pre-season and during the playing season. In *Science and Football III,* edited by Reilly, T., Bangsbo, J. and Hughes, M. (London: E & FN Spon), pp. 106–111.

Reilly, T. and Thomas, V., 1977, Effects of a programme of pre-season training on the fitness of soccer players. *Journal of Sports Medicine and Physical Fitness,* **17**, 401–412.

Thomas, V. and Reilly, T., 1979, Fitness assessment of English league players through the competitive season. *British Journal of Sports Medicine,* **13**, 103–109.

Utter, A.C., Scott, J.R., Oppliger, R.A., Visich, P.S., Goss, F.L., Marks, B.L., Nieman, D.C. and Smith, B.W., 2001, A comparison of leg-to-leg bioelectrical impedance and skinfolds in assessing body fat in collegiate wrestlers. *Journal of Strength and Conditioning Research,* **15**, 157–160.

White, J.E., Emery, T.M., Kane, J.E., Groves, R. and Risman, A.B., 1988, Pre-season fitness profiles of professional soccer player. In *Science and Football,* edited by Reilly, T., Lees, A., Davids, K. and Murphy, W.J. (London: E & FN Spon), pp. 164–171.

21   Physiological Attributes of Professional Players in the Singapore Soccer League

A.R. Aziz, F. Tan, A. Yeo and K.C. Teh
Sports Medicine & Research Centre,
Singapore Sports Council

1. INTRODUCTION

Published literature on soccer players' physiological attributes has mainly focused on European-based teams. While there are some data from Asia, these are limited because the investigations were on small numbers of players and on players representing the national teams, rather than the typical professional players (e.g., Chin et al., 1992; Adhikar and Das, 1993; Aziz et al., 1999; Al-Hazza et al., 2000).

In 1996, the local soccer governing body in Singapore established its own professional league, called the S-League. The present study aims to describe the physiological attributes of a large sample group of players playing in this Southeast Asian professional soccer league. A global comparison between Asian and European-based players is relevant and may reveal pertinent information on the reason(s) behind the widely accepted view of the substantial difference in competitive standards of play between the clubs in the two regions.

2. MATERIALS AND METHODS

Two hundred and thirty-eight injury-free players from all the 12 clubs involved in the S-League were tested. However, only data for professional players (N = 147; 16 goalkeepers, 50 defenders, 54 midfielders and 27 forwards) were reported; the rest were non-professionals or part-time players and their data were excluded.

The tests measures were height, weight and percentage body fat (estimated via the bioimpedance method), maximal aerobic power or estimated $\dot{V}O_{2max}$ (via the 20-m multi-stage shuttle run or Beep test), sprinting ability (5 m and 20-m sprint times using light-cell timing gates) and jumping performance (via Sargeant vertical jump). All testing was conducted either the week prior to or after the start of the clubs' first league match for the season. All clubs would have completed their pre-season fitness programme and players would be at, or close to their highest level of fitness. All performance tests were done in the outdoors on the running track.

The SPSS 10.0 version was used for all descriptive statistical analysis. No attempt was made to compare the variables measured between the different playing positions since this was not the primary purpose of this study.

3. RESULTS

Table 1. Players' physical characteristics and exercise performance tests results *(N = 147)*.

	Goalkeeper	Defender	Midfielder	Forward	Pooled Data of Outfielders
	(N = 16)	*(N = 50)*	*(N = 54)*	*(N = 27)*	*(N = 131)*
Age (years)	25.9 ± 5.0	25.9 ± 4.3	25.5 ± 3.9	23.8 ± 4.4	25.3 ± 4.2
Height (m)	1.748 ± 0.052	1.742 ±0.078	1.722 ± 0.052	1.741± 0.070	1.734 ±0.067
Body mass (kg)	74.5 ± 7.1	71.3 ± 9.3	67.9 ± 7.2	70.4 ± 10.0	69.7 ± 8.7
Body fat (%)	11.9 ± 2.8	11.0 ± 2.8	10.7 ± 2.0	10.9 ± 2.3	10.8 ± 2.4
5-m sprint time (s)	1.06 ± 0.05	1.04 ± 0.05	1.04 ± 0.06	1.01 ± 0.05	1.03 ± 0.05
20-m sprint time (s)	3.07 ± 0.13	3.02 ± 0.09	3.03 ± 0.11	2.95 ± 0.01	3.01 ± 0.10
Vertical Jump (cm)	59.8 ± 6.0	58.1 ± 5.3	57.4 ± 4.8	60.6 ± 5.1	58.4 ± 5.2
Number of Completed shuttles	94 ± 14	108 ± 12	115 ± 13	115 ± 15	112 ± 14
Est. $\dot{V}O_{2max}$ ($ml \cdot kg^{-1} \cdot min^{-1}$)	50.0 ± 4.2	54.2 ± 3.5	56.1 ± 3.7	55.9 ± 4.3	55.3 ± 3.8

Est. $\dot{V}O_{2max}$ = estimated maximal aerobic power.

4. DISCUSSION

Compared with data of professionals from other foreign leagues, the typical S-League player is of a similar age range, but is much shorter and lighter. The typical S-League player possesses a relatively low level of body fat, towards the lower end of the range of 9–16% previously observed in other professional league players. In Singapore, matches are typically played in warm, humid conditions (i.e., temperature 30–34 °C and humidity 65–75%) and having a low body fat might be advantageous since an "overfat" player may suffer early onset of fatigue during matches due to a poorer ability to dissipate heat.

The typical S-League outfielder sprints faster than the Australian Olympic squad, but slower than professional German players. The typical S-League outfielder's vertical jump result falls within the mean values of 50 to 60 cm reported for other foreign league professional players. These data suggest that the S-League players possess good sprinting and jumping capabilities that are comparable to their overseas counterparts.

Table 2. Data for the 20-m multi-stage shuttle run (or Beep) test on soccer players.

Populations	N	Beep test	Est. $\dot{V}O_{2max}$	Reference
		Level:Shuttle		
Singapore S-League clubs	131	12:6[§]	55.3	Present study
English 1st & 2nd Div. clubs	122	13:13[§]	60.4	Davis et al., 1992
Swedish 1st Division club	17	14:1	60.8	Balsom, 1994
Scottish 1st Division club	15	14:8	62.6	Mercer et al., 1997
English 1st & 2nd Div. Clubs	18	14:2	60.7	Dunbar & Power, 1997
English, 3rd Division club	14	13:7	58.8	Dunbar & Power, 1997
Japanese (*status?*)	46	13:5	58.4	Katagiri & Sato, 1999

[§]excluding goalkeepers; *status?*: players' status not reported.

Although soccer activities involve intermittent anaerobic bursts of activity throughout the match, ~90% of activities are aerobic in nature and the majority of energy needed to play soccer is produced via the aerobic pathways (Bangsbo et al., 1991; Balsom, 1999). There is a positive relationship between teams' level of maximal aerobic power and both their success in soccer performance (Wisloff et al., 2001) as well as high placing in the league standing (Apor, 1988). Soccer played at a higher level of competitiveness tends towards a more aerobic nature compared to a lower level of play (Yamanaka et al., 1988) and differences in $\dot{V}O_{2max}$ may also reflect the contrasting standard of play between teams (Nowacki et al., 1988; Ostojic, 2002). Thus the Beep test results of the present outfield players indicate that the local S-League is of a relatively lower standard of play as compared to other foreign leagues (Table 2).

The low aerobic endurance performance may possibly have a negative implication on the S-League players' match performance potential. Research has shown that maximal aerobic power was positively correlated with the distance covered and number of sprints attempted during matches. A high aerobic fitness is critical in maintaining a high work rate as well as ensuring rapid recovery from bursts of anaerobic events and this can have a positive influence on a player's ability to perform maximal anaerobic efforts repeatedly. It is even asserted that a higher level of aerobic fitness may help to maintain the player's technical skills and mental concentration towards the end of the game and this is supported by the observation of an inverse relationship between $\dot{V}O_{2max}$ and decrement in work rate during the second half. In addition, a recent study elegantly showed that gains in aerobic fitness paralleled improvements in players' soccer-specific performance on the playing field (Helgerud et al., 2001). This well-controlled study showed that an 11% enhancement of $\dot{V}O_{2max}$ led to a 20% increase in distance covered, a 100% increase in number of high-intensity sprints, 24% increase in involvement with the ball and greater work-rate during actual matches. All the above appear to suggest that high aerobic fitness in players can make matches more exciting with possibly more "end-to-end goal-mouth" action. Consequently, the relatively low level of aerobic endurance performance of outfield players in the present study may lead to a potentially slower tempo of match-play that could affect the quality or "entertainment-value" of S-League matches. This decline in tempo might be particularly evident in the second half of matches when players experience a greater level of fatigue.

5. CONCLUSION

The present data suggest that Asian-based club professional soccer players are shorter, lighter, and with a lower percentage body fat than players of other professional leagues. They have comparable sprinting and jumping ability but a lower level of aerobic endurance. The latter might be a significant factor that explains the relatively superior performances of European-based clubs.

REFERENCES

Adhikar, A. and Das, S.K., 1993, Physiological and physical evaluation of India National soccer squad. *Hungarian Review of Sports Medicine,* **34**, 197–205.
Al-Hazzaa, H.M., Almuzaini, K.S., Al-Refaee, S.A., Sulaiman, M.A., Dafterdar, M.Y., Al-Ghamedi, A. and Al-Khuraiji, K.N., 2000, Aerobic and anaerobic power characteristics of Saudi elite soccer players. *Journal of Sports Medicine and Physical Fitness*, **41**, 54–61.
Apor, P., 1988, Successful formulae for fitness training. In *Science and Football*, edited by Reilly, T., Lees, A., Davids, K. and Murphy, W.J. (London: E & FN Spon Ltd), pp. 95–107.
Aziz, A.R., Teh, K.C., Lee, H.C. and Yeo, S.H., 1998, Physiological assessment of and comparison between Singapore national junior and senior soccer players. In *Proceedings of the 11th Commonwealth & International Scientific Congress*, 3rd – 8th Sept, Kuala Lumpur, Malaysia, edited by Abdullah, M.S., Saad, J., Zakaria, A.A. and Selvaraj, O., pp. 370–375.
Balsom, P.D., 1994, Evaluation of physical performance. In *Football (soccer)*, edited by Ekblom, B. (Oxford: Blackwell Scientific Publications), pp. 102–123.
Balsom, P.D., 1999, *Precision Football*. (Kempele, Finland: Polar Electro Oy).
Bangsbo, J., Nooregard, L. and Thorsoe, F., 1991, Activity profile of competition soccer. *Canadian Journal of Sport Sciences*, **16**, 110–116.

Chin, M.K., Lo, Y.S.A., Li, C.T. and So, C.H., 1992, Physiological profiles of Hong Kong elite soccer players. *British Journal of Sports Medicine*, **26**, 262–266.

Davis, J.A., Brewer, J. and Atkin, D. 1992, Pre-season physiological characteristics of English first and second division soccer players. *Journal of Sports Sciences*, **10**, 541–547.

Dunbar, G.M.J. and Power, K., 1997, Fitness profile of English professional and semi-professional soccer players using a battery of field test. In *Science and Football III,* edited by Reilly, T., Bangsbo, J. and Hughes, M. (London: E & FN Spon), pp. 27–31.

Helgerud, J., Engen, L.C., Wisloff, U. and Hoff, J., 2001, Aerobic endurance training improves soccer performance. *Medicine and Science in Sports and Exercise*, **33**, 1925–1931.

Katagiri, M. and Sato, T., 1999, Study on the validity of 20-m shuttle run test to estimate endurance performance in soccer players. *Canadian Journal of Applied Physiology,* **24**, 455.

Mercer, T.H., Gleeson, N.P. and Mitchell, J. 1997, Fitness profiles of professional soccer players before and after pre-season conditioning. In *Science and Football III,* edited by Reilly, T., Bangsbo, J. and Hughes, M. (London: E & FN Spon), pp. 112–117.

Nowacki, P.E., Cai, D.Y., Bihl, C. and Krummelbein, U., 1988, Biological performance of German soccer players (professional and juniors) tested by special ergometry and treadmill methods. In *Science and Football,* edited by Reilly, T., Lees, A., Davids, K. and Murphy, W.J. (London: E & FN Spon), pp. 145–157.

Ostojic S., 2002, Anthropometric, physiological and biochemical characteristics of elite Yugoslav soccer players. Doctoral thesis, Medical faculty, University of Belgrade, Belgrade, pp. 1–182 (in Serbian with English abstract).

Wisløff, U., Helgrud, J. and Hoff, J. 2001, Strength and endurance of elite soccer players. *Medicine and Science in Sports and Exercise*, **30**, 462–467.

Yamanaka, K., Haga, S., Shindo, M., Narita, J., Koseki, S., Matsuura, Y. and Eda, M., 1988, Time motion analysis in top class soccer games. In *Science and Football,* edited by Reilly, T., Lees, A., Davids, K. and Murphy, W.J. (London: E & FN Spon), pp. 334–340.

22   Pre-Season Anaerobic Performance of Elite Japanese Soccer Players

Franck Brocherie[1], Tsuguo Morikawa[1], Naoki Hayakawa[1] and Mikinobu Yasumatsu[2]
[1] Scientific Research Commitee – Japan Football Association, Tokyo, Japan [2] Rikkyo St Paul's University

1. INTRODUCTION

It is widely documented that soccer is an high intensity intermittent activity that requires a combination of aerobic capacity with anaerobic factors. Running is consequently the predominant activity, yet explosive type efforts such as sprints, jumps, duels and kicking are important factors for successful soccer performance. These efforts depend on maximal strength and anaerobic power of the neuromuscular system, more particulary of the lower limbs. The evaluation of muscle strength of the lower extremities in soccer has been performed using isokinetic peak torque (Öberg et al., 1986 and Zakas et al., 1995) or free weights (Wisloff et al., 1998). Sprint performance (Brewer and Davis, 1991, Dunbar and Power, 1995 and Odetoyinbo and Ramsbottom, 1995), vertical jumps (Gauffin et al., 1989 ; Bosco, 1990 and Wisloff et al., 1998) have also been used to test the anaerobic power of soccer players. The purpose of such monitoring was to construct individual fitness profiles to indicate strengths and weaknesses for subsequent training prescription. Testing is also conducted to evaluate training adaptations and the efficacy of training programmes utilised. This study aimed to establish normative data for elite Japanese soccer players with an emphasis on their anaerobic factors and secondly to make a comparison with other corresponding level data.

2. MATERIAL AND METHODS

2.1. Subjects

Measurements were performed on 31 professional soccer players, all regular members of the national "A" squad of the Japan Football Association. Descriptive anthropometric data of the subjects are shown in Table 1. There was no significant difference in age between the groups of players. The goalkeepers were significantly heavier and taller than any other group (Table 2). Midfield players were the lightest of the outfield players (71.5 ± 4.4 kg).

Table 1. Main characteristics of the subjects (Means values ± SD); (aa) values for GK significantly higher than for DF (P<0.01); (bb) values for GK significantly higher than for MF (P<0.01); (c) values for GK significantly higher than for FW (P<0.05); (e) values for DF significantly higher than for MF (P<0.05); (ee) values for DF significantly higher than for MF (P<0.01); (l) values for FW significantly higher than for MF (P<0.05); (ll) values for FW significantly higher than for MF (P<0.01).

Group	Age (years)	Height (m)	Mass (kg)
GK (n=7)	24.7 ± 1.8	1.85 ± 0.031 (aa, bb, c)	80.9 ± 2.9 (aa, bb, c)
DF (n=9)	24.0 ± 2.3	1.801 ± 0.034 (ee)	74.8 ± 2.2 (e)
MF (n=8)	24.5 ± 2.5	1.743 ± 0.043	71.5 ± 4.4
FW (n=7)	23.6 ± 2.0	1.813 ± 0.005 (ll)	76.6 ± 2.1 (l)

2.2. Testing

A battery of fitness assessments was administered to all players during the pre-season period. In order to control environmental conditions, all testing took place in an indoor sports hall or in an exercise science laboratory. Prior to testing, each subjects underwent a 10-min warm-up period on a cycle ergometer followed by supervised static stretching of the lower limbs.

2.2.1. Isokinetic test

Muscular strength was measured with an isokinetic dynamometer Biodex (Biodex Corporation, Shirley, NY, USA), which recorded instantaneous muscular torques (expressed in Newton-metres; Nm) at various preset constant angular velocities (Taylor et al., 1991). Measurements were made with the subjects in the sitting position. To minimize hip and thigh motion during all movements, a series of straps was applied across the chest, pelvis, mid-thigh and lower leg. The latter strap secured the leg to the lever arm and for each trial a constant length from the axis of rotation was set. The alignment between the centre of rotation of the dynamometer shaft and the axis of the knee joint was checked at the beginning of each trial. The arms were positioned across the chest with each hand clasping the opposite shoulder. After a period of familiarization with the measurement apparatus, the subjects were asked to repeat three maximal voluntary leg extensions at seven angular velocities (concentric:- 1.05, 2.09, 3.14, 4.19, 5.23 rad.s^{-1} and eccentric:- 1.05 and 2.09 rad.s^{-1}). Only the best performance was retained. A 1-min pause was allowed between each trial. Torques were corrected for gravity at each joint angle, using the maximum torque of the weight of the limb obtained at the joint angle, where the gravity effect was maximal (Taylor et al., 1991). Constant Angle Torques (CAT) computed directly by the Biodex software at 65° were used. The H/Q ratio is given as H_{ecc}/Q_{ecc} and H_{con}/Q_{con} at the corresponding angular velocities and by the method of Aagaard et al. (1995), in which a H/Q ratio is associated with knee extension and flexion (H_{ecc}/Q_{con} for knee extension; H_{con}/Q_{ecc} for knee flexion) at the same angular velocity (1.05 and 2.09 rad.s^{-1}).

2.2.2. Vertical jump test

The jumping capacities of the soccer players were evaluated with a jump mat (TEL.SI s.r.l., Vignola, Italy) controlled by T.A.C. (Test Atletici Computerizzati, TEL.SI s.r.l.) software. The players performed five differents jumps : Squat Jump (SJ), Counter-Movement Jump (CMJ), Counter-Movement Jump and Arm-Swing (WAMJ), Drop Jump from a height of 40 cm (DJ40) and a Repetitive Counter-Movement Jump over 15 s (15J). To avoid errors, all jumps were supervised and incorrect jumps were excluded. Three tests were carried out for each type of jump and the best result retained.

2.2.3. Sprint test

Speeds were measured with infrared photoelectric cells (TEL.SI s.r.l., Vignola, Italy) positioned 05, 10, 15 and 20-m from the start line and controlled by T.A.C. (Test Atletici Computerizzati, TEL.SI s.r.l.) software. The players set off upon a visual signal from a standing position and ran the 20-m distance as fast as possible. Only the best of the three tests was retained.

2.3. Statistical analysis

Results were analysed using standard descriptive statistics, whilst Student's t-test was used to examine differences between subjects according to playing position. In all the statistical procedures, the 0.05 and 0.01 levels of significance were adopted.

3. RESULTS AND DISCUSSION

3.1. Isokinetic test

As shown in Figures 1 and 2, extensor and flexor muscle peak torques were higher in the GK group than in other groups, and were significantly higher than for either DF and MF in eccentric mode ($P<0.05$) and for MF in concentric mode ($P<0.01$ at 1.05 and 2.9 rad.s^{-1}; $P<0.05$ at 3.14, 4.19 and 5.23 rad.s^{-1}). The differences may be explained by differences in training and performance. In fact, vertical jump is to a great extent generated by the knee extensors, which may explain the greater knee extensor strength in this group. Further, the goalkeepers often work with the knees semi-flexed, a position often used for strengthening knee extensors.

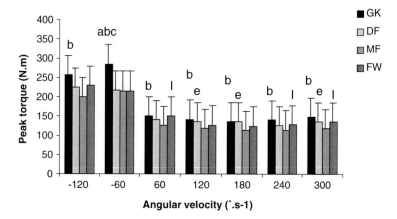

Figure 1. Peak torque developed by the 4 groups for knee extensors, from $120°.s^{-1}$ $(2.09\ rad.s^{-1})$ eccentric to $300°.s^{-1}$ $(5.23\ rad.\ s^{-1})$ concentric. Values are means (± SD); (a) values for GK significantly higher than for DF (P<0.05); (b) values for GK significantly higher than for MF (P<0.05); (bb) values for GK significantly higher than for MF (P<0.01); (e) values for DF significantly higher than for MF (P<0.05); (ee) values for DF significantly higher than for MF (P<0.01); (l) values for FW significantly higher than for MF (P<0.05); (ll) values for FW significantly higher than for MF (P<0.01).

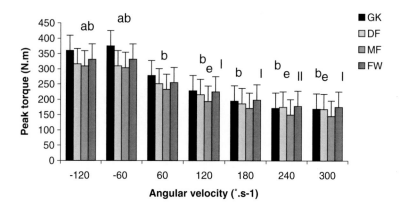

Figure 2. Peak torque developed by the 4 groups for knee flexors, from $120°.\ s^{-1}$ $(2.09\ rad.\ s^{-1})$ eccentric to $300°.s^{-1}$ $(5.23\ rad.\ s^{-1})$ concentric. Values are means (± SD). (a) values for GK significantly higher than for DF (P<0.05). (b) values for GK significantly higher than for MF (P<0.05). (c) values for GK significantly higher than for FW (P<0.05). (e) values for DF significantly higher than for MF (P<0.05). (l) values for FW significantly higher than for MF (P<0.05).

Concerning outfield players, FW players were next, followed by DF and MF (significantly lower than for DF and FW in concentric mode, Figs. 1 and 2). Not surprisingly, it seems logical that DF and FW developed more than MF due to their respective function during effort. However, all the differences disappeared when the results were corrected for body weight. At last, compared with results obtained by other researchers (Davis et al., 1992 and Cometti et al., 2000), the values of this study were higher at all the velocities.

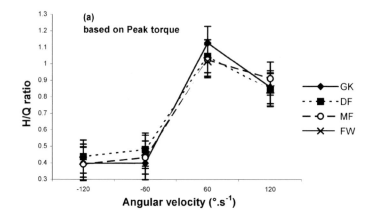

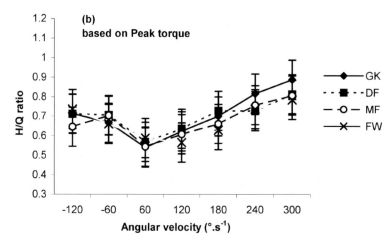

Figure 3. (a) Functional hamstring/quadriceps strength ratio developed by the 4 groups. Positive velocity : Hecc/Qcon representative for knee extension. Negative velocity : Hcon/Qecc representative for knee flexion. (b) Conventional hamstring/quadriceps strength ratio developed by the 4 groups. Positive velocity: concentric muscle contraction (Hcon/Qcon). Negative velocity: eccentric muscle contraction (Hecc/Qecc). Values are means (± SD).

In soccer practice it is normally considered that the quadriceps muscle group plays an important role in jumping and ball kicking while the hamstring group controls running activities and stabilizes the knee during turns or tackles. Moreover, it seems that the contribution of knee flexors to joint stability becomes increasingly important with increasing limb velocity (Hagood et al., 1990). In our study, the four groups of players showed a similar profile at all angular velocities measured (Fig. 2). Expressing the conventional H/Q ratio calculated during concentric and eccentric muscle contractions and also the functional ratio of eccentric hamstrings strength relative to concentric quadriceps strength (H_{ecc}/Q_{con}) indicate important factors for describing the muscular stabilization of the knee joint during active knee extension (Aagaard et al., 1995). It has been demonstrated that the H/Q ratio was significantly higher for soccer players than for untrained subjects (Öberg et al., 1986), but there was no significant difference between different positions (Figs. 3a,b). This may be due to specific training applied to the players where according to the game demands strength between agonist/antagonist is of great importance.

Soccer players are both in training and competition frequently exposed to movement patterns, such as tackles and turns, which require optimum stabilization about the knee joint. During voluntary knee extension such stabilization is provided by both passive and active structures, through ligamentous constraints and antagonist muscle coactivation. The potential capacity of the hamstring muscles to provide stability of the knee joint was increased as a consequence of the high eccentric hamstring strength values (Aagaard et al., 1996). Indeed it seems that eccentric strength of the hamstrings is easily trainable (De Proft et al., 1988). Based on these observations and on our own results, it appears that knee flexor strength is extremely important in soccer players for joint stabilization during various tasks, notably in eccentric action, and systematic strength training is therefore required.

3.2. Vertical jump test

Means and standard deviations for jump test variables are presented in Table 2 and Figure 4. Not surprisingly, goalkeepers were significantly higher than MF and FW players, both in single jump and multiple jump procedures ($P<0.01$ for SJ, CMJ, DJ and 15J; $P<0.05$ for WAMJ and 15J). Differences were also visible between GK and DF in SJ, CMJ and DJ procedures ($P<0.05$). Concerning outfield positions, DF performed better jumps than MF and FW ($P<0.05$ for SJ and WAMJ). The performances obtained in the SJ, CMJ, WAMJ were consistent with those obtained by other researchers (Bosco, 1990; Winkler, 1993 and Cometti et al., 2000). The CMJ-SJ differences reveal, according to Bosco (1990), the elasticity potential of the subjects tested. It can be noted that the CMJ-SJ differences suggest – in accordance with what is usually thought about soccer players – a medium use of their elastic muscular potential. No significant differences were found between the 4 positions (4.20 ± 2.2 for GK, 4.82 ± 2.4 for DF, 4.27 ± 1.7 for MF and 5.06 ± 1.8 for FW).

Table 2. Vertical jump developed by the 4 groups (Means values ± SD). (a) values for GK significantly higher than for DF (P<0.05). (b) values for GK significantly higher than for MF (P<0.05). (bb) values for GK significantly higher than for MF (P<0.01). (c) values for GK significantly higher than for FW (P<0.05). (cc) values for GK significantly higher than for FW (P<0.01). (e) values for DF significantly higher than for MF (P<0.05). (ee) values for DF significantly higher than for MF (P<0.01). (f) values for DF significantly higher than for FW (P<0.05). (ff) values for DF significantly higher than for FW (P<0.01).

Group	SJ (cm)	CMJ (cm)	WAMJ (cm)	DJ (cm)
GK (n=7)	45.56 ± 8.7 (a, bb, cc)	49.76 ± 8.9 (a, bb, cc)	56.71 ± 9.4 (b, c)	49.23 ± 8.6 (a, bb, cc)
DF (n=9)	38.20 ± 2.7 (f)	43.02 ± 4.8	50.91 ± 5.6 (f)	42.62 ± 6.4
MF (n=8)	35.79 ± 5.1	40.06 ± 5.3	47.21 ± 6.0	39.98 ± 4.9
FW (n=7)	32.63 ± 6.0	37.70 ± 4.5	43.76 ± 4.1	39.60 ± 4.7

Results in WAMJ for GK and DF showed a correct segmental coordination and reflect match situations perfectly. On the other hand, FW players showed a weakness in a task compatible with their roles of contesting possession of the ball in the air.

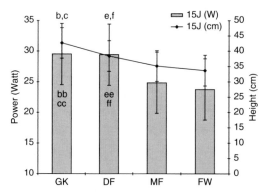

Figure 4. Multiple jump (15J) height and Power developed by the 4 groups (Means values ± SD). (b) values for GK significantly higher than for MF (P<0.05). (bb) values for GK significantly higher than for MF (P<0.01). (c) values for GK significantly higher than for FW (P<0.05). (cc) values for GK significantly higher than for FW (P<0.01). (e) values for DF significantly higher than for MF (P<0.05). (ee) values for DF significantly higher than for MF (P<0.01). (f) values for DF significantly higher than for FW (P<0.05). (ff) values for DF significantly higher than for FW (P<0.01).

The DJ40 describes the reactive capacity of the neuromuscular system of the player. This factor, generally referred to as stretch-shortening cycle, reveals an ability related to storage of elastic energy during pre-stretch and its release (Verkhoshansky, 1988). Performance in DJ40 showed better results than those of previous studies. Goalkeepers were significantly better (P<0.05 vs DF ; P<0.01 vs MF and FW) than the other groups who have researched similar data. This analysis confirmed the usual lack of eccentric loading for playing in outfield positions. Concerning the multiple jump protocol, 15J evaluates the resistive capacities of the knee extensors. Values obtained for the four groups were similar with those reported by Bosco (1990), both in height and power. Comparisons between position revealed differences : GK and DF groups were significantly better than MF and FW (Fig. 4). Due to the stretch-shortening loads employed during intense actions such as sprinting and jumping during games play, it is thought that plyometric training would be of benefit to soccer players. An adequate training programme can develop jumping ability.

3.3. Sprint test

A sprint of 30 m – as recommanded by Föhrenbach et al. (1986) as the best suited distance for assessment of maximal running velocity - is too long a distance and does not mirror actual game situations. Moreover, Kollath and Quade (1993) suggested that in order to perform well in the 30-m sprint, the quick dash at the beginning must be given special attention. On this basis, short-sprinting performance might be an important determinant of match-winning actions and seems more indicative of the level of play than a 30-m sprint.

Table 3. Times over 5, 10, 15 and 20 m for the 4 groups (Means values ± SD). (a) values for GK significantly faster than for DF (P<0.05). (b) values for GK significantly faster than for MF (P<0.05). (c) values for GK significantly faster than for FW (P<0.05). (g) values for MF faster than for GK (P<0.05). (j) values for FW significantly faster than for GK (P<0.05). (k) values for FW significantly faster than for DF (P<0.05).

Group	Reaction Time (s)	5 m (s)	10 m (s)	15 m (s)	20 m (s)
GK (n=7)	0.501 ± 0.01	1.026 ± 0.01	1.737 ± 0.01 (c)	2.333 ± 0.0 (a, b, c)	2.988 ± 0.07
DF (n=9)	0.492 ± 0.04	1.021 ± 0.04	1.768 ± 0.04	2.401 ± 0.05	2.989 ± 0.06
MF (n=8)	0.464 ± 0.03 (g)	1.009 ± 0.04	1.747 ± 0.04	2.393 ± 0.05	3.018 ± 0.03
FW (n=7)	0.372 ± 0.13 (j, k)	1.057 ± 0.01	1.793 ± 0.02	2.468 ± 0.0	3.050 ± 0.02

Table 3 shows better results than those of previous studies (Winkler, 1993, Kollath and Quade, 1993 ; Cometti et al., 2000). Midfield players ran faster over 5 m than any other group, but without showing a significant difference. The GK group reached all interval marks – except the first one, 5 m - earlier than midfield players

(P<0.05 at 15 m), DF (P<0.05 at 15 m) and FW (P<0.05 at 10 and 15 m), respectively. There were no significant differences in the 20-m times among the 4 groups of players. We can also note that the forwards were the last group, but not significantly different from DF, as mentioned by Kollath and Quade (1993). Reaction time values revealed that a quick start does not necessarily reflect a good performance. The first strides of the sprint seem more important for a good performance. Analysis of the sprint capacity, through the relationship between frequency and amplitude of the movement, may contribute to identifying individual strong points and weak points in sprinting performance. Once this kind of information has been provided, the initiative to train acceleration capacities in a fast start, or try to enhance maximal speed, could be taken.

4. CONCLUSION

In view of the scarcity of descriptive data on physiological characteristics of elite Asian soccer players, we can conclude that Japanese players appeared to have better fitness characteristics compared to other international soccer players. Japanese players appeared to be smaller (1.791 ± 0.054 m vs 1.823 ± 0.063 m for the European players) and lighter (75.1 ± 4.9 vs 77.5 ± 6.3 kg for the European players) than those found in Europe, which may be one of the key factors besides tactical experience, that contribute to the lack of success in international competition. In addition, some authors such as Ekblom (1986) and Davis et al. (1992) have suggested that there are limited distinctions in physical characteristics with playing position. In fact, with the exception of the goalkeepers who tended to be the most powerful, the data presented indicated that the specificity of outfield player position was not particularly pronounced in soccer, at least in Japanese players. However, positional roles require different physical demands which may be reflected by some details in their performance during tests. The analysis of these details could provide a better criterion and a better way to specify the training regimens according to positions. Incorporating sports specific testing and evaluation into an overall soccer programme may aid individualized training regimes and players' motivation.

REFERENCES

Aagaard, P., Simonsen, E.B., Trolle, M., Bangsbo, J. and Klausen, K., 1995, Isokinetic hamstring/quadriceps strength ratio : influence from joint angular velocity, gravity correction and contraction mode. *Acta Physiologica Scandinavica*, **154**, 421–427.

Aagaard, P., Simonsen, E.B., Trolle, M., Bangsbo, J. and Klausen K., 1996, Specificity of training velocity and training load on gains in isokinetic knee joint strength. *Acta Physiologica Scandinavica*, **156**, 123–129.

Bosco, C., 1990, *Aspetti fisiologici della preparazione fisicia del calciatore*. ed. Società Stampa Sportiva (Roma).

Brewer, J. and Davis, J.A., 1991, A physiological comparison of English professional and semi-professional soccer players. *In Proceedings of the 2nd World Congress on Science and Football* (Eindhoven), p.141.

Cometti, G., Maffiuletti, N.A., Pousson, M., Chatard, J.C. and Maffulli, N., 2000, Isokinetic strength and anaerobic power of elite, subelite and amateur French soccer players. *International Journal of Sports Medicine*, **21**, 1–7.

Davis, J.A., Brewer, J. and Atkin, D., 1992, Pre-season physiological characteristics of English first and second division soccer players. *Journal of Sports Sciences*, **10**, 541–547.

De Proft, E., Cabri, J., Dufour, W. and Clarys , J.P., 1988, Strength training and kick performance in soccer players. *In Science and Football*, edited by Reilly, T., Lees, A., Davids, K. and Murphy, W.J. (London, New York : E & FN Spon), pp. 108–114.

Dunbar, G.M. and Power , K., 1995, Fitness profiles of English professional and semi-professional soccer players using a battery of fields tests. *Journal of Sports Sciences*, **13**, 501–502.

Ekblom , B., 1986, The applied physiology of soccer. *Sports Medicine*, **3**, 50–60.

Föhrenbach, R., Hollman, W., Mader, A. and Thiele, W., 1986, Testverfahren und metabolisch orientierte intensitätssteuerung im sprinttraining mit submaximaler belastungsstruktur. *Leistungssport*, **5**, 15–24.

Gauffin, H., Ekstrand, J., Arnesson, L. and Tropp, H., 1989, Vertical jump performance in soccer players : a comparative study of two training programmes. *Journal of Human Movement Studies*, **16**, 159–176.

Hagood, S., Solomonow, M., Baratta, R., Zhou, B.H. and D'Ambrosia, R., 1990, The effect of joint velocity on the contribution of the antagonist musculature to knee stiffness and laxity. *American Journal of Sports Medicine*, **18**, 182–187.

Kollath, E. and Quade, K., 1993, Measurement of sprinting speed of professional and amateur soccer players. *In Science and Football II*, edited by Reilly, T., Clarys, J. and Stibbe, A. (London, New York : E & FN Spon), pp. 31–35.

Öberg, B., Möller, M., Gillquist, J. and Ekstrand, J., 1986, Isokinetic torque levels for knee extensors and knee flexors in soccer players. *International Journal of Sports Medicine*, **17**, 50–53.

Odetoyinbo, K. and Ramsbottom, R., 1995, Aerobic and anaerobic field testing of soccer players. *Journal of Sports Sciences*, **13**, 506.

Taylor, N.A.S., Sanders, R.H., Howick, E.I. and Stanley, S.N., 1991, Static and dynamic assessment of Biodex dynamometer. *European Journal of Applied Physiology*, **62**, 180–188.

Verkhoshansky, Y., 1988, Osnovi specialnoi fisiceskoi podgotovki sportmenov (I principi della preparazione fisica speciale degli atleti). Fiskul'tura i sport, Mosca. *In Todo Sobre el Método Pliometrico*, edited by Verkhoshansky, Y. (Barcelona: Editorial Paidotribo).

Winkler, W., 1993, Computer-controlled assessment and video-technology for the diagnosis of a player's performance in soccer training. *In Science and*

Football II, edited by Reilly, T., Clarys, J. and Stibbe, A. (London, New York : E & FN Spon), pp. 73–80.

Wisloff, U., Helgerud, J. and Hoff, J., 1998, Strength and endurance of elite soccer players. *Medicine and Science in Sports and Exercise*, **30**, 462–467.

Zakas, A., Mandroukas, K., Vamvakoudis, E., Christoulas, K. and Aggelopoulou, N., 1995, Peak torque of quadriceps and hamstrings muscles in basketball and soccer players of different divisions. *Journal of Sports Medicine and Physical Fitness*, **35**, 199–205.

23 An Analysis of Fitness Profiles as a Function of Playing Position and Playing Level in Three English Premier League Soccer Clubs

G.M. Joe Dunbar[1] and D.C. Treasure[2]
[1]Joe Dunbar Sport, Teynham, UK
[2]Arizona State University, Phoenix, AZ, USA

1. INTRODUCTION

The English Premier League has become one of the foremost telegenic soccer leagues in Europe and indeed globally. A viewpoint commonly expressed by pundits, coaches and managers associated with this league is that the pace and fitness or physical requirements of the game are constantly increasing.

Intervention of sport science within professional soccer has gathered pace within the last five years, with most clubs within the English Premier League and First Division currently enjoying the benefit of some form of such support. In an applied setting, scientific support can be interdisciplinary or multi-disciplinary in nature, integrating or utilizing sub-disciplines in the specific fields of physiology, fitness/conditioning, nutrition, psychology, biomechanics, immunology, medicine and match analysis.

The formation of a fitness profile is one useful tool as part of an overall interdisciplinary individual and team performance enhancement programme. Not only is this useful for benchmarking and longitudinal monitoring purposes, it also has diagnostic purpose with regards to construction of individual training programme.

We have previously examined fitness profiles of small samples of players in a variety of English leagues and age groups (Dunbar and Power, 1997). More recently, the physiological capacity of elite (predominantly Danish) players has been examined with reference to playing position (Bangsbo and Michalsik, 2002). However, little recent empirical data have been published describing current fitness levels of the English Premier League footballer. The purpose of the current study, therefore, was to examine fitness profiles of a large number (n=89) of elite soccer players drawn from three clubs competing in the English Premier League and assess differences as a function of playing level and position.

2. METHODS

A total of 89 players from three English Premier League clubs were categorized as either first team (n=61) or reserve team (n=28), after consultation with relevant coaching staff and playing appearance records. Playing position was classified either as goalkeeper (n=8), defender (n=34), midfielder (n=30), or forward (n=17). First team players were 25.66 ± 4.47 years of age and 80.39 ± 5.88 kg mass, whilst reserve team players were 20.71 ± 3.04 years and 74.93 ± 7.28 kg. All players completed a battery of fitness tests during the early season period (August-September) of the 2001/2002 season.

On one day, players performed an incremental treadmill test in order to construct a blood lactate profile, via linear interpolation, using the protocol of Dunbar (2002). The running speed ($km.h^{-1}$) at a reference blood lactate concentration of 2 $mmol.l^{-1}$ was determined for each player and taken as an index of aerobic endurance.

On a separate day, a battery of performance tests was completed in an indoor training area consisting of a Fieldturf™ surface, where players could wear their usual soccer specific footwear. After a full and specific warm up, the performance test battery included electronically timed sprints, from a standing start, over 10 m and 20 m, a vertical jump test as a crude indicator of leg power and an Illinois agility run. These were followed finally by an intermittent sprint test, where players ran in pairs seeded according to their 20-m sprint times. The intermittent sprint test consisted of eight, 40-m runs (including two changes of direction) separated by a 20-s recovery period (Dunbar and Woledge, 1995). The mean time of the 8 runs gave an index of anaerobic endurance. Thus the overall fitness profile consisted of measurements of sprint speed, vertical jump (leg power), agility, anaerobic endurance and aerobic endurance.

3. RESULTS

A 2 X 4 (playing level X position) multivariate analysis of variance procedure was conducted with the participants' fitness markers as the dependent variables in the analysis. No significant Playing level by Position interaction effect emerged. Significant main effects for playing level and position did emerge. First team players were older (P<0.001) and had greater body mass (P<0.001) than reserve team players. Follow up univariate analyses for playing level revealed that, although there were no significant differences in either the speed, agility or leg power variables, first team players performed better than the reserve team players in the anaerobic endurance (P<0.05) and aerobic endurance (P<0.01) tests. Specific details of fitness profile results grouped by playing level are summarized in Table 1. In terms of playing position, a post-hoc analysis using Tukey's honestly significant difference test revealed that the goalkeepers (13.49 ± 0.80 $km.h^{-1}$) performed less well in aerobic endurance than the defenders (14.40 ± 1.06 $km.h^{-1}$), midfielders (14.85 ± 1.10 $km.h^{-1}$) and forwards (14.68 ± 1.12 $km.h^{-1}$). No significant differences emerged between the outfield players for any of the fitness variables.

Table 1. Mean (± SD) Fitness profile results as a function of playing level.

Playing Level	10 m	20 m	Vertical Jump	Agility	Anaerobic Endurance	V-2 mmol.l^{-1} (km.h^{-1})
First Team	1.73	2.98	57.37	14.62	8.22*	14.82**
	(0.08)	(0.10)	(7.9)	(0.39)	(0.19)	(1.1)
Reserves	1.71	2.97	54.74	14.76	8.31	13.87
	(0.06)	(0.09)	(7.2)	(0.43)	(0.18)	(0.83)

*P<0.05; **P<0.01.

4. DISCUSSION

The first team players were older and heavier than the reserves team players, which is of little surprise. Since the initial observations of Reilly (1979), it has been widely documented that successful first teams tend to be comprised of players with a mean age of about 25 years and that reserve team players are younger. Squad sizes are currently reducing in English soccer due to the recent financial situation. This means that reserve team squads tend to be even more developmental in nature. The fact that the older players have greater body mass, is likely to be due to muscular development and the continued growth. The first team players from this Premier League sample are, on average, heavier than previous reviews have suggested for players in other leagues or generations (Reilly, 1994). This is likely to be due to a greater muscular component, rather than greater endomorphy. Vertical jump levels are a similar to those seen in English First Division players (Mercer *et al.*, 1997).

The current study suggests that sprint speed over short distances does not discriminate between playing levels. The 20-m sprint performances were slightly quicker than national junior squad players in Australia, whose mean time was 3.01 s (Buttifant et al., 2002), and German National League players, whose mean time was 3.03 s (Kollath and Quade, 1993).

Agility has been shown to be a quite different fitness component to straight line sprinting (Buttifant et al., 2002), but although there was a trend for faster results in the first team players, this did not reach statistical significance. However, the results for the current sample Illinois agility run are by far superior to performances by a squad of First Division first team players (Mercer *et al.*, 1997) who recorded a mean time of 16.5 s before and 16.0 s after pre-season conditioning. Similarly, times of 16.4 s were noted several years ago by White *et al.* (1988) in their investigation into English first division soccer players.

The ability to change direction at speed is a key element of soccer fitness, as is the ability to decelerate rapidly. The average current Premier League player appears competent at both of these factors, as shown by the exceptional agility performances in this sample and the impressive anaerobic performances revealed by the fast average time of the eight shuttle runs. Indeed performance in this test did discriminate between first team and reserve team players, with first team players significantly quicker over the eight runs. Given that the basic speed of the two groups was similar, there were clear differences in the endurance capabilities of the two groups. This is not simply due to current conditioning, as both groups utilized similar training programmes in the pre-season and early season periods. Considering the first team mean age is several years older, there may be the benefit of accumulated training over several years that contributed to superior first team performance.

The same might also be true for aerobic endurance where, again, first team players registered better performances than reserve team players. The actual mean V-2 mmol.l^{-1} speed for the current first team group was the same (14.82 v 14.80 km.h^{-1}) as the mid-season mean of an English First Division side that won the Championship in the year of testing (Dunbar, 2002). The greater aerobic endurance of the first team players could be due to a background of more years of full-time training, given the older age.

The aerobic endurance test was the only component of the fitness profile that revealed a difference between playing positions. That the goalkeepers were less fit than the outfield players for this component was of little surprise, due to the relative physical demands of the respective playing positions. The fact that no other fitness differences existed between playing positions is in contrast to the review by Bangsbo and Michalsik (2002). This may be partly explained by the fact that there was no sub-division between centre backs and full backs in the current study. We have noticed that due to smaller squad sizes in recent years, players have played in a variety of positions, thus making them difficult to categorise in some instances. For example, we have observed two players who have played in the Premier League in the position of full back, wing back, centre half and left wing, all within the same season, albeit in different team formations. Another factor potentially responsible for the lack of fitness differences between playing positions, is the general increase in athleticism required by the demands and competitiveness of the modern game in the English Premier League.

5. CONCLUSIONS

It was concluded that the fitness attributes of speed, leg power and agility are not different between playing positions or playing level in this sample of 89 English Premier League soccer players from three different clubs. However, the aerobic endurance of outfield players was significantly higher than goalkeepers. Furthermore, the aerobic and anaerobic endurance of first team players was significantly better than reserve team players.

REFERENCES

Bangsbo J. and Michalsik L., 2002, Assessment of the physiological capacity of elite soccer players. In *Science and Football IV*, edited by Spinks, W., Reilly, T. and Murphy, A. (London: Routledge), pp. 53–62.
Buttifant, D., Graham, K., and Cross, K., 2002, Agility and speed in players are two different performance parameters. In *Science and Football IV*, edited by Spinks, W., Reilly, T. and Murphy, A. (London: Routledge), pp. 329–332.
Dunbar, G.M.J., 2002, An examination of longitudinal change in aerobic capacity through the playing year in English professional soccer players, as determined

by lactate profiles. In *Science and Football IV*, edited by Spinks, W., Reilly, T. and Murphy, A. (London: Routledge), pp. 72–75.

Dunbar, G.M.J. and Power, K.T.D., 1997, Fitness profiles of English professional and semi-professional soccer players using a battery of field tests. In *Science and Football III*, edited by Reilly, T., Bangsbo, J. and Hughes, M. (London: E & FN Spon), pp. 27-31.

Dunbar, G.M.J. and Woledge, J., 1995, An investigation into the order of tests performed by games players in a battery of field tests. *Journal of Sports Sciences*, **14**, 77–78.

Kollath, E. and Quade, K.,1993, Measurement of sprinting speed of professional and amateur soccer players. In *Science and Football II*, edited by Reilly, T., Clarys, J. and Stibbe, A. (London: E & FN Spon), pp. 31–36.

Mercer, T.H., Gleeson, N.P., and Mitchell, J., 1997, Fitness profiles of professional soccer players before and after pre-season conditioning. In *Science and Football III*, edited by Reilly, T., Bangsbo, J. and Hughes, M. (London: E & FN Spon), pp. 112–117.

Reilly, T. and Thomas, V., 1979, Estimated energy expenditure of professional association footballers. *Ergonomics*, **22**, 541–548.

White, J.A., Emery, T.M., Kane, J.L., Groves, R., and Risman, A.B., 1988, Pre-season fitness profiles of professional soccer players. In *Science and Football*, edited by Reilly, T., Lees, A., Davids, K. and Murphy, W.J. (London: E. & F.N. Spon), pp. 164–171.

24   Off-Season and Pre-Season Changes in Total and Regional Body Composition in Japanese Professional Soccer League Players

Y. Hoshikawa[1], A. Kanno[2], T. Ikoma[3], M. Muramatsu[1], T. Iida[1], A. Uchiyama[1] and Y. Nakajima[1]

[1] Sports Photonics Laboratory, Hamamatsu Photonics K.K., 2150-1 Iwai, Iwata-City, Japan
[2] Yamaha Football Club Co.Ltd, 2044-3 Nishikaizuka, Iwata-City, Japan
[3] Sanfreece Hiroshima Football Club, 4-10-2 Kanonshin-Machi, Nishi-Ku, Hiroshima, Japan

1. INTRODUCTION

The simple task of measuring body weight is a basic element in monitoring the physical condition of professional soccer players. However, body composition plays a far more important role in determining successful performance because excessive fat weight is clearly a disadvantage in soccer. In fact, the percent of body fat in elite soccer players has been reported to be close to 10% (Reilly, 1994) which is just as low as other sports competitors except for elite endurance athletes.

After several months of the competitive season, professional soccer players spend about one month off-season without any soccer games or physical training. Consequently, it is likely that their body composition will shift to an excess fat condition during the off-season. Therefore, when designing a training programme for use after the off-season period, it is essential that coaches understand how much of a change has occurred in the player's body composition rather than just the body weight during the off-season. The first aim of this study was therefore to evaluate off-season total body composition by means of the well known densitometry method as well as regional body composition from magnetic resonance (MR) images of the thigh (Despres *et al.*, 1996;Malina, 1996) in professional soccer players. Secondly, changes resulting from a re-training programme were also evaluated after the following pre-season period.

2. METHODS

Subjects were fifty Japanese professional soccer league (J-League) players and twenty youth team players (Group 1). Most subjects belonged to Jubilo Iwata, which took part in the final Asian club championship matches for three years in a row from 1999 to 2001 during the study. The subjects consisted of 66 players from

Japan, 3 from Europe, and 1 from South America. The competitive season for J-League starts from the middle of March and ends in late December, so that J-League clubs set January as the rest period (off-season) and February to March as the period for preparing for the next game season (pre-season). Thus to make comparisons with off-season, measurements in this study were conducted in December (measurement 1; end of game-season) and late January (measurement 2; beginning of pre-season). In addition, 25 of the 50 professional players (Group 2) were measured again in March (measurement 3; beginning of game season) to confirm the effects of the pre-season training programme (Figure 1). The length of the off-season period in the study was approximately 4 weeks during which there were no soccer games or team training programmes but the subjects were allowed to do any light physical activities that they wished. The length of the pre-season was 7 weeks including 2 weeks in camp and consisted of eight or more training sessions per week. The ages of the subjects were 22.3 ± 5.0 and 24.3 ± 3.8 years, and heights were 1.76 ± 0.061 and 1.783 ± 0.05 m for Group 1 and Group 2.

Total body composition was measured by total-body densitometry with air displacement plethysmography using the Bod Pod (Life Instrument Measurement Inc.). Total percent body fat (TFATP), total fat weight (TFATW) and fat free weight (FFW) were calculated according to the equation by Brozek *et al.* (1963). Since skeletal muscle is known to be the largest fat-free tissue component in the human body, we used FFW as a variable representing the muscle volume of the entire body.

Magnetic resonance images were obtained with a General Electric 0.2-T scanner (Signa Profile) to assess regional fat and muscle volume of the right thigh. Firstly a longitudinal image of the thigh was taken to identify the greater trochanter and lower edge of femur. The length of the femur was measured from the image. Subsequently, a series of transverse slice images of 10 mm thickness with 10 mm gap (TR 350 ms, TE 21 ms, matrix 256×256, field of view 400 mm, 2 NEX) was obtained from the greater trochanter to the lower edge of femur, and the images nearest to 30% (lower), 50% (middle) and 70% (upper) of the femur length were selected in the series. On the selected images a single experienced observer, who did not know the subject's characteristics, outlined femur, subcutaneous fat, quadriceps femoris (QF), hamstrings (HAM), adductor muscles (ADD), sartorius, gracilis, and others to calculate their cross-sectional areas by summing the pixels surrounded by those outlines using dedicated computer software. Regional fat volume index (RFI) and muscle volume index (RMI) in the thigh were calculated as the products of the length of the femur and the average of the area of the lower, middle, and upper thigh fat and overall muscles, respectively. The inter-observer difference for the calculation of cross-sectional area of fat and overall muscles in the same MR image of the thigh was less than 1% in our laboratory testing.

Paired t-tests were performed to compare between the measurements and significance was accepted at the $P < 0.05$ level.

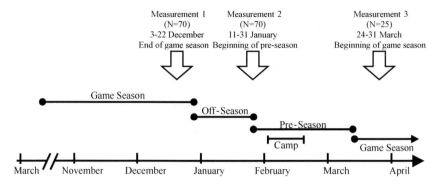

Figure 1. Season profile of J-League and measurement schedule.

3. RESULTS AND DISCUSSION

3.1. Comparison between measurement 1 and measurement 2

Table 1. Total body composition of 70 subjects by Bod Pod at measurement 1 (end of game season) and measurement 2 (beginning of pre-season); 25 of the 70 subjects were measured again at measurement 3 (beginning of game season).

	Group1 (n=70)		Group2 (n=25)		
	Measure.1	Measure.2	Measure.1	Measure.2	Measure.3
	End of game Season	Beginning of pre-season	End of game season	Beginning of pre-season	Beginning of game season
Body mass (kg)	69.4±7.8	70.1±7.8**	72.8±6.4	73.5±6.6**	73.9±6.7**#
Total body percent fat (%)	8.44±3.16	9.68±3.31**	8.73±3.47	10.24±3.56**	9.02±2.70##
Total body fat mass (kg)	5.98±2.83	6.90±2.94**	6.49 ±3.20	7.67±3.35**	6.77±2.61###
Fat free mass (kg)	63.5±6.3	63.2±6.3	66.3±4.8	65.8±4.6*	67.1±5.0*##

*p<0.05, **p<0.01 Compared with the value at measurement1;
#p<0.05, ##p<0.01 Compared with the value at measurement2.

Body mass showed only small increases of about 0.6 kg in both of Group 1 and Group 2 during the off-season. At this time, however, TFATP increased significantly (P<0.01) from 8.4% to 9.7% and from 8.7% to 10.2% for Group 1 and Group 2; TFATW also increased significantly (P<0.01) from 6.0 kg to 6.9 kg and from 6.5 kg to 7.7 kg for Group 1 and Group 2 (Table 1). In line with the total fat increases, the cross-sectional area of fat in all parts of the thigh increased significantly (P<0.01) during the off-season. Consequently, there were significant increases (P<0.01) in RFI from 1173 cm^3 to 1266 cm^3 for Group 1 and from 1192 cm^3 to 1265 cm^3 for Group 2 (Table 2). The percentage of TFATW increase was therefore about 15–18%, which was two times greater than that in the RFI of about

6-8% for both groups, suggesting that fat component increases occurred largely in regions of the body other than the thigh. Figure 2 shows the correlation between the amount of changes in TFATW and RFI among the measurements. No significant correlation was found during the off-season; however, it should be noted that increases in fat components occurred in both the entire body and thigh in 50 of the 70 subjects, and occurred in either location in 66 subjects during the off-season. Since we did not control the physical activities of subjects in the study, the physical condition at measurement 2 probably varied according to the subject since some subjects continued personal physical training even during the off-season. However, it is reasonable to conclude that a short period (4 weeks) of off-season inactivity was likely to increase fat in both the entire body and the legs of soccer players even if their body weight did not increase much.

As for muscle-related variables, there was no significant change in FFW for Group 1, while there was a small but significant decrease (-0.55 kg) for Group 2 during the off-season. The RMI was also not significantly different in the off-season in either group despite significant (P<0.05) decreases in the cross-sectional area of overall muscles of upper thigh in Group 1 and of middle thigh in Group 2. Due to the large inter-individual differences, changes in muscle-related variables during the off-season were not clear in contrast with the changes in fat-related variables mentioned above. Bangsbo and Mizuno (1988) reported that the mean muscle fibre cross-sectional area determined by biopsies from m. gastrocnemius showed a significant decrement of 6.7% during 3 weeks of the off-season in four semi-professional soccer players. It might therefore be possible that several weeks of detraining during the off-season period could cause muscle atrophy in the legs of professional soccer players. Further analysis revealed no significant changes in the cross-sectional area of QF and HAM in any part of the thigh. However, those of ADD showed significant decreases during the off-season for both Group 1 and Group 2 (Table 3). It therefore seemed that adductor muscles (ADD) of the thigh were most susceptible to detraining in soccer players. However, another study is needed to clarify this point since the decreases were too small to establish a firm conclusion.

Table 2. Cross-sectional area (cm^2) of total, fat and overall muscle of lower, middle, and upper thigh measured from MR images. Detailed calculation for regional fat and muscle volume index was described in method.

		Group1 (n=70)		Group2 (n=25)		
		Measure.1	Measure.2	Measure.1	Measure.2	Measure.3
		End of game Season	Beginning of pre-season	End of game season	Beginning of pre-season	Beginning of game season
Total cross-sectional area (cm^2)	Lower	151.9±15.4	153.4±16.5**	156.2±14.3	156.9±16.8	159.4±16.8*[##]
	Middle	206.3±19.0	207.7±19.5**	215.6±16.7	215.3±17.2	220.0±18.4*[##]
	Upper	238.6±24.6	240.9±25.5**	251.3±20.7	252.6±21.9	255.5±22.4[#]
Cross-sectional area of fat (cm^2)	Lower	18.3±5.1	19.3±5.9**	17.6±5.2	18.5±6.1*	17.5±6.0[##]
	Middle	23.7±7.5	25.4±8.3**	23.6±7.9	24.7±8.5**	23.7±8.4[#]
	Upper	37.4±15.0	41.0±16.8**	38.5±15.7	41.4±17.1**	36.3±16.5[#]
Cross-sectional area of overall muscles (cm^2)	Lower	115.9±13.5	116.4±14.0	118.7±12.3	119.4±13.4	121.7±13.2*[##]
	Middle	168.5±16.2	167.9±16.6	175.7±13.6	174.1±13.2*	179.4±14.3*[##]
	Upper	184.6±17.0	183.3±18.5*	192.7±12.5	192.2±13.3	197.4±12.9*[##]
Regional fat volume index (cm^3)		1173±425	1266±476**	1192±447	1265±489**	1158±473[##]
Regional muscle volume index (cm^3)		6910±794	6888±821	7244±567	7221±588	7411±601**[##]

*p<0.05, **p<0.01 Compared with the value at measurement 1:

#p<0.05, ##p<0.01 Compared with the value at measurement 2.

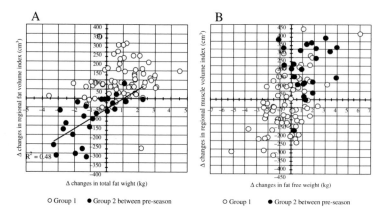

Figure 2. The correlation of changes in fat (A) and muscle (B) component between the entire body and thigh. Significant relation was found only in fat component on Group 2 between the pre-season.

Table 3. Cross-sectional area (cm^2) of quadriceps femoris, hamstrings, and adductor muscles from lower, middle, and upper thigh of MR images.

		Group1 (n=70)		Group2 (n=25)		
		Measure.1	Measure.2	Measure.1	Measure.2	Measure.3
		End of game Season	Beginning of pre-season	End of game season	Beginning of pre-season	Beginning of game season
Quadriceps Femoris (cm^2)	Lower	62.3±7.4	62.7±7.5	63.1±7.2	63.5±7.7	64.0±7.7
	Middle	83.2±8.1	83.0±7.9	86.8±6.3	85.8±6.1	87.9±6.9***##
	Upper	76.6±7.9	76.4±8.2	80.5±6.2	80.5±5.8	82.0±5.7##
Hamstrings (cm^2)	Lower	43.8±6.2	43.8±6.5	45.6±5.0	45.8±5.5	47.4±5.4***##
	Middle	40.9±4.6	40.8±4.8	42.1±4.7	42.1±4.8	43.8±4.8***##
	Upper	15.2±4.0	15.1±4.1	15.7±3.7	15.8±3.8	16.5±3.5***##
Adductor muscles (cm^2)	Lower	1.8±1.4	1.9±1.5	1.8±1.6	1.8±1.6	1.8±1.5
	Middle	33.2±6.1	32.9±6.2*	34.9±5.9	34.4±6.0*	35.8±6.4*##
	Upper	67.8±8.0	66.9±8.5**	70.9±7.4	70.0±7.1	72.8±6.9***##

*p<0.05, **p<0.01 Compared with the value at measurement 1;
#p<0.05, ##p<0.01 Compared with the value at measurement 2.

3.2. Comparison between measurement 2 and measurement 3

Body mass in Group 2 showed a small but significant increase of 0.41 kg (P<0.05) during the pre-season. The increase in body mass at this period was attributable to a significant increase (P<0.01) in FFW from 65.8 kg to 67.1 kg, which over-compensated for possible losses in body weight by a significant (P<0.01) decline in TFATW from 7.7 kg to 6.8 kg (Table 1). The RFI decreased significantly (P<0.01) from 1265 cm^3 to 1158 cm^3, the same way as for total body composition; however, RMI increased significantly (P<0.01) from 7221 cm^3 to 7411 cm^3 (Table 2). The percent changes in TFATW and FFW of the entire body were therefore 11.7% and 2.0 %, or roughly the same level as the respective regional changes in RFI and RMI of 8.5% and 2.6%. While no significant correlation was found between increases in FFW and RMI, there was a significant (P<0.01) correlation between the decreases in TFATW and RFI (Figure 2). As such, unlike the changes observed during the off-season, the change in body composition was similar in both the entire body and thigh during the pre-season period, where the muscle component increased simultaneously with decreases in the fat component, which is certainly a favourable improvement for soccer performance.

Values for TFATP, TFATW and RFI at measurement 3 were not different from those at measurement 1. The magnitudes of changes in the fat component during pre-season were to the same extent inversely observed during the off-season on both the entire body and thigh. Thus, the 7-weeks pre-season re-training served to cancel out marked increases in the fat component caused during the off-season. In contrast, the FFW, RMI, and the cross-sectional area of QF, HAM and ADD at measurement 3 showed significant (P<0.05) increases compared to measurement 1 as well as measurement 2 (Table 3). Therefore, the possible loss in muscle volume caused during the off-season seems to be more than offset by an adequate pre-season training programme allowing recovery to the levels exceeding those at the end of the competitive season.

4. CONCLUSIONS

The primary findings of the study were that the body composition of professional soccer players during off-season and pre-season changed as follows. First, irrespective of body mass changes, most players tended to increase their body fat component totally and regionally in the thigh, and some players lost a portion of their muscle component in the off-season. Second, a physical condition characterized by excess fat and possible muscle atrophy during the off-season can be reversed from by using a well-designed pre-season training programme.

REFERENCES

Bangsbo, J. and Mizuno, M., 1988, Morphological and metabolic alterations in soccer players with detraining and retraining and their relation to performance. In *Science and Football*, edited by Reilly, T., Lees, A., Davids, K. and Murphy, W. J. (London: E. & F. N. Spon), pp.114–124.

Brozek, J., Grande, F., Anderson, T. and Keys, A., 1963, Densitometric analysis of body composition: Revision of some quantitative assumptions. *Annals of the New York Academy of Sciences*, **110**, 113–140.

Despres, J.-P., Ross, R. and Lemieux, S., 1996, Imaging techniques applied to the measurement of human body composition. In *Human Body Composition*, edited by Roche, A.F., Heymsfield, S.B. and Lohman, T.G. (Champaign: Human Kinetics Publishers, Inc.), pp.159–176.

Malina, R.M., 1996, Regional body composition: age, sex and ethnic variation. In *Human Body Composition*, edited by Roche, A.F., Heymsfield, S.B. and Lohman, T.G. (Champaign: Human Kinetics Publishers, Inc.), pp.227–263.

Reilly, T., 1994, Physiological profile of the player. In *Handbook of Sports Medicine and Science-Football* edited by Ekblom, B. (London: Blackwell Scientific Publications), pp.78–94.

25 Fitness Profiles of Elite Players in Hurling and Three Football Codes: Soccer, Rugby Union and Gaelic Football

Noel Brick[1] and Peter O'Donoghue[2]

[1]Causeway Institute of Higher and Further Education, Union Street, Coleraine, Co. Londonderry, BT52 1QA, UK
[2]School of Applied Medical Sciences and Sports Studies, University of Ulster, Jordanstown, Co. Antrim, BT37 0QB, UK

1. INTRODUCTION

Gaelic football and hurling are two of the national sports in Ireland. Both are field games played by two teams of 15 players. Gaelic football is played with a round ball, which may be played with the hands or the feet. Hurling is played with a smaller, tennis-sized ball, which is propelled by striking it from the hand or the ground with a hurley (a stick approximately 80 cm – 90 cm long). These sports contrast with Association Football (soccer), which is played by two teams of 11 players, where any body part, except the arms or the hands, can be used to manipulate the ball. Both Gaelic football and hurling are played on a similar sized pitch, which is about 40% longer than a soccer pitch (Strudwick et al., 2002). Rugby Union is a further code of football played by teams of 15 (8 forwards and 7 backs). The object of the sport is to secure possession of an oval shaped ball and capitalise on possession by scoring more points than the opponents.

Knowledge of demands of these different sports is important during the development of training programmes. The comparison of the activities is important in Ireland, as there are "dual code" players who compete at elite level at both hurling and Gaelic football. Furthermore, there are individuals who have competed at elite level in Gaelic football and soccer (Watson, 1995). It has previously been noted (Strudwick et al., 2002) that there is a lack of research comparing the fitness characteristics of elite level players in each of the football codes. Even less is known about the fitness characteristics of hurlers. The aim of the present study, therefore, was to examine the fitness characteristics of players at an elite level in soccer, Rugby Union backs, Rugby Union forwards, Gaelic football and hurling with the view of making comparisons between them.

2. METHODS

2.1. Subjects

This study used subjects from the leading teams within a chosen county of Northern Ireland (Derry). There were 22 semi-professional soccer players (age 24.6±5.0 years), 9 Rugby Union forwards (age 28.8±3.9 years), 5 Rugby Union backs (age 21.2±2.2 years), 25 senior inter-county Gaelic football players (age

23.6±3.4 years) and 20 senior inter-county hurlers (age 26.6±3.5 years). None of the subjects were goalkeepers.

2.2. Measurement and testing

Measurements were taken during the early-season stage for each of the sports. This was in January for the Gaelic footballers and hurlers, and during September for the soccer players and Rugby Union players. Measurements taken included body mass, percent body fat estimated from three skinfold measurements (chest, abdomen and thigh) using Harpenden™ skinfold calipers, isometric handgrip strength using a handgrip dynamometer (Takei), dynamic upper body strength (1-repetition maximum on the bench press). Flexibility of the body was measured using the sit-and-reach test. Vertical jump was measured as the rise in height of the body using a digital jump dynamometer (Takei). The maximal oxygen uptake $\dot{V}O_{2\,max}$) was estimated from performance on a progressive 20-m shuttle run test.

Running speed as measured using a 40-m split-sprint test on the soccer players and the Gaelic footballers. This test involved a 40-m run composed of a 10-m, a 20-m and a final 10-m segment with a 120° turn at the end of each stage. A straight-line 40-m sprint was used for the Rugby Union players and hurlers. Electronic timing gates (Newtest) were set at the start and end lines of each sprint course.

2.3. Statistical analysis

An independent t-test was used to compare the 40-m split-sprint test performance between the soccer players and Gaelic footballers. A one-way ANOVA was used to compare the straight line 40-m sprint performances of the Rugby Union backs, Rugby Union forwards and the hurlers with Bonferroni adjusted post hoc tests employed to compare individual pairs of groups. The remaining dependent variables were compared between all five groups using a one-way ANOVA with Bonferroni adjusted post hoc tests employed to investigate differences between pairs of groups where group was a significant factor.

Each pair of sports was also compared using the sum of absolute differences between the z-scores of their measures for each variable that was tested or measured for each group (grip strength for each hand weighted as half a variable each). The purpose of constructing this composite variable for the difference between each pair of sports was to allow the most similar sports in terms of player characteristics to be identified.

3. RESULTS

The 40-m split-sprint performances for the soccer players (9.0±0.2 s) and the Gaelic footballers (8.9±0.3 s) were not significantly different ($t_{45} = 0.8$, $P = 0.404$). The straight line 40-m sprint performances were 5.0±0.2 s for the Rugby Union backs, 5.5±0.1s for the Rugby Union forwards and 5.6±0.2 s for the hurlers. Group had a significant effect on 40-m sprint performance ($F_{2,31} = 19.1$, $P < 0.001$) with Bonferroni adjusted post hoc tests revealing that the Rugby Union backs were significantly faster than the Rugby Union forwards ($P < 0.001$) and the hurlers

(P < 0.001). Table 1 shows the results for the remaining variables. There was no significant difference between the five groups for sit-and-reach performance ($F_{4,76}$ = 1.0, P = 0.409). However, there were significant differences between the five groups of subjects for all the other variables ($F_{4,76} >= 4.7$, P <= 0.002). Rugby Union forwards had the highest values for body mass, percentage body fat, grip strength and repetition maximum. Rugby Union backs, on the other hand, had the highest values for vertical jump performance and estimated $\dot{V}O_2$max.

Table 1. Summary of analysis.

Variable	Group					$F_{4,76}$
	Soccer	Hurling	Gaelic Football	Rugby forwards	Rugby backs	
Body Mass (kg)	81.4±8.0$	84.5±10.1$	86.5±8.6$	100.2±9.2	84.5±4.7$	7.7***
Body Fat (%)	12.1±3.6$	15.8±5.3	12.0±4.3$	17.5±4.0	12.1±3.7	4.7**
Grip Str Right (kgf)	42.5±6.7	52.0±8.5$^	55.1±5.4^	61.3±7.6^	54.2±6.1^	15.9***
Grip Str Left (kgf)	42.5±6.6	51.3±7.8^	53.4±5.9^	55.9±8.6^	53.4±4.7^	10.2***
Rep Max (kg)	80.0±11.7$	69.7±12.3$	93.6±12.3$^&	109.7±26.7	88.6±7.0	15.7***
Sit-and-Reach (cm)	27.1±5.3	26.4±8.7	29.8±4.1	27.8±6.4	27.6±5.5	1.0
Vertical Jump (cm)	59.7±6.1	56.6±5.9	62.2±5.1&$	54.1±4.6	64.2±2.9$	6.0***
Estimated $\dot{V}O_2$max (ml.m in^{-1}.kg^{-1})	51.3±4.4	53.2±4.0	57.0±3.9^&	54.1±2.6	59.6±4.7^&	8.6***

ANOVA: * P<0.05, ** P<0.01, *** P<0.001.
Bonferroni adjusted post hoc tests:
$ significantly different from Rugby Union forwards (P<0.05);
^ significantly different from soccer players (P<0.05);
& significantly different from hurlers (P<0.05).

Figure 1 shows the differences between the five groups in terms of the summed absolute difference between z-scores for each pair of groups. The Gaelic footballers and Rugby Union backs were the most similar pair of groups. The hurlers and soccer players were the next most similar pair of groups. Rugby Union forwards were the most different group of subjects to the other four groups; the subjects they were closet to were the Gaelic footballers.

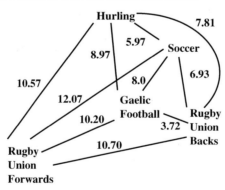

Figure 1. Sum of absolute difference between z-scores between the five groups.

4. DISCUSSION

Rugby Union forwards were the group with the highest body mass, percentage body fat, grip strength and maximal 1-repetition performance of a bench press. The maximal 1-repetition performance of a bench press for the current Rugby Union forwards was lower than the 114 kg of the front row forwards analysed by Tong and Wood (1997) but higher than the 100.5 kg for second row forwards and the 103.5 kg for back row forwards reported by Tong and Woods (1997). Rugby Union is a contact sport involving tackling with the hands, rucks and mauls, all of which require upper body strength. It is surprising that the Rugby Union forwards had the lowest vertical jump performance and Rugby Union backs had the highest vertical jump performance as it is the forwards in Rugby Union who participate in line outs. Second row forwards are usually taller than other players and this may lead to a reduced requirement for vertical jumping ability. Furthermore, players may be assisted by team-mates when they jump during the line out, further reducing the need for vertical jumping ability. Rugby Union backs had the fastest 40-m straight sprint times of the three sets of players tested. The highest estimated $\dot{V}O_{2max}$ was for the Rugby Union backs who are required to participate in running and passing play of an intermittent nature. It is notable that despite their body mass, the Rugby Union forwards had a higher estimated $\dot{V}O_{2\ max}$ than hurlers and soccer players. The forwards spend more time involved in high intensity activity during competition than the other four groups because many forwards can be involved simultaneously in play during rucks and mauls.

The soccer players had a significantly lower grip strength than all of the other groups. The lower grip strength of soccer players may be explained by the fact that outfield soccer players cannot manipulate the ball with their hands whereas the use of hands to manipulate the ball is permitted in Rugby Union, Gaelic football and hurling. In hurling, it is also necessary to hold the hurley stick. The estimated $\dot{V}O_{2}max$ was also lower in the current players than that observed by Tíryakí *et al.* (1997) in Turkish first division soccer players.

The Gaelic football players had the highest sit-and-reach scores of the five groups. The sit-and-reach performance of the current Gaelic football subjects was greater than that reported by Young and Murphy (1994) for the 1993 senior Ulster inter-county champions as well as being greater than that of the inter-county players studied by Donnelly *et al.* (2002). Despite having the lowest percentage body fat estimates of the five groups, percentage body fat of the current Gaelic footballers was higher than the 11.4% (pre-season) of the subjects reported by Young and Murphy (1994) but less than the 12.3% of the inter-county players analysed by both Strudwick et al. (2002) and Donnelly *et al.* (2002). Further comparisons with the results of Donnelly *et al.* (2002) show the current Gaelic football subjects to be heavier, with a marginally lower estimated $\dot{V}O_{2\ max}$ but with a greater vertical jump performance. However, body mass, estimated $\dot{V}O_{2}max$ and vertical jump performance were all greater in the current Gaelic footballers than those values observed by Keane *et al.* (1997).

Within the current study, the Gaelic footballers had the highest estimated $\dot{V}O_{2}max$. Although a Gaelic football pitch is 40% larger than a soccer pitch, Strudwick *et al.* (2002) suggested that the relative intensity of competitive match-play is roughly equivalent in both Gaelic football and soccer. However, the duration of a soccer match (90 minutes) is 20 minutes longer than a senior Championship game in either Gaelic football or hurling (70 minutes). It might therefore be argued that soccer players would need a higher level of endurance to complete a full game. Currently, the Gaelic games are amateur sports and the greater $\dot{V}O_2$max than soccer could be interpreted as resulting from a greater personal commitment than professional soccer players.

The hurlers in the current investigation had the lowest 1-repetition maximal bench press performance. Hurling is less physically demanding in terms of the upper body strength required. However, hurling is a very fast moving game. The ball tends to move up and down the pitch very quickly. It is possible that more emphasis is put on speed and skill in hurling training and less emphasis on endurance. The ball is controlled with the hurley and therefore challenges tend to be made on the hurley rather than on the person. Physical challenges, where one player is required to "hold off" an opponent and protect the ball rarely happens in hurling in comparison with Gaelic football and soccer. The hurling subjects also had the lowest vertical jump performance and highest percentage body fat of the five groups with the exception of Rugby Union forwards. In hurling, players more often use the hurley to bat down a ball, so jumping high may not be as high a priority as in the other sports. In comparing the current hurlers with the inter-county hurlers studied by Donnelly *et al.* (2002), the current hurlers were heavier, had a greater body fat percentage, lower estimated $\dot{V}O_2$max but greater vertical jump and sit-and-reach performances.

Each pair of sports was compared using the sum of absolute differences between the z-scores of their measures for each variable. This showed that Gaelic footballers were more similar to Rugby Union backs and soccer players than they were to hurlers. Similarly, the hurlers were closer to soccer players and Rugby Union backs than they were to Gaelic footballers. However, there are "dual code" players who compete at both Gaelic games, Gaelic football and hurling. The present findings suggest that the fitness demands and conditioning elements of training programmes may be different for these Gaelic sports, and that Gaelic games players may be choosing a second sport to compete in for cultural reasons rather than its similarity to their own sport.

5. CONCLUSIONS

The current results revealed significant differences between the sports investigated suggesting that the demands of the games are different. This difference should be considered by those designing the conditioning elements of training programmes for these sports. Furthermore, those aspiring to participate in more than one of these sports should be aware of the demands of the different activities they are preparing for. In particular, players of Gaelic games who are considering becoming "dual-code" players should be advised of the anthropometric and fitness characteristics of players in alternative sports. It is recommended from the current findings that those Gaelic footballers and hurlers who wish to take up a second sport should consider non-Gaelic alternatives.

REFERENCES

Donnelly, J.P., Doran, D. and Reilly, T., 2002, Kinanthropometric and performance characteristics of Gaelic games players. In *Proceedings of the 12ᵗʰ Commonwealth International Sport Conference*. (London: Association of Commonwealth Universities), pp. 162.

Keane, S., Reilly, T. and Borrie, A., 1997, A comparison of the fitness characteristics of elite and non-elite Gaelic football players. In *Science and Football III*, edited by Reilly, T., Bangsbo, J. and Hughes, M. (London: E & F. N Spon), pp. 3–6.

Strudwick, A., Reilly, T. and Doran, D., 2002, Anthropometric and fitness profiles of elite players in two football codes. *Journal of Sports Medicine and Physical Fitness*, **42**, 239–242.

Tiryaki, G., Tuncel, F., Yamaner, F., Agaoglu, S.A., Gümüda, H. and Acar, M.F., 1997, Comparison of the physiological characteristics of the first, second and third league Turkish soccer players. In *Science and Football III*, edited by Reilly, T., Bangsbo, J. and Hughes, M. (London: E & FN Spon), pp. 32–36.

Tong, R.J. and Wood, G.L., 1997, A comparison of upper body strength in collegiate rugby players. In *Science and Football III*, edited by Reilly, T., Bangsbo, J. and Hughes, M. (London: E & FN Spon), pp. 16–20.

Watson, A.W.S., 1995, Physical and fitness characteristics of successful Gaelic footballers. British *Journal of Sports Medicine*, **29**, 229–231.

Young, E. and Murphy, M., 1994, Off-season and pre-season fitness profiles of the 1993 Ulster Gaelic football champions. *Journal of Sports Sciences*, **12**, 167–168.

26 Physiological and Anthropometric Characteristics of Female Gaelic Football Players

Leanne Tucker and Thomas Reilly
Research Institute for Sport and Exercise Sciences, Liverpool John Moores University, Henry Cotton Campus, 15-21 Webster Street, Liverpool, L3 2ET

1. INTRODUCTION

Gaelic football is the national sport of the island of Ireland and is played by both males and females. Whilst data on male Gaelic football players now provide baseline comparisons for fitness assessments (Reilly and Doran, 2001), there are no corresponding data for female players. This lack of information exists despite the popularity of the woman's game, which typically attracts 23,000 spectators to the inter-county final.

The women's game is played on the same sized pitch as that used by men. The playing time for competition matches is 60 minutes, separated into two halves of 30 minutes each. Male players contest inter-county matches over 70 minutes, with time added on for injury and other stoppages at the discretion of the referee. In women's matches the clock is stopped during each legitimate stoppage and each half is terminated when the 30-minute active playing time runs out.

There are two other instances where rules for women differ from those applying to the men's game. Women can pick the ball directly off the ground with their hands whereas men are penalised if they touch the ball by hand while it is on the ground. Furthermore, shoulder charging is prohibited in the case of women whose game is deemed non-contact as a result. In all other respects the rules of play are similar for the two genders.

The broad similarities in play between the men's and women's versions of Gaelic football cannot be generalised towards common training practices without information about respective demands of match-play and assessments of players. The present study was a first step towards establishing a profile of females specialising in Gaelic football. The purpose was to investigate the physiological and anthropometric characteristics of a sample of female Gaelic footballers.

2. METHODS

Subjects were selected from the Liverpool John Moores University Ladies Gaelic Football team ($n = 12$), who in the year of study were runners up in the British Universities Championships. A group of field-sport and court team players was used as a control ($n = 8$). Their physical characteristics are included in Table 1. All subjects persuaded written informed consent to participate in the study which was approved by the institution's Human Ethics Committee.

Table 1. Physical characteristics of female Gaelic football players and of field sports competitors.

	Gaelic football	**Games players**
Stature (m)	1.65 ± 0.05	1.60 ± 0.08
Body mass (kg)	69.3 ± 5.8	60.3 ± 5.8

Observations included flexibility (sit-and-reach) aerobic capacity (20-m shuttle run according to Ramsbottom *et al.*, 1988), explosive leg strength (vertical jump), anaerobic performance (repeated 30-m sprints) and somatotype (Carter and Heath, 1990). Statistical methods applied for comparison between means were two sample t-tests and Mann Whitney U tests.

3. RESULTS

The main findings included: flexibility of 23.38 ± 4.1 cm *vs* 21.0 ± 6.88 cm (Gaelic *vs* non-Gaelic players); estimated $\dot{V}O_{2max}$ of 42.0 ± 6.76 ml.kg^{-1}min *vs* 42.7 ± 5.20 ml.kg^{-1}.min^{-1}, mean somatotypes of 2.5 ± 1.1 – 4.4 ± 1.5 – 1.7 ± 1.1 *vs* 2.6 ± 0.6 – 4.4 ± 0.9 – 1.4 ± 0.9. Significant differences observed between the groups were as follows: 30-m sprint times of 5.20 ± 0.12 *vs* 5.45 ± 0.08 s (Gaelic *vs* non-Gaelic); vertical jump heights of 44.85 ± 3.16 cm *vs* 39.87 ± 5.96 cm and vertical jump power of 1005.98 ± 82.76 Watts *vs* 822.64 ± 93.76 Watts.

4. DISCUSSION

The Gaelic footballers in the current study were of a good standard, the majority regularly competing in club competition as well as with the University team. They participated in a systematic training programme which was reflected in their somatotype characteristics. They were heavier than the representative games players (from netball, basketball and hockey) chosen as a reference group for comparative purposes. They were heavier and taller than the elite female soccer players studied by Reilly and Drust (1997) and the University players studied by Wells and Reilly (2002).

The Gaelic footballers were low on endomorphy and ectomorphy and higher than average on mesomorphy. The somatotypes were not significantly different from the reference group. The low endomorphy values are likely due to reduced adiposity corresponding to a training response. The figures reported for endomorphy are lower than reported for regional standard female hockey players based on using the same skinfold method (Reilly and Bretherton, 1986). They may reflect the timing of the current observations which were made during the peak period of University competition.

The Gaelic footballers outperformed the reference group in both the sprint tests and the vertical jump. Jumping to catch the ball in the air is an important skill in Gaelic football irrespective of playing position. The figures for jumping were higher than those reported for elite soccer players (Reilly and Drust, 1997) and elite hockey players (Reilly and Borrie, 1992).

Values for estimated maximal oxygen uptake ($\dot{V}O_{2max}$) were similar between the groups. The mean values of the Gaelic footballers were similar to those actually measured (41 ± 6 ml.kg^{-1}.min^{-1}) in county-level hockey players but lower than those (46 ml.kg^{-1}.min^{-1}) in an elite regional squad (Reilly and Bretherton, 1986). Mean values for the Wales national hockey squad (54.5 ml.kg^{-1}.min^{-1}) studied by Reilly *et al.* (1985) demonstrated superior characteristics to the current team of Gaelic footballers.

It seems that female Gaelic footballers are characterised by a lean and muscular physique and possess high qualities in anaerobic performance. This profile differs from that of inter-county male teams whose aerobic fitness measures are similar to those of professional soccer players but are lacking in sprinting over short distances (Strudwick *et al.*, 2001). Whether the modest aerobic fitness measures are replicated in inter-county women's teams is worthy of future investigation. It would be relevant also to establish whether there are differences in work rate and patterns of play which would call for a novel approach to training and preparation among female players.

It is concluded that there were significant differences between the female Gaelic footballers and other games players in stature, body mass, vertical jump height and power production, and 30-m sprint times. Whilst the two groups were similar in somatotype, the Gaelic footballers were superior in 'explosive' power and in sprinting speed. These data provide a reference from which future studies could draw. Future work could usefully be focussed on elite players at inter-country level, with sufficient participants to examine differences between positional roles.

REFERENCES

Carter, J.E.L. and Heath, B.H., 1990, Somatotyping, Development and Applications. (Cambridge: Cambridge University Press).

Ramsbottom, R., Brewer, J. and Williams, C., 1988, A progressive shuttle run list to estimate maximal oxygen uptake. *British Journal of Sports Medicine*, **22**, 141–144.

Reilly,T. and Borrie, A., 1992, Physiology applied to field hockey. *Sports Medicine*, **14**, 10–26.

Reilly,T. and Bretherton, S., 1986, Multivariate analyses of fitness of female field hockey players. In *Perspectives in Kinanthropometry*, edited by Day, J. A. P. (Champaign, Ill: Human Kinetics), pp. 135–142.

Reilly, T. and Doran, D., 2001, Science and Gaelic football: A review. *Journal of Sports Sciences*, **19**,181–193.

Reilly, T. and Drust, B., 1997, The isokinetic muscle strength of women soccer players. *Coaching and Sports Science Journal*, **2**, 12–17.

Reilly, T., Parry-Billings, M. and Ellis, A., 1985, Changes in fitness profiles of international female hockey players during the competitive season. *Journal of Sports Sciences*, **3**, 210.

Strudwick,A., Reilly, T. and Doran, D., 2002, Anthropometric and fitness profiles of elite players in two football codes. *Journal of Sports Medicine and Physical Fitness*, **42**, 239–242.

Wells, C., and Reilly, T., 2002, Influence of playing position on fitness and performance measures in female soccer players. In *Science and Football IV*, edited by Spinks, W., Reilly, T. and Murphy, A. (London: Routledge), pp. 369–373.

Part IV
Performance Analysis

27　Changes in Professional Soccer: A Qualitative and Quantitative Study

Werner Kuhn

Institute of Sport Sciences, Humboldt University, Berlin, Germany

1. INTRODUCTION

Performances in sport have improved tremendously over the past 50 years. This applies not only to individual sports but also to team sports. The purpose of this study is to report important changes in soccer from the 1950s to the present day from a qualitative and quantitative standpoint. The focus is upon developments on the field rather than off the field. The problem was approached from two directions: first, people who followed intensely the last fifty years as players, spectators and licensed soccer coaches were interviewed. Second, a documentary analysis of four international matches spread out over several decades was carried out. The four case studies are more or less only a comparison of four important matches. In order to conduct a valid study of time changes in soccer, samples of 20 to 30 matches for each decade need to be examined. From an economic standpoint this was not feasible and so there are limitations to this study.

Objective data with regard to team games are hard to find in the literature (Reilly et al., 1988; Reilly et al., 1993; Reilly et al., 1997 ; Spinks et al., 2002). Cross-sectional studies carried out mostly in connection with World Cups and European Championships exist in a limited number (Kuhn and Maier 1978; Pollard et al., 1988; Sund, 1997). Longitudinal studies are very scarce. Bisanz (1993) gave an overview of systems of play from the sixties to the nineties. Loy (2002) compared qualitatively and quantitatively all World Cup matches from 1990 to 2002. Van Gool et al. (1988) reported that the distance covered by players on the field as well as the running speed (sometimes broken down into three of four grades of intensity) were investigated most often, unfortunately with different methods, so results are hard to compare. Medical specialists also showed an early interest in the endurance capacity of soccer players. However, conclusions are hard to draw as procedures and protocols fluctuated between research groups.

2. QUALITATIVE STUDY

2.1. Methodology

Twenty licensed German coaches with an average age of 68 (range 60 to 89) years who were active in amateur and professional teams were interviewed by telephone. It was not a random sample. The German Soccer Coaches' Federation provided the telephone numbers of 25 coaches older than 60 years.

Five coaches could not be contacted. None of the remaining 20 coaches refused the interview. They were well suited as time witnesses as they followed soccer very closely as player, coach and spectator for 45 to 50 years on average, in some cases even more than 70 years.

Prior to the interview a suitable date was arranged to avoid time constraints. The interview technique used was narrative. The speaker was only interrupted when the topic was neglected. The time for each interview fluctuated between 4 and 46 minutes depending upon the elaborateness of each speaker. An extensive protocol was written immediately afterwards on the basis of notes taken during the ongoing interview. The analysis was descriptive. The following three questions were asked:

(a) What changes have taken place in today's game compared with the fifties?
(b) Was the standard of play better today or in the fifties?
(c) What would be the result if a top team of the fifties played a top team of the nineties? (for instance the German World Cup team in 1954 versus the World Cup team in 1998).

2.2. Results

Question (a):- All coaches uniformly stated that time and space have dramatically changed over the years. An overview of answers is given in Table 1. Changes in speed were most striking to 85% of the people interviewed. As a result of spatial and temporal constraints on the field and also because of higher levels of speed and strength, today's game requires more explosive actions, speed and cognitive speed. One coach put it this way: 'in former times you could trap the ball, look and play, today you have to look prior to making contact with the ball. Otherwise the ball is lost'. Today's coaches prefer players who have good natural speed, a pronounced speed technique and who can read a game and anticipate the development of offensive and defensive actions two or three moves ahead. Today's game has become more athletic and more physical (60%). Several coaches mentioned the robustness and cleverness in 'duel' situations which sometimes turn into fierce aggression. Further, there was a higher incidence of injury as a result of higher speed and hidden brutal fouls (50%). Ten coaches referred to the greater emphasis on tactics; the older coaches especially criticized the defensive orientation and the offensive line-up with one or two strikers. Five coaches stated that nowadays there is a higher level of tolerance towards unfair play (e.g. pulling shirts, forcing positions). Four coaches mentioned the better equipment now available, two coaches found that today's game is more professional. Nowadays there is enormous pressure on each player in training and competition as top teams have two or three back-ups for each position. The old times with team rosters of 14 to 16 players were more amateur and more fun-oriented.

Question (b): Eighty-five percent of the coaches claimed that today's football has a higher standard of play. The players are much better trained in all areas that dominate performance (technique, tactics, conditioning, mental alertness). Three older coaches held the opinion that the quality of play was not inferior in former times but different from nowadays. They were supported by six other coaches who thought that matches in the 1950s were more pleasing to the eye. Everything was quieter and more comfortable. As ball-possessing players were not attacked so fiercely they had more time and room for dribbling and long penetrating passes. Good teams demonstrated a technical, elegant and artistic football with partially brilliant plays and goals. Two coaches drew parallels between men's football in the 1950s and today's women's top football. Strikers were not covered so intensely and 1 versus 2 or 1 versus 3 situations occurred very seldom.

Table 1. Overview of answers with regard to question 1 (number of hits in parentheses).

Fifties	Today
Slower (1)	Faster (16)
More fighting spirit (1)	More athletic (12)
Less fighting spirit (1)	
Less physical (1)	More physical (12)
	More injury-prone (10)
More technique-centered	More tactic-centered (10)
	More tolerant towards unfair play (5)
More amateur (1)	Better equipment (4)
More fun-oriented (3)	More professional (2)

Five coaches mentioned that more natural talent was available in the 1950s. As soccer was the sole and only sport for youngsters, there was a broad base of players. The pool of talent in those times was practically unlimited. Only the very best succeeded in getting contracts. Today many players compensate their technical-tactical deficiencies with outstanding athletic abilities.

One coach compared the developments in soccer with the general changes in daily life. Everything has become more intense, more dynamic and also more hectic. Embedded in the respective circumstances of life, the achievements in each period were brilliant and deserved the highest respect. A few coaches mentioned that former players would achieve higher performances than today's generation of players if they had had the same conditions relating to training, nutrition, equipment and medical treatment. The pool of talent in those times was practically unlimited. Only the very best succeeded in getting contracts.

Question (c): Although most coaches were unable to put forward an actual match result, they agreed that teams of the fifties would not have a winning chance. Only five coaches came up with an actual result: three predicted 0:5, 0:6 and 0:7, two coaches pointed out that at the beginning of a match teams of the fifties would be superior (1:0 or 2:0 ahead after 30 or 45 minutes) but at the end of a game would be heavily defeated (1:7 or 2:7 after 90 minutes). The remaining 15 coaches predicted a clear defeat (n = 8), a narrow defeat (n = 5) and a draw (n = 2).

3. QUANTITATIVE STUDY

3.1. Methodology

We analyzed video documents of four important matches for a retrospective investigation of the development of performance of world-class soccer teams. The matches studied were England versus Hungary (25.11.1953), Germany versus The Netherlands (7.7.1974), France versus Brazil (12.7.1998) and Brazil versus Germany (30.6.2002). The significance of the games was not equal. The England versus Hungary match was a friendly encounter, whereas the other three matches were World Cup finals. However, in the fifties friendly matches were taken much more seriously than nowadays because there were fewer international competitions. Besides, England was always under pressure as the team had to defend its home record. The England versus Hungary match was originally a film document that was transferred to video later-on. Unfortunately the black and white document is not complete: 3 minutes and 27 seconds are missing from 90 minutes due to foggy conditions at Wembley Stadium in the month of November. Additional time was handled by the referees not always correctly. For instance in the Brazil – Germany encounter three minutes and 20 seconds were allowed in the second half although twice as much time was lost due to injuries treated on the field and due to changing of a jersey. The effective playing times were within the norm of 60 plus/minus 10 min except for the Brazil – Germany game (Table 2).

In order to secure exact times for the analysis, an electronic clock was inserted into the video recordings. Commercial TV broacasts do not give the total picture of a football field. They only show actions involving the ball. This causes serious limitations in analysing data. Based upon the coaches' subjective views, the following game-related variables were investigated per video:- space, time and the relationship of space and time. The following indicators (underlined in Table 3) were examined in our study: for the variable space ball possession in zone 1, 2, 3 and 4 as well as system of play, for the variable time ball-possessing time of field players/goalkeepers and number of successful direct passes, for the variable space/time the speed of successful passes and dribbles. In addition to that, the game structure was measured as follows: analysis of attacking actions (number of interactions, duration and outcome) and several quotients: successful dribbles/successful passes, successful short passes/successful passes, successful medium long passes/successful passes, successful long passes/successful passes, successful short dribbles/successful dribbles, successful medium long dribbles/successful dribbles, successful long dribbles/successful dribbles. The key concepts were defined as follows:

Attacking actions: A team starts an attacking action when it has the ball safely under control. Attacking actions need not alternate between teams. One team can execute several attacking actions in succession. An attacking team always begins a new action when the match is interrupted (e.g. defensive fouls, a defensive action with the ball rolling out of bounds). However, when the ball remains under control of the attacking side after an uncontrolled action of the defending team, the same attacking action continues. It is important to note that a new attacking action always starts when the ball rebounds from a defensive player, from the goalkeeper, from the goal-post or from the cross-bar after a shot at goal.

Ball-possession in zone 1, 2, 3 and 4: The field is divided lengthwise into four zones. Zone 1 covers the area from own goal-line to own penalty line (16.50 m) extended to the sidelines; zone 2 comprises the area from own penalty line to the midfield line (38.50 m of a 110 m long soccer pitch); zone 3 ranges from the midfield line to the extended penalty line of the opposing team (38.50 m); zone 4 covers the area from the extended penalty line of he opposing team to the goal-line of the opposing team (16.50 m). If a player touches or possesses the ball in one of the four zones, the action is recorded. Thus, we can identify if and how often defensive players enter the attacking half of the field as well as if and how often offensive players help out in their own penalty area. Simple penetration into a specific zone without ball contact or possession is not registered.

Successful pass: Every pass (including kick-off, punt, throw, corner-kick and throw-in) that reaches a team-mate is considered successful. The distance between player A and B is estimated on the basis of an outline of the playing field containing exact measurements in metres. The lengths of passes are categorized into short (0–10 m), medium long (11–20) and long (20 and more). The duration of each pass is measured exactly.

Table 2. Descriptive data of the four matches.

Fixture	Match day	Result	Venue	Duration of the matches 1st half 2nd half total	Effective match time 1st half 2nd half total

Table 3. Overview of the variables space, time and space/time and of possible indicators.

Variables	Space	Time	Space/Time
Possible Indicators	Distance covered Working area = length/breadth Match formation Gain in meters	Ball-possessing time Direct passes Number of interactions	Running speed Passing speed Dribbling speed Shooting speed

Successful dribbling: Every dribble (slow or at high speed) is considered successful when the ball is not lost from the beginning of the action to the very end (pass, centre, shot at goal, beginning of a one-on-one situation). The lengths are also estimated and classified into short, medium long and long dribbles. The duration of each dribble is also measured exactly.

Ball-possessing time (field player): It is defined as the time that elapses from the first contact of the ball until delivery (pass, shot) or loss. Direct passes are ignored.

Ball-possessing time (goalkeeper): It is defined as the time that elapses from the first contact of the ball until delivery (kick, throw, pass) or loss. Direct passes are ignored.

The analysis of the four matches was carried out by two trained soccer experts with coaching licenses. In order to determine the coefficients of objectivity and reliability of selected variables, the first 15 min of the European Cup final Real Madrid versus Eintracht Frankfurt (1960) were used. Twice within one week the lengths of passes and dribbles as well as their duration were independently recorded by two experts. Product-moment correlations were much higher for the variable duration than for the variable estimated distance (measurement 1: 0.92 versus 0.81, measurement 2: 0.90 versus 0.80). Test-retest reliability coefficients were 0.88 for the variable duration and 0.78 for the variable estimated distance.

On the basis of the interviews the following hypotheses (H) were derived:

H1: The working area of defenders, midfielder and attackers increases from game 1 to game 3 and 4.

H2: Game formations become more defence-oriented from game 1 to game 3 and 4.

H3: Ball-possessing time for goalkeepers and field players decreases from game 1 to game 3 and 4.

H4: The number of successful direct passes decreases from game 1 to game 3 and 4.

H5: Ball speed of successful passes increases from game 1 to game 3 and 4.

H6: Ball speed of successful dribbles increases from game 1 to game 3 and 4.

H7: The relationship of dribbling to passes develops in favour of passes from game 1 to game 3 and 4.

3.2. Results

Analysis of selected parameters concerning game structure: An overview of number, interactions and duration of attacking actions, broken down into individual errors, fouls (including both defensive and offensive fouls) and shots at goal is given in Table 4 for each team. By far the largest number of attacking actions as well as the lowest number of interactions occur in the match England versus Hungary. However, there was no causal link between these two variables as there was no inverse relationship in the other games. The breakdown of the attacking actions into individual errors, fouls and shots at goal throws some light on the superiority of the Hungarians in this match. It is demonstrated by a relatively small individual error rate of 68% and by a goal-shot percentage of an astonishing 24%. Only 7.53% of attacking actions were stopped through fouls (both offensive and defensive). In contrast the English team produced 81% individual errors and only 6.62% shots at goal. If one considers the other three games individual errors constitute a high percentage whereas fouls and shots at goal decrease percentage-wise. In the England-Hungary match, the overall game strategy of both teams was oriented towards offense whereas in the other three games ball-possession and ball-control were also emphasized. A good indicator of ball-control would be the number of back passes and side passes.

Diverse quotients to characterize changes in the game structure are given in Table 5. The quotient successful dribbling/successful passes demonstrates that there is a tendency in favour of passes from game 1 to game 4. If only successful space-covering long dribbles are considered, the results are even more pronounced. In 2002 the percentage of successful dribbles in relation to successful passes fell below 20% for both teams. Passes have become more and more dominant as they contribute to speed up a game. Dribbles have decreased because the risks of losing the ball are high as a consequence of an enforced defence and uncompromised tackling in one-on-one situations. An analysis of the lengths of passes yields hardly any differences between the first three games. Short and medium long passes (40% each) occurred more often than long passes (about 20%). In the Brazil–Germany game over 50% of the successful passes were in the short range. The medium long passes dropped to about 30%. Changes were even more obvious on analyzing successful dribbling. There was an overall tendency towards short dribbles, but it was very pronounced in 2002.

The reasons are obvious. Medium long and long dribbles occurred relatively seldom as the ball-possessing player is attacked very early by a zone defence and quite often is hunted down by several opposing players.

Analysis of selected space parameters: In 1953 teams used a modified WM-system. The pure WM-system had two defenders, three midfield players and five attackers. In 1953 the centre-half was moved back in line with the two defenders. Hence, the three defenders covered the centre-forward and the right and left winger. The right and left midfield players took care of the inside right and inside left forwards. The English squad used a system that resembled more a 3 : 2 : 5 formation. The Hungarians played with two inside forwards and two outside forwards. Their centre-forward was an outstanding soccer personality. He played behind the forward line. He was playmaker and goal-getter at the same time. Thus, the formation of the Hungarians was a 3 : 3 : 4. In 1974 a more defence-oriented system than the WM-system was dominant:- the formation 4 : 3 : 3 with libero. The midfield consisted of a defensive, an offensive and a creative player (playmaker). The midfield was strengthened at the expense of striking power in 1998 and 2002. Zone defences without libero have become very popular. In 1998 the French team used a 4 : 5 : 1 formation. The Brazilians applied a 4 : 4 : 2 formation in 1998 and 2002. The Germans played a 3 : 5 : 2 formation in the final. Many teams chose flexible formations within a match and between matches depending upon the team line-ups of the opposition. The WM-system is often said to be static with fixed working areas for defence and offence. The 1953 game revealed a completely different picture. Table 6 shows that both English and Hungarian defensive players made contact with the ball in the opponent's half (zone 3), while both English and Hungarian attackers gained ball-possession in their own half (zone 2). Direct comparisons of the four matches with regard to the working areas of the players are difficult to realize because match formations differed for defensive, midfield and attacking players in number. Yet, a look at the frequencies in zone 4 of the defensive players shows that functional areas increased from game 1 to game 2 – 4. It is well documented in the literature that distances covered by players on the field have increased from the fifties to the seventies and also from the seventies to the nineties. From the early 1990s up to the present, no significant changes have been reported. However, there is a tendency towards more intensive running.

Table 4. Number of interactions and duration of offensive actions (broken down into individual errors, fouls, shots at goal).

Teams	Individual errors				Fouls				Shots at goal			
	n	%	Interactions	Duration	n	%	Interactions	Duration	n	%	Interactions	Duration
England	111	81.62	2.46	8.48	16	11.76	2.93	12.16	9	6.62	2.67	12.09
Hungary	99	68.28	2.02	9.96	11	7.53	3.06	13.22	35	24.14	3.83	13.00
Germany	56	59.57	3.14	15.63	25	26.60	3.11	13.18	13	13.83	3.00	11.62
The Netherlands	68	67.33	3.72	17.59	18	17.82	4.48	17.99	15	14.85	3.87	15.20
France	70	70.71	3.30	13.37	14	14.14	2.21	7.90	15	15.15	4.07	14.13
Brazil	78	76.47	4.68	18.82	21	20.59	4.52	15.08	13	12.75	3.54	13.69
Brazil	90	79.65	3.29	11.12	12	10.62	2.34	8.42	11	9.73	3.69	11.62
Germany	95	69.34	3.49	12.57	24	17.52	3.48	10.59	18	13.14	3.90	8.66

Table 5. Diverse quotients to characterize changes in game structure.

Teams	Successful Dribbling/ Successful Passes	S. short passes/s. passes	S. medium long passes/ s. passes	S. long passes/ s. passes	S. short dribbling/ s. dribbl.	S. medium long dribbl./ s. dribbl.	S. long dribbl./ s. dribbl.
England	0.59	0.41	0.41	0.19	0.38	0.35	0.27
Hungary	0.42	0.38	0.42	0.20	0.42	0.40	0.19
Germany	0.58	0.42	0.42	0.16	0.46	0.30	0.23
The Netherlands	0.53	0.39	0.39	0.22	0.46	0.33	0.21
France	0.40	0.39	0.42	0.19	0.42	0.37	0.22
Brazil	0.30	0.32	0.44	0.24	0.47	0.35	0.18
Brazil	0.43	0.59	0.30	0.11	0.72	0.20	0.07
Germany	0.38	0.50	0.31	0.19	0.82	0.13	0.04

Analysis of selected time parameters: An overview of the average ball-possessing time of goal-keepers and field players is given in Table 7. It is obvious that there were sharp increases for goal-keepers from game 1 and 2 to game 3 and 4. The high score of the French goal-keeper was due to the fact that he had several actions in the second half in which he held the ball longer than 10 s. This offence should have been noticed by the referee.

In 2002 it was clear that unchallenged goal-keepers used the back-pass rule to dribble with the ball in the penalty area in order to break up the rhythm opposing team and calm down the game. There are no clear-cut results for ball-possessing time for field players. The times were roughly identical for match 1 and 2 as well as for match 3 and 4. Because of pressing in the half of the opposition, congesting space through ball-oriented defence, a decrease of the ball-possessing time would have been expected from game 1 to game 3 and 4 but this was obviously not the case.

Clearly, successful direct passes decreased from game 1 to game 4. Direct passing is an excellent weapon against an enforced defence as it can speed up the game and create surprise effects. Besides, direct passing becomes a necessity as the player in possession is frequently attacked from several directions. The longer the ball is retained, the greater is the danger of losing the ball, or being fouled or risking an injury. There were more attempts at direct passes but the success rate has dropped tremendously due to congestion on the field. In 2002 only 19% (Brazil) and 27% (Germany) were of all direct pass attempts were successful.

Table 6. Number of ball possessions of defensive, midfield and attacking players in zone 1, 2, 3 and 4.

Teams (Match formation)	Defensive Players				Midfield Players				Attacking Players			
	Z 1	Z 2	Z 3	Z 4	Z 1	Z 2	Z 3	Z 4	Z 1	Z 2	Z 3	Z 4
England (3 : 2 : 5)	29	77	22	0	10	74	86	7	0	68	112	22
Hungary (3 : 3 : 4)	24	70	14	0	8	52	88	17	1	40	132	55
Germany (4 : 3 : 3)	63	106	44	6	15	54	65	18	6	49	52	31
The Netherlands (4 : 3 : 3)	32	150	103	15	9	74	76	23	6	21	47	40
France (4 : 5 : 1)	29	104	43	1	11	116	139	13	1	5	14	6
Brazil (4 : 4 : 2)	20	175	93	18	1	123	159	24	0	13	38	12
Brazil (4 : 4 : 2)	37	67	32	8	7	61	86	11	0	13	82	12
Germany (3 : 5 : 2)	9	102	36	2	9	91	149	28	0	13	44	13

Table 7. Average ball-possessing time (goal-keeper and field player) and number of successful direct passes.

Match	Average ball-possessing time Goal-keeper	Average ball-possessing time Field player	Number of successful passes
England	2.44	2.23	182
Hungary	2.65	2.26	262
Germany	2.84	2.50	112
The Netherlands	2.31	2.57	139
France	7.12	2.22	133
Brazil	2.32	2.21	118
Brazil	6.50	2.74	32
Germany	5.19	2.18	64

Analysis of selected space/time parameters: An overview of the number and average speeds of successful passes and dribbles over different lengths is given in Tables 8 and 9. It was postulated that changes in speed would be observable from 1953 to 1998/2002. This is obviously not the case. Table 8 shows that speed for short successful passes was highest in 1953. Surprisingly, results are not at all clear-cut. There is a weak tendency that ball speed of successful passes increased for medium-long and long passes. With regard to dribbling speed, there has been a sharp drop for short and medium range dribbles in 2002. Goal-keepers as well as defensive and midfield players hold the ball for tactical reasons when they are not attacked.

Table 8. Number (n) and average speed of successful passes of various lengths.

Teams	Length of passing					
	0–10 m		11 – 20 m		> 20 m	
	n	speed	n	speed	n	speed
England	92	7.50	93	9.42	42	13.39
Hungary	99	7.20	109	9.49	51	11.52
Germany	82	6.91	81	9.08	31	11.88
The Netherlands	114	5.55	113	8.88	64	11.47
France	100	7.25	107	10.23	47	12.79
Brazil	131	7.25	181	10.30	101	13.15
Brazil	134	5.90	67	10.00	26	13.22
Germany	147	7.04	90	9.44	56	13.70

Table 9. Number (n) and average speed of successful dribblings over various lengths.

Team	Length of dribbling					
	0 – 10 m		11 – 20 m		> 20 m	
	n	speed	n	speed	n	speed
England	51	5.60	46	5.56	36	5.56
Hungary	45	5.10	43	5.63	20	5.78
Germany	52	3.71	34	4.52	26	5.31
The Netherlands	72	3.31	51	3.82	32	4.23
France	42	3.96	37	5.39	22	5.24
Brazil	57	3.62	43	4.57	22	5.28
Brazil	71	1.86	20	3.55	7	6.05
Germany	92	1.75	15	3.88	5	4.83

4. OVERVIEW

The aim of the study was to point out important changes in soccer in the last 50 years. The focus was on developments on the field, rather than off the field. In the first part of the report, a qualitative analysis was presented. Twenty licensed coaches (age 60–89) were asked to answer a series of questions.

All coaches agreed that time and space have changed tremendously over the past 50 years. Apart from speed robustness and cleverness in duel situations have increased. The majority of coaches agreed that today's soccer has a higher quality and teams of the fifties would not have a winning chance against current teams.

In the second part of the report, four matches between national teams (England versus Hungary, Germany versus The Netherlands, France versus Brazil, Brazil versus Germany) were analysed quantitatively from video recordings. On the basis of the coaches' subjective responses the following variables were investigated:- working area of players, match formation, ball-possessing time of field players and goal-keepers, successful direct passes, passing and dribbling speed.

The following hypotheses were supported:
(a) Match formations become more defence-oriented from game 1 to games 3 and 4.
(b) The number of successful direct passes decreases from game 1 to games 3 and 4.
(c) The relationship of dribbling to passes develops in favour of passes from game 1 to games 3 and 4.

The reason for this meagre output was probably due to the fact that only four games were analyzed. Therefore, a replication of the quantitative analysis with a larger sample of games from the World Cup 1954, 1974 and 1998/2002 would be recommended. As the development of the game has obviously not come to an end and as improvements in all performance-related factors can be expected, important games should be recorded and archived in the future for a total view of he field. With improved measuring devices the dimensions of time and space could be analyzed much better than nowadays.

REFERENCES

Bisanz, G., 1993, Fußball-Taktik im Wandel der Zeit. In *fußballtraining*, **11**, 50–54.
Kuhn, W. and Maier, W., 1978, *Beiträge zur Analyse des Fußballspiels*, (Schorndorf: Hofmann).
Loy, R., 2002, Analyse der 64 Spiele der WM 2002. *Bund Deutscher Fußball-Lehrer Journal*, 24, 23–28.
Pollard, R., Reep, C. and Hartley, S., 1988, The quantitative comparison of playing styles in soccer. In *Science and Football,* edited by Reilly, T.,

Lees, A., Davids, K. and Murphy, W.J. (London: E and F. N. Spon), pp. 309–315.

Reilly, T., Bangsbo, J. and Hughes, M., 1997, *Science and Football III*. (London: E and F. N. Spon).

Reilly, T., Clarys, J. and Stibbe, A., 1993, *Science and Football II*. (London: E and F. N. Spon).

Reilly, T., Lees, A., Davids, K. and Murphy, W.J., 1988, *Science and Football*. (London: E and F. N. Spon).

Spinks, W., Reilly, T. and Murphy, A., 2002, *Science and Football IV*, (London: Routledge).

Sund, B., 1997, The British and continental influence on Swedish football. *The International History of Sport*, **2**, 163–173.

Van Gool, D., Van Gerven, D. and Boutmans, J., 1988, The physiological load imposed on soccer players during real match play. In *Science and Football*, edited by Reilly, T., Lees, A., Davids, K. and Murphy, W.J. (London: E and F. N. Spon), pp. 51–59.

28 The Goal Complete: The Winning Difference

Neil Lanham
Football Performance Analysis,
Helions Bumpstead, Suffolk, UK

1. INTRODUCTION

Scoring a 'goal' is supported by performance. Only the tip of the iceberg is visible. Similarly a goal, being the only factor that is counted, manifests performance which is not fully appreciated as it includes elements which are not quantified or counted. It still exists regardless, in the same way that the remainder of the iceberg is beneath the surface. With the iceberg 8 parts out of 9 are beneath the surface and invisible; similarly there is a "Near Constant Law of Chance" that 180 possessions on average are lost and won back, supporting the single occurrence of 'goal'. At an assumed 240 possessions per match, this figure represents 1.33 goals on average for and against. This figure is the same at all levels of the game, however it is played, and whether fast or slow, and was the subject of the report by Lanham (1991). Reep and Benjamin (1968) reported that there were near constant laws of chance dominating football at every level. Lanham (1991) added a further 'Near Constant Law of Chance' confirming that the figure of 180 possessions on average per goal, with a variation of 10% either way, was 'ideal'. It is the intention of this report to extend the work of Lantham (1991) by looking at the three stages that go to make up the 180 lost possessions of the average goal.

2. LEAGUE PERFORMANCE ANALYSIS

Over 3000 games have been fully recorded by using a previously noted shorthand code of every move in every possession in each match for both "For" and "Against" teams. Since 1985 this information has been fed into a database computer system programmed to average long runs of matches so that rate and quality can be examined. The 15 teams selected for this report were all recorded in long runs and all had success in either achieving promotion or top of the table status. From their figures, the measured difference that brought success can be pinpointed.

Table 1 shows the average number of goals scored per team in the English Premier league season 2001–2002: this average of all goals at 1.31 per team per match shows that this near constant is still current. The less possessions one takes for one's own goal, the more goals are scored per match (Lanham, 1991). It in turn makes the opponents take the equivalent number more than the 180 possessions for their goal and they therefore will score less per match.

Table 1. Premier Division, Season 2001–2002.

Team	F	A	Av. Goals For	Av. Goals Against	Total av. Goal/match
Arsenal	79	36	2.079	0.947	3.026
Liverpool	67	30	1.763	0.789	2.553
Man Utd	87	45	2.289	1.184	3.474
Newcastle	74	52	1.947	1.368	3.316
Leeds	53	37	1.395	0.974	2.368
Chelsea	66	38	1.737	1.000	2.737
W Ham	48	57	1.263	1.500	2.763
A Villa	46	47	1.211	1.237	2.447
Tottenham	49	53	1.289	1.395	2.684
Blackburn	55	51	1.447	1.342	2.789
Southampton	46	54	1.211	1.421	2.632
Middlesbrough	35	47	0.921	1.237	2.158
Fulham	36	44	0.947	1.158	2.105
Charlton	38	49	1.000	1.289	2.289
Everton	45	57	1.184	1.500	2.684
Bolton	44	62	1.158	1.632	2.789
Sunderland	29	51	0.763	1.342	2.105
Ipswich	41	64	1.079	1.684	2.763
Derby	33	63	0.868	1.658	2.526
Leicester	30	64	0.789	1.684	2.474
Total	1001	1001	Overall Av		2.634

A calculated estimate of 240 possessions per match, and 1.317 goals per team per match, equals 182.23 lost possessions/goal average overall. The average goals for and against in other English leagues for season 2001–2002 were Division 1–1.345, Division 2–1.34 and Division 3–1.24.

3. WORLD AND EUROPEAN FINALS

The three stages of the rate of these 180 lost possessions in theory and more importantly in practice in World and European Cup Finals between 1978 and 1996 are shown in Table 2.

Table 2. The three stages of rate.

Team	Season	Goal	THE EQUATION									
			Strike Rate Shots/Goal		Rate of Final 3rd Poss/shots		Total all Final 3rd Poss/Goal		All Poss lost short of final 3rd/Goal		Total all Poss/ Goal
World Cup	90	109	10.62	x	8.27	=	87.82	+	79.62	=	167.44
Euro Cup	88	34	9.59	x	9.00	=	86.31	+	82.94	=	169.25
Euro Cup	92	30	10.80	x	8.92	=	95.73	+	90.00	=	185.00
Euro Cup	96	43	10.74	x	9.24	=	100.25	+	101.53	=	201.76
Various Internationals	to 02/94	96	8.83	x	9.76	=	86.18	+	85.39	=	171.57
		312	9.99	x	9.00	=	89.91	+	85.77	=	175.68

In theory our ideal would be:- 10.00 x 9.00 = 90.00 + 90.00 = 180.00. This value proves the recorded figures to be a good fit. Table 2 shows World Cup and European Cup Finals, and averages of all teams, i.e. both For and Against. The most important thing to note is that where the shot to goal ratio is higher, the Final Third to shot ratio is accordingly lower so there is a near constant of Final Third possessions to goal and not just shot/goal ratio or Final Third possessions to shot ratio. Table 3 shows the 1820 goals from 15 teams of promotion/top of the table standard; it is apparent how they made the opposition take more possessions per goal and with it less possessions per goal themselves to score more goals on average per match. From this observation, it becomes clear that of the three rates making up the 180, one was largely variable and the other two together remained near constant.

4. HISTORICAL LEAGUE ANALYSIS

Table 3. Where the winning difference lies.

Team	Season	Div	Final	Games	Goals	Strike rate shots/go	x	Rate of final 3rd poss/shots	=	Total all final 3rd poss/goal	+	All poss lost short of final	=	Total all poss/goal	Av. all lost poss/goal both teams
Wimbledon	86/87	1	6	47	67	9.52	x	10.85	=	103.29	+	73.45	=	176.70	} 195.28
Opp					55	9.24	x	10.40	=	96.09	+	121.84	=	217.93	
Difference					12					−7.20	+	48.39	=	41.19	
Wimbledon	87/88	1		24	35	8.00	x	12.00	=	96.00	+	79.60	=	175.90	} 197.00
Opp					26	9.30	x	11.10	=	103.23	+	127.30	=	232.50	
Difference					9					7.23	+	47.70	=	54.93	
Arsenal	87/88	1		10	19	6.60	x	10.80	=	71.28	+	69.00	=	140.28	} 179.57
Opp					11	6.60	x	17.10	=	112.86	+	137.00	=	249.86	
Difference					8					41.58	+	68.00	=	109.58	
Watford*	82/83	1	2	49	87	9.70	x	9.84	=	95.45	+	60.45	=	155.90	} 177.10
Opp					72	12.36	x	7.99	=	98.97	+	106.02	=	204.99	
Difference					15					3.52	+	45.57	=	49.09	
Wolver W*	94/95	1	4	46	77	8.48	x	9.52	=	80.72	+	72.36	=	153.08	} 168.95
Opp					61	10.18	x	7.91	=	80.52	+	104.30	=	184.82	
Difference					16					−0.20	+	31.94	=	31.74	
Watford*	81/82	2	2	50	92	8.53	x	9.87	=	84.19	+	55.35	=	139.54	} 177.76
Opp					52	10.56	x	9.32	=	98.42	+	142.41	=	240.83	
Difference					40					14.28	+	87.06	=	101.29	
Crystal Plce	87/89	2	6	54	95	7.71	x	9.93	=	76.59	+	74.96	=	157.55	} 171.47
Opp					73	7.15	x	12.06	=	86.25	+	111.33	=	197.58	
Difference					22					9.66	+	36.37	=	46.03	
Sheffield U	89/90	2	2	55	104	8.57	x	10.20	=	87.44	+	73.80	=	161.24	} 184.15
Opp					66	9.91	x	9.50	=	94.15	+	121.60	=	215.75	
Difference					38					6.71	+	47.80	=	54.51	
Charlton A*	85/86	2	2	41	80	7.48	x	10.98	=	82.13	+	67.40	=	149.53	} 195.77
Opp					49	9.32	x	11.22	=	104.57	+	137.45	=	242.02	
Difference					31					22.44	+	70.05	=	92.45	
Plymouth*	86/87	2	8	42	62	8.85	x	10.24	=	90.64	+	76.64	=	167.28	} 173.67
Opp					57	7.74	x	10.44	=	80.80	+	99.26	=	180.00	
Difference					5					−9.84	+	22.62	=	12.78	
Cambridge U	90/91	3	1	60	97	7.78	x	11.73	=	91.29	+	71.03	=	162.32	} 204.00
Opp					57	10.63	x	11.08	=	117.77	+	161.65	=	279.42	
Difference					40					26.48	+	90.62	=	117.10	
Wimbledon	83/84	3	2	12	20	8.28	x	10.54	=	87.28	+	63.32	=	150.60	} 182.66
Opp					15	9.51	x	10.21	=	97.10	+	106.15	=	203.25	
Difference					5					9.82	+	42.83	=	52.65	
Preston NE	93/94	3	4	55	98	6.48	x	14.00	=	90.68	+	68.94	=	159.62	} 174.84
Opp					82	7.65	x	9.90	=	75.70	+	117.58	=	193.28	

Difference					16					−14.98	+	**48.64**	=	33.66	
Sheffield U	88/89	3	2	55	110	7.57	x	9.83	=	74.45	+	63.27	=	137.72	} 170.80
Opp					67	7.70	x	11.51	=	88.66	+	137.44	=	226.10	
Difference					33					14.21	+	**74.17**	=	88.37	
Cambridge U	89/90	4	4	23	39	6.63	x	11.90	=	78.90	+	69.80	=	147.80	} 179.81
Opp					25	7.92	x	12.40	=	98.21	+	129.70	=	227.90	
Difference					14					19.31	+	**59.90**	=	80.10	

* figures supplied by Simon Hartley

Average of all 28 teams together (14 home team and 14 opposition against)

Arsenal excluded as it is considered that 10 games constitute an insufficient sample for this purpose

Total Goals	Strike rate shots/goal		Rate of final 3rd poss/shots		Total all final 3rd #poss/goal		All poss lost short of final 3rd/goal		Total all poss/goal
1820	8.57	x	10.53	=	89.01	+	91.22	=	180.23

If we separate the difference in possessions taken by the successful teams scoring 1063 goals as against the 757 in the same 1226 games, another picture emerges.

Table 4. Observations on all home teams and the opposition.

	Total Goals	Strike Rate Shots/Goal	Rate of final 3rd poss/shots	Total all final 3rd poss/goal	All poss lost short of final 3rd/Goal	Total all poss/goal
All home teams	1063	8.11 x	10.75 =	86.42 +	68.83 =	155.24
The opposition	757	9.21 x	10.22 =	92.65 +	122.66 =	215.31
				6.24 +	53.84 =	60.07

This represents a near constant of 90 Final Third possessions per goal for all teams. It shows that 89.62% of all wins were achieved by simply not losing the ball short of the Final Third as much as the opposition.

It should be noted that where, for example, the goal/shot ratio has decreased (see Cambridge United 90–91, 89–90 and Preston North End 93–94) the Final Third to shot ratio has accordingly increased, keeping the number of Final Third possessions to goal as a near constant of 90. Piecemeal studies without comparison to the "big picture" of all possessions can yield false conclusions.

Referring now to Table 3, the 10 games at Arsenal show that 10 games are an insufficient sample on which to base any important conclusion because there is a freak figure of 17.1 Final Third possessions to shots for the opposition over this short period where chance does not average out as it does over the longer runs of games. Too small a sample can give rise to false interpretations in soccer analysis. The figures for Arsenal have not therefore been included in the final average.

Of these 15 examples it is evident that winning teams' figures for their Final Third possession/goal varied but little however. The difference that brought them almost their total success is shown in all possessions lost short of the Final Third column, where it was losing possession less times short of the Final Third that brought all of these teams almost all (90%) of their success.

A good example is Team A Wimbledon 1986–87, having progressed from Division IV with many players in the team who joined the club when in this Division. The team was on a shoestring budget and was playing against opposition with world-class strikers. Wimbledon scored at the rate of 1 goal in every 9.52 shots whereas all opposition teams, with their expensive world-class players in their team, could score at almost no greater rate per goal i.e. 1 in 9.24 over the season. This was indeed similar for the Final Third Possession to Shot ratio resulting in Wimbledon taking 103.29 Final Third possessions to score a goal and the opposition over the whole season similar at 96.09. Yet for possessions lost short of the Final Third per goal, Wimbledon lost the ball only 73.45 times on average/goal. The seemingly more formidable opposition lost the ball short of the Final Third 121.84 times on average/goal i.e. 48.39 possessions more per goal lost short of the Final Third and it was this near enough alone that brought Wimbledon 66 goals to the opposition's 55 and took the team into its highest ever position of 6th in the old Division I – now known as The Premier League.

The success of all other 14 teams is similarly based on losing the ball less times than the opposition short of the Final Third and not in scoring at any greater rate than the opposition for Final Third possessions.

There is therefore a Near Constant Law of Chance of 90 with a deviation of 10% either way of Final Third possessions, for each and every team at every level, to score a goal. Teams are successful by simply losing the ball less times short of the Final Third as the 89.62% of the success rate in this report shows for the 14 recorded winning teams.

Table 5. The 1950s picture of goal.

Team	Season	Division	Games	Goals	Strike rate shots/goal		Rate of Final 3rd poss/shots		Total all Final 3rd poss/goal		All poss lost short of final 3rd/Goal		Total all poss/goal	Av. all lost poss/goal both teams
									EQUATION					
Sheffield W	55/56	1	42	101	8.62	x	7.11	=	61.29	+	54.00	=	115.29	} 143.40
Opp			42	62	11.27	x	7.46	=	84.07	+	103.93	=	188.00	
Difference				39					22.78	+	**49.93**	=	72.71	
Wolver W	53/54	1	25	56	10.13	x	6.45	=	65.27	+	56.39	=	121.66	} 155.47
Opp			25	26	10.34	x	8.41	=	86.87	+	128.32	=	215.19	
Difference				30					21.74	+	**71.93**	=	93.67	

The above figures were computed from those supplied by Charles Reep who allowed the author access to his work. They show that scoring was easier in the 1950s i.e. it took less than 180 lost possessions on average to score a goal. The principle that winning was achieved by losing the ball less times than one's opposition short of the Final Third remains the same. It is believed that further runs of successful teams in longer samples would have confirmed this more decisively.

REFERENCES

Benjamin, B. and Reep, C. ,1968, Skill and chance in association football. Journal of the Royal Statistical Society, A, **131**, 581–585).

Benjamin, B., Pollard, R. and Reep, C., 1971, Skill and chance in ball games Journal of the Royal Statistical Society, A, **134**, 623–629.

Lanham, N., 1991, Figures do not cease to exist because they are not counted. In *Science and Football II*, edited by Reilly, T., Clarys, J. and Stibbe, A. (London: E and FN Spon), pp. 180–185.

29   Analysis of a 16-Game Winning Streak in Australian Rules Football

Brian Dawson[1,2], Brendyn Appleby[2,3] and Glenn Stewart[2]
[1] School of Human Movement and Exercise Science, The University of Western Australia, 35 Stirling Highway, Crawley, 6009, Western Australia, Australia
[2] West Coast Eagles Football Club, PO Box 508, Subiaco, 6008, Western Australia, Australia
[3] Western Australian Institute of Sport, Mt. Claremont, 6010, Western Australia, Australia

1. INTRODUCTION

Despite a good deal of notational and/or statistical analysis of football matches (of all codes) which have been presented at the four previous Science and Football Congresses, very few prior analyses of a prolonged winning streak by a single side have been reported. For example, previous studies have investigated factors such as home ground advantage (Nevill and Holder, 1999), travel and time zone shifts (Jehue et al., 1993), patterns of play of successful and unsuccessful teams in tournament play (Hughes et al., 1988) and goal scoring patterns (Garganta et al., 1997), but not the winning streaks of successful sides.

One of the rare studies to attempt this was the work of Luhtanen et al. (1997) who compared Brazil (the winners) and its respective opponents in the 1994 soccer World Cup. They reported that Brazil had the highest number of successful attacking trials to the attacking third, the highest number of scoring chances in the "vital" area and the highest number of shots for scoring goals. How successful teams achieve these types of results is obviously of interest to other sides for planning tactics to use against such high ranking opponents, as well as to the successful teams themselves, in order to help them maintain their standing.

In the 2001 Australian Football League (AFL) season, the Brisbane Lions Football Club made history by winning their first ever premiership. The club entered the League in 1987 and had made the finals on five previous occasions, but 2001 was the first season in which they qualified for the Grand Final. Making the achievement of their first premiership win all the more meritorious was the fact that their Grand Final victory was the 16th win in succession. After the first nine rounds of the season the side had won four games (by margins of 60, 49, 55 and 32 points) and lost five games (by margins of 6, 22, 53, 74 and 5 points). In the remainder of the regular season the team won the next 13 games (by between 21–87 points, $\bar{x}$ of 39 points) and then three finals (by 32, 68 and 26 points) to take the premiership title.

Analysing the match performances of the Brisbane Lions, both before and during the 16-game winning streak, might highlight results and trends that underpin their sustained winning phase.   General indicators of successful performance in Australian Rules football as well as specific pointers to the style of play practised by Brisbane might be uncovered.   Therefore, using the comprehensive match statistics made available by the AFL to all clubs on all games (Prowess systems), a detailed analysis of the 2001 season game performances by Brisbane was undertaken to attempt to isolate some objective reasons for its long winning streak.

2. METHODS

The game performance analysis was done by comparing Brisbane's own match statistics, averaged over the first nine regular season games (rounds 1–9) (pre-streak) and the last 13 regular season games (rounds 10–22) (winning streak) with the mean match statistics of the other seven sides that made the finals, as well as the mean match statistics of the other 15 teams in the League combined.   The three finals that Brisbane won to extend the winning streak to 16 were not analysed here, as less total teams were involved.   The match statistics used for comparison purposes were as follows:

(a)   Offensive statistics:

   (i)   possessions per goal scored;

   (ii)   total number of points scored;

   (iii)   number of individual goal scorers in each game;

   (iv)   number of entries into the forward 50-metre zone;

   (v)   number of unbroken chains of possession (2 or 3 or 4 or 5 or 6);

   (vi)   how the goals were scored (distance from goal, angle from centre of goal and whether a "set" kick or a "general play" kick was used to score).

(b)   Defensive statistics:

   (i)   the respective number of tackles;

   (ii)   bumps, spoils shepherds ('blocks or screens");

   (iii)   smothers of opposition kicks.

(c)   Errors:

   (i)   the respective number of fumbles;

   (ii)   kicks which directly led to opposition possession (turnovers);

   (iii)   number of dropped marks.

The data were analysed by t-tests utilising Bonferroni corrections, such that significance was only accepted when $P<0.01$ was reached.

3. RESULTS

The results of the mean match performance analyses for rounds 1–9 and 10–22 for Brisbane, the other top seven teams and the other 15 teams combined, are presented in Table 1. Due to the large volume of data analysed, only the match performance statistics where significant differences were observed are reported.

For rounds 1–9 (pre-streak), no significant differences in any of the match statistics were found between Brisbane, the other top 7 teams and the other 15 sides combined. During their winning streak (rounds 10–22) Brisbane recorded significantly better results (P<0.01) than both the other top 7 and other 15 teams combined in: (i) possessions per goal; (ii) total points scored; (iii) number of spoils; (iv) number of kicks to opposition.

Significant results were also recorded for Brisbane versus the other 15 teams combined for rounds 10–22 in: (i) number of individual goal scorers; (ii) number of smothers (of kicks).

Although not significantly different, in relation to the other 15 teams combined in rounds 10–22, Brisbane tended to have more tackles (64 to 60) and more "shepherds" (9 to 7), less fumbles (9 to 7) and score more goals from distances of 10–30 metres (44% to 37%) and from greater than 50 metres (11.2% to 9.4%). In addition, it was noted that Brisbane had the most stable playing squad of any side in the competition (21 players who played 75% or more of the 25 games that they played in the season) and also the most individual players (9) who scored 20 goals or more for the year.

Table 1. Mean ± SD match performance statistics.

Statistic	Rounds 1–9			Rounds 10–22		
	Brisbane	Top 7	Other 15	Brisbane	Top 7	Other 15
Possessions/goal	22±12	23±10	24±12	19±4	23±7**	25±13**
Total points scored	108±29	103±30	96±32	120±21	102±31**	97±31**
No. of goal scorers	9±3	8±2	8±3	10±1	8±2	7±2**
No. of spoils	30±5	27±6	27±6	28±6	23±7**	23±6**
No. of smothers	5±3	5±4	5±4	4±3	5±2	6±2**
No.of turnovers	11±5	12±5	12±5	11±4	14±5**	13±5**

** = P<0.01: Significantly different from Brisbane.

4. DISCUSSION

Long winning streaks are often attributed to "having the best players and/or team" and "good luck with injury". While such factors may ultimately be very important, they are extremely difficult to objectively analyse. The study performed here of Brisbane's 2001 winning streak was an attempt to analyse objectively the team performance during this season. Such information may highlight general current indicators of success in Australian football, as well as specific characteristics of the style of play used by Brisbane.

A very large volume of statistical data is available on the Internet for every game played in the AFL. Therefore, several offensive, defensive and error statistics were chosen for use in this study, to limit the analysis. For many of these selected statistics, no significant differences were found between Brisbane and either the other top 7 sides or the other 15 teams combined. However, as shown in Table 1, six statistics were found to show significant differences and four of these saw Brisbane record superior results to the other Top 7 teams. Of these, Brisbane players were seen to be more "efficient' in their play (less possessions per goal), to have less "turnovers" (by kick) than their opponents and to spoil the ball (in marking contests) more often. These results may point to better defensive discipline and decisions (spoiling) and a better skill level, (and option taking) in retaining possession of the ball more often (less possessions per goal and less turnovers). Although not statistically analysed, from rounds 1–9 (where Brisbane won four and lost five games) to rounds 10–22 (where the team won 13 games), the important changes may have been improved efficiency in play (possessions per goal decreased from 22–19) and the slight increase in the number of individual goal scorers (from 9 to 10) per game. It is probably noteworthy that Brisbane had the most players (9) who scored 20 or more goals for the season, which indicates that the players had several individual scoring options within their side, making it more difficult for opposing sides to defend. While these suggestions and interpretations are necessarily subjective in nature, the findings reported here assist in objectively explaining why Brisbane was able to produce a 16-game winning streak in the 2001 AFL season, and eventually claim its first ever premiership. While Brisbane players may have been "the best team" and had "good luck with injury", analysis of their pre-streak and winning streak match performances also shows that they became superior in certain offensive, defensive and error statistics, which may also help to explain their long successful run.

REFERENCES

Garganta, J., Maia, J. and Basto, F., 1997, Analysis of goal scoring patterns in European top level soccer teams. In *Science and Football III,* edited by Reilly, T., Bangsbo, J. and Hughes, M. (London: E. and F.N. Spon), pp. 246–250.

Hughes, M., Robertson, K. and Nicholson, A., 1988, Comparison of patterns of play of successful and unsuccessful teams in the 1986 World Cup for soccer. In *Science and Football,* edited by Reilly, T., Lees, A., Davids, K. and Murphy, W. J. (London: E. & F.N. Spon), pp. 363–367.

Jehue, R., Street, D. and Huizenga, R., 1993, Effect of time zone and game time changes on team performance: National Football League. *Medicine and Science in Sports and Exercise,* **25,** 127–131.

Luhtanen, P.H., Korhonen, V. and Ilkka, A., 1997, A new notational analysis system with special reference to the comparison of Brazil and its opponents in the World Cup 1994. In *Science and Football III,* edited by Reilly, T., Bangsbo, J. and Hughes, M. (London: E and F.N. Spon), pp. 229–232.

Nevill, A.M. and Holder, R.L., 1999, Home advantage in sport. *Sports Medicine,* **28,** 221–236.

30   Activity Profile of Men's Gaelic Football

Peter O'Donoghue and Shane King

School of Applied Medical Science and Sports Studies, University of
Ulster, Jordanstown, County Antrim, BT37 0QB, UK

1. INTRODUCTION

Time-motion analysis has determined the work-to-rest ratio of Gaelic football competition together with the duration of the average high intensity burst and average low intensity recovery period between bursts (McErlean *et al.*, 2000). However, the bursts performed have a wide range of durations as do the recovery periods. Previous experimental studies have failed to find conditioning programmes based on an average burst duration and an average recovery duration to be effective. One such study consisted of a training programme of 40 repetitions of a 6-s sprint with a 30-s jog recovery performed by club hockey players once a week for 8 weeks (Huey *et al.*, 2001). A further study tested a training programme of 3 sets of 8 repetitions of a 40-m agility run with a 90° direction change every 5 m with a 30-s recovery interval performed once a week by an international netball squad for 8 weeks (O'Donoghue and Cassidy, 2001). Both of these experimental studies employed training sessions that were based on time-motion analysis findings. One of the reasons why they failed to improve relevant fitness variables above control conditions could be the fact that both were based on an average burst duration and an average recovery duration. Such specific training sessions need to use a profile of burst and recovery durations that is more representative of the range experienced in competition. This is because demands placed on energy sources will be different where there are occasional long bursts of over 10 s and short recoveries of under 30 s. There are few studies that have determined the profile of bursts and recoveries in team games. O'Donoghue (2002) did find a wide variety of burst durations from under 2 s to over 12 s in FA Premier League soccer with a wide range of recoveries from under 2 s to over 90 s. However, there are no time-motion analysis studies for Gaelic football to provide such information.

The purpose of the current investigation, therefore, was to determine the profile of durations of both high intensity bursts and low intensity recoveries that occur during men's Gaelic football competition. A further objective was to determine if there was a relationship between the duration of the burst and the duration of the following recovery period.

2. METHODS

The study used time-motion history files for 55 senior male players whose activity had been observed and verbally coded using portable dictation machines during competitive inter-university Gaelic football matches. The players were 12 full backs, 15 full forwards, 14 wing halves (8 wing half backs and 6 wing half forwards), as well as 14 central players (7 midfielders, 3 centre half backs and 4 centre half forwards). During observation of players' movements, activity had been classified into the following seven movement classes:

- *Stationary* - where the player is standing still, sitting, stretching or lying in a prone position.
- *Walking* - walking in a forward direction.
- *Backing* - walking backwards or sideways.
- *Jogging* - slow running in a forward direction without acceleration.
- *Running* - purposeful running with obvious effort or all-out sprinting.
- *Shuffling* - a sideways, backwards or on-the-spot movement requiring effort and shuffling movements of the feet. This category includes jogging backwards and sideways.
- *Game-related activity* - where the subject is involved in an on-the-ball event or travelling with the ball during game time. Such events include striking the ball at a free kick, tackling, passing, being tackled, aerial challenges and 'soloing'.

Of these activities, running, shuffling and game-related activity were classified as high intensity activity with all other activities being classified as low intensity activity. A computer program was specifically designed to capture and analyse sequences of activities that occur during Gaelic football. The on-field activity for each subject was entered into this system during playback of the audio-cassette which had been used to record the subject's movements during the match. A Siemens Nixdorf PCD 4N notepad computer was used, with a keyboard overlay identifying the movement classifications represented by each function key. The system strung together consecutively performed high intensity movement instances into individual bursts of high intensity activity. It also strung together consecutively performed low intensity movement instances into individual recovery periods of low intensity activity. The time-motion history files were processed by the computerised time-motion analysis system to extract the following information:

1. The percentage of match time spent performing high intensity activity.
2. The number of high intensity bursts performed.
3. The duration of the average high intensity burst performed and average low intensity recovery period taken.
4. The frequency of bursts of under 2 s, 2–4 s, 4–6 s, 6–8 s, 8–10 s, 10–12 s and over 12 s.
5. The frequency of recovery periods of under 2 s, 2–4 s, 4–8 s, 8–12 s, 12–20 s, 20–45 s, 45–90 s and over 90 s.
6. The frequency of burst and following recovery period of all 7 × 8 of the burst × recovery category listed in 4 and 5 above.

These durations of bursts and recoveries are the same as those used by O'Donoghue (2002) to allow comparisons to be made with elite soccer competition. An inter-observer reliability study revealed no significant difference between the two observers for the profile of bursts ($\chi^2_6 = 3.5$, P = 0.746) or the profile of recoveries recorded ($\chi^2_7 = 2.5$, P = 0.929). A series of Kruskal Wallis H tests were used to compare the four broad positional groups in terms of the variables produced by the computerised time-motion analysis system. A chi-squared test was applied to test whether the recovery duration was independent of the preceding burst duration. Chi-squared tests were also used to compare the profile of bursts performed as well as recoveries taken between the four positional groups.

3. RESULTS

The players performed 95.7 ± 25.7 bursts of high intensity activity with an average duration of 5.7 ± 1.6 s followed by an average recovery of 36.7 ± 14.1 s. The work-to-rest ratio was 1 : 6.6 ± 2.2 with the players spending $14.4\pm4.7\%$ of match time performing high intensity activity. Table 1 summarises the durations of bursts and following recovery periods. A chi-squared test was used to compare the profile of recoveries that followed bursts of different durations. In order to achieve an expected count of 5 or more in each cell, 2 broad classes of burst (under 6 s or 6 s and longer) and four broad classes of recovery (under 8 s, 8 s to 20 s, 20 s to 45 s and 45 s or longer) were used. There was no significant difference in the profile of the recoveries that followed the bursts of under 6 s and the bursts of 6 s and longer ($\chi^2_3 = 1.3$, P > 0.05).

Table 1. Frequency of bursts and following recovery periods of different durations

Burst	Following Recovery								
	0–2 s	2–4 s	4–8 s	8–12 s	12–20 s	20–45 s	45–90 s	90 s+	All
0–2 s	3.0±3.6	2.4±2.8	2.7±2.7	1.3±1.5	1.9±1.9	4.4±3.4	2.7±2.0	1.5±1.9	20.0±14.9
2–4 s	3.1±2.9	2.5±2.1	3.2±2.2	2.0±1.6	3.1±2.4	6.3±3.3	3.7±1.8	1.8±1.4	25.6±10.3
4–6 s	1.3±1.3	1.9±1.5	2.1±1.7	1.2±1.2	2.4±1.8	4.8±2.3	2.9±1.7	1.4±1.3	18.0±6.3
6–8 s	0.9±1.2	1.0±1.1	1.3±1.1	1.0±1.2	1.3±1.2	3.4±2.4	1.9±1.4	1.1±1.2	11.9±4.6
8–10 s	0.3±0.5	0.5±0.8	0.7±0.9	0.5±0.7	0.8±0.9	2.0±1.7	1.5±1.3	0.6±0.7	7.0±3.5
10–12 s	0.3±0.8	0.5±0.7	0.5±0.7	0.3±0.6	0.7±1.0	1.1±1.1	0.8±0.9	0.5±0.7	4.7±3.1
12 s+	0.4±0.7	0.6±1.0	0.7±1.0	0.6±1.0	1.3±1.4	2.3±2.6	2.1±1.7	0.7±1.0	8.6±6.4
All	9.4±7.4	9.5±5.7	11.1±5.5	6.9±4.0	11.6±5.5	24.2±8.3	15.5±3.5	7.6±3.8	95.7±25.7

Table 2 compares the four broad positional groups in terms of work rate and average burst and recovery duration. There was no significant difference between the four positional groups for the duration of the average high intensity burst performed. However, the 4 central players (the centre-half back, centre-half forward and 2 midfielders) performed more bursts with shorter recoveries contributing to a higher percentage of match time spent performing high intensity activity than the other 3 positional groups.

Table 2. Summary of high intensity (HI) activity for the 4 positional groups

Variable	Position				H_3
	Full Back	Central	Wing Half	Full-Forward	
%Time performing HI activity	12.8±2.9	19.8±4.2	14.2±3.8	10.7±1.5	27.4***
Frequency of HI bursts	85.1±16.7	120.5±17.7	88.4±28.4	88.5±22.2	17.7**
Duration Average Bursts (s)	5.7±1.1	6.2±1.8	6.3±1.2	4.9±1.7	7.6
Duration Average Recovery (s)	70.5±11.8	24.7±3.4	41.2±15.7	40.8±14.7	22.4***

- $P < 0.05$, ** $P < 0.01$, *** $P < 0.001$.

Table 3 shows the profile of burst durations performed by the 4 positional groups while Table 4 shows the profile of recoveries performed by the 4 positional groups. The Kruskal Wallis H tests revealed some significant differences between the four positional groups for the frequency of bursts and recoveries of some durations. However, the fact that the average central player performed 120.3 high intensity bursts compared with 84.8 to 88.3 for the average member of the other 3 positional groups is largely responsible for these differences.

Table 3. Profile of high intensity bursts.

Burst (s)	Position				H_3
	Full Back	Central	Wing-Half	Full-Forward	
0–2	13.0±9.1	24.2±17.3	15.8±11.5	7.2±16.7	7.2
2–4	22.9±7.8	29.9±12.2	24.3±11.4	24.9±8.7	3.0
4–6	19.0±5.7	21.4±5.5	16.1±7.1	15.9±5.7	6.6
6–8	13.3±4.1	14.4±4.5	10.8±4.3	9.3±3.8	11.4*
8–10	5.3±3.0	9.8±3.5	7.7±3.1	5.0±1.9	17.2**
10–12	4.2±1.9	7.4±3.5	4.0±2.4	3.1±2.6	13.6**
12±	7.1±5.3	13.1±8.0	9.6±3.8	4.6±4.7	13.8**
Total	84.8±16.6	120.3±17.5	88.3±28.4	88.3±22.0	17.8***

* $P < 0.05$, ** $P < 0.01$, *** $P < 0.001$.

Table 4. Profile of low intensity recovery periods.

Recovery (s)	Position				H_3
	Full-Back	Central	Wing-Half	Full-Forward	
0–2	5.7±3.6	13.1±8.6	8.6±7.7	9.7±7.6	6.8
2–4	8.7±5.5	13.5±5.1	7.5±6.6	8.1±3.6	12.0**
4–8	10.7±4.6	14.9±5.5	8.2±4.8	10.4±5.0	10.8**
8–12	5.6±2.5	10.6±4.2	5.9±3.7	5.4±3.2	15.5**
12–20	9.7±4.5	17.0±3.6	10.6±6.0	8.9±3.5	19.7***
20–45	20.0±6.8	31.4±4.3	22.3±10.0	22.8±6.6	17.1**
45–90	15.4±3.4	16.1±2.9	17.0±3.6	13.6±5.6	19.4***
90±	9.0±2.5	3.8±2.0	8.1±4.5	9.5±2.7	6.7
Total	84.8±16.6	120.3±17.5	88.3±28.4	88.3±22.0	17.8***

$P < 0.05$, ** $P < 0.01$, *** $P < 0.001$.

A chi-squared test compared the frequencies of the different burst durations between the four positions. It was necessary to consider all bursts of over 10 s together to avoid expected counts of under 5. The chi-squared test revealed that there was no significant difference between the profile of bursts performed between the 4 positional groups ($\chi^2_{15} = 9.9$, $P > 0.05$). A further chi-squared test revealed no significant difference between the profile of recoveries taken between the 4 positions ($\chi^2_{21} = 10.2$, $P > 0.05$).

4. DISCUSSION

When comparing the intermittent nature of Gaelic football with that of soccer, the average burst of 5.7 s performed by the Gaelic footballers is greater than the 3.2 s average bursts performed in FA Premier League soccer (O'Donoghue, 2002). Furthermore, 68% of the high intensity bursts performed by soccer players are under 4 s in duration compared with 46% of the bursts performed by the Gaelic footballers in the current study. O'Donoghue (2002) found that only 4% of high intensity bursts performed by FA Premier League soccer players were 8 s or more in duration compared with 34% of the bursts performed by the Gaelic footballers in the current study. The percentage of recovery periods of under 20 s, 20–45 s and over 45 s was 51%, 25% and 24% for the Gaelic footballers in the current study compared with 57%, 23% and 20% for the FA Premier League soccer players analysed by O'Donoghue (2002). This shows that despite being a 15-a-side game with more players contributing to a team performance, Gaelic football requires players to perform longer bursts with shorter recovery than in soccer.

The current study has found that Gaelic football is an intermittent high intensity team game like soccer but with a higher work-rate. The range of bursts performed during men's Gaelic football competition has implications for the sources of energy utilised during high intensity activity. Degradation of muscle creatine phosphate (CP) and stored muscle adenosine triphosphate (ATP) provides most of the energy for short high intensity bursts performed in soccer (Bangsbo, 1997). Previous research into the energy sources used for short bursts of high intensity activity also gives an indication of the sources used in Gaelic football competition. Glycolytic and aerobic sources have been shown to contribute to the energy required during a Wingate test after the first 5 s of exercise (Smith and Hill, 1991).

There is also a full range of recovery periods between bursts of high intensity activity with 51% of recoveries taking less than 20 s and 8% of recoveries lasting 90 s or longer. The range of recoveries between bursts may also have implications for the energy systems that are utilised during high intensity bursts. Previous experimental research has shown that blood lactate accumulation and performance decrements over five 6-s maximal sprint bouts performed on cycle-ergometer equipment were greater when a recovery of 30 s was taken between bouts than when the recovery was 60 s (Wootton and Williams, 1983). Further work has shown that muscle CP may not be sufficiently replenished after recovery periods of under 45 s (Balsom *et al.*, 1992).

While the current study has shown a similar profile of bursts and recoveries between the 4 positional classes, the total number of bursts performed by the central players was almost 50% greater than that of any other positional group. This has led to a significantly higher proportion of match time being spent performing high intensity activity by the central players than the other positional groups. The wing-halves also perform much more high intensity activity than players in the full forward line and full back line.

5. CONCLUSIONS

The current study has provided new information for Gaelic football. The results show that male players perform bursts of high intensity activity of a range of durations. There is also a range of recovery periods that follow these bursts of high intensity activity. The central players perform significantly more bursts of high intensity activity than the other positional groups. It is therefore recommended that the full range of bursts performed and the variation in recovery periods for players' positional roles are taken into consideration when designing the conditioning elements of players' training programmes.

REFERENCES

Balsom, P.D., Seger, J.Y., Sjodin, B. and Ekblom, B., 1992, Maximal-intensity intermittent exercise: effect of the recovery duration. *International Journal of Sports Medicine,* **13**, 528–533.

Bangsbo, J., 1997, The physiology of intermittent activity in football. In *Science and Football III,* edited by Reilly, T., Bangsbo, J. and Hughes, M. (London: E & FN Spon), pp. 43–53.

Huey, A., Morrow, P. and O'Donoghue, P.G., 2001, From time-motion analysis to specific intermittent high intensity training, *Proceedings of the World Congress of Performance Analysis, Sports Science and Computers (PASS.COM),* (Cardiff: UWIC), pp. 29–34.

McErlean, C.A., Cassidy, J. and O'Donoghue, P.G., 2000, Time-motion analysis of gender and positional effects on work-rate in elite Gaelic football competition. *Journal of Human Movement Studies,* **33**, 269–286.

O'Donoghue, P.G., 2002, Time-motion analysis of work-rate in English FA Premier League soccer. *International Journal of Performance Analysis of Sport (e),* **2**, 36–43.

O'Donoghue, P.G. and Cassidy, D., 2002, The effect of specific intermittent training on the fitness of international netball players. *Journal of Sports Sciences,* **20**, 56–57.

Smith, J.C. and Hill, D.W., 1991, Contribution of energy systems during a Wingate power test. *British Journal of Sports Medicine,* **25**, 196–199.

Wootton, S.A. and Williams, C., 1983, The influence of recovery duration on repeated maximal sprints. In *Biochemistry of Exercise,* edited by Knuttgen, H.G., Vogel, J.A. and Poortmans, J. (Champaign, IL: Human Kinetics), pp. 269–273.

31 Applications of Logistic Regression to Shots at Goal in Association Football

Jake Ensum[1], Richard Pollard[1] and Samuel Taylor[2]
[1]California Polytechnic State University, San Luis Obispo, California
[2]Research Institute for Sport and Exercise Sciences, Liverpool John Moores University

1. INTRODUCTION

Pollard and Reep (1997) introduced the use of logistic regression to analyse shots at goal in soccer. This approach allowed researchers to investigate factors thought to affect the chance of scoring from a shot. Factors identified as significant were utilised to quantify a shooting chance by estimating a shot's scoring probability. These shot probabilities were then used as an outcome measure to quantify the effectiveness of playing strategies and to construct contour diagrams for scoring probability. The following study expands upon Pollard and Reep's approach. More factors are analysed to investigate their importance in scoring from shots and shot probabilities are used as a comparative tool to evaluate shooting performance of 2002 World Cup semi-final teams (the quality of chance a team creates/concedes and the individual efficiency in scoring/saving these chances). Some limitations of logistic regression analysis are discussed and some directions for future work are suggested.

2. METHODS

Altogether, 1099 shots and 117 goals from 48 matches in the 2002 World Cup were recorded by five observers. For each shot, 9 factors were entered into Excel. Factors comprised those at the moment of the shot (definitions 1–5 (Table 1)) and those preceding the moment of the shot (6–9). A shot was defined as "an attempt to propel the ball into the opposition's goal".

Inter-reliability studies were conducted on 2.5 matches. These revealed that the shooting technique of kicked shots and the event preceding the shot (other than a cross) were not consistently recorded by observers and were rejected from the analysis. Other factors excluded were the number of passes involved in the movement, the match time and the match position (whether a team was winning, losing or drawing) as they were unsuitable for logistic regression. As in Pollard and Reep's study, shots blocked within 1 m of their origin were not included in the analysis. Shots taken directly from free kicks and penalties were excluded due to their infrequency and differing characteristics from other types of shot (both are closed rather than open skills). In total 729 kicked shots with 77 goals and 163 headed shots with 27 goals remained. Due to the technical differences between kicked and headed shots, both were analysed separately. The GLIM program was used to perform the logistic regression analyses. Semi-final teams' performances were used for evaluation purposes as they provided the most data.

Table 1. Definitions of variables.

Variable	Definition
1. Distance	The distance between the shot position and the nearest goal-post.
2. Angle	The angle between the shot position and the nearest goal-post.
3. Space	The shot-taker had >1 m of space from an opposition player.
4. GK position	The goalkeeper was positioned between the shot-taker and goal.
5. # players	The number of outfield players between the shot-taker and goal.
6. SP origin	The movement leading to the shot originated from a dead ball.
7. RP area	The pitch position from which possession is regained, divided into attacking, midfield and defending thirds.
8. Cross	A pass directed towards the opposition's penalty box from a wide area (this is from the by-line to 2 m inside the penalty box).
9. # touches	The number of touches completed by the player to take the shot, including the final touch to shoot.

3. RESULTS AND DISCUSSION

3.1. Investigation and quantification of factors

An initial logistic regression analysis showed that no second order interactions were significant. Subsequent analyses therefore omitted interaction terms.

The factors of 'distance', 'angle', 'cross', 'space' and '# players' all had a significant effect (where $P<0.05$) on the success of a kicked shot (Table 2). For headed shots, only 'distance' and 'space' were significant factors (Table 3).

Table 2. Significant factors for kicked shots.

Variable	Coefficient	P value	Odds Ratio
Distance	−0.115	0.001	0.89
Angle	−0.021	0.003	0.98
Cross	0.695	0.038	2.00
Space	0.734	0.019	2.08
# players	−0.311	0.004	0.73

Table 3. Significant factors for headed shots.

Variable	Coefficient	Pvalue	Odds Ratio
Distance	−0.522	0.000	0.59
Space	1.140	0.019	3.13

3.1.1. Significant factors

For most significant factors, their importance to shot scoring is self-evident and will not be discussed further. However, the 'cross' factor warrants further examination. Whilst the odds of scoring increase when a shot originates from a cross, this does not mean that crosses are the most effective means of penetrating a defence; many fail to meet their target. Principally, a cross changes the angle and area of play more than any other type of preceding event, thus placing greater attentional and decision making demands on defending players. For the defending players, attention has to take account of, and change to, this new area of play. Attention may also need to be directed towards the multiple points at which the ball might be met across the goal. Consequently, defenders and goalkeepers may have less time to organise and pick up cues that help them to anticipate play and there may be more space for shot-takers. For goalkeepers, the situation may also require them to move across the goal so that they have momentum in one direction. Therefore, they may not be well balanced to save in all potential directions. A further development in examining crosses would be to compare cross types. Partridge and Franks (1989, a and b) provided an interesting analysis of this question.

3.1.2. Non-significant factors

It was unexpected that 'GK position' was not significant, perhaps due to the small number of instances where the goalkeeper was not in the goal. Most factors preceding the shot were not significant. This result emphasises the importance of measuring factors as close as possible to the moment of the shot. In addition, the '# touches' factor may have been multi-modal and thus unsuitable for logistic regression as the data would violate the assumption of a sigmoidal relationship with the dependent variable (a goal).

3.1.3. Quantification of factors

Whilst most of the significant results might be expected, another value of logistic regression is to quantify factors, so informing coaches how important these factors are. The odds ratios in Tables 2 and 3 indicate this. For instance, for kicked shots, for each yard (0.9 m) the shot is taken away from goal, the odds of scoring reduce by 11%, or, if a player has space, the odds of scoring double. A coach may choose to use these figures to motivate players and aid their understanding.

When comparing kicked and headed shots, 'distance' and 'space' become more important for headed shots. This may be due to headers generally having less power and their technique being impeded more easily through contact than for kicked shots.

3.2. Comparison with Pollard and Reep's (1997) study

Pollard and Reep's results of the 1986 World Cup are provided in Table 4. The '# touches' was recorded as a dichotomous variable of one touch or greater than one touch. The 'angle' measurement was originally reported in radians. This has been converted into degrees for ease of comparison. The '# touches' was not analysed (NA) for headed shots as all but one shot involved one touch.

Table 4. Pollard and Reep's results (1997).

Sample	Constant	Distance	Angle	Space	SP Origin	# Touches
410 kicked shots	1.245	−0.219	−0.026	0.947	−1.069	NS
74 headed shots	1.520	−0.237	−0.052	NS	−1.784	NA

Direct comparison is not wholly appropriate as different combinations of factors were analysed. Nevertheless, for kicked shots, both studies have broad agreement in their findings of significant factors, bar the factor of whether the movement originated from a dead ball ('SP origin'). It may be that as set plays are usually associated with an increased number of players advancing or retreating into attacking or defensive positions, the 2002 sample may more accurately account for the negative effect 'SP origin' has on scoring from shots by recording the number of players in front of goal.

For headed shots, 'distance' was significant for both samples. The other discrepancies may best be explained by the small sample size.

When comparing coefficient values for kicked shots, 'angle' and 'space' were similar. However, for the 2002 sample, 'distance' was half that of the 1986 sample (−0.113 compared to −0.219 (Tables 2 and 4)). This observation is hard to account for. It may be due to improvements in accuracy and power in 2002 and/or climatic locational differences. Less consistent recording of shots from distance in the 2002 sample is also possible, due to the number of observers involved. It may also indicate that more data are required for the values to stabilise.

For headed shots, coefficient values varied between samples but are not discussed further due to the small sample size. In general, analysis of all factors would have benefitted from greater reliability testing (no intra-reliability tests were conducted and only 2.5 matches were tested for inter-reliability whilst the data were recorded by 5 observers). Also, given the inconsistent findings between the two samples, it would be inappropriate to make generalisations for universal soccer performance at this stage.

3.3. Calculation of shot scoring probabilities

Despite the inconsistency of the results, calculating shot scoring probabilities may still provide useful information for this particular sample and their method of calculation and their applications are of interest.

The equations for calculating the 'y' value of kicked (1) and headed (2) shots are outlined below where 'y' is the dependent variable, 'D' represents the distance factor, 'A' angle, 'C' cross, 'S' space and 'P' the number of players.

$$y = 0.325 - (0.115*D) - (0.021*A) + (0.695*C) + (0.734*S) - (0.311*P) \qquad (1)$$

$$y = 2.239 - (0.522*D) + (1.14*S) \qquad (2)$$

'y' can be converted into a probability of scoring using the formula below (3).

$$p = \frac{\exp y}{1 + \exp y} \tag{3}$$

These probabilities for shot scoring can be applied in a number of ways. As previously stated, they have been utilised as an outcome measure to evaluate the effectiveness of playing strategies and to estimate scoring probabilities at set co-ordinates in a given situation, so enabling the construction of a visual contour diagram (Pollard and Reep, 1997). In this study they are utilised to evaluate performance associated with shooting.

3.4. Evaluation of 2002 Semi-Final teams

Tables 5 and 6 indicate the potential of logistic regression to provide useful information on performance associated with shooting. The sum of all shot probabilities from kicked and headed shots for each team provides an estimate of the total number of goals that were expected to be scored. Those directly taken free kick shots and penalties were not analysed. Comparing the aggregate shot probabilities to those actually scored gives an indication of striking or saving ability. This may provide useful information when preparing to play other teams, evaluating longitudinal player performance or recruiting players. For instance, a characteristic of most semi-final teams was their opposition's low conversion of estimated chances (against Germany, Turkey and Brazil teams scored 60–70% of estimated goals (Table 6), where 100% would represent the expected conversion rate for all teams in the sample). This may be attributed to poor shooting accuracy and/or goalkeeping performance (to measure a goalkeeper's saving ability only the shots on target should be analysed). In addition, Turkey's success in the World Cup can in part be attributed to the players' striking efficiency (154% of estimated goals were scored (Table 5)). With a greater amount of data this analysis could also be applied to individual strikers.

The mean shot probability, combined with the total number of shots, indicates how well a team has performed in creating or conceding shots. Brazil's players created the best quality chances in the World Cup (their shots had a mean scoring probability of 13.5% (Table 5)), suggesting that they were the most adept at penetrating defences. Also, 8 of their 18 goals were created from crosses (which has been found to improve the chance of scoring). This quantitative analysis may prove useful to teams in understanding the relative importance of a team's attacking strategies when preparing to play them, developing their own attacking strategies and training players. This finding could also be applied to the conceding of chances to assess defensive weaknesses but may require more data due to the variation of opposition teams' attacking strategies.

Table 5. Semi-final teams' attacking performance for kicked and headed shots.

Team	Shots Taken	Mean Shot Probability	Estimated Total No. of Goals	Goals Scored	Estimated Goals to Goals (%)
Germany	87	12.2	10.58	12	113
S Korea	76	6.6	5.04	6	119
Turkey	57	10.3	5.86	9	154
Brazil	79	13.5	10.69	14	131

Table 6. Semi-final teams' defending performance for kicked and headed shots.

Team	Shots Conceded	Mean Shot Probability	Estimated Total No. of Goals	Goals Conceded	Estimated Goals to Goals (%)
Germany	45	10.0	4.51	3	67
S Korea	57	11.1	6.3	6	95
Turkey	79	8.4	6.6	4	61
Brazil	65	9.0	5.84	4	68

A further value of calculating shot probabilities in addition to shots and goals is that accurate information is provided. For instance, when comparing South Korea's and Brazil's shots to goals (Table 5), South Korea created a similar number of shots but it misleadingly appeared that the team's conversion of chances was not half as good as Brazil's (6 compared to 14 goals were scored). However, the aggregate shot probability analysis would suggest that the cause of South Korea's poor conversion of shots to goals was due to an inability to create as many *good quality* chances, rather than poor finishing ability (this was actually above the tournament average (119%) and close to Brazil's (Table 5)). The implications for effective training time may therefore have been to improve the creation of shooting opportunities rather than finishing ability.

4. LIMITATIONS

The most pertinent limitations to logistic regression are briefly discussed below.

4.1. Relationships between dependent and independent variables

The model assumes that each factor affects the chance of scoring in a monotonically increasing manner. However, some factors do not have the assumed sigmoidal relationship with the dependent variable and so they are unsuitable for logistic regression. Equally, some factors may have fluctuations within their broadly sigmoidal relationships that are not accurately accounted for. For instance, it might be expected that there are certain thresholds at which 'distance' deviates from this relationship, i.e. when players change technique to increase accuracy or power when closer or further away from goal, or, at a certain distance where a goalkeeper's reaction time is not quick enough to react to the shot.

4.2. Inclusion of all relevant factors

If all relevant factors are not analysed, a significant predictor's variance may be wrongly attributed as it may be shared with the variance of factors that are not included. Equally, some factors cannot be appropriately analysed, as above, which suggests that there is always the possibility for error when analysing shots at goal with logistic regression. In addition, some factors may not be included in the analysis as further work is required to identify all the factors that are significant to scoring from shots and some of these factors may be difficult to record, e.g. the goalkeeper's anticipation speed.

4.3. Net effect

The coefficients for each factor give a net effect. In some situations factors can have both positive or negative effects on scoring from a shot. For example, the number of players in front of goal would reduce the amount of the goal area available although, in some instances, they might also unsight the goalkeeper.

5. FUTURE WORK

Given the inconsistency in findings between the two samples studied and the utility of the information which logistic regression could provide, it would be desirable to record an appropriate sample in terms of validity and reliability for elite soccer. This would enable the reliable quantification of factors and comparison of performance between competitions, teams and players. With this sample, it might not be necessary for more practical match analysts (who wish to assume the study's reliability and validity or are unable to collect a large enough sample size) to collate and analyse data for logistic regression. The process could be 'short-cut' by using the study's coefficient values with the chosen sample so that performance could be compared as desired.

6. CONCLUSION

Despite the issues of reliability, sample size and the problems inherent in logistic regression, the present report has demonstrated some useful applications of logistic regression to shots at goal in soccer. Factors important to scoring goals can be identified and quantified and the probability of a shot scoring estimated. The calculation of shot scoring probabilities allows evaluation of the effectiveness of playing strategies, construction of scoring probability contours and assessment of performance associated with shooting. In this latter regard, the value of measuring shot-scoring probabilities over merely shots and goals was highlighted whilst evaluating 2002 World Cup teams. Future work may be directed towards analysing an appropriate sample for elite football so that reliable comparisons can be made and match analysts have greater access to this method of analysis.

REFERENCES

Partridge, D. and Franks, I.M., 1989a, A detailed analysis of crossing opportunities from the 1986 World Cup. Part I. *Soccer Journal*, **34** (2), 47–50.

Partridge, D. and Franks, I.M., 1989b, A detailed analysis of crossing opportunities from the 1986 World Cup. Part II. *Soccer Journal*, **34** (3), 45–48.

Pollard, R. and Reep, C., 1997, Measuring the effectiveness of playing strategies in soccer. *The Statistician*, **46**, 541–550.

32   Attacking Profiles of Successful and Unsuccessful Teams in Copa America 2001

Mike Hughes and Steve Churchill
Centre for Performance Analysis, UWIC, Cardiff CF23 6XD

1. INTRODUCTION

After analysing the 1986 World Cup for shots and crosses, Partridge and Franks (1989a,b) concluded that the success of a team is considered in terms of being able to score more goals than the opposition in a particular game. The importance of scoring goals is paramount for any team's success. To achieve the highest success, coaches use performance analysis to examine attacking play, in particular, and also identify the strengths and weaknesses of their own team and their opposition.

Match analysis can provide coaches with information regarding successful patterns of play compared with unsuccessful patterns of play, player movements and individual contributions and from the results attempts to employ tactics that create goal scoring opportunities can be made. The majority of soccer analysis has been focused upon goal scoring and patterns of build-up play leading to shots. Hughes (1996) stated that soccer has followed a basically negative and defensive trend for the last thirty or so years. Game statistics illustrate this completely. The 1954 World Cup produced 140 goals in 26 matches, averaging 5.4 per game. In 1986 only 132 goals were scored in twice as many games, an average of 2.5 per game. With the rarity of goals in the game, it is vital that teams take their chances and create goal-scoring opportunities frequently.

The aim of this study was to develop a reliable hand notation system to compare the patterns of play of successful and unsuccessful teams leading to shots and goals during the Copa America Tournament of 2001. The results were then compared to previous studies such as those by Hook and Hughes (2001), Jinshan et al. (1993) and Reep and Benjamin (1968) to define patterns of play of South American international teams.

2. METHODS

A hand notation system was designed based on the work of Hook and Hughes (2001), tested for reliability and used to record variables of playing patterns in the 2001 Copa America. The largest percentage errors, of 5.4%, were accepted on variations in 'duration of attack', and 'position in goal' as being within the critical aims of the analysis. All other error values for the other variables were less. Matches involving successful teams (n=19) and unsuccessful teams (n=11) were analysed, and the performances were compared using performance indicators from 10 variables. Chi-squared tests were used, where appropriate, to determine whether there were any significant differences between the two sets of data.

3. RESULTS AND DISCUSSION

Jinshan et al. (1993) found that for every 15 minutes that the match progressed, the number of goals increased gradually with time, the peak being located between 75–90 minutes. The results of this study of patterns of play leading to shots are similar to those of Jinshan and co-workers. Although not every 10-min period produced more shots than the previous, there was a trend that showed an increase in shots as time progressed, with the last period (80–90 min) producing the most shots (88). There were three periods of play (0–10, 30–40 and 70–80 min) that produced noticeably lower amounts of shots than other times. The reason for this could be that these times of the match are considered to be bad times to concede goals (at the start, just before and after half time and nearing the end) which causes teams not to commit as many players forward in fear of a counter-attack, thus restricting their attacking options.

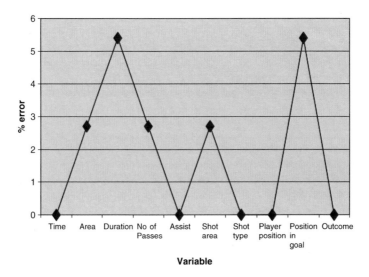

Figure 1. An adapted Bland and Altman (1986) plot showing error within the system.

Possession gained in area 4 (attacking quarter) resulted in 41.63% of the shots that were made and 68.42% of shots came from possession being gained in areas 3 and 4 (attacking half) of the pitch. Reep and Benjamin (1968) found that 50% of all goals came from possession being gained in the final attacking quarter; this study found similar results that showed 50% of the goals scored came from possession being gained in area 4 and 58% came from possession being gained in areas 3 and 4.

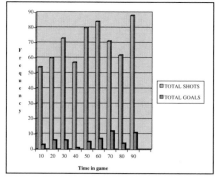
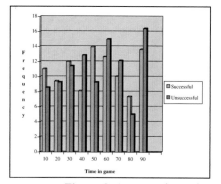

Figure 2. The total shots and goals for each 10 minute period of the match.

Figure 3. A comparison of the percentages for the time of shots for successful and unsuccessful teams.

Table 1. The total shots and goals produced in different possession lengths.

Duration	Shots	Goals	Conversion ratio
0–4	272	18	15.11
5–9	179	19	9.42
10–14	101	11	9.18
15–19	37	4	9.25
20+	37	4	9.25

Table 1 shows that the shorter the duration of possession, the more likely it is that a shot will be made. Similarly the longer the duration of possession, the less likely a shot or goal is. There were 272 (43.5%) shots taken from possessions of 4 s or less, and 72% of all shots resulted from possessions of 9 s or less. Altogether, 66% of goals were scored from moves of 9 s or less.

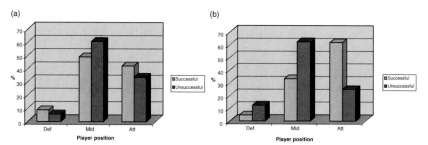

Figure 4. A comparison of the percentages for player position of shots taken and goals scored.

Figures 4a,b show that midfielders took the most shots for both successful and unsuccessful teams, although considerably more so for unsuccessful teams. Their midfielders took over 60% of the shots compared to 33% from their attackers, whereas successful teams' midfielders took 49% and attackers took 42%. This finding indicates that successful teams were able to get the ball to their attackers in shooting range of the goal more frequently and did not rely on the midfield players to take longer shots as the unsuccessful teams had to. The attackers for the successful teams, although taking less shots, converted more chances to goals than their midfielders (10% compared to 4.6%). This could be because they are more skilful players in taking chances than midfielders or maybe the shots they took were from an easier position or angle. The inability of the unsuccessful teams to score could be due to the poor standard of their attackers, as they only converted 1 in 23.5 of their shots to goals compared to midfielders who scored 1 in 17.

From Table 2 it can be seen that short passes led to the most shots (255) and from those shots 12 were converted to goals (4.7%). Crosses led to 21 goals from 108 passes which produced a 19.4% conversion rate. This shows that the cross is a much more effective route to creating goals, as it is hard to defend if played with power and accuracy. The chip proved to be a very successful way of scoring with 4 goals being scored from 6 shots; this could be because the chip is an excellent way of putting an attacker through on goal in a central position. The reason that it was not used more frequently may be because it is hard to execute against elite defences.

The most frequently used type of shot was the drive, which contributed to 49.6% of all shots taken. However, it was only the third most successful shot for producing goals. The placed shot accounted for 15 goals from 52 shots which shows that opting for accuracy is more effective than going for power; this demonstrated a conversion rate of 28.8%. Additionally 14 goals were scored from headers, one more than the drive produced, but from only 82 shots. The reason that the drive had a poor conversion rate is because many shots from outside the area are driven in hope of the power beating the goalkeeper, although by maximising power some accuracy is lost.

The total conversion of shots for the tournament was 8.9% or 1 goal for every 11 shots.

Table 2. The total shots and goals according to each preceding assist pass.

Assist pass	Total Number of Shots	Total Number of Goals
Cross	108	21
Header down	22	2
Through ball	49	4
Chip over top	6	4
Short pass	255	12
Long pass	27	4
Back heel	2	0
Flick (head)	4	1
Flick (feet)	3	1
Throw-in	5	0
Set piece	74	1
Rebound	44	4
Chest	3	1
None	27	1

Table 3. The totals and percentages of the outcomes of shots.

Successful		Outcome	Unsuccessful	
Total shots	% of shots		Total shots	% of shots
29	9.41	Goal	12	8.57
150	48.70	Missed	70	50
86	27.92	Saved	35	25
8	2.60	Deflected	7	5
26	8.44	Blocked	14	10
7	2.27	Post	1	0.71
2	0.65	Crossbar	1	0.71

When analysing the outcomes of shots, it was expected that successful teams scored more goals than unsuccessful teams, and this was the case. Table 3 shows that successful teams scored 29 goals (9.41%) and unsuccessful teams scored 12 goals (8.5%). There were no significant differences ($P<0.05$) found for the outcome of shots between successful and unsuccessful teams. Both sets of teams had approximately 50% of shots off target and roughly 25% saved.

4. CONCLUSIONS

It was concluded that there were no significant differences ($P>0.05$) between the successful and unsuccessful teams' patterns of play leading to shots. However, successful teams adopted effective styles of play to a greater degree than unsuccessful teams. These styles of play are to gain the ball in the attacking quarter as often as possible as possessions gained here produce more goals. The shorter the duration and the less the number of passes in a possession, the more

It can be concluded that the less time the defence has to
session, the better is the chance of scoring.
from closer range and because of this were more accurate
because they were more able to pass the ball and break
et into better positions.
vere able to score from a wider variety of passes and shots,
ore skilful players and could adapt to different situations if
ams used limited types of passes and shots to score and so
were more predictable in their play.

REFERENCES

Hook, C. and Hughes, M., 2001, Patterns of play leading to shots in Euro 2000. In
Pass. Com. edited by Hughes, M. and Franks, I.M. (Cardiff: Centre for
Performance Analysis, UWIC).

Hughes, C., 1996, *Soccer Skills: Tactics and Teamwork.* (London: Diamond
Books).

Jinshan, X., Xiaoke, K., Yamanaka, K. and Matsumoto, M. 1993, Analysis of the
goals in the 14th World Cup. In *Science and Football II,* edited by Reilly, T.,
Clarys, J. and Stibbe, A. (London: E & FN Spon), pp. 203–205.

Partridge, D. and Franks, I.M., 1989a, A detailed analysis of crossing opportunities
in the 1986 World Cup Part I. *Soccer Journal*, May/June, pp. 47–50.

Partridge, D. and Franks, I.M., 1989b, A detailed analysis of crossing opportunities
on the 1986 World Cup Part II. *Soccer Journal*, June/July, pp. 45–48.

Reep, C. and Benjamin, B., 1968, Skill and chance in association football. *Journal
of the Royal Statistical Society,* Series A, **131**, 581–585.

33   Notational Analysis of Corner Kicks in English Premier League Soccer

J.B. Taylor, N. James and S.D. Mellalieu
Department of Sports Science, University of Wales Swansea,
Singleton Park, Swansea, SA2 8PP, Wales, UK

1. INTRODUCTION

Notational analysis is commonly used in many sports and is viewed as a vital process in allowing coaches to collect objective information that can be employed to provide feedback on performance (Franks, 1997). Without this type of analysis coaches are prone to being subjective in their judgements and unable to recall events reliably (Franks and Miller, 1986; Franks and McGarry, 1996). Hence, it is to the benefit of both the coach and the athlete that objective feedback on performance is provided via analysis systems. Recent advances in sports science and progress in technology, particularly audio/visual and computer, have led to the development of these systems (Vivian *et al.*, 2001), with some success in monitoring and improving soccer performance (Olsen and Larsen, 1997).

Empirical research in soccer has covered a diverse range of areas including tactical, technical and physiological aspects. In particular the way that goals are scored has been a focus of attention for over half a century (e.g. Reep and Benjamin, 1968). It has been suggested that over 40% of goals in soccer are scored from set-pieces (Hughes, 1999) and that goals from this source are important at all levels of the game (Bate, 1988). Jinshan *et al.* (1993), for example, found that set-pieces accounted for between 27% and 32% of goals in the 1986 and 1990 Soccer World Cups respectively, while Grant *et al.* (1999) reported a figure of 24.6% at the 1998 tournament. Among set pieces, free kicks and corner kicks have been shown to be the greatest source of goals, producing 46% and 13% of goals respectively at the 1994 Soccer World Cup (Sousa and Garganta, 2001) and 50% and 47.6% at the 1998 competition (Grant *et al.*, 1999).

Although various groups have examined set-pieces, there is limited research into any one component of this match area. In a study of the Norwegian national soccer team and their opponents, Olsen and Larsen (1997) reported a mean of 10.4 corner kicks per game and found that swinging corner kicks had the best chance of creating an attempt on goal (1:5 and 1:3 for inswing and outswing corner kicks respectively). Hill and Hughes' (2001) investigation of corner kicks during the 2000 European Championship indicated a mean of 10.9 corner kicks per game, with one in every five producing an attempt at goal. The authors concluded by suggesting that in order to increase the chance of scoring, corner kicks should be played with curl, above head height and with few actions, that is, an attempt on goal should be made as soon as possible.

Given the lack of research into such an influential aspect of soccer performance, the aims of the present investigation were to present an in-depth analysis of corners in English Premier League soccer and further explore the key indicators of successful corners. Specifically, it was intended to examine the frequency of corner kicks, the incidence of corner kicks with regard to match time, the type of corner kick, the critical area where the corner kick was played into and the team making the first contact.

2. METHODS

Twenty English Premier League matches from the 2001-02 season were randomly sampled and recorded from terrestrial and digital television. A hand-based system was utilised to record information and data were transferred to SPSS for analysis. Each corner kick was notated until four separate actions had taken place or a defining action occurred. A defining action was deemed as any action that produced an obvious end to the corner kick phase, such as a defender clearing the ball, a loss of attacking possession, or a goal. Each corner kick was analysed with regard to the time of incidence during the match, the side of the pitch it was played from, style of corner kick played (i.e. inswing, outswing, straight, short or chipped), the area of the action on the pitch, the player performing the action, and type of action (e.g. shot, clearance, pass). The number of actions, defender and attacker numbers and the relative success of the corner kick were also recorded. Each corner kick was therefore assessed with regard to between 15 and 27 factors depending on the number of actions. Successful corner kicks were defined as any corner kick resulting in an attempt on goal. Figure 1 displays the pitch divisions used to identify the locations of actions at corner kicks. A chi-squared test was used to examine the data with alpha levels set at $P=0.05$.

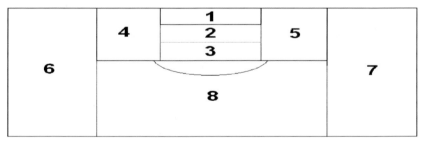

Figure 1. Pitch representation of areas used in analysis of corner kicks.
(Note: as if all corner kicks are from the left side as looking towards goal).

3. RESULTS

3.1. Preliminary analysis

The analysed matches resulted in 59 goals scored with 6 (10.2%) as a direct result of corner kicks. In total 217 corner kicks were examined, with 68 (31%) resulting in an attempt on goal (i.e. successful). Of these, 8% resulted in goals, 49% in shots off-target and 43% in shots on-target. Comparing the incidence of corners over six 15-min periods of the game no significant differences were observed for either all corners (Chi-squared = 10, df = 5, P>0.05) or successful corners (chi-squared = 7.951, df = 5, P>0.05). The analysis produced a total of five corner kick styles (Table 1) with the number of corner kicks swerved (in or out) found to be significantly greater than any of the other styles (Chi-squared = 75.696, df = 4, P<0.01). The outswing corner kick produced the most attempts at goal, with the majority off-target (60.7%). The inswing corner kick was found to produce the greatest number of goals scored (66%).

Table 1. Breakdown of corner kick styles with special reference to attempts on goal.

Style	Frequency	Unsuccessful Outcomes	Success Rate (%)	Goals	On-target Shots	Off-target Shots
Inswing	79	57	28	4	11	7
Outswing	66	38	42	1	10	17
Straight	36	28	22	0	3	5
Chipped	9	6	33	0	3	0
Short Corner	27	20	26	1	2	4

An indication of the area into which the ball was played was obtained by investigating the area of first contact by a player (Figure 2). The area along the front of the six-yard box (Area 2) was found to have the greatest frequency of first contacts (41%) and a high success rate (42%), and was deemed the critical area for further analysis.

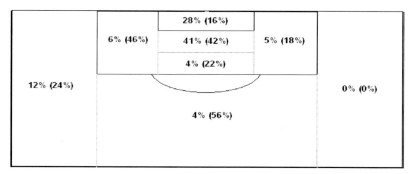

Figure 2. Percentage of corner kicks into each area (relative percentage of attempts on goal in brackets). (Note: as if all corner kicks are from the left side as looking towards goal).

3.2. The critical area

Similar to the preliminary analysis, swinging corners were found to be the most frequent style into the critical area (Table 2). The outswinging kick was the most successful in creating a goal scoring chance (55%) although 65% of these were off-target.

Table 2. Further analysis of corner kick styles and outcomes into the critical area.

Style	Frequency	Unsuccessful Outcomes	Success Rate	Goals	On-target Shots	Off-target Shots
Inswing	30	21	30%	1	5	3
Outswing	42	19	55%	1	7	15
Straight	13	10	23%	0	1	2
Chipped	3	2	33%	0	1	0

Players were classified as attackers or defenders and no significant difference was found in the number of first contacts in the critical area by each of these player types (Chi-squared = 2.909, df = 1, P>0.05). When only the successful corner kicks into the critical area were considered, attackers made significantly more first contacts (n=29) than defenders (n=8; Chi-squared = 11.919, df = 1, P <0.01; Table 3).

Table 3. Success of corner as a function of corner style and the player making the first contact.

	Attacker makes 1st contact		Defender makes 1st contact	
	Successful outcome	Unsuccessful outcome	Successful outcome	Unsuccessful outcome
Inswing	17	1	2	20
Outswing	7	5	6	14
Chipped	2	0	0	1
Straight	3	1	0	9

4. DISCUSSION

Corner kicks occurred frequently (mean = 10.85) in the English Premier League and provided many goal-scoring opportunities (1 in 3) although these opportunities were only converted 1 in 11 times. These findings were similar to Hill and Hughes (2001) and Olsen and Larsen (1997). Interestingly, the 1:11 ratio is the same as Partridge and Franks (1989a, 1989b) found for crosses, suggesting communality between the two aspects of play.

In line with previous studies, corner kicks played with swing were found to be the most frequent with the outswing style producing most goal-scoring chances, although the inswing corner kick resulted in the most goals. This may explain why this type of corner, especially one which is played to the near post, is commonly perceived as the biggest provider of goals (Hughes, 1999). In the current study the most critical area to play the ball into from corner kicks was along the front of the six-yard box (named as area 2). Corner kicks swinging into this area were again likely to provide the most attempts at goal, although the inswing style appeared to present the best chance of creating a shot on-target or a goal. Due to the high success rate of playing corner kicks towards the area in front of the penalty box (area 8), this would seem to provide a good alternative strategy. It is also apparent that regardless of the style of kick adopted, the player type making the first contact (i.e. attacker/defender) is critical in defining the corner kick outcome. Specifically, an attacker was found to make first contact with the ball 80% of the time at successful corners and 27% at unsuccessful corners.

The findings from the study present several practical implications for coaches and players. First, it appears that there are many chances created by corner kicks but relatively few goals scored, suggesting this is an area for practice and improvement. With regard to corner kick tactics, playing the ball into the critical area with swing, in particular inswing, or pulling it back to the front edge of the penalty area appear to present good opportunities to produce an attempt at goal. In addition, it is paramount that an attacking player makes the first contact in order to maximise the chance of creating a goal attempt. Finally, although the current study indicated that corners played with swing into the critical area were the most successful, it should be noted that corners should be varied in order to avoid predictability and enhance uncertainty in the defending side.

REFERENCES

Bate, R., 1988, Football chance: Tactics and strategy. In *Science and Football*, edited by Reilly, T., Lees, A., Davids, K. and Murphy, W. J. (London: E. & FN. Spon), pp. 293–301.

Franks, I.M., 1997, Use of feedback by coaches and players. In *Science and Football III*, edited by Reilly, T., Bangsbo, J. and Hughes, M.D. (London: E. & FN. Spon), pp. 267–278.

Franks, I.M. and McGarry, T., 1996, The science of match analysis. In *Science and Soccer*, edited by Reilly, T. (London: E. & FN. Spon), pp. 363–375.

Franks, I.M. and Miller, G., 1986, Eyewitness testimony in sport. *Journal of Sport Behaviour*, **9**, 39–45.

Grant, A.G., Williams, A.M. and Reilly, T., 1999, Analysis of goals scored in the 1998 World Cup. *Journal of Sports Sciences*, **17**, 826–827.

Hill, A. and Hughes, M.D., 2001, Corner kicks in the European Championships for Association Football, 2000. In *PASS.COM*, edited by Hughes, M.D. and Franks, I.M., (Cardiff, UWIC), pp. 284–294.

Hughes, C., 1999, *Football Tactics and Teamwork*, 8th Ed., (Harpenden: Queen Anne Press).

Jinshan, X., Xiaoke, C., Yamanaka, K. and Matsumoto, M., 1993, Analysis of goals in the 14th World Cup. In *Science and Football II*, edited by Reilly, T., Clarys, J. and Stibbe, A. (London: E. & FN. Spon), pp. 203–205.

Olsen, E. and Larsen, O., 1997, Use of match analysis by coaches. In *Science and Football III*, edited by Reilly, T., Bangsbo, J. and Hughes, M. (London: E. & FN. Spon), pp. 209–220.

Partridge, D. and Franks, I.M., 1989a, A detailed analysis of crossing opportunities in the 1968 World Cup Part I. *Soccer Journal*, May/June, pp. 47–50.

Partridge, D. and Franks, I.M., 1989b, A detailed analysis of crossing opportunities in the 1986 World Cup Part II. *Soccer Journal*, June/July, pp. 45–48.

Reep, C. and Benjamin, B., 1986, Skill and chance in association football. *Journal of the Royal Statistical Society, Series A*, **131**, 581–585.

Sousa, T. and Gargantua, J., 2001, The importance of set-plays in soccer. In *Proceedings of the IV World Congress of Notational Analysis of Sport*, edited by Hughes, M.D. and Tavares, F. (Portugal: University of Porto), pp. 53–57.

Vivian, R., Mullen, R. and Hughes, M.D., 2001, Performance profiles at League, European Cup and international levels of male Rugby Union players, with specific reference to flankers, no 8 and no 9. In *PASS.COM*, edited by Hughes, M.D. and Franks, I.M. (Cardiff: UWIC), pp. 284–294.

34 Analyses of Intensity of Physical Load during a Soccer Match

Vihren Bachev[1], Plamen Marcov[2], Petar Georgiev[3] and Mihail Iliev[2]
[1]Middle East Technical University, Ankara, Turkey
[2]Bulgarian National Soccer Team
[3]National Sports Academy, Sofia, Bulgaria

1. INTRODUCTION

The intensity of physical exercise refers to the qualitative component of performance in a given period of time (Bompa, 1994). When exercise has a similar motor structure and form of realisation (i.e. locomotion), it can be easy to analyse its intensity. Analysis of changes in velocity, power output or physiological responses such as heart rate (HR) can then be used.

In soccer, which is characterised by lots of technical skills, movements and activities, the partial type of measurement, including only one type of parameter, cannot give complete information. For that reason, specialists have tried to do complex analyses of players' activities during matches (Malomsoki, 1993; Ohashi et al., 1993; Capranica et al., 2001; Bachev et al., 2002).

Accepting this type of research, the purpose of the present study was to establish a model for evaluating the physical load on soccer players, utilising objective criteria from complex registration of mean parameters and activities during the match.

2. METHODS

Field research and apparatus for observation of game activities were used for complex registrations of parameters. The measurements were carried out in parallel with measurement of *blood* lactate concentration (Lactate Pro-LT-1710) every 10 min), HR changes ("Polar S 810"; "S 710") registered every 5 s and kinematic characteristics of player movements ("Sony" video camera and recorder, Digital video creator and "SIMI" motion analysis system). One example from field observations (striker, member of senior National Team, first half of control match, 26.03.2003) is presented in Table 1.

Table 1. Parallel changes of HR (beats. min⁻¹), blood lactate concentration (mmol.l⁻¹) and game activities (speed m.s⁻¹) for a striker, during a time interval 42–44 minutes within a game.

Time (s)			42 min					43 min				44 min				
			5	10	-	30	35	-	45	50	55	-	20	25	-	35	40	-
HR			184	180	-	190	188	-	182	188	180	-	182	188	-	175	177	-
La			10.3	10.3	-	10.3	10.3	-	10.3	10.3	10.3	-	10.3	10.3	-	10.3	10.3	-
Game Activities	A	A			-			-				-			-			-
		B	4	3.7	-		2	-	2		3	-			-	3	2.5	-
		C			-	7		-		5		-			-			-
	B	D			-			-				-	3		-			-
		E			-			-				-		4	-			-
		F			-			-		X		-			-			-
		G			-		X	-				-		X	-		X	-

Note: A= Walking; B=Middle speed running; C= Sprint running; D= Middle speed dribbling; E= Sprint dribbling; F= Shooting heating; G= Others- passing, crossing ball, ball loosing, ball winning.

The participants were 16 juniors (19.5 ± 1.7 years) and 14 other (24 ± 2.1 years) male soccer players, members of the Bulgarian National Team. They were divided into groups of defenders, midfield players and strikers. The research was conducted during training and friendly matches in the years 2002 and 2003.

Distance, duration, and velocity of running and dribbling, different types of shooting and some other ball activities were recorded. These observations were compared with changes in HR and blood lactate concentrations measured in parallel. After collection of significant amounts of data, statistical methods (ANOVA, ANCOVA, t-tests) were used for quantitative analyses and comparisons.

3. RESULTS AND DISCUSSION

According to the results of systemised data related to the HR changes during reference games, mean values of heart rate were 169 ± 15 beats. min^{-1} for the male adult players and 165 ± 19 for the junior players. Additionally, blood lactate concentrations were found to be very different and general systemisation was not informative. An example from the first half of the juniors' game (26.03.2003 – Sofia) is presented in Table 2.

Comparisons of the game activities of the same players showed some differences. Moreover, parallel changes of external and internal characteristics of physical load were not found at every occasion. Based on the results derived from the study, one of the main ideas was to establish a complex model and assessment scale of the intensity of exercise during a soccer match.

The first problem, which was solved, was time duration of assessment of changes in lactate concentration. The variability scores showed that it is possible to have exact information in a short period of time – one minute before and one minute after a particular event.

The proposal for the assessment of lactate concentration changes was: – 1 point, for 2 $mmol.l^{-1}$ concentrations. Scientific arguments for this proposal were found in publications of Nowacki and Preuhs (1993), who measured blood lactate concentration during a soccer match; they reported a mean value of 5.5 $mmol.l^{-1}$ and a maximum of 7.5 $mmol.l^{-1}$. Gerisch et al. (1988) registered mean values of 6.0 $mmol.l^{-1}$ and a maximum 12.4 $mmol.l^{-1}$ blood lactate concentration. Smith et al. (1991) recorded during a soccer match a mean blood lactate concentration of 5.23 $mmol.l^{-1}$ and a maximum of 11.63 $mmol.l^{-1}$. The highest value reported for a male sportsmen was measured using a maximal test on a cycle (Grancharov, 1997), being a blood lactate concentration of 24 $mmol.l^{-1}$ in basketball players. This result suggested that the theoretical maximum of points can be 12, and in a soccer match it is up to 7 points. Point assessment of intensity over 5 points could be deemed *maximal* according to blood lactate concentration.

Table 2. Individual and mean HR (beats.min^{-1}) and blood lactate (mmol.l^{-1}) concentration, during a reference match (Juniors National Team).

Parameter	Player	2'		43'		MAX	MEAN
		HR	La	HR	La	HR	HR
Defender (1)		124	1.1	168	8.8	196	148
Defender (2)		131	1.2	159	5.1	197	155
Defender (3)		128	3.7	182	5.3	189	157
Mean D.		128	1.7	170	6.4	194	153
Striker (1)		118	1.2	157	10.3	188	158
Striker (2)		136	2.2	174	7.9	190	156
Striker (3)		114	0.8	169	5.8	196	163
Mean S.		123	1.2	163	8.0	191	159
All Players		126	1.5	166	7.2	193	156

Decisions about point assessment of HR changes were based on different HR zones of exercise intensity: HR < 120 - 1 point; HR >120 <140 - 2; HR >140 <160 - 3; HR >160 <170 - 4; HR >170<180 - 5 points and + 1 point for every 10 HR beats min^{-1} over. The maximal HR values during a soccer match, according to Winkler (1993), Ogushi et al. (1993), Smith et al. (1993), were 200 beats.min^{-1}. From our measurements, maximal HR values of 230 beats.min^{-1} were observed (Bachev et al., 2001). According to the model presented the level of 200 beats.min^{-1} corresponded to 7 points. That means that an intensity over 5 points can be classed as maximal.

The assessment of game activities (GA) parallel to the physiological scale was indicated by speed (m.s^{-1}) of movements. A coefficient of 1.5 is allocated for activities with the ball. The arguments for this proposal are based on results of comparisons between multiple running and energy metabolism during dribbling using a laboratory model (Reilly, 2002).

Observations in a real soccer match showed a maximal speed of running without the ball of 7.8 m.s^{-1} (Erdmann, 1993) and 7–8 m.s^{-1} in a 30-m test run (3.95 s time) by professional German soccer players (Kollath and Quade, 1993). On the other hand, the average distance covered by soccer players in a match is between 7–13 km, and <15% of it is at maximal speed (Ohashi et al., 1993).

The model and assessment of physical load were established as a function of changes presented for these three parameters. The points were summed every 5-s interval and then divided by the numbers of intervals. The higher result means a higher intensity. Suggestions are systemized in Table 3.

Table 3. Model of quantitative point assessment of intensity of physical loads.

Parameters Points	Intensity	Blood lactate concentration $(mmol.l^{-1})$	Heart Rate $(beats.min^{-1})$	Game Activities	
				A- outball game activities speed $(m.s^{-1})$	B-ball game activities Speed $(m.s^{-1})$
1	Very Low	2	<120	1	0.7
2	Low	4	120–140	2	1.35
3	Middle	6	140–160	3	2
4	High	8	160–170	4	2.65
5	Very High	10	170–180	5	3.65
6	Maximal	12	180–190	6	4
7	Up to Maximal	12	190–200	7	4.65
>7	Limit	>14	>200	>7	>5

The summary showed a middle level of intensity of physical load. During the game analysed the intensity increased from the beginning to the last third and the more active player was a midfielder. After that assessment, the information presented was analysed together with visual game information and individual characteristics of the players. These observations and expert evaluations of the coaches and medical staff provided useful feedback to the players.

4. CONCLUSION

The two main observations to observe can be summarized as follows:-
- The maximal HR was 197 beats.min^{-1} and the mean was 165±19 beats.min^{-1} for junior soccer players during a match. The maximal blood lactate concentration was found to be 10.3 mmol.l^{-1} for the same group.
- First results of the data on HR, La and Game Activities and quantitative assessments of intensity, showed middle and high level loads on average during soccer games by junior players.

Measurements and analyses of physical load during a match are important factors in effective management of the training process in soccer. On that background, established model of point assessment of exercise intensity can be useful.

Acknowledgments

The assistance of the following is gratefully acknowledged:- Petar Miladinov – Head Coach of Bulgarian National Seniors Soccer Team, Dr. Petar Bonov – National Sports Academy, Sofia, Leyla Saraç – Middle East Technical University Physical Education and Sports Department, Turkey; Timur Atalay – Middle East Technical University Physical Education and Sports Department, Turkey.

REFERENCES

Bachev, V., Çiçek, Ş. and Bizati, Ö., 2001, Characteristics of variability of heart rate during the match by elite soccer players. Balkan Scientifis Conference "Nature and Optimisation of Training Loads" National Sports Academy- Sofia, Bulgaria 26.04. 2001.

Bachev, V., Bizati, Ö., Cicek, Ş. and Iliev, M., 2002, System of registration of physical load during a soccer match - National Sports Academy, Anniversary Scientific Conference, Traditions, Current Trends and Perspectives, Sofia, Bulgaria, 30.05.2002.

Bompa, T., 1994, Theory and Methodology of Training (Third Edition). (U. S. A: Kendall/Hunt Publishing Company), p.77.

Capranica, L., Tessitore, A., Guidetti, L. and Figura, F., 2001, Heart rate and match analysis in pre - pubescent soccer players, Journal of Sports Sciences, **19**, 379–384.

Erdmann, V., 1991, Quantification of games - preliminary kinematic investigations in soccer. In Science and Football 11, edited by Reilly, T., Clarys, J. and Stibbe, A. (London: E & FN Spon), pp. 174–179.

Grancharov, N., 1997, Anaerobic Threshold - Nature and Applied Value in Sport. (Sofia: NSA Press).

Kollath, E. and Quade, K., 1993, Measurement of sprinting speed of professional and amateur soccer players. In Science and Football 11, edited by Reilly, T., Clarys, J. and Stibbe, A. (London: E and F. N. Spon), pp. 31–36.

Malomsoki, E., 1993, Physiological characterization of physical fitness of football players in field conditions. In Science and Football 11, edited by Reilly, T., Clarys, J. and Stibbe, A. (London: E & FN Spon), pp. 81–85.

Nowacki, P. and Preuhs, M., 1993, The influence of a special endurance training of the aerobic and anaerobic capacity of soccer players tested by the soccer treadmill methods. In Science and Football 11, edited by Reilly, T., Clarys, J. and Stibbe, A. (London: E & FN Spon), pp. 86–91.

Ogushi, T., Ohashi, J., Nagahama, H., Isokawa, M. and Suzuki, S.,1993, Work intensity during soccer match - play (a case study). In Science and Football 11, edited by Reilly, T., Clarys, J. and Stibbe, A. (London: E & F. N Spon), pp.121–123.

Ohashi, J., Isokawa, M., Nagahama, H. and Ogushi, T., 1993, The ratio of physiological intensity of movements during soccer match – play. In Science and Football 11, edited by Reilly, T., Clarys, J. and Stibbe, A. (London: E & FN Spon), pp. 124–128.

Reilly, T., 2002, Physiological demands in soccer play. 7. Uluslararası Spor Bilimleri Kongresi, 27–29 Ekim 2002, Kemer Antalya.

Smith, M., Clarke, G., Hale, T. and McMorris, T., 1993. Blood lactate levels in college soccer player during match – play. In Science and Football 11, edited by Reilly, T., Clarys, J. and Stibbe, A. (London: E & FN Spon), pp.129–134.

Winkler, W., 1993, Computer controlled assessment and video -technology for the diagnosis of a player's performance in soccer training. In Science and Football 11, edited by Reilly, T., Clarys, J. and Stibbe, A. (London: E & FN Spon), pp.73–80.

35   Evolving Penalty Kick Strategies: World Cup and Club Matches 2000–2002

Edgard Morya[1], Hamilton Bigatão[1], Adrian Lees[2]
and Ronald Ranvaud[1]
[1]Institute of Biomedical Sciences, Department of Physiology and
Biophysics, University of São Paulo, Av. Lineu Prestes 1524,
05508-900, São Paulo, Brazil
[2]Research Institute for Sport and Exercise Sciences, Liverpool John
Moores University, Webster Street, Liverpool, L3 2ET, UK

1. INTRODUCTION

It is important to understand the factors that limit performance both in kicking and in defending penalties so as to determine the best strategies to prepare for this often critical moment of the game. Relatively little research has addressed penalty kicks, however, and most of it has dealt with goalkeepers' anticipatory strategies (Kuhn, 1988; Morris and Burwitz, 1989; McMorris et al., 1993; Williams and Burwitz, 1993; McMorris and Colenso, 1996; McMorris and Hauxwell, 1997; Franks et al., 1999; Savelsbergh et al., 2002). Kuhn's (1988) study of European league club matches found that 20% (13/66) of penalties were saved and also identified two types of goalkeeper strategy. In the first ("late strategy"), which Kuhn called GA, goalkeepers initiated their dive at the moment the kicker made contact with the ball or immediately afterwards (23% or 15/66), whereas in the second (GB, or "early strategy") goalkeepers dived *before* kicker-ball contact (77% or 51/66). Kuhn recommended the GA strategy, since it led to a higher probability of saving the penalty (GA: 60% saves vs. GB: 8%). Franks et al. (1999) analysed 138 penalty kicks in World Cups between 1982 and 1994, reported that 14.5% of the shots were saved. Without separating early and late diving goalkeepers, they concluded that expert goalkeepers overall were not successful in predicting ball direction because in their data goalkeepers went the same direction as the ball only 41% of the time. It is important to remember, however, that both goalkeepers and kickers have (and use) a third option down the middle, different from sideways, right or left. Thus, if goalkeepers were only capable of wild guesses one would predict less than 50% chance of a "correct anticipation" and, depending on the relative probabilities of the three options, perhaps even less than 40%.

   Ball velocity depends on the conservation of linear momentum in football collision (Luhtanen, 1994), but is also influenced by the elastic efficiency of ball materials. World Cups have stimulated improvements in ball technology, aiming at increased speed and accuracy, while maintaining basic specifications for circumference (68–70 cm), weight (410–450 g) and pressure (600–1100 g.cm^2 at sea level) (FIFA, 2002). Approximate values of ball velocity in penalty kicks were given by Franks et al. (1999) (around 22 m.s^{-1}), and Kuhn (1988) (between 14 and 28 m.s^{-1}). In the World Cup 2002, ball velocities were much higher as described below, perhaps because of both new ball design and deliberate use of force by kickers. Suzuki *et al.* (1987) claimed that performance of goalkeepers depends on the ability to throw the body faster and further so as to move the centre of gravity quickly toward the ball. Considering the accuracy with which professional soccer players can kick the ball (Lees and Nolan, 2002), the performance of goalkeepers in international competitions such as club matches and the World Cup have been quite remarkable. Goalkeepers appear to have been limited largely by physical constraints, whereas kickers appear to have been performing below their best capabilities.

From an analysis of penalties kicked in the World Cup 2002 (**WC**) and in European and South American Club Matches (**CM**) between 2000 and 2002, we tried to determine how the penalty kick has evolved in recent years by comparison to previously reported data. Further, we tried to identify common factors which might be key to performance, from both the kicker's and the goalkeeper's points of view.

2. MATERIALS AND METHODS

Starting from videotapes, a total of 75 penalty kicks were digitised using a computer analysis system composed of VisionTek Xtasy video card with a 64MB AGP GeForce2 MX400 based graphics accelerator, 512 RAM and a 650 MHz processor. The software (Video Wave 4SE) permitted frame by frame (30 Hz) analysis of the digital videos. The following parameters were measured:- ball speed; whether the goalkeeper dived and, if so, when, relative to the instant of kicker-ball contact; whether the goalkeeper anticipated correctly the ball's trajectory; whether it was a save, a miss (woodwork or out) or a score; and finally where the ball hit the plane of the goalmouth. The goalmouth was divided into 24 rectangles 0.91 m wide by 0.81 m high (Figure 1), as adopted by Graham-Smith *et al.* (1999), to identify where the ball hit the goalmouth on each shot. The convention is to define ball direction and goalkeeper movement (right or left) always with respect to the kicker's perspective (Figure 1). Data were submitted to a Student's t-test ($\alpha=0.05$) or chi-square analysis of contingency tables ($\alpha=0.05$).

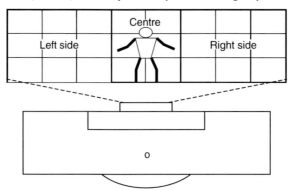

Figure 1. Kicker's view of the goalmouth, divided into 24 rectangles, and the convention to define the laterality of ball direction and goalkeeper movement.

3. RESULTS AND DISCUSSION

We analysed all 37 penalties kicked in World Cup 2002 and a random sample of 38 penalties from Club Matches 2000–2002 and compared to prior reports. The most striking difference was ball speed, with an average of 32 ($\pm$ 6) m.s^{-1} in the WC2002 (flight time to goalmouth only 344 ms!), much higher than the 26 ($\pm$ 3) m.s^{-1} from the CM2000–2002, and also higher than reported in previous studies (21 m.s^{-1} by Kuhn, 1988). The information available about "Fevernova", the official ball of World Cup 2002, was that it is faster and improves accuracy (Roach, 2002). Perhaps higher ball speeds in the WC data here reported might, at least in part, be due to the technology of the new ball. On the other hand, higher ball speed in the 2002 World Cup, not only relative to Kuhn's (1988) data, but also relative to CM2000–2002 (t=8.57; df=71; P<0.001), could also be a result of kickers deliberately hitting the ball very hard. One might then expect the high speed to be accompanied by relatively low accuracy, as pointed out by Lees and Nolan (2002).

A goal was scored in 76% (57/75) of the attempts we analysed, with slightly higher kicker success in club matches (82% or 31/38) than in the World Cup (70% or 26/37), not a statistically significant difference (x^2=1.314; df=1; P=0.252).

In part, the higher success of CM2000–2002 kickers relative to WC2002 kickers could have been due to better ball placement: CM kickers placed 39% (15/38) of their shots within 0.91 m (one yard) of the post, as opposed to only 19% (7/37) for WC kickers (x^2 = 3.82; df = 1; P=0.050). Furthermore, in our sample CM kickers did not miss (woodwork or out), as opposed to 3 misses for WC kickers (Figure 2). The higher ball speeds of penalties in the World Cup compared to club match penalties are indeed consistent with deliberate use of force by the kickers, at the cost of accuracy (Lees and Nolan, 2002).

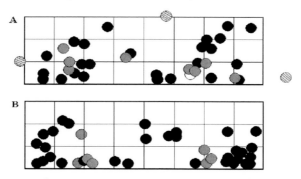

Figure 2. ● = scored, ◐ = saved; ◎ = out/lost; ○ = goalkeeper touched the ball but was not able to save. A – Represents the shots in the goalmouth of World Cup 2002. B – Represents the shots in the goalmouth of Club Matches 2000–2002.

In both WC and CM, goalkeepers dived on contact or later (Kuhn's GA strategy) about 40% of the time (WC: 15/37 and CM: 14/38), considerably more often than Kuhn's (1988) 23% (15/66) as shown in Figure 3 (x^2=3.644; df=1; P=0.056).

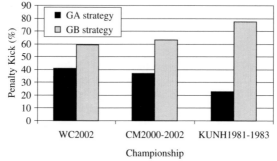

Figure 3. Diving strategy used by goalkeepers. GA strategy – goalkeepers dive after or at kicker-ball contact. GB strategy – goalkeepers dive before kicker-ball contact. A noticeable increase in adopting the GA strategy is evident in the World Cup 2002, Club Matches 2000-2002 and relative to Club Matches reported by Kuhn (1988).

Overall, we confirm Kuhn's report that late-diving GA goalkeepers were more likely to save penalties than early diving GB goalkeepers (GA: 36% (10/29) saves vs. GB: 11% (5/46); x^2=6.2; df=1; P=0.013). The difference, however, (Figure 4) is less than that reported by Kuhn. This is consistent with higher ball speeds, which leave less time for the goalkeepers to reach the ball especially when they dive late.

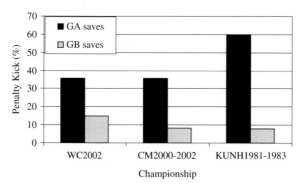

Figure 4. Saving success for GA and GB strategies.

Looking more closely at how good goalkeepers were in anticipating ball direction, we found that when adopting the GB strategy goalkeepers went in the same direction as the ball (right, left or middle) on about 30% (13/46) of occasions (probably about chance level) with no differences between WC (27% or 6/22) and CM (29% or 7/24, x^2 = 0.02; df = 1; P = 0.887). On the other hand when adopting the GA strategy goalkeepers performed much better, going the correct way on 69% (20/29) of occasions, certainly higher than chance level (Figure 5). Thus, in spite of the difficulty in getting to faster balls, goalkeepers still saved significantly more shots when diving relatively late because of the higher probability of going in the correct direction.

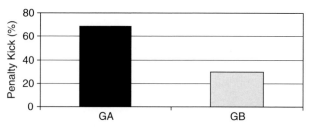

Diving to ball direction

Figure 5. GA strategy – goalkeepers dive after or at kicker-ball contact. GB strategy – goalkeepers dive before kicker-ball contact. GA strategy was more effective in enabling goalkeepers to dive to the same direction as the ball.

In WC2002 and CM2000-2002 a majority of penalty kicks were taken with the right foot (77% – 58/75 against 23% – 17/75 of left footed kicks). In contrast to McMorris and Colenso (1996), who indicated that goalkeeper anticipation to right footed kicks was significantly more accurate, in our data goalkeepers anticipated ball direction in 52% (30/58) of right footed shots, no different from the 47% (8/17) of left footed shots ($x^2 = 0.114$; df = 1; P = 0.735).

It would appear important for goalkeepers to take advantage of all resources at their disposal, to improve their anticipatory abilities, such as through the observation of videos of players taking penalties (McMorris *et al.*, 1993; McMorris and Colenso, 1996; McMorris and Hauxwell, 1997; Savelsbergh et al., 2002).

4. CONCLUSIONS

In the last two years the rate of success in scoring penalties in top level professional football has not changed appreciably from previously reported values, around 70% (give or take 10%). We confirm Kuhn's (1988) finding that strategies that include diving relatively late give goalkeepers a better chance of making a save. This is because they are more likely to dive in the correct direction (or correctly stay put). According to our data, however, and probably because of higher ball speeds, the advantage of such late diving strategies was less than it was in the Club Matches of the 1980s analyzed by Kuhn. A somewhat better scoring average in Club Matches 2000–2002 than in the World Cup 2002 suggests WC goalkeepers were better prepared for penalties than WC kickers. Compared with earlier reports, the higher incidence of late diving, which follows Kuhn's (1988) recommendation, corroborates the idea of improved technique on the part of goalkeepers. The superior placement of the ball, near the posts and not outside, by CM kickers would suggest WC kickers tended towards blasting the ball, thus sacrificing accuracy. This does not appear to be an effective strategy. Further research is needed to help kickers develop effective strategies and take best advantage of improved technology, and to help goalkeepers to glean as early as possible which way the ball will go.

REFERENCES

FIFA, 2002, Fédération Internationale de Football Association. *Laws of the Game*, pp. 1-17.

Franks, I. M., McGarry, T. and Hanvey, T., 1999, From notation to training: analysis of the penalty kick. *Insight: the FA Coaches Association Journal*, **2**, 24–26.

Graham-Smith, P., Lees, A. and Richardson, D., 1999, Analysis of technique of goalkeepers during the penalty kick. *Journal of Sports Sciences*, **19**, 916.

Kuhn, W., 1988, Penalty-kick strategies for shooters and goalkeepers. In *Science and Football*, edited by Reilly, T., Lees, A., Davids, K. and Murphy, W.J. (London: E & FN Spon), pp. 489–492.

Less, A. and Nolan, L., 2002, Three dimensional kinematic analysis of instep kick under speed and accuracy conditions. In *Science and Football IV*, edited by Spinks, W., Reilly, T. and Murphy, A. (London: E & FN Spon), pp. 16–21.

Luhtanen, P., 1994, Biomechanical aspects. In *Handbook of Sports Medicine and Science: Soccer*, edited by Ekblom, B. (London: Blackwell Scientific Publication), pp.59–77.

McMorris, T and Colenso, S., 1996, Anticipation of professional soccer goalkeepers when facing right and left-footed penalty kicks. *Perceptual and Motor Skills*, **82**, 931–934.

McMorris, T. and Hauxwell, B., 1997, Improving anticipation of soccer goalkeeper using video observation. In *Science and Football* III, edited by Reilly, T., Lees, A., Davids, K. and Murphy, W. J. (London: E & FN Spon), pp. 290–294.

McMorris, T., Copeman, D., Corcoran, D., Saunders, G. and Potter, S., 1993, Anticipation of soccer goalkeepers facing penalty kicks. In *Science and Football II*, edited by Reilly, T., Clarys, J. and Stibbe, A. (London: E & FN Spon), pp. 250–253.

Morris, A. and Burwitz, L., 1989, Anticipation and movements strategies in elite soccer goalkeepers an penalty kicks. Paper presented at the *Britsh Association of Sports Science Annual Conference*, Exeter, September.

Roach, S., 2002, Players bawl over ball. BBC. http://news.bbc.co.uk/sport3/worldcup2002/hi/other_news/newsid_2001000/2001924.stm.

Savelsbergh, G. J. P., Williams, A. M., Der Kamp, J. V. and Ward, P., 2002, Visual search, aticipation and expertise in soccer goalkeepers. *Journal of Sports Sciences*, **20**, 279–287.

Suzuki, S., Togari, H., Isokawa, M., Ohashi, J. and Ohgushi, T., 1988, Analysis of the goalkeeper's diving motion. In *Science and Football I*, edited by Reilly, T., Lees, A., Davids, K. and Murphy, W.J. (London: E & FN Spon), pp. 468–475.

Williams, A. M. and Burwitz., 1993, Advance cue utilization in soccer. In *Science and Football II*, edited by Reilly, T., Clarys, J. and Stibbe, A. (London: E & FN Spon), pp. 239–243.

36   Defence Performance Analysis of Rugby Union: The Turnover-play Structure

Koh Sasaki, Jun Murakami, Hironobu Simozozno, Takuo Furukawa, Masahiko Miyao, Taketoshi Saito, Takumi Yamamoto, Mituyuki Nakayama, Seiji Hirao, Nobuaki Hanaoka, Takasi Katuta and Ichiro Kono
Research Centre of Health, Physical Fitness and Sports, Nagoya University, Nagoya, Japan

1. INTRODUCTION

In the first weekend of the Six-Nations Championship in 2001, there were 19 tries scored, 17 of which came directly from "turnover ball". Does this mean that on 17 occasions the wrong decision was made or did the errors occur in execution? Both of these outcomes are possible. However, had several players used "brain rather than brawn" the total number of turnovers might well have been significantly decreased (Askew, 2001).

The tactics of Rugby Union have strong relations to the changes that correspond to the World Cup competition. After the 1st competition in 1987, defensive skills and strategies for winning were developed worldwide. In the mid-1990s, the 2nd and 3rd World Cup competition years, the changes in the rules encouraged and enforced the development of attacking strategies.

Then, the game of rugby was characterised by a more dynamic competition after 1999, the 4th World Cup including interactive situations and their continuation. Due to rule changes the competitive conditions can be altered quickly and the offence and defence are reversed momentarily. In other words, Rugby Union in the 21st century is being shaped in the perspective of a non-stop game. So, the systematic development of tactics is not only applied to the offence but also the defence is directly connected with getting a score (Katsuta, 2003).

As a performance analysis of defence in Rugby Union, the turnover play structure is considered in this study. The operational definition of turnover play is the act of getting the ball by tackle, loose-ball possession or pass-interception from the opposite team's attack (Sasaki et al., 2002) (Figure 1). The turnover play is essential to a team for total game management. Also, a team that has a disadvantage because of inferior physical strength - like Japan compared to New Zealand or England - must create a systematic defence.

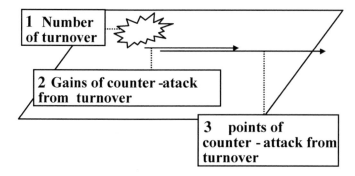

Figure 1. The factors of defense performance analysis in this study.

2. METHODS

Turnover plays in ten games between Under-21 Rugby World-Cup semi-final teams and "the other teams" in 2002 were analysed. The total number of turnovers occurring was over 200 which means there were approximately 20 turnovers in one game.

Items analysed included spot/time, start of play situations in each area of pitch, what kind of play (tackle, loose ball possession or pass-interception) occurred. The unique factors analysed in this study were the kind of play that was selected (punt or pass) in the counter-attack (attacking-after-turnover), the gain distance of the counter-attack from turnover and the points of the counter-attack from turnover (Try points, Penalty Goal points) that contributed to the game result or not (Duthie, Pyne and Hooper, 2003).

Multiple regression analysis was used for the examination of the turnover effects (the independent variables: turnover plays variation and the number, the gains and the points; the dependent variable: team point's balances).

Variations in turnover plays were considered by comparison between the top teams (Semi-finalists) and the lower teams ("The others"). The positional factors (Forwards, FW; Backs, BK and more sub-divided positions) are added in discussion because Rugby Union players' positions are each determined by differences in body size and play patterns.

3. RESULTS AND DISCUSSION

The average values of turnover-times, turnover-gains and turnover-points for the top teams and the other teams are shown in Table 1. The top teams displayed the more effective values of performance on the turnover than the other teams. The number of turnover-times was high. The acquisition gain was also long. The top teams' one turnover produces almost one point on a calculation value.

Table 1. The average value of turnover-times, turnover-gain and turnover-points on the upper teams and the others.

	Turnover-times	Turnover-Gains	Turnover-points
Upper teams	16.1	25.4	0.9
Others	10.7	17.1	0.5
	(times/game)	(metres/turnover)	(points/turnover)

The regression equation between 'the team-point balance' and 'the contribution factors of the defensive performances are shown in Table 2.

Table 2. Regression equation between 'Team points balance' and the defence (counter-attack) performance.

Team Points Balance =	2.07 * TO +	0.05 * CAG +	3.90 * CAP
S →¨	(1.82)	(0.06)	(0.91)
t →¨	(1.13)	(0.82)	(4.79)*
R^2 =0.85	s =21.87	F = 18.67*	*p<0.01

TO; numbers of turnover, CAG; counter-attack gain (m),
CAP; counter-attack point.

High regression values were obtained in this analysis (R square=0.85, s = 21.87, F = 18.67, P < 0.01). The findings presented in Table 2 indicate that the three independent variables of performance in defence (counter-attack) explain the contributing factors for the positive points balance. Furthermore, a statistically significant correlation was found between the independent variable 'Counter-attack points (CAP)' and the index 'Team points balance'. These result suggested that the performance in defence, not only the 'number of turnover (TO)' and 'the counter-attack gain (CAG) but also 'counter-attack points (CAP)' which means getting 'TRY (5 points)' or 'Penalty Goal (3 points)' after the turnover would be more important to the team points balance, in effect securing 'a Win'. More practically, when the turnover has occurred, the counter-attack should be executed with a more effective strategy for securing points.

Selected turnover plays had some consequences for the game results. Positional factors also had some influences on the games (Figure 2). It becomes a negative situation for the 'HB' (Half-Back) positions in the poorer teams to participate in defensive performance. If the half-backs, who usually have the important function of the team's decision-making plays, must attend to defence, then they cannot play in the next counter-attack strategy. In other words, by participating in defence, the team loses the opportunity for an effective game-making response.

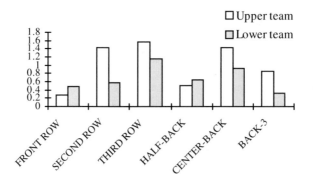

Figure 2. Comparison of the players' turnover
average per one game between the top teams and
the lower teams.

Many important games in the past have been won on the basis of sound defensive patterns (Katsuta, 2003). This study suggests that teams should create systematic turnover play to get points from the counter-attack, and not occupy the decision making players solely with the defence.

REFERENCES

Askew, T., 2001, Defence performance. *England Rugby Football Union Technical Journal*, Winter.

Duthie, G., Pyne, D. and Hooper, D., 2003, The reliability of video based time motion analysis. *Journal of Human Movement Studies*, **44**, 259–272.

Katsuta, T., 2003, The rule changes of Rugby Union. Conference of science committee in Japan Rugby Union.

Sasaki, K., Murakami, J., Shimozono, H., Furukawa, T., Katuta, T. and Kono, I., 2002, Contributing factors to successive attacks in Rugby football games. In *Science and Football IV*, edited by Spinks, W., Reilly, T. and Murphy, A. (London: Routledge), pp.167–170.

37 Patterns of Play of Successful and Unsuccessful Teams in Men's 7-a-side Rugby Union

Mike Hughes and Rhys Jones
Centre for Performance Analysis, UWIC, Cardiff CF23 6XD

1. INTRODUCTION

During the past 20 years, seven-a-side rugby has become both an established and very important aspect of the international rugby scene. It has been boosted by the popularity of the Rugby Sevens World Cup, every four years, and the new annual 10-tournament IRB World Sevens Series. The latest and most ambitious addition to the international rugby scene, the IRB World Sevens Series sets in place another important element in the IRB's drive to establish rugby as a truly global sport. New Zealand was crowned the inaugural IRB World Sevens Series champion for 1999/2000 after winning tournaments in Dubai, Punta del Este, Suva, Hong Kong and Paris. The 2000/2001 IRB World Sevens Series was also won by New Zealand, after being victorious in Durban, Dubai, Hong Kong, Tokyo, London and Cardiff.

Both northern hemisphere and southern hemisphere teams compete in these tournaments. However the southern hemisphere teams, such as New Zealand, Australia and Fiji, have dominated the competitions recently.

At present, very little research in terms of notational analysis has been carried out in seven-a-side rugby, unlike the fifteen-a-side game. Most of the notational analysis studies in rugby union are statistical compilations (Potter, 1996) or time-and-motion analyses (Docherty et al., 1988), but also there have been studies examining law changes (Hughes and Clarke, 1994) and refereeing (Thomas, 1995). Hughes and Williams (1988) made a comparison between French, Scottish and Irish compared to the English and Welsh patterns of play. They found no significant differences between the patterns of play for successful and unsuccessful teams.

Notational analysis has rarely been used to study patterns of play in seven-a-side rugby. Hence the aim of the study was to determine if there were any significant differences in patterns of play between successful and unsuccessful seven-a-side rugby teams.

2. METHODS

A specifically designed hand notation system was used to gather data from video recordings of the 2001 IRB World Sevens Series. An intra-operator reliability test was conducted on the match. The error calculated was 3.9%, which was considered an acceptable level of reliability. Normative profiles (Hughes et al., (2001) showed that a sufficient number of games were analysed to provide averages for the main actions, as all the profiles apart from tackling by successful teams stabilize. In all of the other profiles, the means of 6th, 7th and 8th matches fell within a 5% limits of error variation. %Error = (Σ(mod [V1 – V2]) /ΣV1) x 100; %Error = 9/232 x 100; %Error = 3.9**%**

Sixteen matches were analysed, with eight of the games involving successful teams and eight of the games involving unsuccessful teams. The successful teams included New Zealand, Australia and Samoa, having a winning profile of 70% or more. The unsuccessful teams included Wales, England and Canada; these teams have a winning profile below 70% (N=16, 8 in each group). A Wilcoxon signed-rank test was used to identify significant differences between the two groups.

3. RESULTS AND DISCUSSION

Table 1. Reliability test results.

Performance Indicator	Test 1	Test 2	Difference	Module
Ball in play %	49	49	0	0
Territory %	44	43	−1	1
Possession %	33	34	+1	1
Restart (own)	0/4	0/4	0	0
Restart (opp)	½	1/2	0	0
Lineout (own)	½	1/2	0	0
Lineout (opp)	0/0	0/0	0	0
Scrum (own)	2/2	2/2	0	0
Scrum (opp)	0/2	0/2	0	0
Ruck/maul (own)	5/6	5/6	0	0
Ruck/maul (opp)	4/9	4/9	0	0
Goal kicking	1/3	1/3	0	0
Passes	26	25	−1	1
Loop passes	2	2	0	0
Miss passes	0	0	0	0
Dummy passes	2	1	−1	1
Switch passes	0	0	0	0
Offloads	4	4	0	0
Line kicks	0	0	0	0
Wipers kicks	0	0	0	0
Drop kicks	0	0	0	0
Chip kicks	2	2	0	0
Grubber kicks	1	1	0	0
Penalty taps	6	6	0	0
Clean breaks	3	3	0	0
Sidesteps	1	2	+1	1
Swerves	2	3	+1	1
Knock ons	3	3	0	0
Forward passes	0	0	0	0
Incomplete passes	3	2	−1	1
Penalties conceded	3	3	0	0
Tackles made	15	15	0	0
Missed tackles	8	7	−1	1
Attacking efficiency	11 passes per. try	10 passes per. try	−1	1
Total	**232**	**229**	**−3**	**9**

Table 2. Match averages of successful and unsuccessful teams.

Successful teams	Performance Indicators	Unsuccessful teams
41%	Ball in play %	40%
62%	Territory %*	51%
51%	Possession %*	43%
19%	Own restarts won	23%
77%	Opp. restarts won	82%
50%	Own lineouts won	94%
25%	Opp. lineouts won	33%
81%	Own scrums won	79%
7%	Opp. scrums won	10%
91%	Own rucks/mauls won	84%
22%	Opp. rucks/mauls won	24%
6	No. of rucks/mauls formed/game. *	9
62%	Goal kicking %	57%
29	No. of passes/game	33
17	No. of normal passes/game*	24
1	No. of loop passes/game*	1
2	No. of miss passes/game*	1
2	No. of dummy passes/game*	1
1	No. of switch passes/game	2
6	No. of offloads/game	4
2	No. of kicks/game*	3
21%	Line kick %	21%
5%	Wipers kick %	0%
5%	Drop kick %	9%
21%	Chip kick %	35%
48%	Grubber kick %	35%
3	Penalty taps per. Game	3
18	Evasive runs/game*	11
7	Clean breaks/game*	4
7	Sidesteps/game*	5
4	Swerves/game*	2
8	Errors/game*	6
4	Handling errors/game	4
4	Penalties conceded/game*	2
27%	Knock on %	30%
2%	Forward pass %	2%
21%	Incomplete pass %	28%
50%	Penalties conceded %	40%
16	Tackles/game*	19
2	Missed tackles/game*	4
86%	Tackling success %	83%
7 passes per try	Attacking efficiency*	11 passes per try

* Significantly different at $P < 0.05$.

The game between England and France, during the Cardiff Sevens 2001, was used for the reliability test. An intra-operator reliability test was conducted on the match; Table 1 displays the results. The error % equation (Hughes et al., 2001) was used to enable the reliability of the hand notation system to be calculated. The error % produced was 3.9%, which was considered an acceptable level of reliability, as it is below the our accepted limits of error (5%).

Comparing the two sets of data in Table 1, there were 9 differences between test 1 and test 2. There were no differences between test 1 and test 2 in the following performance indicators:- restarts, set pieces, breakdowns, goal kicking, tackles and kicks. These actions were found easier to observe. The differences between test 1 and test 2 occurred when collecting open play actions, such as passing and evasive moves. A considerable proportion of seven-a-side games is spent in open play, with most of the actions and movements performed very fast; the operator might have missed some actions due to the pace of the game.

The Wilcoxon signed-rank test results show both sign of the differences and the magnitude of the differences between the groups. The sign of the differences shows which group obtained the higher values.

Most of the significant differences between the two groups were open play actions, and also there was a high average ball-in-play % found during the seven-a-side games. These results suggest that the reason why successful teams like New Zealand and Australia dominate the game, is due to the actions performed in open play. There were 15 significant differences in open play and two significant differences of general success percentages between successful and unsuccessful teams. Bass (1981) identified that there are two playing styles in Rugby sevens; the results suggest that successful teams tended to play a 'cat and mouse' style and that unsuccessful teams tended to play a 'cut and thrust' style. Bass (1981) stated that the 'cat and mouse' style is "a waiting game, with the side in possession probing, changing pace, bluffing, with a feint, a dummy or sleight of hand for the chance of that vital overlap", and the 'cut and thrust' style is a "fast, aggressive and direct" style.

The suggestion that successful teams play a 'cat and mouse' style and unsuccessful teams play a 'cut and thrust' style, is because the successful teams when in possession performed significantly more miss passes, dummy passes, total evasive moves, clean breaks, sidesteps and swerves per game and performed significantly fewer rucks/mauls, kicks, normal passes, loop passes and passes per try per game than unsuccessful teams. Also, the successful teams obtained a significantly higher territory % and possession % than unsuccessful teams. These results indicated that successful teams had better control of the games, with the patterns of play being more fluent as they would rather keep the ball alive than go into contact and had more width, patience, deception and evasion in attack, whilst being clinical try scorers. So, it seems that playing with a 'cat and mouse' style may contribute to success in seven-a-side rugby.

However, the successful teams conceded significantly more penalties per game, which suggests that these teams have poor discipline, but may also be due to penalties against the unsuccessful teams, although given, not being taken because of the successful team utilising the advantage rule. This finding is not too worrying in

Rugby sevens though, as no points are conceded via penalty kicks in "sevens", as tap penalties are normally used to keep the ball alive.

It is impossible to have possession for the whole game, so defence is just as important as attack. A good defence is a crucial factor for success in seven-a-side rugby as there is so much time and space for attackers. In defence, successful teams performed significantly better in defence and had significantly fewer miss tackles than unsuccessful teams. Together with this, as the successful teams had a better percentage of possession, so they made significantly fewer tackles per game.

The similarities between the two groups included all of the set piece, breakdown, tackling and goal kicking success percentages. There were also similarities in number of passes, switch passes, offloads in the tackle, line kicks, drop kicks, chip kicks, grubber kicks, penalty taps, total handling errors, forward passes, knock-ons and incomplete passes per game. It seems that there are significant differences in patterns of play, in attack and defence between successful and unsuccessful teams, which could be the reasons why successful teams dominate the game. However, there are other factors to be considered, such as size, fitness levels, skill and technique which can all be reasons for success in games; so these differences in patterns of play can not be the only reasons why some teams are more successful than others.

4. CONCLUSIONS

The main conclusions drawn from this study are that successful teams play a 'cat and mouse' style as they perform in significantly fewer rucks/mauls and kicks and perform significantly more dummy passes, sidesteps, swerves, clean breaks, whereas unsuccessful teams play a more direct style. It was also concluded that the successful teams obtained significantly higher territory % and possession % during the games. The successful teams performed significantly more "miss passes" and significantly fewer normal passes, loop passes and passes per try than the unsuccessful teams, which suggest successful teams played with more width and were clinical in attack. Finally, in defence, the successful teams had to make significantly fewer tackles, and missed significantly fewer tackles than the unsuccessful teams. It was concluded that successful teams are dominant in defence, as well as attack.

REFERENCES

Bass, J.C.S.,1977, *Seven-a-side Rugby: Including Tactics Suitable for Mini Rugby.* (London: Pelham).

Docherty, D., Wenger, H.A. and Neary, P., 1988, Time-motion analysis related to the physiological demands of Rugby. *Journal of Human Movement Studies*, **14**, 269–277.

Hughes M.D. and Clarke, A., 1994, Computerised notation analysis of rugby union to examine the effects of law changes upon the patterns of play by international teams. *Journal of Sports Sciences*, **12**, 180.

Hughes, M.D. and Williams, D., 1988, The development and application of a computerised Rugby Union notation system. *Journal of Sports Sciences,* **6**, 254–255.

Hughes, M., Evans, S. and Wells, J., 2001., Establishing normative profiles in performance analysis. eIJPAS, **1,** 4–27.

Potter, G., 1996., A case study of England's performance in the five nations championship over a three year period (1992–94). In *Notational Analysis of Sport – I and II*, edited by Hughes, M.D. (Cardiff:UWIC), 193–202.

Thomas, C., 1995, Rugby's penalty problem – myth or reality? *In Science and Football III,* edited by Reilly, T., Bangsbo, J. and Hughes, M. (London: E & FN Spon), pp.330–336.

38 Measurement of a Soccer Defending Skill Using Game Performances

K. Suzuki[1] and T. Nishijima[2]

[1] Doctoral Program in Health and Sport Sciences, University of Tsukuba, Japan

[2] Institute of Health and Sport Sciences, University of Tsukuba, Japan

1. INTRODUCTION

In conventional game performance analyses, the investigators focus on data concerning the frequency with which techniques are used, the success and failure of performance and the behaviour patterns (e.g., Hughes, 1996; Hughes and Franks, 1997; Reilly et al., 1997; Spinks et al., 2002). However, in order to evaluate the overall team skill by considering game statements such as field positions of team mates and opponents, there is a need to develop a team skill scale which has causal structures according to the attacking or defending phase (Hughes, 2002). Additionally, the team skill scale should be able to evaluate multi-dimensional abilities of (a) the phases, and (b) objects of attacking or defending. Data based on such a scale will provide coaches with useful information for designing training programmes. Moreover, conventional game performance analyses take too long to return the information to players. However, the automatic measurement of the location of players in games owing to advances in motion analysis techniques (Taki et al., 1996) will be able to decrease the time required to return the information to players and to reduce the hard work of analysts in collecting data.

The purpose of this study was to examine the validity of "a soccer defending skill scale" (SDSS) measured on the basis of the location of players in soccer games using structural equation modelling (SEM).

2. METHODS

2.1. Samples

The samples were 469 defending performances in the final of FIFA World Cup Korea-Japan 2002™ (Brazil versus Germany), which were determined by distances and angles between attackers and defenders, and the number of players (Table 1).

Table 1. Measurement items of defending skills.

Points of measurement	Defending phases	Defending objects	Measured movements	Measurement items
Point of receiving a pass (1st)	Delaying attack	Attacker with the ball	Delay	1) Position of a 1st defender to the attacker with the ball 2) Body shape to direction of attack of the attacker with the ball
		Attackers without the ball	Marking	3) Open players in attack 4) Circumstances of attackers trying use the space behind the defence
		Attacking space	Covering of attacking space	5) Positioning of defenders 6) Circumstances of back-line defender
Point of receiving a pass (2nd) Point of passing	Forcing play in one direction	Attacker with the ball	One side cutting	7) Direction of a pass of the attacker with the ball 8) Number of pass courses which a 1st DF stops
		Attackers without the ball	Pass courses cutting	9) Number of pass course which defenders except a 1st DF stops 10) Open players in attack
		Attacking space	Balance control	11) Circumstances of back-line defender 12) Side space 13) Control of a back-line
Point of receiving a pass (2nd)	Squeezing working space of attackers	Attacker with the ball	Challenge	14) Challenge of a 1st DF on the attacker with the ball 15) Body shape to direction of attack of the attacker with the ball
		Attackers without the ball	Concentration in defence	16) Challenge of a 2nd DF on the attacker with the ball 17) Direction of squeezing space
		Attacking space	Reducing width and depth in attack	18) Width 19) Depth

2.2. Data collection

Defensive game performances were measured using the following 19 items: distances between attackers and defenders (8 items), angles between attackers and defenders (4 items), and the number of the players (7 items) in the tactical defending area. These items were evaluated using 5-point interval scales (Table 2). Game performances were measured using the reduced map of the pitch for the purpose of suppressing measurement error to a minimum (Suzuki and Nishijima, 2002). Basically, measurement items such as distances and angles should be evaluated using ratio scales. However, these items were actually measured using interval scales for reasons of measurement error and practicality in the context of coaching. In applying the automatic measurement method, these items could be measured directly using ratio scales.

Table 2. Measurement methods of defending skills.

Measurement items	Units	Scales					
		1	2	3	4	5	6
1) Position of a 1st defender relative to the Attacker	Angle	>= 150	150 > >= 120	120 > >= 90	90 > >= 60	60 > >= 30	30 >
2) Body shape to direction of attack of the attacker with the ball	Angle	< 30	60 > >= 30	90 > >= 60	120 > >= 90	150 > >= 120	>= 150
3) Open players in attack	Person	>= 5	4	3	2	1	0
4) Circumstances of attackers trying to use space behind the defence	Person	>= 5	4	3	2	1	0
5) Positioning of defenders	Person	0	1	2	3	4	>= 5
6) Circumstances of back-line defenders	Distance (m)	>= 10	10 > >= 8	8 > >= 6	6 > >= 4	4 > >= 2	2 >
7) Direction of a pass by the attacker with the ball	Angle	< 30	60 > >= 30	90 > >= 60	120 > >= 90	150 > >= 120	>= 150
8) Number of pass courses which a 1st DF stops	Person	0	1	2	3	4	>= 5
9) Number of pass course which defenders (except a 1st DF) stops	Person	0	1	2	3	4	>= 5
10) Open players in attack	Person	>= 5	4	3	2	1	0
11) Circumstances of back-line defenders	Distance (m)	>= 10	10 > >= 8	8 > >= 6	6 > >= 4	4 > >= 2	2 >
12) Side space	Distance (m)	>= 30	30 > >= 25	25 > >= 20	20 > >= 15	15 > >= 10	10 >
13) Control of a back-line	Distance (m)	>= 25	25 > >= 20	20 > >= 15	15 > >= 10	10 > >= 5	5 >
14) Challenge of a 1st DF on the attacker with the ball	Distance (m)	>= 9	9 > >= 7	7 > >= 5	5 > >= 3	3 > >= 1	1 >
15) Body shape to direction of attack of the attacker with the ball	Angle	< 30	60 > >= 30	90 > >= 60	120 > >= 90	150 > >= 120	>= 150
16) Challenge of a 2nd DF of the attacker with the ball	Distance (m)	>= 11	11 > >= 9	9 > >= 7	7 > >= 5	5 > >= 3	3 >
17) Direction of squeezing space	Person	>= 5	4	3	2	1	0
18) Width	Distance (m)	>= 50	50 > >= 40	40 > >= 30	30 > >= 20	20 > >= 10	10 >
19) Depth	Distance (m)	>= 25	25 > >= 20	20 > >= 15	15 > >= 10	10 > >= 5	5 >

2.3. Scaling procedure

It was hypothesized that defending game performances are determined by defending skills which have a causal structure according to the defending phases. Therefore, the scaling procedures of the defending performances were as follows: (a) construct a hypothetical structure of the defending performance using previous studies (Hughes, 1973, 1980a, 1980b; Wade, 1967), a qualitative cause and effect analysis, a brain storming method and a matrix diagram; (b) test content validity of 19 measurement items; (c) select the measurement items using item analysis and confirmatory factor analysis (CFA) for each defending phase; (d) test construct validity of SDSS using CFA; (e) test the causal structure of SDSS using structural equation modelling with a multiple-indicator (MI) model; (f) test multi-dimensionality of SDSS using SEM with a multi-dimensional model consisting of the defending phases and the defending objects; and g) compare the two models (i.e., the CFA and multi-dimensional models). The CFA, the MI and the multi-dimensional models were tested using Amos statistical software, version 4.02J (Arbuckle, 1997) with the maximum likelihood estimation procedure. An overall goodness of fit of the models was tested using Adjusted Goodness of Fit Index (AGFI), Comparative Fit Index (CFI), Root Mean Square Error of Approximation (RMSEA), and Akaike Information Criterion (AIC).

3. RESULTS AND DISCUSSION

Figures 1 and 2 show the defending phases and a qualitative causal structure of the defending performances. Defending game performances consisted of 9 performances combining with the defending phase and defending objects.

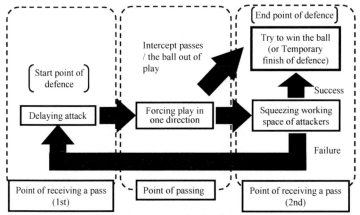

Figure 1. Cycle structure in the defending phases.

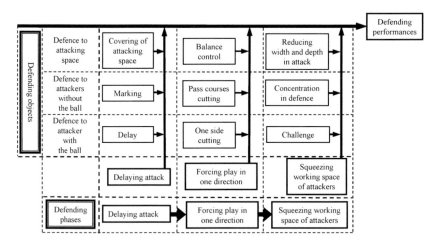

Figure 2. Hypothetical structure of defending performances.

Tables 3 and 4 indicate the results of CFA. Items whose mode was 1 or 5 were excluded from the subsequent analysis in advance. Based on the results of

CFA models for each defending phase, 9 items with high factor loadings were selected from 19 items in order to enhance practicality.

Table 3. Factorial structure of each defending phase in CFA models: standardized solution.

Variable (n=469)	Factor loadings			
	Defence to attacker with the ball	Defence to attackers without the ball	Defence to attacking space	Correlated uniqueness [a]
Phase of delaying attack	(F1)	(F2)	(F3)	
Delay2	1.00	0	0	
Marking1	0	0.92	0	
Marking2	0	0.23	0	0.10
Covering of attacking space1	0	0	0.99	
Covering of attacking space2	0	0	0.28	
Factor correlations				
Factor	F1	F2	F3	
F1	1.00			
F2	0.30	1.00		
F3	0.24	0.44	1.00	
Phase of forcing play in one direction	(F1)	(F2)	(F3)	
One side cutting1	0.99	0	0	0.26
One side cutting2	0.05	0	0	
Pass courses cutting1	0	0.17	0	
Pass courses cutting2	0	0.54	0	
Balance control1	0	0	0.08	
Balance control2	0	0	0.82	
Factor correlations				
Factor	F1	F2	F3	
F1	1.00			
F2	0.19	1.00		
F3	0.62	0.11	1.00	
Phase of squeezing working space of attackers	(F1)	(F2)	(F3)	
Challenge1	0.94	0	0	
Challenge2	0.64	0	0	
Concentration in defence1	0	0.72	0	
Concentration in defence2	0	0.60	0	0.36
Reducing width in attack	0	0	0.77	
Reducing depth in attack	0	0	0.78	
Factor correlations				
Factor	F1	F2	F3	
F1	1.00			
F2	0.97	1.00		
F3	0.95	0.82	1.00	

a: The three correlated uniquenesses posited are between marking2 and covering of attacking space, one side cutting1 and pass courses cutting2, concentration in defence2 and reducing depth in attack.

Table 4. Goodness of fit indices of CFA models.

Fit indices	Model of each defending phase		
	Delaying attack	Forcing play in one direction	Squeezing working space of attackers
Chi-square values	6.862	6.821	9.915
P values	0.076	0.338	0.078
GFI	0.994	0.995	0.993
AGFI	0.971	0.984	0.971
NFI	0.964	0.931	0.992
TLI	0.929	0.975	0.988
CFI	0.979	0.990	0.996
RMSEA	0.052	0.017	0.046

Note. CFA = confirmatory factor analysis; GFI = goodness-of-fit index; AGFI = Adjusted GFI; NFI = normed fit index; TLI = Tucker-Lewis index; CFI = comparative fit index; RMSEA = root mean square error of approximation.

Results of CFA consisting of the selected 9 items indicated a good fit to the data (e.g., AGFI = 0.968, CFI = 0.994, RMSEA = 0.032, AIC = 80.739) (Fig. 3). The causal structure model of the defending skills was also statistically valid (AGFI = 0.966, CFI = 0.991, RMSEA = 0.037, AIC = 83.061) (Fig. 4). These results indicated that SDSS was statistically valid for measuring defending skills in soccer, and that the defending skills of soccer were constructed from 3 sub-domains of "Delaying attack", "Forcing play in one direction", and "Squeezing working space of attackers".

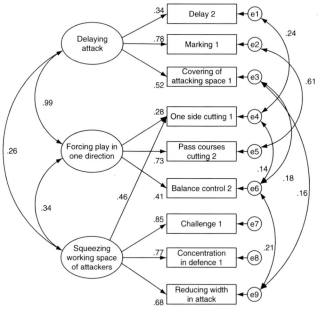

GFI = .987 AGFI = .968 NFI = .981 TLI = .988 CFI = .994
RMSEA = .032 Chi-square = 26.739 (P = .084) AIC = 80.739

Figure 3. The CFA model of the defending skills: standardized solution.

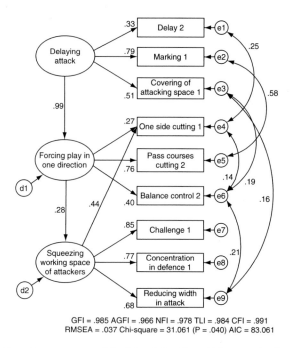

GFI = .985 AGFI = .966 NFI = .978 TLI = .984 CFI = .991
RMSEA = .037 Chi-square = 31.061 (P = .040) AIC = 83.061

Figure 4. Causal structure model of the defending skills: standardized solution.

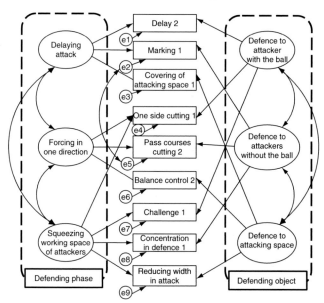

Figure 5. Multi-dimensional model of the defending phases and the defending objects of a SDSS.

The multi-dimensional model (Fig. 5), in which three factors of the defending phases were combined with three factors of the defending objects, indicated a much better fit to the data than the three factor defending skill model (AGFI = 0.980, CFI = 1.000, RMSEA = 0.000, AIC = 79.361) (Tables 5 and 6). Additionally, the chi-square difference for these models was significant (chi-square = 17.378, $df = 8$, $P < 0.05$).

Table 5. Factorial structure of multi-dimensional model: standardized solution.

Variable (n=469)	Factor loadings						
	Delaying attack	Foring play in one direction	Squeezing working space of attackers	Defence to attacker with the ball	Defence to attackers without the ball	Defence to attacking space	Correlated uniqueness [a]
Phase of delaying attack	(F1)	(F2)	(F3)	(F4)	(F5)	(F6)	
Delay2	0.51*	0	0	0.20	0	0	
Marking1	0.64*	0	0	0	0.41*	0	0.61*
Covering of attacking space1	0.49*	0	0	0	0	0.37*	
One side cutting1	0	0.43*	0.30*	0.49*	0	0	
Pass courses cutting2	0	0.59*	0	0	0.38*	0	
Balance control2	0	0.24	0	0	0	0.63*	
Challenge1	0	0	0.78*	0.38*	0	0	
Concentration in defence1	0	0	0.70*	0	0.37*	0	
Reducing width in attack	0	0	0.64*	0	0	0.38*	
Factor correlations							
Factor	F1	F2	F3	F4	F5	F6	
F1	1.00	1.00*	0.11				
F2	1.00*	1.00	0.18				
F3	0.11	0.18	1.00				
F4				1.00	0.74*	0.56*	
F5				0.74*	1.00	0.61*	
F6				0.56*	0.61*	1.00	

Note. *: $P < 0.05$. a: The two correlated uniquenesses posited are between marking1 and pass courses cutting2.

Table 6. Comparison of fit indices in two models.

Fit indices	Competing models	
	CFA model consisting of the defending phase	Multi-dimensional model consisting of the defending phase and object
Chi-square values	26.739	9.361
p values	0.084	0.498
GFI	0.987	0.996
AGFI	0.968	0.980
NFI	0.981	0.994
TLI	0.988	1.002
CFI	0.994	1.000
RMSEA	0.032	0.000
Comparison indices		
AIC	80.739	79.361
BCC	81.918	80.890
BIC	252.130	301.535
ECVI	0.173	0.170

Note. CFA = confirmatory factor analysis; GFI = goodness-of-fit index; AGFI = Adjusted GFI; NFI = normed fit index; TLI = Tucker-Lewis index; CFI = comparative fit index; RMSEA = root mean square error of approximation; AIC = akaike information criterion; BCC = Browne-Cudeck criterion; BIC = Bayes information criteiron; ECVI = Expected value of the cross-validation index.

Based on the overall results, it was concluded that SDSS with 9 items was able to measure the game performance according to the causal structure of the tactical defending phase. It was further concluded that SDSS was able to measure multi-dimensional abilities consisting of the defending phases and defending objects.

REFERENCES

Arbuckle, J. L., 1997, *Amos Users Guide Version 3.6.* (Chicago: Smallwaters Corporation).

Hughes, C., 1973, *Football Tactics and Teamwork.* (London: EP Publishing).

Hughes, C., 1980a, Defending (1) as an individual. In *The Football Association Coaching Book of Soccer Tactics and Skills,* edited by Hughes, C. (London: British Broad Corporation), pp. 179–202.

Hughes, C., 1980b, *The Winning Formula Soccer Skills and Tactics.* (London: William Collins Sons & Co).

Hughes, M., 1996, Notational analysis. In *Science and Soccer, edited by Reilly, T.* (London: E & FN Spon), pp. 343–361.

Hughes, M., 2002, The use of performance indicators in performance analysis. *Journal of Sports Sciences,* **20**, 739–754.

Hughes, M. and Franks, I. 1997, *Notational Analysis of Sport.* (London: E & FN Spon).

Reilly, T., Bangsbo, J. and Hughes, M., 1997, *Science and Football III,* (London: E & FN Spon).

Spinks, W., Reilly, T. and Murphy, A., 2002, *Science and Football IV.* (London: Routledge), pp. 101–170

Suzuki, K. and Nishijima, T., 2002, Causal structure of the attacking skill in soccer games [in Japanese]. *Japan Journal of Physical Education, Health and Sport Sciences,* **47**, 547–567.

Taki, T., Matsumoto, T., Hasegawa, J. and Fukumura, T., (1996), Evaluation of teamwork form soccer game scenes [in Japanese]. *The Institute of Electronics, Information and Communication Engineers, Technical report of IEICE* PRMU96-10, 67–74.

Wade, A., 1967, *The Football Association Guide to Training and Coaching.* (London: Heinemann).

39   The Effect of the Wheeled Scrum Law in Rugby Union

Jason Williams, Corris Thomas, Rhodri Brown and Naomi Jones
IRB Game Analysis, University of Wales Institute Cardiff, Cardiff
CF23 6XD

1. INTRODUCTION

In 1999, the International Rugby Board introduced the "use it or lose it" law with regards to the wheeled scrum in Rugby Union. Firstly, this change involves the referee calling "use it, lose it" when the ball does not emerge immediately from the scrum. Secondly, if the scrum rotates over 90 degrees it is called to an end by the referee and it is reset, with the ball being put in by the opposition. This was meant to improve the scrum, reducing the time being used up in reformations, collapses, wheels and injury (Silver, 1992). These problems have largely been answered with the introduction of this change (Thomas, 2002). However, it may be argued that there have been changes with other aspects of the scrum, such as winning the scrum through fair competition. It is hypothesised that that the amount of possession gained through winning or losing in the scrum, with a clean strike of the ball, is decreasing. The present aim was to investigate this rule change within Rugby Union and measure the effect on the amount of possession gained through winning or losing the ball at the scrum.

The reasons for changing a particular rule within a sport have been defined by a number of researchers. Hammond et al. (1999) in their work on netball, attributed rule changes to three main factors:- player performance, technological advancement and commercial pressures. They concluded that rule changes should be analysed systematically to gauge their effect. Kew (1987) researched rule changes in basketball, hockey and different codes of football. It was found that rules change frequently, but little is known of the processes through which such changes are impelled. The work categorised two types of rule change; the first is the definitive rule – a concern to re-establish and re-emphasise the key characteristics of that specific sport. The second category was defined as a shared concern about what must be preserved, enhanced or enabled in order to sustain the viability of the sport.

It is argued that the effect of rule changes on a sport cannot be objectively determined unless there is some form of measure associated with it. Presently, little formal use is made of notation in tracking changes to a sport after a rule change. There have been various research projects that have used notation to examine the effect of changes on game play. Much of the work undertaken measures the intentional change that a particular rule is required to resolve, such as the time that a ball is in play, or the number of kicks in a game. Hughes (1995) used notational analysis to investigate a change in scoring with squash and found that the game became more interesting for players and spectators. There are other areas within a sport that may unintentionally change with the introduction of a new rule. For example, Doggart *et al.* (1993) examined Gaelic football and a number of rule changes that were introduced to improve the game. The time that the ball was in play increased by 2% but also there was a noticeable increase in the number of possessions gained and tackles made. They concluded that the intended increase in the ball-in-play time also introduced other changes within the game that the authorities may not have foreseen.

2. METHODS

Matches in the Six-Nations (n=15) and Tri-Nations (n=6) tournaments were analysed over a period of 4 years, between 1999 and 2002. Data captured from the year preceding the law change (1999) were compared with the three following years. The research concentrated on the terminating events that signal the end of a scrum. For the purposes of this study, the end of a scrum was defined as when the ball is either won, lost or another occurrence takes place, such as a penalty or a free kick. These events were categorised into clean or unclean scrums (Figure 1). A clean scrum was defined as when the scrum is either won by the team putting the ball in, or won by the team not putting the ball in. Scrums that were unclean were defined as a scrum ending due to any other condition, which may be a penalty, free kick, wheeled or stationary scrum. Table 1 defines the type of information captured by the software:

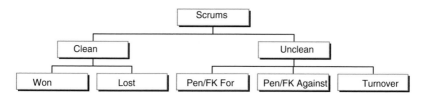

Figure 1. Hierarchy of definition of terms.

Table 1. Definition of terms.

Won	A clean win of the ball by the team introducing the ball to the scrum
Lost	A clean win of the ball by the team not introducing the ball to the scrum
Pen/FK For	A Penalty or Free Kick to the team introducing the ball to the scrum
Pen/FK Against	A Penalty or Free Kick to the team not introducing the ball to the scrum
Turnover	A scrum where the referee indicates that the scrum has turned over 90 degrees or where the team does not play the ball when instructed. A new scrum is then awarded to the defending team.

The data were collected using a real-time data capture system, which had been written for the notational analysis of Rugby Union (Williams, 1998). This software captured a number of game actions as the game progressed in the real time of the game (Figure 2). For the purpose of this study, all games were notated from video, but in a real-time environment. The data were written to an Access database, which was interrogated for the required information through a series of queries (Figure 2). The system had been tested for reliability using percentage differences for inter- and intra- operator reliability (Hughes et al., 2002). This scored error percentages of less than 5%, which was considered acceptable given the analytical goals of the study. The data were examined for significant differences using a Kruskal-Wallis test and were then interrogated further using a post-hoc application of a Mann-Whitney test.

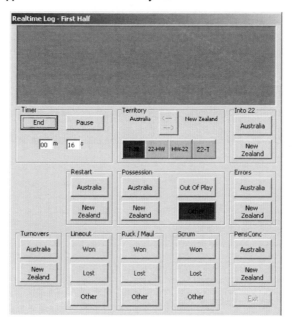

Figure 2. RealLog data capture screen from analysis software.

3. RESULTS

Figure 3 indicates that there had been an increase in the number of unclean scrums in the six Nations (9%) and a decrease in the Tri-Nations (8%) competitions. Further analysis of the data using Kruskal-Wallis indicated that there was a significant difference in the data (H <0.01). The post-hoc application of a Mann-Whitney test denoted that there was a significant difference (P< 0.05) in the six Nations (6N) and Tri-Nations (3N) with the year preceding the law change (1999) and the year after (2000). There was also a mean difference of 16% between the two game groupings in this year. The following years did not show any significant differences from before the law change. These two years (2001 and 2002) appeared to indicate that they were returning to the levels found in 1999. The mean difference between the two competitions had reduced to 2% in 2001 and 1% in 2002 (Figure 3).

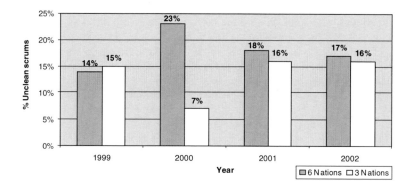

Figure 3. The mean of unclean scrums in six-Nations and Tri-Nations events over a 4-year period.

The research highlighted a decrease in the number of scrums in three years following the law change at the end of 1999. The application of a Kruskal-Wallis test indicated that there were significant differences (H > 0.01) in the Six-Nations and Tri-Nations competitions. A post-hoc application of a Mann-Whitney test indicated that there was a significant difference (P > 0.05) in the Six-Nations, but not in the Tri-Nations.

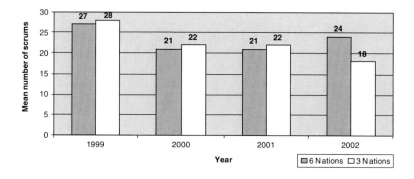

Figure 4. The mean number of scrums in Six-Nations and Tri-Nations over a 4-year period

4. DISCUSSION AND CONCLUSION

The data highlighted the effect that the law change had on the scrum in the Six-Nations and Tri-Nations matches. Using Kruskal-Wallis it was found that there was a significant difference (H < 0.01) in the first year of the law change both with the Six-Nations and Tri-Nations competitions. There was a percentage increase in the number of unclean scrums in the Six-Nations and a decrease in the Tri-Nations. It was also found that there was a decrease in the number of scrums in a game in both competitions. The application of the new law appeared to differ as well, with more incidences of its application in the Six-Nations than the Tri- Nations.

The reason why the there was a difference between the competitions in the first year is unclear. It is suggested that this may be due to one of three possible reasons. Firstly, it may be due to different interpretations of the law by the referees within each competition, which adds to the popular argument that northern hemisphere referees officiate differently to their colleagues in the south and vice versa. This argument may be considered meaningless as referees from both hemispheres may referee in either of the competitions (Thomas, 2000). Secondly, it may be that the Six-Nations competition takes place a few months before the Tri-Nations, and so the new law was interpreted in a more relaxed manner in the latter competition with referees becoming accustomed to it. Finally, it may be evidence that the scrum in the Six-Nations is more competitive than the Tri-Nations, with teams trying to turn the new law to their advantage. The mean number of unclean scrums differed significantly in the first year after the law change, but the number in 2002 returned to the same level before the law change. There appeared to be an effect, then a process of familiarisation, followed by a return to the level before the law change.

Analysis of the number of scrums in a game indicated a decrease in the mean number of scrums. Although this was not one of the main aims of the study, the information does suggest that there should be some investigation into why there was a decrease. Further analysis of the data may include the analysis of competition within the scrum and the number of penalties conceded by the team putting in and the team not putting the ball into the scrum. Additionally, research should be undertaken with regards to the effect of the law change on different levels of the game, such as Super 12, European Cup and domestic leagues.

In conclusion, the new law had the effect of decreasing the number of clean scrums, but appears to have had less of an effect on the game as the new law became established. The amount of possession gained through winning or losing in the scrum, with a clean strike of the ball, decreased in the Six-Nations but increased in the Tri-Nations. Although the problems within the scrum appeared to have been resolved with some aspects of the scrum, the research appears to indicate that there was another change that may not have been predicted by the game administrators. It is possible to speculate as to why these changes occurred, but a more detailed study needs to take place to determine why the changes occurred.

REFERENCES

Doggart, L., Keane, S., Reilly, T. and Stanhope, J. 1993, A task analysis of Gaelic Football. In *Science and Football II*, edited by Reilly, T., Clarys, J. and Stibbe, A. (London: E. & F. N. Spon), pp. 186 – 189.

Hammond, J., Hosking, D. and Hole, C., 1999, An exploratory study of the effectiveness of rule changes in netball. Journal of Sports Sciences, **17**, 916–917.

Hughes, M., Cooper, S.M. and Nevill, A., 2002, Analysis procedures for non-parametric data from performance analysis. *International Journal of Performance Analysis in Sport,* **2** (1), 6–20.

Hughes, M. and Sykes, I., 1994, Computerised notational analysis of the effects of the law changes in soccer upon patterns of play. *Journal of Sports Sciences,* **12**, 180.

Kew, F., 1987, Contested rules: An explanation of how games change, *International Review for the Sociology of Sport,* **22**(2), 125–135.

Silver, J.R., 1992, Injuries of the spine sustained during rugby. *British Journal of Sports Medicine,* **26**, 253–258.

Thomas, C., 2000, The myth crusher. *Oval World,* **15**, 42.

Thomas, C., 2002, An examination of all scrums in matches played at senior international level between 1999 and 2002. *IRB Game Analysis.* (Cardiff, UK: UWIC).

Williams, J.J., 1998, *IRB Game Analysis.* (Cardiff, UK: UWIC).

40 Effects of Time of Day on the Performance of Soccer-Specific Motor Skills

T. Reilly, K. Farrelly, B. Edwards and J. Waterhouse
Research Institute for Sport and Exercise Sciences, Liverpool John Moores University, Henry Cotton Campus, 15-21 Webster Street, Liverpool, L3 2ET

1. INTRODUCTION

Previous research has indicated that many aspects of human performance vary according to a circadian rhythm (Atkinson and Reilly, 1996). The majority of measures follow a curve closely corresponding to the rhythm in core temperature, which peaks at about 18:00 hours. Since football training and matches are held at various times during the day, ranging from 10:00 to 20:00 hours, the study of diurnal variation in skilled tasks related to soccer is relevant.

2. METHODS

Eight male soccer players (age 19.1 ± 1.9 years; height 1.78 ± 0.04 m; body mass 75.9 ± 7.9 kg) with 10.8 ± 2.1 years (means $\pm$ SD) experience of playing the game participated in the study. Measurements were made on different days at 08:00, 12:00, 16:00 and 20:00 hours in a counterbalanced manner. Intra-aural temperature, grip strength, reaction times and flexibility (forward flexibility and sit-and-reach) were used as markers of circadian rhythms. Soccer-specific skills included separate juggling and dribbling tasks and a wall-volley test (Reilly and Holmes, 1983). The data were examined for diurnal variation using repeated measures ANOVA.

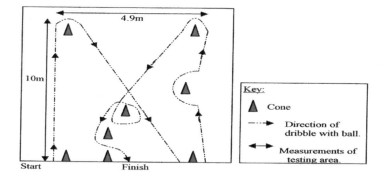

Figure 1. The path travelled in the dribbling test.

3. RESULTS

In general, superior performances were evident late afternoon and evening compared to morning and mid-day values. This observation applied across the range of variables that was monitored.

Table 1. Summary of significant diurnal variation in core temperature, subjective states and in performance. The peak time is indicated for each variable.

Valuable	Time of Peak	P value
Body Temperature	20:00	<0.0001
Alertness	20:00	<0.0001
Fatigue	08:00	<0.0005
Reaction Time	16:00	<0.05
Grip Strength (Right)	20:00	<0.02
Forward flexion	16:00	<0.02

A significant diurnal variation was found for body (intra-aural) temperature ($F_{3,7} = 19.16$; $P < 0.0005$), choice reaction time ($F_{3,7} = 4.07$; $P < 0.05$), rating of alertness ($F_{3,7} = 8.59$; $P < 0.001$), fatigue (see Figure 2), forward flexion and right grip strength ($P < 0.05$) but not for left grip strength and sit-and-reach flexibility (see Table 1). Juggling performance showed a significant peak ($P < 0.05$) at 16:00 hours whereas the variations in the wall-volley test just failed to reach significance (see Figure 3). Performance in dribbling was non-significant (see Table 2).

Table 2. Performance on the soccer-specific tasks.

Task	Time of Peak	Observed power	P value
Juggling	16:00	0.71	0.03
Wall Volley	20:00	0.56	0.06
Dribbling	08:00	0.11	0.55

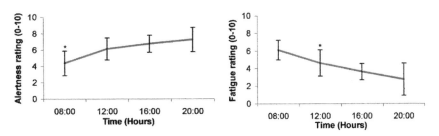

Figure 2. Diurnal variation in alertness and fatigue ratings.

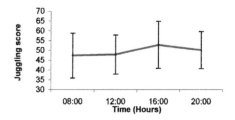

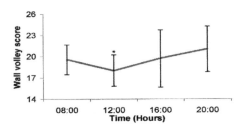

Figure 3. The influence of time of day on juggling and wall-volley tests

4. CONCLUSIONS

The results indicate that some but not all components of soccer skills exhibit diurnal variation. The variations with time of day suggest that changes in performance do not rely solely on the body temperature rhythm.

REFERENCES

Atkinson, G. and Reilly, T., 1996, Circadian variation in sports performance. *Sports Medicine*, **21**, 292–312.

Reilly, T. and Holmes, M., 1983, A preliminary analysis of selected soccer skills. *Physical Education Review*, **61**, 64–71.

41 Time of Day and Performance Tests in Male Football Players

Thomas Reilly, Emma Fairhurst, Ben Edwards and Jim Waterhouse
Research Institute for Sport and Exercise Sciences, Liverpool John
Moores University, Henry Cotton Campus, 15–21 Webster Street,
Liverpool, L3 2ET

1. INTRODUCTION

Circadian rhythms refer to cyclical changes occurring over the solar day. Human
circadian rhythms influence many aspects of human performance (Waterhouse *et al.*,
2002). In the main, changes in performance follow closely the circadian curve in
body temperature with a peak at about 17:00 hours and a trough at 05:00 hours.
Football games may take place at various times throughout the day whilst training
may be held in the morning or afternoon. Whilst many physiological functions
related to football, for example muscle strength and self-paced endurance
performance, have been studied (Reilly et al., 1997), there has been no attention
given to the study of time-of-day effects on game-related skills. The main purpose
of the study was to analyse the effects of the time of day on specific performance
tests in football players.

2. METHODS

Eight university male football players volunteered to take pace in the study after
signing a voluntary informed consent form. They were aged 23 ± 0.7 years, body
mass 77 ± 2.7 kg with stature 1.81 ± 0.09 m. They all avoided physical exercise
before testing. Each subject had at least 6 hours sleep the night before and a light
snack was pemitted 2 hours prior to exercising.

    Subjects completed 5 sessions of testing, two at 08:00 hours, and one
session at each of 12:00, 16:00 and 20:00 hours using a counterbalanced design.
Intra-aural temperature (Genius, Ballymoney) and alertness were also recorded.
The profile of mood states (McNair et al., 1971) and chronotype questionnaire
(Horne and Ostberg, 1976) were also completed. Performance tests included
football chipping, dribbling time, flexibility (sit-and-reach and spinal hyper-
extension), grip strength (Takei-kigi Kogyo, Tokyo), vertical jumping and the
standing long jump.

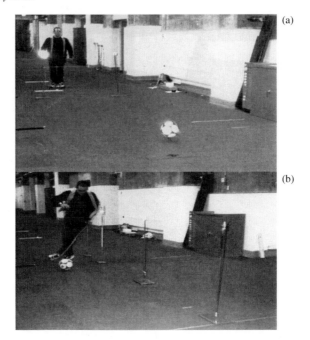

Figure 1. Subject performing (a) football chip and (b) straight dribble tests.

3. RESULTS

Test-retest reliability determined at 08:00 hours for all components showed no significant (P>0.05) changes (CV=4.0–4.5%). Intra-aural Body temperature showed a significant time-of-day effect (see Table 1) with mean temperature at 16:00 (36.4°C) higher than at 08:00 hours (35.4°C) (P<0.001). There was no significant effect of chronotype on the temperature acrophase (P>0.05). The football chip test was significantly more accurate at 16:00 hours (mean error = 0.75 m) than at 08:00 hours (mean error = 1.01 m) (P<0.001). A significant time-of-day effect was also found for dribbling speed, the test performance being evident at 20:00 hours (P<0.001)

Significant diurnal rhythms were found for most other performance tests including sit-and-reach (P<0.01), spinal hyper-extension (P<0.05), grip strength and jump tests (P<0.05). Peaks in the early evening between 16:00 and 20:00 hours were computed. The forward flexion test did not reveal a significant time-of-day effect (P>0.05). All performance components conformed closely in phase to the temperature rhythm (see Table 2).

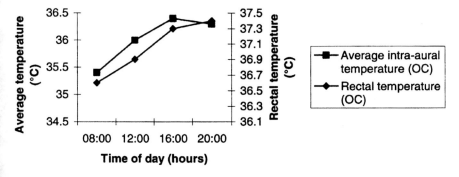

Figure 2. Intra-aural temperature in comparison with rectal temperature taken from Reilly et al. (1997, p. 16).

Table 1. Mean and standard deviation for body temperature and soccer-specific performance at the four times of day.

	08:00	12:00	16:00	20:00
Aural temperature (^{0}C)	35.36±0.16	36.08±0.28	36.44±0.44	36.37±0.83
Chipping accuracy (m)	1.01±0.34	0.83±0.30	0.75±0.26	0.85±0.28
Dribbling time (s)	13.60±3.57	12.54±4.13	12.15±2.46	11.99±4.43

Table 2. Means (±SD) for flexibility (cm), strength (kg) and jump (cm) tests.

	08:00	12:00	16:00	20:00
Forward flexion	−15.3 ± 6.8	−14.4 ± 7.6	−13.9 ± 4.3	−13.3 ± 7.3
Spinal hyperextension	24.9 ± 5.9	25.8 ± 5.2	26.8 ± 7.7	28.1 ± 6.3
Sit-and-reach (cm)	12.5 ± 11.5	15.2 ± 12.8	15.9 ± 10.9	17.2 ± 11.2
Grip (Right)	44.5 ± 9.5	46.4 ± 10.2	47.6 ± 10.6	51.8 ± 10.8
Grip (Left)	40.6 ± 8.6	44.8 ± 8.3	44.8 ± 8.7	46.0 ± 8.5
Vertical jump	45 ± 1.5	48 ± 1.6	50 ± 0.9	50 ± 1.0
Broad jump	206 ± 4.9	213 ± 6	217 ± 5.1	218 ± 5.8

Alertness and mood states both revealed significant time-of-day effects ($P<0.05$) with a strong link between the fatigue and vigour sub-scales ($P<0.05$) that reflected on performance. Peaks were found to occur between 12:00 and 16:00 h for both components.

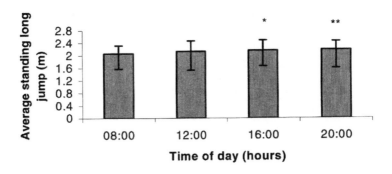

** Significantly different from 08:00 P=0.02 and 12:00 P=0.03
* Significantly different from 0800 P=0.03

Figure 3. Standing long jump and time of day.

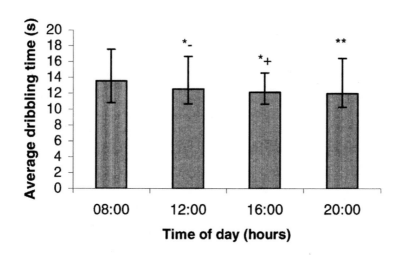

** Significantly different from 08:00 P=0.001 and 12:00 P=0.002
*+ Significantly different from 08:00 P=0.007
*- Significantly different from 08:00 P=0.005

Figure 4. Average dribbling time and time of day.

4. CONCLUSIONS

Results indicate that the present sample of football players performed at their optimum between 16:00 and 20:00 hours, due to all performance components peaking between these times. Performances were closely related to body temperature rhythms. It is suggested that other variables such as alertness and mood state may also have a role in influencing performance.

REFERENCES

Horne, J. A. and Ostberg, C. O., 1976, A self-assessment questionnaire to determine morningness – eveningness in human circadian rhythms. *International Journal of Chronobiology*, **4**, 97–110.
McNair, D. M., Lorr, M. and Droppleman, L. F., 1971, *Profile of Mood States Manual*. (San Diego: Educational and Industrial Testing Service).
Reilly, T., Atkinson, G. and Waterhouse, J., 1997, *Biological Rhythms and Exercise*. (Oxford: Oxford University Press).
Waterhouse, J., Minors, D. S., Waterhouse, M. E., Reilly, T. and Atkinson, G, 2002, *Keeping in Time with your Body Clock*. (Oxford: Oxford University Press).

42 Specificity of Acceleration, Maximum Speed and Agility in Professional Soccer Players

Thomas Little[1] and Alun Williams[2]
[1]Head of Conditioning, Newlife Fitness, Nottingham Forest, UK
[2]Department of Exercise and Sport Science,
Manchester Metropolitan University, UK

1. INTRODUCTION

The capability of football players to produce varied high-speed actions is known to impact upon soccer match performance (Luhtanen, 2000). While high speed actions only contribute to 11% of total distance covered, high-speed movements constitute the more crucial moments of the game and contribute directly to winning possession of the ball and to the scoring or conceding of goals (Bangsbo, 1994). Superior performance in varied speed tests of professional players compared to the general population, and within higher standards of soccer, would indicate that certain speed attributes would be advantageous for elite soccer (Kollath and Quade, 1993). While developed tactical sense and high technical ability can certainly compensate for deficiencies in speed elements, it is clear that excelling in acceleration, top speed and agility will help predispose a person towards elite soccer, and improving these attributes will enhance the performance of players.

High-speed actions during soccer competition can be categorised into those requiring maximal speed, acceleration and agility. Acceleration is the rate of change of velocity that allows a player to reach maximum velocity in a minimum amount of time. Maximum speed is the maximal velocity at which a player can sprint. Agility does not have a global definition, but is often recognised as the ability to change direction and start and stop quickly (Gambetta, 1996).

The range of sprint distances recorded during games (1.5–105 m) indicates the requirements of both acceleration and maximum speed capacities during a game. Although the average sprint distance is only small (14 m) the fact that players are often moving to pace when initiating a sprint, indicates that top speed will be achieved more than distance, or time parameters might otherwise predict. Many instances in soccer play demand rapid changes of direction. Withers et al. (1982) have shown that players make an average of 50 turns per game. Some common physiological determinants of agility performance as for acceleration and maximum speed, such as fibre type proportion, may lead to the assumption that these three qualities are highly related.

Research concerning the interrelationship of the three speed qualities has been inconsistent in its findings. Delecluse (1997) found maximal speed and acceleration to be specific qualities in sprint athletes. However, participants in field sports are believed to have different running mechanics to sprint athletes (Sayers, 2000) and significant correlations between acceleration and maximum speed in professional rugby players have been reported (Baker and Nance, 1999). Buttifant and Graham (1999) and Young et al. (1996) reported non-significant correlations between straight sprinting and agility speed tests in Australian soccer, and Australian Rules football players, respectively. However, Pauole et al. (2000) found significant correlations between performance in an agility T-test and 40-yard sprint time, in both men and women. No study to date has specifically examined the relationships between specific components of straight sprinting speed (acceleration and maximum speed) and agility.

Therefore, the purpose of this study was to determine the extent that top speed, acceleration and agility are distinct physical attributes in professional soccer players. The findings have potential implications for the training and assessment of physical performance in elite soccer players.

2. METHODS

2.1. Subjects

Thirty-five professional soccer players, from an English League Division 1 team, were tested as part of their athletic training programme at the completion of their pre-season training period. All subjects gave their informed consent and the study was approved by the Local Ethics Committee.

2.2. Testing

At the present time, there is no "gold standard" criterion measure for agility, and scarce literature exists concerning the validity of agility tests. However, the T-test has been found to be a valid predictor of the level of sports participation and has excellent reliability scores (Pauole et al., 2000). To be a valid representation of agility in the present study, the T-test should be representative of typical actions observed within soccer. In the test, subjects sprint 10-m out to point B, where they touch a cone and then break at $90°$ to sprint 5-m left or right, touch either cone C or D and turn $180°$ to sprint 10-m to the far cone (D if originally touched C, and vice versa). Subjects then again turn $180°$ and sprint past point B, where the test terminates. Turns of both $90°$ and $180°$ are common to the test and soccer performance. The performance of the T-test in the present study was adapted from the traditional version described by Semenick (1990) by using constant forward based running, whereas the original test utilised lateral movements after the initial 10-m sprint. The logic was to use as similar musculature as possible to that engaged in the acceleration and maximum speed tests. In this manner, variation in test performance will be mainly attributed to speed and strength qualities of the major muscle groups used during forward running. The use of lateral movement would utilise partly different musculature to the acceleration and top speed tests, which may oversimplify the mechanisms of specificity.

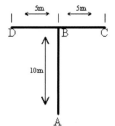

Figure 1. Layout of the T-test

Acceleration was tested using a stationary 10-m test and maximum speed was assessed using a flying 30-m test, both of which had been used previously for their respective measures (Mero et al., 1981; Wilson et al., 1993; Faccioni, 1994). 'Stationary 10 m' involved sprinting 10 m as fast as possible from a stationary start position. 'Flying 30 m' involved sprinting 30 m as fast as possible from a maximum speed start. All tests were performed on an indoor synthetic pitch and electronic timing gates were used to record completion times (Brower Timing System, Salt Lake City, UT). Subjects performed two maximal attempts at each exercise with at least 2 min rest between tests and trials. The best times were used for analysis.

2.3. Analysis

The relationships between the acceleration, maximum speed and agility tests, were determined by Pearson correlations (r) and the coefficient of determination (r^2) was used for interpreting the meaningfulness of the relation.

3. RESULTS

Mean times (± SD) for all the tests are shown in Table 2. The correlations, and coefficient of variations between the various tests are outlined in Table 3.

Table 1. Mean time (± standard deviation) results for the various speed tests.

Stationary 10-m Test	1.87 (± 0.08) s
Flying 30-m test	3.58 (± 0.15) s
T-Test	6.87 (± 0.20) s

Table 2. The relationships between the various speed measurements.

Speed Attributes	r	r^2	P-value
Acceleration & Max speed	0.440	0.194	0.008
Acceleration & Agility	0.550	0.302	0.001
Maximum speed & Agility	0.336	0.120	0.042

4. DISCUSSION

Results showed that the stationary 10-m test, flying 30-m test and T-test, were all significantly correlated (P<0.05). This would suggest that acceleration, maximum speed and agility share common determining factors. However, the coefficient of determination calculations show that even the most significantly correlated tests share only 30% common variance. Thomas and Nelson (1990) stated that "when common variance between the two variables is less than 50%, it indicates that they are specific or somewhat independent in nature". It appears that acceleration, maximum speed and agility are relatively independent attributes in professional footballers. The requirement of high power production for each speed component, which is partly dependant on muscle fibre size, length and proportion, means that the different speed components show some significant relationships. However, it is clear that several distinct factors contribute to successful performance in each speed discipline.

A potential problem with this conclusion relates to the small range of values for the performance measures. When the range within the data is small, as it is in the present study, the likelihood of producing a high correlation between two variables is decreased (Thomas and Nelson, 1990). The small range of data dictates that a large number of subjects need to be sampled in order to obtain sufficient statistical power (Hopkins et al., 1999). Therefore, the findings of the present study may be a derivative of a relatively small sample size and range of measures. However, we have unpublished data on a far greater number of subjects (107) showing similar results to this study, supporting the current conclusion.

A further problem of the current and previous research concerning speed specificity is that cross-sectional analysis has been utilised. Such analysis is limited because external factors that can influence results are difficult to control and causal mechanisms may only be inferred from the results. Recently, Young et al. (2001 a) conducted a longitudinal study examining the specificity of the training response to straight sprint and agility training. Six weeks of straight sprint training (20-40 m) significantly improved 30-m sprint performance, but performance improvements were lower on agility courses as the number and severity of directional changes increased. Conversely, the agility training resulted in significant improvements in the tests incorporating change of direction but no significant improvement in straight sprint performance. It was concluded that straight speed and agility training methods are specific and produce limited transfer to the other. Such training response specificity supports the current findings and suggests that specific test procedures for each speed component should be utilised in support work with elite players. Testing of individual players should allow specific training programmes to be employed to address specific weaknesses, and ultimately improve match performance. In order to design training programmes aimed at improving specific speed components we must first decipher which differential elements are important to performance, and thereby the cause of the specificity in the different speed components. The specificity may be attributable to differences in the musculature utilised, strength qualities required, and complexity of motor control, between the different speed components.

Biomechanical (Young et al., 2001b) and electromyographic analyses (Wiemann and Tidow, 1995) have revealed differences in the relative importance of different muscles to acceleration and maximum speed. During acceleration the quadriceps and gluteus maximus appear to be of particular importance but as the sprint progresses quadriceps involvement decreases. As speed increases and the body becomes more upright, the hip extensor involvement becomes more prominent, of which the hamstrings appear to be of particular importance. Scant research exists on the musculature utilised during various agility tasks. The short sprint distances would indicate that a significant portion of the forward propulsion would stem from the driving, pushing action generated from the quadriceps and gluteus muscles, as when accelerating. When turning, the foot is invariably placed at 90° to the intended direction and as such hip abductors of the plant leg, and hip adductors of the front leg will be important when changing direction.

In addition to different muscles, there appears to be variation in the relative importance of strength qualities to the different speed elements. Correlation analysis showed that acceleration ability is best related to relative strength (strength divided by body weight) in purely concentric contractions (Young et al., 1996; Baker and Nance, 1999). This is a simple reflection of Newton's second law, where acceleration= force/mass. During the initial acceleration eccentric loading of the muscles, although apparent, will be low and therefore the concentric strength qualities may have greater relative importance compared to reactive strength (stretch-shortening cycle qualities). As speed increases, the increased velocity and stride length result in greater eccentric loads on ground contact (Delecluse, 1997). Therefore, reactive strength, in order to minimize ground contact time, should become increasingly important as speed increases. This is reflected in the findings that counter-movement, and drop-jump performance, both indicative of reactive strength, were highly correlated to maximum speed capabilities (Mero, 1985; Young et al., 2001a). Both acceleration and maximum speed capabilities have been found to be highly correlated to rate of force development (Young et al., 1985). The short straight sprint distances involved in the agility test would suggest that the muscular requirement for forward propulsion would be similar to acceleration (i.e. relative concentric strength from the quadriceps and gluteus maximus). This is reflected in the current findings, as agility and acceleration showed the strongest relationship. However, the strength requirement involved in turning rapidly should be very different. In order to produce a fast change of direction, it would be desirable to achieve a relatively short ground contact time, where reactive strength is essential. Studies have shown significant, although limited correlations between reactive strength measures and agility performance (Djevalikian, 1993; Young et al., 1996). However, no studies have examined the correlation between reactive strength and specifically turning ability.

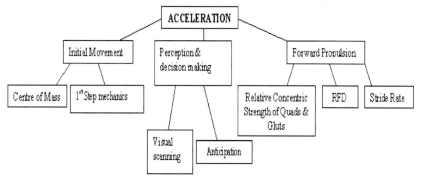

Figure 2. Factors that affect acceleration.

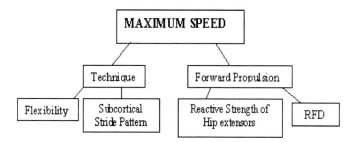

Figure 3. Factors that influence maximum speed.

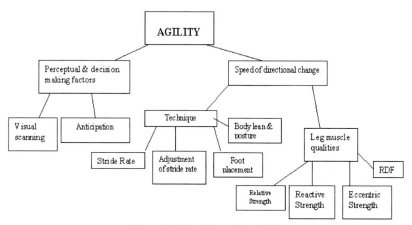

Figure 4. Factors determining agility.

Research concerning which characteristics are important to performance of the speed components has utilized cross-sectional analysis. Such analysis can only provide suggestive mechanisms for the factors that limit performance. To elucidate true cause and effect relationships, longitudinal studies are required, where potential limiting factors are specifically trained. Until such time, speed training should be biased to the suggested limiting factors for each speed component, represented in Figures 2, 3 and 4, in areas where the player is weak or the speed component is of particular importance.

REFERENCES

Baker, D., and Nance, S., 1999, The relation between running speed and measures of strength and power in professional rugby league players. Journal of Strength and Conditioning Research, **13**, 230–235.

Bangsbo, J.,1994, The physiology of soccer: With special reference to intense physical exercise. *Acta Physiologica Scandinavica*, **150**, 1–156.

Buttifant, D. and Graham, K., 1999, Agility and speed measurement in soccer players are two different performance parameters. *Fourth World Congress of Science and Football. (*Abstract). Sydney, Australia. p 57.

Delecluse, D., 1997, Influence of strength training on sprint running performance: current findings and implications for training. Sports Medicine, **24**, 147–156.

Djevalikian, R.,1993, *The relationship between asymmetrical leg power and change of running direction.* Master's Thesis, University of North Carolina, Microform publications, University of Oregon, Eugene Oregon.

Faccioni, A., 1994. Assisted and resisted methods for speed development, part 11. *Modern Athletes and Coach*, 32(3), 8–12.

Gambetta, V., 1996, How to develop sport-specific speed. *Sports Coach,* **19**, 22–4.

Hopkins, W., Hawley, J. and Burke, L., 1999, Design and analysis of research on sport performance enhancement. *Medicine and Science in Sports and Exercise,* **31**, 472–485.

Kollath, E.and Quade, B., 1993, Measurement of sprinting speed of professional and amateur soccer players. In *Science and Football II*, edited by Reilly, T., Clarys, J. and Stibbe, A. (London: E and FN Spon), pp. 31–36.

Luhtanen, P., 2000, Mechanical aspect of running and speed. Retrieved July 16, 2001 from the World Wide Web: http://www.education.ed.ac.uk/soccer/papers/pl-6-html.

Mero, A., 1985, relationship between the muscle fibre characteristics, sprinting and jumping of sprinters. *Biology of Sport*, **2**(3), 155–161.

Mero, A., Luhtanen, P., Viitasalo, J. T. and Komi, P. V., 1981, relationship between the maximal velocity, muscle fibre characteristics, force production and force relaxation of sprinters. *Scandinavian Journal of Sports Science,* **3**, 16–2.

Pauole, K., Madole, K. and Lacourse, M., 2000, Reliability and validity of the T-test as a measure of agility, leg power and leg speed in college aged men and women. *Journal of Strength and Conditioning Research,* **14**(4), 443–450.

Sayers, M., 2000, Running techniques for field sport players. *Sports Coach,* **23**,(1) 26–27.

Semenick, D., 1990, The T- test. *NSCA Journal,* **12** (1): 36–37.

Thomas, J. R. and Nelson, J. K., 1990, *Research Methods in Physical Activity.* (Champaign: Human Kinetics).

Wiemann, K. and Tidow, G., 1995, Relative activity of hip and knee extensors in sprinting – implications of training. *New Studies in Athletics,* **10**(1), 29–49.

Wilson, G. J., Newton, R.U., Murphy, A.J. and Humphries, B.J., 1993, The optimal training load for the development of dynamic athletic performance. *Medicine and Science in Sports and Exercise,* **25**, 1279–1286.

Withers, R., Maricic, Z., Wasilewski, S. and Kelly, L., 1982, Match analysis of Australian soccer players. *Journal of Human Movement Studies,* **8**, 159-76.

Young, W. B., McLean, B. and Ardagna, J., 1996, Relationship between strength qualities and sprinting performance. *Journal of Sports Medicine and Physical Fitness,* **35**, 13–19.

Young, W.B., McDowell, M.H. and Scarlett, B.J., 2001a, Specificity of sprint and agility training methods. *Journal of Strength and Conditioning Research,* **15** (3), 315–319.

Young, W., Benton, D., Duthie, G. and Pryor, J., 2001b, Resistance training for short and maximal speed sprints. *Strength and Conditioning,* **23** (2), 7–13.

Young, W., Hawken, M. and McDonald, L., 1996, Relationship between speed, agility and strength qualities in Australian rules football. *Strength and Conditioning Coach,* **4**, (4), 3–6.

Part V

Medical Aspects of Football

43 Sports Science Support for the England Amputee Soccer Team

D. Wilson, P. Riley and T. Reilly

Research Institute for Sport and Exercise Sciences, Liverpool John Moores University, 15–21 Webster Street, Liverpool, L3 2ET, UK

1. INTRODUCTION

Amputee football involves players who have classes A2/A4 and A6/A8 amputation. An A2 amputation is above the knee (see Figure 1.1), and A4 is below the knee of one leg. Conversely, A6 denotes that one arm is amputated above or through the elbow joint, and an A8 indicates one arm amputated below the elbow, but through or above the wrist joint. The A2 and A4 classes make up the outfield players and A6/A8 amputees can only play in goal. During match-play the wearing of a prosthetic device is not permitted and all outfield players must use crutches. Furthermore, the game includes 'Les Autres players'; these are players with congenital limb impairments to either a single leg or arm (Figure 1.2). To ensure equality between various types of disability, both outfield players and goalkeepers are not permitted to control or touch the ball with the residual limbs. In addition, crutches may not be used to advance the ball. Blocking, trapping, or touching the ball with a crutch, and any intentional contact between non-playing limb and ball, are considered the same as a "handball" in able-bodied football (Wilson, 2001).

The game consists of two halves each of 25-min with a 10-min half time interval. Game surfaces range between astroturf, grass, and indoor (sports hall) flooring. Normal F.I.F.A. rules apply with some minor alterations to accommodate the disability of the players. Officiating is carried out using two referees, adjudicating half a pitch each. The 'off-side' rule does not exist and kick-ins are applied instead of throw-ins. Goalkeepers are not permitted outside the goal area and slide tackling is prohibited. Substitutions are unlimited and any one player can be utilised on several occasions during a game. Finally, both teams can use one 'time out period' in each half lasting 1 min (similar to basketball).

Figure 1.1. Above knee amputation reference to A2 lesion.

Figure 1.2. Congenital arm impairment in a goalkeeper.

Table 1. International game and pitch regulations.

Pitch Trait	Dimension
Length	55–70 m
Width	30–60 m
Goal area	10x6 m
Penalty spot	7 m
Goal height	2.2 m
Goal breath	5 m

The aim of this investigation was to i) quantify the physiological demands of outfield amputee soccer players and ii) analyse responses of players in a tournament context.

2. METHODS

Ten English international outfield amputee players were investigated during all the games in the amputee World Cup (n=7). The mean (SD) age of the subjects was 29 (± 7) years and their mean (SD) body mass was 71.2 (± 13.2) kg. Heart rate (HR) data were collected for all subjects using short-range radio telemetry (Polar, Kempele, Finland) during each half of all seven games.

The World Cup was hosted by Russia in the town of Sochi. Six teams played five games each in a preliminary league. The top four teams competed in the semi-finals, final, and third/fourth place play-off. During England's seven games, recovery HR was recorded at 1, 2, and 5 min after participation. This timing took into consideration the "roll on" "roll off" substitutions and the varying nature of intensity from game to game.

3. RESULTS

Table 2. Players (n=10) mean HR (beats.min^{-1}) over seven games from first and second halves.

Games	First Half	Second Half
1	182	182
2	182	179
3	182	177
4	178	174
5	178	176
6	175	176
7	169	169
SD	4.80	4.60

There was no significant difference found between first and second half in mean HR of the players. The first half produced a mean HR of 178 beats.min^{-1} compared to the 176 beats.min^{-1} of the second half. The data highlight the need for developments in measurement tools that estimate a player's maximal heart rate.

Table 3. Peak heart rate (beats.min^{-1}) following the end of each half of games, compared to maximal value reached in the matches.

	Heart Rate (beats.min^{-1})	
	First Half	Second Half
HRmax	189	186
1 min	167	163
2 min	150	147
5 min	134	135
SD	23.57	22.05

4. DISCUSSION

To understand the nature of amputee soccer it is important to understand the players' physiological responses to the game. Amputee soccer is played at a high intensity with short rest periods. Table 3 indicates that in the first and second half there was only an 11–14% (22–23 beats.min^{-1}) decrease in HRpeak with a 1-min recovery. In contrast, a 2-min recovery produced a 21% (39 beats.min^{-1}) reduction in heart rate after both first and second halves. This observation suggests that not enough time is provided from the players to recuperate for high-intensity play. Nevertheless, Table 2 indicates that the 10-min half time period was sufficient for player recovery, because there is a 29–27% (55–51 beats.min^{-1}) reduction in HR after 5 min of recovery. It is conceivable that a 2-min "time out" period better suits players to recover permitting them to rehydrate and refuel. This intermission should decrease the likelihood of physiological stresses such as heat exhaustion, glycogen depletion and subsequent hypoglycaemia (which was apparent in two English players in the tournament). The heart rates of players during games highlight the high and intense physiological demands that players experience during games.

Table 4. Mean HR of one player over seven games in the amputee World Cup.

Game	HR
1	194
2	188
3	184
4	185
5	184
6	185
7	179
Average	186

The work-rate profile of a player (see Table 4) indicates an average heart rate of 186 beats.min^{-1} over seven games and a HRpeak value of 194 beats.min^{-1}. This indicates the intensity that players perform at during a game. It is clear that in order for this particular player to develop and maintain fitness, the nature of the training or practice games must replicate and at times exceed this intensity.

A number of players achieved between 10 and 20 beats.min^{-1} higher in games, compared to games previously monitored during training sessions. Without a true maximal value obtained in test conditions, it is inappropriate to present a definitive percentage of HRmax in training of international amputee soccer players. Additionally, due to lack of players competing within the English game, it is not possible to compare international and domestic intensity of full 7-a side games.

The seven games were played on consecutive days, and average HR decreased by 13 beats.min^{-1} from 182 to 169 beats.min^{-1} over this time-span of the tournament. The trend suggests that playing seven games on consecutive days leads to a cumulative state of fatigue. This fatigue does not allow players time to recover from game to game, which has detrimental effects on players' performances. As a result of metabolic and neuromuscular strain, the game intensity decreased over the successive games (see Table 4). This resulted in players not performing to their best due to the fatiguing responses that the competition places on the players.

5. CONCLUSION

It is evident from heart rate data that amputee soccer is an intense activity. During the amputee World Cup 2002, players' average heart rates decreased throughout each game. Moreover, players displayed increased signs of fatigue as the tournament progressed. The use of heart rate monitoring proved to be a useful tool for assessing physiological demands on amputee soccer players. Observations from successful games in tournament conditions suggested a cumulative fatigue effect over successive matches. The use of heart rate monitoring in training contexts is recommended, especially to evaluate the physiological similarities of game related drills among this group of players. More detailed research is required to investigate the circulatory responses to intense intermittent exercise.

REFERENCES

Wilson, D. 2002, Sports science support for the England amputee team. *Insight: The F.A. Coaches Association Journal*, **5 (2)**, 31–33.

44   Modelling the Impact of Heading: Influence of Inflation Pressure, Contact Mass, Ball Size and Velocity

Robin M. Harrell, Paul S. Weinhold, Bing Yu and
Donald T. Kirkendall
Department of Orthopaedics, University of North Carolina-Chapel
Hill, Chapel Hill, NC 27599-7055

1. INTRODUCTION

The popularity of soccer brings increased concern about injuries sustained while playing soccer. Soccer is the only sport in which the head is used to gain control of the ball, score goals, and pass the ball between players (Barnes et al., 1998; Baroff, 1998). Head injuries account for between 10% and 13% of all soccer injuries, with concussions accounting for 20% of the head injuries (Tysvaer, 1992; Baroff, 1998; Green and Jordan, 1998; Collins et al., 1999). There are a few possible causes of head injuries in soccer such as unexpected collisions between players, or between the player and another object such as the goal post, ground, or soccer ball, or repetitively heading the soccer ball that could lead to neurocognitive impairment (Jordan et al., 1996; Baroff, 1998; Matser et al., 1998). Some controversy exists in the literature concerning possible neurocognitive impairment in soccer players. Some studies have reported that repeated heading resulted in a decreased score on memory, planning, and IQ (Intelligence Quotient) tests (Tysvaer, 1992 and Matser et al., 1999) while more recent work reports that repeated soccer heading did not lead to a decrease in neurocognitive test scores (Guskiewicz et al., 2002).

Other studies have reported that the impact force from heading could be significantly increased as a result of improper heading technique, which in 32% to 43% of players has been associated with headaches and in some cases has resulted in amnesia (Barnes et al., 1998; Green and Jordan, 1998). Previous studies focused on the effect soccer heading had on adults, not children. When compared to older players, improper heading technique, inexperience and skeletal immaturity may significantly increase the risk of children sustaining head injuries. The purpose of this study was to investigate the effects of contact speed, ball size, inflation pressure, and contacting mass on the estimated peak impact force in purposeful and accidental heading.

2. METHODS

Ball-to-head impact was modeled using the principles of classical elastic theory and the following assumptions: (1) the player's head and the soccer ball were linearly elastic isotropic materials; (2) the contact surface between the two bodies was flat, and (3) the contact duration was long as compared to the natural frequency of the system, hence the system vibrations could be neglected. Our model was based on that of Crisco et al. (1997).

The elastic modulus of the size 3, 4 and 5 soccer balls at 10 psi, 12 psi, and 14 psi were determined from compression tests performed using a 8500 plus servo-hydraulic materials testing system (Instron Corporation, Canton, MA). The compression tests were performed at a deformation rate of 30,000 mm.min^{-1}. The compressive stiffness was calculated as the slope that was tangent to the force-deformation curve at a load level of 450 N. The details of the calculation of the elastic modulus from the compressive stiffness can be found in the literature (Crisco et al., 1997). Head and trunk masses for three age groups (6-9, 10-13 and 14–18 years) were estimated from growth chart data containing children's body weight and height, in conjunction with children's head and trunk anthropometric data (Jensen, 1989)

To determine the effects of the relative velocity of the ball-to-head on the peak impact force and the head injury criteria (HIC), both the peak impact forces and the HIC values were calculated by altering the relative velocity of the ball-to-head from 0.1 m.s^{-1} to 80 m.s^{-1} in increments of 0.1 m.s^{-1}. The head mass was altered from 1.08 kg to 7.88 kg in increments of 0.1 kg, in order to generate a HIC value of 1000 at game velocities. To determine the HIC value and then to determine the safe maximum ball velocity relative to the head (safe velocity is defined below a HIC of 1000), the 50th percentile head mass of the oldest boys and girls and the 50th percentile head mass of the youngest boys and girls in the age group were used. The head-to-ball mass ratio was determined using the head mass at the 50th percentile for a given age group, while the peak impact force was computed for a given ball size at all 3 pressures over a range of ball velocities (0-30 m.s^{-1}). To determine the effect of head mass on the peak impact force, the peak impact force was determined at an inflation pressure of 12 psi over a range of ball velocities (0-30 m.s^{-1}), with the low, middle, and high head masses in each age group. The low, middle, and high head masses in each age group were defined as he 3rd percentile, 50th percentile, and the 97th percentile of the head masses in a given age group.

Finally, intentional heading was defined as heading the ball while the muscles of the neck are contracted so that the ball is effectively the combined mass of the head, the neck and the upper trunk. In order to determine the effect of intentional impacts, the trunk mass was added to the head mass to calculate the HIC values for comparison with the accidental ball-to-head impact with appropriate techniques. The safe velocities for heading were determined by using the 50th percentile head mass and trunk masses of the youngest and oldest boys and girls for each age group.

3. RESULTS

The peak impact force increased as the ball velocity relative to the head increased, in essentially a linear manner (Figure 1). There was a slight increase in the slope of the peak impact force versus ball velocity relative to the head curve as the inflation pressure was increased (Figure 1). The ball inflation pressure effect was more obvious when the ball inflation pressure was increased from 12 psi to 14 psi.

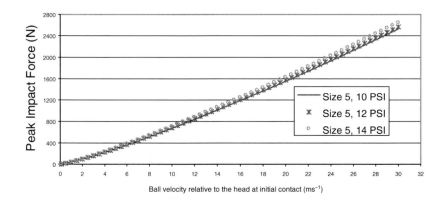

Figure 1. Peak impact force for size 5 ball at different pressures.

We arbitrarily selected a HIC of 1000 as a cut-off for a head injury (Schneider and Zernicke, 1988). For example for boys in the 6–9 year old age group the safe maximum ball velocity relative to the head varied from 8.06 m.s^{-1} to 8.44 m.s^{-1} for the 50th percentile 6 year old and the 50th percentile nine year old, respectively. In the case of the girls in the same age group the safe maximum ball velocity relative to the head varied from 7.87 m.s^{-1} for the 50th percentile 6-year old and 8.44 m.s^{-1} for the 50th percentile 9-year old. Table 1 shows these estimated velocities independent of sex.

The maximum safe velocity was significantly different between accidental impact and intentional heading with appropriate technique (Table 1). The maximum safe ball velocity is relative to the head in accidental impacts and significantly lower than those in intentional heading with appropriate techniques. The safe maximum ball velocities relative to the head increased in accordance with age and as a result the head mass of the player increased, which was consistent for both genders.

Table 1. Estimated ball velocity for an HIC=1000.

Age (years)	H/B mass ratio	Accidental Impact	H+T/B mass ratio	Intentional Impact
6	8.20	7.06 m.s^{-1}	28.71	20.44 m.s^{-1}
9	9.14	7.72 m.s^{-1}	37.90	26.05 m.s^{-1}
10	9.62	8.04 m.s^{-1}	42.14	28.59 m.s^{-1}
13	10.09	8.37 m.s^{-1}	55.10	36.18 m.s^{-1}
14	10.09	8.37 m.s^{-1}	58.40	38.09 m.s^{-1}
18	9.34	7.88 m.s^{-1}	63.59	41.05 m.s^{-1}

*H/B mass ratio=head-to-ball mass ratio (accidental impact).

*H+T/B mass ratio=head+trunk-to-ball mass ratio (intentional impact).

4. DISCUSSION

The results of this study provide significant information for future studies on head injuries in soccer. The results of this study that a change in the inflation pressure between 10 psi and 14 psi has little effect on the peak impact force. The similarity between the peak impact force curves allow the HIC curves to be created using the properties of a 12-psi ball. The results of this study indicate that 18-year old boys can sustain head injuries from accidental ball impact when the ball is traveling close to 9.5 m.s^{-1} and for 18-year old girls injuries can occur at velocities close to 8 m.s^{-1}. In both cases, the velocities are below the reported ball velocities observed in professional (25.60 m.s^{-1}) and unskilled (19.92 m.s^{-1}) soccer games. However, the ball velocities in children's games are not well known, but would be below the reported velocities for both professional and adult players (Levendusky et al., 1988). An important result to emerge from this work is the difference between accidental and intentional impact. By increasing the contacting mass, the risk of head injuries is decreased; hence the player with a prepared head (i.e. neck muscles contracted to fix head to the truck) has less chance of incurring head injuries as compared to the player with an unprepared head. In addition, these results indicate the importance of teaching players to use proper technique when heading the soccer ball, meaning the player should tighten the muscles around the neck and actively head the ball instead of allowing the ball to hit him or her.

This model seemed to be valid as linear head accelerations, impact forces, and estimated impacts were similar to others in the literature (Armstrong et al., 1988; Levendusky et al., 1988; Schneider and Zernicke, 1988; Naunheim et al., 2000).

This study supports results from the area of neurocognitive testing that indicated there was no significant difference between collegiate soccer players and the study controls in term of their results on neurocognitive tests (Putukian et al., 2000; Guskiewicz et al., 2002). It appears that a single impact from heading a soccer ball is not strong enough to cause neurocognitive impairment, which might be inferred from the present study. The mathematical model generated and used for this study only addressed acute injuries and does not consider the problems associated with injuries that could result from repeatedly heading the soccer ball.

Future directions for this research might include the addition of an angular acceleration and rotational head motion into the model to investigate the chances of head injuries under more game like conditions. With the consideration of the angular acceleration of the head, it would be interesting to investigate alternative heading techniques to reduce the risk of head injuries, and to consider if there is an appropriate age for children to begin heading the ball under controlled conditions. Also, more sophisticated models are needed in order to study the cumulative effect of soccer heading and the incidence of head injuries that may result from these repeated impacts.

In conclusion, this study demonstrated that ball size has a significant effect on the peak impact force and the HIC, while the inflation pressure of the ball does not have an effect. Based on these conclusions, children should not head a soccer ball larger than the one for their age group. Finally, there may be an increased risk of sustaining an acute head injury when a head impact is accidental as opposed to when it is intentional.

Acknowledgements

The authors thank Nike, Inc for supplying the balls used in this study. Details on the mathematical details of the method can be obtained by writing to the authors (DTK).

This study funded in part by a grant from Nike, Inc.

REFERENCES

Armstrong, C.W., Levendusky, T. A., Eck, J. S. and Spyropoulos, P., 1988., Influence of inflation pressure and ball wetness on the impact characteristics of two types of soccer balls. In *Science and Football,* edited by Reilly T., Lees, A., Davids K. and Murphy, W.J. (New York, NY, E.& F. N. Spon), pp. 394–398.

Barnes, B.C., Cooper, L., Kirkendall, D.T., McDermott, T.P., Jordan, B.D. and Garrett, W.E., Jr., 1998, Concussion history in elite male and female soccer players. *American Journal of Sports Medicine,* **26**, 433–438.

Baroff, G.S., 1998, Is heading a soccer ball injurious to brain function? *Journal of Head Trauma Rehabilitation,* **13**(2), 45–52.

Collins, M.W., Grindel, S.H., Lovell, M.R., Dede, D.E., Moser, D.J., Phalin, B.R., Nogel, S., Wassik, M., Cordry, D., Daugherty, M.K., Sears, S.F., Nicolette, G., Indelicato, P. and McKeag, D.B., 1999, Relationship between

concussion and neuropsychological performance in College
Journal of the American Medical Association, **28**, 964–970

Crisco, J.J., Hendee, S.P. and Greenwald, R.M., 1997, The infl
modulus and mass on head and chest impacts: a theoretica
and Science in Sports and Exercise, **29**, 26–36.

Green, G.A. and Jordan, S.E., 1998, Are brain injuries a signif
soccer? *Clinics in Sports Medicine,* **17**, 795–809.

Guskiewicz, K.M., Marshall, S.W., Broglio, S.P., Cantu, R.C. and Kirkendall,
D.T., 2002, No evidence of impaired neurocognitive performance in collegiate
soccer players. *American Journal of Sports Medicine,* **30**, 157–162.

Jensen, R., 1989, Changes in segment inertia proportions between 4 and 20 years.
Journal of Biomechanics, **22**, 529–536.

Jordan, S.E., Green, G.A., Galanty, H.L., Mandelbaum, B.R. and Jabour, B.A.,
1996, Acute and chronic brain injury in United States National team soccer
players. *American Journal of Sports Medicine,* **24**, 205–210.

Levendusky, T.A., Armstrong, C.W., Eck, J.S., Jeziorowski, J. and Kugler,
L.,1988, Impact characteristics of two types of soccer balls. In Science and
Football, edited by Reilly, T., Lees, A., Davids, K. and Murphy, W.J.
(New York, NY: E.& F.N. Spon), pp. 385–393.

Matser, J. T., Kessels, A.G., Lezak, M.D., Jordan, B.D. and Troost, J., 1999,
Neuropsychological impairment in amateur soccer players. *Journal of the
American Medical Association,* **28**, 971–973.

Naunheim, R.S., Standeven, J., Richter, C. and Lewis, L.M., 2000, Comparison of
impact data in hockey, football, and soccer. *Journal of Trauma Injury,* **48**,
938–941.

Putukian, M., Echimendea R. and Mackin S., 2000, Acute effects of heading in
soccer: a prospective neuropsychological evaluation. *Clinics in Sports
Medicine,* **10**, 104–109.

Schneider, K. and Zernicke, R.F., 1988, Computer simulation of head impact:
estimation of head-injury risk during soccer heading. *International Journal of
Sports Biomechanics,* **4**, 358–371.

Tysvaer, A.T., 1992, Head and neck injuries in soccer: Impact of minor trauma.
Sports Medicine, **14**, 200–213.

45 Mechanisms and Characteristics of Injuries in Youth Soccer

N. Rahnama[1,2] and L.K. Manning[1]
[1]Research Institute for Sport and Exercise Sciences, Liverpool John Moores University, Liverpool, UK
[2]Physical Education Department, Isfahan University, Isfahan, Iran

1. INTRODUCTION

Soccer is a contact sport and due to the specific mechanics of the game it leads to a relatively high incidence of injuries (17–24 injuries per 1000 playing hours) with injury being defined as 'a lesion which prevents a player from participating in a game or training session' (Ekstrand and Gillquist, 1982). Furthermore, the risk of injury in professional soccer is around 1000 times higher than that observed in other occupations. For example, construction and mining, with 0.02 injuries/1000 hours, are generally regarded as high risk (Health and Safety Commission, 1997). The costs of injuries to soccer players are enormous; the cost of treatment and loss of production through time off work has been estimated at about £1 billion in the United Kingdom each year (Ball, 2000).

It is therefore important, and a legal requirement, for managers of professional soccer clubs to reduce this level of risk wherever possible and to ensure, so far as is reasonably practicable, the health and safety of their players. To assist with this process, medical and coaching staff require detailed knowledge about injury risk associated with different aspects of the game within their own clubs as well as within other clubs for comparative purposes. Few prospective studies have been carried out that both involve junior-professional players and that provide the level of detailed, statistically accurate information on injuries that is required for this purpose.

The aim of this study was to establish the mechanisms and characteristics of injury to male players in an English youth-professional soccer team during competition and training over a period of seven months. This information would allow medical and coaching staff to develop personalised injury prevention strategies.

2. MATERIALS AND METHODS

2.1. Participants

Lost time resulting from injuries to 24 male, youth-professional soccer players was entered into an injury surveillance log-sheet by the club physiotherapist at an English League Academy over the period 01.07.2000 to 01.02.2001. Altogether

43.5 hours of match-play and 364 hours of training were monitored resulting in an overall total of 31 injuries being recorded.

Twenty-four youth-professional soccer players (age 17 ± 0.81 years, height 1.77 ± 0.05 m, body mass 73.4 ± 3.2 kg) were involved in the study. Their playing positions were: - forwards (6), midfield players (5), wingers (2) central defenders (5), full backs (4) and goalkeepers (2). Data included information related to the injury, date and place of occurrence, playing surface conditions, injury diagnosis, severity of injury, mechanism of injury, whether a foul was committed or not. Also, relevant details concerning injury rehabilitation or previous injury were recorded during the 2000–2001 English competitive soccer season. Players also completed a questionnaire containing 27 questions relating to injury prevention practices and advice received on these issues.

2.2. Statistical analysis

The majority of the statistical analysis consisted of using the independent Kruskal-Wallis test to indicate the significance of any difference noted between different groups of variables at the same time. When a significant difference was observed, post-hoc, independent students t-tests were also carried out. The level of significance on all tests was set at $P < 0.05$.

3. RESULTS

Complete responses to the questionnaire were received from 20 players. The main deficiencies identified were related to an appreciation of the benefits of the use of shin pads during training, carbohydrate intake before and after training, cool down after training and matches, and strength and flexibility exercises to reduce the risk of injury.

The overall injury frequency rate was 3.2 injuries per player per 1000 h, with the injury rate during competition (16.3) being higher than that during training (1.3). An average of 19.9 days absence per injury was noted. Moderate injuries (52%) were found to occur more frequently than slight (3%), minor (16%) or major (29%) injuries ($P < 0.05$). Injuries were found to occur more frequently ($P < 0.05$) on pitches of poor (wet/soft or hard/dry) condition (75%) than on pitches of good condition (25%). Only 23.5% of all injuries resulted from foul play, although player-to-player contact was involved in 48% of all injuries identified. Tackling was the most frequent mechanism of injury ($P < 0.05$). Running, striking and turning accounted for 42% of all injuries identified. Strains (29%), sprains (26%) and contusions (29%) represented the major types of injury. The ankle (28%), foot (13%) and hip (13%) represented the major locations of injury. Re-occurrence of injuries accounted for 16% of all injuries. Wingers had the highest ($P < 0.05$) injury rate.

4. DISCUSSION

Injury frequency results support findings by Arnason *et al.* (1996) who reported that youth players (of varying skill levels and ages below 18 years) have an overall injury incidence ranging from 0.5 to 5.6 injuries for each 1000 h of activity. This figure confirms the high risks to which players, especially youth players, are exposed and emphasises the need to reduce this risk by introducing prevention strategies based on personal injury data.

Hunt and Fulford (1990) reported that players directly involved in attack or defence are most likely to be injured. This finding was confirmed by the high injury frequency noted amongst wingers in this current investigation. Reilly and Thomas (1976) demonstrated that in competitive professional football, midfielders are responsible for covering the greatest overall distance among outfield players during match play. Wingers, however, were not analysed in their study and as these players combine attacking and defensive findings, they may have a high overall work-rate. The work-rate, i.e. distance covered, and player profile of each academy squad player in relation to injury frequency warrant further investigation.

The large injury risk associated with player-to-player contact gives some cause for concern. Questions should be raised about whether the amount of allowable contact between players should be reviewed and whether minor changes to the laws of the game could reduce injury. Competent and responsible officiating is one of the major factors in controlling practices which may contribute to injury.

A soccer player spends large quantities of time running as well as having frequent contact with other players; thus, the value of optimum footwear and protective equipment in injury prevention has been stressed. Shin-guards, shoes and insoles are important items of equipment in soccer. It has been demonstrated that shock-absorbent, anatomically shaped shin guards, protecting a large area of the lower leg, can prevent injuries to the shin in soccer players (Ekstrand, 1982).

The stiffness properties of a playing surface have an influence on some chronic overuse injuries as shown in this study. Clubs must ensure that playing surfaces are in good condition and do not pose undue hazards to the players from unseen objects, uneven playing surfaces, and inadequate safety margins around fields. Surfaces which are too dry/hard or too soft/wet should be regarded as high risk and training or match-play should not be allowed to take place in such conditions.

Ekstrand and Gillquist (1982) have discussed the relation between muscle tightness and a player's propensity for muscle strains. They showed the benefits of warm-up and cool-down programmes for reducing muscle tightness and the number of muscle strains. Since the majority of soccer injuries affect the lower extremities, stretching exercises for the leg muscles (adductors, hamstrings, quadriceps, iliopsoas and triceps surae) must be included in warm-up and cool-down regimens. Players with muscle tightness can be detected by measurements of range of motion during pre-season examinations and individual stretching exercises should be recommended.

It is possible that the attention paid to general body co|
and flexibility training) in English clubs is less than that founc
clubs, thus making players at these clubs more liable to muscl|
1994). Injury prevention in soccer requires competent coaching
sound conditioning and training techniques with the teaching o
in the various facets of the game.

5. CONCLUSIONS

Detailed analysis of injury causation is essential for the successful development of specified injury prevention strategies. More efficient implementation of injury prevention strategies by coaching and medical staff of football clubs should lead to a greater reduction in injury and optimise the health, safety and welfare of professional soccer players, which remains the ultimate goal.

REFERENCES

Arnason, A., Gudmundsson, A. and Dahl, H.A., 1996, Soccer injuries in Iceland. Scandinavian Journal of Medicine and Science in Sports, **6**, 40–5.

Ball, D.J., 2000, Risks of injury: an overview. In ABC of Sports Medicine, edited by Harries, M., McLatchie, G., Williams, C. and King, J. (London: BMJ Books), pp. 88–91.

Bangsbo, J., 1994, Fitness Training in Football: a Scientific Approach, (Bagsvaerd: HO + Storm).

Ekstrand, J., 1982, Soccer injuries and their prevention. Linkoping University Medical Dissertations, no 130, Linkoping, Sweden.

Ekstrand, J. and Gillquist, J., 1982, The frequency of muscle tightness and injuries in soccer players. *American Journal of Sports Medicine*, **10**, 75–88.

Health and Safety Commission, 1997, Health and safety statistics: statistical supplement to the 1996/1997 annual report. (London: HMSO).

Hunt, M. and Fulford, S., 1990, Amateur soccer; injuries in relation to field position. *British Journal of Sports Medicine,* **24**, 265.

Reilly, T. and Thomas, V., 1976, A motion analysis of work rate in different positional roles in professional football match-play. *Journal of Human Movement Studies*, **2**, 87–97.

Injury Incidence in Youth Soccer: Age and Sex-Related Patterns

Donald T. Kirkendall, Patricia M. Marchak and
William E. Garrett, Jr.
Duke University Medical Center Durham, NC 27710 and
The Department of Orthopaedics University of North Carolina
Chapel Hill, NC 27599

1. INTRODUCTION

It is estimated that there are nearly 3 million youth (under 19 years of age) registered players in the United States as of 1998 (J. Cosgrove, US Youth Soccer Association, personal communication) and this figure represents a 235% increase since 1980 (Soccer Industry Council of America, personal communication). The Council survey of all soccer participation in 1996 showed that there are 7.7 million frequent (>25 and less than 52 days/year) of which there are 3.2 million "core" (>52 days/year) participants. In the youngest ages (6–11 years of age), participation in soccer ranks 2nd and ranks 3rd for older children (12–18 years of age).

Our purpose was to attempt to determine the typical injuries that are seen in competitive youth soccer. Injuries from 3 consecutive years of highly competitive youth (U12-U18) soccer in North Carolina were reported by the team coach or manager. Multiple years removed the limitation of a single season or single tournaments. This statewide survey offered significant numbers of players and injuries reported by the team allowed us to collect data on minor injuries that might be missed in insurance claim or emergency department data. By following a wide range of youth ages and both genders, our data should be applicable to a large spectrum of the soccer playing community.

2. METHODS

The North Carolina Youth Soccer Association (NCYSA) oversees soccer in the following primary levels: recreational, Challenge (1st level of travelling play), Classic (highest level of travelling play), and the Olympic Development Program (the highest calibre statewide team). The Medical Center Institutional Review Board approved the project. Operational definitions for this project are contained in Table 1.

Table 1. Operational definitions.

Reportable Injury	Any injury that requires the player to be removed from play. There were no constraints on time out of play.
Body Categories	Head (includes scalp or global head injuries such as concussion) Face (includes cheek, nose), Eyes, Mouth/jaw/teeth (collectively), neck, clavicle, shoulder, upper arm, elbow, lower arm, wrist, hand/fingers, chest, back, trunk, abdomen, hip/pelvis, groin, front thigh, back thigh, knee, patella, leg/shin/calf, ankle, foot, toes, other (e.g. asthma, cramps, heat illness)
Exposure	Any coach-directed session (practice or game) where the athlete was exposed to the opportunity for injury. A practice exposure was any training session. A game exposure was any competitive match. An athletic exposure was all practice and game exposures.
Type of Injury	Contusion, sprain, strain, fracture, overuse, cartilage damage dislocation, laceration/abrasion, other
Season	From the first day of training through the last scheduled league game/tournament. Games outside of the season (i.e. summer tournaments) were not included in the study.

Each season, a player must register with the NCYSA. Each coach/team manager received a detailed description of the project that outlined their responsibilities plus a set of injury reporting cards. Each week during the Classic season, the coach/team manager was to return a card stating which player had been injured that week, what body part was injured, whether the injury occurred during practice or a game, and the player's home phone number. A card was to be returned even if no injuries had occurred. This card was to accompany the game report that was returned to the NCYSA each week.

A season was defined as all practices and Classic league games/tournaments. Summer tournaments outside of the State-directed Classic season were not considered. The annual playing year for the NCYSA is August to May. The fall season began in late August and concluded in November. The spring season began in February and concluded in May. Players were registered according to age into U12, U13, U14, U15, U16, U17, and U18 age groups based on birth year at the start of the season. The U12-U14 boys and girls played both a fall and spring season, therefore, the fall and spring seasons were considered as separate seasons. If reports were obtained from a team both seasons, the team was 'counted' twice, but if a team sent in reports for one season, but not the other, that team was 'counted' only once. The U15-U18 boys played a single spring season to avoid conflicts with their fall scholastic season. The U15-U18 girls played a single fall season to avoid conflicts with their spring scholastic season. Each season, a stratified random sample representing 20% of the teams (within age group and sex) was selected to record practice and game exposures.

The data were recorded according to player, date of injury, player age, sex, site of injury and type of injury (if reported). Routine descriptive statistics and contingency tables summarized the data. Injury rates and 95% confidence intervals were determined per 1000 practice-exposures (PE), per 1000 game-exposures (GE) and per 1000 athletic-exposures (AE).

3. RESULTS

There were 1233 team-seasons during the 3-year study with a total of 18,924 player-seasons (table 2). Not all teams reported to us, so we obtained data on a total of 756 team-seasons and 11,580 player-seasons. Altogether 1810 injuries were reported. Based on the gross injury rate (#/100 players) the injury rate for girls was 23% greater than the injury rate for boys (Table 2).

Table 2. General participation data.

	Male	Female	Male	Female
Team seasons	504	252	836	397
Player seasons	7589	3991	12644	6280
Reported injuries	1098	712		
Injury rate/100 players	14.47	17.84		
IRR*	1.23			

team seasons = the total number of teams for the 3 years.
player seasons = the total number of players for the 3 years.
injury rate/100 players = reported injuries/number of player-seasons multiplied by 100.
*Injury rate ratio (IRR) = the injury rate for girls/injury rate for boys.

Table 3 indicates the fraction of total injuries by anatomical location of injury and gender for the 10 most frequent locations of injury. With minor differences, the rank order of injuries was similar for both males and females. The top 4 locations accounted for over 50% of all injuries.

Table 3. Percentage of all injuries by location and gender.

	Males %	Females %	Overall %
Ankle	22.02	29.00	24.65
Knee	15.30	16.29	15.67
Leg.shin/calf	9.29	6.95	8.41
Head	6.13	7.15	6.52
Foot	6.25	3.77	5.32
Face/nose	5.60	3.87	4.95
Front thigh	4.35	3.97	4.21
Wrist	4.05	3.97	4.02
Back	3.69	4.37	3.95
Hand/fingers	3.10	3.38	3.20

Table 4 is the summary of injury rates per 1000 practice, game, and athletic exposures by sex and age group. Overall, the rate of game injury was 18.2 and 10.3 times the practice injury rate in females and males, respectively. When looking just at the injury rates for females, there appears to be an increase in injury rate from the U12 to the U13 age group, then the rates stay relatively constant for practices, games and overall. For males, the practice, games and overall injury rates are fairly constant for all age groups.

Table 4. Injury rate (95% confidence intervals) by gender, play setting and age group.

	Females		Males	
	/1000GE	/1000AE	/1000GE	/1000AE
U12	6.32 (4.39-8.26)	2.92 (2.09-3.77)	10.13 (8.49-11.78)	4.54 (3.84-5.25)
U13	11.18 (9.55-14.26)	5.25 (4.52-6.58)	9.83 (8.40-11.27)	4.39 (3.77-5.00)
U14	13.99 (11.62-16.36)	6.66 (5.62-7.71)	11.65 (10.30-13.00)	5.23 (4.65-5.82)
U15	9.11 (6.28-9.96)	4.3 (3.23-4.96)	10.08 (8.56-11.60)	4.39 (3.75-5.04)
U16	10.17 (8.17-12.18)	4.61 (3.75-5.48)	8.33 (6.89-9.79)	3.68 (3.06-4.29)
U17	12.17 (9.57-14.77)	6.08 (4.91-7.27)	7.32 (5.83-8.80)	3.27 (2.63-3.91)
U18	12.14 (9.80-14.48)	5.44 (4.43-6.44)	9.73 (7.37-12.10)	4.19 (3.20-5.19)
Overall	9.81	4.16	10.89	5.08

PE=practice exposures, GE=game exposures, AE=overall athlete exposures.

Another way to look at injury rates is the injury rate per team per season (e.g. "How many ankle injuries am I likely to see in a season?"). Table 5 lists these rates by injury location and sex. The column labelled incidence rate ratio shows the ratio of female injuries/male injuries. A ratio of 1.0 indicates a similar injury rate. Ratios below 1.0 indicate the injury rate for males exceed that of females, while the converse is true for ratios above 1.0. Using this method of looking at differences in injury rates between males and females, it appears that the rate of injury for females is 13% greater than the injury rate for males.

Table 5. Injury rates (#/team-season) by injury location and sex.

	Injury/team-season		
	Males	Females	IRR*
Ankle	0.78	1.16	1.49
Knee	0.54	0.65	1.21
Leg: shin/calf	0.33	0.28	0.85
Head	0.22	0.29	1.32
Foot	0.22	0.15	0.68
Face/nose	0.20	0.16	0.78
Front thigh	0.15	0.16	1.03
Wrist	0.14	0.16	1.11
Back	0.13	0.18	1.34
ALL INJURIES	3.54	4.01	1.13

*IRR=Injury Rate Ratio (Female rate/Male rate).

Table 6 lists the injury rates (per 1000 exposures) by anatomical location, gender, and setting (game or practice). To demonstrate the relative increase in injury rate between the (safer) practices and the (riskier) games, the game rate is divided by the practice rate. For example, in males, the risk of a game-related knee injury in males is 25 times that of a practice-related knee injury while for females, the risk is a factor of 10. An incidence rate ratio for games and practices is also included in the table. For game-related knee injuries, the females carry a 124% increased risk, but a 300% risk of a practice-related injury.

Table 6. Injury rates (per 1000 exposures) of the 10 most frequent injuries by anatomical location, gender and setting (game or practice).

	Males			Females			IRR*	
	Game	Practice	G/P*	Game	Practice	G/P*	Game	Practice
Ankle	2.04	0.14	14.42	3.38	0.29	11.61	1.66	2.06
Knee	1.64	0.06	25.43	2.03	0.19	10.45	1.24	3.02
Leg/shin/calf	0.78	0.17	4.67	0.83	0.07	11.43	1.06	0.43
Head	0.60	0.11	5.46	0.90	0.05	18.57	1.51	0.44
Foot/toes	0.70	0.15	4.52	0.54	0.11	4.92	0.77	0.71
Face/nose	0.48	0.13	3.71	0.40	0.00		0.83	0
Wrist	0.40	0.02	20.48	0.43	0.01	35.71	1.1	0.63
Front thigh	0.36	0.06	6.19	0.43	0.07	5.95	1.21	1.26
Back thigh	0.22	0.05	4.90	0.21	0.07	2.86	0.94	1.62
Back	0.43	0.03	16.79	0.47	0.05	9.64	1.08	1.88

*IRR = Female rate/Male rate; G/P = game rate / practice rate

Tables 7 and 8 show the injury rates by anatomical location for males and females by age group. Pick any anatomical location and observe the change in rate with age. As the vast majority of the reported injuries were in games, only the game rate is reported here.

Table 7. Injury rates (per 1000 game-exposures) of the 10 most frequent injury locations by age group, and setting in males.

	u12	u13	u14	u15	u16	u17	u18
	Game	Game	Game	Game	Game	Game	Game
Ankle	2.08	1.20	2.20	2.27	2.04	2.20	2.85
Knee	1.67	1.86	1.63	1.61	1.51	1.26	2.10
Leg/shin/calf	0.62	1.09	1.26	0.36	0.72	0.31	0.60
Head	0.62	0.71	0.69	0.66	0.66	0.31	0.15
Foot/toes	0.14	0.98	0.61	0.90	0.46	0.63	1.65
Face/nose	0.49	0.77	0.45	0.60	0.20	0.47	0.15
Wrist	0.28	0.44	0.65	0.42	0.33	0.16	0.15
Front thigh	0.35	0.33	0.53	0.54	0.20	0.16	0.15
Back thigh	0.28	0.22	0.29	0.12	0.00	0.31	0.45
Back	0.35	0.22	0.77	0.54	0.26	0.39	0.15

Table 8. Injury rates (per 1000 exposures) of the 10 most frequent injury locations by age group, and setting in females.

| | U12 | U13 | u14 | u15 | u16 | u17 | u18 |
	Game	Game	Game	Game	Game	Game	Game
Ankle	1.85	3.40	2.72	3.04	3.70	5.65	3.42
Knee	1.54	1.46	1.98	0.97	2.26	2.75	3.18
Leg/shin/calf	0.31	1.34	1.36	0.61	0.10	1.01	1.06
Head	0.31	0.97	1.88	0.61	0.62	0.72	0.94
Foot/toes	0.31	0.36	0.94	0.61	0.51	0.43	0.47
Face/nose	0.31	0.49	0.52	0.12	0.62	0.14	0.47
Wrist	0.77	0.85	0.63	0.12	0.31	0.43	0.00
Front thigh	0.31	0.36	0.84	0.12	0.41	0.14	0.71
Back thigh	0.00	0.00	0.31	0.12	0.31	0.00	0.59
Back	0.00	0.36	0.94	0.85	0.21	0.58	0.24

4. DISCUSSION

This project was unique in a number of ways. First, we chose a liberal definition of 'injury' that should be more applicable to the practicing coach. When a situation occurs and the player has to leave the field, the coach considers the player 'injured'. Many other publications use more conservative definitions of injury such as time lost or an insurance claim.

Second, our anatomical breakdown was more detailed than most studies. We may understate injuries when comparing rates between studies when other studies combine body parts leading to a greater injury rate. For example, if we calculate the gross injury rate (injuries/100 players seasons) for ankle/foot injuries by Powell and Barber-Foss (2000), that rate would be 9.03 whereas our rate of ankle injuries alone would be 4.9.

Third, we chose to study this wide age range of youth, but a wide range of ages has been reported in the literature. This makes generalization of injury frequencies fairly strong. Trying to extrapolate from professional athletes (as reported in Ekstrand and Tropp, 1990; Hawkins and Fuller, 1996; Hawkins and Fuller, 1998) to youth is tenuous at best.

In studies where game and practice injury rates are calculated, the game injury rate always exceeds the practice injury rate. Competition is more intense, at a faster pace potentially leading to higher force collisions.

The data from some studies allow for gender comparisons to be made. Again, using a very gross statement of rate, injuries/player (#injuries/#player-seasons) or rates/1000 player-hours, the rate of injury for females exceeds that of males. In this project, the injury/player rate was over 25% greater in females than in males.

Table 6 also lists an injury rate ratio (IRR) for the female rate divided by the male rate for both practices and games. The game IRR ranges from a low of 0.25 (groin) to 2.96 (chest), but if these two extremes are ignored, the IRR ranges from a low of 0.69 (shoulder) to a high of 1.88 (elbow). The IRR from practices differs with a low of 0.38 (shoulder) to a high of 3.02 (knee), suggesting that females have a three-fold risk of injuring a knee in training than do males and a 2-fold risk of injuring an ankle.

These data are not specific diagnoses. A knee injury means that the knee sustained some injury be it a sprain, contusion and so on. A head injury does not mean concussion. The reading and interpretation of these data, as well as data in the literature, are limited to overall rates of injury to a location and not a rate of a specific diagnosis.

A common perception has been that the incidence of injury increases as the age of the player increases. Our data suggest that this may be the case in females as the injury rate increases from 12 to 13 year old players, but then is somewhat stable for the subsequent years. The rate for boys is fairly stable, with some variation, throughout the age ranges reported. By combining these data with the literature, it appears that the increase in injury rate is more likely to occur when players move up in competitive class, not just by becoming older. However, Backous et al. (1988) pointed out that the most likely candidate for injury in males is the tall, weak player whose muscular development has not yet caught up with linear growth - a maturation factor somewhat age-dependent.

Our project does have some limitations. First, we did not have reporting on all teams. Second, the person recording the injury was probably not a health care professional. Third, comparisons between studies are difficult as different rate denominators are used. Fourth, studies like this tend to focus on acute injuries. Overuse injuries may be diagnosed by a physician, but may not be sufficient to remove a player from play; therefore, injuries of overuse can be underestimated. Finally, our estimates of the type of injury (sprain, strain, etc.) were made from either the injury reporting card or phone call with the player. As not all injury types were reported on the cards, and not all injured athletes were reached by telephone, the spectrum of injuries may not be fully representative of what actually occurred.

Our data indicate that the injury rate in greater than that reported in studies of multiple age and skill levels of soccer, but less than that reported in highly competitive and professional athletes. Games are far more risky than training and females have a greater risk of injury than males. Over half of the injuries to females occur from the knee to the foot while males add injuries to the head to this list. From a practical standpoint, coaches and team officials should be educated about and prepared to deal with acute injuries to the lower leg and head.

In summary, we show that nearly 2/3 of all injuries in this level of youth player is between the knee and the foot plus the head and that for most injuries, females have a greater rate of injury than males and that games carry to most risk.

Acknowledgements

A study of this breadth could not be completed without the assistance of many colleagues. We acknowledge the administration of the NCYSA (Kathy Robinson-president, Tom Mosier-database manager, Rachael Jones-administrative assistant, and Mark Moore-Classic program coordinator). All of the Classic team coaches and administrators are to be thanked. We asked a lot of them and they performed very well. This work would not have been completed without their help.

At the K Lab, data collection and reduction were assisted by Tony Francisco, Kyle Leonard, Uttama Sharma, Jason Hurst, Trina Sanatmauro, Wesley Dowd, and Scott Colby. Dr. Steven W. Marshall of the Injury Prevention Research Center at the University of North Carolina was instrumental in the statistical summary. Erez Morag and Mario LaFortune of the Nike Sport Research Lab were advisors in the design, development and conduct of this project.

This project was funded by a grant from NIKE, Inc.

REFERENCES

Backous, D.D., Friedl K.E., Smith, N.J., Parr, T.J. and Carpine, Jr., W.D., 1988, *Soccer injuries and their relation to physical maturity.* American Journal of Diseases of Children, **142**, 839–842.

Ekstrand, J. and Tropp, H., 1990, *The incidence of ankle sprains in soccer.* Foot & Ankle, **11**, 41–44.

Hawkins, R.D. and Fuller, C.W., 1996, *Risk assessment in professional football: an examination of accidents and incidents in the 1994 World Cup finals.* British Journal of Sports Medicine, **30**, 165–170.

Hawkins, R.D. and Fuller, C.W., 1998, *An examination of the frequency and severity of injuries and incidents at three levels of professional football.* British Journal of Sports Medicine, **32**, 326–332.

Powell, J.W. and Barber-Foss, K.D., 2000, *Sex-related injury patterns among selected high school sports.* American Journal of Sports Medicine, **28**, 385–391.

47   Balance Exercises Reduce Lower Extremity Injuries in Young Soccer Players

G. Pafis, A. Gioftsidou, P. Malliou, A. Beneka, I. Ispirlidis
and G. Godolias
Department of Physical Education and Sports Science, Democritus
University of Thrace, Komotini, Greece.

1. INTRODUCTION

In soccer, musculo-skeletal injuries to the lower limb are frequently observed, although soccer represents one of the most popular sports. Sixty-eight to 88% of all soccer injuries involve the lower extremity, especially the knee and ankle (Heidt *et al.*, 2000). The incidence of soccer injuries in adult male players is estimated to be 10 to 35 per 1000 game hours (Dvorak, 2000).

With respect to the incidence of injuries, many studies have been carried out to determine the injury patterns in soccer, but only a few have been undertaken prospectively in young players. Nilsson and Roaas (1978) found the incidence of injury in boys to be 14 injuries per 1000 hours of tournament play. Most injuries involved the lower extremities, especially the knee and ankle (Tucker, 1997). Only a few of them were severe. Also, Nielsen and Yde (1989) reported that the incidence of injury in adolescent players is similar to that of senior players.

Muscular imbalances between hamstrings and quadriceps muscles are thought to be possible factors contributing to injury (Hewett *et al.*, 1999), meaning that strengthening of those muscles must be emphasised in order to prevent many lower-limb injuries (Fried and Lloyd, 1992). Similar results were reported by Cometti *et al* (2001): they found that hamstring strength in soccer players is extremely important in joint stabilisation during various tasks. Also, muscle tightness and loss of flexibility have been mentioned as predictive factors for injuries in soccer (Inklaar, 1994).

Proprioception is an important element of both static and dynamic balance, which are determining factors for preventing injuries in soccer (Barret et al., 1991; Aune *et al.* 1995). Proprioception may be defined as the ability to acquire information from muscle spindles, tendon organs, and joint receptors and to convey this information to the central nervous system (Irrgang *et al.*, 1994). This means that proprioception is the awareness of posture, movement and changes in equilibrium as well as the knowledge of position, weight, and resistance to objects in relation to the body (Davies, 1989).

Balance exercises have been used for lower extremity proprioception testing and training. The ability to quantify balance would help the clinician in objectively determining proprioception deficits (Andrews *et al.*, 1998).

It is frequently reported that athletes with poor postural control are more prone to injuries (Hoffman and Payne, 1995). Training on specially designed plates enables injured and non-injured subjects to improve proprioception and increase postural control (Gauffin et al., 1988; Hoffman and Payne 1995). Numerous studies have been carried out using force-plate balance testing to determine a quantitative measure of postural equilibrium. Patients with functional instability have been found to have significant deficits in balance compared to controls (Osborne *et al.*, 2001). Therefore, a decrease in all types of injuries but especially of the lower extremities, may be expected after specific training of proprioception, balance and functional strength.

Some studies report the use of a proprioceptive training programme to assist in the rehabilitation of the proprioceptive mechanism to minimise coordination problems (Freeman *et al.*, 1965; Tropp *et al.*, 1984; Tropp *et al.*, 1985; Gauffin et al., 1988). The results were associated with low injuries occurrence and research has suggested that during ankle disk coordination training, damaged afferent joint receptors are possibly re-educated while the muscles may be strengthened (Glencross and Thornton, 1982). Also many authors reported that balance measurement is serving as a predictor of ankle sprain (McGuine *et al.*, 2000). More specifically Lephart *et al.* (1998) reported that proprioception may play an important role in preventing acute injuries. Furthermore, they mentioned that the incidence of re-injury and the cause of chronic injuries may be attributed, to a greater extent, to proprioceptive deficits.

The aim of the present study was to investigate the effect of a balance training programme on proprioception ability of young soccer players, as a means of preventing lower limb injuries.

2. METHODS

The sample of the study comprised of 50 young soccer players (age: 16.8±0.9, mass: 64.77±6.34, height: 1.75±0.064 m), from two different teams, playing in the first Greek division (2001–2002 championship). One team was the experimental group (N=25), and the other the control group (Table 1) (n=25). The experimental group followed a gradually increasing proprioceptive training programme of 20 minutes, 3 times per week for 3 months. The programme included balance exercises performed: a) on a "Biodex Stability System" balance device, b) on a mini trampoline and c) on balance boards. More specifically, the soccer players were trying to maintain their balance while they were performing soccer agility exercises. The control group did not participate in any proprioception training programme.

Before the beginning of the training period, the balance ability was evaluated using tests performed on the balance device (Biodex Stability System) and on balance boards. Two different tests were performed on the balance device: a) the "static" test, where the dependent variables were the Stability Indices (Anterior-Posterior, Medial-Lateral and Total) which represented the variance of platform displacement in degrees from the initial level, and b) the "dynamic" test, where the dependent variable was the time needed to complete a dynamic agility (achieve the targets).

For the balance boards tests, two different kind of boards were used. The dependent variable was the time that balance was maintained (for the Anterior-Posterior, Medial-lateral motion and Total). Balance was defined as the ability of the subject to maintain equilibrium while keeping the board from contacting the ground.

All the tests were performed: 1) before the beginning of the training programme (initial measures), 2) after 45 days of training (intermediate measures), 3) after 90 days of training (final measures) and 4) 45 days after the completion of the intervention programme (maintenance measures). Repeated measures ANOVA was used in order to determine possible statistically significant differences among the four measurement times and between the experimental and control group. Also chi squared (X^2) was used to check the differences between the injury rates. The level of statistical significance was set at $P<0.05$.

Table 1. Age and the anthropometric characteristics of subjects.

Athletes characteristics	Experimental Group (n=25)	Control Group (n=25)
Age (years)	16.7 (±0.5)	16.9 (±0.7)
Mass (kg)	65.94 (±7.9)	63.50 (±5.3)
Height (m)	1.77 (±4.13)	1.73 (±0.073)

3. RESULTS

According to the results, the incidence rate through the 12-month period involved mild injuries of 78%, moderate injuries 11% and major injuries 11% for the experimental group and for the control group 63%, 24% and 13% respectively (Table 2). The experimental group reported 30 lower limb injuries and the control group 44 injuries for the 12-month period (Table 3).

Comparing the initial performance with the other three measurements for the experimental group, improvements appeared in all dependent variables for the tests performed on the balance system and those performed on balance boards (Table 4, 5).

Table 2. Severity of injuries reported.

Rate (cases)	Mild	Moderate*	Major
Experimental	78% (24)	11%(3)	11%(3)
Control	63% (28)	24%(11)	13%(5)

* statistically significant differences between adult - young soccer players

Table 3. Lower limb injuries reported for the 12-month period.

	Experimental	Control
Hamstring strains	4	4
Ankle sprains	11	19
Adductors strains	5	4
Knee ligament strains	7	14
Quadriceps strain	3	3

Table 4. Balance stability indices for the two groups through Stability System measurements.

	Initial	Inter/te	Final	Maintenance
Total Index (°) Control	7.9±3.2	7.7±3.2	7.8±3.2	7.9±3.8
Experimental	8.1±3.5	5.2±2.1*	5.1±1.9***	5.2±2.2**
A-P Index (°) Control	6.7±3.1	6.4±3.1	6.5±3.1	6.8±3.1
Experimental	6.9±3.2	3.8±1.7*	3.8±1.7***	4.2±1.9**
M-L Index(°) Control	3.9±1.5	4.1±1.5	3.6±1.5	3.8±1.5
Experimental	4.2±1.7	3.6±1.4*	3.2±1.1***	3.5±1.2**
1st target (s) Control	12.8±4	11.5±3	12.2±4	12.6±4
Experimental	13.8±5	10.3±4*	7.5±1.7***	8.7±1.7**
6st target (s) Control	70.3±8	69.3±9	77.1±8	67.3±9
Experimental	67.8±8	51.3±14*	43.7±5***	47.5±9**

Table 5. Time of balance for the two groups through balance-board measurements.

		Initial	Inter/te	Final	Maintenance
Total(s)	Control	2.3±1.2	2.4±1.3	2.5±1.3	2.5±1.2
	Experimental	2.4±1.2	4.1±0.6*	4.3±1.3***	4.1±1.7**
A-P (s)	Control	2.9±1.4	2.6±1.4	2.7±1.5	2.6±1.7
	Experimental	2.8±1.1	7.5±4.4*	9.6±6.9***	8.7±2.3**
M-L (s)	Control	2.6±1.3	2.9±1.3	2.7±1.3	2.6±1.5
	Experimental	2.6±1.1	18.9±7*	18±13***	12.2±4**

* $P<0.05$ **$P<0.01$ ***$P<0.001$

4. DISCUSSION

The results of this study suggest that the balance training protocol used in this study is an effective means of improving proprioception ability, as assessed through single-leg standing ability and reduction of lower limb injury rates.

Similarly, Carrafa *et al.* (1996) in a prospective controlled study of 600 soccer players in 40 semi-professional or amateur teams, studied the possible preventive effect of a gradually increasing proprioceptive training on four different types of wobble-board during three soccer seasons. Three hundred players were instructed to train 20 min per day with 5 different phases of increasing difficulty. The first phase consisted of balance training without any balance board; phase 2 was training on a rectangular balance board; phase 3 consisted of training on a round board; phase 4 was training on a combined round and rectangular board; phase 5 comprised of training on a so-called BAPS board. A control group of 300 players from other, comparable teams trained "normally" and received no special balance training. They found an incidence of 1.15 ACL injuries per team per year in the proprioceptively trained group (P<0.001). The authors concluded that proprioceptive training can significantly reduce the incidence of ACL injuries in soccer players, being in accordance with the results of the present study.

In contrast, Soderman *et al.* (2000) showed no significant differences between soccer players who applied 10–15 min balance-board training and the control group with respect either to the number, incidence, or type of traumatic injuries of the lower extremities. However, the participants in this study were exercising at home, and not in a controlled environment like in the present study. This may provide evidence that the efficiency of the programme applied may be dependent on the place where it is developed.

Heidtkamp *et al.* (2001) studied the isolated effect of balance training on muscle strength of the flexors and extensors of the knee. They concluded that balance training might be an important factor for preventing injuries. The results indicated balance training to be effective in gaining muscular strength, and that, in contrast to strength training, equalisation of muscular imbalances may be achieved after balance training.

Another prospective study regarding injury prevention and balance training was conducted with volleyball players in Norway. The authors applied an injury prevention programme, and demonstrated a substantial decrease in the incidence of ankle sprains with no change in the occurrence of other injuries. The interventions focused on the prevention of ankle sprains, including a 1-hour didactic session on risk factors, treatment, rehabilitation, and ankle disk training, and a 2-hours training session on the ankle disk and safe side-to-side and take-off techniques (Bahr *et al.,* 1997).

5. CONCLUSION

Considering the global results of the present study, we propose to include a sport specific balance training as a part of the normal soccer training programme, in order to improve the proprioception ability and prevent lower limb injuries.

REFERENCES

Andrews, J.M., Harrelson, G.L. and Wilk, K.E., 1998, Physical Rehabilitation of the Injured Athlete. (Philadelphia: W.B. Saunders Company, Second Edition).

Aune, A.K., Nordsletten, L., Skjeldal, S., Madsen, E. and Edeland, A., 1995, Hamstrings and gastrocnemius co-contraction protects the anterior crucuate ligament against failure: an in vivo study in the rat. *Journal of Orthopaedic Research*, **13**, 147–150.

Bahr, R., Lian, O. and Bahr, I.A., 1997, A twofold reduction in the incidence of acute ankle sprains in volleyball after the introduction of an injury prevention program: A prospective cohort study. *Scandinavian Journal of Medicine Science and Sports*, **7**, 172–177.

Barrett, D.S., Cobb, A.G. and Bentley, G., 1991, Proprioception and function after anterior cruciate reconstruction. *Journal of Bone and Joint Surgery*, **73B**, 833–837.

Caraffa, A., Cerulli, G., Projetti, M., Aisa, G. and Rizzo, A., 1996, Prevention of anterior cruciate ligament injuries in soccer. A prospective controlled study of proprioceptive training. *Knee Surgery Sports Traumatology Arthroscopy*, **4** (1), 19–21.

Cometti, G., Maffiuletti, N.A., Pousson, M., Chatard, J.C. and Maffulli, N., 2001, Isokinetic strength and anaerobic power of elite, subelite and amateur French soccer players. *International Journal of Sports Medicine*, **22**, 45–51.

Davies, C., 1989, *Taber's Encylopedic Medical Dictionary* (16th ed, F.A Davies Company).

Dvorak, J., 2000, Football injuries and physical symptoms. *American Journal of Sports Medicine*, **28**(5), 69–74.

Freeman, M., Dean, M. and Hanham, I., 1965, The etiology and prevention of functional instabilities of the foot. *Journal of Bone and Joint Surgery*, **47B**, 678–685.

Fried, T. and Lloyd, G.J., 1992, An overview of common soccer injuries: Management and prevention. *Sports Medicine*, **14**, 269–275.

Gauffin, H., Tropp, H. and Odenrick, P., 1988, Effect of ankle disk training on postural control in patients with functional instabilities of the ankle joint. *International Journal of Sports Medicine*, **9**, 141–144.

Glencross, D. and Thornton, E., 1982, Position sense following joint injury. *Journal of Sports Medicine*, **21**, 23–27.

Heidt, R.S, Sweeterman, L.M, Carlonas, R.L, Traub, J.A. and Tekulve, F.X., 2000, Avoidance of soccer injuries with preseason conditioning. *American Journal of Sports Medicine*, **28**, 659–662.

Heitdkamp, H.C., Horstmann, T., Mayer, F., Weller, J. and Dickhuth, H.H., 2001, Gain in strength and muscular balance after balance training. *International Journal of Sports Medicine*, **22**, 285–290.

Hewett, T.E., Lindenfeld, T.N., Riccobene, J.V. and Noyes, F.R., 1999, The effect of neuromuscular training of the incidence of knee injury in female athletes. *American Orthopaedic Society for Sports Medicine*, **27**, 699–706.

Hoffman, M. and Payne, G., 1995, The effects of proprioceptive ankle disk training on healthy subjects. *Journal of Orthopedic Sports Physical Therapy*, **21**(2), 90–93.

Inklaar, H., 1994, Soccer injuries, II: Aetiology and prevention. *Sports Medicine,* **18**, 81–93.

Irrgang, J., Whitney, S.L. and Cox, E.D., 1994, Balance and proprioceptive training for rehabilitation of the lower extremity. *Journal of Sport Rehabilitation*, **3**, 68–83.

Lephart, S.M., Pincivero, D.M. and Rozzi, S.L., 1998, Proprioception of the ankle and knee. *Sports Medicine*, **25**, 149–155.

McGuine, T.A., Greene, J.J., Best, T. and Leverson, G., 2000, Balance as a predictor of ankle injuries in high school basketball players. *Clinical Journal of Sport Medicine*, **10**, 239–244.

Nielsen, A.B. and Yde, J., 1989, Epidemiology and traumatology of injuries in soccer. *American Journal of Sports Medicine*, **17**, 803–807.

Nilsson, S. and Roaas, A., 1978, Soccer injuries in adolescents. *American Journal of Sports Medicine*, **6**, 358–361.

Osborne, M., Chou, M., Laskowski, E., Smith, J. and Kaufman, K., 2001, The effect of ankle disk training on muscle reaction time in subjects with a history of ankle sprain. *American Journal of Sports Medicine*, **29**, 627–632.

Soderman, K., Werner, S., Pietila, T., Engstrom, B. and Alfredson, H., 2000, Balance board training: prevention of traumatic injuries of the lower extremities in female soccer players? A prospective randomized intervention study. *Knee Surgery, Sports Traumatology, Arthroscopy*, **8**, 356–363.

Tropp, H., Askling, C. and Gillquist, J., 1985, Prevention of ankle sprains. *American Journal of Sports Medicine*, **13**, 1259–1262.

Tropp, H., Ekstrand, J. and Gillquist, J., 1984, Stabilometry in functional instability of the ankle and its value in predicting injury. *Medicine and Science in Sports and Exercise*, 16, 64–66.

Tucker, A.M., 1997, Common soccer injuries. Diagnosis, treatment and rehabilitation. *Sports Medicine*, **23,** 21–32.

48   Restoration of Muscle Imbalances with a Specific Strength Training Programme in Young Soccer Players

A. Beneka, P. Malliou, A. Gioftsidou, I. Ispirlidis and G. Godolias
Department of Physical Education and Sports Science,
Democritus University of Thrace, Komotini, Greece

1. INTRODUCTION

Soccer is one of the most popular sports in the world (Soderman *et al.*, 2001). It attracts many participants but leads to a substantial number of injuries, also (Lyon, 2001), both in senior and in sixteen- to eighteen-year old soccer players (Schmidt-Olsen *et al.*, 1991).

Soccer training has an effect on the development of muscle strength. The quadriceps and hamstring muscle groups are considered to be the primary movers of the movements involved, because the quadriceps play an important role in jumping and ball kicking (kicking the ball itself tends to develop the quadriceps muscles, as it requires resisted extension of the knee with considerable force), while the hamstrings control running activities and stabilize the knee during turns (Fried and Lloyd, 1992). In addition to ball practice, coaches concentrate on training the quadriceps, as they recognize the importance of a strong kick, while exercising the hamstrings remains secondary (Fried and Lloyd, 1992).

The normal ratio for quadriceps and hamstring strength is around 3 to 2, but because of the neglect of hamstring training, much higher ratios are found frequently (Davies, 1984). Also, this ratio varies within different athletic groups (Zakas *et al.*, 1995). The differentiation of the muscle group ratios is important because muscle strength asymmetry seems to contribute not only to injury risk in athletes but also to injury prediction. The flexor-extensor balance plays an important role in articular stabilization and may be an injury factor if the ratio is abnormal (Stafford and Grana, 1984). Notably, Knapik and co-workers (1991) found that knee flexor/extensor ratio of 75% or less at 3.14 rad.s^{-1} was associated with increased lower extremity injury risk in collegiate female athletes.

Bilateral differences in isokinetic movement have also been considered as an important predictor of injury in soccer players (Fowler and Reilly, 1993). Isokinetic testing of both legs may be helpful in the identification of muscle strength weaknesses (Baltzopoulos and Kellis, 1998). Similarly, knee flexor strength differences between limbs (15% and more) were also associated with increased risk (Brown, 2000).

The aim of the present study was to investigate the effect of a muscular training programme on young soccer players who demonstrated muscle imbalances, in order to restore the "normal" quadriceps and hamstrings strength ratios and to prevent lower limb injuries.

2. MATERIAL AND METHODS

The sample of this study comprised of 35 young soccer players (age: 16.8±0.9, mass: 64.77±6.34 kg, height: 1.75±0.064 m), playing in the Greek first division (2000–2001 period). A Cybex Norm (Lumex Corporation, Ronkonkoma, NY) dynamometer was used for the isokinetic strength measurements. All tests were performed in a seated position (hip flexion =110°). Each subject underwent 15 min warm-up of cycling and stretching exercises. The trunk, waist and thigh of the tested leg were stabilized with hook and loop fastener straps to prevent any movement that could affect the measurements. Subjects were also instructed to cross their arms on their chests. The resistance pad was placed proximal to the ankle joint.

Each subject spent 15 min in warm-up cycling without resistance. Then the subject performed a submaximal effort on each leg where the lower and upper limits in the range of motion were defined. For all subjects, the motion ranged from 0° (full extension) to 110° of knee flexion. This was followed by two submaximal efforts and one maximal effort of the knee extensors and flexors at angular velocities of 1.05 and 3.14 rad.s^{-1}. The main test protocol consisted of three maximum concentric efforts of knee extensors and flexors at the above velocities and the one with the highest peak torque value was used. The subjects were instructed to perform as maximally as possible in both movements. They had also visual feedback of the recorded performance. Following the testing of one leg, there was a 5-min rest after which testing of the other leg was initiated. The order of testing the legs was random across subjects. The leg used most often to kick the ball was considered as the preferred leg. This decision was based on the questionnaire responses of the players and after consultation with the coaches.

Thirteen soccer players appeared to have muscular imbalances and were considered to follow a specific isokinetic training programme in order to restore muscle strength imbalances, three times per week and over 2 months (Table 1).

"Manova Repeated Measures" was used in order to determine possible statistically significant differences between the initial and the final measurement in the muscle strength ratios. Data were analyzed using the SPSS PC (version 8.0) programme for Windows. Also, means (± SD) were calculated. The level of statistical significance was set at $P < 0.05$.

Table 1. The isokinetic exercise programme.

Angular Velocity	Set	Rep.	Muscle group
2.60 rad.s^{-1}	1	15	Extensors / flexors
3.14 rad.s^{-1}	2	15	Extensors / flexors
3.60 rad.s^{-1}	1	15	Extensors / flexors
4.19 rad.s^{-1}	1	15	Extensors / flexors
2.60 rad.s^{-1}	1	15	Extensors or flexors
3.14 rad.s^{-1}	1	15	Extensors or flexors
3.66 rad.s^{-1}	1	15	Extensors or flexors
4.19 rad.s^{-1}	1	15	Extensors or flexors

3. RESULTS

Anthropometric characteristics of the study sample are shown in Table 2. At 1.05 rad.s^{-1}, mean bilateral difference was 22% ($\pm$12) in the knee extensors and 15% ($\pm$10) in the knee flexors. At 3.14 rad.s^{-1} mean bilateral differences of the knee extensors were 24% ($\pm$12) and 18% ($\pm$12) in knee flexors (Table 2). Mean hamstrings to quadriceps ratios were 60% ($\pm$22) at 1.05 rad.s^{-1} and 67% ($\pm$15) at 3.14 rad.s^{-1} (Table 3).

The results showed statistically significant differences in flexor/extensor peak torque ratio between initial and final measurements. The ratio ($F_{1,11}$=15.26) significantly increased from 60 % ($\pm$15) to 70 % ($\pm$7) at 1.05 rad.s^{-1}. Also, the ratio ($F_{1,11}$=18.34) significantly changed from 64 % ($\pm$15) to 71 % ($\pm$8) at 3.14 rad.s^{-1}.

In addition, significant decreases between the initial and final measurements were detected with respect to the peak torque differences at both the movement speeds used (Table 4).

Table 2. Anthropometric characteristics of the selected participants.

Athletes characteristics	N= 13, Mean ($\pm$SD)
Age (years)	27.24 ($\pm$5.2)
Mass (kg)	80.24 ($\pm$6.3)
Height (m)	1.868 ($\pm$0.084)

Table 3. Peak torque (means and standard deviations) for knee extensors and flexors of the soccer
players at pre-measurement assessments.

	Extensors of the knee	Flexors of the knee
	Means (±SD)	Means (±SD)
1.05 rad.s^{-1} R(Nm)	233.76 (±49,91)	155.94 (±34.15)
1.05 rad.s^{-1} L(Nm)	230.88 (±42,04)	162.29 (±32.15)
3.14 rad.s^{-1}R(Nm)	155.94 (±26,15)	115.94 (±21.15)
3.14 rad.s^{-1} L(Nm)	153.29 (±29,15)	113.29 (±19.15)

Table 4. Bilateral differences (diff) before and after the intervention period.

Angular velocity	Bilateral diff. Means (±SD)		Bilateral diff. Means (±SD)	
Muscle group	Extensors		Flexors	
	Initial	Final	Initial	Final
1.05 rad.s^{-1}	24(±15)	10(±5)	18 (±6)	8(±6)
3.14 rad.s^{-1}	18(±12)	8(±6)	17(±5)	4(±4)

4. DISCUSSION

The results of the present study support the belief that isokinetic testing can
provide safe and accurate information for the knee joint muscular performance on
which an injury prediction can be based. Thirteen of the 35 soccer players
appeared to have deficits and/or imbalances in knee joint muscles, corroborating
the statement that muscle imbalances are frequently found in soccer players
suffering recurrent injuries (Inklaar, 1994). The isokinetic knee flexor/extensor
balance is reported to play an important role in joint stabilization and might be an
injury factor if the ratio is abnormal (Stafford and Grana, 1984). It could even
predict injury risk (Brown, 2000).

Studies on the association between isokinetic strength and subsequent
hamstring injury have been somewhat scarce. The study of professional Australian
Rules footballers by Orchard and co-workers (1997) demonstrated an association
between pre-season Cybex 340 concentric peak torque of the knee extensors and
flexors and hamstring injury during the subsequent season. Sixteen percent of the
37 players studied suffered a hamstring injury. The bilateral knee flexor ratios at
1.05 rad.s^{-1} were significantly lower in the injured compared to the uninjured
players (means of 88% versus 100%, respectively). A significant difference in the
reciprocal knee flexor/knee extensor ratio (hamstring-to-quadricep ratio) was a
secondary finding in this study, explained by the bilateral knee flexor imbalance
mentioned previously and the absence of a bilateral difference in knee extensor
strength. Also the study by Jonhagen *et al.* (1994) on sprinters with a history of
very severe hamstring strains did show those athletes to be weaker than uninjured
sprinters.

Rochcongar *et al.* (1988) found that young French elite soccer players had
greater isokinetic leg strength compared with high school students, indicating that
soccer training has an effect on the development of muscle strength. However, the
soccer training has not only an effect on the development of muscle strength.

Monitoring specific soccer techniques, De Proft *et al.* (1988) found that during the kicking motion, antagonist muscle (hamstring) contractions were greater in soccer players than in non-soccer players. Soccer players kicked the ball farther and with greater control (De Proft *et al.,* 1988). Kicking the ball itself tends to develop the quadriceps muscle, as it requires resisted extension of the knee with considerable force. In addition to ball practise, coaches concentrate on training the quadriceps, as they recognise the importance of a strong kick, while exercising the hamstrings is secondary (Fried and Lloyd, 1992).

Also the nature of the soccer game probably enhances the existence of such imbalances. Over-emphasis on one-sided activities such as kicking may lead to asymmetry or dominance of one leg, i.e. greater than normal differences in strength between contra-lateral muscle groups. An unfavorable difference between agonist and antagonist muscle groups is also considered to leave the weaker muscle group at a disadvantage, e.g. hypertrophy of the quadriceps at the expense of the hamstrings may be a factor in causing hamstring injuries (Davies, 1984; Fried and Lloyd, 1992). When these factors are identified, injuries may be effectively reduced or prevented by appropriate modifications to the training regimens.

The results of the present study suggest that applying a specific muscular strength training programme on an isokinetic device at the beginning of the training period is an effective means of restoring quadriceps and hamstrings strength ratios. Based on Knapik and co-workers' (1991) recommendations, thirteen soccer players of our sample appeared to have muscular imbalances. Their flexors/extensors ratios were 60% at 1.05 $rad.s^{-1}$ and 67% at 3.14 $rad.s^{-1}$. These authors reported that when those players followed a specific isokinetic training programme, three times per week for 2 months, they restored their imbalances effectively. Similar conclusions were revealed by Giannakopoulos and co-workers (2003) for the shoulder joint. They applied different training modes for strengthening the rotator cuff muscle group. The authors assessed the performance of the internal and external rotators of the shoulders using the isokinetic device before and after the completion of the strength programme in order to evaluate the effectiveness of each treatment.

In conclusion, it can be stated that the nature of the soccer game probably enhances the existence of knee muscle strength imbalances. Therefore, testing and exercising programmes have to be implemented in order to avoid these possible imbalances and injury rates.

REFERENCES

Baltzopoulos, V. and Kellis, E., 1998, Isokinetic strength during childhood and adolescence. In *Pediatric Anaerobic Performance*, edited by Van Praagh, E. (Champaign, IL: Human Kinetics), pp. 225–240.

Brown, L., 2000, *Isokinetics in Human Performance.* (Champaign, III: Human Kinetics).

Davies, G.J., 1984, *A Compendium of Isokinetics in Clinical Usage and Rehabilitation Techniques*. (Publishers, La Crosse).

De Proft, E., Cabri, J., Dufour, W. and Clarys, J.P., 1988, Strength training and kick performance in soccer players. In Science and Football, edited by Reilly, T., Lees, A., Davids, K. and Murphy, W.J. (London: E and F.N. Spon), pp. 108–113.

Fowler, N. and Reilly, T., 1993, Assessment of muscle strength assymetries in soccer players. In *Contemporary Ergonomics*, edited by Lovesey, E. (London: Taylor and Francis), pp. 327–366.

Fried, T., and Lloyd, G., 1992, An overview of common soccer injuries. Management and prevention. *Sports Medicine*, **14**, 269–275.

Giannakopoulos, K., Beneka, A. and Malliou, P., 2003, Isolated versus complex exercise in strengthening the rotator cuff muscle group. *Journal of Orthopedic Sports Physical Therapy*, In press.

Inklaar H., 1994, Soccer injuries, II: Aetiology and prevention. *Sports Medicine*, **18**, 81–93.

Jonhagen, S., Nemeth, G. and Eriksson, E., 1994, Hamstring injuries in sprinters: The role of concentric and eccentric hamstring muscle strength and flexibility. *American Journal of Sports Medicine*, **222**, 262–66.

Knapik, J., Bauman, C., Jones, B., Harris, J. and Vaughan, L., 1991, Preseason strength and flexibility imbalances associated with athletic injuries in female collegiate athletes. *American Journal of Sports Medicine*, **19**, 76–81.

Lyon, R., 2001, Prevent Injuries in Young Soccer Players. (*Medical College of Wisconsin: Physicians & Clinics*, MCW Health Link).

Orchard, J., Marsden, J., Lord, S. and Garlick, D., 1997, Preseason hamstring muscle weakness associated with hamstring muscle injury in Australian Footballers. *American Journal of Sports Medicine*, **251**, 81–85.

Rochcongar, P., Morvan, R., Jan, J., Dassonville, J. and Beillot, J., 1988, Isokinetic investigation of knee extensors and knee flexors in young French soccer players. *International Journal of Sports Medicine*, **9**, 448–450.

Schmidt-Olsen, S., Jorgensen, U., Kaalund, S. and Sotersen, J., 1991, Injuries among young soccer players. *American Journal of Sports Medicine*, **19**, 273–275.

Soderman, K., Werner, S., Pietila, T., Engstrom, B. and Alfredson, H., 2001, Balance board training: prevention of traumatic injuries of the lower extremities in female soccer players? A prospective randomized intervention study. *Knee Surgery, Sports Traumatology, Arthroscopy*, **8**, 356–363.

Stafford, M. G. and Grana, WA., 1984, Hamstring/quadriceps ratios in college football players: high velocity evaluation. American Journal of Sports Medicine, **12**, 209–211.

Zakas, A., Mandroukas, K., Vamvakoudis, E., Christoulas, K. and Aggelopoulou, N., 1995, Peak torque of quadriceps and hamstring muscles in basketball and soccer players of different divisions. *Journal of Sports Medicine and Physical Fitness*, **35**, 199–205.

49   Injury Profiles in Soccer during the Championship Period: A Comparison between Adult and Young Players

P. Malliou, I. Ispirlidis, A. Gioftsidou, G. Pafis, E.M.
Papakostas, X. Bikos, G. Godolias and P. Alexopoulos
Department of Physical Education and Sport Science,
Democritus University of Thrace, Komotini, Greece

1. INTRODUCTION

Soccer is described as the most popular team sport in Europe but also as a sport with a high incidence of acute and chronic sports injuries. In many European countries, injuries sustained in soccer account for 40% of all sports injuries. Risk factors that predispose to injury are the training regimen, contact with the opponent and other external factors such as field conditions and so on (Inklaar, 1994).

The ultimate goal of sports medicine is the prevention of injury. Preventive medicine is best approached by an analysis of the epidemiology of disease or injury (Nicholas and Hershman, 1990). In the case of sports injuries, the agent (immediate causative factor), the host (the athlete sustaining the injury) and the environment (conditions which may predispose or prevent the injury) need to be analyzed (Nicholas and Hershman, 1990). The incidence of soccer injuries has been investigated in several studies (Peterson et al., 2000). The results differ because of differences in population characteristics, injury definition, and research design. There are also great differences among the various age groups and levels of skill. Inklaar (1994) stated that senior players sustain more injuries than young players. Sixteen to 18-year-old players seem to have an incidence similar to that of senior players (Nielsen and Yde, 1989). Also Tucker (1997) reported that the risk of injury increases with the age of the participants. One survey reported a 7.7% injury rate for high school players and 8.7% for players 19 and under in a community league (McCaroll et al., 1984). Maehlum and Daljord (1984) found that injuries peaked in the 20 to 24 year old age group, then declined with increasing age.

The location and type of injury in players of all ages have been studied extensively. The lower extremity is the most commonly injured limb, with the ankle, knee and shin accounting for more than two-thirds of all injuries (McCaroll et al., 1984).

In Greece, soccer is the most popular sport involving a great number of participants all over the country. In addition, during the last decade the game rapidly increased in popularity among Greek athletes (GSF News Greek soccer Federation, 2000). As is the case for the adult professional championship in soccer, young players (until the age of 21 years old) have a similar organization of competitions. The selected youth players of each soccer team follow the same competition programme as the adults. This means that the need for more information concerning occurrence of injuries during practice and games for both adults and younger soccer players is evident.

The aim of the present study was to investigate the incidence rate of injuries and their characteristics in adult and young soccer players. The main purpose of the study was to screen and study the incidence of sports injuries during practice and competition. This study was conducted on two soccer teams: these were a professional adult male soccer team that obtained fifth place in the national championship and a young soccer team that also participated in a year-round championship, finishing in sixth place.

2. MATERIAL AND METHODS

The sample of this study comprised of 35 young soccer players (Table 1) competing in the Greek first division (2001–2002 period). An orthopedic surgeon, a physiotherapist and a trainer formed the "injury assessment" team. The authors have conducted personal consultations with the team physicians, twice a week, to register any injury occurring during scheduled games or practices, which prevented the athlete from playing in the next game or practice. The injury incidence rate, characteristics (severity, diagnosis) and anatomical location of musculo-skeletal injuries, which occurred during practice and competition in all the championship period, were recorded. Injury was defined as "any incident that occurred during scheduled games or practices causing an athlete to miss a subsequent game or practice session". Injuries were classified in relation to severity in three grades: minor (absence of training or games less than a week), moderate (absence of training or games one to two weeks) and major (absence of training or games more than two weeks). This classification is in accordance with other studies reported in the literature (Morgan and Oberlander, 2001). The statistical tests used were the χ^2 and the level of significance was $P<0.05$.

Table 1. Age and the anthropometric characteristics.

Athletes characteristics	N= 35, Mean (±SD)
Age (years)	16.5 (±1.5)
Body mass (kg)	70.8 (±6.3)
Height (m)	1.81 (±0.06)

3. RESULTS

The total sample reported 81 acute injuries and nine overuse syndromes for the 12-month experimental period (Table 2). Their severity was reported in terms of absence from the game or practice after injury. According to the descriptive analysis, the rate involved mild, moderate and severe injuries for the adult and the younger team as shown in Table 3. In relation to the anatomical location of injury, the lower extremity was significantly more frequently injured in both age categories (Table 4). According to the clinical diagnosis, the type of injury rates was differently classified for the adult and the young team (Table 5). A positive result was that young soccer players did not report any chronic injury; however, adult players reported 9 overuse syndromes. In relation to the time of injury occurrence (during practice or game), the results revealed that, in both age categories, the players were injured significantly more frequently during practice than during competition (Table 6).

Table 2. Acute injuries recorded for young and adult players.

	Adult	Young
Cases	51	30
Rate*	63%	37%

* statistically significant differences between adult and young soccer players (P<0.05)

Table 3. Severity of injuries reported.

Rate(cases)	Mild*	Moderate*	Major
Adult	54.9% (30)	21.5%(13)	13.7%(8)
Young	78% (26)	11%(2)	11%(2)

* statistically significant differences between adult and young soccer players (P<0.05)

Table 4. Injury rates according the anatomical location.

Rate (cases)	Back region	Lumbar spine	Knee	Ankle	Shoulder
Adult	1.9% (1)	9.9% (5)	58.8%(30)	27.5% (14)	1.9% (1)
Young	1% (3)	-	46.6%(14)	40% (12)	1% (1)

Table 5. Clinical diagnosis for injuries reported.

	Adult	Young
Hamstring strains	15	2
Ankle sprains	14	12
Adductors strains	6	4
Shoulder girdle strain	1	1
Knee ligament strains	9	8
Lumbar spine injuries	6	3
Chronic overuse syndrome	9	0

Table 6. Injuries occurrence during practice or game.

	Game	Practice*
Adults	12	39
Young	8	22

* statistically significant differences between adult and young soccer players (P<0.05)

4. DISCUSSION

Based on the results of the present comparative study between two different age-groups, soccer may be considered as a relatively low-risk and safe sport in young players, with an injury pattern just slightly different from the seniors and with only a few severe injuries. The present study supports the view that adult players are more frequently injured than youngsters, which is in accordance with results of previous studies. Youth games are probably less aggressive with less stress than in adult games (Schmidt-Olsen *et al.,* 1991). Concerning the type of injury, the proportion of acute and overuse injuries was also similar to findings reported in other studies for adult players. The majority of soccer injuries are acute and the proportion connected with overuse varies from 9% to 34% (Nielsen and Yde, 1989; Arnason *et al.,* 1996). The fact that, in adult players, chronic injuries exist, is related to the nature of soccer. Various overuse injuries of the knee are reported to be common in soccer (Schmidt-Olsen *et al.,* 1991). These include quadriceps and patellar tendinitis, illiotibial tract syndrome and patellofemoral syndrome.

The present study revealed that the majority of the injuries were of minor severity, which is in agreement with other studies. More specifically, Morgan and Oberlander (2001) found that of the 256 injuries in adult soccer players, 60% were categorized as minor, 26% as moderate and only 14% as major injuries. Similarly, Schmidt-Olsen (1991) found slightly lower incidence rates in youngsters in comparison to the adults.

With respect to the anatomical location of injuries, the present study confirms that most soccer related injuries affect the lower extremity, both in adults and in young soccer players. Given the demands of the game, one would expect that a disproportionate percentage of its participants would suffer injuries in the ankles, knees and hips. With regard to lower extremity injuries, researchers have identified the knee and ankle as the most frequently injured joints (Ekstrand and Gilliquist, 1983; Poulsen *et al.,* 1991). These results are in agreement with previous studies reporting the most common injuries in soccer as involving the ankle and knee joints, and the muscles and ligaments of the thigh and calf (Fried and Lloyd, 1992; Inklaar, 1994; Tucker, 1997). Kicking the ball itself tends to develop the quadriceps muscle group, as it requires resisted extension of the knee with considerable force. In addition to ball practice, coaches concentrate on training the quadriceps, as they recognize the importance of a strong kick, while exercising the hamstrings is secondary. Even if it is rare to suffer a sprain of the quadriceps, a tear of the hamstring muscle group is a frequent occurrence and once it has occurred it is usually quite disabling for a long period.

In contrast with other authors, the present study revealed that most injuries occurred during practice and not during competition. Many other studies concluded that more injuries occur during games than in training sessions (Peterson *et al.*, 2000). This argument may be due to the fact that in the present study injury is defined as "causing an absence from at least one training session or match" meaning that minor injuries and complaints which are usually related to overuse syndromes were also included. Nevertheless, Albert (1983) found that, in a five-year study, 47% of injuries occurred during games and 53% were associated with practice.

Studies of the incidence and severity of soccer injuries have produced a variety of (sometimes conflicting) results because of the differences in collecting the data, the definition of injury or the selection criteria. As a general conclusion it may be stated that the incidence of injury depends on the population age. Further epidemiological studies have to be carried out in order to learn more about intervention strategies for the prevention of soccer injuries.

REFERENCES

Albert, M., 1983, Descriptive three year data study of outdoor and indoor professional soccer injuries. *Athletic Training, 18*, 218–220.

Arnason, A., Gudmundsson, A., Dahl, H.A. and Johannsson, E., 1996, Soccer injuries in Iceland. *Scandinavian Journal of Medicine and Science in Sports*, **6**(1), 40–45.

Ekstrand, J. and Gilliquist, J., 1983, The avoidavility of soccer injuries. *International Journal of Sport Medicine*, **4**, 124–128.

Fried, T. and Lloyd, G.J., 1992, An overview of common soccer injuries: Management and prevention. *Sports Medicine*, **14**, 269–275.

GSF News, 2000, (Athens, Greece: Greek Soccer Federation).

Inklaar, H., 1994, Soccer injuries, I: Incidence and severity. *Sports Medicine*, **18**, 55–73.

Maehlum, S. and Daljord, O.A., 1984, Acute sports injuries in Oslo: a one year study. *British Journal of Sports Medicine*, **18**, 181–185.

McCaroll, J.R., Meaney, C. and Sieder, J.M., 1984, Profile of youth soccer injuries. *Physician and Sportsmedicine*, **21**, 126–129.

Morgan, B. and Oberlander, M., 2001, An examination of injuries in major league soccer. *American Journal of Sports Medicine*, 29, 426–430.

Nicholas, J. and Hershman, E., 1990, *The Lower Extremity & Spine*. (St Louis: Mosby Company), pp. 1510–1511.

Nielsen, A.B. and Yde, J., 1989, Epidemiology and traumatology of injuries in soccer. *American Journal of Sports Medicine*, **17**, 803–807.

Peterson, L., Chomiak, J., Graf-Baumann, T. and Dvorak, J., 2000, Incidence of football injuries and complaints in different age groups and skill-level groups. *American Journal of Sports Medicine*, **28**, Suppl. 5, S51–57.

Poulsen, T.D., Freund, K.G and Madsen, F., 1991, Injuries in high-skilled and low-skilled soccer: A prospective study. *British Journal of Sports Medicine*, **25**, 151–153.

et al.

S., Jorgensen, U., Kaalund, S. and Sotersen, J., 1991, Injuries
ig soccer players. *American Journal of Sports Medicine,* **19**, 273–

1997, Common soccer injuries. Diagnosis, treatment and
n. *Sports Medicine,* **23**, 21–32.

Part VI

Football Training

50   Cross-Training for Junior Soccer Players

Werner Kuhn

Institute of Sport Sciences, Humboldt University Berlin

1. INTRODUCTION

According to Moran and McGlynn (1994) cross-training can be defined as "using another sport, activity or training technique to help improve performance in the primary sport or activity". Cross-training is described by the authors as a powerful training tool which can help to improve performance in the primary sport and also avoid over-training and burnout. Cases in point are downhill skiers bicycling or mountain-biking during the off-season in order to maintain or improve the strength and endurance of their leg muscles, and volleyball players using weight training to enhance their leg and arm strength. Cross-training has successfully been applied not only in top-level sport, but also in rehabilitation and in health and fitness training programmes for a longer time.

2. REVIEW OF LITERATURE

Cross-training is not a new principle of training invented in the 20th century. Cross-training has always played a role in top-level sport and can be traced back to the ancient times. Moran and McGlynn (1994) developed sport-specific cross-training options for 26 different sports, including soccer. In their activity matrix for cross-training the following exercises were mentioned for soccer:- treadmill, rowing machine, cross-country skiing machine, stair master, versa climber, bicycling, swimming, aqua jogging, aerobics, lateral sports, weight training, plyometrics, arm ergometry, roller blading, rope jumping, agility exercises, flexibility exercises and running. Motor abilities (such as strength, muscular endurance, aerobic endurance, anaerobic endurance, flexibility, ability and balance) are mixed with such concepts as warm-up/cool-down and rehabilitation. The significance of the exercises for different abilities was expressed in two grades:- recommended and highly recommended. For instance weight training was highly recommended for the development of strength and muscular endurance as well as in rehabilitation.

Moran and McGlynn also offered aerobic/anaerobic sample training programmes for three, five and seven days. Apart from training frequency the programmes vary according to the muscle groups and exercises used. The focus can be laid either on the lower body (LB), the upper body (UB) or on both (UB/LB). In the last chapter of their book, the authors presented a valuable multisportive matrix of compatibility which detailed the benefits of different sports for soccer.

Another North-American monograph was published by Jaconda (1995) under the name Fitness-Cross-Training. Although the presentation was not geared to specific sports, soccer coaches and players of all ability levels can draw useful information for a variable training programme.

A review of the extensive soccer literature in German-speaking countries revealed that the emphasis is on soccer-specific training. There are a few exceptions. In the official book of the German Soccer Federation authored by Bisanz and Vieth (1999), the concept of polysport education is touched upon briefly. Agility should be improved with relays, catch games and tasks involving other sports equipment. Bauer (2001 a, 2001 b), author of several soccer books, referred to compensatory sports (such as basketball, European handball, basic games, table tennis, volleyball) which should be incorporated into the training programme to maintain a high level of psychological readiness for training and to reduce the total physical strain.

3. DO JUNIOR SOCCER PLAYERS NEED CROSS – TRAINING?

3.1. Arguments in favour of cross-training

There are a few studies that have demonstrated a positive effect of non-specific activities on the primary sport. Zimmerman and Nicklisch (1981) showed that performances in Olympic Gymnastics and European handball significantly improved in the experimental group after a coordination-based cross-training of 20 hours. The control group made no progress. Hirtz and Wellnitz (1985) could also prove that an intensive and variable training of coordination reduced the learning time of a skill in Olympic Gymnastics and in high jumping. In order to support the scarce empirical evidence further, replications for soccer are necessary.

In 2002 standardized interviews (live or by telephone) were conducted with 120 licensed soccer coaches in Germany. All interviewees were in favour of some kind of cross-training at the junior level. Seventy-six per cent of the coaches claimed to make use of cross-training in their annual planning especially during the pre-season and off-season once or twice per week. Those coaches who do not use cross-training in their training plan (24 %) mentioned time constraints. They focus entirely on soccer-specific training and on elements of coordination. They believed that cross-training should be offered by the schools on a larger scale. With regard to the contents of cross-training, running (track, field, woods) and other sports games (such as basketball, European handball, hockey, volleyball) dominated the list. Strength training on stationary apparatus, cycling, cross-country skiing and mental training forms were mentioned to a much lesser extent. The main goals of cross-training were to improve endurance, strength, speed as well as coordination and tactics. The reasons put forward in favour of cross-training can be classified into four categories: (1) Enhancement of performance in soccer. As the dynamics of the game will further develop in the future at all skill levels, an effort must be made to train neuromotor co-ordination. (2) Avoidance of muscular imbalances, reduction of total load on the skeletal and neuromuscular system by using alternative muscles and joints. (3) Improvement of training motivation in the long-range training process. Cross-training can be a pleasant alternative to the normal specific training routine. Thus, it may help to diminish the drop-out rate of junior soccer players. (4) One coach stated that cross-training can also contribute to identify the potential of talent for other sports.

3.2. What kind of sports and exercises are suitable?

Based upon four characteristic phases of training (age group 6–9: elementary education; age group 10–12: basic training; age group 13–15: build-up training; age group 16–18: high performance training) a breakdown of percentages for specific and non-specific training for soccer is given in Table 1. In the elementary education phase, sport-specific training and general training should be about 50% each. In the following three phases of training there is a shift towards specific training: about 60% to 40%, about 70% to 30% and about 80% to 20%. About one fifth of the training time should still be devoted to cross-training in high performance training.

Table 1. Percentages of sportspecific training and general training in elementary education, basic training, build-up training and high performance training.

Phases of training	Sport-specific training	General training
Elementary eduction (age group 6 – 9)	About 50 %	About 50 %
Basic training (age group 10 – 12)	About 60 %	About 40 %
Build-up training (age group 13 – 15)	About 70 %	About 30 %
High performance training (age group 16 – 18)	About 80 %	About 20 %

The goal of the elementary education phase is to lay down the foundation, so the youngster can play the game of soccer in its final form later-on. Besides developing general coordination structures, soccer is practised in a game-like fashion. Soccer must be the focus of the training sessions as the game itself holds the interest of the kids. Further, research on expertise has shown that many world-class soccer players acquired their basic technical and tactical skills of the game at a very young age. If a child did not have the chance to get a decent elementary education, parts of it will have to be integrated in the basic training phase. The reservoir of sports and exercises for cross-training in the different phases of training is huge. The coach of the age group 6–9 years can choose between basic games, other sports games (e.g. basketball, European handball, hockey etc.), swimming, track and field, Olympic gymnastics (especially floor exercises), mini-trampoline, judo and general coordination training. In the age group 10–12 years aerobics with and without music, acrobatics and functional gymnastics are added, in the age group 13–15 general strength training and in the age group 16–18 basic endurance training (cycling, swimming, cross-country skiing etc.).

Coaches should be aware of trade-offs. If too much of total training time is allotted to cross-training, performance in soccer may stagnate or deteriorate. Hence, the implementation of cross-training must be well gauged. In case of injury the training must be carried out quite often entirely with cross-training exercises.

It is important to note that sport-specific training must not be neglected. An overview of possible curricula for the four age groups is given. Age group 6–9: learning elementary technical and tactical skills without opponent and without time constraints, match practice with 4 vs 4 or 7 vs 7. Age group 10–12: mastery of elementary technical skills under pressure from opposition and with time constraints, mastery of elementary tactical actions in lead-up games (1 vs 1, 2 vs 2 etc.), team tactics in matches 11 vs 11. Age group 13–15: mastery of complex technical skills, learning of complex tactical actions in lead-up games and in matches 11 vs 11, soccer-specific speed training and strength training. Age group 16–18: mastery and variable use of all technical skills under extreme pressure from opposition, mastery of complex tactical actions in matches 11 vs 11, soccer-specific strength, speed and endurance training.

A compatibility matrix of contents of cross-training and soccer-specific abilities for junior players is presented in Table 2. It can serve as a point of orientation for all phases of training. The majority of training tools on the left-hand side have a positive influence on conditioning, coordination and tactical skills. They improve or stabilize the energy systems of the primary sport, the compatible muscular systems and muscular coordination. Cycling and swimming are excellent from an energy perspective for the training of basic endurance. Although muscle mechanics are different from the running pattern of a soccer player, both sports are beneficial from a coordination standpoint as they tax other muscles. A positive transfer towards tactical abilities can be expected primarily through basic games, sports games and judo. As soccer is already a high impact sport, negative aspects of physical strain must be taken into consideration when basic games, sports games, running programmes, strength and speed training are carried out with high intensity, high volume and high frequency. One goal of cross-training is injury prevention. Therefore individualized load conditions and careful selection of activities are necessary.

Ten and eleven-year old school children specializing in soccer sometimes cannot participate in training because of injury or muscle soreness. It is obvious that massed training practices may be responsible for an overload: typically on Tuesdays and Thursdays there were training sessions in the morning and evening and sometimes a physical education lesson in between. A distribution of training practices over the whole week would be more sensible.

Table 2. Compatibilty matrix of contents of cross-training and soccer specific abilities.

Contents of cross-training	Conditioning skills	Coordinative skills	Tactical skills	Physical load conditions
Basic games/sports games	+	+	+	−1
General coordinative training	+	+	+	
Judo	+	+	+	
Basic endurance training				
Running	+	+		−1
Cycling	+			+
Swimming	+			+
Aquajogging	+	+		+
In-line skating	+	+		+
XC skiing	+	+		+
Strength training	+	+		−1
Speed training	+	+		−1
Flexibility training/ Functional gymnastics	+	+		+

1High impact in case of high training volume, high training intensity, high training frequency.

3.3. Organisation of cross-training

An excellent school sport programme could serve as a cross-training stimulus almost over the whole year. Unfortunately this is not always the case. Hiking and cycling excursions initiated by the school system can also be advantageous for the ambitious junior soccer player. Holidays are also good occasions to try out or work on alternative sports (e.g. mountain walking, ice skating, in-line skating, cycling, snowsports, swimming, sailing). A sporting environment (parents, brothers and sisters, peers) can be very helpful to engage in new activities. In sportsclub training the transition period (off-season) and preparatory period (pre-season) are most suitable for cross-training. Microcyles geared to cross-training with one or more sports occur very seldom in training organized by sportsclubs or federations. Training sessions can either be mixed or geared to one specific aspect of training (e.g. endurance-, strength-, speed- or flexibility oriented). In mixed training units activities of cross-training can be efficiently worked into the warm-up and warm-down program. For warm-up basic games, basketball, European handball, hockey, rope-skipping are recommended, for warm-down walking, jogging, cycling and swimming with reduced intensity. An adequate level of technique should exist in all cross-training exercises. At the beginning, the intensity and scope of training are reduced. If the goal is to improve the energetic component of the primary sport, intensity and scope of training must be steadily increased to a similar level.

4. OVERVIEW

The main purpose of cross-training is to integrate alternative sports or exercises into the primary sport in order to enhance performance. If activities for cross-training are sensibly selected and cross-training sessions are carefully planned, the following goals can be achieved: (1) Development of a player with outstanding athletic-coordination abilities. This is especially important as the dynamics of the game will further develop in the future at all skill levels. (2) Protection of the skeletal and neuromuscular systems from overuse. (3) Breaking the monotony of training which may lead to higher motivation in training. (4) Avoidance of overtraining and burnout. (5) Extension of the sports career. (6) Checking out the potential of talent for other sports.

Unfortunately there is a lack of studies in soccer to test these suppositions. Hence, there is a need for further research. Cross-training can be a useful and powerful training tool. Nevertheless, we should be aware that there are trade-offs. If too much time is devoted to cross-training, performance in the main sport will stagnate or deteriorate. We should not forget that acquisition of soccer skills is highly specific. Being able to play excellent soccer at the junior and adult stage requires early and extensive exposure with the activity itself.

REFERENCES

Bauer, G., 2001a, *Lehrbuch Fußball,* (München: BLV).

Bauer, G., 2001b, *Richtig Fußball,* (München: BLV).

Bisanz, G. and Vieth, N., 1999, *Grundlagen- und Aufbautraining,* (Münster: Philippka).

Hirtz, P. and Wellnitz, J., 1985, Hohes Niveau koordinativer Fähigkeiten führt zu besseren Ergebnissen im motorischen Lernen. *Körpererziehung,* **35,** 314–318.

Jaconda, J., 1995, *Fitness Cross-training.* (Champaign: Human Kinetics).

Moran, G.T. and McGlynn, G.H., 1994, *Cross-training for Sports.* (Champaign: Human Kinetics).

Zimmermann, K. and Nicklisch, R., 1981, Die Ausbuilding koordinativer Fahigkeiten und ihre Bedeutung fur die technische bzw. technisch-taktische Leistungsfahigkeit der Sportler. Im: *Theorie und Praxis der Korperkultur,* **30,** 764–768.

51   Using Situational Probabilities to Train Perceptual and Cognitive Skill in Novice Soccer Players

A. Mark Williams[1], Paul Ward[2], Kevin Herron[1] and
Nicholas J. Smeeton[1]
[1]Research Institute for Sport and Exercise Sciences, Liverpool John
Moores University, UK
[2] Department of Psychology, and Institute for Simulation and
Training, University of Central Florida, USA.

1. INTRODUCTION

The ability to 'read the game' is one of the strongest predictors of skill in soccer (Reilly *et al.*, 2000). This is particularly the case at elite level where players become more homogenous as far as physical and physiological characteristics are concerned (Williams and Reilly, 2000).

The process of anticipation involves selecting the most important information cues in order to determine effectively an opponent's likely intentions. The cues can be used to 'weigh up' potential events from a diverse repertoire of likely scenarios and actions that are stored in long-term memory.

Skill-based differences in anticipation skill are evident as early as 8-9 years of age (see Ward and Williams, 2003). These skills continue to improve with practice throughout childhood and early adulthood. Previous research has also shown that elite soccer players have more accurate expectations of likely events within any given scenario (i.e., knowledge of situational probabilities), and that this skill helps guide their search for relevant information when attempting to anticipate an opponent's intentions (Williams, 2000). For example, Ward and Williams (2003) required elite and sub-elite soccer players to watch a video containing a series of attacking sequences. Players had to highlight the passing options available to the player in possession of the ball and attribute a likelihood ratio to each of these passing opportunities. The elite players were able to identify the best passing option and were more accurate than sub-elite players in assigning probabilities to the most likely outcome.

The aim in this study was to try and improve novice soccer players' ability to anticipate opponents' intentions. Using video simulation, instruction, and feedback, an attempt was made to improve players' knowledge of situational probabilities and likely event outcome using simulated 11 v 11 action sequences.

2. METHODS

2.1. Participants

Sixteen novice male soccer players were allocated to a Placebo (n = 8, Mean age = 23.5 years, SD = 4.5) or a Training group (n = 8, Mean age = 19.38 years, SD = 1.38). The participants had all played a limited amount of recreational soccer.

2.2. Procedure and apparatus

2.2.1. Pre- and post-test

The experimental and training videos were based on attacking sequences taken from international and English Premiership games filmed from an elevated position behind the defending team's goal.

All participants watched 3 practice and 18 attacking sequences projected on to a large screen (2.7 m × 3.7 m). Each trial lasted approximately 10 s. The video image was frozen for 20 s at a point 120 ms prior to a pass being made by an attacking player. Participants were required to highlight three attacking players likely to receive the ball and rank the attackers according to their perceived importance. A panel of expert coaches determined the correct responses (inter-observer agreement = 0.79).

2.2.2. Training

Instruction was based on a task analysis of the key cues that determine the significance of the attacking players. These included:
- Typical options facing the player in possession of the ball;
- The use of space;
- Types of forward runs made by attacking players;
- The shape of defending teams.

The training group received 45 min of instruction separated into four phases. The tuition phase taught the instruction points identified from the task analysis (15 min). Examples of attacking sequences were provided with descriptive feedback in the demonstration phase (10 min). Personal instruction about the ability to identify features of an attack was provided on an individual basis. Finally, the group discussion phase allowed individuals to debate expected outcomes of attacking sequences with the rest of the group (10 min). The placebo group watched an instructional video on defensive techniques for 45 min.

2.3. Design and analysis of data

The dependent variables were the number of key players highlighted and accuracy of the rankings assigned to these players. Data were analysed separately using a two-way ANOVA for each dependent variable. The within-subject factor was Test (Pre-, Post-) and Group (Training, Placebo) was the between-participants factor. Effect sizes are reported for all significant effects.

3. RESULTS

The ANOVA revealed a significant Group × Test interaction for the number of key players highlighted, $F_{(1,14)} = 13.856$, $P = 0.02$. Pre-to post- test scores increased for the training group (Pre-test Mean = 0.59, SD = 0.14, Post-test Mean = 0.69, SD = 0.09, ES = 0.54) and decreased for the placebo group (Pre-test mean = 0.62, SD = 0.18, Post-test mean = 0.55, SD = 0.15, ES = 0.3). These interactions are represented in Figure 1.

The ANOVA revealed a non-significant Group x Test interaction for the accuracy of the rankings assigned to these players, $F_{(1,14)} = 3.354$, $P = 0.09$. Pre to post-test scores increased for the training group (Pre-test Mean = 0.33, SD = 0.12, Post-test Mean = 0.46, SD = 0.06, ES = 0.97) and decreased for the placebo group ((Pre-test Mean = 0.46, SD = 0.16, Post-test Mean = 0.31, SD = 0.10, ES = 0.79). The data are presented in Figure 1.

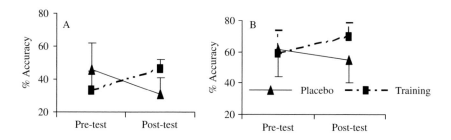

Figure 1. Mean accuracy in assigning ranks to players (A) and percentage of key players highlighted (B) on the pre- and post-tests for the Placebo and Training groups.

4. DISCUSSION

The training programme improved the ability of novice soccer players to highlight key attacking players more accurately. A trend towards an improvement in their ability to rank these players in order of importance was also observed. The participants in the Placebo group on the other hand did not improve their performance from pre- to post-test. It is possible that the decrease in scores for the Placebo group was due to a reduction in motivation. The results suggest that the training programme was partially successful in developing novice soccer players' ability to use situational probabilities.

After a brief training period the novice players developed knowledge that was used to identify key players and, to a lesser degree, rank their perceived importance accurately. The specifics of the training programme may have developed their knowledge of situational probabilities. Successful task performance requires players to identify potential events and evaluate their likely occurrence. A knowledge base regarding the important cues was acquired during the 'tuition' stage. The 'demonstration' stage showed players how to use the knowledge base. Finally, skills in evaluating the likely passing options were developed through the 'individual feedback' and 'group discussion' stages. It is possible the training period was not long enough to develop more complex ranking skills and this factor may be responsible for the non-significant result on this variable. With further training the novices' knowledge may become more detailed, enabling them to assign hierarchical judgements to players already correctly identified as important.

Further research is needed to establish whether the observed improvements in 'game reading' skills transfer to 'real-life' situations. Although the training programme contains appropriate information and instructional strategies for a laboratory-based test, it is currently unclear if the knowledge developed could be used to enhance decision-making in game situations.

REFERENCES

Reilly, T., Williams, A.M., Nevill, A. and Franks, A., 2000, A multidisciplinary approach to talent identification in soccer. *Journal of Sports Sciences,* **18**, 695–702.

Ward, P. and Williams, A.M., 2003, Perceptual and cognitive skill development in sport: The multidimensional nature of expert performance. *Journal of Sport and Exercise Psychology*, **25,** 93–111.

Williams, A.M., 2000, Perceptual skill in soccer: Implications for talent identification and development. *Journal of Sports Sciences,* **18**, 737–750.

Williams, A.M. and Reilly, T., 2000, Talent identification and development in soccer. *Journal of Sports Sciences*, **18**, 657–667.

52   A Comparison of Small-Sided Games and Interval Training in Elite Professional Soccer Players

R. Sassi[1], T. Reilly[2] and F. Impellizzeri[3]

[1]Valencia Football Club, Spain

[2]Research Institute for Sport and Exercise Sciences, Liverpool John Moores University

[3]Laboratario Valutazioni Funzionali, Sport Service MAPEI srl, Italia

1. INTRODUCTION

In the training programmes of professional soccer players, a main concern is the proper regulation of the training intensity. The trainer has to consider the stage of the season, the fitness levels of individual players, the days between competitive engagements and the overall training plan. Furthermore, a choice must be made as to whether the activity concerned will be conducted without the ball or in group drills. Technical and tactical training elements may be focused on strategic aspects of planning for forthcoming games to the neglect of the exercise intensity at which this training is conducted.

Small-sided games provide an alternative to intermittent running. The intensity of exercise can be monitored by means of heart rate and blood lactate responses. By these approaches it is possible not only to record responses to training but also to use the responses to regulate the training stimulus (see Reilly and Bangsbo, 1998). The players' needs may therefore be catered for by considering recovery days after match-play, strenuous sessions and programmes for tapering prior to impending matches (Sassi, 2001).

In the present study the acute physiological responses to a variety of training practices were monitored. The purpose was to compare responses to repetitive internal running, small-sided games (4 *vs* 4 and 8 *vs* 8) and drills for technical-tactical training.

2. METHODS

The observations were made on elite professional players in a top European League. Altogether 9 players were monitored during each of the activities. These were conducted during the course of normal training times and the players provided oral consent to participate.

The repetitive running consisted of 4×1000 m runs with 150 s between bouts of activity. The details of each activity are outlined in Table 1. Heart rate was monitored using radio telemetry (Sport Tester, Finland). Blood samples were obtained post-exercise from fingertips for lactate analysis by photometric methods. The details of each of the conditions are outlined in Table 1.

Table 1. The five conditions compared as training stimuli.

The repetitive running consisted of:

- 4 × 1000 m runs; average time 250 s
        rest 150 s between bouts of activity

Work the ball consisted of:

- 4 vs 4; ball possession; 4 × 240 s
        rest 150 s; area 30 × 30 m
- 4 vs 4; + two goalkeepers; 4 × 240 s
        rest 150 s; pitch: 33 × 33 m

- 8 vs 8; + two goalkeepers; ½ pitch; free touch
- 8 vs 8; + two goalkeepers; ½ pitch: free touch
        with pressing

3. RESULTS AND DISCUSSION

Both of the 4 *vs* 4 and one of the 8 *vs* 8 conditions produced higher average HR responses than the interval running session (see Table 2). The average time for 1000 metres was 250 s .

Table 2. Heart rate (mean $\pm$ SD) in beats.min^{-1} and blood lactate in mmol.l^{-1} responses to different training drills.

4 × 1000 m	4 vs 4		8 vs 8 (1/2 pitch)			Technical-tactical drills
	Without Goalkeeper	With Goalkeeper	Free Touch	Free Touch (Pressing)		
Heart rate	167±4	178±7	174±7	160±3	175±4	140±5
Blood lactate	7.9±3.4	6.4±2.7	6.2±1.4	3.3±1.2	-	2.9±0.8

The heart rate responses in Table 2 indicate the highest intensity was experienced in the 4 vs 4 condition when players averaged 91% of the HRmax. A similar intensity was reached in 8 vs 8 only when pressing was employed. The lowest intensity was observed in the session that focused on technical-tactical training, values averaging 72% HRmax. The variability of responses to the repetitive runs was 3%, mean values being 85% HRmax. Both of the 4 vs 4 and one of the 8 vs 8 conditions produced higher average HR responses than the interval running session.

The minimum and the maximum efforts obtained from individual players were compared when doing the same exercise. The different levels of effort could depend on the attitude and the fitness levels of the participants, i.e. those with greater aerobic capacity needed to us less effort.

Differences in HR and blood lactate were evident on comparing 4 x 1000 metre runs with 4 vs 4 games, 8 vs 8 games and "Technical and Tactical" drills. The latter would be preferred when a day of low-intensity exercise is recommended to avoid 'over-reaching'. It is particularly interesting to notice the difference in HR in 8 vs 8 games with free touch play on the same size pitch when pressing was prohibited, and when it was allowed. Note also the difference in HR when 4 vs 4 games are played with or without goalkeepers. These results show the importance of different exercises and how the drills can be manipulated with specific physiological aims in mind.

Note that the blood lactate concentrations varied between individuals. The lactate values are highly dependent on the activity of the player immediately prior to obtaining the blood sample (Bangsbo, 1994). The variability was greater for the small-sided games in 4-a side matches without a goalkeeper. The higher exercise intensity when the goalkeeper was not used was reflected also in the greatest elevation in mean heart rate.

4. CONCLUSIONS

It is concluded that small-group work with the ball can present physiological training stimuli comparable with and sometimes exceeding interval running without the ball. In contrast, technical-tactical training presents a moderate challenge to the circulatory system, more compatible with maintenance programmes or recovery on days following competitive engagements.

REFERENCES

Bangsbo, J., 1994, The physiology of soccer; with special reference to intense intermittent exercise. Acta Physiologica Scandinavica, **150**, Suppl. 619.
Reilly, T. and Bangsbo, J., 1998, Anaerobic and aerobic training. In Training in Sport: Applying Sports Science, edited by Elliott, B. (Chichester: John Wiley), pp. 351–409.
Sassi, R., 2001, La Preparazione Atletica nel Calcio. (Perugia: Calzetti –Mariucci).

53   Small-Sided Games as an Alternative to Interval-Training for Soccer Players

Thomas Reilly and Craig White

Research Institute for Sport and Exercise Sciences, Liverpool John Moores University

Henry Cotton Campus, 15-21 Webster Street, Liverpool L3 2ET

1. INTRODUCTION

Soccer play places heavy demands on the aerobic pathways whilst at the same time requiring intermittent high-intensity activity. The ability to sustain exercise at high intensity is an important component of fitness for soccer. Whilst various forms of aerobic interval-training have been used traditionally for developing this ability, the use of soccer-specific drills has been advocated for the training of soccer players (Reilly and Bangsbo, 1998). The physiological responses to small-sided games testify to the potential of using this form of play for its training effects (MacLaren et al., 1988).

The attainment of desired fitness levels by means of appropriate training, is a continuous process. Targets are altered as the competitive season progresses, according to a planned periodised programme. Allowances must be made for individuals returning to full training after injury and for players moving into the top squad. There tends to be seasonal effects on fitness during the competitive period (Reilly and Thomas, 1980). A priority must be the maintenance of aerobic fitness whilst at the same time keeping up practice of game skills.

The aims in this study were:- i) to compare the effects of conventional aerobic interval-training with small-sided games; ii) to evaluate the latter as a means of soccer-specific fitness training.

2. METHODS

An exercise training study was performed to assess the effects of aerobic interval training (AITG) or small-sided games training (SSGG) on explosive power, agility and skill, anaerobic and aerobic capacity. Subjects were 18 professional Academy football players, from a Premier League club, aged 17-20 (18.2 ± 1.35) years, randomised to either SSGG or AITG and performed the training twice per week for 6 weeks. The SSGG involved small-sided games (5 v 5) of 6 x 4 min, with 3-min rest, jogging at 50-60% HR_{max}. The AITG involved 6 x 4 min periods of running at 85-90% HR_{max} with 3-min rest, jogging at 50-60% HR_{max}. The sessions were incorporated into the normal weekly programme of the players, who provided oral consent to participate in the study.

Measurements were taken both before and after training. These included a counter-movement jump (C.M.J) and a static squat jump (S.S.J) to measure explosive power; a T-shaped test course to measure agility (TTL or TTR): a dribbling test to measure football skill (FSkT) according to Reilly and Holmes (1983), a repeat 30-s shuttle test (completed 6 times, 30-s recovery interval) to measure anaerobic capacity and a multi-stage shuttle-run test to estimate $\dot{V}O_{2max}$ (Ramsbottom et al., 1988). Heart rate (Polar Electro, Finland) and lactate levels (Lactate Pro, Birmingham) were also monitored during training and at the end of the shuttle-run. Differences between groups were examined using Student's t-test. A probability level of 0.05 was taken to indicate statistical significance.

3. RESULTS

The maximal heart rates were 186 (range 176-203) beats.min^{-1} and 186 (range 176-192) beats. min^{-1} for the SSGG and AITG groups, respectively. Therefore the training zones indicating 85-90% HR$_{max}$ were individualized but averaged 159-168 and 157-166 beats.min^{-1} for the two respective groups.

Table 1. Peak blood lactate (mmol.1^{-1}) concentrations reached at the end of all-out exercise over the six weeks of training. Data are missing for Week 5.

	Week 1	Week 2	Week 3	Week 4	Weeks 6
Small-sided games	13.1 ± 1.5	13.5 ± 1.8	12.9 ± 0.9	12.7 ± 1.3	13.2 ± 0.9
Aerobic interval training	12.3 ± 2.7	11.7 ± 2.1	12.5 ± 1.3	13.0 ± 1.8	13.0 ± 1.3

There were no differences between groups in the highest lactate concentrations reached in all-out exercise. The values ranged from 11.9 – 15.2 and 8.9 – 15.5 mmol.1^{-1} for SSGG and AITG respectively in week 1 to 12.2 – 14.3 and 11.5 - 14.2 mmol.1^{-1} in week 6. These values indicate a high anaerobic competent towards the end of the training session for each group (see Table 1). None of the test items demonstrated a significant effect of training. This result means that there was no deterioration in any aspect of performance measured in either group. The loss of body mass was relatively small, amounting to 0.4 kg and 0.1 kg in the groups doing small-sided games and interval training, respectively.

Table 2. Effects of the two forms of training on body mass and performance measures.

	Small-sided games		Aerobic interval group	
	Pre-Training	**Post-Training**	**Pre-Training**	**Post-Training**
Body mass (kg)	71.8±5.7	71.4±5.5	73.5±4.0	73.4±4.1
Counter-movement jump (cm)	39.2±4.2	39.6±3.4	39.2±6.0	37.8±6.6
Squat-jump (cm)	33.6±3.3	34.7±3.2	32.2±4.2	32.1±3.9
Sprint:10 m (s)	1.71±0.06	1.71±0.05	1.69±0.08	1.70±0.06
Sprint: 30 m (s)	4.08±0.12	4.10±0.12	4.13±0.12	4.10±0.11
Anaerobic capacity test (m)	755±13.7	760±11.5	759±20.3	763±13.6
Agility – left (s)	4.71±0.07	4.73±0.12	4.80±0.13	4.81±0.17
Agility – right (s)	4.72±0.12	4.72±0.13	4.72±0.12	4.72±0.12
Skills test (s)	14.6±0.5	14.1±0.6	14.4±0.9	14.2±0.8

4. DISCUSSION

The physiological training stimulus implicated both aerobic and anaerobic mechanisms, irrespective of whether the session was a conventional 'interval training' model or small-sided games. The training intensity was intended to be high and the mean heart rates reached values exceeding the average encountered in a competitive situation (Reilly, 1997). Such intensities can be presented by means of intermittent exercise regimes, the recovery period of 3 min in the current study allowing for oxidation of the lactate produced during the high intensity bouts of exercise. An efficient oxygen transport system facilitates recovery from intense exercise in such circumstances (Reilly and Bangsbo, 1998).

The present study was conducted during the competitive season when the participants could be considered as already well trained. The maximal oxygen uptake ($\dot{V}O_{2max}$) is relatively insensitive to further training effects when the group is homogeneous and deemed aerobically fit. In this case the maintenance of acquired fitness levels is the main objective of training. Performance capabilities were maintained in all of the measures employed in this study and the small-sided games were equally as effective as the running regimes in achieving this aim. A corollary of this argument is that without the inclusion of systematic physical training, fitness levels may have fallen with likely adverse consequences for match performance.

In the current study the exercise period was slightly longer than the intermission used for recovery. In view of the heart rate and blood lactate concentrations reached during exercise, a 3-min off, 3-min on protocol would appear to be adequate to maintain the training stimulus within the desired training zone. In such events groups of players could alternate exercise and rest periods in a training context, rendering the session as a whole very efficient.

The overall conclusion from this study is that small-sided games are acceptable substitutes for formal interval training to maintain fitness during the competitive season.

REFERENCES

MacLaren, D., Davids, K., Isokawa, M., Mellor, S. and Reilly, T., 1988, Physiological strain in 4-a-side soccer. In Science and Football, edited by Reilly, T., Lees, A.., Davids, K. and Murphy, W. J. (London: E. and Spon, F. N.), pp. 76–80.

Ramsbottom, R., Brewer, J. and Williams, C., 1998, A progressive shuttle run test to estimate maximal oxygen uptake. *British Journal of Sports Medicine*, **22**, 141–4.

Reilly, T., 1997, Energetics of high intensity exercise exercise (soccer) with particular reference to fatigue. *Journal of Sports Sciences*, **15**, 257–263.

Reilly, T. and Bangsbo, J., 1998, Anaerobic and aerobic training. In *Training in Sport: Applying Sport Science*, edited by Elliot, B. (Chichester: John Wiley), pp. 351–409.

Reilly, T. and Holmes, M. (1983). A preliminary analysis of selected soccer skills. Physical Education Review, 6, 64–71.

Reilly, T. and Thomas, V., 1980, The stability of fitness factors over a season of professional soccer as indicated by serial factor analyses. In *Kinanthropometry 11*, edited by Ostyn, M., Beunen, G. and Simons, J. (Baltimore: University Park Press), pp. 247–257.

54 Reliability of Heart Rate Recorded during Soccer Training

E. Rampinini, A. Sassi and F.M. Impellizzeri
Physiology Laboratory, SSMAPEI, Italy

1. INTRODUCTION

Heart rate (HR) is commonly used to monitor and to design aerobic training (Gilman, 1996). Recently, Hoff et al. (2002) have been shown that the HR-$\dot{V}O_2$ relationship in soccer-specific exercises (five-a-side, dribbling track) was not significantly different from HR-$\dot{V}O_2$ relationship found in the laboratory. Using this relationship it is possible to analyze the metabolic demands and the energy cost of sport-specific exercises or competitions. Furthermore, HR itself was suggested to be indicative of physiological effort (Reilly, 1997). These findings support the use of HR in aerobic soccer training. In fact, aerobic endurance training, using interval training performed at a target HR (90-95% of HR_{max}) improved soccer performance by increasing distance covered during a match, work intensity, the number of the sprints and involvements with the ball (Helgerud et al., 2001). In addition, Hoff et al. (2002), have shown that is possible to reach a similar exercise intensity as match-play by using games and a soccer-specific circuit track as in interval training.

However, many coaches and athletic trainers cannot use HR telemetric systems during all training session. For example, they do not often have at their disposal HR monitors for all players. Moreover a lot of time is required to download and to analyze recorded HR data and the high cost of a large number of HR monitors for all the team can limit their use.

Consequently, it could be possible to estimate the physiological load imposed on a single player, using the HR data recorded during soccer-specific exercises performed by the same subject but at different times (for example, during pre-season training camps). In this way, coaches could use these HR reference data to determine the exercise intensity of players during the following training session.

To our knowledge, there is no literature about HR reliability in soccer specific training. Thus, the aim of this study was to determine the reliability of typical soccer specific exercises, with and without the ball, commonly included in the soccer training programme of an Italian junior team.

2. METHODS

2.1. Subjects

Fifteen elite junior soccer players were involved in the study [mean (standard deviation): age 17.4 (0.5) years, body mass 70.4 (5.2) kg, height 1.793 (0.041) m]. All the subjects were part of the same team (Pro Patria Beretti).

2.2. Laboratory test

All subjects performed a preliminary incremental treadmill test. The protocol used was that suggested by Helgerud et al. (2001): 1 $km \cdot h^{-1}$ increment every 5 min, using a treadmill inclination of 3%. Both $\dot{V}O_{2\ max}$ and maximal HR were determined. Respiratory gases were analyzed breath by breath using a VMAX29 system (Sensormedics, CA, USA).

2.3. Field measurement

Subjects performed two training sessions within one week. During the whole training session, HR was recorded every 5 s using a HR monitor (VantageNV and mod. S710, Polar Electro, Finland) but the players had no possibility to observe their HR. They followed technical and tactical indications of the coach. Training duration was 120 min and included warm up with technical exercises using the ball, 4vs4 (4×4 min with 3 min recovery, free touch without goalkeepers, field dimension 25×30 m), 4vs2 (3×4 min with 3 min recovery, free touch without goalkeepers' field dimension 25×30 m), 10vs10 (10 min, free touch with goalkeepers' field dimension 50×60 m) and two circuit tracks (A and B) without the ball (2×8 min) very similar to each other, including changes in direction, backward and lateral running, sprints, jumps, slalom and hills.

2.4. Statistical analysis

Reliability was determined using Bland and Altman scatterplots (difference between the two HR training sessions expressed in % HR_{max} plotted against the measurements of the mean). Reference lines were determined as the mean difference $\pm$ 1.96 SD (Bland and Altman, 1986). Intra-class correlation coefficients (ICC) were also calculated (Hopkins, 2000).

3. RESULTS

Maximal HR was 188 (7) $beats.min^{-1}$ and $\dot{V}O_{2\ max}$ was 53.3 (4.2) $ml \cdot kg^{-1} \cdot min^{-1}$. The exercise intensities expressed as % HR_{max} during the first training session were 76.6 ± 7.4 (warm up), 87.3 ± 3.4 (4vs4 set 1), 87.9 ± 4.6 (4vs4 set 2), 89.2 ± 2.8 (4vs4 set 3), 89.2 ± 4.3 (4vs4 set 4), 88.3 ± 3.0 (4vs4 mean), 75.5 ± 4.6 (4vs2 mean), 84.3 ± 3.5 (10vs10), 89.5 ± 2.5 (circuit A), 89.2 ± 2.2 (circuit B) and 89.4 ± 2.4 (Circuit mean). The exercise intensities expressed as % HR_{max} during the second training session were 73.1 ± 5.5 (warm up), 87.1 ± 4.0 (4vs4 set 1), 88.6 ± 6.6 (4vs4 set 2), 88.9 ± 6.2 (4vs4 set 3), 87.7 ± 4.8 (4vs4 set 4), 88.1 ± 4.5 (4vs4 mean), 80.1 ± 6.2 (4vs2 mean), 86.0 ± 5.6 (10vs10), 87.0 ± 2.7 (circuit A), 88.8 ± 2.1 (circuit B) and 87.9 ± 2.4 (Circuit mean). The ICC values for exercises with the ball are presented in Table 1 and Table 2, while ICC values for exercises without the ball are presented in Table 3.

Table 1. The ICC values for some exercises with the ball.

Exercises	Warm up	4vs2 mean	10vs10
ICC	0.38	0.62	0.48

Table 2. The ICC values for 4vs4 side-a-game.

Exercises	4vs4 set1	4vs4 set2	4vs4 set3	4vs4 set4	4vs4 mean
ICC	0.60	0.72	0.32	0.37	0.62

Table 3. The ICC values for exercises without the ball.

Exercices	Circuit A	Circuit B	Circuit mean
ICC	0.89	0.83	0.90

The bias ± random error component (SD of the differences multiplied by 1.96) expressed as % HRmax for warm up with the ball was 3.5 ± 14.2, for 4vs4 set1 was 0.1 ± 6.5, for 4vs4 set2 was -0.7 ± 8.3, for 4vs4 set3 was 0.3 ± 11.0, for 4vs4 set4 was 1.5 ± 10.2, for Circuit A was 2.5 ± 2.4 and for Circuit B was 0.5 ± 2.5. Bland and Altman scatter plots for 4vs4 mean, 4vs2 mean, 10vs10 and circuit mean are shown in Figures 1, 2, 3 and 4.

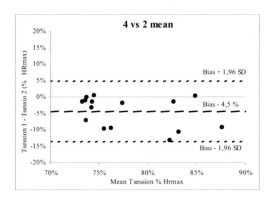

Figure 1. Bland and Altman plot demonstrating the limits of agreement (± 1.96). Bias was significantly different from zero (P<0.05). Bias –4.5 % ± 9.3 %.

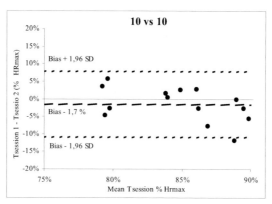

Figure 2. Bland and Altman plot demonstrating the limits of agreement (± 1.96). Bias was not significantly different from zero. Bias–1.7 % ± 9.3 %.

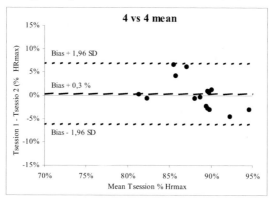

Figure 3. Bland and Altman plot demonstrating the limits of agreement (± 1.96). Bias was not significantly different from zero. Bias 0.3 % ± 6.5 %.

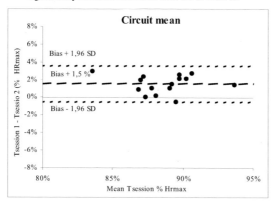

Figure 4. Bland and Altman plot demonstrating the limits of agreement (± 1.96). Bias was not significantly different from zero. Bias 1.5 % ± 2.1 %.

4. DISCUSSION

The results of this study showed poor reliability of exercises with the ball as suggested by the low ICC (from 0.38 to 0.72) with 95% of HR differences within ± 6.5 % to ± 14.2 % of HR_{max}. On the contrary, the circuit track HR performed without the ball used in the present investigation showed a higher reliability with ICCs ranging from 0.83 to 0.90 (from moderate to high) with total error for HR within ± 2.1% and ± 2.5% of HR_{max}.

In this study players followed only technical and tactical instructions of the coach who was asked to manage small-sided games as he commonly does. No other interventions from the researchers were conducted in order to verify the reliability in the most typical and actual situations. A possible reason for the poor reliability of the small-sided games found in this investigation, could be the lack of coach- specific actions aimed to increased and to maintain a high intensity. The use of motivation is very important as reported by Hoff et al. (2002) who suggested that, during games, continuous encouragement and constructive messages are necessary to reach sufficient exercise intensity to improve aerobic fitness. The lack of this involvement by the coach could have allowed players to self-select the intensity, thereby diminishing the reliability between the two sessions, but this suggestion needs to be confirmed by further studies. This kind of supervision is very common and so we strongly suggest that coaches control their soccer-specific exercises with the ball in order to achieve a training stimulus and, especially, to keep training stimuli sufficiently high.

In conclusion, these findings suggest that exercise intensity during aerobic training (circuit running track) is reliable and could be performed without continuous HR monitoring during the season. Instead, soccer-specific exercise training using the ball, if not well directed, needs to be controlled continuously by means of HR monitoring. This could allow coaches to determine the actual individual cardiovascular load in order to optimise the training sessions, or to control the compliance of the physiological stimuli imposed on players with the training previously planned.

REFERENCES

Bland, J.P. and Altman, D.G., B.G., 1986, Statistical methods for assessing agreement between two methods of clinical measurement. *Lancet*, **1**, 307–310.

Helgerud, J., Engen, L.C., Wisloff, U. and Hoff, J., 2001, Aerobic endurance training improves soccer performance. *Medicine and Science in Sports and Exercise*, **33**, 1925–1931.

Hoff, J., Wisloff, U., Engen, L.C., Kemi, O.J. and Helgerud J., 2002, Soccer specific aerobic endurance training. *British Journal of Sports Medicine*, **36**, 218–221.

Hopkins, W.G., 2000, Sportscience: A new view of statistics. *http://www.sportsci. org/resource/stats/index.html.*

Reilly, T., 1997, Energetics of high-intensity exercise (soccer) with particular reference to fatigue. *Journal of Sports Sciences*, **15**, 257–263.

55   Biomechanical Analysis of the Load Imposed on Under-19 Soccer Players during Some Typical Football Training Drills

Javier Mallo Sainz and Enrique Navarro Cabello
Sports Biomechanics Laboratory,
Instituto Nacional de Educacion Fisica,
Polythecnical University of Madrid, Spain

1. INTRODUCTION

Football (soccer) is a high intensity intermittent exercise (Ekblom, 1986). During a 90-minute match, a football player can perform over 1000 changes in activity with a mean duration of about 6 seconds (Reilly and Thomas, 1976), thus needing a specific development of the physical capacity of the player linked to technical, tactical and psychological training programmes.

The demands of playing competitive football have been described in several studies regarding external – what the player does during the game (Mayhew and Wenger, 1985) - and internal – the physiological response to the work done (Ali and Farrally, 1991) - points of view.

From all of these studies, it may be concluded that the mean distance covered during a game is around 10 km (range: 9–12 km), in a non-continuous motion mode, with over 3% of the total playing time running at a linear velocity higher than 5 m.s^{-1} (Ohashi *et al.*, 1988). Average oxygen consumption during a game has been estimated to be around 75% of the maximal oxygen uptake (Van Gool *et al.*, 1988) and the mean heart rate registered during the first half of a competitive game was 164 beats. min^{-1}, while in the second half it decreased to 154 beats.min^{-1} (Bangsbo, 1994). Anaerobic metabolism plays a qualitative role as high intensity activities are a characteristic of top-level games, with a frequency of 19 sprints per game for a player, with an average duration of 2 s (Bangsbo *et al.*, 1991). However, little has been studied considering football training drills.

The purposes of this study were therefore:
a)   To develop and apply an objective methodology for match-analysis based on the calculation of the position of the football players by computerized means.
b)   To assess the differences between three common football training drills (according to kinematic, physiological and technical parameters).
c)   To relate the kinematic and physiological parameters registered during the training drills with real match-play.

2. METHODS

Ten semi-professional male football players (18.4 ± 0.6 years, 1.782 ± 0.051 m and 71.5 ± 1.4 kg) from an U-19 top-class football team (Spanish champions in the 2001 - 2002 season) participated in the study. All the players were experienced in playing the game (with an average practice of 9.3 ± 1.4 years) and they had training sessions at least four days a week plus a competitive match every weekend.

After a standardized match-day warm-up, the players performed the following drills in a rectangular 33x20 m artificial turf surface:

  a) Drill 1 (D1): 3-a-side game with the aim of keeping the ball in possession as much time as possible.
  b) Drill 2 (D2): 3-a-side game with 2 "outer" players who can pass the ball to a player from the team it was received from. Aim: keep possession of the ball.
  c) Drill 3 (D3): 3-a-side game with goalkeepers (3vs3+2) and ordinary football rules. Aim: score goals.

In each of the games, when the ball went out of the playing pitch it was immediately replaced by a new one. Before the training drills, the players were informed of the objectives of each drill and verbally encouraged to play at their maximal intensity.

The method used for the kinematic analysis is very similar to one reported previously (Van Gool *et al.*, 1988) which allows the game to be analyzed by means of a digitization process. The drills were video taped using a JVC GY-DV500E digital camera placed in the stand, so the whole playing pitch was televised, using the sidelines (of known length) for the calibration of the images.

The tape was played back and the frames captured by a specific software developed in the Biomechanics Laboratory at the I.N.E.F. of Madrid (Photo23D), which allows digitizing the position of the players at a sample rate of 2 Hz and then obtaining the coordinates (x,y) of the position, the distance covered and the linear velocity of the players during the games. This method is a DLT-based two-dimensional photogrametric analysis.

Heart rate was recorded at 5-s intervals throughout the drills for three of the players using Polar Accurex Plus heart rate monitors (Polar Electro Oy, Kempele, Finland). Data were transmitted to the computer with the Polar Interface Plus.

A notation sheet was specifically designed to register the technical parameters (passes, shots at goal, etc.) and the video recording was used to review the drills at the same time as total real playing time was calculated.

Microsoft Excel 2000 and SPSS 9.0. statistical software were used for the analysis of the football players´ data.

3. RESULTS AND DISCUSSION

The mean distance covered in D1 for the six players was 746.858 ± 24.032 m, in D2 748.566 ± 29.406 m and in D3 637.838 ± 33.839 m (significantly lower than D1 and D2 ($P<0.05$)).

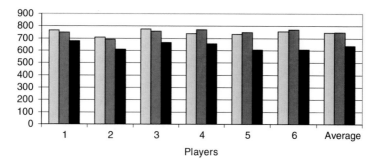

Figure 1. Distance covered by the six football players during the three training drills.

To gain a qualitative approach of the relative intensity of the games, the displacements of the players were divided into five categories (standing still, walking, jogging, running and sprinting) according to their linear velocity. No significant differences were found in the time spent in each type of movement between the drills. Low intensity activities (linear velocity <3 m.s^{-1}) accounted for 67% of the total time, medium intensity activities (from 3 to 5 m.s^{-1}) for 27% and high intensity activities (>5 m.s^{-1}) for 6%.

Table 1. Distribution of the displacements into categories according to the linear for the six players that took part in the three training drills.

Linear Velocity (m.s^{-1})	Drill 1	Drill 2	Drill 3
0–1 (Standing Still-Walking)	12.18 %	11.27 %	17.85 %
1–3 (Jogging)	51.41 %	53.03 %	55.45 %
3–5 (Medium intensity running)	30.47 %	29.48 %	22.33 %
5–7 (High intensity running)	5.35 %	6.11 %	4.15 %
+7 (Sprinting)	0.62 %	0.17 %	0.22 %

There was no significant difference between mean heart rate for the three drills (D1: 173 ± 13,; D2: 166.33 ± 17.67; D3: 166.67 ± 17.04 beats.min^{-1}).

The technical data registered during the three drills showed that Drill 1 was characterized by the use of short-distance passes by players, while Drill 2 required the players to use medium and long distance passes, in order to reach the outer players. In Drill 3, there was the option to shoot to goal, another technical parameter recorded at the same time requiring a different tactical behaviour of the players, who organized themselves to defend their goal once they lost possession of the ball.

When comparing the results obtained during the training drills with real match-play, it could be observed that the relative intensity of the drills was slightly higher than competition matches as total distance covered (extrapolated to 90 minutes) was higher: 12,800 vs. 10,800 m (Bangsbo *et al.*, 1991), as well as time spent in high-intensity running (>5 m.s^{-1}): 6 vs. 3.9% (Ohashi *et al.*, 1988), real playing time: 85 vs. 65% (Bangsbo, 1994) and mean heart rate: 169 vs. 164 beats. min^{-1} (Bangsbo, 1994).

4. CONCLUSIONS

The methodology developed in this study of match-analysis allows objective data about the players' behaviour to be obtained during the games, without interfering with the players' performances. The information obtained with this method concerning the training load may be very useful for coaches in order to control the process.

The drills analysed may represent an important training stimulus for football players as they reproduce the demands of the game. Total distance covered, linear velocity of the displacements and mean heart rate were in the range of data previously published with respect to the demands of 11-a-side football. At the same time, these games require technical and tactical responses of the players and are more motivating than the traditional conditioning schemes without a ball.

REFERENCES

Ali, A. and Farrally, M., 1991, Recording soccer players´ heart rates during matches. *Journal of Sports Sciences*, **9**, 183–189.

Bangsbo, J., 1994, The physiology of soccer with special reference to intense intermittent exercise. *Acta Physiologica Scandinavica*, **151** (Suppl. 619), 1–156.

Bangsbo, J., Norregard, L. and Thorsoe, F., 1991, Activity profile of competition soccer. *Canadian Journal of Sports Science*, **16**, 110–116.

Ekblom, B., 1986, Applied physiology of soccer. *Sports Medicine*, **3**, 50–60.

Mayhew, S.R. and Wenger, H.A., 1985, Time-motion analysis of professional soccer. *Journal of Human Movement Studies*, **11**, 49–52.

Ohashi, J., Togari, H., Isokawa, M. and Suzuki, S., 1988, Measuring movement speeds and distances covered during soccer match-play. In *Proceedings of the First World Congress on Science and Football*, Liverpool, edited by Reilly, T., Lees. A., Davids, K. and Murphy, W.J. (London: E. & F.N. Spon), pp. 329–333.

Reilly, T. and Thomas, V., 1976, A motion analysis of work-rate in different positional roles in professional football match-play. *Journal of Human Movement Studies*, **2**, 87–97.

Van Gool, D., Van Gerven, D. and Boutmans, J., 1988, The physiological load imposed on soccer players during real match-play. In *Proceedings of the First World Congress on Science and Football*, Liverpool, edited by Reilly, T., Lees, A., Davids, K. and Murphy, W.J. (London: E. & F.N. Spon), pp. 51–59.

56   The Effects of a 10-day Taper on Repeated-Sprint Performance in Females

D. Bishop and J. Edge

School of Human Movement, The University of Western Australia

1. INTRODUCTION

Team-sport players and coaches are constantly seeking methods by which to improve performance. In many sports, a common practice designed to elicit maximal performance is to reduce the training stimulus 5 to 21 days prior to an important competition. This reduction in the training stimulus is incremental and is commonly termed 'taper'. The goal during taper periods is to maintain the physiological adaptations achieved during intensive training, while reducing the negative impact of training (i.e., residual fatigue). Under ideal circumstances, this change will result in an athlete who has made maximum physiological adjustments at the exact same time as the negative influences of training have diminished, resulting in an optimal performance potential.

While there have been very few studies of the influence of taper on athletic performance, most have reported improved performance. A consistent improvement of approximately 3% in swim performance (50–1500 m) has been reported following 14-day tapers (Costill et al., 1988). A similar improvement in 5-km run time has also been reported following a 7-day, high-intensity taper (Houmard et al., 1994). Improvements in cycling performance (3–8%) have also been reported following 7–14 day tapers (Martin et al., 1994). While taper is a well-established practice for continuous exercise, no previous study has investigated the effects of taper on repeated-sprint performance. The purpose of this study was to investigate the influence of a 10-day taper on repeated-sprint performance.

2. METHODS

2.1. Subjects and procedures

Eleven physically active female subjects (mean $\pm$ SD: age = 19 $\pm$ 3 years, mass = 59.3 $\pm$ 9.6 kg, $\dot{V}O_2$ max = 39.0 $\pm$ 6.4 ml·kg^{-1}·min^{-1}) participated in this study. Subjects were informed of the study requirements, benefits and risks before giving written informed consent. Approval for the study's procedures was granted by the Research Ethics Committee of the University of Western Australia.

Following a familiarisation session for all tests, subjects performed a graded exercise test (GXT) to determine both their lactate threshold (Tlac) and. The $\dot{V}O_2$ max following week subjects began the training programme which consisted of 4–12 $\times$ 2-min efforts at 130–180% Tlac, interspersed with a 1-min rest period, three times per week for six weeks. Each week (on a non-training day), subjects performed a repeated-sprint ability (RSA) test (5 x 6-s sprints every 30 s) in an attempt to ensure that no learning effect was evident following the 10-day taper. Following the initial six-week intensive training period, subjects were then given a 10-day taper followed by a final RSA test. Based on previous research (Banister et al., 1999), we used a fast exponential taper that consisted of approximately 33% reduction in training load (intensity x duration) on each subsequent training session performed during the taper.

2.2. Statistical analyses

The mean and standard deviation ($\pm$ SD) for the dependent variables of each study were calculated. One-way repeated measures ANOVAs were used to test for changes in repeated-sprint ability. Least-squares linear regression analysis was used to calculate correlation coefficients between independent variables and repeated-sprint performance variables, using Pearson's product moment (r). The level of statistical significance was set at $P<0.05$.

3. RESULTS

The effects of the six-week training period and the 10-day taper procedure on repeated-sprint ability are summarised in Figures 1 and 2. Total work (kJ) during the 5 x 6-s test tended to increase from week 1 to week 4, with a plateau in performance being evident from week 4 to week 6. After six weeks, there was, on average, a 26.5% increase in total work (kJ). Following the 10-day taper, the group averaged a 4.4% increase in total work during the 5 x 6-s test, but this was not significant ($P = 0.157$). Similar results were also reported for average peak power (Figure 2). Following the 10-day taper, the group averaged a 3.2% increase in average peak power (W) during the 5×6-s test, but again this was not significant ($P = 0.178$). For both total work and average peak power, performance post-taper was the only occasion when performance was greater than that recorded in week 3. There was a significant relationship between change in performance from week 5 to week 6 and post-taper change in performance (r=0.76; $P<0.05$). However, there was no significant correlation between aerobic fitness (either Tlac or $\dot{V}O_2$ max) and post-taper change in performance (r=0.1 and r=0.2 respectively; $P>0.05$). There was no significant change in body mass throughout the study.

The effects of the 10-day taper procedure on each sprint of the repeated-sprint ability test are summarised in Figures 3 and 4. While there was no significant difference in sprint performance for any of the sprints between week 6 (pre-taper) and week 8 (post-taper), there was a trend for better recovery of sprint performance following the taper. This is supported by the significant decrease in work decrement (Wk 6: $10.2 \pm 3.5\%$ v Wk 8: $7.9 \pm 4.3\%$; $P < 0.05$) following the 10-day taper. The change in peak power decrement following the 10-day taper also approached significance (Wk 6: $7.7 \pm 3.5\%$ v Wk 8: $6.5 \pm 4.3\%$; $P = 0.08$).

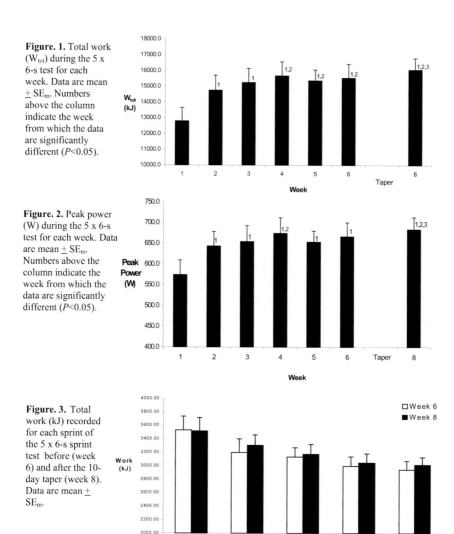

Figure. 1. Total work (W_{tot}) during the 5 x 6-s test for each week. Data are mean ± SE_m. Numbers above the column indicate the week from which the data are significantly different ($P<0.05$).

Figure. 2. Peak power (W) during the 5 x 6-s test for each week. Data are mean ± SE_m. Numbers above the column indicate the week from which the data are significantly different ($P<0.05$).

Figure. 3. Total work (kJ) recorded for each sprint of the 5 x 6-s sprint test before (week 6) and after the 10-day taper (week 8). Data are mean ± SE_m.

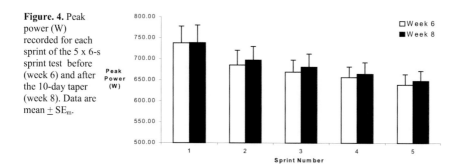

Figure. 4. Peak power (W) recorded for each sprint of the 5 x 6-s sprint test before (week 6) and after the 10-day taper (week 8). Data are mean ± SE_m.

4. DISCUSSION

This is the first study to document the effects of taper on repeated-sprint ability. Although not significant, following the taper there was a 4.4% increase in total work (kJ) during the RSA test. This improvement appeared to be related to an improved ability to maintain sprint performance, as there was a significant decrease in work decrement across the five sprints following the taper. The plateau in performance from week 4 to week 6 and the non-significant change in sprint 1 performance suggest that the observed changes following the taper were not due to a learning effect.

We have previously reported that interval training can significantly improve repeated-sprint performance (Edge et al., 2002). However, the results of the present study demonstrate that most of this improvement occurs in the first few weeks of interval training. Similar to the results of Martin et al. (1994), changes in performance were most pronounced in the first two to four weeks. From week four to six there appeared to be a plateau in performance. This plateau may indicate a training stimulus that was either not adequate in progressively overloading the subjects or was excessive and produced a residual fatigue that impaired RSA (Fry et al., 1991). The 4.4% improvement in performance associated with the 10-day taper supports the latter explanation. Furthermore, there was a progressive increase in training load each week.

The 10-day taper used in the present study was associated with a significant decrease in work decrement during the RSA test. Furthermore, although not significant, the 4.4% improvement in performance in the present study is comparable in magnitude to previously reported significant improvements in performance following similar taper protocols. It is likely that the large variance in the present study made it difficult for group means to reach statistical significance. Previous seven-day tapers, consisting of high-intensity exercise, have been reported to improve running performance (5 km) in trained runners by 2.8% (Houmard et al., 1994). A 14-day taper, including high-intensity exercise, has also been reported to improve performance by a similar percentage ($\sim$ 3%) in competitive swimmers throughout a wide variety of racing distances (50 -1560 m; 23 - 1020 s in duration) (Costill et al., 1985). It therefore appears that a taper that includes high-intensity exercise can improve performance. Furthermore, this is the first study to suggest that tapering can improve RSA.

The 4.4% improvement in total work appeared to be attributable to an improved ability to maintain sprint performance during the RSA test. There was a significant decrease in work decrement across the five sprints following the taper. The decrease in power decrement also approached significance ($P=0.08$). While no previous study has investigated the effects of a taper on RSA, a case study has previously indicated that power loss during a 30-s cycle sprint test was 2.3% less following a 7-day taper in a national team pursuitist (Shepley et al., 1992). While further research is required, it may be that taper improves the ability to maintain work and power output.

The response to the taper was variable with 8 out of the 11 subjects exhibiting a performance improvement. While performance change following the taper was not correlated with aerobic fitness (Tlac or $\dot{V}O_2$ max), it was significantly correlated with the change in performance from week 5 to week 6 (r= 0.76; P<0.05). That is, the larger the increase in performance from week 5 to week 6 (the final two weeks of training), the smaller the increase in performance post-taper. A continued increase in performance during training may indicate that the subject is adapting to the training stimulus, whereas a plateau or a decrease in performance may indicate residual fatigue and inability to cope with the training demand (Fry et al., 1991). Thus, the results of the present study suggest that a taper is more beneficial to individuals whose performance is stagnating or declining.

In summary, tapering from high-intensity interval training appears to be a useful strategy for promoting improved repeated-sprint ability. In particular, tapering seems to improve the ability to maintain work output during repeated sprints, as evidenced by the significant decrease in work decrement following taper. Further research is required to identify the mechanisms by which a taper may improve RSA, in sports such as football. While we used a common taper strategy involving a reduction in both weekly training time and intensity, further research is needed to investigate optimal taper strategies for athletes requiring good RSA.

REFERENCES

Banister, E.W., Carter, J.B. and Zarkadas, P.C., 1999, Training theory and taper: validation in decathlon athletics. *European Journal of Applied Physiology, 79*, 182–191.

Costill, D.L., Flynn, H.G., Kirwan, J., Houmard, J.P., Mitchell, R. and Park, S.H., 1988, Effects of repeated days of intensified training on muscle, glycogen and swimming performance. Medicine and Science in Sports and Exercise, **20**, 245–254.

Costill, D.L., King, D.S., Thomas, R. and Hargreaves, M., 1985, Effects of reduced training on muscular power in swimmers. *Physician and Sportsmedicine, 13*, 94–101.

Edge, J., Bishop, D., Goodman, C. and Dawson, B., 2002, The effects of training intensity on muscle buffer capacity and repeated sprint ability. *European Congress of Sport Science*, Athens, Greece, 622.

Fry, R.W., Moreton, A.H. and Kent D., 1991, Overtraining in athletics! An update, *Sports Medicine*, **12**, 32–65.

Houmard, J.A., Scott, B.K., Justice, C.L. and Chenice, T., 1994, The effects of taper on performance in distance runners. *Medicine and Science in Sports and Exercise*, **26**, 624–631.

Martin, D.T., Scifres, J.C., Zimmerman, S.D. and Wilkinson, S.D., 1994, Effects of interval training and a taper on cycling performance and isokinetic leg strength. *International Journal of Sports Medicine*, **15**, 485–491.

Shepley, B., MacDougall, J.D., Gipriano, N., Sutton, J.R., Tarnopolsky, M.A. and Coates, G., 1992, Physiologic effects of tapering in highly trained athletes. *Journal of Applied Physiology*, **72**, 706–711.

57 Effect of Repeated Sprints on Hamstring Quadriceps Torque Ratios

W. Andrews[1], B. Dawson[1,2] and G. Stewart[2]

[1] School of Human Movement and Exercise Science, The University of Western Australia, 35 Stirling Highway, Crawley, WA 6009
[2] West Coast Eagles Football Club, P.O. Box 508, Subiaco, 6008, Australia

1. INTRODUCTION

In Australian Rules Football (ARF), players must perform numerous near-maximal sprints with little recovery between each effort (McKenna et al., 1988). Heavy demands are placed on the phosphate and glycolytic energy pathways to produce energy rapidly for both hamstrings and quadriceps muscle contractions when sprinting. Research has identified the hamstrings as containing a greater proportion of fast-twitch (type II) muscle fibres than the quadriceps (Garrett et al., 1983; Garrett et al., 1984), therefore suggesting faster torque production (Aagaard et al., 1998). However, over a series of repeated sprint efforts, this may lead to an earlier onset and greater degree of fatigue in the hamstrings, therefore potentially altering the strength (torque) balance between these two muscle groups.

Early research by Dorman (1971) identified a possible relationship between fatigue and hamstrings muscle injury. More recently, Seward and Patrick, (1992) conducted a three-year survey on Australian Football League (AFL) injuries and found hamstrings strains were the most common muscle strain. They also found that hamstrings strains occurred most often towards the end of the third and fourth quarters, suggesting player fatigue as a possible causal factor for injury.

Hamstrings muscle strength and its proposed relationship with hamstrings injury have been studied for many years (Burkett, 1970; Heiser et al., 1984). Researchers have examined the strength balance between the hamstrings and quadriceps muscle groups through the calculation of the isokinetic hamstrings to quadriceps (HQ) torque ratio. Initially, only a traditional HQ ratio was used (Klein and Allman, 1973), whereby peak knee flexion strength (hamstrings torque) is divided by peak knee extension strength (quadriceps torque) at a given angular velocity and contraction mode (concentric or eccentric). Later researchers examined muscle strength properties of the knee joint by employing a functional HQ torque ratio method which more closely simulates the skill of running (Aagaard et al., 1995; Aagaard et al., 1998; Bennell et al., 1998). Eccentric hamstrings (He) muscle strength is divided by concentric quadriceps (Qc) muscle strength to reflect the role of the hamstrings in controlling knee extension and hip flexion (HeQc). Conversely, concentric hamstrings (Hc) muscle strength is divided by eccentric quadriceps (Qe) muscle strength when the quadriceps are controlling knee flexion and hip extension (HcQe).

Orchard et al. (1997) compared peak conventional HQ ratios of hamstrings injured and uninjured ARF players and found injured players recorded significantly lower values at a slow 1.05 rad.s^{-1} angular velocity. In contrast, Bennell et al. (1998), who also compared muscle strength and subsequent hamstrings injury of ARF players, found no significant reduction. Both of these studies, however, compared pre-season muscle strength ratios of injured and uninjured ARF players and not the "on-field" strength values directly after fatiguing exercise, when injury to the hamstrings is more likely to occur in this type of game (Seward and Patrick, 1992). Therefore, the aim of this study was to examine the effects of acute running fatigue on hamstrings (and quadriceps) strength levels. Both traditional (HcQc) and functional (HeQc and HcQe) ratios were calculated.

2. METHODS

2.1. Subjects

Nine elite ARF players were recruited from one AFL team. All participants reported that they had not suffered any hamstrings or quadriceps muscle injury in the three months prior to the study. Testing was conducted over a four-week period during the AFL off-season (October-November).

2.2. Experimental design

The format of the experimental design consisted of one familiarisation session, followed by four sessions for testing the torque of the hamstrings and quadriceps muscles. Sessions 1 and 3 were completed in a non-fatigued state, and sessions 2 and 4 were performed in an acutely fatigued condition. A minimum of three days separated session 1 from the familiarisation session and a similar time was permitted between each of the subsequent torque testing sessions.

2.2.1 Familiarisation session

After a 5-minute jog and 10-minute stretch, each subject attempted the first of two 40-metre maximal sprint efforts on a grassed oval while wearing football boots. Time was recorded using an electronic Speed Timing Light System (Omron Electronics Pty Ltd, North Ryde, N.S.W). After ten minutes of walk recovery, the second maximal sprint effort was completed. Both times were recorded to the nearest 0.001 second.

After a further 15 minutes of walk recovery, each subject was then taken into the laboratory and given further verbal instruction in regard to using the Biodex 2000 isokinetic dynamometer (Model 900–350, Shirley, N.Y.). Each subject then performed four sub-maximal, followed by three maximal concentric and eccentric hamstrings and quadriceps muscle actions at an angular velocity of 1.05 rad.s^{-1}.

Session 1 and 3 (Non-fatigued torque testing)

Following a 5-minute jog and 10-minute stretch, the subject was positioned into the Biodex and the gravity correction moment was obtained at a knee joint angle of 30° knee flexion. The subject then performed three maximal concentric hamstrings and quadriceps actions and three maximal eccentric hamstrings and quadriceps actions (order assigned by the toss of a coin) through a range of 10° to 95° knee flexion and extension, at an angular velocity of 1.05 rad.s^{-1}.

Session 2 and 4 (Fatigued torque testing)

After an identical 15-minute warm-up procedure (as for session 1 and 3), each subject completed 6 x 40-metre maximal sprint efforts. Each subject was given a total of 30 s to complete each of the 40-metre sprints and jog back to the start of the timing gates ready for the next maximal effort. Subjects were required to complete only the first of the six efforts within 95% of their best effort recorded during the familiarisation session. Upon completion of the sixth effort, the subject was taken directly into the laboratory and positioned into the Biodex device, whereby the torque testing protocol identical to session 1 and 3 was immediately initiated (approximately 30 s after finishing the final sprint).

2.3. Statistics and data analysis

2.3.1 Muscle torque

The torque value at three angle specific (30°, 40° & 50° flexion), and peak variables were extracted from the data and recorded for each of the three concentric and three eccentric hamstrings and quadriceps attempts on the Biodex dynamometer. The mean torque from the three attempts, (at 30°, 40°, 50° and peak) for each contraction type was calculated. The values determined from the two non-fatigued and fatigued sessions were corrected for gravity using the following formula, which incorporated the Biodex generated 30° static gravitational torque value as the reference angle:-

cos (knee angle i.e., 40°, 50°, peak angle) x (M $_{reference\ angle\ torque\ value}$ (at 30°) / cos 30°)
(Westing and Seger, 1989)

Eccentric and concentric hamstrings torque values for each variable required the subtraction of the corresponding angles' gravitational moment, whereas the identical gravitational moment was added to all eccentric and concentric quadriceps variables. Mean values of session 1 and 3 and session 2 and 4 torque values were calculated for analysis.

Paired samples t-tests were used to determine whether any significant differences ($P<0.05$) existed when comparing non-fatigued concentric and eccentric torque to fatigued concentric and eccentric torque, for both muscle groups, at each of the three angle specific (30°, 40°, 50°) and peak variables.

2.3.2 Muscle Torque Ratios

The mean gravity corrected torque at each variable over the three attempts was then calculated to determine the conventional HcQc torque ratio, and/or the functional HeQc and HcQe torque ratios using the following formulae:-

$$
\text{HcQc} = \frac{\text{Concentric hamstrings torque} - (\text{correction for gravity at } 30°, 40°, 50° \text{ and peak})}{\text{Concentric quadriceps torque} + (\text{correction for gravity at } 30°, 40°, 50° \text{ and peak})} \times 100
$$

$$
\text{HeQc} = \frac{\text{Eccentric hamstrings torque} - (\text{correction for gravity at } 30°, 40°, 50° \text{ and peak})}{\text{Concentric quadriceps torque} + (\text{correction for gravity at } 30°, 40°, 50° \text{ and peak})}
$$

$$
\text{HcQe} = \frac{\text{Concentric hamstrings torque} - (\text{correction for gravity at } 30°, 40°, 50° \text{ and peak})}{\text{Eccentric quadriceps torque} + (\text{correction for gravity at } 30°, 40°, 50° \text{ and peak})}
$$

(From Aagaard et al., 1998)

Paired samples t-tests were again performed on all four conventional (HcQc) ratios and seven functional (4 HeQc & 3 HcQe) torque ratios, to identify whether there was any significant difference between the non-fatigued and fatigued ratios.

3. RESULTS

The 6 × 40-m sprints resulted in a mean performance decrement of approximately 8% (time for first to last sprint).

Concentric and eccentric hamstrings and quadriceps torque values

These values are presented in Table 1. No data for the peak eccentric quadriceps torque were recorded, as all subjects stopped the Biodex (cut off at $\approx$ 245 Nm) in both the fatigued and non-fatigued conditions.

Table 1. Mean ($\pm$SD) concentric hamstrings (Hc), concentric quadriceps (Qc), eccentric hamstrings (He), and eccentric quadriceps (Qe) torques (Nm), non-fatigued and fatigued, for the three angle specific and peak torque variables.

	Hc Torque	Qc Torque	He Torque	Qe Torque
30° NF	137.16 ($\pm$25.21)	133.52 ($\pm$39.64)	169.95 ($\pm$44.98)	159.12 ($\pm$32.67)
30° F	120.03 ($\pm$21.85)**	130.22 ($\pm$28.94)	160.68 ($\pm$52.01)	155.59 ($\pm$32.06)
40° NF	137.33 ($\pm$30.97)	170.73 ($\pm$45.73)	161.85 ($\pm$43.37)	201.75 ($\pm$33.7)
40° F	117.29 ($\pm$24.92)**	169.63 ($\pm$39.85)	154.28 ($\pm$47.11)	195.14 ($\pm$36.36)
50° NF	134.68 ($\pm$33.87)	203.73 ($\pm$54.27)	164.05 ($\pm$42.58)	218.02 ($\pm$34.15)
50° F	110.2 ($\pm$25.06)**	201.2 ($\pm$46.04)	151.08 ($\pm$41.2)*	213.97 ($\pm$17.62)
peak NF	156.33 ($\pm$27.13)	251.58 ($\pm$50.04)	171.18 ($\pm$40.4)	
Peak F	133.98 ($\pm$23.88)***	234.49 ($\pm$46.36)*	160.81 ($\pm$46.89)	

NF : non-fatigued (no prior acute running fatigue)
F   : fatigued (with acute running fatigue)
*   significant difference (P<0.05), NF versus F
** significant difference (P<0.01), NF versus F
***significant difference (P<0.001), NF versus F

Concentric hamstrings torque significantly ($P<0.01$) decreased after the fatiguing exercise protocol for the three angle specific and also the peak torque ($P<0.001$) variables.   The concentric quadriceps torque variable showed a significant decrease ($P<0.05$) at one (peak) of the four variables following the 6 x 40-metre maximal sprint efforts, when compared to the non-fatigued condition. There was also a significant decrease ($P<0.05$) in eccentric hamstrings torque after the fatiguing exercise for the 50° angle specific variable when compared to a non-fatigued condition.

Conventional HcQc and functional HeQc and HcQe torque ratios

These values are presented in Table 2.

Table 2. Mean (±SD) HcQc, HeQc, and HcQe torque ratios, non-fatigued and fatigued, for three angle specific and peak torque variables.

	HcQc Torque Ratio %	HeQc Torque Ratio	HcQe Torque Ratio
30° NF	108.41 (±24.2)	1.51 (±0.37)	0.88 (±0.18)
30° F	94.24 (±15.16)*	1.37 (±0.45)	0.80 (±0.21)*
40° NF	82.23 (±10.44)	1.09 (±0.21)	0.67 (±0.09)
40° F	70.08 (±9.53)**	1.03 (±0.3)	0.60 (±0.13)*
50° NF	67.46 (±10.21)	0.87 (±0.14)	0.51 (±0.03)
50° F	55.36 (±8.99)*	0.80 (±0.21)	0.44 (±.0.07)
peak NF	62.69 (±5.63)	0.77 (±0.14)	
peak F	57.78 (±7.05)*	0.79 (±0.21)	

NF : non-fatigued (no prior acute running fatigue)
F   : fatigued (with acute running fatigue)
* significant difference ($P<0.05$), NF versus F
** significant difference ($P<0.01$), NF versus F

There was a significant decrease between the non-fatigued and fatigued conventional (HcQc) torque ratios at all four (30°, 40°, 50° & peak) variables. Conversely, there was no significant reduction in any of the four HeQc functional ratios analysed following the fatiguing exercise protocol, although there was a significant decrease ($P<0.05$) in the fatigued HcQe functional ratio for the 30° and 40° variables when compared to a non-fatigued condition.

Traditional concentric hamstrings to concentric quadriceps ratios of less than 61% (or 0.61) were common in all subjects tested. No subjects had a ratio less than 0.61 at 40° non-fatigued, and only one when fatigued. Two players had <61% ratios at 50° non-fatigued, which increased to seven when fatigued. Also, seven of the nine players had a ratio <61% at the peak torque variable in a fatigued condition as well as three in a non-fatigued condition. No subject had a HcQc ratio less than 61% at the 30° angle, whether in a fatigued or non-fatigued condition.

4. DISCUSSION

Of the eleven angle specific and peak torque variables analysed, six produced ratios that were significantly lower after the 6 × 40-metre maximal sprint efforts, when compared to a non-fatigued state. To date there is no published research that compares conventional and functional HQ torque ratios measured without prior fatigue, with ratios measured directly after fatiguing repeated sprint exercise.

Conventional HcQc torque ratio

The three angle specific (30°, 40°, 50°) and peak conventional HcQc torque ratios analysed in the present study were significantly lower following the maximal sprint efforts, when compared to those recorded in a non-fatigued state. These results indicate that acute, fatiguing, repeat sprint exercise has a measurable detrimental effect on the concentric muscle strength relationship of the hamstrings and quadriceps muscle groups.

The fatigued concentric hamstrings torques for the 30°, 40°, 50° and peak variables were significantly lower than those recorded in a non-fatigued condition. There was no significant decrease shown for the three angle specific concentric quadriceps torque values following the fatiguing exercise protocol. However, there was a significant reduction in the peak concentric quadriceps torque in a fatigued condition. These results suggest the repeated sprint running exercise protocol used here was sufficient to reduce concentric muscle strength in the predominantly fast fatiguing type II fibre hamstrings muscles, but with only minimal torque performance decrement to the predominantly more type I fibre quadriceps muscles.

Functional HeQc torque ratio

None of the four angle specific and peak torque functional HeQc ratios had significantly lower values following the fatiguing exercise when compared to a non-fatigued state. These results indicate that the acute fatiguing sprint exercise had no marked detrimental effect on the eccentric hamstrings to concentric quadriceps strength relationship.

There was no significant decrease for three of the four fatigued eccentric hamstrings torque values (30°, 40° & peak) when compared to a non-fatigued condition. These results are in support of the data of Hortobagyi et al. (1996), who found no detrimental effect on the isokinetic production of eccentric hamstrings torque following repeated eccentric and concentric actions. In comparison, all four angle specific and peak concentric hamstrings torques were significantly lower after the 6 x 40-metre sprints.

Functional HcQe torque ratio

Two of the three angle specific, functional HcQe torque ratios (30°, 40°) analysed were significantly lower following the fatiguing repeat sprint exercise, when compared to those measured in a non-fatigued condition. Further investigations are required to substantiate that acute fatiguing exercise has a measurable detrimental effect on the concentric hamstrings and eccentric quadriceps strength relationship.

As already identified, the fatigued concentric hamstrings torque means for the 30°, 40°, 50° and peak variables were significantly lower than the non-fatigued counterparts. There was no significant decrease recorded for the three angle specific, eccentric quadriceps torques following the 6 × 40-metre maximal sprint efforts.

Prediction of hamstring injury

In the present study, three of the nine subjects displayed HcQc peak torque ratios of less than 0.61 (or 61%) in a non-fatigued condition, increasing to seven following the 6 × 40-metre sprints. Similar findings were evident in the study of Bennell et al. (1998), where 77% of the subjects had a HcQc ratio less than 0.60 for the peak torque variable at an angular velocity of $60^\circ \cdot s^{-1}$ when non-fatigued. Orchard et al. (1997) found that players are at an increased risk of hamstrings strain when the HcQc peak ratio is less than 0.61. According to this standard, most of the subjects used in the present study are susceptible to hamstrings injury predominantly when in a fatigued condition. However, Bennell et al. (1998) did not support a significant relationship between non-fatigued pre-season muscle strength (weakness) and subsequent hamstrings injury.

5. CONCLUSIONS

On the basis of the results of this study, it was concluded that :
- An 8% performance decrement (increase in sprint time) was recorded across the 6 × 40-metre sprints, indicating that this task produced an acute state of fatigue.

- Acute sprint fatigue reduced the conventional, but only partially reduced the functional torque ratios of the hamstrings and quadriceps muscles.

Repeated sprint efforts resulted in the reduction of concentric hamstrings torque values when compared to a non-fatigued state, but there was no decrease recorded for the eccentric hamstrings and concentric and eccentric quadriceps torque values (excluding Qc 30°).

The fatiguing repeated sprint exercise protocol used in this study attempted to simulate a brief period of team sport play. Acute running fatigue may increase the susceptibility of the hamstrings to injury. Future research of this type may further increase knowledge regarding injury rehabilitation and strength and conditioning programme for injury prevention for the hamstrings. The best way to train the hamstrings in order to increase their resistance to fatigue is unknown, as having to contract forcefully in a fatigued state is likely to predispose these muscles to injury. According to previous research (Orchard et al., 1997), the subjects in this study, with peak conventional HcQc ratios of <0.61, are at an increased risk of hamstrings strain, and the acute running fatigue further reduced this ratio. Therefore, training modalities to limit or prevent the running-induced decline in hamstrings / quadriceps strength ratios, need to be further investigated.

REFERENCES

Aagaard, P.M., Simonsen, E.B., Trolle, M.M., Bangsbo, J. and Klausen, K., 1995, Isokinetic hamstring/quadriceps strength ratio: influence of joint angular velocity, gravity correction and contraction mode. *Acta Physiologica Scandinavica, 154*, 421–427.

Aagaard, P., Simonsen, E.B., Magnusson, S.P., Larsson, B. and Dyhre-Poulsen, P., 1998, A new concept for isokinetic hamstrings: quadriceps muscle strength ratio. *American Journal of Sports Medicine, 26*, 231–237.

Bennell, K., Wajswelner, H., Lew, P., Schall-Riaucour, A., Leslie, S. and Cirone, J., 1998, Isokinetic strength testing does not predict hamstring injury in Australian rules footballers. *British Journal of Sports Medicine, 32*, 309–314.

Burkett, L.N., 1970, Causative factors in hamstring strains. *Medicine and Science in Sports and Exercise, 2*, 39–42.

Dorman, P., 1971, A report on 140 hamstring injuries. *Australian Journal of Sports Medicine, 4*, 30–36.

Garrett, W.E., Califf, J.C. and Bassett, F.H., 1984, Histochemical correlates of hamstring injuries. *American Journal of Sports Medicine, 12*, 98–103.

Garrett, W.E., Mumma, M. and Lucareche, C.L., 1983, Ultrastructural differences in human skeletal muscle fibre types. *Orthopaedic Clinics of North America, 14*, 413–25.

Heiser, T.M., Weber, J., Sullivan, G., Clare, P. and Jacobs, R.R., 1984, Prophylaxis and management of hamstring muscle injuries in intercollegiate football players. *American Journal of Sports Medicine, 12*, 368–70.

Hortobagyi, T., Barrier, J., Beard, D., Braspenninex, J., Koens, P., Devita, P., Dempsey, L. and Lambert, J., 1996, Greater initial adaptations to submaximal muscle lengthening than muscle shortening. *Journal of Applied Physiology, 81*, 1677–1682.

Klein, K. and Allman, F.L., 1973, *The Knee in Sports*. (Saint Louis: CV Mosby Co).

McKenna, M.J., Patrick, J.D., Sandstrom, E.R. and Chennells, M.H.D., 1988, Computer video analysis of activity patterns in Australian rules football. In *Science and Football*, edited by Reilly, T., Lees, A., Davids, K. and Murphy, W. J. (London: E. and F.N. Spon), pp. 274–281.

Orchard, J., Marsden, J., Lord, S. and Garlick, D. 1997, Preseason hamstring muscle weakness associated with hamstring muscle injury in Australian footballers. *American Journal of Sports Medicine, 25* (1), 81–85.

Seward, H.G. and Patrick, J., 1992, A three year survey of Victorian football league injuries. *Australian Journal of Science and Medicine in Sport, 24* (2) 51–54.

Westing, S.H. and Seger, J.Y., 1989, Eccentric and concentric torque-velocity characteristics, torque output comparisons, and gravity effect torque corrections for the quadriceps and hamstring muscles in females. *International Journal of Sports Medicine, 10*, 175–180.

58 The Influence of Pre-Warming on the Physiological Responses to Soccer-Specific Intermittent Exercise

W.A. Gregson[1], B. Drust[1], A. Batterham[2] and N.T. Cable[1]

[1] Research Institute for Sports and Exercise Sciences, Liverpool John Moores University, Liverpool, UK

[2] Department of Sport and Exercise Science, University of Bath, Bath, UK

1. INTRODUCTION

Preliminary "warm-up" strategies are often used to promote an increase in temperature of the core and working muscles, an elevation in cardiovascular and respiratory functioning and neuromuscular rehearsal of the subsequent performance (DeVries and Housh, 1994). Physiological changes resulting from pre-exercise warming protocols (e.g., increased body temperature and body water loss) have, however, been shown to reduce the capacity to perform prolonged periods of continuous (Gonzalez-Alonso et al., 1999; Gregson et al., 2002b) and intermittent (Gregson et al., 2002a) exercise in ambient temperatures of 21–22 °C. These changes in prolonged exercise capacity are suggested to be mediated through mechanisms associated with the earlier development of high internal body temperature and/or alterations in the body's capacity to store heat (Gonzalez-Alonso et al., 1999; Gregson et al., 2002a; Gregson et al., 2002b).

Warm-up routines remain an integral part of pre-match preparation. However, no study to date has determined the influence of pre-exercise warming strategies on the physiological responses to soccer-specific intermittent exercise performance. The aim of the current investigation was therefore to examine the effects of two different pre-exercise warming strategies on the metabolic and thermoregulatory responses to soccer-specific intermittent exercise.

2. METHODS

2.1. Subjects

Six male university soccer players (mean ± s age 24 ± 6 years; height 1.81 ± 0.3 m; body mass 76.8 ± 6.4 kg; maximal oxygen uptake [$\dot{V}O_{2\ max}$] 4.52 ± 0.2 l·min^{-1}) were studied. All subjects were well trained and were not acclimatised to heat.

2.2. Procedures

Each subject was required to complete a 90-min soccer-specific intermittent exercise treadmill protocol (2 x 45 min halves separated by a 15-min intermission period) following both active pre-warming (AH) and passive pre-warming (PH).

A third trial with no prior manipulation of body temperature was also included as a control (Cont). All trials were undertaken without the use of fan-assisted air movement in laboratory ambient (dry bulb) temperatures of 19 ± 0.6 °C (Relative humidity 36.7 ± 5.0 %).

Active warming required subjects to perform treadmill running at an exercise intensity of 70% $\dot{V}O_{2max}$, until the attainment of a rectal temperature (T_{rec}) of 38 °C. During the PH procedure, subjects were immersed in a heated water tank (44 °C) to the level of the gluteal fold until an identical T_{rec} was reached. In the control condition subjects rested in a seated position for 30 min.

Following an elevation in T_{rec} to 38 °C, subjects were removed from the treadmill/water tank and placed in a seated position for 10 min (Figure 1). At the cessation of the 30-min standardisation period in the control condition, subjects undertook a further 10-min resting period, to maintain consistency in experimental methodology in all trials. Subjects then completed the soccer-specific intermittent exercise protocol. The intermittent protocol was performed on a motorised treadmill and based on work-rate profiles of elite South American international soccer players (Rienzi *et al.*, 2000).

Rectal temperature, mean skin temperature (T_{skin}) and heart rate (HR) were continually monitored during the intermittent protocol with mean values recorded at 5-min intervals (Figure 1). The T_{rec} and T_{skin} measurements were used to calculate mean body temperature (T_b) (Burton, 1935) and the thermal gradient (T_{rec}-T_{skin}) during each experimental condition. The rate of heat storage (HS; $W \cdot m^{-2}$) was calculated as previously described by Lee and Haymes (1995): HS = $0.97 \cdot m \cdot (\Delta T_b/\Delta t)/A_D$ where 0.97 is the specific heat capacity of body tissue ($W \cdot kg^{-1}$), m is body mass, $\Delta T_b/\Delta dt$ is the change (Δ) in T_b from the beginning to the end of exercise divided by the duration of exercise (Δt), and A_D is body surface area (m^2) calculated according to DuBois and DuBois (1916).

Venous blood samples for determination of glucose, lactate and free fatty acids (FFA) along with muscle temperature (T_m) recordings were obtained at the onset and cessation of each 45-min exercise period. Ratings of perceived exertion (RPE) were recorded at 5-min intervals throughout the protocol. Following exercise, the subject's nude weight was measured and weight loss, corrected for respiratory (Mitchell *et al.*, 1972) and metabolic water loss (Kenney, 1998), was taken to represent sweat loss.

2.3. Analysis

All data are presented as mean $\pm$ SD. A two-way (condition x time) analysis of variance (ANOVA) with repeated measures, was undertaken for the pre-warming and exercise periods to determine any treatment differences. Following observation of a main effect of pre-warming, a one-way ANOVA test was employed to determine at which time points a significant effect was observed. *Post-hoc* analysis by paired t-tests (with Bonferroni correction of alpha) was undertaken to examine which trials were significantly different from each other. A one-way ANOVA was used to determine any difference in total sweat loss between conditions. Simple effect size, estimated from the ratio of the mean difference to the pooled standard deviation, was also calculated. This was used to provide a measure of the magnitude of difference between conditions, where failure to observe statistical significance may have reflected the small sample size currently utilised (Vincent, 1995). A correction factor for effect sizes derived from small samples was also applied (Becker, 1988). The alpha level for the evaluation of statistical significance was set at $P < 0.05$.

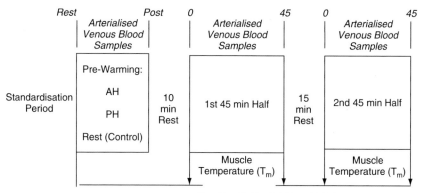

Figure 1. Diagrammatic representation of sampling points for the metabolic and thermoregulatory variables.

3. RESULTS

Mean T_{rec} (AH, 38.4 ± 0.3 °C, PH, 38.3 ± 0.3 °C, Cont, 37.9 ± 0.3 °C) and T_b (AH, 37.5 ± 0.3 °C, PH, 37.4 ± 0.2 °C, Cont, 37.1 ± 0.2 °C) for the first 45 min of the protocol, were significantly greater under both pre-warming conditions compared with the control ($P < 0.05$). No differences were observed between the two pre-warming conditions. Both T_{rec} (Figure 2) and T_b were significantly higher during the initial 25 min of the first half under both AH and PH conditions compared with Cont ($P < 0.05$). Both T_{rec} and T_b also remained significantly elevated at 35 and 40 min of exercise in the AH condition compared with Cont ($P < 0.05$).

During the second half of the protocol, T_{rec} and T_b were not significantly different at any time point between experimental conditions (Figure 2). Mean T_{rec} and mean T_b responses for the second 45 min of the protocol were significantly higher than corresponding values in the first half under the control condition only ($P < 0.01$). Mean T_{rec} (AH, 38.5 ± 0.3 °C, PH, 38.4 ± 0.3 °C, Cont, 38.2 ± 0.4 °C) and mean T_b (AH, 37.6 ± 0.3 °C, PH, 37.5 ± 0.2 °C, Cont, 37.4 ± 0.2 °C) responses representative of the full 90-min intermittent protocol, were significantly greater following AH compared with Cont ($P < 0.05$).

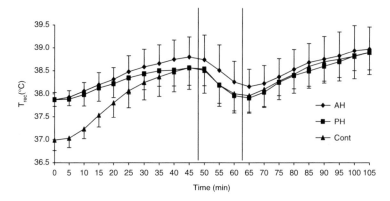

Figure 2. Mean ± SD T$_{rec}$ (Rectal temperature) during the soccer-specific intermittent protocol (including 15-min intermission period) under AH (Active Heating), PH (Passive Heating), and Cont (Control) conditions N = 6. Significant difference ($P < 0.05$): - b, between AH and Cont, c, between PH and Cont.

Muscle temperature (AH, 37.7 ± 0.3 °C, PH, 37.9 ± 0.2 °C, Cont, 34.5 ± 0.7 °C) was significantly higher at the onset of first half in the AH and PH conditions compared with the control ($P < 0.05$). No further differences in T$_m$ were observed at the end of the first half (AH, 38.5 ± 0.4 °C, PH, 38.7 ± 0.6 °C, Cont, 38.7 ± 0.6 °C) or at the onset (AH, 36.9 ± 0.7 °C, PH, 37.0 ± 0.5 °C, Cont, 37.1 ± 0.5 °C) and cessation of the second half (AH, 38.6 ± 0.9 °C, PH, 38.6 ± 0.7 °C, Cont, 38.6 ± 0.4 °C) between any condition. Mean skin temperature and the T$_{rec}$ -T$_{skin}$ gradient were similar throughout the intermittent protocol under all experimental conditions.

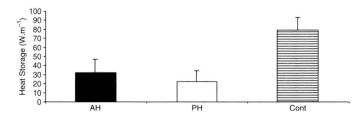

Figure 3. Mean ±^{b}SD heat storage responses during the first 45-min half of the soccer-specific intermittent protocol under AH (Active Heating$_c$), PH (Passive Heating), and Cont (Control) conditions. N = 6. Significant difference ($P < 0.05$):- b, between AH and Cont, c, PH and Cont.

The rate of heat storage during the first half was significantly reduced under both AH and PH conditions compared with the control ($P < 0.05$) (Figure 3). A significant decline in the rate of heat storage was observed during the second half compared with the first in the control condition ($P < 0.05$). During the second half the rate of heat storage was similar under all experimental conditions. The rate of heat storage representative of the 90-min intermittent protocol (AH, 19.2 ± 7.0 W.m^{-2}, PH, 16.8 ± 5.0 W.m^{-2}, Cont, 40.7 ± 7.0 W.m^{-2}) was significantly reduced following AH and PH compared to Cont.

At the onset of the first half, HR was significantly elevated under both AH (106 $\pm$ 5 beats·min^{-1}) and PH (92 $\pm$ 17 beats·min^{-1}) conditions compared with the control (61 $\pm$ 5 beats·min^{-1}) ($P < 0.01$). During the first half, HR remained significantly higher in the AH condition compared with Cont at 10 min, 15 min and 20 min of exercise ($P < 0.05$) (Figure 4). No significant difference in HR was observed between the PH and Cont or the two pre-warming conditions at the onset of exercise or at any time point during the first half of the protocol (Figure 4). No significant difference in HR was observed between any condition during the second half (Figure 4). Heart rate during the second half of the protocol was significantly greater compared with the first half under control conditions (P < 0.01). Heart rate under both AH (Effect Size 0.7) and PH (Effect Size 0.9) conditions also remained higher during the second half exercise period compared with the first, but did not reach statistical significance. Mean HR for the 90-min intermittent protocol was not significantly different between any condition (AH, 159 $\pm$ 5 beats·min^{-1}, PH, 155 $\pm$ 6 beats·min, Cont, 156 $\pm$ 7 beats·min^{-1}).

Total sweat production estimated from changes in body mass, was not significantly different between conditions (AH, 2.1 $\pm$ 0.4 l, PH, 1.9 $\pm$ 0.3 l; Cont, 1.7 $\pm$ 0.3 l).   A moderate (Effect Size 0.6) and large effect size (Effect Size 0.9) for sweat production was, however, observed between the PH and Cont and the AH and Cont conditions respectively, indicating that differences in total sweat production were apparent between the pre-warming conditions and the control. No significant differences in the concentration of blood glucose, blood lactate and plasma FFA were observed between any condition during the soccer-specific protocol (Table 1). Mean RPE values (AH, 5 $\pm$ 2, PH, 4 $\pm$ 1, Cont, 4 $\pm$ 2) during the intermittent protocol were also similar under all experimental conditions.

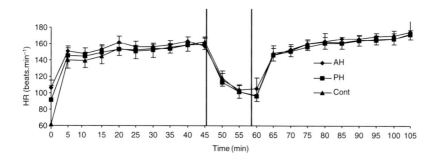

Figure 4. Mean $\pm$ SD HR (Heart rate) responses during the first 45-min half of the soccer-specific intermittent protocol under AH (Active Heating), PH (Passive Heating), and Cont (Control) conditions. N = 6. Significant difference ($P < 0.05$): - b, between AH and Cont.

Table 1. Metabolic responses to exercise under AH (Active Heating), PH (Passive heating) and Cont (Control) conditions.

	End of 1st Half			End of 2nd Half		
	Cont	AH	PH	Cont	AH	PH
Lactate (mmol.l^{-1})	4.3 ± 1.6	4.2 ± 1.1	4.2 ± 1.6	4.0 ± 1.6	4.0 ± 1.2	3.4 ± 0.4
Glucose (mmol.l^{-1})	4.7 ± 0.8	4.7 ± 0.5	5.2 ± 1.7	4.9 ± 0.6	5.0 ± 0.8	4.8 ± 0.5
FFA (mmol.l^{-1})	0.5 ± 0.3	0.6 ± 0.3	0.5 ± 0.2	0.7 ± 0.3	1.1 ± 0.3	1.0 ± 0.4

Values are Mean ± SD lactate (Blood lactate), glucose (Blood glucose) and FFA (Plasma free fatty acids) responses to the soccer-specific intermittent protocol under AH (Active heating), PH (Passive heating), and Cont (Control) conditions: N = 6.

4. DISCUSSION

The data from the current investigation demonstrate that active (AH) and passive pre-warming (PH) strategies increase the short-term thermoregulatory strain during soccer-specific intermittent exercise in ambient temperatures of 19 °C, compared with pre-exercise rest. Current findings also indicate that the effects of pre-warming on the physiological response to soccer-specific intermittent exercise are independent of the pre-warming strategy utilised. The present observations suggest that the physiological changes arising as a result of pre-warming strategies are unlikely to have detrimental effects on the performance of a 90-min soccer-specific simulation under the current environmental temperatures.

Increased thermoregulatory and cardiovascular strain, characterised by a significantly higher T_{rec}, T_b, HR and a reduced heat storage capacity, has previously been shown to reduce time to exhaustion during prolonged continuous (Gregson *et al.*, 2002b) and intermittent (Gregson *et al.*, 2002a) exercise under ambient temperatures of 21–22 °C. In the current study, changes in short-term thermoregulatory strain were associated with the performance of 90 min of soccer-specific intermittent exercise, following AH and PH. This increased thermoregulatory strain was characterised by a significantly higher mean T_{rec} (Figure 2) and mean T_b along with a decline in heat storage capacity (Figure 3) during the first half of the intermittent protocol under both AH and PH conditions, compared with the control. These physiological changes did not, however, impact on the performance of this mode of exercise under the current environmental conditions. Such observations are supported by a similar mean subjective perception of effort (RPE) reported by subjects throughout the intermittent protocol under all experimental conditions.

Pre-warming induced alterations in both body hydration status and the level of body temperature *per se*, are likely to have contributed to the increased T_{rec}, HR and the reduced heat storage capacity observed during the first half of the protocol under both AH and PH conditions. Previous observations have shown that AH and

PH are associated with alterations in plasma volume (used as an indication of changes in hydration status) (Jimenez *et al.*, 1999; Gregson *et al.*, 2002b). The observed effect sizes in the current study, suggest that a greater rate of sweat loss (estimated from changes in body mass) was associated with the performance of the intermittent protocol under both AH (Effect Size 0.9) and PH (Effect Size 0.6) conditions compared with the Cont. As the duration of the exercise was constant under all experimental conditions, these differences in body water loss reflect the sweat loss associated with the active and passive pre-warming procedures completed prior to exercise. Core temperature is the primary stimulus to the sudomotor centre with alterations in skin temperature and the rate of change in skin temperature being of secondary importance (Wyss *et al.*, 1974). Consequently, a higher rate of sweat loss may have been associated with the increased T_{rec} observed in both AH and PH conditions during the initial stages of the first half. Sweat production rate in the current study was, however, estimated from changes in nude body mass at rest to completion of the intermittent protocol. As a result of these sampling times, it is therefore not possible to determine whether differences in sweat production rates were evident between conditions during the initial stages of the protocol.

A significantly higher mean HR, T_{rec} and a decline in heat storage capacity was observed during the second half of the protocol under the control condition, compared with the first. The moderate (Effect Size 0.7) and large (Effect Size 0.9) effect size observed under the AH and PH conditions respectively, suggest that mean HR during the second half of the protocol was also increased under these conditions. Such physiological changes are likely to have been mediated primarily by the increased demand for skin blood flow (for the dissipation of heat), and evaporative sweat loss with continuation of the intermittent protocol (Hamilton *et al.*, 1991; Gonzalez-Alonso *et al.*, 1997). In contrast, mean T_{rec}, T_b and the rate of heat storage were not significantly different between the two 45-min periods in the pre-warming conditions. Consequently, the increased internal temperature observed during the first half of exercise under both AH and PH conditions, was not maintained throughout the intermittent protocol. It would appear therefore, that for a given metabolic heat load there is a reduction in the magnitude of increase in T_{rec} (during the latter stages of prolonged exercise) when pre-warming precedes exercise.

Findings from the present investigation suggest that preliminary warm-up procedures are unlikely to affect the capacity to perform exercise patterns that simulate the demands of soccer. These observations contrast with findings from previous investigations using prolonged continuous (Gonzalez-Alonso *et al.*, 1999 and Gregson *et al.*, 2002b) and intermittent exercise (Gregson *et al.*, 2002a) patterns. During the current mode of exercise, the 15-min static recovery period reduced the level of thermal strain by approximately 0.6 °C under all conditions (Figure 2). In addition, in contrast with responses observed during the first 45 min of the protocol, the subsequent level of thermoregulatory strain during the second half of the protocol remained similar under all conditions. Such observations indicate (under the current environmental conditions), that the presence of a half-time period (15 min) may therefore prevent pre-warming strategies from promoting a sustained increase in thermoregulatory strain that has detrimental effects on performance.

On the basis of the results from the current study, it is concluded that pre-exercise active (AH) and passive warming (PH) increase the level of thermoregulatory strain during the first half (45 min) of a 90-min soccer-specific intermittent exercise protocol under ambient temperatures of 19 °C compared with pre-exercise rest. Such thermoregulatory changes are closely associated with a decline in heat storage capacity during the initial 45 min of exercise. Current findings also indicate that the effects of pre-warming on the physiological response to soccer-specific intermittent exercise are independent of the pre-warming strategy utilised. These findings suggest that pre-warming strategies are unlikely to promote physiological alterations that have detrimental effects on the performance of prolonged soccer-specific intermittent exercise under the current environmental temperatures. This appears likely to reflect predominately the effects of the half-time period.

REFERENCES

Becker, B.J., 1988, Synthesizing standardized mean-change measures. *British Journal of Mathematical and Statistical Psychology*, **41**, 257–278.

Burton, A., 1935, Human calorimetry II. The average temperatures of the tissues of the body. *Journal of Nutrition*, **9**, 261–280.

DeVries, H.A. and Housh T. J., 1994, *Physiology of Exercise for Physical Education, Athletics and Exercise Science, 5th ed.* (Wisconsin: Brown & Benchmark Publishing).

DuBois, D. and DuBois, F., 1916, Clinical calorimetry; a formula to estimate the approximate surface area if height and weight be known. *Archives of Internal Medicine*, **17**, 863–871.

Gonzalez-Alonso, J., Rodriguez, R., Below, P.R. and Coyle, E.F., 1997, Dehydration markedly impairs cardiovascular function in hyperthermic endurance athletes. *Journal of Applied Physiology*, **82**, 1229–1236.

Gonzalez-Alonso, J., Teller, C., Andersen, S.L., Jensen, F.B. and Nielsen, B., 1999, Influence of body temperature on the development of fatigue during prolonged exercise in the heat. *Journal of Applied Physiology*, **86**, 1032–1039.

Gregson, W.A., Batterham, A. Drust, B. and Cable, N.T., 2002a, The effects of pre-warming on the metabolic and thermoregulatory responses to prolonged intermittent exercise in moderate ambient temperatures. *Journal of Sports Sciences*, **20**, 50.

Gregson, W.A., Drust, B., Batterham, A. and Cable, N.T., 2002b, The effects of pre-warming on the metabolic and thermoregulatory responses to prolonged sub-maximal exercise in moderate ambient temperatures. *European Journal of Applied Physiology*, **86**, 526–533.

Hamilton, M.T., Gonzalez-Alonso, J., Montain, S.J. and Coyle, E.F., 1991, Fluid replacement and glucose ingestion during exercise prevent cardiovascular drift. *Journal of Applied Physiology*, **71**, 871–877.

Jimenez, C., Melin, B., Koulmann, N., Allevard, A.M., Launay, J.C. and Savourey, G., 1999, Plasma volume changes during and after acute variations of body hydration level in humans. *European Journal of Applied Physiology*, 80, 1–8.

Kenney W.L., 1998, Heat flux and storage in hot environments. *International Journal of Sports Medicine*, 19, S92–S95.

Lee, D. and Haymes, E., 1995, Exercise duration and thermoregulatory responses after whole body pre-cooling. Journal of Applied Physiology, **79**, 1971–1976.

Mitchell, J.W., Nadel, E.R. and Stolwijk, J.A.J., 1972, Respiratory weight losses during exercise. *Journal of Applied Physiology*, **32**, 474–476.

Rienzi, E., Drust, B., Reilly, T., Carter, J.E.L. and Martin, A., 2000, Investigation of anthropometric and work-rate profiles of elite South American international soccer players. *Journal of Sports Medicine and Physical Fitness*, **40**, 162–169.

Vincent, W.J., 1995, *Statistics in Kinesiology.* (Champaign, Illinois: Human Kinetics).

Wyss, C.R., Brengelmann, G.L., Johnson, J.M., Rowell, L.B. and Niedderberger, M., 1974, Control of skin blood flow, sweating and heart rate: role of skin, vs. core temperature. *Journal of Applied Physiol*ogy, **36**, 726–733.

59   The Effects of Different Modes of Stretching during Warm-up on High Speed Motor Capacities in Professional Footballers

Thomas Little[1] and Alun Williams[2]

[1]Head of Conditioning, Newlife Fitness/ Nottingham Forest, UK
[2]Department of Exercise and Sport Science, Manchester Metropolitan University, UK

1. INTRODUCTION

The inclusion of static stretching as part of a pre-exercise warm up routine has been commonplace in a multitude of sports, including soccer. This stemmed from the belief that static stretching will aid performance and decrease injury risk (Wydra, 1997). However, new research has challenged some long held concepts about common stretching practices. In particular, research suggests that a regime of stretching provides an acute inhibition of maximal force production by the stretched muscle group (Walsh and Wilson, 1997; Kokkonen et al., 1998; Church et al., 2001; Jones and Surlive, 2001; Nelson et al., 2001a; Nelson et al., 2001b; Young and Elliot, 2001). Such findings have prompted recommendations that static stretching be omitted or be replaced by dynamic stretching, during warm-up (Murphy, 1994; Mann and Whedon, 2001; Anderson, 2003). Although well intentioned, such recommendations may be premature, as many aspects relating to the effects of static stretching remain unclear. Large discrepancies between warm-up protocols used in a sport environment and those used in research studies, and problems inherent in performance measures, indicate further research is warranted. Furthermore, despite the widespread use of dynamic stretching, scant research exists on the on the effects of this mode of stretching on performance parameters.

Thus, the aim of the present study is to examine the effects of different modes of stretching as opposed to no stretching on motor qualities that are important to football success, placed within a warm-up protocol that is typical of that used before competition in professional soccer.

2. METHODS

Eighteen professional soccer players, from an English League Premier Division were tested as part of their athletic training programme. All subjects gave their informed consent and the study was approved by the local Ethics Committee.

Three warm-up protocols differentiated by their stretching content were used – Static, Dynamic and No-Stretch. Aside from the stretching, each warm-up followed the same general design:
- 4 min jogging/varied movements
- 6.20 min flexibility work (except for No-Stretch protocol)
- ~4 min incremental intermittent sprint and agility runs
- 2 min rest.

The principal locomotive leg muscle groups were stretched (gastrocnemius, hamstrings, quadriceps/hip flexors, gluteals, adductors). Between each stretch there was 20 s rest. For static stretching, each stretch was held for 30 s on each leg, changing immediately to the contralateral side. Subjects were told to stretch until they approached end range of motion (ROM) but within the pain threshold. The dynamic stretches were performed for 60 s for each muscle group at a rate of approximately one stretch cycle every 2 s. Subjects were instructed to try and attain maximal ROM with each repetition. In the No-Stretch protocol, instead of stretching, subjects rested for 1 min following the general warm-up and then proceeded to complete the incremental intermittent sprint and agility runs.

Vertical jump, stationary 10 m, flying 20 m and a zig-zag course were used to assess leg power, acceleration, maximum speed and agility capacities. Vertical jump involved a two-footed counter-movement jump from a stationary position with the intension of attaining maximum height. Subjects were instructed to maintain hands on the hips and keep the legs straight once they had left the ground. "Stationary 10 m" involved sprinting 10 m as fast as possible from a stationary start position. "Flying 20 m" involved sprinting 20 m as fast as possible from a maximum speed start. The zig-zag course consisted of four 5-metre sections set out at 100° angles. It was chosen because the angle changes are similar to those experienced in competitive football situations and because its relative simplicity meant learning effects would be minimal. During the test session each subject first performed the vertical jump test, stationary 10 m test, flying 20 m test, and finally the agility test. Subjects performed two maximal attempts at each exercise and the best time was retained . A rest of at least 2 min between trials and tests was included to minimise the effects of fatigue. The tests were conducted > 48 hours following a match or hard physical training to minimise the fatiguing effects of previous exercise. Tests took place on three non-consecutive days, one for each warm-up protocol. The different protocols took place in the order:- Static, No-Stretch and Dynamic. All tests were performed in an indoor synthetic pitch. Newstart Electronic timing gates and jumping mat (Brower Timing System, Salt Lake City, UT) were used to measure completion times and vertical jump, respectively.

Repeated-measures ANOVA was used to compare the three warm-up/stretching conditions. Newman-Keuls post-hoc analysis was used to identify pairwise differences. Statistical significance was accepted at $P \leq 0.05$.

3. RESULTS

The mean scores (± SD) for the performance measures following the different warm-up procedures are presented in Table 1 and Figures 1, 2 and 3.

There was no significant difference between the different warm-up protocols for vertical jump performance (ANOVA $P=0.074$). There were significant differences between the different warm-up protocols for acceleration with Dynamic stretching resulting in significantly superior performance than the No-Stretch protocol (ANOVA $P=0.025$, No-Stretch and Static $P=0.079$, No-Stretch and Dynamic $P=0.011$, Static & Dynamic $P=0.350$).

Table 1. Mean scores (± SD) for the performance measures with the different warm-up procedures.

	No-Stretch	**Static**	**Dynamic**
Vertical Jump (cm)	40.4 ± 4.9	39.4 ± 4.5	40.2 ± 4.5
Acceleration (s)	1.87 ± 0.09	1.85 ± 0.08	1.83 ± 0.08
Max Speed (s)	2.41 ± 0.13	2.37 ± 0.12	2.37 ± 0.13
Agility (s)	5.20 ± 0.16	5.22 ± 0.18	5.14 ± 0.17

In tests for maximum speed, Static and Dynamic stretching protocols produced significantly better performance than no stretching (ANOVA $P<0.0005$, No-Stretch and Static $P<0.0005$, No-Stretch and Dynamic $P<0.0005$, Static & Dynamic $P=0.92$). There were significant differences between the warm-up protocols for agility with the Dynamic protocol resulting in significantly better performance than the Static and No-Stretch protocols (ANOVA $P<0.0005$, No-Stretch and Static $P=0.232$, No-Stretch and Dynamic $P=0.01$, Static and Dynamic $P<0.0005$).

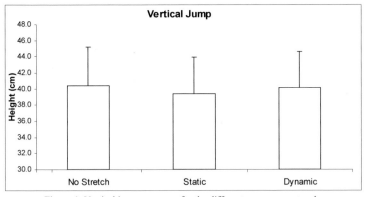

Figure 1. Vertical jump measures for the different warm-up protocols.

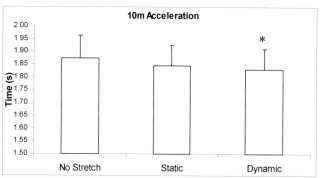

Figure 2. The 10-m acceleration times for the different warm-up protocols. * significantly faster than the No stretch condition.

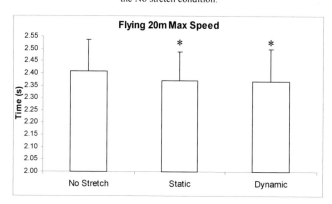

Figure 3. The 20-m maximum speed times for the different warm-up protocols. * significantly faster than the No stretch condition.

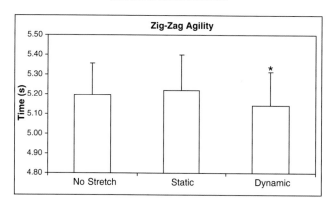

Figure 4. Zig-zag agility times for the different warm-up protocols. * significantly faster than the No stretch and static condition.

4. DISCUSSION

Static stretching did not result in any significant performance decrements compared to the No-Stretch protocol. In fact, the Static stretching protocol resulted in significantly quicker maximum speed performance compared to No-Stretch. Therefore, the recommendation that static stretching should be omitted from warm-ups may be inappropriate, with little consideration for injury and performance aspects related to static stretching, aside from absolute force potential. Dynamic stretching resulted in the best scores in all but the vertical jump test. Therefore, the use of dynamic stretching in warm-ups is probably optimal for high speed soccer performance.

Discrepancies between the current protocol and that of previous studies may explain why the static stretching produced no performance decrements in the present study. Previous protocols (Kokkonen et al., 1998; Nelson et al., 1998, Fowles et al., 2000, Behm et al., 2001; Nelson et al., 2001a; Nelson et al., 2001b) stretched muscles for far greater durations than those used in typical warm-ups. Such stretching durations may elicit neural, and excessive mechanical force inhibitory mechanisms that are not apparent during typical warm-ups. Further, performance analysis was often conducted immediately following the stretching (Kokkonen et al., 1998; Fowles et al., 2000; Behm et al., 2001; Church et al., 2001; Nelson et al., 2001a; Nelson et al., 2001b). However, in practice, there is typically further warm-up activity after the stretching. Rosenbaum and Hennig (1995) reported that additional physical activity subsequent to stretching attenuated the decreases in peak force, RFD, relaxation rate and EMG amplitudes of the Achilles tendon reflex following stretching. Furthermore, Young and Behm (2002) showed that four practice jumps subsequent to stretching resulted in significantly higher vertical jumps compared to when the practice jumps were omitted from the warm-up protocol. Therefore, inclusion of further activity post-stretching appears beneficial to subsequent performance.

Research indicating that a bout of static stretching is detrimental to performance has involved relatively slow action such as 1RM tests, some isokinetic testing and vertical jump for height (Walsh and Wilson, 1997; Kokkonen et al., 1998; Nelson et al., 2001a; Nelson et al., 2001b), yet most important motor actions in soccer, such as sprinting and shooting, are dependent on high velocity movements and RFD. The absence of inhibitory effects on the high velocity movements used in the present study suggests that the deleterious impact of stretching activities on force production might be limited to movements performed at relatively slow velocities. Recent findings from Nelson et al. (2001b) support this notion. The authors reported that attenuation in force post-stretch decreased as movement speed increased, to the point where at the fastest movement speed (4.71 $rad.s^{-1}$) post-stretch force was greater, although not significantly. Powerful movements in soccer involve even greater movement velocities than the highest 4.71 $rad.s^{-1}$ reported by Stone et al. (2002) suggesting that static stretching may not reduce the force capacity of high speed motor actions typically required in soccer.

Dynamic stretching resulted in the best performances in all but the vertical jump test, with significant improvements in the acceleration and maximum speed tests compared to no stretching, and in the agility test compared to static stretching. This may be due to facilitated motor control as a result of actively taking the joints through the full range of motion (Clark, 2002). Active contractions of the muscles will improve active stiffness (ability to actively absorb energy; Safran et al., 1988) and improvements in muscular compliance may enhance performance via mechanisms affecting rate of force development. The active process of dynamic stretching also helps to elevate body temperature and increase blood flow to muscles to be exercised.

The results suggest that the sole use of dynamic stretching, as opposed to static stretching or no stretching during warm-ups, is optimal for high speed soccer performance. However, this conclusion may not adequately reflect requirements for football performance and injury prevention in players presenting with inadequate ROMs. Research has shown that, in general, soccer players have poor flexibility values (Oberg and Ekstrand, 1984) which have been shown to increase the risk of injury (Inklaar et al., 1996; Witvrouw et al., 2002). Based on current research, forms of static stretching appear to have the greatest effects on factors relating to ROM (Bandy et al., 1998; Shrier, 1999). Therefore, if a player presents an inadequate ROM or muscular tightness, bouts of static stretching should be used on specific musculature in the warm-up. This practice can then be combined with general dynamic stretching for optimal preparation.

REFERENCES

Anderson, O., 2003, Does stretching help prevent injuries. Sport Injury Bulletin, **28**, 6–9.

Bandy, W.D., Irion, J.M. and Briggler, M., 1998, The effects of static stretch and dynamic range of motion training on flexibility of the hamstring muscles. *Journal of Orthopedic Sport Physicians,* **27**, 295–300.

Behm, D., Button, D. and Butt, J., 2001, Factors affecting force loss with prolonged stretching. *Canadian Journal of Applied Physiology*, **26**, 262–272.

Church, B., Wiggins, M., Moode, E. and Crist, R., 2001, Effect of warm-up and flexibility treatments on vertical jump performance. Journal of Strength and Conditioning Research, **15**, 332–336.

Clark, M.A., 2000, *Intergrated Training for the New Millennium.* (Thousand Oakes, CA: National Academy of Sports Medicine).

Fowles, J., Sale, D. and MacDougall, J., 2000, Reduced strength after passive stretch of the human plantarflexors. *Journal of Applied Physiology*, **89**, 1179–1188.

Inklaar, H., Bol, E. and Mosterd, W.L., 1996, Injuries in male soccer players: Team risk analysis. *International Journal of Sports Medicine*, **17**, 229–234.

Jones, K. and Surlive, V., 2001, An independent replication of the Kokkonen et al. (1998) study: Acute muscle stretching inhibits maximal strength. *Research Quarterly for Exercise and Sport*, **S21**, A16.

Kokkonen, J., Nelson, A. and Cornwell, A., 1998, Acute muscle stretching inhibits maximal strength performance. *Research Quarterly for Exercise and Sport*, **69**, 411–415.

Mann, D. and Whedon, C., 2001, Functional stretching: Implementing a dynamic stretching program. *Athletics Therapy Today,* **6**, 10–13.

Murphy, D.R., 1994, Dynamic range of motion training: An alternative to static stretching. *Chiropractic Sports Medicine*, **8**, 59–66.

Nelson, A.G., 2001a, Inhibition of maximal voluntary isometric torque production by acute stretching is joint angle specific. *Research Quarterly for Exercise and Sport*, **72**, 68–70.

Nelson, A.G., Guillory, I.K., Cornwell, A. and Kokkonen, J., (2001b), Inhibition of maximal voluntary isokinetic torque production following stretching is velocity specific. *Journal of Strength and Conditioning Research*, **15**, 241–246.

Oberg, H. and Ekstrand, J., 1984, Muscle strength and flexibility in different positions in soccer players. *International Journal of Sports Medicine,* **5**, 213–216.

Rosenbaum, D. and Hennig, E.M., 1995, The influence of stretching and warm-up exercises on Achilles tendon reflex activity. *Journal of Sports Sciences*, **13**, 481–490.

Safran, M.R., Garrett, W.E., Seaber, A.V., Glisson, R.R. and Ribbeck, B.M., 1988, The role of warm-up in muscular injury prevention. *American Journal of Sports Medicine,* **16,** 123–129.

Shrier, S., 1999, Stretching before exercise does not reduce the risk of muscle injury: A critical review if the clinical and basic science literature. *Clinical Journal of Sports Science*, **9**, 221–227.

Stone, M. H., Moir, G. and Glaister, M., 2002, How much strength is necessary? *Physical Therapy in Sport*, **3**, 88–96.

Walsh, A. and Wilson, G., 1997, The influence of musculotendon stiffness on drop jump performance. *Canadian Journal of Applied Physiology*, **22**, 117–132.

Witvrouw, E., Witvrouw, E., Danneels, L., Asselman, P., D'Have, T. and Canbier, D., 2002, Muscle flexibility as a risk factor for developing muscle injuries in male professional soccer players. *American Journal of Sports Medicine*, **31**, 41–46.

Wydra, G., 1997, Stretching - a survey of the present state of research. *Sportwissenschaft*, **27**, 409–427.

Young W.B. and Behm, D.G., 2002, Should static stretching be used during a warm-up for strength and power activities? Strength and Conditioning, **24**, 33–37.

Young, W. and Elliot, S., 2001, Acute effects of static stretching, proprioceptive neuromuscular facilitation stretching and maximum voluntary contractions on explosive force production and jumping performance. *Journal of Sports Medicine and Physical Fitness*, **72**, 273–279.

60 Predictors of Changes in $\dot{V}O_{2max}$ during Periods of Intense Training in Rugby League Players

Aaron Coutts[1,2], Peter Reaburn[2], Terrence Piva[3] and Aron Murphy[1]
[1]School of Leisure, Sport and Tourism,
University of Technology, Sydney
[2]School of Health and Human Performance,
Central Queensland University
[3]School of Chemical and Biomedical Sciences,
Central Queensland University

1. INTRODUCTION

Many high-level athletes complete large volumes of intensive physical training to improve performance. Unfortunately for the athlete, excessive physical training, incomplete recovery and high general stress may manifest in the form of reduced performance and poor health which is now referred to as overreaching. Symptoms of overreaching and overtraining have been reported to occur in 30–50% of high level soccer players during a competitive season (Lehmann et al., 1992; Naessens et al., 2000). However, there is a lack of consensus as to what are valid and reliable early identifiers of overreaching in the findings of most previous studies examining this area (Urhausen and Kindermann, 2002). Furthermore, to date, there have only been a few studies that have reported on physiological or biochemical changes with overreaching and overtraining in team sport performances (Naessens et al., 2000; Filaire et al., 2001). Therefore, the aim of this research was to identify predictors of changes in $\dot{V}O_2$ max as an early identifier of excessive fatigue in team sport participants.

2. METHODS

2.1. Subjects

Eighteen semi-professional rugby league players (age:23.3±3.3 years; $\dot{V}O_2$max: 50.5±3.5 ml·kg^{-1}·min^{-1}; body mass index: 27.5±1.8) from the same semi-professional team were divided into two groups matched for $\dot{V}O_2$max, playing position and BMI were randomly assigned to complete 6 weeks of being well-trained (WT) or deliberately overreached (OR).

2.2. Physical training

Both training groups completed 6 weeks of physical training during the specific preparatory training phase of the Rugby League training year. All subjects completed 6 weeks, of 5–7 sessions per week of physical training that included field-based specific Rugby League training, endurance development, resistance and speed and agility training. These subjects were matched according to physical characteristics and playing position and then divided into either a group that were deliberately overreached (OR) or a group that were well trained (WT) during the 6-week overload training period. Physical training was planned so that the OR group completed progressively more training load than the WT group. During the final week of the 6-week overload training period, approximately 12.5 and 10.2 h of physical training was completed by the OR and WT group, respectively. The training load for each subject during each training session was calculated according to the methods of Foster et al. (2001).

2.3. Physiological tests

Before and after the 6-week training period, all participants were tested for various physiological characteristics following a day of rest. Anthropometry measures were taken by a trained anthropometrist using the methods of Gore (2000). A 10-s 'all-out' cycle sprint capacity was measured on a magnetically braked cycle ergometer (LODE, Groningen, Holland). Total work and peak power achieved over the 10-second period were recorded using an AMLAB computer system (AMLAB, Peak Performance Technologies, Inc., USA). A vertical jump test was used as a test of leg power and was assessed according to the methods described by Gore (2000) using the Vertec® jumping device (Sports Imports, Columbus, USA).

Maximal oxygen uptake ($\dot{V}O_2$max) was determined using an incremental treadmill test to exhaustion on a motorised treadmill (Precor, USA), using a Medgraphics® CPX-D Gas Analysis System (Medgraphics®, Parkway, USA). Criteria for attainment of $\dot{V}O_2$max were according to the methods described by Gore (2000). Maximal aerobic running speed and peak blood lactate ($[La^-]_{b,peak}$) measures were at the completion of the treadmill test.

The subjects also completed a submaximal, field-based warm-up heart rate test at the commencement of every field training session. For this test, subjects were required to run back and forth on a 20-m course and touch the 20-m line with the foot at the same time that a sound signal was emitted from a pre-recorded compact disk. The frequency of the sound signals was set so that the subjects completed the following work:

- Stage 1: 160 m·min⁻¹ (9.6 km·h⁻¹) for 2 min followed by 60 s rest;
- Stage 2: 180 m·min⁻¹ (10.8 km·h⁻¹) for 2 min followed by 60 s rest;
- Stage 3: 200 m·min⁻¹ (12.0 km·h⁻¹) for 2 min.

At the completion of each stage, individual peak heart rates were recorded using Polar NV heart rate monitors. This test was completed as part of a standardised team warm-up on a freshly mown grassed surface at the same time of day before each training session. The heart value–velocity relationship (i.e. HR and velocity) was determined from the final HR value at the end of each stage.

2.4. Biochemistry

Testosterone, cortisol, ACTH, prolactin, glucose, CK, urea, ferritin, full blood count, haemoglobin, haematocrit, total leukocyte and five cell differential counts, glutamine, glutamate, urinary catecholamines and branched chain amino acid measures were taken prior to, and at fortnightly intervals during the 6-week overload training period. All haematological measures were taken in a fasted state between 05:30 and 07:30 hours in the mornings of testing. The urine voided during the 12-hours prior to blood sampling was also collected for later analysis. All biochemical analyses were completed immediately on the day of collection at Dr T.B. Lynch Research and Diagnostic Laboratories, Rockhampton, Qld.

2.5. Psychology

Self-reported stress and recovery were measured using the RESTQ-76 Sport questionnaire using the methods described by (Kellmann and Kallus, 2001). The subjects completed the RESTQ-76 on the same testing days as the biochemistry measures. The subjects completed the RESTQ-76 Sport in a quiet laboratory at standardised times prior to blood sampling.

2.6. Statistical analyses

The training load and aerobic power data were analyzed by a two-factor (group, testing occasion) multivariate repeated measures analysis of variance. Simple contrasts were used to determine global changes relative to the previous measure.

A step-down regression analysis using the linear regression model was used to develop a predictive equation for changes in $\dot{V}O_2$max during the taper from the population of subjects (N=18). For each subject, the change in $\dot{V}O_2$max and each important physiological, biochemical and psychological variable measured before and after both the loading periods were calculated as a percent (%) change. SPSS statistical software package (SPSS Inc., Chicago, USA) was used for all statistical calculations. The level of significance was set at 0.05.

3. RESULTS

3.1. Training

During the 6-week overload training period the OR group also completed a significantly greater training load (21.6%) than the WT group (*P*<0.05) (See Table 1). During the last week of the progressive overload training, the OR group spent significantly more time training (*P*<0.01) (746 ± 41 min) than the WT group (617 ± 18 min) (see Table 2).

Table 1. Mean training load measured for both OR (N=9) and WT (N=9) groups during the 6-week overload training period and the seven-day taper period (mean ± SD).

Measure	Condition	Week 1	Week 2	Week 3	Week 4	Week 5	Week 6
Training	OR	1391 ±	1764 ±	2270 ±	2410 ±	2654 ±	3107 ±
Load		160†	160*†	103*†	223*†	214*†	289*†
(AU)	WT	1238 ±	1413 ±	1831 ±	1992 ±	24153	2556 ±
		131	160*	121*	156*	± 169*	143*

* Sig. different to previous measure (*P* <0.05); †Sig. different to WT group (*P* <0.05).

Table 2. Training time (h:min) for the field and resistance training for both the OR (N=9) and WT (N=9) groups during the final week of overload training (mean ± SD).

Measure	Condition	Pre-taper	Post-taper
Field training	OR	$8{:}00 \pm 0{:}14^{\dagger}$	$3{:}09 \pm 0{:}04^{\#}$
(h:min)	WT	$6{:}57 \pm 0{:}09$	$3{:}07 \pm 0{:}04^{\#}$
Resistance training	OR	$4{:}28 \pm 0{:}10^{\dagger}$	$2{:}25 \pm 0{:}04^{\#}$
(h:min)	WT	$3{:}16 \pm 0{:}20$	$2{:}24 \pm 0{:}04^{\#}$
Combined training	OR	$12{:}29 \pm 0{:}19^{\dagger}$	$5{:}34 \pm 0{:}04^{\#}$
(h:min)	WT	$10{:}13 \pm 0{:}25$	$5{:}31 \pm 0{:}07^{\#}$

$^{\#}$ Significantly different to previous pre-taper ($P < 0.05$); †Significantly different to WT group ($P < 0.05$).

3.2. Physiology

Table 3 displays the physiological variables that changed significantly during the 6-week overload training period. There were significant main effects observed in $\dot{V}O_2$max over time ($P<0.05$) and between groups ($P<0.05$) during the 6-week training period. Repeated contrasts demonstrated a significant decrease $\dot{V}O_2$max over time, with the OR group being significantly lower $\dot{V}O_2$max compared to the WT group at the end of the 6-week overload training period. No significant differences were observed between groups with 6 weeks of overload training in any of the other physiological variables. However, significant reductions were observed at the completion of the 6-week overload training period in maximal aerobic speed, HRmax, body mass, skinfolds and peak cycling power ($P<0.05$). No significant changes were observed in vertical jump, $[La^-]_{b,peak}$, or mean power output, and mean relative anaerobic capacity measured during a 10-s sprint. Table 4 shows the physiological, biochemical and psychological variables that changed significantly as a group (i.e. OR and WT groups combined) during the 6-week training period.

Table 3. Physiological variables of OR and WT Rugby League players during 6 week of overload training (mean ± SD).

Measure	Condition	Pre-training	Post-training
$\dot{V}O_{2max}$	OR	51.2 ± 2.5	$47.9 \pm 3.7^{\dagger\#}$
$(ml{\cdot}kg^{-1}{\cdot}min^{-1})$	WT	51.8 ± 4.8	51.6 ± 3.8
	Group	51.6 ± 3.2	$49.8 \pm 3.8^{\#}$

$^{\#}$ Sig. different to previous measure ($P<0.05$); †Sig. different to WT group ($P<0.05$).

Table 4. Group (N=18) changes in physiological, biochemical and psychological measures during the 6-week overload training period.

Measure	Change (%)
Physiological	
$\dot{V}O_2$max	−3.9 ± 9.1*
Maximal aerobic running speed	−3.7 ± 6.7*
Time to fatigue	−4.3 ± 9.1*
HRmax	−3.6 ± 4.9*
$[La^-]_{b,peak}$	4.2 ± 37.9*
Body mass	0.8 ± 1.5*
Σ9 skinfolds	−6.2 ± 3.1*
Peak power during 10 s cycle sprint	0.2 ± 14.0*
Biochemical	
Testosterone	−15.1 ± 17.2*
Testosterone:Cortisol ratio	−14.8 ± 29.7*
Prolactin	94.1 ± 70.2*
CK	169.1 ± 152.1*
Neutrophils	5.2 ± 29.0*
Lymphocytes	8.3 ± 27.5*
Immunoglobulin A	−11.8 ± 12.1*
Glutamate	112.9 ± 21.4*
Glutamine:Glutamate ratio	−149.0 ± 67.3*
Urinary BCAA	−12.8 ± 31.8*
Psychological	
Social relaxation	−104.2 ± 101.6*
Sleep Quality	104.2 ± 110.2*
Fatigue	104.2 ± 133.2*

Values are mean ± SD; negative signs indicate reduced values. * Significantly change with 6-week progressive overload training (only variables with significant changes shown).

3.3. Multiple regression

Multiple regression analysis revealed the change in $\dot{V}O_2$max was predicted from changes in self-regulation (β=−0.381), the heart rate-velocity relationship from stage three of the warm up test (β=0.537), plasma IgA levels (β=−0.477) and blood urea (β=0.357). This model accounted for 95% of the variance in $\dot{V}O_2$ max. The partial correlations of these predictors are shown in Table 5.

Table 5. Partial correlations of predictors of change in $\dot{V}O_2$max with progressive overload training.

	Self Regulation	HR-Velocity Slope	Plasma IgA	Blood Urea
$\dot{V}O_2$max	0.701	0.852	−0.806	0.698

4. DISCUSSION

The purpose of this study was to identify markers of recovery in team sport participants during 6 weeks of progressive overload training. This was achieved by progressively increasing the physical training volume in 18 semi-professional Rugby League players from 5.7 and 5.1 h of physical training in the OR and WT groups respectively, to 12.5 and 10.0 h for the OR and WT groups, respectively. The training loads in the present study appear to be similar to those reporting overreaching (Halson et al., 2002).

In the present study $\dot{V}O_2$max was used as the criterion measure of adaptation. Although this physiological measure is not a direct measure of 'on-field' performance, it has been shown to be strongly related with key performance indicators such as distance covered during a competitive match, involvement with the ball and number of sprints completed during a game in elite soccer players (Helgerud et al., 2001). Therefore, for the purposes of the present study, $\dot{V}O_2$max changes are considered to be a valuable indicator of performance in Rugby League players.

The present result of a decreased $\dot{V}O_2$max in the OR group with 6-weeks of training designed to overreach deliberately are in agreement with recent studies reporting a reduction in $\dot{V}O_2$max with over-reaching in endurance athletes (Halson et al., 2002). Furthermore, peak cycling power was significantly decreased in both experimental groups which may be related to increased peripheral fatigue. Similarly, the progressive overload training did lead to a decreased body mass and skinfolds in both experimental groups. This was most likely due to the increased energetic demands of training. However, in accordance with previous investigators (Filaire et al., 2001; Halson et al., 2002), there does not appear to be a clear biochemical explanation for these changes in physiological measures.

In agreement with many previous investigators (Rowbottom et al., 2000; Halson et al., 2002), the present results suggest that there are no specific biochemical markers of overreaching. The present results show that compared to baseline measures the testosterone, T:C ratio, prolactin, CK, immunoglobulin A, neutrophils, lymphocytes, glutamine, glutamine to glutamate ratio and summed urinary BCAAs demonstrated a significant change at the end of the 6 weeks of progressive overload training. These findings suggest that overreaching is most likely due to the cumulative effect of fatigue in a number of pathophysiological systems, rather than exhaustion in one or a few systems.

The multiple regression equation demonstrated that the combination of the self-reported measure of the use of mental skills (i.e. the use of mental skills for athletes to prepare, push, motivate, and set goals for themselves), the change in the HR-velocity relationship during stage three of the warm up test, changes in resting plasma IgA and changes in blood urea concentration were accurate predictors of change in $\dot{V}O_2$max during 6 weeks of progressive overload training. This equation may be applied practically to select measures that may be useful for predicting changes in $\dot{V}O_2$max in team sport performers during periods of heavy physical training. However, caution must be taken when interpreting these results due to the large number of variables relative to the total subject number.

The present finding of psychological measures being the strongest contributor to the predictor of aerobic power decrement is in agreement with previous researchers who have reported psychological measures to be the most valuable predictor of performance in three stale elite swimmers (Hooper et al., 1995). These investigators observed that self-reported sleep, fatigue and stress were the best predictors of swim time trial performance change. The best self-reported measure in the present study was self-regulation. Self-regulation refers to the athlete's motivation and desire to complete physical training as well as the ability to use mental skills training. These present results are in agreement with previous investigators who have suggested that self-assessment tools may provide useful data for monitoring fatigue, overreaching and overtraining (Hooper et al., 1995).

Another important finding in the present study is the change in the HR-velocity relationship established during an incremental work test during a field-based warm-up test is a strong predictor of performance change as measured by $\dot{V}O_2$max. A possible explanation for the change in the HR-velocity relationship measured during the increased physical training is most likely dysfunction of the neuroendocrine system. However, the observed urinary adrenaline and noradrenaline results from the present study were unable to confirm this suggestion.

In the current investigation, the elevated resting plasma IgA levels associated with the performance change was an unexpected finding. Most previous researchers have not observed relationships between immune measures and athletic performance (Mackinnon, 2000). However, one study has reported elevated plasma IgA levels with increased training loads in elite swimmers (Gleeson et al., 1995), but no association with actual swim performance was established. It is therefore recommended that future studies be conducted to examine the relationship between $\dot{V}O_2$max and immune system measures.

Blood urea changes reflect increased protein use with increases in this measure indicating a state of catabolism. The multiple regression analysis shows that changes in blood urea levels, in combination with changes in self-regulation, the heart rate-velocity relationship and resting plasma IgA levels, can accurately be used to predict changes in $\dot{V}O_2$max. Therefore, the present data suggest that changes in blood urea may be useful in detecting fatigue during periods of heavy training when taken with other measures.

5. CONCLUSION

The present findings suggest that biochemical measures in blood and urine are variable and only give a general indication of fatigue rather than a clear diagnosis of overreaching. Therefore it appears that measuring one or few biochemical markers of fatigue is not useful for identifying the early stages of overtraining in team sport participants in a practical setting.

The present multiple regression suggests that the change in $\dot{V}O_2$max during 6 weeks of progressive overload training in Rugby League players may be predicted by a few psychological and physiological variables. These findings show that self-regulation, heart rate-velocity relationship changes, blood urea and plasma IgA may be useful in monitoring decreases in $\dot{V}O_2$max in team sport players. The small sample size in the present study suggests that further research is warranted before firm conclusions based on these measures are made.

REFERENCES

Filaire, E., Bernain, X., Sagnol, M. and Lac, G., 2001, Preliminary results on mood state, salivary Testosterone: Cortisol ratio and team performance in a professional soccer team. *European Journal of Applied Physiology,* **86**, 179–184.

Foster, C., Florhaug, J.A., Franklin, J., Gottschall, L., Hrovatin, L.A., Parker, S., Doleshal, P. and Dodge, C., 2001, A new approach to monitoring exercise training. *Journal of Strength and Conditioning Research,* **15**, 109–115.

Gleeson, M., McDonald, W.A., Cripps, A.W., Pyne, D.B., Clancy, R.L. and Fricker, P.A., 1995, The effect of immunity of long term intensive training in elite swimmers. *Clinical and Experimental Immunology,* **102**, 210–216.

Gore, C., 2000, Physiological Tests for Elite Athletes, 1st ed. (Champaign, Illinois: Human Kinetics).

Halson, S.L., Bridge, M.W., Meeusen, R., Busschaert, B., Gleeson, M., Jones, D.A. and Jeukendrup, A.E., 2002, Time course of performance changes and fatigue markers during intensified training in cyclists. *Journal of Applied Physiology,* **93**, 947–956.

Helgerud, J., Christian Engen, L., Wisløff, U. and Hoff, J., 2001, Aerobic endurance training improves soccer performance. *Medicine and Science in Sports and Exercise,* **33**, 1925–1931.

Hooper, S.L., Mackinnon, L.T., Bachmann, A.W., Howard, A. and Gordon, D., 1995, Markers for monitoring overtraining and recovery. *Medicine and Science in Sports and Exercise,* **27**, 106–112.

Kellmann, M. and Kallus, K.W., 2001, *Recovery-Stress Questionnaire for Athletes: User Manual.* (Champaign, Illinois: Human Kinetics).

Lehmann, M., Schnee, W., Scheu, R., Stockhausen, W. and Bachl, N., 1992, Decreased nocturnal catecholamine excretion: parameter for an overtraining syndrome in athletes? *International Journal of Sports Medicine,* **13**, 236–242.

Mackinnon, L.T., 2000, Overtraining effects on immunity and performance in athletes. *Immunology and Cell Biology,* **78**, 502–509.

Naessens, G., Chandler, T.J., Kibler, W.B. and Driessens, M., 2000, Clinical useful of nocturnal urinary noradrenaline excretion patterns in the follow-up of training processes in high-level soccer players. *Journal of Strength and Conditioning Research,* **14**, 125–131.

Rowbottom, D.G., Morton, A.R. and Keast, D., 2000, Monitoring for overtraining in the endurance performer. In *Endurance in Sport,* 2nd ed., edited by Shephard, R.J. and Åstrand, P.O. (Oxford: Blackwell Science Ltd.), pp. 486–506.

Urhausen, A. and Kindermann, W., 2002, Diagnosis of overtraining. What tools do we have? *Sports Medicine,* **32**, 95–102.

61 On the Relationship of Fitness to Running Volume and Intensity in Female Soccer Players

Donald T. Kirkendall, Kyle Leonard and W.E. Garrett, Jr.
Duke University Medical Center Durham, NC 27710 and
The Department of Orthopaedics University of North Carolina
Chapel Hill, NC 27599

1. INTRODUCTION

That fitness is an important component of success is soccer is not an issue. The game's hybrid nature of changing directions and velocities every 5–6 s is well known (Ekblom, 1986; Bangsbo, 1991), yet also means that there are numerous aspects of fitness that must be addressed in training. These include speed, endurance, power, strength, agility, flexibility and balance.

While there are many reasons to assess the fitness level of an athlete, one purpose might be to predict eventual performance of that athlete. This has been a common aspect of individual sports like running, swimming, and cycling. However, little attention has been paid to team sports because of the multitude of variables dictating the flow of the game that could affect running performance during competition. The present purpose was to see if field tests of fitness might predict the amount and intensity of running in women soccer players.

2. METHODS

We tested the women's soccer team at the University of North Carolina upon their arrival at training camp in August. The project was approved by our Institutional Review Board. The tests performed were the vertical jump (VJ, 1-step approach), Illinois Agility Run, 7×30 m sprints with a 25-s recovery between each run, Cooper's test, and the Intermittent Recovery Yo-Yo test. Game running volume (practice game, n=9) was determined by global position system (GPS) tracking of the players, then solving a two-dimensional distance formula. Data from GPS were saved every 2 s. The game was against another university, but was a pre-season game. The university system in the USA allows a restricted form of free substitution.

Data were summarized using routine descriptive statistics. Field test performances were correlated with the running volume (m), running intensity ($m.s^{-1}$) for each half and the full game. Specific regression models were tested. Individual P values will be reported.

3. RESULTS

Means of the tests and running volume are reported in Table 1.

Table 1. Descriptive summary of field test and game running distance.

	Mean ($\pm$ s.d.)
Distance run (m)	5240 (605)
Yo-Yo test (m)	1470 (232)
V.J. (cm)	51.05 (3.8)
Agility (s)	15.42 (.43)
Cooper (m)	2956 (48) [7.4 laps]

Table 2 shows the relative fraction of the total distance covered according to running velocity for the 9 players.

Table 2. Average fraction (% of total game distance) by half and velocity.

	1st half	2nd half
0–2 m.s^{-1}	61	64
2–4 m.s^{-1}	32	28.5
4–6 m.s^{-1}	4.5	5.4
6+ m.s^{-1}	0.7	1.1

The 7 × 30-m sprint test presents a number of results. We placed a timer at 10 m to obtain times for a 10-m sprint, a 20-m sprint (with a 10 m running start), and the full 30-m time. For the 7 sprints, we collected each player's best time, the average of all 7 runs and an index of fatigue where the percent decline in time from the fastest sprint (usually the 1st or 2nd sprint) to the slowest sprint (usually the 6th or 7th sprint) was determined. This was done for each sprint distance. Table 3 presents these values for the players studied.

Table 3. Average sprint times (s) and velocity (m.s^{-1}) by sprint distance and computed value.

	Best	Avg	%decline
10 m (s) (m.s^{-1})	1.86 (5.4)	1.95 (5.1)	−8.01
Flying 20 m (s) (m.s^{-1})	2.74 (7.3)	2.88 (6.9)	−8.44
30 m (s) (m.s^{-1})	4.60 (6.5)	4.84 (6.2)	−8.06

Out of all the 14 values tested, there were few significant correlations with running velocity by half. There were a possible 52 correlations for each half. Most 1st half correlations were between the 4–6 m.s^{-1} velocity and the various sprint times from the 7×30-m sprints. There were no 2nd half correlations.

When the tests were correlated with overall running distance, to our surprise, the agility test had the highest correlation with running total running distance ($R^2 = 0.92$). Adding the Yo-Yo test and the vertical jump increased the R^2 to 0.95 ($P=0.0014 \pm 151$ m).

When adding the sprint factors to the model of agility, vertical jump and Yo-Yo tests, the best model added the fastest time for the 20-m sprint ($R^2=0.98$, $P=0.0011 \pm 81$ m), but the use of any of the sprint values increased the R^2.

4. DISCUSSION

We were unable to find any reports that attempted to correlate running volume with fitness test data. Claiming that these are the 'first' data on the topic is always risky, but to our knowledge such results are new.

The most significant finding in this project was that agility had the best correlation with total running distance. A priori, we predicted that the Yo-Yo test would show the best correlation. This test has been shown to be a reliable and valid test of fitness for soccer (Krustrup et al., 2003). Yet the use of this particular agility test that is longer than most other agility tests was highly correlated with running performance in the game.

A second important finding was that a model of multiple aspects of fitness produced a model that accounted for an astonishing 98% of the variance in the project.

In considering these findings, we must consider some potential limitations. First, the total running volume was fairly low for this calibre of player. In the USA, a national collegiate championship has been contested for 20 years. This university team has been to every final weekend (of 4 teams) and won the championship 16 times. We have monitored running volume by GPS a number of times and typically record distances of around 8500 m with a couple of midfield players covering over 10,000 m in highly competitive games (unpublished observations). The nature of the match (being a pre-season game) and the amount of substitutions lowered the typical running volume of this level of female player. Second, these running volumes were obtained before the random error signal on the GPS system had been removed by order of President Clinton. We obtain a 'map' of the field each game by walking the perimeter of the field and then correct the values for the known distance around the field. There is the chance that the error signal affected our results. Third, the Illinois Agility Run is longer than most agility tests that typically take around 5 s. This test was chosen because our use of one of the shorter tests showed little discrimination between youth players, college players, and national team players. This longer run seems to be a better discriminator between levels of performers.

The length of the agility test might be a factor in these results. The shorter agility tests may have 2–4 changes of direction in 5 s, but in soccer the agility requirements suggest changes in speed or direction every 5–6 s. Therefore the shorter tests might not be the best test to choose given specificity arguments.

Of interest was the complete lack of any relationship of the Cooper 12-min run with any factor in this study. This result might suggest that using this test to monitor soccer-specific endurance is not advisable.

These results show that the single test of fitness that best predicted running volume is agility, but that a multi-component model gives a more accurate estimation. As agility is a known requirement of soccer, more emphasis on assessment of, and training for, agility might be warranted.

Acknowledgement

Thanks to Anson Dorrance and his players of the University of North Carolina women's soccer team. This project was funded in part by a grant from Nike Inc.

REFERENCES

Bangsbo, J., Norregaard, L. and Thorsoe, F., 1991, Activity profile of competition soccer. Canadian Journal of Sport Science, **16,**110–116.
Ekblom, B., 1986, Applied physiology of soccer. Sports Medicine, **3,** 50–60.
Krustrup, P., Mohr, M., Amstrup, T., Rysgaard, T., Johansen, J., Steensberg, A., Pedersen, P.K. and Bangsbo, J., 2003, The yo-yo intermittent recovery test: physiological response, reliability, and validity. Medicine and Science in Sports and Exercise, **35**, 697–705.

62   Beating the Hesitation or "Stutter" Step

Doug McClymont

Christchurch College of Education, New Zealand

1. INTRODUCTION

1.1. Background

In most team ball games the concept of faking, or "selling the dummy", is an integral part of an offensive strategy. Defensive coaches attempt to teach players how to avoid "buying the dummy" but in the game situation, if the move is well constructed, then the dummy is almost always effective. This report is of an intervention designed to defend against one particular dummy, the hesitation, or as it is often described, the stutter step. It includes some detail of the motor control theory underlying both the hesitation and its defence, and the results of a trial of the intervention in a practice environment. The intervention was developed within the structure of the Rugby Union game and is described as such, but the process is equally relevant in any game in which the hesitation ploy is used.

The hesitation defines a situation in which an attacking player running with the ball is attempting to beat a single defender by running around him/her. As the two approach each other the attacking player hesitates in his/her running, presented as a slight pause or slowing, often with an exaggerated movement of the legs and known as a goose or stutter step. The move may also include a pronounced leaning back of the upper body and, in a few cases, may even be accompanied by a deliberate confusing ball movement. Whatever the accompanying actions, the pause in fast running is always followed immediately by the resumption of fast running. The defender invariably responds to the slowing of the attacking player by slowing also. However, the defender is unable to respond immediately to the resumption of fast running by the attacking player who, having sold the dummy, is now able to run around the defender and gain an advantage. The slowing response along with the inability to respond immediately to the second stimulus is known as the double-stimulation paradigm. First, it is appropriate to present some motor control background.

1.2. Decision making

The motor control process by which Rugby Union players receive information from the environment, interpret that information, decide on a course of action and respond may be known as the decision making process. It may also be referred to as stimulus-response time, but more commonly, the time between the presentation of the stimulus and the first response is referred to as reaction time. Reaction time may be further divided into simple, choice, and discriminant, but for present purposes reaction time is assumed to be the time taken to react to the stimuli in the game, regardless of their type.

Figure 1 illustrates the decision making process. Information is received from the environment (e.g. other players, the ball, action in the game) through the player's sensory receptors of vision, hearing, and touch. The player begins the decision making process by identifying the appropriate stimulus from a number of competing environmental stimuli. The player is able to identify several stimuli at one time, but choosing the correct stimulus is a skill influenced by knowledge and experience of the game (Schmidt and Wrisberg, 2000).

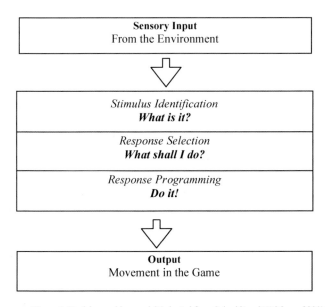

Figure 1. Decision making model (adapted from Schmidt and Wrisberg, 2000).

Once the appropriate stimulus is identified, the player then searches his/her stored knowledge for a suitable response (taking care to eliminate the possibility of misidentification) and selection of the appropriate response is made. Processing at this stage may be time consuming and attention demanding (known as controlled processing), or it may be very fast, or automatic. Automatic processing is the result of considerable practice and is thought to be determined by the ability of the athlete to form production units, groups of stimuli which, when presented in a particular combination, elicit an immediate or automatic response. Interference or conflict at the response selection stage may be caused by inability to identify the important stimulus or combination of stimuli, and will increase the processing time and thus, the time to react.

When the response has been selected, it is programmed and the command delivered to the player's motor control system for the action to take place. This stage is known as response programming and takes place in a very short time.

However, in each phase there may be interference, and the total response time increased. If the total processing time (the reaction time) is increased then the defensive player is disadvantaged. The practiced defensive player may reduce that time, thus minimising the advantage of the attacking player. The hesitation defence is based specifically on avoiding the delay that occurs in the response selection phase.

The total processing time (RT) of the player is the total time from the stimulus to the first movement of the response. With only a single response available this time may be anywhere between 150 and 200 ms. The time taken for each of the three parts will be increased if there is any interference or decreased as a result of good coaching and game experience. If decision making time can be reduced, then an advantage is gained.

1.3. Influences on reaction time

There are well documented factors in motor learning literature (Schmidt and Wrisberg, 2000; Magill, 2001) that influence reaction time. While some of those influences on the decision making process have been described, success of the hesitation is determined by the speed of the game in conjunction with two further motor control principles, the double-stimulation paradigm and consistent stimulus-response mapping.

1.4. The speed factor

A fast running rugby player may approach a speed of 10 m.s^{-1}. At that speed, if reaction time is 200 ms, then a player will travel 2 m before he/she even begins to change direction or slow down in response to a stimulus. An example is seen with a fast running player chasing a kicked ball. Faced with a stationary player, who has retrieved the ball and steps aside as the runner approaches, the chasing player runs right past the ball carrier, as he/she is unable to begin to change direction for at least 2 m.

1.5. The double-stimulation paradigm

The double stimulation paradigm describes a situation in which two closely spaced stimuli are presented and there is a response to first one, then the other. Research indicates (Schmidt and Wrisberg, 2000) that while response to the first stimulus may be of normal duration, response to the second is delayed. This is known as the psychological refractory period.

During decision making, stimulus identification and response selection may occur in parallel. However, at the response programming stage, where the instruction is delivered to the motor system, operation is serial. Once the response to the first stimulus has begun to be delivered, it is as if the instructions for the second must wait in a queue to proceed through a bottleneck in single file. For example, the reaction time of a particular player is 200 ms, 100 ms of which is taken up by the identification and response selection process of the first stimulus, and a second stimulus is presented 60 ms after the first, then while the defender may identify and select a second response, the programming of the second response does not begin until the first is completed. Thus, the first movement in the correct direction occurs 260 ms after the original stimulus. In that time, the attacking player has accelerated and gained a distance advantage over the defender whose response was delayed.   Research into the precise parameters of the psychological refractory period and faking (Schmidt and Wrisberg, 2000) indicates that if the second stimulus is delivered up to 40 ms after the first, the two stimuli are treated as one. If, however, the second stimulus is delivered at 60 ms after the first, then the response delay is maximised. Figure 2 illustrates the effect of the psychological refractory period.

It is the delay of the psychological refractory period that is the basis of "selling the dummy". While rugby examples abound, a very fine visual example of the process in action is seen in the game of cricket, when a bowler stumbles as he begins his/her delivery. The TV bowling action replay shows very clearly that even as the player is falling towards the ground, the bowling arm continues the bowling action. The stimulus of the stumble has been identified and the decision made to cease bowling and protect oneself from the ground. The instruction to save oneself from falling, however, is queued up in the bottleneck waiting for the "bowling" instruction to finish.

Every rugby player who has been sold a good dummy experiences the same inevitable reaction. For example, while the instruction to move to the right in response to the first stimulus is being run, the player is aware that the attacker is in fact moving to the left (the second stimulus) but is unable to respond.

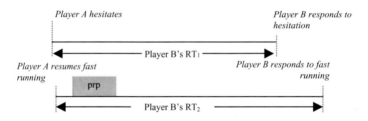

Figure 2. Player A hesitates but resumes fast running before Player B has responded. Player B is unable to respond to the second stimulus until the first RT has been completed. Time between the two responses is greater than time between the two stimuli.

1.6. Stimulus – response mapping

One of the significant influences on reaction time concerns the compatibility of the stimulus and the response. Schmidt and Wrisberg (2000) used the example of a laboratory situation in which the subject responds more quickly to a stimulus if the response is on the same side of the body and closely associated with the stimulus. They described it as a natural response.   Traffic lights provide a good example of a learned natural response. The well learned response to stop for a red signal is known as consistent stimulus-response mapping, in which the same response is made to the same stimulus consistently. If the law were changed so that we were to go on red, and stop on green, it would take some time and many hours of practice under varied conditions for the new response to become consistent. In all faking situations in sport the natural response of the defender is to do as the attacker does. In the case of the hesitation, the attacker slows and the defender slows in response. The hesitation defence intervention, through practice, proposes to replace the natural slowing response with another, learned response.

1.7. Time to contact (tau)

In situations in which a person moves towards an object or the object moves towards the person, vision plays an important role in specifying when to initiate the action to make contact with the object. The important visual information in these situations is the time to contact, which is the amount of time remaining until the object contacts the person (or vice versa) from a specific distance. Time to contact (tau) is specified according to the relative rate of change of size of the image of the object on the retina of the eye. In a rugby game as two players approach each other, there is a change in the size of the retinal image. As this image reaches a certain critical size, it triggers the action/tackle required by the situation.

The predictive function of tau is time based, which allows action initiation and contact to occur at a specific time regardless of the speed of the object or person. In a rugby game, the player lines up a tackle based on the time to contact, rather than cognitive knowledge of the distance to and velocity of the other player. Velocity, however, is a function of time and distance, so in reality the time to contact may well be interpreted as specifying a predicted point of contact. As illustrated in Figure 3, if there is a perceived change in the predicted point or time, then the player will adjust his/her velocity to make the tackle at the new point or time.

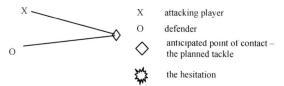

Figure 3. The hesitation: the attacking player X is running with the ball and the defender O plans to make contact at ◊.

With some understanding of the underlying motor control principles related to hesitation, it is appropriate to discuss the theory of the hesitation as it appears in the rugby game.   The change of pace, stutter step, or hesitation, provides a stimulus to the defender that the attacker has slowed, and the anticipated time to contact has changed. The compatible response to that stimulus is that the defender slows also (see Figure 3). Unfortunately, in the hesitation move, the attacker has planned a more complex motor pattern, to slow momentarily, and then accelerate immediately. As discussed, the double-stimulus paradigm determines that the defender does not respond immediately to the second stimulus (the speeding up again) until after the first instruction has completed its travel through the bottleneck, leaving the defender waiting to respond while the attacker is back to fast running. The attacker then gains a time/speed advantage and the time to contact for the defender is no longer attainable and he/she is left grasping (see Figure 4).

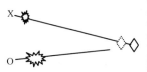

The attacking player X hesitates, and even though taking a slightly longer time to reach the anticipated point of contact, will still reach the new point well before the defender O, who has paused for an even longer time, the psychological refractory period.

Figure 4. The missed tackle.

1.8. The theory of the hesitation defence

Utilising this theory of the hesitation, the following defence against the move is proposed:- That the "natural" slowing response to the hesitation be replaced with a change of direction toward the attacker. In motor learning terms, this means a change to the stimulus response compatibility (Magill, 2001).

2. METHODS

To determine whether the proposed hesitation defense was possible 12 academy level Rugby Union players (ages 18–20 years and identified as probable elite performers within three years) were invited to participate in a one-day trial. Players warmed up as for a standard practice session that usually includes a short game of touch. Prior to the warm-up game, players and researcher discussed various methods of beating a defender in a one-on-one situation and the players indicated a familiarity with the hesitation technique and its variations. The discussion was presented in rugby parlance and based around the theory presented earlier. Players then took part in a 10-min game of touch within a 22×30 m area of a grass playing field in which they were encouraged to use the run around or hesitation if the appropriate situation arose.

After the Touch, game players were paired with one taking the part of the attacker, and the other, the defender. Using demonstration and discussion, the defending player of each pair was then instructed in the theory of the hesitation defence. Each was instructed to respond to the hesitation of the attacking player with a change of directions towards the ball carrier (see Figure 5). In individual 10 m x 10 m areas of the field each pair practised the hesitation move with, in the first instance, only the defender aware of the proposed defence. Each pair performed the new technique five times, the result self-recorded after each trial using X or O to indicate success or failure (see Table 1).

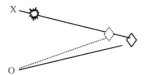

The attacking player hesitates, and the anticipated contact is now at a point slightly closer than before. The defender however has not hesitated, simply changed direction ...... to meet the new anticipated point of contact.

Figure 5. The new scenario.

Success was described as:- the defender responding to the ball carrier's hesitation with a change of direction towards the ball carrier, and making contact with the ball carrier. This outcome was recorded as 0.

Failure was described as:- the defender responding to the ball carrier's hesitation with hesitation, and being beaten. This result was recorded as X.

After five attempts the results were discussed with all participants. Then the roles reversed and the new defenders instructed in the change of direction technique. Each pair then performed the new technique five times, the result being self-recorded as previously (see Table 1).

3. RESULTS

Players were numbered in pairs. In each pairing the uneven number (see Table 1) took the role of ball carrier for the first five trials. While the ball carrier was unaware of the defender's instructions for the first trial, within two trials the changed response was obvious to the ball carrier. As a consequence of participation in the first series both players were aware of the defensive strategy in the second set of trials (see Table 1, Column B).

When players used the change of direction technique in a one-on-one simulated game, the ball carrier was able to beat the defender in only 10 of 60 attempts. In the first set of five trials, 22 out of 30 attempts were successful. In the second set of five trials, when players were more aware of the requirements and had been caught by their partner when carrying the ball, 28 of 30 trials were successful. Players 5-6 were an unevenly matched pairing with player 6 being considerably faster and more mobile than player 5. Ignoring their results, in every instance in the first pairing the defender was able to tackle the attacking player more often than not. For the second pairing when the attacker was aware of the defence response, success was almost complete.

Table 1. Self-reported scores of hesitation defence.

Change of Direction Response by Defender												
Ball Carriers 2-12 Unaware							**Ball Carriers 1-11 Aware**					
Defending Player	1	3	5	7	9	11	Defending Player	2	4	6	8	10	12
Trial 1	O	X	X	O	X	X	Trial 1	O	O	O	O	O	O
2	O	O	O	O	O	O	2	O	O	O	O	O	O
3	O	O	X	O	O	O	3	O	O	O	O	O	O
4	O	O	X	O	O	O	4	O	O	O	O	X	O
5	O	X	O	O	O	X	5	O	O	O	X	O	O
Success	5	3	2	5	4	3	**Success**	5	5	5	4	4	5

4. DISCUSSION

It is difficult to quantify the magnitude of the change of direction of the defender as in each trial the direction and speed of both players varied. This variation altered the parameters of the change of direction. Informed observation by three interested coaches of the game of "touch" prior to the testing confirmed that all players used some variation of the hesitation at least once while carrying the ball. In all cases where the technique was appropriate and there was space, the ball carrier was able to beat the defender. It is thought that the key to the hesitation defence is that what has really changed is the anticipated time to contact (tau). To counter the hesitation, the defending player learned to respond to the slowing of the attacker with a new response. When the attacking player hesitated, the defender responded with a change of direction toward the attacking player. As the slowing response seems to be a natural and consistent response built up over many years of playing contact type games, there is a very strong stimulus-response compatibility and making this change should be a difficult task for the learner. It would seem that by practising the hesitation defence in a one-on-one situation and then incorporating the move in a simulated game that it is possible to replace the existing compatibility with a new response, which, with practice, may become automatic. Figure 5 illustrates the mechanics of the move.

There are several significant changes that take place in the hesitation defence scenario (see Figure 5), all benefiting the original defending player. The attacker has hesitated, knowing from experience that the defender will slow, and so has pre-planned an immediate return to full speed. This instruction has been delivered as a single motor command (see Figure 1, Response Programming) with no provision for feedback, and must run its course before a second program may be initiated (see double stimulation paradigm). In this new scenario, however, when the attacker has hesitated and the defender responded with a change of direction (see Figure 5), the advantage is with the defender. For the attacker, the original motor program has continued (like the cricket bowler whose arm continued to bowl while falling) and he/she is unable to respond to the unexpected change of direction of the defender until the second part of the motor command has run its course. Inevitably, in that short time the attacker is tackled.

5. CONCLUSION

This study was designed to test a hypothesis and while there are limitations such as the simulated game environment and the observer's interest in the outcome, this first attempt at making a change to the natural hesitation response in a simulated game appears to have been successful. Success in the rugby environment, however, is only measured in the competitive arena and it remains to be seen whether the new response to the original stimulus can be practised in the game situation. Further research on the hesitation defence is required, with particular emphasis on the design of practice to ensure correct learning of the new skill and the transfer of the defence from the practice arena to the game environment.

REFERENCES

Magill, R.A., 2001, *Motor Learning: Concepts and Applications.* 6th ed. (Boston, Mass: McGraw-Hill).
Schmidt, R. A., and Wrisberg, C.A. 2000, *Motor Learning and Performance*(2nd ed). (Champaign, Ill: Human Kinetics Books).

63 Use of the Reactive Strength Index (RSI) as an Indicator of Plyometric Training Conditions

Doug McClymont
Christchurch College of Education

1. INTRODUCTION

1.1. Background

The Reactive Strength Index (RSI) is one component of the Strength Qualities Assessment Test (SQAT). This test is used at the Australian Institute of Sport (Young, 1995) to differentiate between the various strength qualities of sprinters and jumpers. Using a contact mat with drop jump protocol the RSI value is derived by dividing the height jumped by the time in contact prior to take-off (height jumped/time). Tests are conducted from a range of drop heights to impose increasing stretch loads on the leg extensors and RSI is interpreted as an indicator of the ability of the athletes to withstand those stretch loads during the plyometric component of their conditioning and general preparation. This report is based on use of the RSI in monitoring the drop heights of players in a professional Rugby Union Franchise (Study 1), and as a secondary consideration (Study 2), the effects of pre-season training on the Reactive Strength Index.

1.2. Reactive strength

Reactive strength can be defined as the ability to change quickly from an eccentric to a concentric contraction (Young, 1995). It includes utilisation of the stretch-shorten cycle (SSC), movements classified as either fast (a contact time between 100 and 250 ms), or slow (contact time >250 ms). Slow SSC is utilised in activity such as a basketball jump shot, whereas fast SSC is utilised in the contact time or support phase during activity such as sprinting (Schmidtbleicher, 1992). The SSC tested in the drop jump is common in all ballistic actions, (e.g. throwing a ball, stepping into a jump) and is commonly known as pre-stretch. There is increased activation of the muscle fibres from the pre-stretch and this results in an increase in maximal force production. Specifically, force enhancement occurs in the dynamic concentric contractions after stretch, with the force-velocity relationship shifting toward increasing forces at any given velocity (Bartlett, 1999). If the time available for this stretch-shorten action is less than 300 ms, the rate of force development, rather than maximal strength, is the deciding factor in the power outcome (Zatsiorsky, 1995). While the contact time of sprinters may be as short as 80 ms (Wiemann and Tidow, 1995), utilisation of fast SSC is recognised as an essential component of testing for the specific strength characteristics required by jumpers (Young, 1995).

1.3. Plyometrics

Plyometric training has been an integral part of athletic conditioning since the 1960s. The word plyometric was coined by in 1966 (Zanon, 1989) and depth jumping techniques proposed by Verkhoshanski (1966) in the same year. There have been many proponents of the activity and while it is recognised (Horrigan and Shaw, 1989) that young athletes should progress in stages from light jumping exercises to depth jumping, there have been some prominent detractors amongst elite performers in both track and field and American football who blame career ending injury on plyometric training (Brzycki, 1986; Wikgren, 1988).

Rugby coaches, in the preparation of players, attempt to develop a high level of competence with specific rugby skills and a high level of specific rugby fitness. The modern professional rugby player is intelligent, agile, strong, powerful, coordinated and has an ability to run fast. In developing these characteristics, specialist coaches teach and hone the specific game skills, while the fitness coach or trainer prepares the individual player for the physical requirements of the game. Given the specific requirements of Rugby Union players at the elite level, the ability to utilise the fast SSC during running and jumping is an essential part of that preparation. Hence all components of preparation include an element of eccentric-concentric work (including depth jumping and bounding) that may be described as plyometrics.

2. STUDY 1 - THE RSI MONITORING PROCESS

2.1. Importance

While the athletes involved in this study were mature adults performing at an elite level, it was felt that monitoring of the RSI to determine optimal drop heights of individual plyometric training would minimise injury to the musculotendinous complex of the legs during this phase of preparation. It was decided that box heights would be confined to a maximum height of 45 cm and players would be encouraged to achieve contact times close to 200 ms.

2.2. Methods

Twenty-three professional Rugby Union players were tested three times over a period of 10 weeks prior to the start of the 2002 'Super 12' season (weeks 1, 6 and 10). The test was conducted when players were in a fatigued state, within 30 min of the completion of the standard NZRFU phosphate decrement test. Players stepped from a bench from three increasing measured heights (15, 30, 45 cm), and upon contact with the mat/floor performed a maximal jump, with a minimum contact period. No restriction was placed on arm movement. Three jumps from each of three drop heights were performed with drop height recorded manually and time in contact and height jumped recorded by the portable version of Multi-Timer©. Players were offered the option of repeating one attempt at each drop height if not satisfied with their own performance. Data were recorded in Excel and RSI was calculated using the formula, height jumped divided by time in contact (mm/ms).

In measuring height jumped from a contact mat, results will be significantly lower than standard jump-and-reach scores. Jump-and-reach measures the vertical displacement of the outstretched hand from a flat-footed position to full extension at peak flight. It therefore includes in the height measured almost the full length of the athlete's foot. The contact mat, however, records the time from the athlete leaving the mat at full extension until landing at full extension. Therefore almost the full length of the athlete's foot is not included in the result. Athletes in this test were informed of this length of foot difference and advised not to compare these results with jump-and-reach scores.

While variations in lean body mass will influence the results of this type of testing it was decided that as that measure was monitored regularly by the team dietician and fitness trainer as an integral component of the conditioning process, recommendations made on the basis of RSI testing would not incorporate any correction for lean body mass. It was assumed that the player was within the lean body mass parameters required by the fitness trainer and dietician.

Any plyometric training injury was recorded specifically as such, as part of ongoing monitoring by medical staff.

2.3. Results

Tables 1 and 2 below are examples from the first testing session. The RSI for each jump is calculated as is the average RSI for each series of three jumps from each drop height.

Data in Table 1 demonstrate contact times well within the parameters required by the fitness trainer (<200 ms) but with jump heights considered low.

Table 1. Sample of RSI testing results – low jump height.

	Position #8										
Drop Height(cm)	15			Mean	30			Mean	45			Mean
Height Jumped(mm)	336	352	336	341	389	368	336	364	400	368	341	370
Contact Time(ms)	223	188	194	202	196	177	171	181	208	175	165	183
RSI	1.51	1.87	1.73	1.70	1.98	2.08	1.96	2.01	1.92	2.10	2.07	2.03

Table 2. Sample of RSI testing results – long contact times.

Variable	Position prop										
Drop Height(cm)	15			Mean	30			Mean	45			Mean
Height Jumped(mm)	3 8 9	3 8 4	368	3 8 0	395	3 8 9	400	3 9 5	417	412	4 17	4 1 5
Contact Time(ms)	3 0 1	2 5 6	225	2 6 1	251	2 4 0	257	2 4 9	246	260	2 74	2 6 0
RSI	1.29	1.50	1.64	1.48	1.57	1.62	1.56	1.58	1.70	1.58	1.52	1.60

Data in Table 2 demonstrate acceptable jump heights. Average contact times were close to or greater than 250 ms.

While the prevention of training injury was the basic reason for the use of RSI monitoring there was no comparative data from previous seasons with which to compare injury rates. In this pre-season period there were no player injuries that could be attributed to plyometric activity during conditioning.

2.4. Discussion

To gauge an individual's SSC abilities, the reactive strength index (RSI) is used with incremental drop jump protocols. Thus, if RSI increases or is at least maintained as the drop height is increased, it is assumed that an individual's reactive strength capabilities are sound. In Table 1 the contact times were well within the required 200 ms and RSI increased as the drop height. This was interpreted to mean that SSC capabilities were sound and plyometric activity up to 45 cm would not expose the athlete to injury. However, the actual height jumped – apart from the first jump at 45 cm - was low in comparison to international norms in which healthy male physical education students who jumped an average height of 40.3 ± 6.9 cm from a drop height of 63 ± 22.7 cm, and male volleyball players 41.0 ± 14.5 cm from a drop height of 66.0 ± 16 cm (cited in Logan et al., 2000). The data in Table 1 indicate that while the player was utilising SSC he was not jumping as high as might be expected of, in this case, a professional number 8 forward whose role in the game of rugby includes fast open field running, agility, and application of power in the scrummage. Observation during testing indicated that this player was not competing full leg extension in the jumping phase. Information was presented about this individual with the results (Table 1) and the following recommendation:-

"Contact times are almost all <200 ms indicating use of fast SSC. Although average jump height increases with drop height the best jump of 400 mm is the only performance at the expected level of a power athlete. It is recommended that plyometric drop heights of up to 45 cm be utilised. It was observed during testing that the subject did not fully extend, there should be an emphasis on height jumped with full extension of all three joints."

Table 2 contains data from a player in the front row of the scrum who demonstrated satisfactory height jumped – an indicator of power – but whose contact times were all greater than the targeted 200 ms. This information was presented with the results (Table 2) as:-

"Contact times are all >220 ms indicating that fast SSC is not being used consistently. While RSI increases with drop height the index is low in comparison with others. It is recommend that drop heights be restricted to 30 cm max with an emphasis on the rebound."

Recommendations based on RSI results provided the fitness trainer with another source of data with which to monitor progress of players through the pre-season period. There were no injuries during this period attributable to plyometric or eccentric-concentric training activity, suggesting that the test provided an effective and useful tool in the preparation of elite athletes. All recommendations were reviewed after the next testing in six weeks.

3. STUDY- THE PLYOMETRIC CONDITIONING PROGRAMME

Investigation of the effects of training on the RSI of elite level Rugby Union players was a secondary consideration of this study.

3.2. Methods

3.2.1. Subjects

Thirty-five professional Rugby Union players undertook a physical conditioning programme over 10 weeks immediately prior to the 2002 'Super 12' season. The programme included elements of plyometric activity (see Table A). In recognition of conflicting views of the cost/benefits of plyometrics, a programme of RSI testing (see Study 1) was undertaken to monitor reactive strength development and 23 of the players were tested at least once over the pre-season period. While the conditioning of the athletes involved in this study included all aspects of rugby-specific fitness, the plyometric component can best be described as eccentric-concentric work leading to plyometric conditioning activity. In every activity in which a raised platform or box was used, the drop height was determined by the RSI report. Players did not exceed a target maximum of sixty rebound contacts per session.

3.2.2. Strength and power

Pre-season strength training was conducted 3–4 times per week with generally two days between each body part. The first four weeks of the period under discussion was generally core contrast while weeks 5–10 consisted of a power contrast phase. Those with "good core" strength completed the power contrast phase in the earlier four-week period.

3.2.3. Speed instruction

This work was done under the supervision of a specialist sprint coach (track athletics), by those players new to the squad and who required sprint instruction. Essentially, they were taught how to run efficiently. In the early part of the period this involved acceleration mechanics and drills designed to give players a feeling of applying force into the ground from the correct body position. With some success at acceleration, players were introduced to maximum velocity mechanics and associated issues of flexibility and stability. This component included the concept of turnover and fast response or rebound.

The six-week programme of 1–2 sessions per week was completed with rugby specific movements such as sidestepping, accelerating from a rolling start, change of direction etc. The only specific rebound activity included in the speed instruction programme was a series of two-footed jumps with an emphasis on fast rebound.

The content of the conditioning programme

The conditioning programme included elements of plyometrics. The drop heights of those activities were determined by the RSI testing programme.

Strength & Power

In the general preparation phase there was an emphasis on increasing strength and body mass. Athletes performed a large volume of work with high numbers of sets and reps and sufficient mass to work to exhaustion/failure. Strength training was undertaken on two days per week, with speed and/or rugby specific work on another four days.

During weeks 1–4 of the strength programme there was one plyometric activity.

Bungy Abduction
> A bungy cord was attached at the ankle and fixed to the wall at ankle height on both sides of the athlete. The athlete was required to bound sideways from one leg to the other providing a rebound upon landing while at the same time the free leg acted against the resistance of the bungy on that side. The emphasis was on the fast rebound and pulling the free leg across to the landing leg against the bungy resistance.

In the specific preparation phase (weeks 5–8) there was still an emphasis on increasing strength but the intensity was raised to increase the endurance effect. Within this phase there were a number of eccentric-concentric activities, some of which may be described as ballistic stretches, or formal plyometrics.

Power Clean
> Lift all the way to the shoulders with a maximum effort and jump off the ground as the bar reaches the shoulders.

Caber Toss
> Using a medicine ball in both hands, swing the ball back between the legs then throw for maximum height.

Cone Hops
> Three cones were adjusted for individual requirements. The athlete was required to hop laterally over the row of three cones, out and back, and repeated for each leg. *The height of the cones was adjusted individually as determined by the RSI report.*

Alternating Power Press
> From a front support or push up position the athlete jumps hands up and down a 5-cm step.

Weighted Power Rotation
> With heavy dumbbell, hips square to the front, rotate through ¼ turn and return.

Speed Ladder In/Outs

Single leg rebounds, in and out for two lengths of the ladder with the emphasis on rebound speed.

The power phase of the conditioning programme (weeks 5–10), has an emphasis on speed with lighter weights (50–70%RM). These exercises were included in the phase leading into the playing season.

Power Clean

As above

Side Medicine Ball Throw

With ball in front, pass and sprint 6 steps.

Alternating Medicine Ball Press

Jump press ups alternating one hand on medicine ball.

Lineout Jump with Sprint

Step forward into maximum jump, land facing forward, and turn and sprint 6 steps.

Box Hops

Use 3 boxes of varying height, step off and rebound onto next box. *Box heights determined by RSI report.*

External Boxing

One foot on box, other alongside. Hop onto box with other foot landing and rebounding back onto box. *Box height determined by RSI report.*

While RSI monitoring did not continue into the playing season, plyometric activity remained an integral component of the fitness programme. During this time the emphasis is on multi-joint exercise specific to the playing position, using contrast activities. Plyometric type activities in this phase include:-

Calf Bounds with Pass

Ball in hand, one foot on box, with small bounce swap feet quickly and pass to partner. *Box heights determined by final RSI report.*

Box Hop into Sprint

Hop off raised box and immediately sprint, receiving pass in first/second step. Also performed as Box Step onto alternate leg. *Box height is determined by final RSI report.*

External Tyre Toss

From ¼ squat position and straight arms, rotate and throw tyre across body.

Bungy Jumps

Bungy attached at waist, double foot jumps to maximum height.

Resisted Tow onto Ball

Bungy attached at waist, partner resists acceleration, player released and runs onto pass from another partner.

Bungy Abduction

As described above

Lower Ab Dynamic Swings

On back in pike position, partner throws legs down, player rebounds without feet hitting ground.

In every activity in which a raised platform or box is used, the height of the drop is determined by the RSI report. Just as players become accustomed to using appropriate weight in the free and machine weight exercises so they quickly become accustomed to checking their personal box heights.

3.2.4. Speed training

These sessions included the complete squad and while the emphasis was on repetition sprints it included single leg bounds, medicine ball throws, run-jump-throw, and two-footed jumps with an emphasis on fast rebound.

3.2.5. Rugby practice

Bounding is used in preparation for specific speed activity, otherwise the only eccentric-concentric work is that involved in normal running and specific rugby activity.

3.3. Results

Table 3. Mean scores of nine players tested in weeks 1 and 10 of the pre-season programme.

Drop Height	Height Jumped (cm)		Contact Time (ms)		RSI	
(cm)	*Week 1*	*Week 10*	*Week 1*	*Week 10*	*Week 1*	*Week 10*
15 cm	364.5	338.2	213.0	218.3	1.81	1.65
30 cm	399.7	372.0	213.3	216.6	1.99	1.84
45 cm	416.0	381.2	214.0	220.1	2.03	1.84

Paired sample t-tests were used to compare RSI performances before and after the period of plyometric training, a ten-week period (Table 2). Following the conditioning programme a lower index was observed at each of the three drop heights (15 cm, 30 cm, and 45 cm), though all differences were statistically non-significant ($P > 0.05$). Responsible for the reduced RSI were both lowered jump heights and increased contact times (non-significant).

3.4. Discussion

While the full squad of players numbered 35, only nine were tested at both the beginning and end of the pre-season training period. The unexpected decreases in the RSIs, although small, are difficult to explain. The results might reflect the high volume of non-plyometric training engaged in close to the periods of testing although this possible confounding factor was not directly tested.

4. CONCLUSION

To determine the effectiveness of plyometric training would require an experimental design with both test and control groups. In a professional rugby franchise if the fitness trainer requires plyometric activity as an integral part of the conditioning programme, then it would be difficult to convince a group of players that they would not be disadvantaged in their career by training in a non-plyometric environment. The results of this study indicate that if the development of reactive strength is a major component of player preparation, then further research in the area is required.

Acknowledgments

The author wishes to acknowledge the assistance of Dr. Darren Cole of the Christchurch College of Eduction, for his statistical analysis advice.

REFERENCES

Bartlett, R. M., 1999, *Introduction to Sports Biomechanics*. (London: E. & F. N. Spon).

Brzycki, M., 1986, Plyometrics is a giant step backwards. Athletic Journal, **66** (9), 22–23.

Horrigan, J. and Shaw, D., 1989, Plyometrics: think before you leap. Track and Field Quarterly Review, **89** (4), 41–43.

Logan, P., Fornasiero, D., Abernethy, P. and Lynch, K., 2000, Protocols for the assessment of isoinertial strength. In Physiological Tests for Elite Athletes, edited by Gore, C. J. (Champaign, Ill: Kinetic Books), pp. 213–214.

Schmidtbleicher, D., 1992, Training for power events. In Strength and Power in Sport, edited by Komi, P.V. (Oxford: Blackwell), pp. 381–395.

Verkhoshanski, V., 1966, Perspectives in the improvement of speed-strength preparation of jumpers. Review of Soviet Physical Education and Sports, **4** (2), 28–29.

Wiemann, K. and Tidow, G., 1995, Relative activity of hip and knee extensors in sprinting – implications for training. New Studies in Athletics, **10** (1), 29–49.

Wikgren, S., 1988, The plyometrics debate: safe and beneficial, or dangerous and unproven? Coaching Volleyball, **1** (5), 8–12.

Young, W., 1995, Laboratory strength assessment of athletes. New Studies in Athletics, **10** (1), 88–96.

Zanon, S., 1989, Plyometrics: past and present. New Studies in Athletics, **4**, 7–17.

Zatsiorsky, V. M., 1995, *Science and Practice of Strength Training*. (Champaign, IL: Human Kinetics Books).

Part VII
Paediatric Exercise Science

64   Youth Football Players: Number of Participants, Growth and Maturity Status

Robert M. Malina,
Tarleton State University, Stephenville, TX, USA

1. INTRODUCTION

The scope of Science and Football includes all football codes - soccer (association football), American football (tackle, touch, flag, Canadian), rugby (Union, League), and Australian Rules and Gaelic football. Soccer is generally conceded as the most popular sport in the world, and this is reflected in the research on football in general and in research on youth participants. This review provides an overview of the extent of youth participation in the different football codes, and then focuses on the growth and maturity status of youth participants primarily in soccer and to a lesser extent in American football.

2. ESTIMATED NUMBERS OF PARTICIPANTS

Participation statistics are at best estimates. Participation rates in youth sports increase with age during childhood, but subsequently decline during the transition into adolescence, i.e., after about 12–13 years of age, and through adolescence. The distribution of youth sports participants has the shape of a pyramid with a broad base. Numbers are largest during childhood – the broad base - but decline with increasing age through adolescence as sports become more demanding and specialized, and as interests of children and adolescents change. The structure of youth sport programmes varies among countries, which makes it difficult to compare participation rates. Nevertheless, it is reasonably well established that significant numbers of children and adolescents throughout the world are involved in organized sports, including the different football codes.

 England. England is generally accepted as the cradle of modern football. A national survey of participation trends of young people 6 to 16 years of age (curriculum years 2 to 11) in England in 2002 estimated that 57% of boys and 18% of girls participated in soccer (including 5-a-side) frequently (at least 10 times) outside of school time (Sport England, 2003). Using school attendance statistics for 2001 (Statistics of Education, 2001), these percentages translate to about 1.75 million boys and 536,000 girls who participated frequently in soccer. Corresponding estimates of participation for Rugby Union, Rugby League and "rugby" (includes touch rugby and new image rugby) were 9%, 6% and 10%, respectively, among boys, and one percent in each code among girls, which translates to about 770,000 boys and 89,000 girls who participated frequently in some form of rugby. Estimated participation rates in soccer declined from 41% in curriculum years 2–6 to 32% in curriculum years 7–11, whereas the opposite was true for the different rugby codes, 4% to 6% in Rugby Union and 4% to 7% in "rugby" (Sport England, 2003).

Such estimates provide a glimpse of the relative popularity of soccer and rugby among English youth. However, potentially talented youth players, the elite, are often the focus of attention in research on football. In this case, the pool of athletes is considerably smaller. Registration statistics for professional club academies and centres of excellence development programmes in England suggest a pool of about 10,000 boys between 9 and 16 years of age (Simmons, 2001). This figure represents 0.46% of boys 9–16 years of age enrolled in maintained primary and secondary schools in England in January 2001 (Statistics of Education, 2001). The probability of moving from the academies and centres of excellence to the Premier League needs to be established.

United States. Among United States youth 6–17 years of age, it was estimated that about 9.6 million participated in organized soccer programmes, 5.4 million boys and 4.2 million girls, and 4.3 million participated in American football in 2000 (Sporting Goods Manufacturers Association, 2001). American football includes tackle, touch and flag rules, and 95% of participants are boys. Comparison of these estimates with those for American youth 6–16 years in 1977 (Martens, 1978), 1.24 million participants in soccer (0.72 million boys, 0.52 million girls) and 3.32 million participants in tackle and flag football (2.67 million boys, 0.65 million girls), highlights the incredible growth in the popularity of organized soccer programmes for youth.

The United States also has highly organized interscholastic sport programmes at the high (secondary) school level, in contrast to most countries in the world. Estimates from the 2002 High School Participation Survey indicated that 339,101 boys and 295,265 girls participated in soccer, and 1.02 million boys participated in 11-player American football. An additional 25,766 boys participated in modified American football - 6-, 8- and 9-player football (National Federation of State High School Associations, 2003). Participants in American football represent about 14% of the male school population in grades 9–12, while participants in soccer represent about 4.6% and 4.0% of the male and female school population.

Soccer was not an inter-scholastic sport for girls in the mid-1970s, but rapidly expanded in the late 1970s and 1980s when the regulations implementing Title IX of the Education Amendments Act of 1972 were put into effect in 1975. The relevant section of the act stated as follows: "No person in the United States shall, on the basis of sex, be excluded from participation in, be denied the benefits of, or be subjected to discrimination under any education program or activity receiving Federal financial assistance..." (as quoted by Pieronek, 1994, p. 353). The regulations included inter-scholastic and inter-collegiate sport programmes, among others, and contributed to the expansion of sports available for girls and women. This is reflected in the dramatic increase in the number of high school female soccer participants, 247% since the 1985–1986 school year, compared to an increase of 73% in male high school soccer participants. In contrast, the number of American inter-scholastic football participants (all forms) has increased by about 10% over this interval. An additional factor in the rapid growth of soccer in the

United States is increased immigration, especially from Latin American countries, in the 1990s. The influx of immigrants and population mobility in some neighbourhoods has resulted in the elimination of American football in some schools (Peabody, 2003).

Although the numbers of participants in American football and soccer are large, relatively few make it to the inter-collegiate and professional levels. About 6% of high school seniors (grade 12) will play American football at the inter-collegiate level and only 0.09% will be drafted by a National Football League team. Corresponding estimates for men's soccer are quite similar, about 6% of high school seniors will play inter-collegiate soccer and only 0.08% will be drafted by a professional soccer club (National Collegiate Athletic Association, 2000).

Australia. Information about youth participation in Australian Rules and Gaelic football is limited. A national survey of activities of Australian youth 5–14 years of age over 12 months to April 2000 indicated that about 20% of boys (265,000) and 3% of girls (37,300) participated in outdoor soccer, 13% of boys (170,300) and 0.3% of girls (4,100) participated in Australian Rules football, and 7% of boys (92,500) and 0.2% of girls (2,500) participated in Rugby League (Australian Bureau of Statistics, 2003). Information about numbers of participants at more competitive levels is lacking.

3. GROWTH AND MATURITY STATUS OF YOUTH FOOTBALL PLAYERS

Data about the growth and maturity status of youth football players are available primarily for male participants in soccer, and are relatively limited for participants in American football and female participants in soccer. No corresponding data for youth participants in rugby and Australian Rules and Gaelic football are available.

Male Soccer Players. Mean heights and weights of youth soccer players 9 through 18 years of age were previously summarized (Malina, 2003). Mean heights and weights of an additional 20 samples of players reported in the abstracts of the World Congress on Science and Football (2003) were added to this compilation. The samples are primarily from Europe with several from Latin America. The majority of mean heights of young soccer players fall within the bounds of the 25th and 75th percentiles of United States reference data (Centers for Disease Control and Prevention, 2000). The resulting line of a fourth degree polynomial fit the reference medians quite closely throughout the age range. This contrasted with the line of the earlier fit in later adolescence (Malina, 2003), which was slightly below the reference medians at these ages.

Mean body weights for the expanded sample of soccer layers also fall within the bounds of the 25th and 75th percentiles of United States reference data. A fourth degree polynomial was fit to the data points. The resulting line of a fourth degree polynomial approximated the reference medians from about 9–14 years and then was above the reference medians through late adolescence. This trend is consistent with the earlier analysis (Malina, 2003).

Corresponding data for young soccer players from other areas of the world are apparently limited (Malina, 2003). There is a need for data from young soccer players in different areas of the world. Such data are probably available in the medical and training records of soccer clubs, but do not ordinarily make their way into the scientific literature.

The trend for the body size of young soccer players suggests, in general, appropriate weight-for-height during childhood and early adolescence, but more weight-for-height in later adolescence. Although the body mass index (BMI, wt/ht^2) is commonly used to describe weight-for-height relationships, it is of limited utility for adolescent males in general and athletes in particular given adolescent growth in fat-free mass and the generally larger fat-free mass of adolescent athletes. The BMI is more appropriately an index of heaviness (Malina et al., 2003a).

Weight-for-height relationships in adolescent soccer players are consistent with data for somatotype. Soccer players tend to be muscular or mesomorphic as assessed by the Heath-Carter somatotype protocol and this is already apparent in adolescent players (Table 1). Mean somatotypes of adolescent soccer players are generally similar to and fall within the ranges of somatotypes of national and international calibre players (Carter and Heath, 1990), although the latter are, on average, more mesomorphic and less endomorphic and ectomorphic (Table 1). This trend emphasizes the potentially important role for physique in the selection or exclusion process for soccer. Soccer players are also leaner than the general population, so that the proportionally high weight-for-height most likely reflects a greater amount of lean tissue, specifically muscle mass.

Available data dealing with the biological maturity status of youth soccer players are based on skeletal age and secondary sex characteristics, with limited data for the age at peak height velocity. Boys of all maturity levels are represented among soccer players 10–13 years of age, i.e., advanced (early), average ("on time") and delayed (late), and elite players tend to be somewhat more advanced in sexual and skeletal maturity status than non-elite players. With increasing age during adolescence and presumably more rigorous selection and training, boys advanced in skeletal and sexual maturity are more commonly included in samples of soccer players 14+ years of age (Malina, 2003). Some 15–16 year old players attain skeletal maturity at a younger chronological age than the reference samples, which has implications for the use of "bone age" to verify chronological ages in some international competitions.

Table 1. Mean Heath-Carter anthropometric somatotypes of several samples of adolescent male soccer players, with comparative values for professional players.

	Age, years	Endomorphy	Mesomorphy	Ectomorphy
Argentina (Barbieri	13+	2.4	4.4	3.5
and Rodriguez Papini, 1996)	14+	2.5	4.5	3.3
	15+	2.6	4.5	3.3
	16+	2.3	4.4	3.3
	17+	2.5	4.8	2.8
	18+	2.8	4.8	2.6
Copa America* (Carter et al., 1998)	25.8	2.0	5.3	2.2

*Except goalkeepers

Differences in body size associated with variation in biological maturity status in adolescent players have implications for performance. Within an age group of early adolescent boys (e.g., 11–13 years), players advanced in maturity status are taller and heavier and excel in power tasks; in contrast, players delayed in maturity status tend to perform better in aerobic tasks. As adolescence progresses (e.g., 14–15 years), size and power differences favouring boys advanced in maturity status persist, although they are reduced, whereas aerobic performance favours boys delayed in maturity status, though the number of late maturing players is small at these ages. Size and performance differences associated with variation in maturity status during early and mid-adolescence virtually disappear among soccer players as maturity is approached, e.g., 16–17 years of age (L. Horta and R.M. Malina, unpublished data). Maturity-associated variation in size and performance among soccer players is, thus, transient, but advantages associated with advanced maturity status may influence the selection process, especially in early adolescence.

Variation in position is also associated with maturity status in early- and mid-adolescent elite Portuguese soccer players (L. Horta and R.M. Malina, unpublished data). Forwards, central defenders and goalkeepers tend to be advanced in maturity status compared to midfielders and lateral defenders. There is an interesting change in the gradient of body size among positions as adolescence progresses. Among 11–13 year old players, the difference in height between forwards and defenders is small, and midfielders are shortest and lightest. This reflects the maturity differences among players by position. Among players 14–15 years, forwards are, on average, the shortest, followed in order by midfielders and lateral defenders, central defenders and goalkeepers. The weight of forwards is, on average, midway between weights of midfielders and lateral defenders on one hand, and central defenders and goalkeepers, on the other. This trend in height is also evident among players 16–17 years, although body weights are reasonably similar among forwards, midfielders and lateral defenders. Central defenders and goalkeepers are, on average, the heaviest players in this age group.

A question of interest relates to the contribution of variation in body size and maturity status to performance on functional and soccer-specific skills tests. This question was addressed in a sample of Portuguese players 13–15 years of age (Malina et al., no date a,b). Multiple linear regression was used to estimate the relative contribution of chronological age, stage of sexual maturity (pubic hair), height, weight, the height X weight interaction, and years of formal training in soccer to three functional variables (aerobic resistance, power, speed) and six soccer skill tests. Body size, sexual maturity and years of training accounted for 18% to 49% of the variance in the three functional tasks. In contrast, age, size, maturity and experience accounted for relatively little of the variation in performances on soccer-specific skill tests, 10% to 19% in three tests (ball control with head and body, dribbling speed with a pass), and no significant contributions to three other tests (passing and shooting accuracy, dribbling speed). Though only suggestive, the results highlight the potential interactions among age, body size, maturity status and experience in the physical fitness and sport-specific skills in a sample of elite adolescent soccer players.

Female Soccer Players. Given the relatively recent prominence of soccer among girls, information on the growth and maturity characteristics is limited. Trends based on 100 elite players from central Texas, including a youth club, Olympic development programme teams, and a university team, indicate mean heights and weights that approximate United States reference medians, but mean weights that are slightly above the reference medians between 10 and 16 years and clearly above the medians in late adolescence and young adulthood (Siegel, 1995). Mean somatotypes of this sample of soccer players and three comparative samples of adult players are summarized in Table 2.   Endomorphy increases and ectomorphy decreases, on average, with age in the adolescent sample.   The two samples of more elite players from South Australia and Bulgaria are more mesomorphic than the sample from central Texas.

Data for maturity status are limited to the age at menarche. In the sample from Texas, all players 14 years and older were post-menarcheal. Status quo and retrospective estimates for the Texas sample were identical, 12.9 years (Siegel, 1995).   These estimates are slightly later than the current estimate for the United States population, but generally similar to means based on retrospective data for two other samples of soccer players, 12.4 and 13.1 years (Malina et al., 2003b).

More information on the growth, physique and maturity status of elite soccer players will presumably become available as the popularity of the sport for girls increases throughout the world.   Comparisons of elite male and female youth players should provide potentially important information for the talent detection and development processes.

Table 2. Mean Heath-Carter anthropometric somatotypes of several samples of female adolescent soccer players, with comparative values for adults.

	Age, years	Endomorphy	Mesomorphy	Ectomorphy
U.S.A. (Siegel et al., 1996)	10–13	3.6	3.4	3.1
	14–18	4.1	3.1	2.7
	19–24	4.7	3.6	1.8
S. Australia (Withers et al., 1987)	22.1	4.2	4.6	2.2
Bulgaria (Toteva, 1992)	-	4.0	4.2	2.6

American Football Players.   Although American football is a popular sport among American boys, information on the growth, maturity and physique of young participants is relatively sparse.   Youth football leagues ordinarily have weight ranges for overlapping age categories.   Pop Warner Football, which had 240,000 participants in 2001, has 7 divisions ranging from 7–9 to 13–15 years. Each division has a certification weight range, e.g., 8–10 years, 55–95 lbs (24.9–43.1 kg) and 12–14 years, 115–160 lbs (52.2–72.6 kg), and provision is made in each division for "older but lighter" players.   Weight changes during the season are also monitored; a player may gain 1 pound (0.45 kg) per week after the second game up to a maximum of 9 pounds (4.1 kg) during the 7 to 9 game season (Pop Warner Football, 2003).   Other youth football programmes are organized by grade level in school, and the range of body size in such competitive units is considerable (Table 3).

Table 3. Ranges of age, body weight, height, and the body mass index in youth football players by grade in school, the competition unit.

Grade	n	Age, yrs	Weight, kg	Height,cm	BMI, kg/m^2
4th–5th	251	8.7 – 11.5	23.4 – 79.2	121.8 – 163.2	14.0 – 33.8
6th	174	10.1 – 12.9	31.0 – 93.6	131.2 – 172.2	15.6 – 40.1
7th	176	11.4 – 14.1	31.6 – 104.0	138.1 – 180.5	15.6 – 39.6
8th	73	12.7 – 14.6	38.6 – 105.0	148.7 – 181.7	16.9 – 36.1

R.M. Malina (unpublished data; see Malina et al., 2003b).

Mean heights of the sample of youth football players described in Table 3 moved from the reference median for the United States at 9 years of age towards the 75th percentile at 14 years. Mean body mass, on the other hand, moved from the 75th percentile of the reference at 9 years and was just below the 90th percentile at 14 years. As a result, the BMI, on average, was slightly below the 85th percentile of the reference (the cut-off for classification of overweight) from 10 to 14 years of age (Malina et al., 2003b). Clearly, a good number of the youth players would be classified as overweight and obese!

Data for biological maturity status are rather limited. In an early study (Rochelle et al., 1961), proportionally fewer inter-scholastic players 13–16 years of age were classified as late or delayed (11, 18%) in skeletal age compared to those classified as average or "on time" (24, 39%) and early or advanced (27, 43%). Other data from the 1960s show advanced skeletal maturity at all ages between 10 and 15 years in inter-scholastic football players compared to non-participants, and greater advancement in maturity among outstanding players than other players (Clarke, 1971). Corresponding data for an index of sexual maturity among prospective football players 13–16 years of age show small differences between those who subsequently played for the school teams and those who did not play (Violette, 1976). At older chronological ages, skeletal age does not differ between football players and non-players, reflecting the catch-up of late maturing boys and attainment of skeletal maturity by many boys.

American football is, of course, a sport in which large body size is an advantage, and many boys are selected for a position by their body size. By the junior high school years (about 12–15 years), boys assigned to line positions (interior linemen and linebackers) are generally taller and especially heavier than boys who are receivers, running backs and quarterbacks, and it is not uncommon for position specialization to start at these ages. There is also more discussion of the size, specifically the massiveness, of elite lineman at the high school (and also inter-collegiate and professional) levels, especially in the sports media. Using reported heights and weights for high school linemen (Parade "All Americans"), the BMI has increased more or less linearly from the early 1970s, about 30 kg/m^2, through 1989, 32.0 kg/m^2 (Wang et al., 1993). For the most recent sample of 17 high school "All American" linemen for the 2002 season (Parade Magazine, 2003), the mean BMI was 33.4 kg/m^2 and five of the players had weights above 136 kg. Data from the media, of course, need to be interpreted with caution. Media guides often inflate the body sizes of athletes. Such inflation occurs in the general population for height, but the opposite occurs for body weight; individuals tend to overestimate height and underestimate weight.

4. IMPLICATIONS

The limitations of the presently available data need to be recognized. Soccer is the only football code that includes relatively large numbers of girls, and the data are quite limited on the growth, maturity and performance status of young soccer players. Corresponding data are reasonably extensive for male soccer players and less so for American football players. There is a need for data on female participants in soccer, and on male and female participants in the other football codes.

Implications of the presently available data have been discussed at length for young male soccer players (Malina, 2003a). Soccer appears to favour early maturing boys as adolescence progresses, and the same trend is suggested for American football. American football shows more variation in body size by position compared to soccer. Large size is an advantage and is often a selective factor in American football. Soccer, in contrast, shows less variation in size by position, and the smaller, skilled youngster often succeeds in soccer. A question that needs serious consideration by soccer trainers is the following. How can the small, late maturing boy who is skilled be nurtured and in some cases protected so that he will persist in the sport? On the other hand, youngsters who are large for age are often treated as being chronologically older. Thus, how can such a youngster be nurtured through a sport keeping in mind his needs as a child and without exploiting his size for immediate success?

Those who work with young players in the different football codes should be aware of individual differences in growth status and in the tempo and timing of the adolescent growth spurt and sexual maturation. Among boys, maturity-associated variation in size and performance is especially marked in early adolescence (under 14 years of age), is reduced with progress through adolescence, and is negligible as maturity is attained. Corresponding data for girls are consistent for size, but show less maturity-associated variation for performance (Malina et al., 2003b). However, data relating performance to the maturity status in young female athletes are not available.

Most of the presently available data for male soccer players are derived from Europe and the Americas. Ethnic variation in the growth and maturation has not received systematic consideration in the soccer community. This may have relevance to problems associated with documenting chronological age of participants in international competitions. Birth certificates are not readily available in many parts of the world. "Bone age" has been used in an attempt to verify ages in international competitions (Soccer News, 2001). Note, however, that some 15-year old elite youth soccer players are already skeletally mature and would be penalized by use of "bone age." Methods of assessing skeletal maturity are not identical and vary in sensitivity of assessments in late adolescence. Moreover, there is ethnic variation in skeletal maturation and use of reference values based on European and American (largely American White children) may not be appropriate for samples of Asian and African ancestry (Malina et al., 2003a).

Many factors are involved in successful athletic performance during childhood and adolescence. Physical characteristics as reflected in growth and maturity status are important, but they are not the only determinants of successful performance. Rather, they are part of a complex matrix of biocultural characteristics related to the demands of a specific sport. Those who work with young athletes need to be patient; the youngsters are children and adolescence with the needs of children and adolescents.

REFERENCES

Australian Bureau of Statistics, 2003, Year Book Australia 2003: Culture and recreation, Children's participation in sports and leisure activities, www.abs.gov.au.

Barbieri, C. and Rodriguez Papini, H., 1996, Proyecto Antropometrico Torneos Juveniles Bonaerenses Final Provincial 1996: Informe Final. (La Plata, Argentina: Instituto Bonaerense del Deporte).

Carter, J.E.L. and Heath, B.H., 1990, Somatotyping - Development and Applications. (Cambridge: Cambridge University Press).

Carter, J.E.L., Rienzi, E.G., Gomes, P.S.C. and Martin, A.D., 1998, Somatotipo y tamano corporal. In Futbolista Sudamericano de Elite: Morfologia, Analisis del Juego y Performance, edited by Rienzi, E. and Mazza, J.C. (Rosario, Argentina: Biosystem Servicio Educativo), pp. 64–77.

Centers for Disease Control and Prevention, 2000, National Center for Health Statistics, CDC growth charts: United States, www.cdc.gov/growthcharts.

Malina, R.M., 2003, Growth and maturity status of young soccer (football) players. In Science and Soccer, 2nd edition, edited by Reilly, T. and Williams, A. M. (London: Routledge), pp. 287–306.

Malina, R.M., Barron, M., Morano, P., Miller, S.J., Cumming, S.P. and Kontos, A.P., 2003a, Incidence and Player Risk Factors for Injury in Youth Football. (Dallas, TX: National Athletic Trainers' Association Foundation).

Malina, R.M., Bouchard, C. and Bar-Or, O. 2003b, Growth, Maturation, and Physical Activity, 2nd edition. (Champaign, IL: Human Kinetics).

Malina, R.M., Cumming, S.P., Kontos, A.P., Eisenmann, J.C., Ribeiro, B. and Aroso, J., no date. Maturity-associated variation in sport-specific skills of youth football (soccer) players 13–15 years (submitted for publication).

Malina, R.M., Eisenmann, J.C., Cumming, S.P., Ribeiro, B. and Aroso, J., no date b. Maturity-associated variation in the growth and functional capacities of youth football (soccer) players 13–15 years (submitted for publication).

Martens, R., 1978, The emergence of children's sports. In Joy and Sadness in Children's Sports, edited by Martens, R. (Champaign, IL: Human Kinetics), pp. 6–11.

National Center for Education Statistics, 2001, Digest of education statistics, 2001, www.nces.ed.gov.

National Collegiate Athletic Association, 2000, Probability of competing in athletics beyond the high-school interscholastic level. The NCAA News Digest, 14 August, www.ncaa.org/news.

National Federation of State High School Associations, 2003, 2002 high school participation survey, www.nfhs.org.

Parade Magazine, 2003, Parade All-America football team, www.all-americans.parade.com.

Peabody, Z., 2003, No football, just futbol. Houston Chronicle, 5 May, pp. 1A, 8A, www.houstonchronicle.com.

Pieronek, C., 1994, A clash of titans: College football v. Title IX. Journal of College and University Law, **3**, 351–381.

Pop Warner Football, 2003, Pop Warner football structure, www.popwarner.com.

Rochelle, R.H., Kelliher, M.S. and Thornton, R., 1961, Relationship of maturation age to incidence of injury in tackle football. Research Quarterly, **32**, 78–82.

Siegel, S.R., 1995, Growth and maturity status of female soccer players from later childhood through early adulthood. Unpublished master's thesis, University of Texas at Austin.

Siegel, S.R., Katzmarzyk, P.T. and Malina, R.M., 1996, Somatotypes of female soccer players 10–24 years of age. In Studies in Human Biology, edited by Bodzsar, E., and Susanne, C. (Budapest: Eotvos Lorand University Press), pp 277–285.

Simmons, C., 2001, Football and age appropriate learning. Insight: The F.A.Coaches Association Journal, **4** (autumn), 58–60.

Soccer News, 2001, Cheating does not pay. Asia bans teams, players for over-age infractions. www.sportsillustrated.cnn.com/soccer/news/2001.

Sport England, 2003, Young people and sport in England: Trends in participation 1994–2002. (London: Sport England), www.sportengland.org.

Sporting Goods Manufacturers Association, 2001, US. Trends in Team Sports, 2001 edition. (North Palm Beach, FL: Sporting Goods Manufacturers Association).

Statistics of Education, 2001, Schools in England 2001, www.dfes.gov.uk.

Toteva, M., 1992, Somatotypology in Sports. (Sofia: National Sports Academy).

Violette, R.W., 1976, An epidemiologic investigation of junior high school football injury and its relationship to certain physical and maturational characteristics of the players. Doctoral dissertation, University of North Carolina, Chapel Hill.

Wang, M.Q., Downey, G.S., Perko, M.A. and Yesalis, C.E., 1993, Changes in body size of elite high school football players: 1963–1989. Perceptual and Motor Skills, **76**, 379–383.

Withers, R.T., Whittingham, N.O., Norton, K.I. and Dutton, M., 1987, Somatotypes of South Australian female games players. Human Biology, **59**, 575–584.

World Congress on Science and Football, 2003, Book of Abstracts. (Lisbon:Faculty of Human Kinetics, Technical University of Lisbon).

65   Physical Performance Tests in Young Soccer Players with Reference to Maturation

C. Capela, I. Fragoso, F. Vieira, P. Mil-Homens, J. Gomes Pereira,
C. Charrua, N. Lourenço and Z. Gonçalves
Faculty of Human Kinetics, Technical University of Lisbon, Portugal

1. INTRODUCTION

Soccer (more formally known as association football) is unarguably the world's most popular sport. The FIFA World Cup finals of 1998 attracted an estimated 40 thousand million television spectators (Hillis, 1998).

Management of the top teams is continually on the look out for emerging star players, either mature players on opposition teams, or those developing in under-age and youth ranks. The economic benefits of being able to recruit talented players and develop them to full potential are obvious. Recognition of financial gains associated with early development of footballing talent has led to the institution of "academies" as centres of excellence attached to the major professional soccer clubs worldwide (Reilly *et al.*, 2000).

To remain competitive, clubs now endeavour to invest significant amounts of money in attempting to identify and nurture potential elite players. Identifying potential at an early age ensures that players receive specialized coaching and training to accelerate their development process (Williams and Reilly, 2000). The reliable identification of future elite players permits clubs to focus their expenditures on developing a much smaller number of players, and a more effective management of their resources.

The identification and selection of young talented soccer players is not an easy operation. It is more complex in team games than in individual sports, where there are more objective ways to measure their performance.

In soccer, a large range of physical performance tests has been used as indicators of good preparation for demands of the game. Due to the predominance of the involvement of the lower extremities in soccer actions, different types of tests have been used to measure motor abilities, such as running speed and muscle strength.

The aim of this study was to measure muscle strength and speed, of young soccer players, with different tests in order to find the ones most influenced by biological age and morphological characteristics.

2. METHODS

This study assessed a total of 62 male soccer players aged between 13 and 16 years, who attended the Sporting Club of Portugal. Time spent in sport-specific training was on average 8 hours per week. Anthropometric measures were obtained according to Fragoso and Vieira (2000). Speed was measured with two tests: a 30-metre linear running test with light barriers (5-15-25-30 m) and with a T-type test with changes in directions (6×5=30 m). Muscle strength (maximal strength and the rate of force development) was evaluated based on an isometric force-time curve, produced in an instrumented leg press machine. Additionally, the long stretch-shortening cycle was evaluated with a squat jump (SJ) and a counter-movement (CMJ) jump on a contact mat. Skeletal maturity based on radiographs of the hand and wrist bones, was accessed according to Tanner-Whitehouse III Method (TW3). Descriptive statistics (mean and standard deviation) were used to characterize the variables. Correlation coefficients were calculated for all variables in the three age groups. ANOVA and Scheffé techniques were used to assess significant differences in anthropometric and maturational variables. The probabilities of F for entrance and removal of the variables were set at P <0.05 and 0.10 for all the variables.

3. RESULTS AND DISCUSSION

Table 1 summarizes the observed mean and standard deviation values of some anthropometric and motor variables and maturational indicators. In general, anthropometric measures, especially mid-thigh and calf girths, increased with age. The U-15 boys were 5.34 cm higher than U-14 boys but 6.82 cm shorter than U-16 years old boys. The velocity results showed a great variability especially linear speed at U-16 years. Physical test results were better when performed by the right side of the body.

Table 1. Means and standard deviations of anthropometric, motor variables and bone age results.

	Mean (17)	SD	Mean (21)	SD	Mean (27)	SD
Bone Age	13.2	1.56	14.7	1.4	16.1	1.0
Height (m)	1.610	0.08	1.664	0.102	1.732	0.064
Mass (kg)	51.5	8.9	57.7	10.4	64.4	5.2
Mid-thigh Girth	46.1	3.7	47.4	4.2	50.3	2.4
Calf Girth	33.4	3.1	35.4	2.5	36.5	1.5
Linear Speed	16.1	7.0	24.9	10.0	29.9	7.9
Linear Speed (R)	8.7	0.3	8.3	0.2	8.0	0.3
Linear Speed (L)	8.5	0.3	8.1	0.3	8.0	0.2
T Speed Test	15.0	7.2	12.5	7.0	12.0	10.8
Max. Strength (R)	1403	370.2	1675	347.7	1805	358.0
Max. Strength (L)	1342	369.9	1599	346.1	1780	409.5
Rate Force Dev. (R)	6168	1750	6827	1588	7513	1591
Rate Force Dev. (L)	5651	1009	6440	1643	7328	1692
Squat Jump (cm)	25.9	3.2	28.6	3.4	31.7	4.2
CMJ (cm)	30.5	3.5	32.8	3.9	36.3	4.6

As expected, for the U-14 ($R^2 = 0.23$) and U-15 ($R^2 = 0.36$) age groups, linear running speed showed a negative correlation with skeletal maturity ($P < 0.01$), which means that more mature boys are faster than less mature (Figure 1).

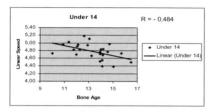
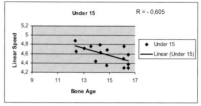

Figure 1. Graphs of correlations between linear speed and bone age for U-14 and U-15.

In line with previous results, isometric maximal strength ($P < 0.01$), also showed in the same groups a positive relationship with bone age. These results were significant for the right ($R^2 = 0.42$) and left leg ($R^2 = 0.45$) for U-14, and for right ($R^2 = 0.42$) and left leg ($R^2 = 0.33$) for U-15 as illustrated in Figure 2. Under 14 years, it can also be observed there was a positive and significant correlation between skeletal maturity and rate of force development ($P < 0.05$), for both the right ($R^2 = 0.29$) and the left ($R^2 = 0.23$) leg.

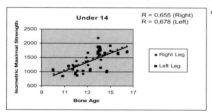
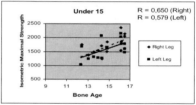

Figure 2. Graphs of correlations between isometric maximal strength and bone age for U-14 and U-15.

On the other hand, the U-14 and U-15 groups did not demonstrate any significant correlations between the speed test of the right side ($R^2 = 0.06$) and left side ($R^2 = 0.02$), the SJ ($R^2 = 0.04$), the CMJ ($R^2 = 0.01$), and skeletal maturity. In other words, there was not any relationship between bone age and other tests normally used to access the same or related motor qualities.

Instead of using bone age as a maturational indicator to explain performance, we used two anthropometric measures both of them very important to evaluate muscular development, respectively mid-thigh and calf girth. Table 2 summarises the results of Pearson Product Moment correlations. Mid-thigh and calf girths showed a significant relationship with linear running speed, isometric maximal strength and with the rate of force development in the U-14 and U-15 age groups.

Table 2. Pearson correlations results.

Motor variables	Girths	R^2 U-14	Sig.	R^2 U-15	Sig.
Linear Speed	Calf girth	0.39**	0.000	0.30*	0.010
	Thigh girth	0.26**	0.006	0.21*	0.033
Isometric MS right leg	Calf girth	0.59**	0.000	0.57**	0.000
	Thigh girth	0.44**	0.000	0.62**	0.000
Isometric MS left leg	Calf girth	0.72**	0.000	0.29*	0.011
	Thigh girth	0.41**	0.000	0.52**	0.000
Rate of force	Calf girth	0.42**	0.000	0.62**	0.000
development right leg	Thigh girth	0.25**	0.000	0.52**	0.000
Rate of force	Calf girth	0.36**	0.001	0.57**	0.000
development left leg	Thigh girth	0.17*	0.032	0.78**	0.000

** Correlation is significant at the 0.01 level (2-tailed)
* Correlation is significant at the 0.05 level (2-tailed)

The muscle volume of the mid-thigh and calf of U-14 and U-15 groups did not show any correlation between the T-speed test and the right side calf (R^2= 0.03), left side calf (R^2= 0.01), right side thigh (R^2= 0.01), left side thigh (R^2= 0.02), and between the squat jump and the calf girth (R^2= 0.01) the thigh girth (R^2= 0.01) and between the counter-movement jump and the calf girth (R^2= 0.00) and the thigh girth (R^2= 0.03). It is important to note that, for the U-16 age group almost all the subjects had already achieved the last degree of skeletal maturation and as a consequence, there were no correlations between bone age and the different tests evaluated in this study.

Physical exercise during growth depends on the morphological characteristics and growth stage of the body (Kemper et al., 1997). Motor skill levels and physical fitness tend to be optimized during adolescence, especially strength which depends on lean body mass (Carter, 1988; Malina and Bouchard, 1991; Vieira et al., 2003). The possible association between the anthropometric measures, bone age and strength performance was confirmed through the results described above. On the other hand, mid-thigh and calf girths showed the same relationship, with the selected motor performance tasks, as bone age. Muscular girth variability is related to hormonal variability and though skeletal and sexual maturation are not necessarily synchronous, it seems that maturation can also be expressed through muscular volume.

4. CONCLUSIONS

Maturity level of the subjects, as expected, influenced the performance on linear running speed, isometric maximal strength and the rate of force development. However, when considering more specific tests normally used to access the same or related motor qualities, like the T-speed test, the SJ and CMJ, maturation seemed to have a considerably lesser influence. In other words, the T-speed test together with the SJ and CMJ, are also probably influenced by other factors, like the intermuscular coordination level of the subject.

In line with the observations described above, muscle circumferences of the mid-thigh and calf showed correlations with linear running speed, isometric maximal strength and rate of force development, and did not show any association with SJ, CMJ, and speed with changes in direction. We suggest that linear running speed, isometric maximal strength and rate of force development are more influenced by muscular development. Maturation can be measured through several methods, and it may possibly be expressed through muscular volume variability.

REFERENCES

Carter, J.E.L., 1988, Somatotypes of children in sports, In *Young Athletes. Biological, Physiological and Educational Perspectives,* edited by Malina, R.M. (Champaign, IL: Human Kinetics), pp. 153–165.

Fragoso, I. and Vieira, F., 2000, *Morfologia e crescimento. Curso prático,* (Cruz Quebrada, Portugal: Faculdade de Motricidade Humana).

Hillis, S., 1998, Preparations for the World Cup. *British Journal of Sports Medicine,* **32**, 95.

Kemper, H.C., Post, G.B. and Twist, J.W., 1997, Rate of maturation during the teenage years: nutrient intake and physical activity between ages 12 and 22. *International Journal of Sports Nutrition,* **7**, 229–240.

Malina, R.M. and Bouchard, C., 1991, *Growth Maturation and Physical Activity.* (Champaign, IL: Human Kinetics).

Reilly, T., Bangsbo, J. and Franks, A., 2000, Anthropometric and physiological predispositions for elite soccer. *Journal of Sports Sciences,* **18**, 669–683.

Vieira, F., Fragoso, I., Silva, L. and Canto e Castro, L., 2003 in, Morphology and sports performance in children aged 10–13 years: Identification of different levels of motor skills. In *Kinanthropometry VIII,* edited by Reilly, T. and Marfell-Jones, M. (London: Taylor and Francis), pp. 93–103.

Williams, A. M. and Reilly, T., 2000, Talent identification and development in soccer. *Journal of Sports Sciences,* **18**, 657–667.

66   Anthropometric and Physiological Profile of Successful Young Soccer Players

S.M. Gil[2], J. Gil[1], A. Irazusta[2], F. Ruiz[1] and J. Irazusta[1]

[1]Instituto Médico Basurto, [2]School of Nurses and the Department of Physiology, School of Medicine and Dentistry, University of The Basque Country, Spain

1. INTRODUCTION

Identification of talented young soccer players is not easy. Besides, finding out which ones will perform at elite level is even more difficult. For sure, many physical and physiological factors are involved in this matter.

Franks *et al.* (2002) did not find any anthropometric or physiological differences between international players (aged 14–16 years) who became professionals and the players who did not. However, Reilly *et al.* (2000) using a multivariate analysis of anthropometric, physiological, psychological and soccer specific characteristics, observed that elite footballers (aged 16) compared to their non-elite (aged 15) counterparts, were leaner, faster, had more aerobic power and better tolerance to fatigue, and performed better on psychological and anticipation tests. The most discriminating measures were sprint time, ego orientation, anticipation skills and especially agility

Viviani *et al.* (1993) observed differences in height, weight, body fat and the endomorphy and ectomorphy of a group of "experienced" soccer players compared to "beginners" aged 12–13.

On the other hand, soccer players with more advanced skeletal age compared to their chronological age were described by Malina *et al.* (2000). They found that among Portuguese players aged 15–16, the percentage of early maturing was higher (65%) than for late maturing boys.

The objective of this study was to describe the anthropometric and physiological characteristics of young soccer players that are important in making them successful or not.

2. METHODS

2.1. Participants

Different measurements were taken on 49 young footballers (aged 14.04±0.28 years) who entered a football team. After a year playing in that level some players were selected to join the main team and some were rejected. The main team plays at the main provincial category level.

The technical staff made this selection based on the footballers' skills and performance during training and games. The technical staff was not aware of the results of our studies.

2.2. Measurements

2.2.1. Anthropometry

Each player was weighed (Añó Sayol, Barcelona), his stature determined (Añó Sayol, SL, Barcelona) and the Body Mass Index (BMI) calculated.

Skinfold measurements were taken at six sites:- triceps, subscapular, abdominal, suprailiac, thigh and lower leg, using a skinfold calliper (Harpenden, England). Each measurement was individually used for analysis and also the sum of the six measures was computed.

The circumferences in the upper arm, thigh and lower leg were taken, and also four diameters:- biepicondylar humerus (elbow), biestyloid at the wrist, biepycondilar femur (knee) and bimaleolar in the ankle. All these measurements were taken following the guidelines outlined by the ISAK (International Society for the Advancement of Kinanthropometry).

Afterwards body composition (fat, bone and muscle: weights and percentages) and the somatotype were calculated (Heath and Carter, 1967).

2.2.2. Aerobic capacity

2.2.2.1 Åstrand's test

All the players completed Åstrand's test (Åstrand and Rodahl, 1986) on a cycle ergometer for calculation of their maximal oxygen uptakes, absolute ($l \cdot min^{-1}$) and relative ($ml \cdot kg^{-1} \cdot min^{-1}$).

2.2.2.2. Endurance test

They also performed a rectangular progressive test on the athletics track. They ran 800 m at an increasing pace (6:30 min, 5:30 min, 5 min, 4:30 min, 4 min and 3:40 min), and recovered for 1 min between the runs. Heart rates were measured during the runs and resting times using a pulsemeter (Polar Electro OY, Finland).

2.2.3. Anaerobic capacity

2.2.3.1. Sprint time

They performed two tests:- 30-m flat sprint and 30-m sprint with 10 cones (turns). All sprint times were recorded using electronic timing lights (Seiko, Japan).

2.2.3.2. Jump tests

Participants also jumped twice in each of the three jumping modalities: squat jump, counter-movement jump and drop jump, the best jumps were selected. This test was measured using a jump mat (Bosco Systems, Italy).

2.2.4. Date of birth

We also looked at the footballers' date of birth (month), and the months of the year were divided in two semesters (January to June and July to December). Another variable was the age in months.

2.2.5. Statistical methods

The results of these tests were compared using students' t-tests between the two groups; when the variances were not equal a Mann-Whitney test was applied. For categorical variables (date of birth) a Chi^2 test was used. Logistic regression analysis was used to ascertain which variables discriminated best between the two groups. A statistical significance was set at a P<0.05.

3. RESULTS

Players (n=29) were selected and 20 were not. Table 1 shows that selected players were taller and they had larger elbow (6.70±0.47 cm *vs* 6.48±0.45 cm, P<0.05) and wrist (5.47±0.43 cm *vs* 5.26±0.40, P<0.05) diameters (Figure 1). They also had bigger bone weight (11.20±1.00 kg *vs* 10.27±1.4 kg, P=0.01).

Table 1. Anthropometric characteristics of young soccer players.

	Group	Mean	S. D.
Height (cm)	R	166.50*	8.80
	S	172.13	9.70
Mass (kg)	R	57.44	9.40
	S	60.62	10.60
Sum skinfolds (mm)	R	71.37*	29.9
	S	69.35	30.66

R= rejected, S= selected
*P<0.05

Selected footballers were leaner, their skinfolds at suprailiac, thigh and lower leg were lower together with the sum of the six skinfolds (Figure 1). Fat percentage was lower but this difference was not statistically significant (Figure 2). The endomorphy was also lower in the selected group: 2.25±0.71 *vs* 2.84 ±1.14, P<0.05.

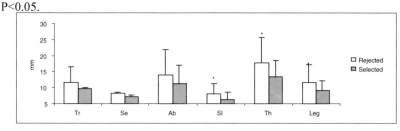

Figure 1. Skinfold measurements at six sites.

Tr= trizeps, Se= subscapular, Ab= abdominal, SI= suprailiac, Th= thigh *P<0.05

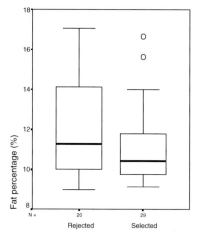

Figure 2. Whisker plot of the fat percentage in both groups of soccer players.

Besides, as shown in Figure 3 selected footballers were faster in the flat 30-m sprint (3.95±0.24 s *vs* 4.20±0.26 s, P<0.01), and in the cone dash (5.08±0.36 *vs* 5.25±0.28, P>0.05).

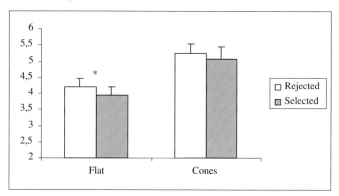

Figure 3. Sprint performance in the selected and non-selected players.

Åstrand's test also showed higher oxygen uptakes in the selected footballers: 3.36±0.57 *vs* 2.84±0.70 l·min^{-1}, P<0.05 and 55.73±7.86 *vs* 47.72±10.25 ml·kg·min^{-1}, P<0.05.

There were no statistically significant differences in the endurance test. However, as is shown in Figure 4, selected players had lower heart rates at the end of the runs and during the recovery periods.

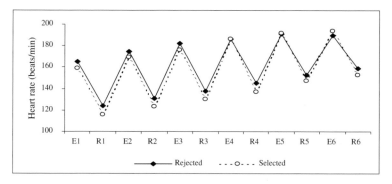

E= exercise, R= recovery time
Figure 4. Aerobic performance in the selected and rejected group.

There were no significant differences between the groups in any of the jump tests.

On the other hand, 35 (71.4%) subjects were born in the first semester of the year and 14 (30%) in the second. From those rejected, 12 (60%) were born in the first semester and (79.3%) were from the selected group.

In order to find if age alone or other factors related to age such as height and body mass were responsible for this selection, median values of height (170.45 cm), weight (59.05 kg) and muscle weight (27.21 kg) were calculated. Both groups were divided in the first and second semester and these in subgroups of low or high for each characteristic.

In the rejected group all players born in the second half were below the median height, and in the selected group 69.6% of those born in the first half were above the median height (P<0.05), see Table 2.

Table 2. Number of players and percentages (%) above or below the median height (170.45 cm), median mass (59.05 kg) and median muscle mass (27.21 kg). Within each group (rejected or selected) it is shown those born in the first or the second semester.

		Height		Mass		Muscle Weight	
	Semester	Low	High	Low	High	Low	High
Rejected	1	6(50%)*	6(50%)*	6(50%)	6(50%)	6(50%)	6(50%)
	2	8(100%)*	0(0%)*	7(87.5%)	1(12.5%)	6(75%)	2(25%)
Selected	1	7(30.4%)	16(69.6%)	7(30.4%)	16(69.6%)	9(39.1%)	14(60.9%)
	2	3(50%)	3(50%)	4(66.7%)	2(33.3%)	4(66.7%)	2(33.3%)

Low= below the median, High= above the median.
*P<0.05

Regression modelling indicated that three variables successfully discriminated between the two groups:- height, sprint time and $\dot{V}O_{2\ max}$. The model explained 85.7% of the criterion variance, with the $\dot{V}O_2$ being the largest contributor (P<0.05).

4. CONCLUSIONS

This research showed there were relevant differences between the selected and rejected soccer players. All players followed the same training programme; thus differences were unlikely to come from differences in training which may have happened in other studies where different teams with different training sessions were compared.

Selected players were taller, bigger and had larger bone weight. Height especially appears as a very distinctive parameter. It is also emphasised in the model created by logistic regression. When controlling for the effect of having been born in the first or second half of the year, it was found that none of the rejected players born in the second semester was higher than the median.

It is relevant that in the present study height and weight were positively correlated to sprint time ($r = -0.525$, P<0.05 and $r = -0.462$, P=0.002, respectively) even when controlling for age.

The soccer players who were selected were also leaner than the other. This has been seen earlier by Viviani *et al.* (1993) and Reilly *et al.* (2000). It is also relevant that as it is shown in Figure 1 most players had fat percentages between 10–12%, which is considered appropriate for this level of soccer, whereas in the rejected group many were well above 12% fat percentage. Having a higher than adequate fat mass is correlated with a poor performance. Carrying an excess of weight makes running, sprinting, dribbling more difficult. Moreover, the cause of this overweight should be taken into account, because it could be due to poor training or an inadequate diet.

Selected individuals were also faster than those rejected. Although a soccer player is sprinting only 8–13% of whole football match (Tumilty, 1993), these high intensity runs are of most importance for deciding many balls.

Selected players had better endurance, which cannot be explained by different training regimens. Current figures for elite adult players, except the goalkeeper, are in the range of 60–70 ml·kg^{-1}·min^{-1}, with a minimum of 65 ml·kg^{-1}·min^{-1} (Shephard, 1999). In the present work players were young non-elite, and goalkeepers were also included.

Moreover in the regression analysis $\dot{V}O_{2\ max}$ was the most important characteristic of the model to differentiate both groups. Oxygen consumption together with height and velocity were the more relevant parameters.

On the other hand, it is noticeable that from the whole group of players, most of them were born in the first part of the year (71.6%). Within the selected group there was more that had been born earlier in the year than in the non-selected group. This phenomenon was observed before by Simmons and Paull (2001) and in a study of a group of 247 footballers of different levels where 67.4% players were born in the first semester of the year. Players (aged 14) born in the first half of the year were taller, heavier, and had bigger diameters and muscle weight (Gil *et al.,* 2002).

The selection process should be taken very carefully: the selection may be limited mainly to older and early maturing individuals, whereas talented players with late maturity or younger may be discarded. On the other hand, early maturing players may be close to their best physical and physiological status, and smaller players may reach better performances at the end of their growth. Malina *et al.* (2000) found that 15–16 year-old soccer players had older skeletal maturation compared to their chronological age. Thus, much of what coaches see as early talent may be explained by physical precocity associated with a relative age advantage (Helsen *et al.,* 2000).

Technical staff made the selection based on the players' technical skills and their performance during the games and training sessions. Although they were unaware of the results of these tests, they recognised the footballers with the best anthropometric and physiological profiles.

In summary, selected players were taller, leaner, faster and had better endurance compared to the rejected footballers.

This project was made by an agreement between the Arenas Club de Getxo and the University of the Basque Country, and supported by the Bizkaia-Bizkaialde Foundation.

REFERENCES

Åstrand, P.O. and Rodahl, K., 1986, In *Fisiología Del Trabajo Físico.* 2nd ed., edited by Editorial Médica Panamericana, Buenos Aires.

Franks, A.M., Williams, A.M., Reilly, T. and Nevill, A.M., 2002, Talent identification in elite youth soccer players: physical and physiological characteristics. In *Science and Football IV*, edited by Spinks, W., Reilly, T. and Murphy, A. (London: Routledge), pp.165–270.

Gil, S.M., Irazusta, A., Ruiz F., Gil, J. and Irazusta, J., 2002, Oral comunication In the 3rd *International Congress on Soccer and Sports Sciences*, Madrid 12–14 September.

Heath, B.H. and Carter, J.E.L., 1967, A modified somatotype method. *American Journal of Physical Anthropology* 27, 57–74.

Helsen, W.F., Hodges, N.J., Van-Micnkel, J. and Starkes, J.L., 2000, The roles of talent, physical precocity amd practice in the development of soccer expertise. *Journal of Sports Sciences,* **18**, 727–736.

Malina, R.M., Peña Reyes, M.E., Eisenmann, J.C., Horta, L., Rodrigues, J. and Miller, R., 2000, Height, mass and skeletal maturity of elite Portuguese soccer players aged 11–16 years. *Journal of Sports Sciences*, **18**, 685–693.

Reilly, T., Williams, A.M., Nevill, A.M. and Franks, A.M., 2000, A multidisciplinary approach to talent identification in soccer. *Journal of Sports Sciences*, **18**, 695–702.

Shephard, R.J., 1999, Biology and medicine of soccer: an update. Journal of Sports Sciences, **17**, 757–786.

Simmons, C. and Paull, G.C., 2001, Season of birth bias in association football. *Journal of Sports Sciences,* **19**, 677–86.

Tumilty, D., 1993, Physiological characteristics of elite soccer players. *Sports Medicine,* **16**, 80–96.

Viviani, F., Casagrande, G. and Toniutto, F., 1993, The morphotype in a group of peripubertal soccer players. *Journal of Sports Medicine and Physical Fitness.* 33, 178–183.

67   Bilateral Isokinetic Knee Strength Profiles in Trained Junior Soccer Players and Untrained Individuals

John Iga, Thomas Reilly, Adrian Lees and Keith George
Research Institute for Sport and Exercise Sciences, Liverpool John Moores University, Liverpool, L3 2ET, UK

1. INTRODUCTION

Asymmetries in strength both between antagonistic muscle groups and bilateral limbs have been deemed predisposing factors towards injury in soccer players (Fowler and Reilly, 1993). Isokinetic dynamometers provide a relatively easy means of assessing these relationships. Although the ratio of peak eccentric hamstrings torque to peak concentric quadriceps torque (H_{ECC}:Q_{CON} ratio) may be the most accurate means of describing the strength properties about the knee (Aagaard et al., 1998), combining such data with conventional hamstrings to quadriceps ratios (H:Q ratio) and absolute values of isokinetic strength provides a more detailed description. While these variables have been studied in the dominant and non-dominant legs of young soccer players (Kellis et al., 2001), no direct comparisons have been made between trained and untrained individuals in order to elucidate the effects of soccer involvement on the bilateral strength profiles of the knee musculature. The aim of this investigation was therefore to compare the bilateral isokinetic strength characteristics of the knees flexor and extensor muscles in trained junior soccer players to an untrained control group.

2. METHODS

Twenty-eight male children matched for chronological age, height and body mass participated in the present study (chronological age 15.5 ± 0.6 years; height 1.74 ± 0.05 m; body mass 65.3 ± 6.9 kg). Fifteen of the subjects trained under the talent development programme of a club in the English professional soccer leagues and had been involved in accelerated training programmes for 4.7 ± 0.6 years prior to testing. They trained three times a week for two hours and played competitive matches once a week. Thirteen boys made up the untrained group. These individuals were not participating in any organized training or sport at the time of testing.

A Lido-Active isokinetic dynamometer (Loredan Biomedical Inc., Davis, Ca) was used to measure the strength of the knee flexor and extensor muscles in both the dominant and non-dominant limbs. Limb dominance was determined through interview and was defined as the preferred leg when kicking a ball. All measurements were performed from a seated position (hip flexion angle approximately 90°). Stabilization straps were applied across the trunk, waist and distal femur of the leg being tested to eliminate additional movements and to provide constant conditions for all subjects. The axis of the dynamometer was visually aligned with the approximate axis of knee rotation and the resistance pad placed proximal to the medial malleolus. Range of motion was 90° flexion to 0° extension. Fifteen minutes of cycling and stretching exercises preceded measurement. Measurements were made during concentric and eccentric muscle actions at slow (1.08 rad s^{-1}) and fast (4.32 rad s^{-1}) angular velocities. At each test condition four warm-up trials were followed by three maximal efforts. Subjects were instructed to grip the side of the seat and to keep the non-involved leg still during testing. Standardised verbal encouragement was given before each maximal effort and visual feedback of the recorded torque was provided. A rest of 30 s was allowed between consecutive efforts and 3 min between angular velocities. Gravity corrected peak torque values were collected and H:Q ratio and $H_{ECC}:Q_{CON}$ ratios later calculated.

Factorial analysis of variance (ANOVA) designs were applied to examine the effects of training status, angular velocity and muscle action on the peak torque of the hamstrings and quadriceps, H:Q ratios and $H_{ECC}:Q_{CON}$ ratios in both the dominant and non-dominant leg. Further factorial ANOVA designs were used to assesses the effects of training status, angular velocity and limb dominance on absolute isokinetic strength, H:Q ratios and $H_{ECC}:Q_{CON}$ ratios. Statistical analysis was performed in SPSS for windows software package (Chicago, Ill) and the level of significance was set at $P < 0.05$.

3. RESULTS

Table 1 illustrates that trained soccer players were stronger than their untrained counterparts in both limbs ($P < 0.05$). Differences were higher in the knee extensors (25–37%) than the flexors (9–21%) during both concentric and eccentric actions and were generally greater at faster (33–37%) than slow speeds (25–29%). No significant bilateral dominance was observed in isokinetic leg strength in either the trained (2–13%) or untrained (1–9%) individuals. Conversely H:Q ratios were significantly higher in the dominant and non-dominant legs of the untrained individuals (Table 2). Differences ranged between 15–28% for the concentric ratios and 13–18% for the eccentric ratios. No significant bilateral differences were observed in H:Q ratios of the trained individuals in all test conditions (4–7%); however, significant differences were present in the eccentric H:Q ratio of the untrained subjects (2–10%). The $H_{ECC}:Q_{CON}$ ratios were also greater in the untrained subjects than the trained ($P < 0.05$). In the untrained group $H_{ECC}:Q_{CON}$ ratios of about 1.00 were observed at fast angular velocities in both limbs. In the trained players ratios of 0.83 and 0.78 were found in the dominant and non-dominant legs at fast extension velocities. No significant bilateral differences were observed in the $H_{ECC}:Q_{CON}$ ratios of both the trained and the untrained individuals across the testing conditions.

Table 1. Mean (±SD) concentric (CON) and eccentric (ECC) peak torque (Nm) in dominant and non-dominant legs of trained and untrained soccer players.

Angular velocity (rad s^{-1})	Dominant		Non-dominant	
	Trained	Untrained	Trained	Untrained
Quadriceps CON				
1.08	222 ± 30	$141 \pm 58^\dagger$	205 ± 23	$144 \pm 54^\dagger$
4.32	169 ± 38	$107 \pm 30^\dagger$	159 ± 41	$105 \pm 38^\dagger$
Quadriceps ECC				
1.08	290 ± 48	$207 \pm 55^\dagger$	279 ± 39	$209 \pm 50^\dagger$
4.32	237 ± 28	$152 \pm 39^\dagger$	232 ± 28	$155 \pm 55^\dagger$
Hamstrings CON				
1.08	112 ± 20	$91 \pm 25^\dagger$	108 ± 27	$89 \pm 28^\dagger$
4.32	94 ± 15	$82 \pm 17^\dagger$	82 ± 15	$75 \pm 21^\dagger$
Hamstrings ECC				
1.08	139 ± 32	$114 \pm 25^\dagger$	127 ± 26	$110 \pm 31^\dagger$
4.32	140 ± 26	$111 \pm 29^\dagger$	124 ± 27	$102 \pm 23^\dagger$

† indicates difference ($P<0.05$) between trained and untrained players

Table 2. Mean (±SD) H:Q ratios and $H_{ECC}:Q_{CON}$ ratios in dominant and non-dominant legs of trained and untrained soccer players.

Angular velocity (rad s^{-1})	Dominant		Non-dominant	
	Trained	Untrained	Trained	Untrained
CON H:Q ratio				
1.08	0.51 ± 0.08	$0.64 \pm 0.45^\dagger$	0.53 ± 0.16	$0.62 \pm 0.29^\dagger$
4.32	0.56 ± 0.15	$0.77 \pm 0.19^\dagger$	0.52 ± 0.16	$0.72 \pm 0.23^\dagger$
ECC H:Q ratio				
1.08	0.48 ± 0.11	$0.55 \pm 0.15^\dagger$	0.45 ± 0.09	$0.54 \pm 0.13^\dagger$
4.32	0.60 ± 0.12	$0.73 \pm 0.31^\dagger$	0.54 ± 0.11	$0.66 \pm 0.16^{\dagger\ddagger}$
$H_{ECC}:Q_{CON}$ ratio				
1.08	0.62 ± 0.12	$0.81 \pm 0.45^\dagger$	0.62 ± 0.12	$0.77 \pm 0.21^\dagger$
4.32	0.83 ± 0.20	$1.04 \pm 0.27^\dagger$	0.78 ± 0.27	$0.97 \pm 0.19^\dagger$

† indicates difference ($P<0.05$) between trained and untrained players; ‡ indicates differences ($P<0.05$) between dominant and non-dominant limbs.

4. DISCUSSION

During many activities in soccer the knee joint flexes and extends actively with both the hamstrings and quadriceps muscles engaged. Much attention has focused on the role of the knee flexors during knee extension movements (i.e., Baratta *et al.*, 1988). During these actions the hamstrings are activated eccentrically exerting an opposing force to the anterior drive of the quadriceps, thereby assisting the anterior cruciate ligament in maintaining knee joint stability. Excessive quadriceps strength may create unwanted stress to the internal structures of the knee, resulting in episodes of joint instability and forced stretching of the hamstrings causing muscle damage.

Present results demonstrate soccer involvement induces significant developments in the isokinetic strength of the knee musculature. The gains in strength were more pronounced in the knee extensors than the flexors and generally more marked at faster angular velocities. These observations may be attributed to the specific muscle loading patterns experienced during soccer related activities. For example, during kicking actions the quadriceps extend the knee rapidly and speeds may approximate 24.4 rad s^{-1} (Orchard *et al.*, 2002). At ball contact, momentum is transferred from the kicking foot/ankle complex to the ball. In return the ball transmits an opposing torque, loading the quadriceps. Over time this loading process would result in the strengthening of the extensors particularly at the faster velocities but also influences muscle strength at lower velocities.

The unbalanced development of knee muscle strength in the soccer players was further reflected in both the H:Q ratio and H_{ECC}:Q_{CON} ratio. The H:Q ratios have typically been used to describe the strength relationships between the knee flexor and extensor muscles in soccer players (e.g., Kellis *et al.*, 2001). Although a range of values has been reported, it is generally believed at slower speeds H:Q ratios lower than 0.60 may indicate an increased risk to muscle strain injury (Renström, 1998). Lower conventional H:Q ratios were observed in the trained than the untrained individuals in all test conditions. At slow speeds, sub-optimal H:Q ratio were observed in the soccer players in both concentric and eccentric muscle actions. The higher H:Q ratios found in the untrained group further suggest soccer training enhances the strength of the knee extensor far more than the flexors.

While H:Q ratios have, by convention, been used to describe the muscle strength properties of the knee, H_{ECC}:Q_{CON} ratios may better reflect the potential of the knee flexors to provide muscular stabilization (Aagaard *et al.*, 1998). In the untrained subjects at fast speeds, a H_{ECC}:Q_{CON} ratio of about 1.00 was observed suggesting the 'braking force' of the hamstrings was equal in magnitude to the maximal contractions of the quadriceps during knee extension. In the trained group significantly lower H_{ECC}:Q_{CON} ratios were found at slow and fast angular velocities and point towards a reduced capacity for the knee flexor to provide knee joint stabilization during knee extension movements.

Collectively these findings suggest impaired knee function and stability with soccer involvement. Nonetheless suitable strength training can improve the joint stabilization capacity of the knee flexors. Aagaard *et al.* (1996) demonstrated in adult soccer players that heavy resistance training (4 sets of 8 reps at 8 RM) improved the potential for muscular joint stabilization. However, such training programmes should not be used directly by adolescents. Further study is needed to establish appropriate training loads in youth soccer players that augment the joint stabilizing capabilities of the hamstrings. In addition to reducing the risk of ligamentous and muscle strain injury, eccentric hamstrings training may also improve kicking performance in adolescents. De Proft *et al.* (1988) noted improved kicking performance with eccentric hamstring strengthening in adolescent soccer players and Cabri *et al.* (1988) reported kicking performance to be positively associated with eccentric hamstring strength.

Since the game of soccer involves many one-sided activities it may be possible to develop asymmetries in muscle strength between the dominant and non-dominant limbs. Athletes with bilateral differences greater than 15% are believed to be at greater risk of musculotendonous injury (Knapik *et al.*, 1991). Non-significant bilateral differences were observed in isokinetic leg strength in both groups (range 4–13%). These findings are comparable with those of Capranica *et al.* (1992) who found non-significant differences in isokinetic strength between the preferred and non-preferred leg of young soccer players. It would therefore appear that the performance of repetitive techniques in soccer does not result in the unbalanced stressing of the lower limbs.

No previous study has reported on the bilateral H:Q ratio of junior soccer players. Non-significant bilateral differences were observed in the H:Q ratios in the trained soccer players; however, significant bilateral differences were found in the fast eccentric H:Q ratio of the untrained groups. The latter finding is unexpected and difficult to explain. Non-significant differences in bilateral $H_{ECC}{:}Q_{CON}$ ratio were also found in both groups. Similar results have been reported by Kellis *et al.* (2001) and indicate soccer involvement does not affect the bilateral balance of strength between the knee flexor and extensor muscles.

5. CONCLUSION

Involvement in soccer by junior players does not result in the significant asymmetrical strengthening of the lower limbs. Gains are induced in the isokinetic strength of the knee muscles in both legs. These gains are more pronounced in the knee extensors than the flexors and thereby reduce the capacity of the hamstrings to provide joint stability during knee extension movements. These findings therefore support a recommendation for eccentric strength training of the hamstrings together with the periodic screening of muscle strength balance in junior soccer players.

REFERENCES

Aagaard, P., Simonsen, E.B., Trolle, M., Bangsbo, J. and Klausen, K., 1996, Specificity of training velocity and training load on gains in isokinetic knee joint strength. *Acta Physiologica Scandinavica*, **156**, 123–129.

Aagaard, P., Simonsen, E.B., Magnusson, P., Larsson, B. and Dyhre-Poulsen, P., 1998, A new concept for isokinetic hamstring: quadriceps muscle strength ratio. *American Journal of Sports Medicine*, **26**, 231–237.

Baratta, R., Solomonow, M., Zhou, B.H., Letson, D., Chuinard, R. and D'Ambrosia, R., 1988, Muscle coactivation: The role of the antagonist musculature in maintaining knee stability. *American Journal of Sports Medicine*, **16**, 113–123.

Cabri, J., De Proft, E., Dufour, W. and Clarys, J.P., 1988, The relation between muscular strength and kicking performance in soccer players. In *Science and*

Football I, edited by Reilly, T., Lees, A., Davids, K. and Murphy, W.J. (London: E&FN Spon), pp. 185–193.

Capranica, L., Cama, G., Fanton, F., Tessitore, A. and Figura, F., 1992, Force and power of preferred and non-preferred leg in young soccer players. *Journal of Sports Medicine and Physical Fitness*, **31**, 358–363.

De Proft, E., Cabri, J., Dufour, W. and Clarys, J.P., 1988, Strength training and kicking performance in soccer players. In *Science and Football I*, edited by Reilly, T., Lees, A., Davids, K. and Murphy, W.J. (London: E&FN Spon), pp. 108–113.

Fowler, N.E. and Reilly, T., 1993, Assessment of muscle strength asymmetry in soccer players. In: *Contemporary Ergonomics*, edited by Lovesey, E.J. (London: Taylor and Francis), pp. 327–332.

Kellis, S., Gerodimos, V., Kellis, E. and Manou, M., 2001, Bilateral isokinetic concentric and eccentric strength profiles of the knee extensors and flexors in young soccer players. *Isokinetics and Exercise Science*, **9**, 31–39.

Knapik, J.J., Baumann, C.L., Jones, B.H., Harris, J.M. and Vaughan, L., 1991, Preseason strength and flexibility imbalances associated with athletic injuries in female collegiate athletes. *American Journal of Sports Medicine*, **19**, 178–182.

Orchard, J., Walt, S., McIntosh, A. and Garlick, D., 2001, Muscle activity during the drop kick. In *Science and Football IV*, edited by Spinks, W., Reilly, T. and Murphy, A. (London: Routledge), pp. 32–43.

Renström, P.A.F.H., 1998, An interaction of chronic overuse injuries. In: *Oxford Textbook of Sports Medicine*, 2nd ed, edited by Harries, M., Williams, C., Stanish, W.D. and Micheli, L.J. (Oxford: Oxford Medical Press), pp. 633–648.

68   Age and Maturity-Related Variability in Body Size and Physique among Youth Male Portuguese Soccer Players

António Figueiredo[1], Manuel Coelho e Silva[1], João Dias and Robert M. Malina[2]

[1]Youth Sports Institute. Faculty of Sport Science and Physical Education – University of Coimbra, Portugal
[2]Research Professor, Department of Health and Physical Education, Tarleton State University, Stephenville, TX, USA

1. INTRODUCTION

Variation in size, physique and maturity characteristics of young athletes in a variety of sports is reasonably well documented (Malina, 1994, 1998). Further, young athletes often have somatotypes that are generally similar, though not identical, to adult athletes within the same sport or event within a sport (Carter and Heath, 1990). On the other hand, maturity-associated variation in size and physique within specific age groups of young athletes in a sport is less well documented. Boys advanced in biological maturity are, on average, taller and heavier, and perform better in strength, speed and power tasks compared to average ("on time") and later maturing chronological age peers (Malina et al., 2003).

Boys advanced in maturity status tend to predominate among youth soccer players as adolescence advances so that late maturing boys are relatively under-represented among elite soccer players 13–16 years of age (Peña Reyes et al., 1994; Malina et al., 2000). These studies are based on two-year age groups so that maturity-associated variation among players is masked in part by chronological age. This study considers the size and maturity characteristics of male Portuguese soccer players 10.9–16.6 years of age, and focuses on maturity-associated variation in single year chronological age groups.

2. MATERIAL AND METHODS

Ninety five players from a single club in the midlands of Portugal were grouped into three age/playing categories used in the country: CA1, infants, 11–12 (n=29); CA2, initiates, 13–14 (n=37); and CA3, juveniles, 15–16 (n=29) years. Somatic characteristics included the dimensions needed to estimate somatotype (Carter and Heath, 1990) and the androgyny index ([3 X biacromial breadth] - bicristal breadth), an estimate of the degree of masculinity in physique (Tanner et al., 1951). Stage of pubic hair development was assessed at clinical examination using the criteria of Tanner (1962).

3. RESULTS

3.1. Comparisons between age/playing groups

Table 1. Descriptive statistics of anthropometric variables and comparisons between age groups.

Variable	CA1 11.0–12.9 (n=29)	CA2 13.0–14.9 (n=37)	CA3 15.0–16.9 (n=29)	$F_{(2,94)}$	p
Age (years)	12.0±0.5	13.9±0.6	16.1±0.5		
Stature (m)	1.456±0.053	1.640±0.093	1.725±0.051	110.09	**
Body Mass (kg)	37.8±4.8	52.5±8.3	63.8±5.8	111.40	**
Androgyny index	75.2±3.6	84.1±5.4	92.9±4.6	10.29	**
Endomorphy	2.2±1.3	2.8±1.0	2.8±0.7		
Mesomorhy	4.4±0.9	4.3±0.9	4.5±0.9		
Ectomorphy	3.3±0.9	3.6±1.0	3.1±0.7		

** ($P \leq 0.01$), * ($P \leq 0.05$), n.s. (non-significant)

Age, size and somatotype of athletes in the three age/playing groups are summarized in Table 1. As expected, the groups differ significantly in height, mass and the androgyny index, and mean values increase with age. Somatotypes of players in the three groups differ significantly (MANCOVA, F=4.098, P<0.001). Pairwise comparisons indicate that CA2 is higher in endomorphy than CA1 ($P \leq 0.05$), and that CA3 is lower in ectomorphy than CA2 ($P \leq 0.05$). All other pairwise comparisons are not significant.

Table 2. Distribution of the soccer athletes by chronological age and pubic hair status (N=95).

Age group	Maturational status (pubic hair)					Total
	1	2	3	4	5	
11.0–11.9	8	6	-	-	-	14
12.0–12.9	1	9	5	-	-	15
13.0–13.0	-	5	8	5	-	18
14.0–14.9	-	-	4	15	-	19
15.0–15.9	-	-	-	6	1	7
16.0–16.9	-	-	-	11	11	22
Total	9	20	17	37	12	95

3.2. Variation by single year age groups within each age/playing group

Distributions of stages of pubic hair (PH) development in single year chronological age groups are summarized in Table 2, while characteristics of players by stage of puberty within each age/playing group are summarized in Table 3. Among CA1 Players, the majority of 11-year-old players are pre-pubertal (PH1). Among CA2 players, the majority are classified as mid-pubertal (PH3 and

PH4), but 15 of 19 14-year old players are already in late puberty (PH4). Among CA3 players, there are only seven 15-year old players, and one-half of 16-year-old players are post-pubertal (PH5).

Variation in size and somatotype by stage of pubic hair within each age/playing group is summarized in Table 3. Within CA1, the least mature boys (PH1) are, on average, younger, shorter and lighter, followed by early (PH2) and mid-pubertal (PH3) boys. Within CA2, early pubertal boys (PH2) are younger, shorter and lighter than players of more advanced pubertal status (PH3 and PH4). In the oldest age group, CA3, players in late puberty (PH4) are younger, shorter , and especially lighter than post-pubertal players (PH5). Differences in body size by maturity status are greatest among CA2 players.

Given the small sample sizes within each group, somatotype does not significantly differ by maturity status. However, several trends are suggested. Among CA1 players, ectomorphy increases, on average, with stage of pubic hair, and among CA2 players, ectomorphy increases from PH2 to PH3. Players classified as PH3 are probably in the midst of the growth spurts in height as the majority of boys are in stages PH3 and PH4 at the time of peak height velocity; moreover, peak growth of body mass and muscle mass occur, on average, after peak height velocity (Malina *et al.*, 2003). The latter would explain the decline in ectomorphy and increase in endomorphy and mesomorphy in CA3 boys in PH5 compared to those in PH4, whereas CA2 boys in PH3 and PH4 have, on average, virtually identical somatotypes.

Table 3. Descriptive statistics and significance tests within each age/playing group.

	CA1: 11–12 yr (n=29)				CA2: 13–14 yr (n=37)				CA3: 15–16 yr (n=29)		
	PH1	PH2	PH3	p	PH2	PH3	PH4	p	PH4	PH5	p
N	9	15	5		5	12	20		17	12	
Age (years)	11.6	12.0	12.5		13.2	13.7	14.2		16.0	16.3	
Stature (m)	1.427	1.452	1.520	**	1.495	1.614	1.693	**	1.708	1.750	*
Body Weight (kg)	36.6	37.6	40.4	ns	43.2	48.7	57.0	**	60.7	68.2	**
Androgyny index	74.5	74.9	77.7	ns	79.3	82.7	86.1	*	92.0	94.1	ns
Endomorphy	2.1	2.4	2.0	ns	3.1	2.6	2.8	ns	2.6	3.1	ns
Mesomorhy	4.8	4.4	4.2	ns	5.2	4.2	4.2	ns	4.3	4.7	ns
Ectomorphy	2.9	3.3	3.9	ns	2.7	3.8	3.7	ns	3.3	2.8	ns

** ($P \leq 0.01$), * ($P \leq 0.05$), n.s. (non-significant)

Figures 1 and 2 compare the heights and body mass values of boys in the same stage of pubic hair but who are in different age/playing groups. Although CA2 players in PH2 are 0.7 years older than CA1 players in PH3, they are shorter. The CA3 players in PH4 are only 1.5 cm taller than CA2 players in PH4, although they are 1.8 years older. The same trends are apparent for boys' mass.

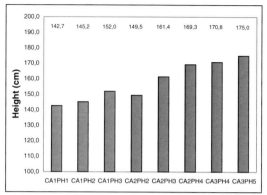

Figure 1. Mean height by stage of pubic hair (PH) within age/playing groups: Legend: CA1PH1 (n=9, 11.6 years), CA1PH2 (n=15, 12.0 years), CA1PH3 (n=5, 12.5 years), CA2PH2 (n=5, 13.2 years), CA2PH3 (n=12, 13.7 years), CA2PH4 (n=20, 14.2 years), CA3PH4 (n=17, 16.0 years), CA3PH5 (n=12, 16.3 years).

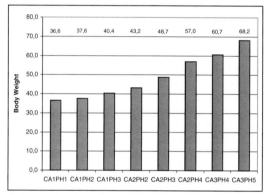

Figure 2. Mean body mass by stage of pubic hair (PH) within age/playing groups: Legend: CA1PH1 (n=9, 11.6 years), CA1PH2 (n=15, 12.0 years), CA1PH3 (n=5, 12.5 years), CA2PH2 (n=5, 13.2 years), CA2PH3 (n=12, 13.7 years), CA2PH4 (n=20, 14.2 years), CA3PH4 (n=17, 16.0 years), CA3PH5 (n=12, 16.3 years).

4. CONCLUSIONS

Variation in body size associated with stage of puberty is more evident among players in CA1 and CA2 than among players in CA3. This reflects the reduced range of variation in sexual maturity status among CA3 boys which is related to the reduced representation, or perhaps elimination of later maturing boys at age and specialization in soccer increase. Maturity-associated variation in body size is greatest among players in CA2, 13–14 years. This is the age range when the majority of boys are in the growth spurt and many are approaching maximal growth or peak height velocity. In contrast, variation in somatotype is less, and is more apparent between boys in PH2 and PH3; somatotype of CA2 boys in PH3 and PH4 do not differ.

Variation in the size of youth soccer players should be recognized by coaches/trainers. It may be more realistic to place players in single year age/playing groups to reduce the range of maturity-associated variation among youth players as they make the transition into puberty and the adolescent growth spurt.

REFERENCES

Carter, J.E.L. and Heath B., 1990, *Somatotyping – Development and Applications.* (Cambridge: Cambridge University Press).

Malina, R.M., 1994, Physical growth and biological maturation of young athletes. *Exercise and Sports Science Reviews*, **22**, 389–433.

Malina, R.M., 1998, Growth and maturation of young athletes – Is training for sport a factor. In *Sports and Children*, edited by Chan, K. M. and Micheli, L.J. (Hong Kong: Williams and Wilkins Asia Pacific), pp. 133–161.

Malina, R.M., Bouchard, C. and Bar-Or, O., 2003, *Growth, Maturation, and Physical Activity*, 2nd edition. (Champaign, IL: Human Kinetics).

Malina, R.M., Peña Reyes, M.E., Eisenmann, J.C., Horta, L., Rodrigues, J. and Miller, R., 2000, Height, mass, and skeletal maturity of elite Portuguese soccer players 11-16 years of age. *Journal of Sports Sciences*, **18**, 685–693.

Peña Reyes, M.E., Cardenas-Barahona, E. and Malina, R.M., 1994, Growth, physique, and skeletal maturation of soccer players 7–17 years of age. *Humanbiologia Budapestinensis*, **5**, 453–458.

Tanner J.M, 1962, *Growth at Adolescence*, 2nd edition. (Oxford: Blackwell Scientific Publications).

Tanner, J.M, Lond, M.B. and Penna, M.D., 1951, Current advances in the study of physique: photogrametric anthropometry and androgyny scale. *The Lancet,* **1**, 574–579.

69   Physiological Demands of Match Play and Training in Elite Adolescent Footballers

Dave Billows, Thomas Reilly and Keith George
Research Institute for Sport and Exercise Sciences, Liverpool John
Moores University, Liverpool. L3 2ET. UK

1. INTRODUCTION

Football match-play and training sessions, both technical and physical, apply particular stresses to the physiological systems. These stresses can vary depending on the intensity of work, environmental conditions, level of ability and physical maturity of the players. Physiological responses to the game and the accompanying training sessions have been well documented in comprehensive studies of adult elite and sub-elite players (Bangsbo, 1993; Reilly, 1994). Methods of analysis have used metabolic responses such as blood lactate and hormonal changes, and movement studies by means of video recordings and motional analysis. Analyses of the concentrations of blood borne or intramuscular metabolites are invasive in nature and can be difficult to administer whereas assessment using video equipment can be expensive and time consuming.

     The demands placed upon both the aerobic and anaerobic energy systems during the course of training and matches can be estimated by analysing heart rate responses as an index of overall physiological strain. This type of analysis has been done on many occasions for elite and sub-elite mature players but there is little or no data relating to elite adolescent players. It is widely accepted that in adults the energy required to sustain exercise at heart rates below 85% of maximum heart rate (HRmax) can be generated aerobically and above 85% HRmax the energy is generated anaerobically. This inference cannot be made for adolescents as the metabolic pathways are still under development with the aerobic pathways developing in advance of the anaerobic pathways and neither being fully mature at the age of the subject population. It would be inappropriate therefore to estimate the physiological strain placed on adolescents during exercise using heart rate parameters that have been developed for use with adults.

     The aims of this study were:- i) To determine the physiological stress placed upon elite adolescent players by analysing heart rate responses during a) match-play and b) training and ii) To compare these data with adult data.

2. METHODS

Twenty male, academy footballers, age 15.5 (± 0.6) years, height 1.73 (± 0.04) m, mass 62.2 (± 5.5) kg had their maximum heart rates (HRmax) determined during a graded exercise test. The Yo-Yo intermittent endurance test by Bangsbo (1996) was used in this study. Heart rates were then monitored during a series of 5 competitive football matches and a total of 15 separate training sessions using Polar Team System heart rate monitors (Polar Ltd, Warwickshire, England). Sample heart rates were taken at 5-s intervals during the course of each match (see Fig 1) and each training session. The resultant data were processed and recorded as a percentage of maximum heart rate for each individual player and were categorised as time spent above and below 85% of HRmax for training and match-play.

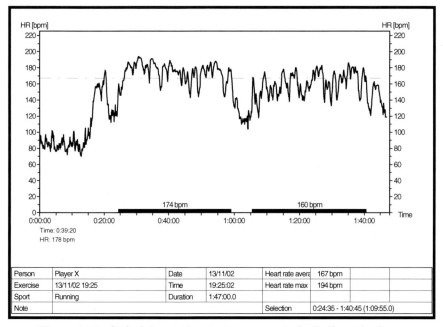

Figure 1. Typical adolescent heart rate response to football match-play.

3. RESULTS

3.1. Match-play

The mean maximum heart rate (HRmax) for the adolescent players was 201 (± 8) beats.min^{-1}. The mean heart rate (mean HR) during the games was 86% of HRmax or 174 beats.min^{-1}. Typical data from an elite adult match show a mean HR of 160 beats.min^{-1} or 82% of HRmax (see Fig.2). The difference in percentage of HRmax between elite adolescents and elite adults is significant (P < 0.01) as is the difference in mean heart rate (p = 0.001). The mean heart rate range during the games was 68–97% of the mean HRmax, which was 137-195 beats.min[-1].

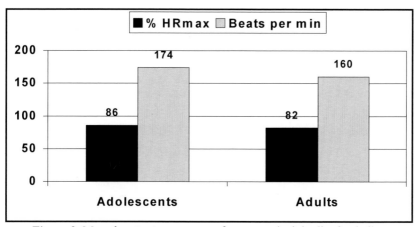

Figure 2. Mean heart rate responses of young and adult elite footballers during match-play.

The mean HR for the first half of the games was 88 (± 3.2)% of HRmax (176 beats.min[-1]). The mean heart rate for the second half was significantly lower (P< 0.01) with a mean heart rate of 85 (± 3.7)% of HRmax (171 beats.min[-1]) (see Fig. 3).

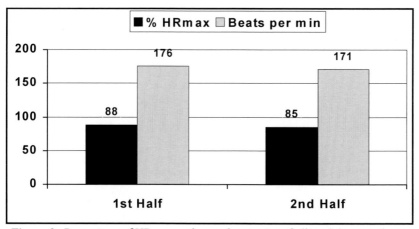

Figure 3. Percentage of HRmax and mean heart rates of elite adolescent players during the first and second half of a game.

The under-15 years age group had a higher but not significantly different (P < 0.05) mean maximum heart rate (202 ± 9 beats min[-1]) compared to the under-16 players (200 ± 9 beats min^{-1}). They also had higher but not significantly different ($P < 0.05$) values for first half mean HR (U15s; $88 \pm 2.1\%$ HRmax - U16s; $87 \pm 3.8\%$ HRmax) for, second half mean HR (U15s; $85 \pm 2.2\%$ HRmax - U16s; $84 \pm 4\%$ HRmax), full game mean HR (U15s; $87 \pm 1.9\%$ HRmax - U16s; $86 \pm 3.4\%$ HRmax) and heart rate range (U15s; 68-98% HRmax - U16s; 67-97% HRmax). The combined mean time spent below 85% HRmax was 27 min or 33% of the total time played and the mean time spent above 85% of HRmax was 53 min or 67% of the time played. The under-15 years age group spent 24 min (30% of total) below 85% of HRmax and 56 min (70% of total) above 85% HRmax compared to 31 min (39%) below and 49 min (61%) above 85% HRmax for the under-16 group (see Table 1).

Table 1. Match-play HR data for Under 16 and Under 15 elite players.

Under 16 Players	Under 15 Players
Mean HRmax – 200 beats.min^{-1}	Mean HRmax – 202 beats.min^{-1}
1st Half – 87% HRmax	1st Half – 88% HRmax
2nd Half – 84% HRmax	2nd Half – 85% HRmax
Full Game – 86% HRmax	Full Game – 87% HRmax
HR range – 67-97% HRmax	HR range – 68-97% HRmax
39% of time <85% HRmax	30% of time <85% HRmax
61% of time >85% HRmax	70% of time >85% HRmax

Match-play statistics for adults based on estimations of energy expenditure from heart rate responses show that elite adult players spend on average 67% of the game exercising at an intensity below 85% HRmax or aerobically. The remaining 33% of the time during a game is spent exercising above 85% HRmax or using anaerobic energy systems. This gives a ratio of slightly greater than 2:1 in terms of aerobic over anaerobic energy expenditure. The results of this study (U15/U16 combined) displayed a mean HR below 85% HRmax for approximately 33% of the game, with the remaining 67% being played at a mean HR above 85% HRmax giving a ratio of 1:2 for aerobic to anaerobic energy expenditure (see Fig.4). This shows that elite adolescent players are exercising above 85% HRmax for twice the percentage of the game compared to elite adult players.

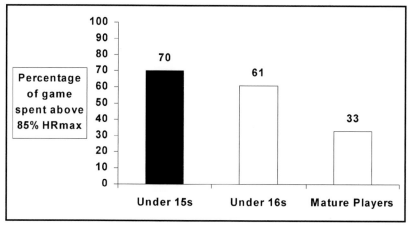

Figure 4. Comparison of time spent above 85% of maximum heart rate for elite adolescent (U15 and U16) and elite mature players during match-play.

3.2 Training sessions

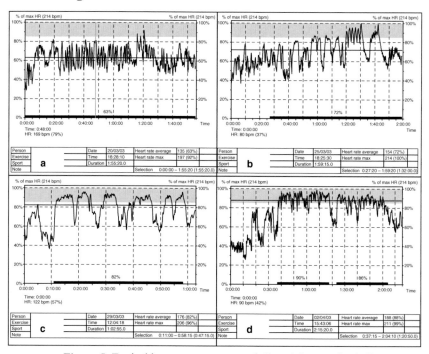

Figure 5. Typical heart rate responses of elite adolescent footballers to various training stimuli.

Heart rate response to training sessions varied according to the type and intensity of work involved. In Figure 5 above, the responses to four different training sessions are displayed. The response to a technical training session where the players are practising passing and shooting is shown in Figure 5a. The intensity is low throughout this session. In the session displayed in Figure 5b the first section is again of a technical nature and the initial intensity is low. The last part of this session involved interval training as can be seen by the regularity of the peaks and troughs in the heart rate response. In this part of the session the intensity was high and the combined effect of the technical and physical components was a medium intensity training session. Figure 5c displays a session that combined technical with physical work in the form of small-sided games. The intensity during the games is high and the rest periods are generally of the same or similar duration to each game (e.g. 3 or 4 min). This session is medium to high in intensity. The final Figure (5d) shows the heart rate response to a practice match within the group and is very similar to the heart rate response to a competitive match shown in Figure 1. This session was of high intensity as can be seen from the HR average line for the session which lies in the grey area representing heart rates above 85% HRmax.

Table 2. Heart rate responses of elite adolescent footballers during training sessions.

- Mean HR of 67 (±5.6)% of HRmax (135 ± 11 beats/min) during training sessions
- HR range during training was 32–97% HRmax
- 85 (± 8.3)% of time was spent exercising below 85% HRmax
- 15 (± 4.2) % of time was spent exercising above 85% HRmax
- Mean time spent above 85% HRmax per training session was 11.2 min
- Time above 85% HRmax per session ranged from 1 min to 26.5 min
- Mean time per week above 85% HRmax was 56 min

Match-play combined with training sessions imposed a mean of 106.3 min per week above 85% HRmax on the players in this study. The under-15 players exercised at a higher percentage of HRmax than did the under-16 players who in turn, exercised at a higher percentage of HRmax than adult players

4. DISCUSSION

Monitoring training load and intensity is very important if the training load is to be optimal for the enhancement of physical development. Continual assessment and, if necessary, adjustment of workload and intensity is required in order to avoid over/under-training and therefore negatively affecting the development of the young athlete. Heart rate responses to exercise are closely coupled to the intensity of the applied workload and provide a valid and reliable method of analysis (Ali and Farrally, 1991). When using HR data to monitor workload in adults, one of the most common methods of estimation is to use the time spent in specific training zones. High intensity exercise is categorised as the time spent exercising above 85% of HRmax and is classed as the red zone. This intensity is deemed high enough to cause the accumulation of lactate in the blood (anaerobic) and is therefore fatigue inducing. Generally 20–30 minutes in the red zone on two separate occasions during a training week (a total of 40–60 min) is considered enough to maintain in-season anaerobic fitness levels for match-play.

In this study the data collected show that boys' heart rates are in excess of 85% HRmax during match-play for much longer periods than adults (67% of the time compared to 33% in adults). From studies on adolescent responses to exercise it is apparent that boys can exercise at these intensities without accumulating lactate in the blood (Reybrouk, 1989; Malina and Bouchard, 1991). The data from this study coupled with previous research lead to the conclusion that adolescent athletes can operate at an intensity above 85% HRmax for long periods without the occurrence of metabolic acidosis. This means that adolescent boys have either a greater capacity than adults to generate energy aerobically, or a more efficient way of dealing with the by-products of anaerobic glycolysis. Studies by Sargeant (1989) and Beneke et al. (1996) have shown that the production of lactate is very limited in pubescent boys and that submaximal energy production is more efficient during adolescence than in adulthood. Differences in the ratios of the glycolytic enzyme phosphofructokinase (PFK) and the oxidative enzyme isocitrate dehydrogenase between children (0.884) and adults (1.633) indicate an enhanced ability for pyruvate oxidation and therefore a greater ability to generate energy aerobically in adolescents compared to adults (Boisseau and Delamarche, 2000). Adolescents can therefore generate enough energy aerobically to elevate their HR above 85% of their individual HRmax values and can operate at a higher relative intensity than adults using predominately aerobic energy sources.

The reasons for this difference between adolescents and adults have not been fully discovered as yet but some of the determining factors include the age-dependant maximum rate of anaerobic energy production. The ability to produce energy via the anaerobic glycolytic pathway increases with age up to physical maturity and so the further from physical maturity a boy is, the more dependant he is on the production of energy aerobically. A major reason for this is the lower level of important glycolytic rate-limiting enzymes such as PFK and lactate dehydrogenase in the muscles of boys compared to men (Eriksson et al., 1973; Naughton et al., 2000). Although the levels of these enzymes are lower in adolescents, they can be increased by training. Fournier et al. (1982) showed that 12 weeks of sprint training generated a 21% increase in the intramuscular concentration of PFK in adolescents, although this was still much lower than adult concentrations and the enzyme activity did return to pre-training levels following detraining. Differences in muscle architecture between adolescents and mature adults could also be a factor in these variations in energy production (Berg and Keul, 1988). It has been shown that muscle fibre type distribution varies between children and adults with a higher proportion of type I (slow-twitch) fibres in the vastus lateralis muscle of children compared to untrained adults (Boisseau and Delamarche, 2000). A higher percentage of type I fibres would reduce the capacity for energy production via anaerobic glycolysis. Another, more basic reason for the higher work-rates in adolescents could be that lower technical ability requires a greater physical effort to achieve the required standards of performance.

5. CONCLUSION

Regardless of the reasons for the higher relative work rate of elite adolescent players compared to elite adult players, it is important to note that the interpretations of markers used to analyse adult HR responses are not appropriate for adolescents. The results of this study highlight the need for these measures to be investigated and adjusted accordingly for adolescent athletes. Future studies should address this fact and attempt to identify workloads and intensities specifically relevant to young and adolescent athletes using HR responses as an "easy to use" guide for the application and prescription of training programmes. Although the ethical problems inherent with studies involving children and adolescents must be addressed, efforts should be made to link metabolic and HR responses to exercise if we are to enhance our understanding and therefore improve the development of young athletes. The fact that adolescent athletes can sustain a HR in excess of 85% HRmax without the development of metabolic acidosis means that estimations of energy expenditure based on HR response used for adults are not applicable to younger athletes.

REFERENCES

Ali, A. and Farrally, M., 1991, Recording soccer players' heart rates during matches. *Journal of Sports Sciences,* **9**, 183–189.

Bangsbo, J., 1993, *The Physiology of Soccer – with Special Reference to Intense Intermittent Exercise.* (Copenhagen: HO + Storm).

Beneke, R., Heck, H. and Schwarz, V., 1996, Maximal lactate steady state during the second decade of age. *Medicine and Science in Sports and Exercise,* **28**, 1474–1478.

Berg, A. and Keul, J., 1988, Biochemical changes during exercise in children. In *Young Athletes: A Biological, Psychological and Educational Perspective,* edited by Malina, R. (Champaign, Illinois: Human Kinetics), pp. 61–67.

Boisseau, N. and Delamarche, P., 2000, Metabolic and hormonal responses to exercise in children and adolescents. *Sports Medicine,* **30**, 405–422.

Eriksson, B., Gollnick, P. and Saltin, B., 1973, Muscle metabolism and enzyme activities after training in boys 11–13 years old. *Acta Physiologica Scandinavica,* **87**, 485–497.

Fournier, M., Ricci, J. and Taylor, A., 1982, Skeletal muscle adaptation in adolescent boys: sprint and endurance training and detraining. *Medicine and Science in Sports and Exercise,* **14**, 453–456.

Malina, R. and Bouchard, C., 1991, *Growth, Maturation, and Physical Activity.* (Champaign, Illinois: Human Kinetics).

Naughton, G., Farpour-Lambert, N., Carlson, J., Bradney, M. and Van Praagh, E., 2000, Physiological issues surrounding the performance of adolescent athletes. *Sports Medicine,* **30**, 309–325.

Reilly, T., 1994, Physiological aspects of soccer. *Biology of Sport,* **11**, 3–20.

Reybrouck, T., 1989, The use of the anaerobic threshold in paediatric exercise testing. In *Advances in Paediatric Sports Sciences,* edited by Bar-Or, O. (Champaign, Illinois: Human Kinetics), pp. 131–150.

Sargeant, A., 1989, Short-term muscle power in children and adolescents. In, *Advances in Paediatric Sports Sciences,* edited by Bar-Or, O. (Champaign, Illinois: Human Kinetics), pp. 41–56.

70   The $\dot{V}O_2$ and HR Response to Training with a Ball in Youth Soccer Players

Carlo Castagna[1,4], Romualdo Belardinelli[2] and Grant Abt[3,4]
[1]Istituto Tecnico Industriale Statale "V. Volterra" Torrette di Ancona, Ancona, Italy [2]Department of Cardiovascular Rehabilitation and Prevention, Azienda Ospedaliera "G.M. Lancisi", Ancona Italy
[3]St. Martin's College, Lancaster, UK
[4]Research Department, Teknosport.com, Ancona, Italy

1. INTRODUCTION

Soccer coaches and players acknowledge the importance of a well-designed physical fitness programme to cope with general and specific match stresses. With the aim to improve preparedness over the last decade, soccer-training science-specific training methodologies have been introduced, with particular attention focusing on the assessment and development of the aerobic abilities of soccer players of different competitive levels.

As many of the aerobic pathway adaptations take place within the muscles involved during training, sport scientists have proposed drills that mimic the playing activity in order to solicit the targeted physiological adaptations that will result in improved soccer performance (Bangsbo, 1993).

Although highly attractive from both a coaching and playing perspective, ball-training can be an unpredictable exercise mode if compared with continuous exercise. Nevertheless, soccer coaches and fitness trainers habitually monitor field training through the use of heart rate monitoring, following the general guidance usually suggested for continuous exercise (Bangsbo, 1993).

Despite the wide acceptance of this training philosophy, the responses of such training have not been extensively investigated, particularly in young soccer players where game-like drills involving the ball are more attractive and potentially more effective.

The aim of this study was to examine the validity of using heart rate as a reflection of the aerobic involvement during ball training aimed at developing aerobic fitness in youth soccer players.

2. METHODS

Participants were 11 provincial level soccer players (age 16.7±0.8 years, height 1.79±0.07 m, body mass 68.0±6.5 kg) randomly chosen among a population of students attending a high school located in the area of Ancona (Istituto tecnico industriale statale Vito Volterra, Torrette di Ancona, Italy) during the 2001–2002 season. All of the subjects were active players at the time of the investigation, training 2–3 times a week with a match played during each weekend of the competitive season. Playing experience of each player was no less than 5 years.

Players were told to refrain from heavy training, alcohol, caffeine and tobacco usage for the two days preceding test sessions. During the two hours preceding the test sessions, only ad libitum water intake was allowed and subjects consumed a light meal at least three hours before the commencement of exercise. All subjects were familiar with the methods and procedures used in this study.

Testing was administrated in a random order and consisted of:-

1. a laboratory test for maximal oxygen uptake (Bruce protocol) performed on a motor-driven treadmill (Cosmed, Rome, Italy);

2. a 5 vs 5 soccer match performed on a 40×20-m team-handball court;

3. a 6-min intermittent exercise protocol consisting of alternating periods of 15-s sprinting and 15-s jogging while dribbling a soccer ball back and forward between two lines set 25 m apart.

In all the test sessions, subjects' expired gases were collected with a portable lightweight breath-by-breath gas analyser (K4 b^2, COSMED, Rome, Italy). Players' expired gases were monitored on-line by telemetry during field-testing. All test sessions took place at a time of day corresponding to the usual training session performed by the provincial level soccer players. Data were stored on a laptop PC (Texas Instruments, Extensa 501T, USA) for analyses following the testing using a dedicated software (K4 b^2, software, COSMED, Rome, Italy). The variables of interest in this study were: oxygen uptake ($\dot{V}O_2$) and heart rate (HR).

3. RESULTS

Players' treadmill average $\dot{V}O_{2peak}$ and HR_{max} were 50.04±6.72 ml kg^{-1} min^{-1} and 192±9 beat min^{-1}, respectively. During the 5 vs 5 session the players attained 53±12% of treadmill $\dot{V}O_{2peak}$ and 72±9% of their HR_{max}. Small-sided game HR vs $\dot{V}O_2$ coefficients of determination (r^2×100) ranged between 27 and 85% (average 70.6±15.7%) ($P<0.001$). Treadmill HR vs $\dot{V}O_2$ r^2 ranged between 89 and 97% (average 92.82±2.48%,) ($P<0.001$). The 15s-15s interval training resulted in an r^2 that ranged between 3 and 90%. The $\dot{V}O_2$ and HR during the 15s-15s protocol averaged 77 and 96% of the treadmill $\dot{V}O_{2peak}$ and HR_{max}, respectively. Estimation of 5 vs 5 and 15s-15s $\dot{V}O_2$ and HR through treadmill HR-$\dot{V}O_2$ regression equations were not significantly different from actual values ($P>0.05$).

4. DISCUSSION

The results of the present study suggest that in this selected population of moderately trained and skilled young soccer players supervised small-sided games have little impact on the development of aerobic power, as revealed by the low average percentage of $\dot{V}O_{2peak}$ attained during the games (53±12%). Interestingly during the 15s-15s protocol players attained 77% of treadmill $\dot{V}O_{2peak}$ despite the attainment of near maximal HR values. This finding is in agreement with that reported by Balsom et al. (1992) who found higher HR responses during high intensity intermittent exercise compared to continuous exercise. As small-sided games are commonly used by coaches to promote soccer fitness, the results of the present study may question the efficacy of using small-sided games with low-trained and skilled young players. However, the HR and $\dot{V}O_2$ response to small-sided games is likely to vary with the dimensions of the playing area, number of players and rules (Flanagan and Merrick, 2002). Consequently, coaches and fitness trainers need to quantify the physiological load (i.e. HR and $\dot{V}O_2$) of different small-sided games before they are used within a training programme for the development of aerobic fitness. Additionally, the treadmill HR-$\dot{V}O_2$ relationship was able to estimate accurately the physiological load imposed during practise. This finding supports the use of the treadmill HR-$\dot{V}O_2$ relationship in training monitoring and prescription and particularly during small-sided games where a fairly good common variance exists between HR and $\dot{V}O_2$ ($r^2 \cong 71\%$ P<0.001).

Acknowledgements

The authors of this study would express their deepest gratitude to Miss Francesca Lacalaprice Bsc PT for her guidance in using the K4 b^2 gas analyser and to all the participants from the Istituto Tecnico Industriale "Vito Volterra" (Torrette di Ancona) for their enthusiastic availability.

REFERENCES

Balsom, P., Seger, J.Y., Sjödin, B. and Ekblom, B., 1992, Maximal-intensity intermittent exercise: Effect of recovery duration. *International Journal of Sports Medicine*, **13**, 528–533.

Bangsbo, J., 1993, Fitness Training in Football- A Scientific Approach. (Copenhagen, Denmark: HO+Storm).

Flanagan, T. and Merrick, E., 2002, Quantifying the workload of soccer players. In Science and Football IV, edited by Spinks, W., Reilly, T. and Murphy, A. (London-New York: Routledge), pp. 341–349.

71 The Importance of Chronological and Maturational Age on Strength, Resistance and Speed Performance of Soccer Players During Adolescence

I. Fragoso[1], F. Vieira[1], F. Canto e Castro[2], P. Mil-Homens[1], C. Capela, N. Oliveira [1], A. Barroso [1], R.Veloso [1]and A. Oliveira Junior[3]

[1]Faculty of Human Kinetics, Technical University of Lisbon, Portugal

[2]Faculty of Science, University of Lisbon, Portugal

[3] Institute of Physical Education and Sport – Rio de Janeiro State University

1. INTRODUCTION

The association between morphological and maturational characteristics and motor performance has been the object of countless research projects. Physical exercise during growth depends on the morphological characteristics and growth stage of the body. Motor skill levels and physical fitness tend to be optimized during adolescence, especially strength which depends on lean body mass (Carter, 1988; Malina and Bouchard, 1991; Vieira *et al.*, 2003). The onset and terminus of adolescence period may vary so much, particularly in boys, that variability can hide the real motor physical value. It is known that during adolescence more mature boys, participating in sports such as baseball, football, soccer, swimming, tennis, and ice hockey, often achieve better results than those less mature (Beunen *et al.*, 1997). However, there are fewer significant motor performance differences between and among maturation groups within specific age groups.

The purpose of this study was to compare the influence of morphological and maturational characteristics on a general strength task such as handgrip with the influence of the same variables on other type of motor abilities such as running speed, resistance and muscle strength, important in soccer actions.

2. METHODS

This study assesses a total of 70 male soccer players aged between 13 and 16 years, who attended the Sporting Club of Portugal. The time spent in sport-specific training was on average 8 h/week. Anthropometric measures were obtained according to Fragoso and Vieira (2000) and included weight, height, BMI, sitting height, arm and leg lengths, biacromial, biiliocristal, biepicondylar humerus and femur, stylion ulnar breadth, biceps, triceps, subscapular, iliac crest, abdominal, thoracic, mid-axila, front thigh and medial calf skinfolds, arm relaxed, and arm tensed, forearm, mid-thigh and calf girths. Aerobic fitness was measured using a 20-m shuttle-run test, and running speed was obtained with a 30-m linear test with light barriers (5-15-25-30 m). Muscle strength was assessed through three different motor tasks: maximal leg strength (MS) was evaluated based on an isometric force-time curve produced in an instrumented leg-press machine; the long stretch-shortening cycle was evaluated with a counter-movement jump (CMJ) performed on a contact mat; and by means of a handgrip (HG) strength test. Handgrip strength was used not only because it is a general strength test but also because it is not particularly influenced by years of experience. Skeletal maturity based on radiographs was assessed according Tanner-Whitehouse III Method (TW3). Sexual maturity was self-evaluated and scored for 5 stages according to Tanner (1962). Age of voice alteration was obtained prospectively according to the proposal of Cameron (personal communication). A new maturation index (SMFS) was created using principal component analysis of sexual maturity variables. Homogeneity of variance was tested to select the variables. With a sample size of 70 elements and a long list of covariates, overfitting and collinearity must be carefully analysed. Consequently an intercorrelation of anthropometric, "bone age", sexual maturity and motor variables was calculated hoping to reduce dimensionality. Descriptive statistics (mean values, standard deviation) were performed for the whole sample and for each variable. Some exploratory statistics and a non-parametric correlation between all maturation indices were performed to understand their association. Finally to know the influence of morphological and maturational variables on performance a linear model was developed for each motor test. The probabilities of F for entrance and removal of the variables were 0.05 and 0.10 for all the variables. Statistical analyses of the data were carried out using SPSS 11.5 software for Windows.

3. RESULTS

The analysis in Table 1 shows that mean bone age was very similar to chronological age until 15 years. At this chronological age, bone age was almost equal to bone age of 16 years old boys. Although the 15 year-old boys were taller than those aged 16 years, their sitting height was smaller. Upper leg length, stylion-ulnar, biepicondylar femur and maleolar breadths were not significantly different (P=0.293; P=0.205; P=0.776) between 13 and 16 years. The same was true for front thigh, medial calf and mid-axilla skinfold (P=0.620; P=0.435; P=0.276). In general, trunk breadths, especially biacromial breadth, arm and mid-thigh girths increased with age. Abdominal skinfold values were really greater at 16 years. At 13 years these boys were late maturers (BA-CA=- 0.23). At 15 years they were almost one year advanced (mean 0.74; sd 0.89) compared to their chronological age. Though only 50% of children were continuously advanced or retarded and could really be considered as early and late maturers (Kemper *et al.*, 1997), these results may mean, that late maturing children may give-up playing sports or may be removed from training.

Table 1. Means and standard deviations of anthropometric, motor and maturational variables.

	Mean	SD	Mean	SD	Mean	SD	Mean	SD
CA	13.6	0.2	14.6	0.2	15.5	0.3	16.5	0.3
Bone Age	13.4	1.5	14.9	1.5	16.2	0.7	16.5	0.0
BA-CA	-0.2	1.5	0.3	1.5	0.7	0.9	0.0	0.3
Height (cm)	162.2	8.5	168.6	10.7	175.2	6.1	174.7	5.4
Mass (kg)	53.4	9.7	59.1	10.7	67.3	4.7	72.1	6.0
Sit. Height	84.2	4.7	88.0	6.0	91.3	2.8	92.2	3.1
Length (cm)								
Upper Arm	33.5	1.9	34.0	2.6	35.7	2.0	39.1	11.4
Upper Leg	41.6	2.3	45.2	12.8	44.3	2.8	44.3	2.6
Breadth (cm)								
B.Humerus	6.4	0.5	6.5	0.5	6.9	0.4	6.9	0.5
Styl.-ulnar	5.3	0.6	5.4	0.6	5.5	0.4	5.6	0.2
B.Femur	9.3	0.9	9.0	0.5	9.6	0.6	9.3	0.4
Malleolar	10.0	14.4	7.4	0.4	8.3	2.7	7.7	0.4
Biacromial	34.9	2.5	36.0	2.6	37.8	1.6	39.0	1.6
Thorax T.	24.8	1.9	25.3	1.8	26.1	1.3	28.5	2.2
Girth (cm)								
Tensed Arm	25.4	2.4	27.2	2.3	29.7	1.7	31.1	1.6
Mid – Thigh	46.5	3.5	47.4	4.0	50.8	2.4	54.4	2.1
Calf	33.7	3.0	35.8	2.4	37.1	1.3	37.9	1.1
Skinfolds (mm)								
Front Thigh	11.5	3.3	11.8	4.0	10.8	3.0	12.4	2.3
Medial Calf	8.0	2.3	8.8	3.1	7.7	2.5	9.1	3.5
Subscapular	6.5	1.3	7.3	2.0	8.0	1.1	9.6	2.4
Mid-Axilla	5.4	1.2	5.3	1.1	5.5	1.0	6.3	2.5
Abdominal	8.4	2.6	9.0	4.1	10.5	3.2	13.0	5.4
Handgrip	33.9	6.4	45.3	9.1	50.5	5.0	52.6	7.3
M.Strength	1481	377.3	1749	358.2	1958	373.0	1997	330.3
CMJ	30.8	3.5	32.9	4.3	37.0	5.4	39.0	4.9
Speed	4.8	0.2	4.6	0.2	4.4	0.2	4.4	0.2
Resistance	16.4	7.2	29.0	8.2	25.4	10.5	27.8	9.0

In Figure 1, it is clear that almost all the subjects are level four and five for pubic hair, have voice changes for less than two years (covering bone ages between 10 to 16 years although quite symmetrically on both directions of the mean), and are between level three and four of genital development.

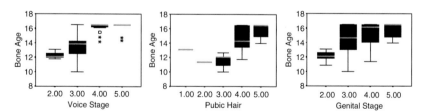

Figure 1. Box-plots for bone age difference in by sexual maturational levels.

The possible association between different measures of sexual maturity development was confirmed through a sexual maturity index based on a weighted vector and some intercorrelation between all maturation measures obtained. The principal component analysis indicates that the first component has a high commonality among the sexual maturity indicators studied, as is reported in the literature (Bielicki *et al.*, 1984; Mueller *et al.*, 2001).

Table 2. Initial eigenvalues and total variance explained by sexual maturational variables (pubic hair, genitalia development and voice alteration).

Component	Initial Eigenvalues		
	Total	% Variance	Cumulative %
1	2.0	67.0	66.9
2	0.6	19.6	86.5
3	0.4	13.5	100.0

After selecting and combining sexual maturity indicators in a principal components analysis, the percentage of variance accounted by the first principal component was 67%. The sexual maturity indictors had higher commonalities among themselves resulting in only one eigenvalue higher than 1, which means that no more than a single factor appeared in the factor analysis (Table 2).

Table 3. Matrix of correlation of different sexual maturation variables.

	BA	VS	PH	GS	SMFS
Bone Age	1.000	.825	.496	.311	.660
Voice Stage	-	1.000	.463	.351	.732
Pubic Hair	-	-	1.000	.549	.840
Genital Stage	-	-	-	1.000	.793
SM Factor Scores	-	-	-	-	1.000

All coefficients were significant at the 0.05 level.

After the construction of a sexual maturity index based on a weighted vector, intercorrelation analysis was conducted to confirm the possible association between different measures of sexual maturity development. Spearman's correlation among voice stage, pubic hair and genital stage was low but significant (Table 3). Skeletal and sexual maturation are not necessarily synchronous, and there was no well-defined correlation between Tanner stages and bone age. We can also observe that sexual maturity measures had great overall bone age variability.

In fact, non-parametric correlations of sexual secondary characteristics and bone age were significant for bone age and voice stage, pubic hair and genitalia development respectively 0.825, 0.496, 0.311. These results show that all the sexual maturity associations were significant and confirm the use of only one indicator, or of a combined sexual variable in a weighted vector. Other sexual maturity measures are redundant. So, since we intended to know the influence of maturation on motor performance we used as explanatory variables SMFS and BA. The choice of SMFS was not only because of the coefficient value observed (0.66) but also because almost the whole sample described themselves as voice stage three and this stage has the greatest variability of bone age.

As observed in Table 4, only the regression models adjusted for handgrip, maximal strength and speed included bone age as an explanatory variable.

Therefore, one of the reasons for the variability of these motor tasks is skeletal age. It seems that for similar biological age groups, CA becomes an important factor of variability for these motor tests. Finally, the measures of mid-thigh and calf girth also influence the results of almost all tests (aerobic fitness is the exception).

Table 4. Five adjusted linear regression models for "motor tests" for all the sample.

	Handgrip	Max. Strength	Speed	Resistance	CMJ
	Coef.	Coef.	Coef.	Coef.	Coef.
(Constant)	-69.395	-589.295	6.670	-36.015	7.034
Bone Age	1.411	-69.049	-0.46		
Sexual Mat. Factor Score		108.287			
Chronological Age	3.074		-0.058		2.414
Calf Girth	1.483		0.033	4.513	
Medial Calf Skinfold	-0.786		0.032		0.504
Abdominal Skinfold				-0.727	
Biep. Femoral breadth					-2.091
Mid – Thigh girth		26.632			0.535
Thorax Transv. breadth					-0.655
R Square	0.701	0.56.2	0.706	0.249	0.578
Adjusted R Square	0.683	0.541	0.681	0.225	0.543
SEE	5.914	282.03	0.149	8.740	3.691
PIN and POUT	0.05-0.10	0.05-0.10	0.05-0.10	0.05-0.10	0.05-0.10

Sexual maturational factor score was only important in explaining maximal strength. Aerobic fitness was only slightly influenced by adiposity. With only four covariates, bone age, chronological age, calf girth and medial calf skinfold, 68% of the variability of the observed "handgrip strength and speed" was explained and, if the model is well adjusted, predicted values will have a standard error of around 6 kg for handgrip and 0.15 seconds for speed. The CA was the most important covariate for the CMJ.

4. CONCLUSIONS

This study showed that SM Factor Score can be used as sexual maturational indicator and appears as an independent variable when studying maximal strength variability. Bone age was an important variable to explain handgrip, maximal strength and speed variability. In similar circumstances of biological age, chronological age becomes, for the whole sample, the most important factor of variability for these motor abilities. Therefore, when two boys have the same biological age but different chronological ages, we presume that the oldest ones have more experience, more years of training, and more learning time (measured by CA). The CA was the most important covariate for CMJ, therefore for this motor ability training makes all the difference in adolescents' performance.

Still, it is important to sustain these findings both with bigger, more specific samples, and with other predefined levels of maturation.

REFERENCES

Beunen, G.P., Malina, R.M., Lefevre, J., Claessens, A.L., Renson, R. and Simons, J.,1997, Prediction of adult stature and noninvasive assessment of biological maturation. *Medicine and Science in Sports and Exercise*, **29**, 225–230.

Bielicki, T., Koniarek, J. and Malina, R.M., 1984, Interrelationships among certain measures of growth and maturation rate in boys during adolescence. *Annals of Human Biology*, **11**, 201–210.

Carter, J.E.L., 1988, Somatotypes of children in sports, In *Young Athletes. Biological, Physiological and Educational Perspectives*, edited by Malina, R.M. (Champaign, IL: Human Kinetics), pp. 153–165.

Fragoso, I. and Vieira, F., 2000, *Morfologia e Crescimento. Curso prático.* (Cruz Quebrada, Portugal: Faculdade de Motricidade Humana).

Kemper, H.C., Post, G.B. and Twisk, J.W., 1997, Rate of maturation during the teenage years: nutrient intake and physical activity between ages 12 and 22. *International Journal of Sport Nutrition*, **7**, 229–240.

Malina, R.M. and Bouchard, C., 1991, *Growth Maturation and Physical Activity.* (Champaign, IL: Human Kinetics).

Mueller, W.H., Cho, S.D., Meininger, J.C., Liehr, P. and Chan, W., 2001, Strategies for combining and scaling sexual maturity indicators: the Heartfelt Study. *Annals of Human Biology*, **28**, 422–430.

Tanner, J.M., 1962, *Growth at Adolescence, with a general consideration of the effects of hereditary and environmental factors upon growth and maturation from birth to maturity*, 2nd edn. (Oxford: Blackwell Scientific Publications).

Vieira, F., Fragoso, I., Silva, L. and Canto e Castro, L., 2003, Morphology and sports performance in children aged 10-13 years: Identification of different levels of motor skills. In *Kinanthropometry VIII*, edited by Reilly, T. and Marfell-Jones, M. (London: Taylor and Francis), pp. 93–103.

72   Passive Smoking and Ventilatory Parameters in Young Soccer Players

Lana Ruzic, Branka R. Matkovic, Bojan Matkovic,
Sasa Jankovic and Goran Leko
Faculty of Kinesiology, University of Zagreb, Croatia

1. INTRODUCTION

The data about paternal or maternal smoking and the children's pulmonary functions have been very inconsistent. Passive smoking, of paternal or maternal origin, is known to influence the development of children's pulmonary function. Passive smoking was associated with reduced FEV, PEFR, and $FEF_{25-75\%}$ (Haby et al., 1994; Beck et al., 1999). Passive smoking is a major contributing factor to the development and persistence of airflow limitation in wheezing children (Sherill et al., 1992).

Even though the findings of previous research are inconsistent, what might be observed is the need for a very large sample in order to obtain reliable results. The problem of a large sample arises if the influence of passive smoking is studied on specific population like particular athletes of a particular age. None of the published studies was performed exclusively on young athletes, even though it may be interesting to compare the data with a non-athletic population of children. Tsimoyianis et al. (1987) pointed out the problem of the relationship between passive smoking and early pulmonary dysfunction in young athletes, but the subjects in that particular study were already teenagers. It would be of interest to investigate the possible attenuation of passive smoking effects in children by means of regular physical activity.

2. OBJECTIVES

The study was performed in order to determine differences in some pulmonary functions in young soccer players that were exposed to cigarette smoke in their homes. The aim of the study was to determine whether young soccer players, that were occasionally exposed to environmental smoke due to paternal or maternal smoking, had impaired pulmonary function, meaning lower values obtained from pulmonary function testing, in comparison to their counterparts from non-smoking homes.

3. METHODS

3.1. Subjects

The study was conducted in the facilities of the First National League team "Dinamo" Zagreb. The subjects were pupils of the Soccer School "Hitrec" which is a training school for possible future "Dinamo" players in older age categories.

The total sample comprised 115 boys between the 11 and 13 years of age (mean age 12.1±0.3). All of the subjects lived with their parents (the subjects living in the attached dormitory were not included).

3.2. Methods

In collaboration with three coaches, the subjects were asked to fill in the questionnaire. The questionnaire was completed prior to the pulmonary function testing. The questionnaire consisted of ten items, multiple choice questions, regarding paternal or maternal smoking at home, guest smoking at home and their own smoking habits. The questionnaire provided the information about whether the subject had his own room at home and whether the family received guests that smoked more then three times a week.

Basic morphological measures included height and body mass. Afterwards, the subjects underwent standardised pulmonary function testing. A portable spirometer (brand COSMED) was used to perform the measurements. The pulmonary function testing encompassed:-
- forced vital capacity (FVC),
- the volume of air expelled in the first second of maximal forced expiration from a position of full inspiration (FEV$_1$),
- FEV$_1$/FVC ratio or Tiffenaou index,
- forced expiratory flow rate between 25 to 75% of FVC (FEF$_{25-75\%}$).

3.3. Data analysis

The data obtained were analysed by means of descriptive statistics, t-test for independent samples and multiple regression analysis was used for data analysis. The statistics software for Windows 5.1 statistical package, licensed to the Faculty of Kinesiology was used.

4. RESULTS AND DISCUSSION

The questionnaire analysis showed that 53% of all of the homes experienced smoking at home. In comparison to the similar studies in other countries those results were neither encouraging nor discouraging. For example, 81% of the children tested in Turkey resided in homes where smoking occurred (Beck et al., 1999), while in Ontario, Canada that percentage was only 34% (Ashley, 1998).

After the analysis of the questionnaires, the sample was divided into two main groups. One group comprised 61 subjects that lived in non-smoking homes. The second group comprised of 54 boys who lived in homes where somebody smoked. The differences between the groups in basic morphological measures were also tested because of the high correlation between height and lung capacities. No statistically significant differences were found in height and body mass between the groups (1.539±0.081 m in "non-smoking homes" group vs. 1.551±0.092 m "smoking homes" group; P=0.487 and 42.4±8.2 kg vs. 43.4±10.2 kg; P=0.605), which enabled future data analysis and comparison of the two groups to be conducted. The mean values of the pulmonary parameters were higher than expected for the age and the height of the subjects, which might be explained by the fact that all of the subjects were athletes.

Differences in forced vital capacity (FVC), the volume of air expelled in the first second of maximal forced expiration from a position of full inspiration (FEV_1), FEV_1/FVC ratio and forced expiratory flow rate between 25 to 75% of FVC ($FEF_{25-75\%}$) were tested by Student t-tests for independent samples. No significant differences in any of the pulmonary function variables were established between the two groups (Table 1). Even though the differences observed were not significant, the subjects from "non-smoking" homes had achieved slightly better results on all measures. The similar studies in this field, utilised much larger samples, so it is difficult to compare the results obtained.

Table 1. Mean values and SD of pulmonary tests and the results of the t-test for independent samples.

	Non-smoking homes		Smoking homes		t-test
	Mean	SD	Mean	SD	P
FVC	2.65	0.632	2.62	0.53	0.785
FEV_1	2.50	0.657	2.40	0.48	0.455
FEV_1/FVC	92.86	5.771	92.17	5.67	0.582
$FEF_{25-75\%}$	3.20	0.874	3.07	0.83	0.499

Multiple regression analysis was used in order to establish possible predictive value of maternal, paternal or guest smoking on pulmonary function measures. Four multiple regression analyses were performed (dependant variables FVC, FEV_1, FEV_1/FVC and $FEF_{25-75\%}$) but none of the models analysed proved to be significant. There was also no predictive power established for any of the independent variables analysed (maternal, paternal or guest smoking at their homes).

5. CONCLUSIONS

Even though the study did not show any significant differences between the young soccer players living in smoking and non-smoking homes, it cannot be concluded that regular exercise contributed to the lack of differences. The subjects from "non-smoking homes" performed somewhat better on pulmonary function testing but the differences were non-significant. We might presume that the sample was too small to obtain significant differences even if present. In future, a larger experimental group would be needed. Also, the future study should include a control group of the same age, comprised of children that are not engaged in any kind of organised sport or recreational activity. In that way it would be possible to establish whether the lack of difference was due to the increased physical activity level of the young soccer players.

REFERENCES

Ashley, M.J., Cohen, J., Ferrence, R., Bull, S., Bondy, S., Poland, B. and Pederson, L., 1998, Smoking in the home: changing attitudes and current practices. *American Journal of Public Health*, **88**, 797–800.

Beck, K., Tomac, N., Delibas, A., Tuna, F., Tezic, H.T. and Sungur, M., 1999, The effect of passive smoking on pulmonary function during childhood. *Postgraduate Medicine Journal*, **75**, 339–341.

Burchfiel, C.M., Marcus, E.B., Curb, J.D., McLean, C.J., Vollmer, W.M., Johnson, L.R., Fong, K.O., Rodriguez, B.L., Maska, K.H. and Buist, A.S., 1995, Effects of smoking and smoking cessation on longitudinal decline in pulmonary function. *American Journal of Respiratory Care Medicine*, **6**, 1778–1785.

Corbo, G.M., Agabiti, N., Forastiere, F., Dell'Orco, V., Pistelli, R., Kriebel, D., Pacifici, R., Zuccaro, P., Ciappi, G. and Perucci, C.A., 1996, Lung function in children and adolescents with occasional exposure to enviromental tobacco smoke. *American Journal of Respiratory Care Medicine*, **3**, 695–700.

Haby, M.M., Peat, J.K. and Woolcock, A.J., 1994, Effect of passive smoking, asthma, and respiratory infection on lung function in Australian children. *Pediatic Pulmonology*, **18**, 323–329.

Sherrill, D.L., Martinez, F.D., Lebowitz, M.D., Holdaway, M.D., Flannery, E.M., Herbison, G.P., Stanton, W.R., Silva, P.A. and Sears, M.R., 1992, Longitudinal effects of passive smoking on pulmonary function in New Zealand children. *American Review of Respiratory Disease*, **145**, 1136–1141.

Tsimoyianis, G.V., Jacobson, M.S., Feldman, J.G., Antonio-Santiago, M.T., Clutario, B.C., Nussbaum, M. and Shenker, I.R., 1987, Reduction in pulmonary function and increased frequency of cough associated with passive smoking in teenage athletes. *Pediatrics*, **80**, 32–36.

Venners, S.A., Wang, X., Chen, C., Wang, B., Ni, J., Jin, Y., Yang, J., Fang, Z., Weiss, S.T. and Xu, X., 2001, Exposure-response relationship between paternal smoking and children's pulmonary function. *American Journal of Respiratory Care Medicine*, **2**, 973–976.

Wang, X., Wypij, D., Gold, D.R., Speizer, F.E., Ware, J.H., Ferris, Jr B.G. and Dockery, D.W., 1994, A longitudinal study of the effects of parental smoking on pulmonary function in children 6–18 years. *American Journal of Respiratory Care Medicine*, **6**, 1420–1425.

73   Correlates of Playing Time in 15- to 16-Year-Old Male Soccer Players

Manuel Coelho e Silva[1], António Figueiredo[1], Hugo Relvas[1]
and Robert M. Malina[2]
[1]Youth Sports Institute. Faculty of Sport Science and Physical
Education – University of Coimbra, Portugal
[2]Research Professor, Department of Health and Physical Education,
Tarleton State University, Stephenville, TX

1. INTRODUCTION

The size, physique, and functional characteristics of young athletes typically reflect the demands of specific sports. Soccer is a sport that requires a high degree of both sport-specific skill and overall athleticism. Motivation of young soccer players to participate in the sport and their satisfaction or dissatisfaction with the sport are also relevant in player selection and development, but such data are generally lacking. The present study compares the physique, motor fitness, sport-specific skill, motivation for sport, and satisfaction with sport of 15–16 year old soccer players classified by level of playing time over the course of a season.

2. LITERATURE REVIEW

2.1. Body size of soccer players

Mean heights and weights of samples of youth soccer players 10–18 years, most of whom could be classified as elite, fluctuate about reference medians for the general population from childhood through mid-adolescence. In later adolescence, mean heights typically fall at or below the reference, while mean weights continue above the reference (Malina, 2003). The greater weight-for-height of soccer players most likely reflects an increase in the proportion of muscle mass, and a dominantly mesomorphic physique (Carter and Heath, 1990).

The English Football Association implemented changes in the way that young players are grouped for the purpose of talent identification (Simmons and Paull, 2001). The new strategy for identifying players with the most potential involves the physical matching of players within selection trials (i.e., players are matched against players of a similar size or physique). Selection is then based upon criteria such as technical skills and tactical awareness.

2.2. Discontinuing sport

An increasing number of young subjects are making a personal decision that organized sport is no longer enjoyable, and the decision is related in part to the size of playing areas, length of games, amount of physical contact, and minimal amount of activity, especially for those who are substitutes, i.e., not on the starting team (Orlick, 1974). Other reasons relate to dissatisfaction with sport organization, e.g., "the season is too long" and "too much travel" (Oldenhove, 1996). Injury is another contributory factor (De Knop *et al.*, 1996). The *Adolescent Injury Control Study*, for example, indicated that one in eleven adolescents 12–16 years of age had experienced an emergency room or hospital visit for a sport-related injury (Aaron and LaPorte, 1997). Coaches are often the target of youth criticism and dissatisfaction with sport (Weinberg, 1981). Reasons for discontinuing sport participation among American youth include the following:- "coach criticizes too much," "coach never let me play," or "coach is not fair." About 30% of Japanese junior and senior high school youth attribute sport discontinuation to preparation for entrance examinations, conflicts with other people, and the club's strong emphasis on winning (Ebihara, 1988).

As interest and motivation for sport change during adolescence, youths develop other interests and find other things to do (Brettschneider and Sack, 1996; Burton, 1988). In the context of Social Cognitive Theory (Bandura, 1986), individuals continue to participate in activities that they enjoy and that they can perform well. Conversely, individuals discontinue an activity in which they feel incompetent or feel pressured to perform.

Although the literature on motivation for and satisfaction with sport is reasonably extensive, issues related to skill and playing time in a specific sport have not been systematically considered in these contexts.

3. METHODS

The sample included 29 male soccer players (16.1±0.5 years of age) who were members of a team among the top 20 in Portugal. Somatotype was estimated with the Heath-Carter anthropometric protocol (Carter and Heath, 1990). Motor fitness was assessed with the 20-m shuttle run, 12-min run, 25-m dash, 10x5-m agility shuttle run, standing long jump, vertical jump, sit-ups, hand grip strength, and sit-and-reach. Two soccer-specific skills were tested, the wall pass and the slalom dribble (Kirkendall *et al.*, 1987). All measurements were taken at the beginning of the season. The players also completed an inventory of motives for participating in sport (Gill *et al.*, 1983) at this time. Official records for playing time of each player in all games of the season (24 games) were used to classify the players by playing time at the end of the season (median split): PT1 - those who played more time and PT2 - those who played less time. Players also completed a questionnaire dealing with sport participation satisfaction at the end of the season.

4. RESULTS

There were no differences between PT1 and PT2 in size and somatotype; those with less playing time, however, were older. Using, height, mass and somatotype as independent variables, it was not possible to predict group membership according to playing time [r_c=0.33, Wilks' Lambda=0.892, Chi-square$_{(5)}$=2.799, P=0.73].

Table 1. Comparisons between groups on morphological characteristics.

	PT1		PT2		P
	Mean	Sd	Mean	Sd	
Age (years)	15.9	0.5	16.4	0.4	**
Stature (m)	1.711	0.049	1.738	0.052	n.s.
Body mass (kg)	62.4	6.1	65.1	5.3	n.s.
Endomorphy	3.6	0.9	3.5	0.5	n.s
Mesomorphy	2.0	0.8	2.0	1.1	n.s.
Ectomorphy	3.5	0.7	3.5	0.8	n.s.
PACER (#)	89	8	102	8	**
12-min run (m)	2534	251	2867	204	**
25-m dash (seconds)	3.98	0.23	3.96	0.15	n.s.
Agility, 10x5 m (seconds)	18.73	0.78	19.09	1.02	n.s.
Standing long jump (cm)	44	7	44	6	n.s.
Vertical jump (cm)	211	18	209	15	n.s.
Sit-ups (#)	55	5	57	9	n.s.
Hand grip strength test (kg)	42.9	8.6	42.3	6.2	n.s.
Sit-and-reach (cm)	13	8	17	11	n.s.
Soccer wall pass test (#)	16.3	1.7	17.9	2.1	*
Soccer dribble test (seconds)	10.69	0.77	10.68	0.96	n.s.

*$P \leq 0.05$, **$P \leq 0.01$, n.s. (non-significant)

Players in PT1 performed significantly better in the PACER, 12-min run and soccer wall pass ($P \leq 0.05$). With motor fitness and soccer-specific skills as predictors, the discriminant function was significant [$r_c = 0.82$, Wilks' Lambda=0.332 Chi-square$_{(11)}$=19.320, $P \leq 0.05$]. The linear combination of variables with significant loadings included the PACER, 12-min run and soccer wall pass, and correctly classified 26 of the 29 players by playing time group.

Players classified as PT1 and PT2 did not differ in motivation for sport with the exception of three items (of 30): "My parents or close friends want me to participate" ($P \leq 0.01$), "I like to compete" ($P \leq 0.05$), and "Influence of coaches"($P \leq 0.05$). Athletes in PT1 reported higher scores on these items.

Results for the sport satisfaction scale at the end of the season showed two contrasts. The PT2 players reported lower satisfaction scores on 3 items: "Challenge given by games and competition" ($P \leq 0.05$), "Number of games during the season" ($P \leq 0.05$), and "Received opportunities to play and compete" ($P \leq 0.05$). The PT1 players indicated less satisfaction in 3 items: "Results in games and competitions" ($P \leq 0.01$), "Friendship in the club" ($P \leq 0.01$), and "Improvement of my technical skills" ($P \leq 0.05$).

Table 2. Comparisons between groups on motives for participating in sports.

	PT1		PT2		P
	Mean	Sd	Mean	Sd	
1. I want to improve my skills	4.1	0.9	4.6	0.6	n.s.
2. I want to be with my friends	3.6	1.2	3.9	0.8	n.s.
3. I like to win	4.3	0.9	4.4	0.9	n.s.
4. I want to get rid of energy	2.9	0.7	3.3	0.7	n.s.
5. I like to travel	2.4	0.9	2.1	1.0	n.s.
6. I want to stay in shape	4.4	0.9	4.6	0.7	n.s.
7. I like the excitement	3.1	1.1	3.5	0.8	n.s.
8. I like the teamwork	4.5	0.8	4.8	0.4	n.s.
9. My parents or close friends want me to participate	3.1	0.9	4.1	0.9	**
10. I want to learn new skills	4.3	0.7	4.7	0.6	n.s.
11. I like to meet new friends	4.1	0.8	4.1	0.8	n.s.
12. I like to do something I'm good at	4.3	0.7	4.2	0.8	n.s.
13. I want to release tension	3.4	0.7	3.2	0.7	n.s.
14. I like the rewards	3.3	1.1	3.0	0.9	n.s.
15. I like to get exercise	4.6	0.5	4.4	0.7	n.s.
16. I like to have something to do	3.5	1.1	3.3	0.7	n.s.
17. I like the action	4.0	1.0	3.7	0.8	n.s.
18. I like the team spirit	4.4	0.8	4.6	0.7	n.s.
19. I like to get out of house	2.4	0.7	2.3	0.6	n.s.
20. I like to compete	4.0	1.1	4.6	0.7	*
21. I like to feel important	2.3	1.1	2.9	1.4	n.s.
22. I like being on a team	3.9	1.4	4.2	1.2	n.s.
23. I want to go to a higher level	4.3	1.1	4.7	0.5	n.s.
24. I want to be physically fit	4.9	0.5	4.7	0.5	n.s.
25. I want to be popular	2.7	1.1	2.6	0.9	n.s.
26. I like the challenge	3.9	1.0	4.2	0.7	n.s.
27. I like the coaches	3.6	1.0	4.3	0.7	*
28. I want to gain status or recognition	3.2	1.1	3.2	1.1	n.s.
29. I like to have fun	3.7	1.1	3.9	0.7	n.s.
30. I like to use the equipment or facilities	3.4	1.3	4.1	1.0	n.s.

*$P \leq 0.05$, **$P \leq 0.01$, n.s. (non-significant)

5. DISCUSSION AND CONCLUSIONS

Although the sample size is somewhat limited, players with more playing time (PT1) performed better on two endurance tests and a soccer-specific skill test. This suggests, perhaps, that coaches promote players (more playing time) on the basis of both motor fitness and soccer-specific skills. Somatotype and body size were not relevant predictors of playing time in this age group. Athletes with more playing time perceived more social support from family and coaches, while athletes with less playing time noted a lack of opportunity to play. It appears that a combination of fitness, skill and perceived social support influence success in soccer viewed in the context of playing time. Providing more playing time for less fit and skilled players may assist in youth player development and perhaps retention.

Table 3. Comparisons between groups on the inventory of attrition with sports

	PT1		PT2		P
	Mean	Sd	Mean	Sd	
1. Level of the opponents in games and competitions	3.7	0.8	3.8	0.7	n.s.
2. Coach's emphasis in the results	4.0	0.9	3.7	1.1	n.s.
3. My friends in sports	4.3	0.8	4.2	0.8	n.s.
4. Emotions given by sport participation	4.6	0.7	4.1	0.9	n.s.
5. Support from family	4.3	0.9	4.7	0.5	n.s.
6. Results in games and competitions	2.8	1.3	1.6	0.5	**
7. Friendship in the club	4.4	0.6	3.3	1.2	**
8. Exigence of training sessions	4.1	0.7	3.7	1.0	n.s.
9. Improvements of my technical skills	4.3	0.5	3.7	1.0	*
10. Travels	3.1	1.0	3.1	1.1	n.s.
11. Behaviour of the coach	2.9	1.1	2.8	1.2	n.s.
12. Support from friends	3.9	1.0	3.6	0.9	n.s.
13. Rewards	4.0	0.7	3.6	0.7	n.s.
14. Time consuming	3.1	1.0	3.0	1.3	n.s.
15. Winnings in games and competitions	2.4	1.2	2.2	1.4	n.s.
16. Quality of facilities	2.2	1.0	1.8	0.9	n.s.
17. Techniques that have been taught to me	3.9	0.8	3.7	1.1	n.s.
18. My physical fitness level	3.9	0.5	4.1	0.5	n.s.
19. Number of training sessions per week	3.9	0.9	4.1	0.9	n.s.
20. Attention given by the coach	3.1	1.2	3.5	1.3	n.s.
21. New friends that I met in sports	4.6	0.7	4.4	0.9	n.s.
22. Enthusiasm during the training sessions	3.7	1.0	3.1	1.4	n.s.
23. Time consuming in training sessions, games and competitions	3.5	1.1	3.4	1.2	n.s.
24. Attained sport level	3.6	0.6	3.2	1.0	n.s.
25. Presence (assiduousness) of my peers in training sessions	3.4	1.0	3.5	0.7	n.s.
26. Exercises and drills in training sessions	3.6	0.8	3.1	1.0	n.s.
27. My health status	4.6	0.7	4.3	1.0	n.s.
28. Duration of sport season	3.8	0.9	3.7	0.7	n.s.
29. Type of training provided by the coach	3.3	1.1	3.1	1.1	n.s.
30. Relationship with my peers	4.1	0.9	4.0	0.9	n.s.
31. Team spirit	3.9	1.0	3.1	1.4	n.s.
32. Weight of sport in my life	4.8	0.4	4.7	0.6	n.s.
33. Support provided by club managers	3.2	0.9	2.7	1.2	n.s.
34. Physical contacts during training sessions and competitions	3.6	0.8	3.5	1.1	n.s.
35. My recognition	3.4	0.7	3.4	0.6	n.s.
36. Duration of training sessions	3.1	1.3	2.9	1.1	n.s.
37. Relationship with the coach	3.6	1.2	3.9	1.1	n.s.
38. The way that my team mates deal with me	3.7	1.3	3.5	1.1	n.s.
39. Challenge given by games and competitions	3.8	1.1	4.4	0.5	*.
40. Balance between sports and school	3.8	0.7	4.0	0.8	n.s.
41. Discipline in the training sessions	3.8	0.9	3.8	0.9	n.s.
42. Improvements that I have done	4.1	0.6	3.9	0.8	n.s.
43. Number of games and competitions during the season	3.3	1.2	4.1	0.9	*.
44. Attention that I receive from the coach	3.1	0.8	3.3	1.1	n.s.
45. Having fun in the training sessions	3.5	0.8	2.9	1.3	n.s.
46. Received opportunities to play and compete	2.4	1.3	3.6	1.3	*
47. Timetable of games and competitions	3.5	1.0	3.7	1.0	n.s.
48. Relationship of the coach with my team mates	3.5	1.0	3.5	1.1	n.s.
49. Enjoyment	4.6	0.5	4.7	0.5	n.s.
50. Referees	3.0	0.8	3.1	0.9	n.s.
51. Regulations of games and competitions	4.0	0.9	3.7	0.8	n.s.

*P$\leq$0.05, **P$\leq$0.01, n.s. (non-significant)

REFERENCES

Aaron, D.J., LaPorte, R.E., 1997, Physical activity and health: an epidemiological perspective. *Exercise and Sport Sciences Reviews*, **25**, 391–405.

Bandura, A., 1986, *Social Foundations of Thought and Action.* (Englewood Cliffs, NJ: Prentice-Hall, Inc), pp. 18–28, 228–282.

Brettschneider, W.D. and Sack, H.G., 1996, Youth sport in Europe - Germany. In *Worldwide Trends in Youth Sports*, edited by De Knop, P., Engstrom, L.M., Skirstad, B. and Weiss, M.R. (Champaign, Illinois: Human Kinetics), pp. 139–151.

Burton, D., 1988, The dropout dilemma in youth sports: documenting the problem and identifying solutions. In *Young Athletes: Biological, Psychological, and Educational Perspectives*, edited by Malina, R.M. (Champaign, Illinois: Human Kinetics), pp. 245–266.

Carter, J. and Heath, B. 1990, *Somatotyping – Development and Applications.* (Cambridge: Cambridge University Press).

De Knop, P., Vanreusel, B., Theebom, M. and Wittock, H., 1996, Youth sport in Europe - Belgium. In *Worldwide Trends in Youth Sports*, edited by De Knop, P. Engstrom, L.M., Skirstad, B. and Weiss, M.R. (Champaign, Illinois: Human Kinetics), pp. 88–100.

Ebihara, O., 1988, Characteristics of sport dropouts from organized sport: a comparison among frequent participants dropouts and non-participants. *Sociological Journal of Physical Education and Sport*, **7**, 107–109.

Gill, D., Gross, J. and Huddleston, S., 1983, Participation motivation in youth sports. *International Journal of Sport Psychology*, 14, 1–14.

Kirkendall, D.R., Gruber, J.J., and Johnson, R.E., 1987, *Measurement and Evaluation for Physical Educators.* (Champaign, Illinois: Human Kinetics Publishers, Inc).

Malina, R.M., 2003, Growth and maturity status of young soccer (football) players. In *Science and Soccer*, 2nd edition, edited by Reilly, T. and Williams, A.M. (London: Routledge), pp. 287–306.

Oldenhove, H., 1996, Youth sport in Oceania: Australia. In *Worldwide Trends in Youth Sport*, edited by De Knop, P., Engstrom, L.M., Skirstad, B. and Weiss, M.R. (Champaign, Illinois: Human Kinetics), pp. 245–259.

Orlick, T.D., 1974, The athletic drop out – a high price for inefficacy. *Canadian Associations for Health, Physical Education and Recreation Journal*, **40**.

Simmons, C. and Paull, G.C., 2001, Season of birth bias in association football. *Journal of Sports Sciences*, **19**, 677–686.

Weinberg, R., 1981, Why kids play or do not play organized sports. *Physical Educator*, **38**, 71–76.

74   The Influential Role of Task Constraints in Acquiring Football Skills

Chris Button, Joanne Smith and Gert-Jan Pepping
Department of Physical Education, Sport and Leisure Studies
University of Edinburgh, St. Leonard's Land
Edinburgh, UK

1. INTRODUCTION

1.1. Background

Co-ordination involves the patterning of limb movements in respect to environmental events and objects (Turvey, 1990). Effective co-ordination of the body in football is essential - how else could players manage to intercept the ball, bring it under control and kick with considerable force whilst still ensuring accuracy. Currently, the physical, mental and competitive demands at the highest levels of the game have increased to such an extent that players who exhibit inefficient and poorly co-ordinated techniques stand little chance of achieving success. Therefore, it is essential for football coaches to have a firm understanding of how appropriate co-ordination can be achieved by players in order that appropriate practice strategies can be devised (Davids, Button and Bennett, 2003).

In this review, the influential role of task constraints will be described with two separate experiments each related to football. In the first experiment, we describe a case study examining the kinematics of a national level player kicking a ball whilst emphasising either speed or accuracy constraints. The emphasis in the second experiment concerns whether learners benefit from practice under altered task constraints (i.e., with a small, heavy ball). Then, summarising both of these experiments, we draw some wider implications for football players and coaches.

1.2. Task constraints in football

Newell's (1986) widely cited constraints model is helpful for researchers and practitioners alike in recognising the multicausative and emergent nature of human movement behavior. Three broad categories of constraint (variables that give rise to coordination patterns) have been proposed. Organismic constraints are structural and functional characteristics of the player, such as strength, flexibility and temperament. Environmental constraints are global informational variables such as the weather, but they also include social-cultural factors (e.g., an expectant manager or crowd). Finally, task constraints are factors that are specific to the objectives and equipment of the game itself such as the offside rule, keeping possession and scoring goals (see Figure 1).

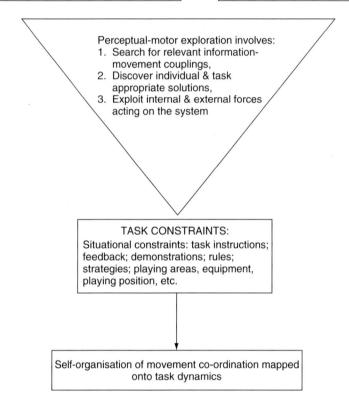

Figure 1. Schematic model to place organismic, environmental and task constraints in context.

Constraints evolve considerably over the course of a game and consequently serve to channel and guide a player's coordination patterns. Task constraints are particularly dynamic and hence can change very quickly (e.g., from having to make a tackle in defence to playing a through-ball for a striker), they are therefore important in terms of moment-to-moment adaptation (see section 2). In previous research there has been an emphasis on finding persistent changes in performance as a function of practice has meant that the transitory changes brought about by task dynamics are often ignored as noise or random variance during task and familiarisation (Newell, Liu and Mayer-Kress, 2001). In fact learners at all levels must undergo an important process of specific attunement to the current environmental and task demands (Button and Pepping, 2003). This period of attunement suggests an important role for perceptual exploration during a warm-up for example, and also whilst performing an action.

Furthermore, an awareness of task constraints can be particularly beneficial for coaches. Subtle manipulations of task requirements can be used to direct perceptual-motor search without overburdening the learner with verbal information (Hodges and Franks, 2002). This strategy can be linked to several other beneficial learning phenomena in which learners are encouraged to engage in various forms of discovery based learning (e.g., analogy learning; external focus of attention; and implicit learning). As an example in football, an altered task constraint such as restricting the number of touches allowed in a game can help to direct the learner's search for more effective ways in which to control the ball (see section 3). The important point is that the responsibility for solving the motor problem is placed upon the learner rather than simply relying upon the coach to provide an ideal solution for everyone.

2. SPEED-ACCURACY DEMANDS UPON COORDINATION OF AN INSTEP KICK

2.1. Theoretical background

Several researchers have examined the kinematics of kicking under a range of task constraints (for a review see Lees and Davids, 2002). Performing an instep kick typically requires a sequential chain of proximal-to-distal (trunk-to-foot) movements through the player's body to be timed relative to the arrival of the ball next to the supporting foot. It should be noted that in many of the studies that have quantitatively analysed the kinematics of an instep kick, an initially stationary ball has been used. Subtle variations of the required movement pattern will be necessary in a game as a function of changing task constraints, such as shooting a moving ball from an indirect free-kick or weighting a pass appropriately for the run of a striker.

The time window in which players must coincide the occurrence of maximum foot velocity with ball-contact is typically very small (i.e. just a few milliseconds) depending on the relative ball and foot speed. As players must also impart force in the appropriate direction for accuracy, a conflict in task demands results in what many researchers have termed the speed-accuracy trade-off (Lees and Nolan, 2002). For novice players, timing an instep kick with a moving ball is noticeably difficult to achieve. However, as a function of practice and improving perceptual guidance, players seem to match their own movements with the ball's trajectory almost effortlessly. The following experiment examines how a skilled, club level player coordinates the instep kick with a moving ball. The role of task constraints was also emphasised with instructions to kick with either maximum speed or maximum accuracy.

2.2. Methods

At the time of testing, the male participant (aged 21 years old, height – 1.78 m, mass – 76 kg) was playing for both a national university and a professional club side in Scotland and had 16 years of playing experience. The player was asked to kick a standard football using a one-step approach, instep kick. The ball was delivered via a sloping ramp so that approach velocity was approximately the same (2 m.s^{-1}) during each trial. During the speed condition, 10 trials were performed with the player instructed to try to achieve maximum ball speed. In the accuracy condition, a further 10 trials were carried out with the player being asked to kick the ball as accurately as possible at a 50 cm x 50 cm target (positioned 4.5 m away).

The trials were filmed using a JVC GR-DV 2000 digital camera at a frequency of 50 Hz and variable shutter speed function of 1/250 to 1/4000. The camera was positioned to the right side of the subject and perpendicular to the primary plane of motion. Five joint markers on the right side of the player's body were used to aid digitisation of the images. These were placed on the player's right shoulder, hip, knee, ankle and the toe. The centre point of the ball was also manually digitised. The start of the movement was taken to be the start of the back swing, that is, when the kicking foot was no longer in contact with the floor. The end of the kick was defined as the end of the follow through of the right leg.

2.3. Results and discussion

The main results are summarised below:
- Increased ranges of joint motion (RoM) in the maximum speed trials enabled the player to increase the momentum of the kicking leg (see Figure 2). In the accuracy condition, RoMs were decreased so as to provide a smaller 'window' of joint space in which a more precise ball contact and resulting ball direction can occur.
- There was evidence of hip and joint coupling (strong correlations) in both the accuracy and maximum speed conditions.
- At ball contact, the hip and knee joints moved in the same direction (in-phase relationship) during the accuracy condition, as opposed to an anti-phase state in the maximum speed condition.

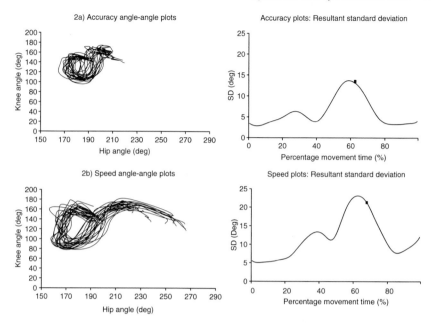

Figure 2a) Speed, 2b) Accuracy. Right knee and hip angle-angle graphs (left) with associated standard deviations as a function of time (right). Several exemplary trials are plotted in each graph overlaying each other.

- In the Maximum Speed trials (Figure 3), the hip peak velocity occurred prior to knee and foot peaks. In both the maximum speed and accuracy trials ball contact occurred within 5 ms of peak foot angular velocity.

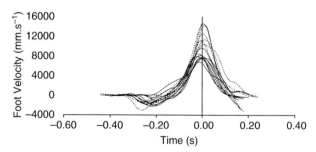

Figure 3. Representative trials from the accuracy (solid line) and maximum speed (broken lines) conditions. The time scale shows the point of ball-foot contact at 0 seconds. Note the clustering of maximum foot velocity around ball contact in both conditions.

The findings of this study indicate that a skilled player used a sensitive form of perceptual control to kick a moving ball In both conditions, peak velocity of the foot occurred within 10 ms of ball contact. However, kicking technique was altered within each trial to satisfy the different demands placed upon the player. For example, in the maximum speed trials the range of motion about the hip and knee was typically increased to generate more force at ball-contact. In the accuracy trials, the hip and knee was extended at the same time (rather than in a chain-like fashion) to impart a more controlled direction of force.

In a related study, Lees and Nolan (2002) examined the role of speed and accuracy constraints on kicking technique in a penalty kick simulation. Two expert players took penalties and were asked to place an emphasis on achieving either maximum accuracy (as in kicking to put the ball exactly in the corner of the goal) or on achieving maximum speed (as in kicking the ball with as great a force as possible). When the footballers focussed on accuracy there was significantly more variability of the foot at ball contact compared to when they focused on speed/force. The authors suggested that this could be due to late modifications in co-ordination during the kicking action to achieve an accurate placement of the foot at contact. In fact, recent research indicates the visual mapping of the moving ball within the brain is assigned to a subconscious neural pathway, allowing the learner to pay (conscious) attention to other factors, such as the position of team-mates on the pitch, at the same time as guiding the kicking leg.

3. MANIPULATING EQUIPMENT TO DIRECT LEARNING

3.1. Studies with learners

Coaches may already be familiar with the concept of manipulating task constraints such as rules, to facilitate learning. The concept of manipulating relevant equipment during practice is, perhaps, less common but is beginning to receive increasing support in the motor learning literature (Araujo et al., 2004). Over the last decade a football designed in South America, the Futebol de Salão (FDS), has been used increasingly during practice. The FDS ball is smaller (i.e., similar in size to a size 3 football) and heavier than a regulation size five football. A regular size five ball has a coefficient of restitution of between 45–48% with a recommended pressure of 11.4 psi (pounds per square inch). The FDS ball has rebound resilience ranging from 10–15% and an inflation pressure of 8.5 psi. Surprisingly, despite its target market, there has also been little previous work evaluating the effects of the FDS ball on children's ball skills, compared to regulation size 4 and 5 balls that are commonly used in junior football.

3.2. Methods

Button et al. (1999) recruited 11-year-old children who were beginners at football and, therefore, more likely to be sensitive to practice over a short period of time. After a pre-test to equate basic skill level, one group practised dribbling and juggling skills with the FDS, while a control group practised with a regulation size 5 football. The aim of the juggling test was to keep the ball in the air for as long as possible using any legal body parts under the laws of association football. The aim of the dribbling test was to examine the participants' ability to complete a course of four cones in a zigzag formation as fast as possible whilst keeping the football under control. The FDS and control groups practised separately over a 5-week training programme, for 2×40-min sessions per week. Each session formed part of a standardised training programme delivered by a qualified coach. All participants undertook post-tests employing the juggling and dribbling skills, conducted one week after the programme. The size 5 football was used for both groups in the pre- and post-tests.

3.3. Results and discussion

Both groups significantly improved in terms of juggling and dribbling performance over the course of the programme. For the juggling test, results indicated that the FDS experimental group juggled with the conventional ball more successfully than the control group (see Figure 4). There were no differential effects between groups for the results of the dribbling test.

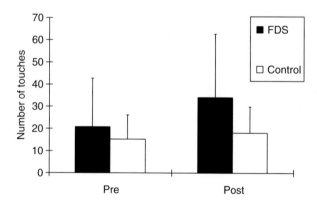

Figure 4. Performance in juggling test before and after practice intervention.

It would seem that the nature of the soccer-specific test mediated the effects. Good performance on the juggling test is achieved by keeping the ball in the air with any part of the body except the arms and hands. Achieving this under the constraints of a ball that is heavier and smaller, may have encouraged a different kind of co-ordination to that used through practice with a regulation ball. The lack of differences between the two groups on the dribbling test suggests that the learning of this skill did not benefit from the constraints imposed by the Futebol de Salao. It is possible that success at the dribbling task was biased more towards running speed rather than ball control. Success at the juggling task was not restricted by the participants' physical abilities. Rather, as noted by two impartial F.A. coaches, that players who practiced with FDS maintained better ball control (i.e., keep the ball close to the body) with a regulation football that resulted in successful performance. The studies of Chapman et al. (2001) and Williams (2000) extended the work of Button et al. (1999) by investigating the effects of ball characteristics on acquisition of ball control in completely novice children and intermediate adult players. In summary, it seems that manipulating the characteristics of football balls can enhance children's ball control, provided the learners are already at the 'control' stage of skill acquisition (Newell, 1986). Stability of task constraints is initially important during learning so that new coordination patterns are assembled, whereas manipulation of equipment characteristics can fine-tune more established actions. Determining how skill level and task constraints mediate the emergence of skilled behaviour poses important challenges for future work.

4. GENERAL IMPLICATIONS

Co-ordination in football involves a mapping of intrinsic dynamics (movement tendencies) onto rapidly changing task constraints. For players this often entails breaking symmetrical movement tendencies that exist both across joints and across limbs. As such, coaches must be aware of how individual players seek to satisfy transitory task constraints within practice (e.g., kicking a moving ball towards a target). Indeed, Newell et al. (2001) pointed out the capability of the learner to develop across different time scales of constraints should be central to any theory of learning. An important objective for future research is to adopt a macroscopic approach and identify which control parameters are used to guide players (and teams) into, and out of, stable patterns (see McGarry et al., 2001). In dynamic sporting environments, such as playing football, it might be argued that movement variability rather than consistency is the key to success. It is important that players are able to perceive information about the dynamic properties of the ball and other players to guide and adjust their own actions continually. Coaches often try to reduce the variability of actions and promote repetitiveness and segmentation of skills. Many practice drills in football are typically conducted either with the ball starting in a static position, or with the ball being fed to the player repetitively from a set position or in a set approach. Such simplified practices mean that the receiving player does not have to deal with the changes in task-related information that are realistic of a game. From a motor control perspective, it is unlikely that the performer's perceptual systems will be as actively engaged (or developed) during interception if practice does not reflect game-like conditions. Davids et al. (2003) indicated that training under random conditions (i.e. in which both the feed and the target are changed unpredictably) could result in a form of experimentation on the part of the athlete which would aid them in their search for optimal co-ordination patterns. In so doing, players would be encouraged to explore which allows them to discover individual appropriate movement solutions rather than simply repeating or copying a solution that they cannot transfer appropriately into a match situation.

REFERENCES

Araújo, D., Davids, K., Bennett, S., Button, C., and Chapman, G., 2004, Emergence of sport skills under constraints, In Skill Acquisition in Sport, edited by Williams, A.M., Hodges, N., Scott, M. and Court, M. (London: Taylor & Francis).

Button, C., Bennett, S., Davids, K. and Stephenson, J., 1999, The effects of practicing with a small, heavy soccer ball on the development of soccer related skills. Invited Communication to British Association of Sport and Exercise Sciences Annual Conference. Leeds Metropolitan University, Sept 9.

Chapman, G., Bennett, S.J. and Davids, K., 2001, The effects of equipment constraints on the acquisition of juggling and dribbling in soccer. Communication to 6th Annual Congress of European College of Sports Science (Perspectives and Profiles), Cologne, Germany.

Davids, K., Button, C. and Bennett, S.J., 2003, Coordination and Control of Movement in Sport: An Ecological Approach. (Champaign, Ill: Human Kinetics).

Hodges, N.J. and Franks, I., 2002, Modelling coaching practice: the role of instruction and demonstration. Journal of Sports Sciences, **20**, 793–811.

Lees, A. and Nolan, L., 2002, 3D kinematic analysis of the instep kick under speed and accuracy conditions. In *Science and Football IV*, edited by Reilly, T., Spinks, W. and Murphy, A. (London: E&FN Spon), pp. 16–21.

Lees, A. and Davids, K., 2002, Co-ordination and control of kicking in soccer. In Interception Actions in Sport: Information and Movement, edited by Davids, K., Savelsbergh, G., Bennett, S. and van der Kamp, J. (London: Taylor & Francis), pp. 273–287.

Newell, K.M., 1986, Constraints on the development of coordination. In Motor Development in Children: Aspects of Coordination and Control, edited by Wade, M., and Whiting, H.T.A. (Dordrecht, Netherlands: Martinus Nijhoff), pp. 341–360.

Newell, K.M., Liu, Y.-T and Mayer-Kress, G., 2001, Time scales in motor learning and development. Psychological Review, **108**(1), 57–82.

Turvey, M.T., 1990, Coordination. *American Psychologist,* **45**, 938–953.

Williams, M., 2000, Transfer of learning in football: From juggling to ball control. *'Insight' - The F.A. Coaches Association Journal,* **4** (3), 30–31.

75   Perceptual-Motor Skills in International Level Youth Soccer Players

P. Luhtanen, M. Blomqvist and T. Vänttinen
KIHU-Research Institute for Olympic Sports, Jyväskylä, Finland

1. INTRODUCTION

Soccer is complex game in nature, with evidence of anthropometric, physiological, psychological, perceptual and technical contributions to performance (Reilly et al. 2000). In addition, there is a requirement for game knowledge to develop strategy and a "game sense" or awareness. Consequently, any attempts to identify early soccer talent must take into account these multiple factors together with the influence of growth and maturation across the development cycle.

A player in a game makes decisions relative to his overall plan assisted by perceptual stimuli, which come from all sides. According to his past experiences the stimuli may have a meaning or not for him. In a game, the player tries to attend only to the important perceptual stimuli such as the opponent in the immediate vicinity or a team-mate anticipating a pass from him. The relevant information is then processed in the central nervous system. On the basis of his perception and interpretation, he makes his decision. It may be to make a pass to his/her teammate or to control the ball and look elsewhere. In any decision, the signals are sent from brain to the appropriate muscle groups to begin a series of movement actions to deal with the intention. The movements are monitored internally.

A player's ability to make movement responses in the game is limited to the speed at which he can react to the stimuli around him. The time taken to begin to respond to a stimulus is called reaction time. This is the period of time it takes to process the information contained in the stimulus. Movement time is the time taken to complete the actual response once the decision has been made to act. The whole event between the presentation of the stimulus to the completion of the movement is called the response time. "Eye hand coordination" involves the integration of the eyes and hand(s) as a unit. Any deficit in these abilities will show itself in slow and clumsy movements or handling of the ball.

There is a physical limit to the visual field. In order to see more the head has to be moved so that another visual field is apparent to the individual. "Peripheral awareness" is the ability to keep focussed centrally while being aware of essential information around and is especially important in team activities such as soccer. The range of visual field varies very little between people, but the ability to notice and pay attention to events within their own visual field varies enormously. It obviously varies also within an individual to the extent of one's concentration of attention.

Skilled players use their superior knowledge to control the eye movement patterns necessary for seeking and picking up important sources of information. The nature of the task plays an important role in constraining the type of search used. Visual search behaviour also differs between defensive and offensive players. These observations have implications for the development of perceptual training programmes and identification of potential soccer players (Williams, 2000).

The purpose of this study was to compare these perceptual-motor skills (reaction time, eye-hand coordination, eye-foot coordination, eye-hand and foot coordination and peripheral awareness) of international level soccer players in different age groups

2. METHODS

2.1. Subjects

Ninety international level Finnish soccer players participated in this study. They represented different age groups and gender as follows: Boys -15 n=23, Girls -15 n=17   Boys -17 n=18 and Girls -17 n=32. Players were tested during their training camp for simple reaction time, eye-hand/foot coordination and peripheral awareness.

2.2. Reaction time measurements

Simple reaction time was assessed using the Wayne Saccadic Fixator (WSF) (Figure 1a). The participant was instructed to extinguish the red signal light as fast as possible and the responses were given in the eye-hand reaction test with the right index finger and in the eye-foot reaction test with the right foot using a special foot switch pad. Reaction time (programme 9–18 was used to measure single reaction time) was measured as the delay between illumination of the stimulus light and the participants' response. In total, 10 trials were presented, with the mean of the last five responses being calculated as dependent measures for hand (RTH, ms) and foot (RTF, ms).

2.3. Eye-hand/foot coordination measurements

In testing eye-hand/foot coordination (programme 9–156 was used to measure eye hand/foot coordination for the target lights located in the directions of 12, 3, 6 and 9 o'clock positions) the participants stood facing the WSF within comfortable reaching distance and the central light was placed at eye level. A proactive test was selected to measure a form of faster eye-hand/foot coordination. In this test the instruction was to distinguish the light, by using hands, feet and both hands and feet, as soon as it was seen, then do the same with the next light that comes on, and so on. After an initial practise trial, two test trials were administered and the best score (number of extinguished lights in 30 s) was derived as dependent measure for hands (EHC), feet (EFC) and hands and feet (EHFC).

Figure 1a. Saccadic fixator.   Figure 1b. Peripheral awareness trainer.

2.4. Measurement of peripheral awareness

The ability of the participants to respond rapidly to peripherally presented stimuli was assessed by using the Wayne Peripheral Awareness Trainer (PAT) (Figure 1b). In this test, the participant was told to fixate on a central constant yellow light and to move a hand-held joystick after detecting peripheral lights in different directions (a control combination of display-testing, mode switch-8 lights and timer 60 seconds – off was used). After an initial practise trial, three test trials were administered and the mean of the best response times in each direction was calculated as dependent measure (PAT, ms).

2.5. Statistical methods

Means and standard deviations of each variable were calculated. A MANOVA was applied to study significant main effects for age groups and gender in reaction time and coordination measurements ($P<0.05$). An independent 2-tailed t-test was used to analyse differences in age and gender groups separately ($P<0.05$). An ANOVA was applied to peripheral awareness test to detect differences between age groups and gender ($P<0.05$).

3. RESULTS

A MANOVA revealed a significant main effect for gender in reaction times (Wilks' lambda=0.84, $F_{1,86}=8.345$, $P<0.001$ and in eye-hand / foot coordination Wilks' lambda=0.96 $F_{1,86}=9.353$, $P<0.001$). Furthermore, an independent t-test indicated that in the younger age group significant differences between genders were found in all measured variables whereas in the older age group significant differences were detected only in RTH and EFC (Table 1). An ANOVA for peripheral awareness indicated a significant main effect for age ($F_{1,86}=5.770$, $P<0.05$), gender ($F_{1,86}=22.221$, $P<0.001$) and interaction ($F_{1,86}=7.174$, $P<0.01$). Moreover, an independent t-test showed that boys were better than girls in the younger age group and that the differences between the age groups were only found in girls.

Table 1. Means and standard deviations for the measured variables.

Group	G-15		G-17		B-15		B-17	
	mean	S.D.	mean	S.D.	mean	S.D.	mean	S.D.
RTH (ms)	237	30	234	29	209	27	214	20
RTF (ms)	256	31	250	26	233	23	245	22
EHC	38.41	3.55	41.09	3.82	42.35	3.26	42.11	3.18
EFC	37.71	6.02	39.34	4.29	44.78	4.70	43.72	5.87
EHFC	35.00	4.09	37.78	3.37	40.04	3.74	39.72	4.10
PAT (ms)	345	76	288	51	261	41	264	37

4. DISCUSSION

The results indicated that in the younger age group boys had significantly faster reactions, better coordination and peripheral awareness when compared to girls. In addition, the findings revealed that older girls had significantly better peripheral awareness when compared to the younger ones. The mean reaction times in RTH and PAT found in this study were faster than those found when studying undergraduate college students (16–25 years) (Wood and Abernethy, 1997). Expert soccer players have also been reported to have faster reactions than novices and intermediate players and better coordination than novices in the corresponding age groups (Blomqvist et al., 2002). It could be argued therefore, that soccer specific training seems to enhance the development of perceptual-motor skills. On the other hand, the gender differences found in this study imply that in coaching girls intensive practices with high tempo might be used more in order to develop reactions (perception and decision-making) as well as coordination.

REFERENCES

Blomqvist, M., Vänttinen, T., Luhtanen, P. and Norvapalo, K., 2002, Differences in perceptual-motor skills in novice, intermediate and expert soccer players. In Proceedings of the 7th Annual Congress of the European College of Sport Science, edited by Koskolou, M., Geladas, N., and Klissouras, V. (Athens: Pashalidis Medical Publisher), pp. 389.

Reilly, T., Williams, A.M., Nevill, A. and Franks, A., 2000, A multidisciplinary approach to talent identification in soccer, *Journal of Sports Sciences*, **18**, 695–702.

Williams, A.M., 2000, Perceptual skills in soccer: Implications for talent identification and development. *Journal of Sports Sciences*, **18**, 737–750.

Wood, J. M. and Abernethy, B., 1997, An assessment of the efficacy of sport training programs. *Optometry and Vision Science*, **74**, 646–659.

76   Temporal Structuring Ability (TSA) in Young Novice, Intermediate and Expert Soccer Players

P. Luhtanen[1], M. Blomqvist[1], T. Vänttinen[1],
K. Norvapalo[1] and H. Selänne[2]
[1]KIHU – Research Institute for Olympic Sports
[2]LIKES – Research Center for Sport and Health Sciences,
Jyväskylä, Finland

1. INTRODUCTION

Skilled soccer players can recall and recognize patterns of play more effectively than their less skilled counterparts. This ability to encode, retrieve, and recognize sport-specific information is due to complex and discriminating long-term memory structures and is crucial to anticipation in soccer. Similarly, experts use their knowledge of situational probabilities to anticipate future events. They have a better idea of what is likely to happen when given a particular set of circumstances (Williams, 2000).

It has been claimed, especially in the Latin American countries, that soccer is more art and music than science. However, there is a belief that science and music can help in soccer. Several researchers (e.g. Hirtz, 1976 and Winter, 1981) have named five basic components of motor skills. These are kinesthetic separating capacity, spatial orientation, balance, reaction capacity and rhythm sense. Sense of rhythm can be an essential part of motor learning and performance (Barsch, 1967). Perceived or reproduced rhythm refers to musical aptitude and performance rhythm to motor skills.

Karma has created a method for measuring musical aptitude. He has devised tests for measuring auditory or visual temporal material (Karma, 1994). Temporal structuring is closely related to rhythm sense. In this case, the stimulus is not sound but temporal visual patterns. Karma has studied if visual temporal structuring shows essential similarities with musical aptitude defined as auditory structuring ability and measured with a modification of Karma's auditory structuring test. A rather high correlation was reported between auditory and visual temporal structuring process (Karma, 1994).

In this study, rhythmic sense is interpreted as an ability to identify structures, which appear in time and are connected to each other forming recognisable periods. The purpose of this study was to describe and compare auditory and visual structuring ability of young novice, intermediate and expert soccer players.

2. METHODS

2.1. Subjects

Novice (n=67), intermediate (n=55) and expert (n=56) Finnish soccer players (15–17 years) participated in this study. The temporal structuring ability (TSA) of participants was tested by using a modification of Karma´s (1990) musical aptitude test. The test procedure consisted of 40 auditory and 30 visual items in which sound patterns (auditory) or temporal visual patterns (visual) were compared. Participants were first tested for auditory and then for visual structuring ability. Prior to both tests, all participants were given the same instructions about how to take the test and were then familiarized with the test by rehearsing three items together with the tester. The test began after the rehearsal and there was a 10-min break between the tests in order to maintain participants´ concentration.

2.2. Measuring auditory structuring

Musical aptitude is defined as the ability to structure sound material. The test has been devised to measure auditory structuring ability by avoiding the effects of culture and training as much as possible. In each item (n = 40) a small pattern of sound is played three times without pause or other indication of where the repetitions end and begin. The participant's task is to divide the series mentally into three similar parts and to form an image of one such part. To test the correctness of the image, a fourth pattern is played after a pause. The subject checks same or different after comparing this pattern with the mental image. The answers were either "yes" or "no" and the scores were summarised to determine participant's auditory structuring ability.

2.3. Measurement of visual structuring

The visual temporal structuring test included 30 items. The test blinks a square on a television screen. The visual test was a parallel version of the auditory test by changing the parameters of the auditory test items according to the following rules. Long and short tones were replaced by long and short durations for the display of the square. An item with duration changes would have the same sequence duration in both tests. The visual item type is very similar to sending Morse code with a lamp. High and low pitched tones were replaced by squares with different light intensities:- bright and dark. In both the auditory and visual test each element of the series (tone or square) consists of approximately 4/5 of presence of the stimulus and 1/5 inter-stimulus silence. The answers were either "yes" or "no" and the scores were summarised to determine the participant's visual structuring ability.

2.4. Statistical methods

A one-way ANOVA was applied to auditory and visual TSA for novice, intermediate and expert groups ($P<0.05$). A Pearson´s correlation coefficient was used to examine the relationship between auditory and visual structuring ability.

3. RESULTS

The mean values of auditory structuring scores were in novice, intermediate and expert groups 31.2±5.7, 32.0±5.7 and 32.4±4.9, respectively. The mean values of visual structuring scores were in novice, intermediate and expert groups 27.0±3.0, 27.3±2.4 and 28.5±1.4, respectively. A significant difference between the groups was detected in visual structuring ability ($F_{2,175}$) = 66.01, P = 0.004. A Bonferroni post hoc analysis indicated that the experts had significantly higher scores in the test of visual structuring ability when compared to novice   (P=0.004) and intermediate groups (P=0.049). A correlation between auditory and visual temporal structuring process was r = 0.47, P<0.001.

4. DISCUSSION

The auditory and visual temporal structuring ability of novices was comparable to the general level of test scores (auditory; good level 36-32 points, visual 26±3.6) (Selänne et al., 2000). The intermediate and expert soccer players represented good level of the auditory structuring ability but the scores were lower when compared to the national levels golf players (33.8±3.6) in the corresponding age group (Selänne et al., 2000). Furthermore, the visual structuring ability of expert soccer players was slightly higher than in national level ice hockey players (27.5±2.2) in the same age group (Selänne et al., 2000). The correlation between the auditory and the visual test obtained in this study was lower than the value of 0.56 reported by Karma (1994).

In future, more information is needed about auditory and visual structuring ability related to "recall pattern recognition", anticipation and different player positions (goalkeepers and field players) in soccer.

REFERENCES

Barsch, R.J., 1967, Achieving Perceptual - Motor Efficiency. (Seattle, Washington: Special Child Publication).

Hirtz, P., 1976, Die koordinative Vervollkommung als wesentlicher Bestandteil der körperlichen Grundausbildung. Körpererziehung, **26**, 8/9, 381–387.

Karma, K., 1994, Auditory and visual temporal structuring: How important is sound to musical thinking? Psychology of Music, **22**, 20–30.

Selänne, H., Kolehmainen, A. and Karma, K., 2000, Is musical sense of rhythm important in space: temporal structuring ability among skilled Finnish ice-hockey juniors and seniors. In Proceedings of the 5th Annual Congress of the European College of Sport Science, edited by Avela, J., Komi, P.V. and Komulainen, J. (Jyväskylä; Gummerus), p. 672.

Williams, A.M., 2000, Perceptual skills in soccer: Implications for talent identification and development. *Journal of Sports Sciences*, **18**, 737–750.

Winter, R., 1981, Grundlegende Orientierungen zur Entwicklungsgemässen Vervollkommung der Bewegungskoordination im Kindes- und Jungendalter. 2.Teil: Schulkindalter. Medizin und Sport, **21**, 8–9, 254–256.

Part VIII
Physiology and Nutrition

77 Electromyographic Analysis of Activity Representative of a Soccer Game

N. Rahnama[1,2], T. Reilly[1] and A. Lees[1]

[1]Research Institute for Sport and Exercise Sciences, Liverpool John Moores University, Liverpool, UK

[2]Physical Education Department, Isfahan University, Isfahan, Iran

1. INTRODUCTION

Surface analysis of muscle activity has received increasing attention in recent years. Electromyography (EMG) has been useful in comparing muscular activity among different movements and it is a valuable tool in evaluating neuromuscular co-ordination. During maximal voluntary contraction several changes are observed in the root mean square (RMS) of the electromyograms. The RMS represents an average of the action potentials recorded at the electrode site. The RMS generally shows a gradual decrement during sustained maximum voluntary contractions, although conflicting results have been reported in this respect (Moritani et al., 1985). Oda and Kida (2001) investigated the occurrence of neuromuscular fatigue during maximal concurrent hand grip, elbow extension and flexion in eight physically fit subjects and reported a significant decrease in the RMS value in biceps brachii but no changes in the triceps.

Most studies of neuromuscular activity and fatigue have evaluated isometric contractions. Isometric contractions may not be representative of muscle activity and fatigue developed during dynamic activities such as human locomotion (Green, 1995). Indeed, available data suggest that the development of fatigue may be specific to contraction type, activity and its duration (Tesch et al., 1990). However, no study appears to have compared neuromuscular fatigue profiles during prolonged exercise representative of a soccer game. So, the present aim was to analyse muscle activity of the major lower extremity muscles during an intermittent exercise protocol designed to simulate the activity of a soccer game.

2. MATERIALS AND METHODS

Ten amateur soccer players (age 21.40 ± 3.13 years; height 1.77 ± 0.06 m; mass 74.55 ± 8.5 kg) volunteered to participate in this study. Participants were recruited if they were not injured or rehabilitating from injury at the time of testing and were aged between 19–30 years. Informed consent was obtained from all subjects in accordance with the University's ethical procedures before data collection. Ethical approval for the study was obtained from the institution's Human Ethics Committee. The EMG activity of major lower limb muscles measured according the procedures that are described in turn.

All tests were performed on a programmable motorised treadmill (Pulsar, HP Cosmos, Nussforf-Traunstein, Germany). The EMG activity was recorded and stored using a Biopac system (MP 100 system, INC, Biopac systems INC, Santa Barbara). Data were collected at 1000 Hz from the rectus femoris, biceps femoris, tibialis anterior and gastrocnemius muscles. Each subject performed a warm-up including some soccer-specific stretching exercises and running at a slow speed on the treadmill. Then the subject performed the test protocol which included speeds of walking (6 km.h^{-1}), jogging (12 km.h^{-1}), running (15 km.h^{-1}) and sprinting (21 km.h^{-1}) for a duration of 10 to 30 seconds in a variable order, during which the sEMG was recorded for 10 seconds. The first record was taken before commencing the soccer simulation. The subject then performed a 45-min soccer-specific intermittent exercise protocol which consisted of the four different exercise intensities. The EMG activity was recorded after finishing the first half of the work-rate simulation. Finally, the EMG activity was recorded for the third time after finishing the second half of the simulated work-rate. The EMG data were analysed using custom written software to derive RMS values over a single gait cycle.

The raw EMG data were low-pass filtered at 350 Hz and high–pass filtered at 10 Hz to eliminate movement artifacts, using a Butterworth fourth-order zero-lag filter. Data were then full-wave rectified and low-pass filtered again at 6 Hz to obtain a linear envelope. The RMS of the EMG signal over 10 cycles was obtained for quantifying the EMG signal. Analyses of variance (ANOVA) for repeated measures with the Least Significant Difference test (LSD) were used where EMG was recorded at three time points (pre-exercise, half-way and post-exercise). The level of significance for all tests was set at $P < 0.05$.

3. RESULTS

The RMS values for the EMG activity per cycle of each muscle [rectus femoris, biceps femoris, tibialis anterior and gastrocnemius] are presented in turn. Each muscle was analysed with a two-factor (condition × speed) repeated measures ANOVA. The three conditions were pre-exercise, half-way and post-exercise. The four speed factors were running at 6 km.h^{-1}, 12 km.h^{-1}, 15 km.h^{-1} and 21 km.h^{-1} on the treadmill.

3.1. Rectus femoris muscle

A significant main effect was found for condition ($F_{2, 18} = 5.39$; $P < 0.05$). The LSD tests indicated a significant difference between the pre-exercise and half-way measures ($\bar{x} = 0.648$ vs 0.594; $P < 0.05$) and between the pre-exercise and post-exercise measures ($\bar{x} = 0.648$ vs 0.587; $P < 005$). A significant main effect was also found for speed ($F_{1.286, 11.577} = 106.35$; $P < 0.001$). The LSD tests indicated a significant difference between the 6 and 12 km.h^{-1} speeds ($\bar{x} = 0.214$ vs 0.545; $P < 0.001$), between the 6 and 15 km.h^{-1} speeds ($\bar{x} = 0.214$ vs 0.682; $P < 0.001$), between the 6 and 21 km.h^{-1} ($\bar{x} = 0.214$ vs 0.997; $P < 0.001$), between the 12 and 15 km.h^{-1} ($\bar{x} = 0.545$ vs 0.682; $P < 0.001$) and between the 15 and 21 km.h^{-1} ($\bar{x} = 0.682$ vs 0.997; $P < 0.001$).

A significant condition × speed interaction was found ($F_{3.36, 30.25} = 6.85$; P < 0.001). The LSD tests indicated a significant difference between the pre-exercise measures and those obtained after the game (P < 0.05) and also between half-way and post-exercise (P < 0.05) at 6 and 21 km.h^{-1}, 12 and 21 km.h^{-1} and 15 and 21 km.h^{-1} speeds. In effect the data became more divergent with increases in speed and as fatigue developed (Figure 1a).

3.2. Biceps femoris muscle

A significant main effect was found for condition ($F_{2, 18} = 7.57$; P < 0.01). The LSD tests indicated a significant difference between the pre-exercise and half-way measures ($\bar{x} = 0.559$ vs 0.479 , P < 0.01) and between the pre-exercise and post-exercise values ($\bar{x} = 0.559$ vs 0.481; P < 0.05).

A significant main effect on the EMG was found for speed ($F_{1.31, 11.79} = 122.33$; P < 0.001). The LSD tests indicated a significant difference between the 6 and 12 km.h^{-1} speeds ($\bar{x} = 0.184$ vs 0.426, P < 0.001), between 6 and 15 km.h^{-1} ($\bar{x} = 0.184$ vs 0.552; P < 0.001), between 6 and 21 km.h^{-1} ($\bar{x} = 0.184$ vs 0.863; P < 0.001), between 12 and 15 km.h^{-1} ($\bar{x} = 0.426$ vs 0.552; P < 0.001) and between the 15 and 21 km.h^{-1} ($\bar{x} = 0.552$ vs 0.863; P < 0.001).

A significant condition × speed interaction was found ($F_{6, 54} = 10.81$; P < 0.001). The LSD tests indicated a significant difference between the pre-exercise and post-exercise values (P < 0.001) in 6 and 21 km.h^{-1} speeds, 12 and 21 km.h^{-1} speeds and 15 and 21 km.h^{-1} speeds. In effect the data became more divergent as speed increased and fatigue became more pronounced (see Figure 1b).

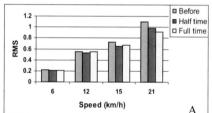 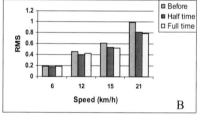

Figure 1. The mean RMS value of EMG activity for (A) the rectus femoris and (b) the biceps femoris for different conditions and speeds for running on a treadmill (EMG is in arbitrary units).

3.3. Tibialis anterior muscle

A significant main effect on RMS was found for condition ($F_{2, 18} = 4.27$; P < 0.05). The LSD tests indicated a significant difference between the pre-exercise and post-exercise measures ($\bar{x} = 0.348$ vs 0.316; P < 0.05).

A significant main effect was found for speed ($F_{1.53, 13.79} = 101.09$; P < 0.001). The LSD tests indicated a significant difference between the 6 and 12 km.h^{-1} speeds ($\bar{x} = 0.202$ vs 0.297; P < 0.001), between 6 and 15 km.h^{-1} ($\bar{x} = 0.202$ vs 0.346; P < 0.001), between 6 and 21 km.h^{-1} ($\bar{x} = 0.202$ vs 0.464; P < 0.001), between 12 and 15 km.h^{-1} ($\bar{x}$ = 0.297 vs 0.346; P < 0.001) and between 15 and 21 km.h^{-1} ($\bar{x}$ = 0.346 vs 0.464; P < 0.001).

A significant condition × speed interaction was found ($F_{2.60, 23.41}$ = 3.53, P < 0.05). The LSD tests indicated a significant difference between the observations made pre-exercise and after the game (P < 0.05) at 6 and 21 km.h^{-1} and 12 and 21 km.h^{-1}, also showing similar divergence as in other muscles (Figure 2a).

3.4. Gastrocnemius muscle

No significant main effect was found for condition using repeated measures ANOVA. A significant main effect was found for speed ($F_{3, 27}$ = 51.93, P < 0.001). The LSD tests indicated a significant difference between 6 and 12 km.h^{-1} ($\bar{x}$ = 0.266 vs 0.488; P < 0.001), between 6 and 15 km.h^{-1} ($\bar{x}$ = 0.266 vs 0.511; P < 0.001), between 6 and 21 km.h^{-1} ($\bar{x}$ = 0.266 vs 0.641; P < 0.001), and between 15 and 21 km.h^{-1} ($\bar{x}$ = 0.511 vs 0.641; P < 0.001). A significant condition × speed interaction was not found using repeated measures ANOVA (see Figure 2b).

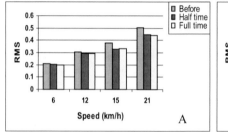 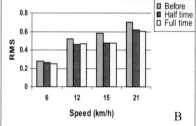

Figure 2. The mean RMS value of EMG activity for (A) the tibialis anterior and (B) the gastrocnemius for different conditions and speeds for running on a treadmill (EMG is in arbitrary units).

4. DISCUSSION

The purpose of this study was to establish the existence of fatigue in the activity of major lower-limb muscles at different speeds of running representing a selected fundamental movement pattern in soccer. In general, the RMS values for rectus femoris, biceps femoris and tibialis anterior decreased significantly as the exercise protocol progressed. These findings showed that fatigue has an effect on muscle activity and is likely to be a cause of reduced activity during a real game decline in muscle torque. This decline in muscle torque has been recognized to be related to both contractile failures during repeated isokinetic efforts (Tesch *et al.*, 1990) and the availability of energy sources within the muscle (Kellis and Baltzopoulos, 1995). Although the studies are fewer in number, changes in EMG activity have also been monitored during repeated dynamic muscle contractions in order to express the effects of fatigue on maximum strength (Potvin and Bent, 1997). The present results (decreases in RMS values as the game progresses) are in agreement with work of Oda and Kida (2001), who found a significant decrease in

RMS values of the biceps brachii muscle following maximal concurrent hand grip and elbow extension. This finding contrasts with work of Psek and Cafarelli (1993) who reported a close relationship between increases in EMG activity in agonist and antagonist muscles as a result of fatigue. Furthermore, the results of this study are contrary to the work of Miller *et al*. (2000), who found no significant differences in RMS activity as the repetitions progressed for any of the quadriceps and hamstring muscles tested. In addition to these observations, Yeung *et al*. (1999) reported an increase in the RMS in M. vastus medialis following 30 maximal voluntary isometric contractions.

The contradictory results of the present study and that of others (Psek and Cafarelli, 1993; Yeung *et al*., 1999; Miller *et al*., 2000 and Oda and Kida, 2001), can be attributed to two major differences. First, there were differences in the test protocol. For example, our study involved 90 min of intermittent exercise, whereas Psek and Cafarelli (1993) used 3-s contractions at 70% of maximal effort, with 7-s rest intervals between each contraction, and Yeung *et al*. (1999) used 30 isometric maximal voluntary contractions while Miller *et al*. (2000) used 30 continuous extension-flexion maximal efforts. Secondly, there were major differences in the types of movements performed: Psek and Cafarelli (1993) evaluated coactivation patterns during static contractions whereas in the previous study the EMG activity was evaluated during 90 min of a simulated soccer game.

In the present study, the RMS values for rectus femoris, biceps femoris, tibialis anterior and gastrocnemius, were increased with increasing speed from 6 $km.h^{-1}$ to 21 $km.h^{-1}$. This finding is in agreement with work of Nilsson *et al*. (1985) who studied the effect of running velocity on EMG. They reported that in absolute terms, the duration of the signal was inversely proportional to velocity, but, in relative terms, muscles were active for a greater percentage of a gait cycle at the higher velocities. In addition, they tended to become active earlier in the cycle. An example of this was the action of the hamstrings in late swing. As the shank velocity increased with increasing running speeds, activity in the hamstrings was required earlier to decelerate the leg effectively. At times these increased demands resulted in an extra burst of activity that was not present at the slower speeds. Vastus medialis and vastus lateralis muscles were normally quiescent in late swing but at the faster running speeds they exhibited a burst of activity during this time. Finally, it appears that velocity can also affect the relative magnitudes of activity. This point was demonstrated in rectus femoris as the bursts during the early swing were larger than that during support. It is expected that with increasing running speed, muscle activity will increase.

5. CONCLUSIONS

In conclusion, the EMG activity in the major lower-limb muscles was greater before than after a simulation of the work-rate of a game. Fatigue was reflected in the electrical activity of the active muscles and is likely to be linked to the reduced strength observed during prolonged exercise. The RMS values increased with increasing speed of running on a treadmill, which indicated that greater muscle activity is required to run at the higher speeds. Therefore, it can be suggested that the decreases in force are related to a reduction of neural activation of muscle, and leads to a decrease in muscle performance.

REFERENCES

Green, H.J., 1995, Metabolic determinants of activity induced muscular fatigue. In *Exercise Metabolism,* edited by Hargreaves, M. (Champaign, Ill: Human Kinetics), pp. 211–256.

Kellis, E. and Baltzopoulos, V., 1999, The effects of fatigue on the resultant joint moment, agonist and antagonist electromyographic activity at different angles during dynamic knee extension efforts. *Journal of Electromyography and Kinesiology,* **9**, 191–199.

Miller, J.P., Ronald, V., Croce, R.V. and Hutchins, R., 2000, Reciprocal coactivation patterns of the medial and lateral quadriceps and hamstrings during slow, medium and high speed isokinetic movements. *Journal of Electromyography and Kinesiology,* **10**, 233–239.

Moritani, T., Muro, M., Kijima, A., Gaffney, F.A. and Parsons, D., 1985, Electromechanical changes during electrically induced and maximal voluntary contractions: surface and intramuscular EMG responses during sustained maximal voluntary contraction. *Experimental Neurology,* **88**, 471–483.

Nilsson, J., Thorstensson, A. and Halbertsma, J., 1985, Changes in leg movements and muscle activity with speed of locomotion and mode of progression in humans. *Acta Physiologica Scandinavica,* **123**, 457–475.

Oda, S. and Kida, N., 2001, Neuromuscular fatigue during maximal concurrent handgrip and elbow flexion or extension. *Journal of Electromyography and Kinesiology,* **11**, 281–289.

Potvin, J.R. and Bent, L.R., 1997, A validation of techniques using surface EMG signals from dynamic contractions to quantify muscle fatigue during repetitive tasks. *Journal of Electromyography and Kinesiology,* **7**, 131–139.

Psek, J.A. and Cafarelli, E., 1993, Behavior of coactive muscles during fatigue. *Journal of Applied Physiology,* **74**, 170–175.

Tesch, P.A., Dudley, G.A., Duvoision, M.R., Hather, B.M. and Harris, R.T., 1990, Force and EMG signal patterns during repetitive bouts of concentric and eccentric actions. *Acta Physiologica Scandinavica,* **138**, 263–271.

Yeung, S.S., Au, A.L. and Chow, C.C., 1999, Effects of fatigue on the temporal neuromuscular control of vastus medialis muscle in humans. *European Journal of Applied Physiology and Occupational Physiology,* **80**, 379–385.

78 Cardio-respiratory Responses of Regional Level Soccer Players to a Progressive Maximal Intermittent Field Test

Carlo Castagna[1,4], Romualdo Belardinelli[2] and Grant Abt[3,4]
[1]Istituto Tecnico Industriale Statale "V. Volterra" Torrette di Ancona, Ancona, Italy
[2]Department of Cardiovascular Rehabilitation and Prevention, Azienda Ospedaliera "G.M. Lancisi", Ancona Italy
[3]St. Martin's College, Lancaster, UK
[4]Research Department, Teknosport.com, Ancona, Italy

1. INTRODUCTION

Aerobic fitness has been reported to affect soccer performance positively (Helgerud *et al.,* 2001). Consequently, many field tests have been proposed for use by soccer coaches and fitness trainers. Due to the nature of soccer, those field tests involving intermittent protocols are particularly interesting.

The Yo-Yo Intermittent Endurance Test (YYIET) is a progressive intermittent shuttle run test that allows 5 seconds recovery following every second 20-m shuttle. Its aim is to elicit progressively a maximal physiological response from players during a soccer specific protocol. The YYIET currently exists in two versions: level 1 and 2. Level 1 has been devised for young and/or amateur athletes or habitually active people while Level 2 is supposed to be used to test the endurance of those who have successfully progressed through all the Level 1 stages (usually well trained athletes) (Bangsbo, 1993).

In Italy, regional level soccer players train two or three times a week only, with a match played during the week-end. This large population of recreational young soccer players is usually tested for endurance throughout the season for fitness and talent selection. Thus, the YYIET Level 1 is particularly interesting for this selected population of young sportsmen.

The existing scientific literature available on this interesting field test (Oliveira and Soares, 2002) has addressed only selected populations of well trained elite athletes who performed the YYIET Level 2 test. To the authors' knowledge, no data are available examining the physiological responses of young soccer players with limited training background during the YYIET. The aim of this study was to examine the cardiovascular response of regional level soccer players while performing the YYIET Level.

2. METHODS

Participants were 18 regional level soccer players (age 16.6±0.8 years, height 1.787±0.062 m, body mass 69.8±6.0 kg) randomly chosen among a population of students attending a high-school located in the area of Ancona (Istituto Tecnico Industriale Statale "Vito Volterra", Torrette di Ancona, Italy) during the 2001–2002 season. All of the subjects were active players at the time of the investigation, training 2–3 times a week with a match played during each weekend of the competitive season. Playing experience of each player was no less than 5 years.

Players were told to refrain from heavy training, alcohol, caffeine and tobacco usage for the two days preceding testing sessions. During the two hours preceding assessments, ingestion of water only was allowed ad libitum and subjects consumed a light meal at least three hours before the commencement of exercise. Eligibility to participate in the study was defined as the inability to progress through all the stages of level 1 YYIET test. This possibility was tested in a pre-experimentation session. All the players were blinded about the admission criteria of this study.

Test sessions were administrated in a random order and consisted of:

1. a laboratory test for maximal oxygen uptake (Bruce protocol) performed on a motor-driven treadmill (Cosmed, Rome, Italy);

2. a YYIET Level 1 test performed indoor on a wooden surface.

In both sessions of testing subjects' expired gases were collected using a portable lightweight breath by breath gas analyser (K4 b^2, COSMED, Rome, Italy). Expired gases were monitored on-line during the field test sessions by telemetry. All test sessions took place at a time of day corresponding to the usual training session performed by the regional level soccer players. Data were stored in a lap-top PC (Texas Instruments, Extensa 501T, USA) for post-test analyses using dedicated software (K4 b^2 software, COSMED, Rome, Italy). The variables of interest of this study were:- peak $\dot{V}O_2$ ($\dot{V}O_2$ peak), maximal heart rate (HRmax), maximal ventilation ($\dot{V}E$peak), respiratory exchange ratio (RER) and oxygen pulse (O_2pulse).

3. RESULTS

The pre-experiment YYIET test distance was not significantly different from that covered during the experimental condition (3052±659 and 2914±748 m respectively, P>0.05). Results of the physiological variables of interest are shown in Table 1.

No significant correlations were found between the distance covered during the YYIET with and without K4b^2 and treadmill $\dot{V}O_2$ peak (r=0.47 and r=0.51 respectively, P>0.05). The YYIET $\dot{V}O_{2\,peak}$ was not related to the distance covered during the test (r=0.38, P>0.05).

Table. 1. Values of the physiological variables of interest. *= significantly different from YYIET Level 1 results (P≤0.05).

Exercise mode	$\dot{V}O_{2\,peak}$ [ml.kg^{-1}.min^{-1}]	HRmax [beats.min^{-1}]	$\dot{V}$Epeak [l.min^{-1}]	O_2pulse [ml.beat^{-1}]	RER
YYIET	50.17±6.08	192±7	133±19	19.41±2.72	1.45±0.21
Treadmill	52.84±7.40	193±8	*148±21	19.43±3.82	1.46±0.23

4. DISCUSSION

The results of the present study have shown that the YYIET elicited maximal physiological responses in the young soccer players. However, the distance covered during the YYIET cannot be considered as a reflection of the individual's maximal aerobic power. The present study has shown the YYIET to be a good field test to elicit peak physiological stress on regional level soccer players and provided the use of a portable gas analyser (K4b^2, COSMED, Rome, Italy) is available, it could be considered as a valuable alternative to a treadmill running test. The lack of a significant relationship between the distance covered during the YYIET and both YYIET and $\dot{V}O_{2\,peak}$ attained on the treadmill shows that running back and forward at increasing speeds is affected by variables other than just maximal aerobic power. Further research is required to investigate the possible factors influencing YYIET performance.

Acknowledgements

The authors of this study would express their deepest gratitude to Miss Francesca Lacalaprice, BSc PT, for her guidance in using the K4 b^2 gas analyser and to all the participants from the Istituto Tecnico Industriale "Vito Volterra" (Torrette di Ancona) for their enthusiastic availability.

REFERENCES

Bangsbo, J., 1993, Fitness Training in Football – A Scientific Approach. (Copenhagen, Denmark: HO+Storm).

Helgerud, J., Engen, L.C., Wisløff, U. and Hoff, J., 2001, Aerobic endurance training improves soccer performance. *Medicine and Science in Sports and Exercise*, **33**, 1925–1931.

Oliveira, J. and Soares, J., 2002, Avaliçao da resistencia em desportos de esforço intermitente. In *A Investigação em Futebol-estudos Ibéricos*, edited by Garganta, J., Suarez, A.A. and Lago Peñas, C. (Universidade do Porto: Faculdade de Ciências do Desporto e de Educação Fisica), pp. 85–101.

79   The Importance of Buffer Capacity for Team-sport Participants

D. Bishop, J. Edge, C. Davis, B. Dawson and C. Goodman
School of Human Movement, The University of Western Australia

1. INTRODUCTION

High-intensity sprints of short duration, interspersed with short recoveries, are the predominant efforts required during most team sports. They apply across the major football codes. Therefore, the ability to recover and to reproduce a high power output in subsequent sprints is an important fitness requirement of team-sport participants. This fitness component has been termed repeated-sprint ability (RSA). However, little is known about what limits RSA and how best to improve RSA.

Depletion of PCr stores has frequently been cited as a limiting factor to the performance of repeated-sprint exercise (Bogdanis et al., 1996). A decrease in muscle pH (pH_m) may also be important. Intracellular acidosis may impair repeated-sprint performance via inhibition of glycolysis and PCr resynthesis, and/or interference with muscle contractile processes. It can be hypothesised therefore, that the restoration of PCr stores and acid-base balance is important to maximise RSA.

The extent of the decrease in pH_m during muscular activity is dependent upon both the production of hydrogen ions (H^+) and on buffer capacity. The decrease in pH_m is reduced through intracellular and extracellular buffering systems. Extracellular buffering systems are important as H^+ efflux out of the muscle cell has been reported to be related to blood buffer (β_{blood}) concentration (Mainwood and Worseley-Brown, 1975). Therefore, an increased β_{blood} should increase H^+ efflux from the muscle, help resist changes in pH_m and thus improve RSA. To our knowledge, no study has investigated the relationship between β_{blood} and RSA (study 1).

In addition to investigating the relationship between β_{blood} and RSA, it is important also to know whether increasing β_{blood} will improve RSA. One way to improve β_{blood} is via ingestion of a buffering agent (e.g., $NaHCO_3$). An improvement in β_{blood} will also increase the rate of H^+ efflux from the muscle into the blood. It may therefore, be hypothesised that the ingestion of a buffering agent such as $NaHCO_3$ improves buffering capacity leading to a decreased accumulation of H^+ in the muscle and improved RSA (study 2).

Changes in intracellular buffer capacity (β_m) may also help to delay fatigue and hence improve performance during repeated-sprint exercise. It appears that training can improve β_m (Sharp et al., 1986). Furthermore, as low-intensity training has been reported not to improve β_m in rats (Weston et al., 1996), it appears that high-intensity training may be necessary to increase β_m. To date, however, no study has compared the effects of training induced increases in βm on RSA (study 3).

The purpose of these three studies therefore, was to assess the relationship between buffer capacity and RSA. It was hypothesised that RSA is related to both intracellular and extracellular buffer capacity.

For the statistical analyses, the mean and standard deviation ($\pm$ SD) for the dependent variables of each study were calculated. Bivariate correlation coefficients between dependent variables were determined using Pearson's product moment correlation coefficient. Repeated measures ANOVA were used to test for interaction and main effects for the dependant variables measured. For all studies, the level of statistical significance was set at $P<0.05$.

2. STUDY 1 – RELATIONSHIP BETWEEN β_{blood} AND RSA

2.1. Methods

Fourteen members of the Australian Women's Hockey squad (Mean $\pm$ SD age: 25 $\pm$ 3 years) participated in this investigation. Their mean ($\pm$ SD) body mass was 61.1 $\pm$ 5.9 kg and $\dot{V}O_{2max}$ 55.1 $\pm$ 3.2 ml·kg^{-1}·min^{-1}. Testing procedures in all studies were approved by the Research Ethics Committee of either The Western Australian Institute of Sport or The University of Western Australia. Each subject gave her written consent for all studies. Upon arrival at the laboratory, resting arterialised capillary blood (100 μl) was sampled from a hyperaemic earlobe. Subjects then warmed up prior to performing the 5 x 6-s cycle test of repeated-sprint ability. Following the fifth sprint, arterialised capillary blood (100 μl) was immediately sampled from a hyperaemic earlobe; subjects then actively recovered for 5 min. Following a 30-min recovery period, each subject performed a graded exercise test (GXT) to determine her $\dot{V}O_{2max}$. For all studies, subjects were asked to not train on the day prior to each test and to be adequately hydrated and not to have eaten for three hours prior to each test.

2.2. Results

There was no significant correlation between power decrement (P_{dec}) during the 5 $\times$ 6-s test and $\dot{V}O_{2max}$ (ml·kg^{-1}·min^{-1} or l.min^{-1}) ($P>0.05$). There was also no significant correlation between total work (W_{tot}) and relative $\dot{V}O_{2max}$ (ml·kg^{-1}·min^{-1}) ($P>0.05$). There were, however, significant correlations between P_{dec} and both change in pH (r=0.75; $P<0.05$) and β_{blood} (r=-0.69; $P<0.05$) and between W_{tot} (J·kg^{-1}) and change in pH (r=0.59; $P<0.05$).

2.3. Discussion

The principal finding of this study was that β_{blood}, but not $\dot{V}O_{2max}$, was a strong predictor of RSA in a homogenous group of elite, female, team-sport athletes. A greater β_{blood} may be related to better RSA by increasing H$^+$ efflux from the muscle cell and facilitating a greater rate of PCr resynthesis and/or decreasing the inhibition of PFK and muscle contractile force. Study 2 was therefore conducted to determine if increasing β_{blood} would improve RSA.

Table 1. Correlation coefficients between RSA and $\dot{V}O_{2max}$, change in lactate concentration (Δ [La⁻]), change in pH (Δ pH) and blood buffer capacity (β_{blood}).

RSA	Mass (kg)	$\dot{V}O_{2\,max}$ (ml·kg⁻¹·min⁻¹)	Blood Variables		
			Δ [La⁻](%)	Δ pH(%)	β_{blood} (mmol.l⁻¹·p^{H}unitv⁻1
P_{dec} (%)	−0.46	0.30	0.20	0.75*	−0.69*
W_{tot} (kJ)	0.91*	0.47	0.37	0.01	0.07
W_{tot} (J·kg⁻¹)	−0.35	0.35	0.06	0.59*	−0.35

* $P<0.05$; P_{dec} (%): power decrement; W_{tot}: total work for 5 x 6-s sprints.

3. STUDY 2 – DO INCREASES IN β_{blood} IMPROVE RSA?

3.1. Methods

Ten physically active female subjects aged between (mean $\pm$ SD: age = 19 $\pm$ 2 years, $\dot{V}O_{2max}$ = 41.0 $\pm$ 8.8 ml·kgv⁻¹·minv⁻¹) participated in this study. Subjects first performed a graded exercise test (GXT) to determine their $\dot{V}O_{2max}$. On subsequent days, and in a double-blind, random, counterbalanced order, subjects performed a RSA cycle test 90 min following the ingestion of either $NaHCO_3$ (0.3 g·kgv⁻¹) or a placebo (NaCl: 0.207 g·kgv⁻¹). Capillary blood was sampled throughout the GXT and prior to and following each 5 x 6-s test and later analysed for blood bicarbonate concentration (HCO_3^-), lactate concentration ([La⁻]$_b$) and blood pH (pH$_b$). Muscle biopsies from the vastus lateralis were also taken prior to and following each 5 x 6-s test to determine muscle [La⁻]$_m$, pH$_m$ and $\beta_{m\ in\text{-}vitro}$ and $\beta_{m\ in\text{-}vivo}$. $\beta_{m\ in\text{-}vitro}$ was determined via titration and expressed as micromoles H⁺ per gram dry muscle per unit pH (μmol H⁺.g muscle dw⁻¹.pH⁻¹) and determined as the subjects $\beta_{m\ in\text{-}vitro}$. $\beta_{m\ in\text{-}vivo}$ was calculated from Δ [La⁻]$_m$/Δ pH$_m$.

3.2. Results

Compared with the NaCl trial, there was a significant increase in resting blood HCO_3^- (23.6 $\pm$ 1.1 vs 30.0 $\pm$ 3.0 mmol·l⁻¹) and resting pH$_b$ (7.42 $\pm$ 0.02 vs 7.50 $\pm$ 0.04), but no significant difference in resting [La⁻]$_b$ (0.8 $\pm$ 0.2 vs 0.8 $\pm$ 0.3 mmol·l⁻¹) during the $NaHCO_3$ trial. There was also no significant difference in resting [La⁻]$_m$, pH$_m$ or $\beta_{m\ in\text{-}vitro}$ between trials (P>0.05; Table 1). Compared with NaCl ingestion, the $NaHCO_3$ trial resulted in a significant increase in total work (15.7 $\pm$ 3.0 vs 16.5 $\pm$ 3.1 kJ), a significant improvement in sprints 3, 4 and 5 (Fig. 1), but no significant change in P_{dec} (8.9 $\pm$ 3.4 vs 8.2 $\pm$ 3.3 %). Post-test values for blood HCO_3^- (15.6 $\pm$ 2.5 vs 20.0 $\pm$ 2.6 mmol·l⁻¹), pH$_b$ (7.27 $\pm$ 0.05 vs 7.34 $\pm$ 0.06) and

$[La^-]_b$ (8.9 $\pm$ 3.7 vs 11.4 $\pm$ 3.3 mmol·l^{-1}) were all significantly higher in the NaHCO$_3$ trial (P<0.05). Despite no significant difference in post-test pH$_m$ between conditions, the NaHCO$_3$ trial resulted in significantly greater post-test $[La^-]_m$ and $\beta_{m\ in\ vivo}$ (Table 2).

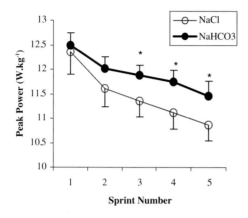

Table 2. $[La^-]_m$ (mmol·kg dm^{-1}), pH, $\beta_{in\text{-}vitro}$ (µmol H$^+$·g dm^{-1}·pH^{-1}) and $\beta_{in\text{-}vivo}$ ($\Delta[H^+]/\Delta[La^-]$) following ingestion of NaCl or NaHCO$_3$.

	$[La^-]_m$		PH$_m$		β_m	
	Pre-	Post-	Pre-	Post-	*in-vitro*	*in vivo*
NaCl	5.4	37.3	7.12	6.89	178.1	144.6
	± 3.5	± 7.8	± 0.06	± 0.06	± 30.0	± 26.0
NaHCO$_3$	7.4	64.1	7.11	6.89	180.0	258.4
	± 3.5	± 14.9*	± 0.04	± 0.03	± 33.2	± 56.4*

* value is significantly different from NaCl trial.

3.3. Discussion

These results support previous findings that NaHCO$_3$ can have an ergogenic effect on RSA, especially during later sprints (5). As NaHCO$_3$ ingestion does not increase resting pH$_m$ or $\beta_{m\ in\text{-}vitro}$, it is likely that the improved performance is a result of the greater extracellular buffer concentration increasing H$^+$ efflux from the muscles into the circulation (4: Mainwood and Worseley-Brown, 1975). Greater H$^+$ efflux may enhance RSA by facilitating a greater rate of PCr resynthesis and/or decreasing the inhibition of anaerobic glycolysis and muscle contractile force. The significant increase in post-test $[La^-]_m$ and $[La^-]_b$ during the NaHCO$_3$ trial suggests that an increased anaerobic energy contribution is one mechanism by which NaHCO$_3$ ingestion improved RSA. These results suggest that increased extracellular buffer can improve RSA. Study three was conducted to determine if increases in intracellular buffer capcity would also improve RSA.

4. STUDY 3 – DO CHANGES IN MUSCLE BUFFER CAPACITY IMPROVE RSA?

4.1. Methods

Twenty active females (mean ± SD: age 19 ± 1 years, mass 60 ± 5 kg) participated in this study. Subjects were matched for RSA and randomly assigned to high-intensity interval training (INT) or moderate intensity continuous (CON) training. Testing pre- and post-training consisted of a graded exercise test (GXT) to determine $\dot{V}O_{2max}$ and lactate threshold (Tlac), followed ~ 48 h later by a RSA test (5 × 6-s cycle sprints departing every 30 s). Capillary blood was sampled at the end of each stage of the GXT and immediately before and after the RSA test to determine blood pH and lactate concentration. Muscle biopsies (vastus lateralis) were taken immediately before and after the 5 × 6-s test to determine muscle lactate ($[La^-]_m$), pH_m and β_m *in-vitro*. Training was matched for total work and consisted of 6 - 10 x 2 min intervals (1 min rest) at 130–140% of Tlac (INT) or 20–35 min of continuous cycling at 85–95% of Tlac (CON), 3 × per week for 5 weeks.

4.2. Results

Both training programmes resulted in a significant improvement in $\dot{V}O_{2max}$ (10–12%), Tlac (8–10%) and peak power during the sprints (5–6%), with no significant difference between groups (Table 3). However, relative to the CON group, the INT group had a significantly greater improvement in β_m *in-vitro* (23%), work performed during sprint 4 (7.5%, Fig. 2) and RSA total work (4.5%). There was no significant difference in $[La^-]_m$ change or pH_m change for either group.

Table 3. Mean ± SD, $\dot{V}O_{2max}$ ($ml\cdot kg^{-1}\cdot min^{-1}$), RSA (total work, $J\cdot kgv^{-1}$), $[La^-]_m$ change, pH_m change and β_m *in-vitro* ($\mu mol\ H^+\cdot g\ dmv^{-1}\cdot pH^{-1}$) before (Pre) and after (Post) 5 weeks of training matched for total work.

| | $\dot{V}O_{2max}$ | | RSA | | $[La^-]_m$ change | | pH_m change | | βm *in-vitro* | |
	Pre-	Post-	Pre-	Post-	Pre-	Post-	Pre-	Post-	Pre-	Post-
CON	41.3	45.6*	257	278*	65.3	60.6	0.23	0.22	130	133
	± 7.3	± 5.7	± 35	± 25	± 11.3	± 16	± .1	± 0.11	± 32	± 19
INT	42.8	48.1*	267	301*‡	45.9	56.9	0.25	0.19	123	153*‡
	± 6.6	± 7.4	± 30	± 28	± 10.1	± 21.7	± 0.06	± 0.07	± 15	± 19

*significantly different to pre-train, ‡significantly different to CON group (P<0.05).

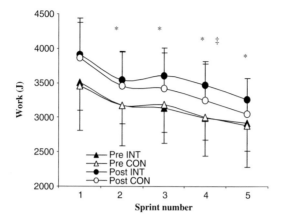

Figure 2. Mean ±SD, total work (J) during each sprint (5 x 6-s cycle test) before (Pre) and after (Post) training (P<0.05). CON = continuous training; INT = interval training.
*significantly different to pre-training;
‡significantly different to CON group (P<0.05).

4.3. Discussion

Consistent with previous research, the two training programmes, matched for total work, produced similar improvements in aerobic fitness ($\dot{V}O_{2max}$ and Tlac) (Cunningham et al., 1979). Despite similar changes in aerobic fitness, the INT group had a significantly greater increase in $\beta_{m\ in\text{-}vitro}$ than the CON group. This suggests that it is the intensity of training, not the total work performed, that is the stimulus for change in $\beta_{m\ in\text{-}vitro}$. Although there was no significant difference between groups for changes in peak power, or work performed in sprint 1, interval training also resulted in significantly greater improvements in work (sprint 4 and total) during the RSA test (Fig. 2). The greater improvements in $\beta_{m\ in\text{-}vitro}$ may in part, explain the greater improvements in RSA following interval training, compared with continuous training.

5. CONCLUSIONS

The purpose of these three studies was to assess the relationship between buffer capacity and RSA. As hypothesised, it appears that RSA is related to both intracellular and extracellular buffer capacity. Intracellular acidosis may impair repeated-sprint performance via a number of mechanisms (e.g., inhibition of PCr resythesis, inhibition of glycolysis or interference with muscle contractile processes). Increased intracellular buffer capacity should help to resist changes in pH_m, while increases in extracellular buffer capacity may increase H^+ efflux out of the muscle cell. Improvements in both intracellular and extracellular buffer capacity may therefore improve RSA in sports such as football codes by helping to resist changes in pH_m.

REFERENCES

Bogdanis, G.C., Nevill, M.E., Boobis, L.H. and Lakomy, H.K.A., 1996, Contribution of phosphocreatine and aerobic metabolism to energy supply during repeated sprint exercise. *Journal of Applied Physiology*, **80**, 876–884.

Cunningham, D.A., McCrimmon, D. and Vlach, L.F., 1979, Cardivascular response to interval and continuous training in women. *European Journal of Applied Physiology*, **41**, 187–197.

Mainwood, G.W. and Worseley-Brown, P. , 1975, The effects of extracellular pH and buffer concentration on the efflux of lactate from frog sartorius muscle. *Journal of Physiology*, **250**, 1–22.

Sharp, R.L., Costill, D.L., Fink, W.J. and King, D.S., 1986, Effects of eight weeks of bicycle ergometer sprint training on human muscle buffer capacity. *International Journal of Sports Medicine*, **7**, 13–17.

Weston, A.R., Wilson G.R., Noakes, T.D. and Myburgh, K.H., 1996, Skeletal muscle buffering capacity is higher in the superficial vastus than the soleus of spontaneously running rats. *Acta Physiologica Scandinavica*, **157**, 211–216.

80 Mineral and Vitamin Intake in the Diets of Male Soccer Players from Three Different Levels of Competition

Cláudio Franco, Nuno Loureiro and Filomena Sousa Calixto
Laboratory of Sports Science, Science Sports School, Politechnic
Institute of Santarém, Portugal

1. INTRODUCTION

There are nutrients that although not contributing directly to enhancing athletes' performance interfere in their health and particularly in some physiological aspects that might, at the end, have a profound effect in performance at a particular time. Athletes in general need more energetic nutrients than sedentary people and so, as several micronutrients interfere in the metabolism of carbohydrates, proteins and fat, it is reasonable to think that micronutrients involved in those processes are increasingly required in the exercising body (Manore and Thompson, 2000). Moreover, many authors have emphasised the role of several micronutrients for athletes' health (for review see Coyle, 2000). It is clear that health and well-being are improved by physical activity and a well balanced diet (Coyle, 2000). Exercise elevates physiological and metabolic stress (Quiles *et al.*, 1999) and both physical activity and diet are interrelated in the fact that optimal adaptation to the stress resulting from exercise requires a balanced diet, containing all its essential components (Suzuki *et al.*, 1999, Coyle, 2000). The immune system is greatly affected by exercise (Nieman, 1995), several cases of immunossupression in elite athletes being related to extreme exercise (Verde *et al.*, 1992; Nieman., 1995, Davis *et al.*, 1997, Shephard and Shek, 1999; Gleeson and Bishop, 2000). Nutrients that have been demonstrated to contribute to a better functioning of the immune system include essential amino acids, the essential fatty acid linoleic acid, vitamin A, folic acid, vitamin B6, vitamin B12, vitamin C, vitamin E, Zn, Cu, Fe and Se. Practically all forms of immunity may be affected by deficiencies in one or more of these nutrients (Calder and Kew, 2002). Moreover, some of these nutrients have been shown to decrease due to exercise (Kobylinski *et al.*, 1990; Quiles *et al.*, 1998, Quiles *et al.*, 1999). The production of energy by the mitochondria results in the formation of reactive molecular species known as free radicals, which in balanced amounts are important in several cellular mechanisms, but if over-increased, they lead to several destructive mechanisms (for review see Fehrenbach and Northoff, 2001). During the course of evolution, the antioxidant system has developed in order to prevent cell damage and to maintain equilibrium between production of free radicals and their neutralization. Many sources of stress including extreme exercise (Mastaloudis *et al.*, 2001) increase production of free radicals and associated reactive oxygen or nitrogen species (ROS/RNS). This is known as the oxidative stress (for review see Jenkins et al., 1984, Fehrenbach and Northoff, 2001). A good nutritional balance, which includes food products rich in antioxidant is a way to ensure adequate removal of radicals during stress and prevent cellular damages (Fehrenbach and Northoff, 2001). Among the nutrients known to have antioxidant effects are micronutrients such as the vitamins A, C and E and selenium (for review see Manore and Thompson, 2000).

The purpose of this study was to investigate the intake of minerals (calcium, Ca; phosphorous, P; sodium, Na; potassium, K and iron, Fe) and vitamins (vitamin A, B1, B2, B6, and C) in the dietary practices of 83 male senior soccer players from three different levels of competition, namely First League, Second and Third Division, from the Portuguese National Teams in the Lisbon area. One-day inquiries were applied during one-day training in the competition period in May, which corresponded to the last weeks of the 2002 season. Results showed that there was a marked difference between the mineral intake of soccer players from the First League and the players from Second and Third Division, although, professional and non-professional soccer players consumed poor sources of all minerals studied. There were differences in the mineral content in the diets of soccer players according to their playing position. In general, the diet of all groups of soccer players studied was poor concerning vitamin A, B2 and C, while reaching or even exceeding the amounts recommended for vitamin B1 and B6. This behaviour leads to the consumption of diets that have deficient amounts of nutrients at a time particularly important concerning nutrient intake, that is the end of the season.

2. METHODS

Subjects: Eight-three senior male soccer players participated in this study. They were from different teams of three different levels of the Portuguese National Teams of the Lisbon area, participating in national and international competitive matches during the all 2002 season. Sixteen soccer players were from the First League, forty-two were from the Second and thirty-two were from the Third Division. The sample included professional (players from First League and half of the Second Division) and non-professional (players from Third Division and half of the Second Division) players.

Study Design: All subjects were instructed to record their food and fluid intake accurately during one all day training by answer an enquiry, which provided detailed information regarding food and fluid consumption, time of meals and supplements used. The enquiry was designed in order to provide clear and comprehensive objectives and quick and easy answers. Data were analysed by considering the menu published by Bangsbo (1998) as a standard. Software used for data analyses was the PIABAD (the Database from the Becel Nutritional Institute for Dietary Analysis, the Portuguese version).

Statistical Analysis: The *Students' t* test and the *Kruskal Wallis* test were used respectively, to compare the data obtained and the standard and the data between the groups analysed. Results are provided as means (±SD).

3. RESULTS

Figure 1 shows the amount of calcium (Ca), phosphorous (P) sodium (Na) and potassium (K) intake for the soccer players from all groups analysed.

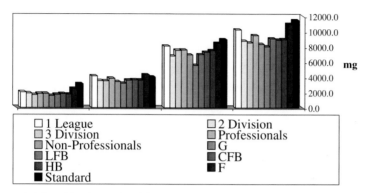

Figure 1. Mineral intake (mg): calcium (Ca), sodium (Na), phosphorous (P) and potassium (K) (respectively from left to right), of soccer players from First League (1 League), Second (2 Division), Third Division (3 Division), professional, non-professional, goalkeepers (G), lateral full-backs (LFB), central full-backs (CFB), half-backs (HB) and forwards (F) and minerals obtained from the menu published by Bangsbo (1998) which was taken as a standard (Standard).

The Recommended Dietary Allowance (RDA) of these minerals are respectively 1000, 700, 500 and 2000 mg, for an adult man, 19-30 years old (Manore and Thompson, 2000), while the values taken as standards, obtained from the menu published by Bangsbo (1998) were respectively 3125, 4024, 8971 and 11483 mg. The intake of P, Na and K of the soccer players from all the groups analysed was higher than the RDAs. Soccer players from the First League took higher amounts of P, Na and K than the other two categories of teams and not different from the standard. Soccer players from both the Second and Third Division as well as non-professional soccer players ingested less of those minerals than the standard, while professional soccer players had less intakes of Na and K and higher (but not significant for Student's t-test, P>0.05) intake of P than the standard. There were differences in the ingestion of these three minerals according to the playing position of the soccer players studied. Goalkeepers (G) ingested significantly less amounts of these minerals. Both lateral full backs (LFB) and half-backs (HB) had significantly lower intakes of Na and K but equal intakes of P, since the difference was not significant (Student's t-test, P>0.05). The differences concerning intake of all these minerals by forwards (F) and central full backs (CFB) were not significant as compared to the standard (Student's t-test, P>0.05). It is possible that the results obtained for the Na intake are underestimated since the salt added to the food according to the Portuguese pattern is normally higher than the amount taken as the standard for each kind of menu described. All the soccer players ingested more Ca than the RDA value but significantly less than the recommended taking the standard menu, except the forwards who also took less calcium but the result was not significantly different from that standard (Student's t-test, P>0.05).

Figure 2 shows that there are differences concerning the intake of iron (Fe) according to the soccer players' league status and professional level.

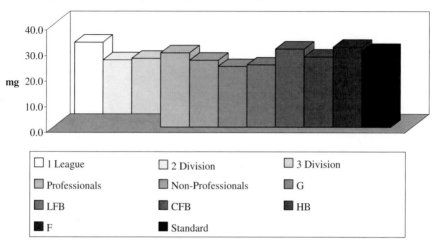

Figure 2. Iron (Fe) intake (mg) of soccer players from First League (1 League), Second (2 Division), Third Division (3 Division), professional, non-professional, goalkeepers (G), lateral full-backs (LFB), central full-backs (CFB), half-backs (HB) and forwards (F) and obtained from the menu published by Bangsbo (1998) which was taken as a standard (Standard).

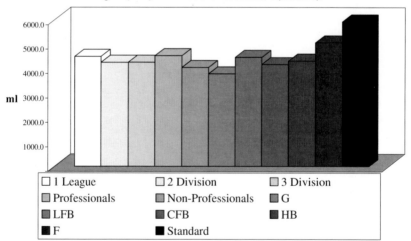

Figure 3. Liquids intake (includes ingested drinks and the watery content of the solid foods, ml) of soccer players from First League (1 League), Second (2 Division), Third Division (3 Division), professional, non-professional, goalkeepers (G), lateral full-backs (LFB), central full-backs (CFB), half-backs (HB) forwards (F) and liquids obtained from the menu published by Bangsbo (1998) which was taken as a standard (Standard).

Soccer players from the first league ingested more Fe than the standard menu (29.7 mg) and even more than the RDA (12 mg), and professional players ingested statistically (Student's t-test, P>0.05) an equal amount of Fe as the standard, while soccer players from the other team levels and non-professional players ingested less of this mineral. The CFB soccer players and the forwards had Fe intake higher than the standard but the difference was not significant (Student's t-test, P>0.05). The results concerning the other playing positions (LFB, HB and G) were lower than the standard although not significantly different (Student's t-test, P>0.05) due the higher SDs obtained.

An analysis of the total liquid intake by the soccer players (Fig. 3), considering the drinks ingested plus the watery content of the solid foods, shows that all the soccer players irrespective of either the team level, the professional level or the playing position took significantly (Student's t-test, P<0.05) less amounts than the standard, the exception being the forwards who had also lower liquid intakes but the difference was not significant (Student's t-test, P>0.05).

Concerning the vitamins A and C intakes (Fig. 4), all the soccer players irrespective of the group analysed took significantly lower amounts of both vitamins than the standard menu (1628.4 mg), except the forwards and CFB players who also took less amounts of vitamin C but the difference was not significant (Student's t-test, P>0.05). Nevertheless, all the soccer players ingested higher amounts of both vitamin A (1000 μg.day^{-1}) and C (60 mg.day^{-1}) than the RDA for adult males. It is interesting to note that the intake of vitamin A decreased with the level of the team from the first to the third league, and from professional soccer players to non-professional players.

Figure 5 shows the soccer players' intake of vitamins from the B group. The vitamin B1 intake of the soccer players from all the groups was significantly higher than the standard menu (2.3 mg) and higher than the RDA (1.2 mg.day^{-1}) except the goalkeepers whose values statistically (Student's t-test, P>0.05) equalled the standard, although higher than the RDA. The result obtained for the CFB although higher than the one obtained for the standard menu was not significantly different (Student's t-test, P>0.05), due to the high SD obtained for this group. Soccer players from all the groups analysed, except forwards, had significantly (Student's t-test, P<0.05) lower vitamin B2 intake than the standard diet (5.1 mg), but higher than the RDA (1.3 mg.day) for adult males.

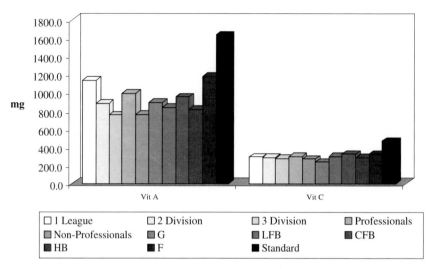

Figure 4. Vitamins intake (mg): vitamin A (Vit A) and vitamin C (Vit C), of soccer players from First League (1 League), Second (2 Division), Third Division (3 Division), professional, non-professional, goalkeepers (G), lateral full-backs (LFB), central full-backs (CFB), half-backs (HB) and forwards (F) and vitamins A and C obtained from the menu published by Bangsbo (1998) which was taken as a standard (Standard).

Forwards took less vitamin B2 but statistically the result was not different from the standard menu (Student's t-test P>0.05). Vitamin B6 intake was different for the different teams level. Soccer players from the First League ingested a higher amount than the standard menu (4.8 mg) but statistically not different (Student's t-test, P>0.05), while teams of the other levels had lower intakes. There was no difference (Student's t-test, P>0.05) between the results obtained for the Third Division and the standard menu. Professional soccer players ingested an equal amount of vitamin B6 while non-professional soccer players took significantly (Student's t-test, P<0.05) less of this vitamin. Soccer players from the different playing positions had vitamin B6 intakes not different (Student's t-test, P>0.05) from the standard menu, but much higher than the RDA (2.0 mg.day^{-1}) for an adult male 19 to 24 years old. Although the results obtained for the different playing positions were not statistically different (*Kruskal Wallis*, P>0.05) between the groups, the result obtained for the goalkeepers was lower with respect to intake of all the vitamins analysed, vitamins A, B1, B2, B6 and C (Fig. 4 and Fig. 5), than for the forwards.

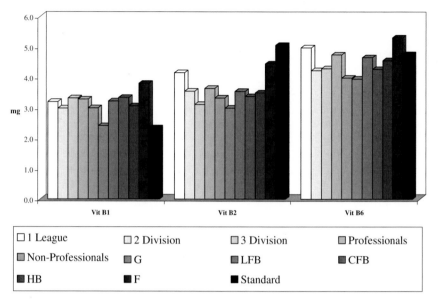

Figure 5. Vitamin intake (mg) from the B complex: vitamin B1 (Vit B1), vitamin B2 (Vit B2) and vitamin B6 (Vit B6), of soccer players from First League (1 League), Second (2 Division), Third Division (3 Division), professional, non-professional, goalkeepers (G), lateral full-backs (LFB), central full-backs (CFB), half-backs (HB) and forwards (F) and vitamins obtained from the menu published by Bangsbo (1998) which was taken as a standard (Standard).

4. DISCUSSION

Minerals and vitamins are not directly related to the body's energy production but they are certainly indirectly related since several enzymes require vitamins or minerals as coenzymes and cofactors. Athletes need more energetic nutrients than sedentary people, they also need different amounts of vitamins and minerals. Because the values stated as Recommended Dietary Allowance (RDA) were established as an average, athletes should look to them as a guide, although knowing that there is a need for the intake of minerals and vitamins to increase with physical training.

It was shown from our results that in general, the diet of the soccer players did not always contain the amount of minerals and vitamins, which was set as reference taking the menu published by Bangsbo (1998) as standard. Important minerals and vitamins are poorly ingested and this is due to the products chosen in their diets. Grouping the products used in the soccer players' diet in the following categories:- group of cereals, group of fruit and vegetables, group of milk and dairy food, group of meat, fish and eggs, group of oil and butter, group of water and juice – we conclude that soccer players ingested preferentially foods from the group of cereals and meat, fish or eggs and ingested low amounts of fruit, vegetables (results not shown) and water. This means that the soccer players consumed low amounts of most of the vitamins and minerals obtained from green leaves, vegetables and fruits. Poor ingestion of liquids (Fig. 3) also decreases the intake of minerals and additionally may have contributed for a dehydrated state of the soccer players.

The lower Ca intake of the soccer players analysed is probably due to the fact that adults do not tend to consume high amounts of milk or dairy products and reaching the Ca recommendations is difficult for athletes who do not regularly consume dairy products or calcium-containing vegetables (Manore and Thompson, 2000). Soccer players from Second and third Division as well as professional and non-professional players had low P, Na and K intakes. There was a difference between the intakes of Ca (although not statistically significant), P, Na, K and Fe between the soccer players from the First League and from the other team levels when compared to the standard menu. This means that there was a difference in the quality of the diets of the different groups, which is probably due to a better nutritional counselling, assessment and supervision of the teams from the First League. The 'forwards' was the only group with optimal intakes of all the minerals analysed, and this is due, at least in part, to a better liquid intake. The Fe intake differed also between professional and non-professional players. Professional soccer players ingested the recommended amounts of Fe, while non-professional players ingested significantly less. Diet intakes, which do not include food products rich in Fe, can have severe consequences to soccer players. Iron (Fe) is a cofactor of the heme group from the haemoglobin, which is present in the erythrocytes or red blood cells. The erythrocytes deliver oxygen to muscles and transport part of the carbon dioxide from the cells to the lungs. Myoglobin is another heme protein found in skeletal muscle, which increases the rate of oxygen transport from the blood to the muscle and constitutes the oxygen reservoir of the muscle. Moreover Fe is a cofactor of enzymes from the electron transport chain, from other enzymes related to carbohydrate and protein metabolism (for review see Manore and Thompson, 2000) and has been demonstrated to have a role in the immune system (Calder and Kew, 2002). Regarding these factors, Fe deficiencies can have severe consequences in soccer players' performance. It is important that soccer players include Fe-rich food products in their diets as well as compounds containing all the other minerals in order to fulfil optimal mineral state and ultimately optimal activity of enzymes and consequently optimal performance.

Soccer players from all the groups analysed had poor vitamin C intakes, with the exception of LFB and forwards, and also poor vitamin A intakes. These two vitamins have an important role as antioxidants. Besides this, vitamin C is essential for amino acid metabolism, increases adsorption of dietary Fe, is essential for collagen synthesis. It has a role in avoiding upper-respiratory tract infection (Manore and Thompson, 2000), and in this stress response (Manore and Thompson, 2000) and possibly prevents the destruction of the red blood cell membrane during exercise (Williams, 1989). Vitamin A and vitamin C have been demonstrated to be required for an efficient immune system function (Calder and Kew, 2002). Vitamin C supplementation was demonstrated to lower both the adrenal stress hormone cortisol and anti-inflammatory polypeptide response to prolonged exercise in runners (Nieman, 1995; Peters *et al.*, 2001). In addition, extra amounts of vitamin A were shown to activate the function of alveolar macrophages preventing pulmonary infection and cancer (Newberne and Conner, 1988; Kishino and Moriguchi, 1992). It has been shown that prolonged exercise reduces the content of vitamin A in the liver (Kobylinski *et al.*, 1990; Quiles *et al.*, 1998, 1999) and muscle (Quiles *et al.*, 1999).

Athletes in general are exposed to acute and chronic stress that has consequences for health. The heavy schedule of training and competition has consequences for the immune system resulting in athletes' greater risk of opportunistic infections (Bishop *et al.*, 1999). Suppression of the immune system and increased generation of oxidative species are some consequences of the exercise related stress. Moreover, the tendency to consume poor amounts of important macro (Loureiro *et al.*, 2003) and micronutrients compromise further the immune system and the antioxidant mechanisms (Sen, 2001). Indeed, the poor nutritional status of some athletes may predispose them to immunosuppression, because enzymes in immune cells require the presence of micronutrients to function properly. The exercise stress is proportional to the intensity and duration of the exercise, relative to the maximal capacity of the athlete. Overtraining and/or under-nutrition leads to an increased risk of infections (Venkatraman and Pendergast, 2002). Nutrient status is a major factor contributing to immune competence because under-nutrition impairs the immune system, suppressing fundamental immune functions, which could be due to insufficient intakes of energy and macronutrients and/or due to deficiencies in, at least certain, micronutrients (Bishop *et al.*, 1999; Calder and Kew, 2002).

Our results concerning soccer players' intake of vitamins from the B complex are also not satisfactory for, at least some of the vitamins studied (Fig. 5). The soccer players from all the groups, except the goalkeepers, took the vitamin B1 excessively and this is probably due to high consumption of products from the group of cereals and pork. On the contrary, the soccer players from all the groups analysed took lower amounts of vitamin B2 when compared to the standard menu (Bangsbo, 1998). Vitamin B6 was consumed in adequate amounts by soccer players from most of the groups analysed, except the second Division and non-professional players. This clearly demonstrates differences in the quality of the diets of players from different professional levels. These three vitamins from the B-Complex are important in the energy metabolism. Vitamin B1 is related to carbohydrate and branch chain amino acid metabolism because it is a coenzyme of several enzymes, as for example pyruvate dehydrogenase (which catalyses the conversion of pyruvate into acetyl-CoA), $\propto$-ketoglutarate decarboxilase (an enzyme of the TCA cycle, interfering in the oxidation of carbohydrates and fat through this cycle). Physical activity stresses the need for this coenzyme since it increases the rate of energy turnover (Manore and Thompson, 2000). The low carbohydrate and high protein intake of the soccer players (Loureiro *et al.*, 2003) combined with high vitamin B1 intake diminishes the role of carbohydrate metabolism and enhances the contribution of amino acid metabolism to the overall energy production. Carbohydrate metabolism is even more compromised due to a low intake of vitamin B2 by the soccer players. This nutrient is a coenzyme of enzymes for the metabolism of glucose, fatty acids, glycerol and several amino acids. Moreover it is involved in the conversion of vitamin B6 to its coenzyme form (for review see Manore and Thompson, 2000). Vitamin B6 is required in the release of glucose from the muscle and liver stores of glycogen and it is involved in the gluconeogenic conversion of amino acids and lactic acid into glucose by the liver cells (Manore and Thompson, 2000). Low vitamin B2 intakes may result in reduction of vitamin B6 in its functional form even though this one is taken in adequate amounts. The differences concerning all sources of vitamins analysed between soccer players from the goalkeeping group and the forwards (although not statistically significant) may be due to the lower total food intake by the goalkeepers (Loureiro *et al.*, 2003), but also to differences in the quality of the diets, which hypothetically can be related to differences in the energy expenditure during training and matches.

Soccer players must be aware of the fact that the exercising body demands different nutritional needs, so their behaviour towards chosen food products is, at least as important as all other aspects. For example, soccer players may give an extreme importance to the shoes they wear during training and matches (as they should), but perhaps they forget to look carefully to what they have eaten and have drank before, during and after training and/or the matches.

Inadequate intake of micronutrients that have a key role in the body's molecular, biochemical and physiological functions has severe consequences not only for health but also for soccer players' performance by accentuating the effects of extreme exercise.

Acknowledgements

The authors wish to acknowledge all the soccer players, trainers and the all teams that participated in this study. We gratefully appreciate the support of the Department of Sports Training, Science Sports School of Rio Maior, Polytechnic Institute of Santarém.

REFERENCES

Bangsbo, J., 1998, *Entrenamiento de la Condición Física en el Fútebol*. 2nd ed., Trad. (Barcelona: Editorial Paidotribo).

Bishop, N.C., Blannin, A.K., Walsh, N.P., Robson, P.J. and Gleeson, M., 1999, Nutritional aspects of immunosuppression in athletes. *Sports Medicine*, **28**, 151–176.

Calder, P.C. and Kew, S., 2002, The immune system: a target for functional foods? *British Journal of Nutrition*, **88**, S165–S177.

Coyle, E.F., 2000, Physical activity as a metabolic stressor. *American Journal of Clinical Nutrition*, **72**, 512S–520S.

Davis, J.M., Kohut, M.L, Colbert, L.H., Jackson, D.A., Ghaffar, A. and Mayer, E.P., 1997, Exercise, alveolar macrophage function, and susceptibility to respiratory infection. *Journal of Applied Physiology*, **83**, 1461–1466.

Fehrenbach, E. and Northoff, H., 2001, Free radicals, exercise, apoptosis, and heat shock proteins. *Exercise Immunology Review*, 7, 66–89.

Gleeson, M. and Bishop, N.C., 2000, Elite athlete immunology: importance of nutrition. *International Journal of Sports Medicine*, **21**, S44–S50.

Jenkins, R.R., Friedland, R. and Howald, H., 1984, The relationship of oxygen uptake to superoxide dismutase and catalase activity in human skeletal muscle. *International Journal of Sports Medicine*, **5**, 11–14.

Kishino, Y. and Moriguchi, S., 1992, Nutritional factors and cellular immune responses. *Nutrition and Health*, **8**, 133–141.

Kobylinski, Z., Gronowska-Senger, A. and Swarbula, D., 1990, Effect of exercise on vitamin A utilization by rats. *Roczniki Panstwowego Zakladu Higieny*, 41, 247–251.

Loureiro, N., Franco, C. and Calixto, F.S., 2003, Energy intake in the diets of male soccer players from three different levels of competition. Poster Presentation at the V World Congress of Science and Footbal – Lisbon 2003.

Manore, M. and Thompson, J., 2000, *Sport Nutrition for Health and Performance.* (Champaign, IL: Human Kinetics).

Mastaloudis, A., Leonard, S.W. and Traber, M.G., 2001, Oxidative stress in athletes during extreme endurance exercise. *Free Radical and Biology & Medicine*, 31, 911–922.

Newberne, P.M. and Conner, M.W., 1988, Dietary modifiers of cancer. *Progress in Clinical and Biological Research*, 259, 105–129.

Nieman, D.C., 1995, Upper respiratory tract infections and exercise. *Thorax*, 50, 1229–1231.

Peters, E.M., Anderson, R., Nieman, D.C., Fickl, H. and Jogessar, V., 2001, Vitamin C supplementation attenuates the increases in circulating cortisol, adrenaline and anti-inflammatory polypeptides following ultramarathon running. *International Journal of Sports Medicine*, 22, 537–543.

Quiles, J.L., Huertas, J.R., Manas, M., Battino, M., Ochoa, J.J. and Mataix, J., 1998, Plasma antioxidants are strongly affected by iron-induced lipid peroxidation in rats subjected to physical exercise and different dietary fats. *BioFactors*, 8, 119–127.

Quiles, J.L., Huertas, J.R., Manas, M., Ochoa, J.J., Battino, M. and Mataix, J., 1999, Oxidative stress induced by exercise and dietary fat modulates the coenzyme Q and vitamin A balance between plasma and mitochondria. *International Journal for Vitamin and Nutrition Research*, 69, 243–249.

Shephard, R.J. and Shek, P.N., 1999, Immune dysfunction as a factor in heat illness. *Critical Reviews in Immunology*, 19, 285–302.

Suzuki, K., Totsuka, M., Nakaji, S., Yamada, M., Kudoh, S., Liu, Q., Sugawara, K., Yamaya, K. and Sato, K. 1999, Endurance exercise causes interaction among stress hormones, cytokines, neutrophil dynamics, and muscle damage. *Journal of Applied Physiology*, 87, 1360–1367.

Sen, C.K., 2001, Antioxidants in exercise nutrition. *Sports Medicine*, 31, 891-908.

Venkatraman, J.T. and Pendergast, D.R., 2002, Effect of dietary intake on immune function in athletes. *Sports Medicine*, 32, 323–337.

Verde, T.J., Thomas, S.G., Moore, R.W., Shek, P. and Shephard, R.J., 1992, Immune responses and increased training of the elite athlete. *Journal of Applied Physiology*, 73, 1494–1499.

Williams, M.H., 1989, Vitamin supplementation and athletic performance. *International Journal for Vitamin and Nutrition Research*, 30, 163–169.

81 Decreased Salivary SIgA Levels before Appearance of Upper Respiratory Tract Infection in Collegiate Soccer Players

Daisuke Nakamura[1], Takayuki Akimoto[2,3], Shigeru Suzuki[1] and Ichiro Kono[4]

[1]Faculty of Economics, Seikei University,
3-3-1 Kichijoujikitamachi, Musashino, Tokyo 180-8633, Japan
[2]Department of Life Sciences, Graduate School of Arts and Sciences, The University of Tokyo,
3-8-1 Komaba, Meguro, Tokyo 153-8902, Japan
[3]Japan Institute of Sports Sciences,
3-15-1 Nishigaoka, Kita, Tokyo 115-0056, Japan
[4]Department of Sports Medicine, Institute of Health and Sport Sciences, University of Tsukuba,
1-1-1 Tennoudai, Tsukuba, Ibaraki 305-5577, Japan

1. INTRODUCTION

Endurance athletes have been suffering from a high incidence of upper respiratory tract infection (URTI) during intense training and after competition. Epidemiological studies have provided some evidence that the amount of exercise and/or its intensity is related to the incidence of URTI (Douglas *et al.*, 1978; Peters et al., 1983; Peters, 1997). Peters and Bateman (1983) have reported that a two-fold higher incidence of URTI symptoms was observed in runners during the two weeks following an ultramarathon compared with age matched non-runners. Douglas and Hansen (1978) have also found that college students who had habitually high intensity training suffered a higher incidence of URTI symptoms compared to control subjects.

Secretory immunoglobulin A (SIgA) is a major effector of mucosal immunity to URTI. It interferes with viral attachment to epithelial surfaces, neutralizes viruses directory within the epithelial cells, binds to antigens in the mucosal lamina propria, and is involved in exertion of viral antigens through the adjacent epithelium into the lumen. It is known that individuals with selective IgA deficiency suffer a high incidence of infections, particularly URTI (Reid *et al.*, 2001).

It has been suggested that decrease of SIgA levels observed after intense exercise may explain a possible mechanism contributing to the increased susceptibility to URTI among athletes (Mackinnon *et al.*, 1989; Mackinnon *et al.*, 1993). Gleeson *et al.* (1999) demonstrated that the lower SIgA levels of pre-training are associated with a number of infections such as URTI. Mackinnon *et al.* (1993) reported that a decline of percent changes of SIgA levels after exercise was found in subjects who exhibited URTI within two days after sampling of saliva. Although the results of these studies have suggested that the decline of SIgA level may relate to incidence of URTI, there are few investigations of the relationship between changes of SIgA level and the appearance of URTI symptoms.

Thus the purpose of the present study was to determine whether changes of SIgA secretion rate are associated with appearance of URTI symptoms of collegiate soccer players. We measured salivary SIgA levels, examined the relationship between daily changes of SIgA from a non-infection period and appearance of URTI symptoms during a training period.

2. METHODS

2.1. Subjects

Thirty-one male collegiate soccer players who belonged to the University football federation of Tokyo participated in this study (19-21 years old). All the subjects were informed of the nature of the study and signed informed consent forms.

2.2. Experimental design

This study was conducted through a period of soccer practice from February 8, 2000 to March 31, 2000. The practice was conducted from Tuesday to Sunday and started at 15:00 hours. Subjects did not have a practice on Monday (off). The subjects came to the laboratory for measurements at 14:30, to measure weight, record subjective condition sheet and provide saliva samples after a 10-min rest. The experiment was conducted in the laboratory at an ambient temperature of approximately 24°C.

2.3. Training programme

All training sessions took approximately two hours. The training was held at the soccer ground of Seikei University. All training sessions were planned by the coach and the physical trainer and included soccer specific training, endurance, sprint, intermittent running exercise and weight training.

2.4. Assessment of URTI

To assess the appearance of URTI, subjects recorded daily physical condition indicating the presence of subjective symptoms of URTI (runny nose, fever, sore throat or coughing). The symptoms of URTI were evaluated by using a five- point scale (1: not at all any symptoms, 5: terribly bad about symptom). An episode of URTI was defined as follows:- the URTI symptoms were two scales up (e.g. from 1 to 3 or 2 to 4), and the URTI symptoms continued for more than 2 days and separated by at least one week from previous episodes. The average of SIgA secretion rate during a period without appearance of any symptoms of URTI was used as baseline in this study.

2.5. Saliva collection

Saliva samples were collected as previously described (Akimoto *et al.*, 2003). Briefly, timed whole mixed saliva samples were collected after rinsing the mouth thoroughly with distilled water, stimulating saliva production by chewing a sterile cotton swab (Salivette; Sersted, Germany) at a frequency of 60/60 s, and saliva was separated from the cotton and centrifuged at 3,000 rev.min^{-1}. After measurement of sample volume, saliva samples were frozen at -80 °C and stored until the end of study period.

2.6. SIgA Assays

Salivary SIgA concentrations were measured by enzyme-linked immunosorbent assay (ELISA) as described elsewhere (Akimoto *et al.*, 2003). Briefly, a 96-well microplate (Immulon II, Dynex Technologies, Chanitilly, VA) was coated with rabbit anti-human secretory component IgG fraction (MBL, Nagoya, Japan) over- night at 4°C. After adding 250 µl phosphate-buffered saline (PBS) containing 1% bovine serum albumin (BSA; Sigma, St.Louis, MO), wells were blocked for 2 hours. Saliva samples were thawed, centrifuged at 10,000 rev.min^{-1} for 5 min and diluted with PBS containing 1% BSA, and 2 µl of each were added and incubated for 1 hour. Using purified human SIgA (Organonteknika, Durham, NC), known concentrations of SIgA were also plated to establish standard values. After washing the plate with PBS-Tween, goat anti-IgA conjugated with HRP (MBL) was added to the plate and incubated for 1 hour. After washing, substrate solution was added and the colour intensity produced after 10 min was measured by a microplate reader (Bio-Rad Laboratories, Hercules, CA) at 490 nm. All samples were assayed in duplicate and the average of absorbance values was used as the representative value. Regression analysis using the relationship of standard SIgA concentrations and amount of absorbance (nm) was used to interpolate the concentration of SIgA in the samples. To avoid interassay variability, all samples from each subject were assayed on the same plate.

2.7. Statistical analysis

All data were expressed as percent changes from baseline. The data of baseline were averaged data of SIgA secretion rate of each subject without any symptoms of URTI. Secretion rate (µg.min^{-1}) of SIgA was calculated by multiplying absolute SIgA concentration (µg.min^{-1}) by saliva flow rate (ml.min^{-1}), which was calculated by dividing the total volume of saliva obtained in each sample (ml) by the time to produce the saliva sample (min).

3. RESULTS

Six of the 31 subjects exhibited URTI during the study period. Two of the six subjects exhibited decreased in SIgA secretion rate below baseline before appearance of URTI (Figure 1 and Figure 2), in contrast two of the six subjects did not exhibit a decline in SIgA secretion rate before appearance of URTI (Figure 3 and Figure 4). Changes in SIgA secretion rate of the remainder who got sick were uncertain, because these subjects had no collected saliva samples prior to the appearance of upper respiratory tract infection.

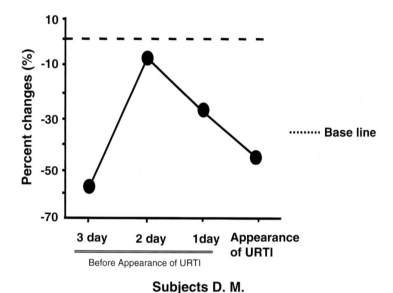

Subjects D. M.

Figure 1. Changes of SIgA secretion rate before Appearance of URTI symptoms. 1-3 day: 1-3 days before appearance of URTI symptoms. Appearance of URTI symptoms: the day URTI symptoms were exhibited.

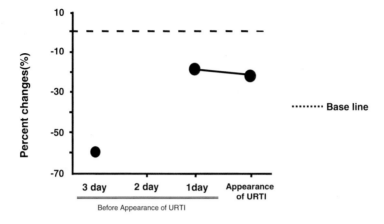

Subject N. N.

Figure 2. Changes of SIgA secretion rate before appearance of URTI symptoms. 1-3 day:1-3 days before appearance of URTI symptoms. Appearance of URTI symptoms: the day when subjects exhibited URTI symptoms.

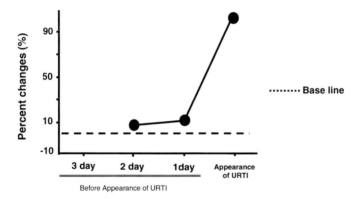

Subject K. I.

Figure 3. Changes of SIgA secretion rate before appearance of URTI symptoms. 1-3 day: 1-3 days before appearance of URTI symptoms. Appearance of URTI symptoms: the day when URTI symptoms were exhibited.

4. DISCUSSION

Our study provides evidence that SIgA secretion rate decreased below baseline prior to the appearance of URTI symptoms. These changes, before appearance of URTI, differed among individuals.

Previous studies (Mackinnon *et al.,*1993; Gleeson *et al.,* 1999) that focused on the relationship between appearance of URTI symptoms and SIgA level assessed the data by absolute value or percent changes from pre-training. In the present study, we assessed the data by the percent changes from baseline. The data of baseline were calculated from the SIgA secretion rate of each subject without any symptoms of URTI. Our present study suggested that daily mucosal immunity particularly SIgA levels changed widely day by day during a training period and this change differed among subjects, if they performed the same protocol. Thus it was necessary to consider the characteristic of individuals when we assessed SIgA level.

Several studies (Mackinnon *et al.*, 1989; Mackinnon *et al*, 1993; Gleeson *et al.*, 1999) reported that decreased salivary SIgA levels are related to appearance of URTI symptoms. In the present study, the mean SIgA secretion rate during the non-infection period used as baseline, demonstrated that the decline of SIgA secretion rate below baseline was found in some subjects who exhibited URTI during the concealment period. On the other hand, Klentrou *et al.* (1995) reported that regular moderate exercise for 12 weeks increased SIgA level at rest and this contributes to a decreased risk of infection compared with control subjects. In the present study the results suggested that the incidence of URTI symptoms was related to SIgA level of each subject and the decline of SIgA secretion rate was found a few days before the appearance of URTI during the training period.

In the present study, the changes of SIgA secretion rate before appearance of URTI differed among individuals. The reason for these results may be related to the difference of judgment for URTI symptoms among individuals. This may have been the cause of the time difference between the changes in SIgA secretion before subjects got sick and appearances of URTI. In the previous studies the incidence of an episode of URTI has been assessed by either self-reported questionnaire (Peters and Bateman, 1983; Heath *et al.*, 1991; Kostka *et al.*, 1995), training logs or diaries (Hooper *et al.*, 1995). While self-questionnaire permit large numbers of athletes to be assessed, some limitations of methodology may exist in terms of judgment of symptoms of URTI as pointed out above. Nevertheless many studies in this field used this method because this method can assess a large number of athletes and is very useful.

Many studies have reported an increase in the incidence of URTI during major competitions, such as Olympic Games, as well as in athletes undergoing high intensity training. The most common infection in highly trained athletes is URTI, which induces a decline of physical performance compared with a non-infection period. Pyne *et al.* (2000) reported that swimmers who had not reported illness during competition tended to have a higher level of performance than those people who had reported illness. Daniels *et al.* (1985) reported decreases in various measures of physical performance, such as isometric muscle strength, isokinetic strength, submaximal exercise during the infectious illness. Therefore, it is very important for athletes to avoid suffering from URTI during competition or intense training. Collecting saliva samples is very easy and non-invasive, thus monitoring SIgA level may be a useful method for risk management of appearance of URTI.

Acknowledgement

We wish special thank to thank Miss Hitomi Kasuga (Skymark Airlines, Co., Ltd.) for skilful assistance and the cooperation of Mr. Koichi Usui and players of Seikei Univ. football club.

REFERENCES

Akimoto, T., Kumai, Y., Akama, T., Hayashi, E., Murakami, H., Soma, R., Kuno, S. and Kono, I., 2003, Effect of 12 months of exercise training on salivary secretory IgA levels in elderly subjects. British Journal of Sports Medicine, **37,** 76–79.

Daniels, W.L., Vogel, A.J., Sharp, D.S., Friman, G., Wright, J.E. and Beisel, W.R., 1985, Effects of virus infection on physical performance in man. Military Medicine, **150,** 8–14.

Douglas, D.J. and Hanson, P.G., 1978, Upper respiratory infections in the conditioned athlete. Medicine and Science in Sports and Exercise, **10,** 55.

Gleeson, M., McDonald, W.A., Pyne, D.B., Cripps, A.W., Francis, J.L., Fricker, P.A. and Clancy, R.L., 1999, Salivary IgA levels and infection risk in elite swimmers. Medicine and Science in Sports and Exercise, **31,** 67–73.

Heath, G.W., Ford, E.S., Craven, T.E., Macera, C.A., Jackson, K.L. and Pate, R.R., 1991, Exercise and the incidence of upper respiratory tract infections. Medicine and Science in Sports and Exercise, **23,** 152–157.

Hooper, S.L., Mackinnon, L.T., Howard, A., Gordon, R.D. and Bachman, A.W., 1995, Markers for monitoring overtraining and recovery. Medicine and Science in Sports and Exercise, **27,** 106–112.

Klentrou, P., Cieslak, T., Macneil, M., Vintinner, A. and Plyley, M., 1995, Effect of moderate exercise on salivary immunoglobulin A and infection risk in humans. European Journal of Applied Physiology, **87,** 153–158.

Kostka, T., Brethouze, S., Lacour, J.R. and Bonnefoy, M., 2002, The symptomatology of upper respiratory tract infections and exercise in elderly people. Medicine and Science in Sports and Exercise, **32,** 46–51.

Mackinnon, L.T., Chlick, T.W., Van, A.A. and Tomasi, T.B., 1989, Decreased secretory immunoglobulins following intense endurance exercise. Sports Training Medicine Rehabilitation, **1,** 1–10.

Mackinnon, L.T., Ginn, E. and Seymour, G.J., 1993, Temporal relationship between decreased salivary IgA and upper respiratory tract infection in elite athletes. Australian Journal of Science and Medicine in Sport, **25,** 94–99.

Peters, E.M., 1997, Exercise immunology and upper respiratory tract infections. International Journal of Sports Medicine, **18,** 69–77.

Peters, E.M. and Bateman, E.D., 1983, Ultramarathon running and upper respiratory tract infections. South African Medical Journal, **64,** 582–584.

Pyne, D.B., McDonald, W.A., Glesson, M., Flanagan, A., Clancy, R.L. and Fricker, P.K., 2000, Mucosal immunity, illness and performance in swimmers. International Journal of Sports Medicine, **21**, 73.

Reid, M.R., Drummond, P.D. and Mackinnon, L.T., 2001, The effect of moderate aerobic exercise and relaxation on secretory immunoglobulin A. International Journal of Sports Medicine, **22,** 132–137

Part IX

Behavioural and Social Sciences

82 Applications of Dynamical Systems Theory to Football

Keith Davids[1], Duarte Araújo[2] and Rick Shuttleworth[3]
[1] School of Physical Education, University of Otago, New Zealand
[2] Faculty of Human Kinetics; Technical University of Lisbon
[3] School of Physical Education, University of Otago, New Zealand

1. INTRODUCTION

Football is a tactically sophisticated sport requiring understanding of coordination processes within and between players during performance of key dynamic interceptive actions such as passing, shooting and dribbling, heading and catching or punching the ball. Dynamical systems theory is an interdisciplinary framework, utilised to study coordination processes in physical, biological and social systems, which has considerable potential for the study of team ball games, including different codes of football. Recent applications of dynamical systems theory to team ball games have examined coordination processes at two different levels. The first level of analysis concerns coordination of dynamic interceptive actions in performers modelled as movement systems (e.g., Davids et al., 2000; Davids et al., 2002). Movement coordination and control in footballers conceived as dynamical movement systems involve two dimensions: (i) coordination between important limb segments to ensure a proximo-distal temporal sequencing in the movements of joint segments of the lower limb when kicking, to facilitate the development of high velocities in the distal segment; and (ii) coordination between a moving ball and an effector that is moved to satisfy the spatio-temporal constraints of interception with a controlled amount of force. The second level of analysis has attempted to model the dynamics of interpersonal coordination within patterns of play emerging in typical sub-phases of team ball games such as attack and defence and 1 v 1 situations (Grehaigne et al., 1997; McGarry et al., 2002; Araújo et al., 2003). These applications are providing useful insights into processes of motor skill acquisition and tactical development for players and coaches. The aims of this review are to: (i) present an overview of the theoretical constructs and concepts of dynamical systems theory which are highly relevant for the study of coordination processes at different levels in the context of football; (ii) review some current data emerging from these modelling attempts; and, (iii) draw some implications for coaching behaviours from the main empirical and theoretical developments in a constraints-led approach.

2. DYNAMICAL SYSTEMS THEORY AND COORDINATION PROCESSES IN FOOTBALL

2.1. General considerations

Generally, nonlinear dynamical systems are highly inter-connected systems composed of many interacting parts, capable of constantly changing their state of organisation (e.g., weather systems; societies; chemical systems). Complex, dynamical systems in nature have several key characteristics important for the study of coordination processes in football. First, fractal analysis in chaos theory has revealed self-similarity between localised sub-system behaviour and global system behaviour. In applications to football, the characteristic of self-similarity implies that the same underlying principles can be used to explain coordination processes in localised sub-systems (e.g., the emergence of patterns of movement coordination in individual players) and the global system (i.e. the emergence of tactical patterns during sub-phases of football including 1 v 1, 3 v 3 and 11 v 11 situations). Second, dynamical systems can display nonlinearity of behavioural output and have a capacity for stable and unstable patterned relationships to emerge between system parts through inherent processes of self-organisation under constraints (i.e., these systems can spontaneously shift between many relatively stable states of coordination (Davids et al., 2004)).

2.2. Constraints on football players as dynamical movement systems

Understanding how coordination emerges in dynamical movement systems, with their huge number of micro-components, was defined as the fundamental question in the human movement sciences and has become known as Bernstein's (1967) degrees of freedom problem (e.g., Turvey, 1990). The degrees of freedom of the human body are the many different parts, for example the muscles, joints and limb segments, which are free to vary in position and movement. Bernstein's (1967) seminal definition of movement coordination neatly captured the fundamental problem. The achievement of coordination between parts of the human body was viewed as "the process of mastering redundant degrees of freedom of the moving organ, in other words its conversion to a controllable system" (p.127). Despite the proliferation of degrees of freedom, dynamical movement systems show a surprising amount of order, and it has been known for some time that functional patterns of coordination emerge in individual performers to satisfy competing and cooperating task, informational and environmental constraints (e.g., Newell, 1986). Such classes of constraints interact to pressure the individual movement system into changing its organisational state during dynamic interceptive actions, such as kicking, punching or catching a ball.

Newell's (1986) model of interacting constraints and self-organisation processes has been applied to the study of coordination and control of dynamic interceptive actions in sport (for many examples see Davids et al., 2002; Davids et al., 2004). According to the model, coordination and control emerge under constraints and a relevant question concerns how the motor system's degrees of freedom are specifically harnessed during the learning of football skills. Bernstein (1967) highlighted the formation of specific functional muscle-joint linkages, later known as coordinative structures, as a method of constraining the large number of degrees of freedom to be regulated in the human movement system. Coordinative structures act as physical constraints, which specify how individual movement system's degrees of freedom can become mutually dependent. Anderson and Sidaway (1994) revealed support for these ideas in soccer players. In their study, novices initially showed joint ranges of motion of lower magnitude during kicking practice, compared to more skilled counterparts who exhibited coordinative structures characterised by greater values of flexion and extension in the knee and hip joints. As a result of a 10-week period of exploratory practice, the novices began to approximate the coordinative structures of the skilled footballers by increasing the joint range of motions for the knee and hip during kicking, increasing the amount of knee flexion prior to hip flexion and by extending the knee earlier with a resultant increase in linear foot velocity at ball contact (see Figure 1).

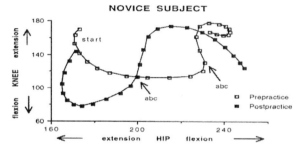

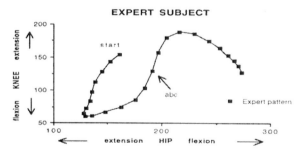

Figure 1. Representative data on coordination of the instep drive towards a target by a novice (top graph) and skilled (bottom graph) performer. Data on pre- and post-practice comparisons are provided for the novice performer. Note the restricted joint ranges of motion in the novice performer prior to practice (open square curve in top graph), the changes in joint ranges of motion after practice for the novice and the increasing similarity with the flexible kicking pattern of the skilled performer, with practice. Data from Anderson and Sidaway (1994). Reprinted with permission from AAHPERD.

These findings supported the dynamical systems interpretation of skill acquisition promoted by Newell (1985), based on Bernstein's (1967) insights. He argued that, early in learning, players typically assemble fairly functional, but rigid, coordination structures to satisfy specific task constraints of football such as passing, dribbling and shooting a ball, whereas later in learning, skilled players practice controlling or varying the parameters of the basic coordinative structure to enhance flexibility of skill performance.

2.3. Coordinative structures and exploration of task constraints

Exploratory practice during discovery learning is valuable at both the coordination and control stage of learning, but for different reasons (Davids et al., 2004). Initially, exploratory practice is useful for football players to assemble functional and unique coordination structures to achieve a specific task goal such as controlling a ball, whereas later in learning exploratory practice allows players to refine and adapt existing basic coordinative structures to enhance flexibility (e.g., control a ball in different ways and under different conditions). In football, exploratory behaviour can be encouraged by manipulating key task constraints to direct the learners' search for effective coordination solutions and an important question concerns the nature of the constraints that learners have to satisfy during motor learning.

One important task constraint that coaches can manipulate is equipment and there have been many claims about the use of smaller and denser footballs, such as the Futebol de Salão (FDS), to enhance the acquisition of ball skills. Araújo et al. (2003) reviewed the evidence surrounding these claims and it appears that there are some benefits to using the FDS to improve ball skills, particularly at the control stage of learning, but not necessarily at the coordination stage. In one study reviewed, Button et al. (1999) examined whether use of the FDS by groups of 11-year-old beginners at soccer would enhance ball control. After a pre-test to equate basic skill level, one group practised dribbling and juggling skills with the FDS, while a control group practised with a regulation size 5 soccer ball. The aim of the juggling test was to keep the ball in the air for as long as possible using any legal body parts under the laws of association football. The aim of the dribbling test was to examine the participant's ability to complete a course of four cones in a zigzag formation as fast as possible whilst keeping the football under control. Results showed that both groups significantly improved juggling and dribbling performance during acquisition. In the juggling test, results indicated that the FDS experimental group juggled the conventional ball more successfully than the control group in the post-test (see Figure 2). Button et al. (1999) suggested that children using a smaller, heavier ball could be guided towards relevant information (such as haptic and proprioceptive sources) for establishing functional coordination structures, enabling effective transfer to other task constraints.

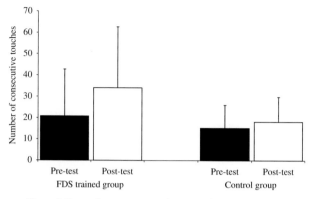

Figure 2. Pre- and post-test comparisons on a ball-juggling test for groups of 11-year old children using a FDS and a size 5 soccer ball (control group). Data reprinted from Araújo et al. (2003).

Pre-test data from Button et al. (1999) in Figure 2 suggested that their learners were at the control stage of learning, and there was a need for further work to understand whether beneficial effects of manipulating ball characteristics would also be observed in children at the coordination stage. Chapman et al. (2001) attempted to extend the work of Button and colleagues (1999) by examining whether the task constraints of using the FDS interacted with skill level of learners and by dissociating the effects of ball size and coefficient of restitution on juggling and dribbling skills. To achieve these aims, completely novice players (at the coordination stage of learning as verified by pre-test scores) aged between 8-11 years old, were investigated, using identical protocols of Button et al. (1999). After the pre-test, all participants were divided into one of three equal, randomly stratified groups. One group practised with the FDS ball, another with the size 3 soccer balls, and a third group of controls was assigned to the size 4 soccer ball. Since the FDS ball approximates the size 3 soccer ball, the comparison of learning to juggle and dribble the FDS, relative to a group practising with a size 4 soccer ball, permitted dissociation of the effects of ball size and ball coefficient of restitution on ball skill acquisition in the children. Means and standard deviations for the dribbling and juggling tests can be seen in Table 1.

Table 1. Means and standard deviations of the juggling and dribbling tests across the time phases. Data are reported in Araújo et al. (2003).

Juggling (Touches)				Dribbling (Seconds)			
	Pre-	Post-	Ret-		Pre-	Post-	Ret-
FDS	2.48	4	3.89	**FDS**	27.62	23.4	25.35
	(± 1.19)	(± 1.63)	(± 2.18)		(± 3.84)	(± 2.48)	(± 3.49)
Size 3	2.66	3.85	3.42	**Size 3**	28.05	24.35	25.64
	(± 0.98)	(± 1.46)	(± 1.53)		(± 6.13)	(± 3.39)	(± 3.35)
Size 4	4.38	6.33	5.33	**Size 4**	26.30	24.21	24.84
	(± 3.77)	(± 4.83)	(± 2.78)		(± 3.11)	(± 2.83)	(± 2.90)

All three groups significantly improved their juggling and dribbling performance between the pre- and post-tests. The results revealed no significant relative benefits for the acquisition of ball control skills among novice children when practising with the FDS ball, compared to conventional size 3 and 4 soccer balls.

Araújo et al. (2003) pointed out that differences in data on ball control, observed in previous studies of equipment constraints in football, were likely due to the differences in skill level between the groups of children involved in the studies. In the study by Button et al. (1999) the participants were at the control stage (Newell, 1985), having already assembled a basic coordination pattern for juggling and dribbling a ball. In the study by Chapman et al. (2001), the lower pre-test means implied that subjects were at the co-ordination stage because they had not yet assembled a stable co-ordination pattern for successfully juggling and dribbling a ball. A more precise definition of the learners in the study by Button et al. (1999) may be 'beginners', whereas the children investigated by Chapman et al. (2001) have been aptly described as complete 'novices'. Although there is a need for further research, it appears that manipulating the characteristics of footballs can enhance children's ball control, as long as the learners are already at the control stage of skill acquisition. Stability of equipment constraints seems important to allow exploration of new coordination structures to be assembled, whereas later in learning, exploration of equipment can refine established coordination patterns. Determining how skill level and task constraints mediate the emergence of skilled behaviour poses important challenges for future work in football. Moreover, refined analyses should assess how movement coordination changes with learning in football players.

Given the fractal nature of some dynamical systems, an interesting question concerns whether similar characteristics of self-organisation and emergence under constraints can be found in analyses of the tactical and strategic formations of football teams, conceptualised as dynamical systems. Evidence suggests that the same processes of self-organisation and emergence do exist at the tactical and strategical level of analysis of football.

3. FOOTBALL TEAMS AS DYNAMICAL SYSTEMS

3.1. Characteristics of football

Team ball sports in general, and football in particular, can be considered as dynamical systems composed of many interacting parts (e.g., players, ball, referees, court dimensions). Macroscopic patterns of behaviour spontaneously emerge from nonlinear interactions of various components at a more microscopic level of organization, the former being clearly different from the behaviour of each component considered separately (Gréhaigne, 1997; McGarry et al., 2002; Araújo, et al., 2003). In football, the game rhythm is characterized by exchanges of the ball in unequal measure. The game is characterised by an opposed relationship, where each "team must coordinate its actions to recapture, conserve and move the ball so as to bring it within the scoring zone and to score a goal" (Gréhaigne et al., 1997, p.137). The self-organizing dynamical pattern of between-person rhythmic coordination investigated by Schmidt and colleagues not only modelled the equilibrium of coordinative states but also how these coordinative states could spontaneously de-stabilise and change form (Schmidt et al., 1990, 1999). It was proposed that principles of pattern formation underlay between-person dynamics, and the same ideas have been applied to the study of player movements on the football field, since there may be transitions in the state of a competitive game, caused by key events that McGarry et al. (2002) called 'perturbations' (i.e., a key event or aspect of skill that disrupted the "normal" rhythm of the game).

From this viewpoint, the game can be characterized by order-order transitions, where individual actions may destabilize or (re)stabilize the system accordingly. These ideas fit well with tactical considerations in football since, at one level of analysis, the game can be described as a series of sub-phases, such as attacking and defending, and goals within each sub-phase constrain the coordination of movements between attackers and defenders to different extents. Sub-phase work (e.g., 1 v 1; 2 v 2; 3 v 3) is typical of practice organisation in soccer. Important loci of perturbations are 1 v 1 sub-phases of football where attackers and defenders are involved in an interpersonal dyad, where the constant adjustment between the positioning of the opposing players is a characteristic of dribbling, and can be understood as a type of interpersonal coordination. Although McGarry et al. (2002) speculated that the quality of an attacker or a defender could be seen in the facility with which he or she disrupts or (re)equilibrates the system, there has been little work examining 1 v 1 sub-phases as processes of maintaining or breaking symmetry in a dynamical system.

3.2. Interpersonal dynamics in football

One study of team ball games by Araújo et al. (2002) considered the relative positioning of an attacker with the ball and a marking defender near the scoring area. Attackers and defenders formed closely interacting dyads in which both parties did not typically seek to coordinate actions. In soccer, the aim of dribbling attackers is to 'destroy' the symmetry of this system by "getting rid" of defenders to score, while defenders seek to remain between attackers and the goal in order to stop the attacker from scoring and to recover the ball. When the defender matched the movements of an opponent and remained in position between the attacker and the goal, the form or symmetry of the system remains stable. When an attacker dribbled past an opponent, near the goal, he/she destroyed system stability.

At this level of analysis, therefore, 1 v 1 situations can be described as the creation, maintenance, and dissolution of a dyad, which relies on information about its ongoing coordinative state, that is, its kinematics and its kinetics. According to Araújo et al. (2003), due to the dynamics of competitive games there is typically not enough information to specify a goal path completely in advance for attackers. Consequently, goal path selection, or decision-making in de-stabilising dyads formed with defenders, can be viewed as an emergent process for attackers.

3.3. Emergent decision making in football

Gréhaigne et al. (1997) argued that changes in the momentary configuration of the game have to be examined in the light of the previous configurations, an example of the concept of conditional coupling in dynamical systems theory (Davids et al., 2004). They concluded that: "Choices are made based on position, movement and the speed of one's teammates and opponents. (…) With the opposition relationship, order and disorder can emerge from the play at any moment. In this way, the energy and choices of the players serve to create the conditions for transitions between configurations of play and thus transform the play" (p.148). These transitions may be best understood in terms of the interactions of multiple local factors (place of the players and of the ball, their speed, the player's cognitions and morphology, the slipperiness of the floor, etc.).

This characteristic is known as a process of *soft-assembly*, meaning that the decisions and moves that emerge in 1 v 1 situations are tailored to the immediate performance context, yet they satisfy some general goal. Of particular interest is the intrinsic metric or specific measurement system that attackers use for making decisions such as the critical location on court, relative to the defender's position, at which they need to change direction during their drive towards the goal area. Dynamical systems theory would predict that this decision would not occur at an absolute critical distance every time (e.g., 1.5 m from the defender), but rather would emerge from the intrinsic metric of the specific system formed by each individual attacker and defender. Analysis of the coaching literature (e.g., Bain et al., 1978) reveals that a candidate control parameter for an attacker-defender dyadic system could be the intrinsic metric of the *interpersonal distance* between the attacker and defender in a 1 v 1 situation. Additionally, the literature on team ball games literature reveals that a potential order parameter could be the median point of the distance of both players to the goal area. In order to test these assumptions, Araújo et al. (2002) investigated whether the equilibrium in attacker-defender dyads is broken when a critical value of interpersonal distance is reached. Obviously, during competition, other factors will constrain the strength of interpersonal coordinative states formed on the court or pitch (e.g., skill level, fitness levels, injuries, relying on non-functional information), but the proposal remains that a basic principle of decision-making in dribbling during team ball games is a symmetry-breaking process, resulting from the interaction of multiple constraints.

To exemplify these arguments we refer to data from studies of the interaction of an attacker and a defender in a 1 v 1 situation in team ball games (exemplified by the task vehicle of basketball), conceptualised as an interpersonal coordinated system, which can result in a stable interactive dyad, since the defender counteracts any movement towards the goal by the attacker (Araújo et al., 2002), as previously described.

In Figure 3a, it can be seen that the attacker-defender-basket system exhibited initial symmetry, which was broken during the transition to a new state (in around 4 seconds) at a specific value of the control parameter (i.e. interpersonal distance). A dynamical systems interpretation of this transition process showed that the attacker-defender system exhibited initial symmetry, which was broken during transition to a new state at a certain value of the control parameter. Analysis of the interpersonal dynamics showed that the attacker was attempting to break the system symmetry by altering the direction of the dribble in front of the defender, but the defender was counter-moving in order to maintain the initial steady state. The emergence of the decision on when to drive past the defender was a result of the breaking of symmetry within the dyad. Alternatively, it can be seen in Figure 3b that when the defender has supremacy, the system maintains its symmetry. These findings suggest that dribbling in team ball games can be described as processes of maintaining or breaking system symmetry, as argued by Schmidt et al. (1999) and questions for future research concern acquisition of skill in emergent decision-making, the nature of control parameters, the bodyscaling of dribbling actions by attackers, and the influence of previous plans for action.

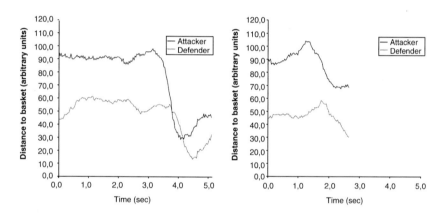

Figure 3. Distinction between individual attacker and defender's distance to basket: (a) Right graph showing a slight attacker's advantage; (b) Left graph showing defender's supremacy. Data are reprinted from Araújo et al., 2003.

4. A CONSTRAINTS-LED PERSPECTIVE IN FOOTBALL: IMPLICATIONS FOR COACHES

What are the implications of a dynamical systems approach to understanding learning and performance of football skills and tactics? First, there is a clear emphasis on discovery learning. Exploratory practice encompasses problem solving behaviours and is commonly referred to as active learning, because players participate actively in the learning process rather than passively receiving knowledge. Players are encouraged to explore and assemble their own tentative solutions to motor problems during exploratory practice. Experience of 'discovering' various solutions to the task, whether successful or not, is essential in learning to explore and exploit movement and sub-phase system dynamics (Davids et al., 2004). Discovery learning occurs in a practice context similar to the performance context enabling the player to become more attuned to the available information sources. Discovery learning promotes variability in practice and exploration of movement dynamics, enhancing the search process by increasing learner's exposure to varieties of task solutions (Newell and McDonald, 1991). There are also other important benefits for the learner. While a player actively participates in learning, he or she is able to concentrate on exploring potentially important sources of information as opposed to independently satisfying task demands prescribed by the coach. This active involvement in practice provides a foundation whereby coordinative structures can be assembled in the early stages of learning so that later in practice they can be strengthened and optimised for skilful performance. Appropriately constrained learning environments provide the player with the opportunity to receive relevant intrinsic feedback necessary for refining movement responses to perceptual and other information constraints.

An important issue with augmented informational constraints is that, in practice, instructions and feedback from the coach are often provided in a way that induces an internal focus of attention within the player. Focus of attention in motor learning relates to the learner's attention to either limb and body movements (an internal-focus on movement dynamics) or on the effects of a motor pattern on the environment (an external focus) such as the ball's trajectory in flight after being kicked (e.g., Wulf et al., 1999; Shea and Wulf, 1999; Wulf et al., 2002). With respect to football, Wulf et al. (2002) examined the effects of an internal/external focus and frequency of feedback on the learning of a lofted pass in football. Statements were provided to reinforce the attention of the learners to either an internal or external focus. Internal-focus feedback comprised such statements as 'Position your foot below the ball's midline to lift the ball' and 'Position your body weight and the non-kicking foot behind the ball' and external-focus feedback comprised statements such as 'Strike the ball below its midline to lift it; that is, kick underneath it' and 'To strike the ball, create a pendulum-like motion with as long a duration as possible'.

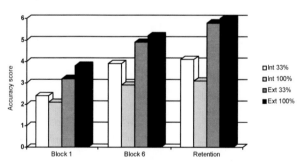

Figure 4. Graph adapted from Wulf et al., 2002.
Accuracy scores of the Int - 33, Int - 100, Ext – 33
and Ext - 100 groups.

As the results show in Figure 4, there was clear evidence of an immediate effect on performance outcome and learning experienced by both external-focus feedback groups. Generally, providing information about a function solution (goal-relevant information) accelerates learning more efficiently than providing information about "correct" means to achieve a solution (i.e., on one of the possible pathways to achieve a functional solution). Furthermore, the interaction between feedback frequency and attentional focus resulted in more effective performance during both practice and retention in the group receiving reduced (33% of trials) external-focus feedback relative to the constant (100% of trials) external-focus feedback group. These data indicated that receiving external focus feedback once in every three trials is as functional for learning as receiving external focus feedback on every trial. These findings highlight the detrimental effects that an internal focus on body parts and movement dynamics has on learning and performance in a dynamic sport such as football. Furthermore, these findings support the idea that discovery learning affords the player more opportunity to explore other potentially important external sources of information using an external focus of attention as opposed to providing the player with an internal focus of attention.

Instructions that direct a player's attention to an internal focus might deprive him/her of the opportunity to discover and satisfy the multiple task constraints unique to each individual. Instructions relating to task goals early in practice should attempt to direct the search toward relevant feedback sources that take into account their movement effects on the environment. A less prescriptive and more self-regulated feedback mechanism, which complements discovery learning and encourages the player to explore the task environment, seems to be a more appropriate instructional technique.

A constraints-led approach to coaching creates an environment that facilitates discovery by guiding a player through a range of potential movement solutions in the search for an optimal movement response. Individual responses are unique to each player, and result in effective retention and transfer of movement skills that require a less prescriptive 'hands-off' approach to coaching (Handford et al., 1997). This can be achieved through the manipulation of key constraints on the player leading to a change in the interaction between constraints, which in turn leads to changes in movement behaviour. It is argued that a thorough grounding of the principles of task constraints forms the basis for a constraints-led approach to practice in sport (Davids et al., 2004). The constraints-led approach is learner-centered, individual specific and involves a minimum of coach-player interaction, in sharp contrast to more traditional, didactic methods that emphasise verbal instructions, technique and task decomposition, generalising learning strategies across groups of individuals.

The primary task of the coach is to identify the key task, environmental and organismic constraints acting on the player and to understand how each one can *bias* the self-organization of the outcome movement. The ability of the coach to manipulate key constraints in a imaginative but functional way is seen as a fundamental principle toward creating an effective learning environment and one that is central to further task development. The process involves skill progression through task development rather than skill reductionism through task decomposition. Task solutions emerge from the time when the player first perceives relevant information for action to a point after which information about action (movement effect feedback) has been received. With the linking of information for action and action for information between player and environment, perception-action couplings emerge with practice and form the principal basis for structuring progressive task development practices. Variability in discovery learning is encouraged in players within the limits imposed by system constraints and consideration should be given to the function and purpose of intra- and inter-individual variability when manipulating constraints for group practices and games (e.g., Teaching games for understanding, TGFU, and conditioning games). Recent developments in thinking games for understanding have been brought about by a perceived need for less technique-based coaching and an increased emphasis on game-related skills, which are individually specific and encourage maximum participation. Coaches are challenged to adopt creative ideas, even borrowing from other sports, to manipulate the interaction of constraints on players, leading to challenging and exciting learning environments.

Progressive task development is achieved by altering the balance of interacting constraints on movement behaviour by manipulating one or several of the specific task constraints but also environmental and individual constraints too. Having identified the key individual constraints on the player, the coach designs a succession of progressive changes to task constraints and may even consider implementing environmental and individual constraints to facilitate and guide the learning process. For example, during dribbling variability of movements is to be encouraged as attackers explore ways to break the symmetry of dyads. Task constraints available for manipulation include changing the task goal over time and making subtle regulatory modifications to elicit desired changes in behaviour and appropriate decision making. Altering the practice rules that apply to attack and defence will initiate many of these changes for the coach. These include constraints on types and number of passes, tackles and contacts on ball, number of players involved, sub-units of the team, units and teams each with differing task goals, duration and time allowed in/out of a zone, channel or game, player roles and positions, the number, dimension and strategic positioning of goals and also boundaries and markings which can provide implicit rules for modified and conditioning games.

The exploratory activities of the players can be made against defenders with different body dimensions such as lower limb lengths or against defenders with different displacement velocities, or with different laterality preferences, or at different distances and spatial positions in relation to the goal area. It is possible to focus more on perception (i.e, in detecting action possibilities), or on actions (i.e., in the execution of action possibilities), but keeping the link present. A third possibility is to provide the formation of new links between perception and action (i.e. creating new action possibilities) (Araújo et al., 2003). The different focus means that, practice must be holistic (i.e., maintaining perception-action coupling) but must set different priorities (i.e., goals) according to players' skills. In sum, coaches should provide tasks where players learn how to soft-assemble adaptive behaviours in ways that respond to local context and exploit intrinsic dynamics.

5. CONCLUSIONS

The theoretical analysis of skill acquisition in sport as an emergent process under constraint is in its infancy, but it is becoming clear that concepts such as body-scaling of actions and symmetry-breaking during dribbling in order to seek phase transitions are potentially useful ideas that need to be fully investigated during practice and in future research programmes. In particular, manipulation of important variables such as practice structure and organisation and the nature of equipment used during learning will be key to understanding the emergence of skilled behaviour. It is clear that the role of the coach from a constraints-led viewpoint is likely to differ in subtle ways from traditional conceptualisations. For example, in the important task of providing feedback to athletes, a focus on functional solutions (i.e. the goal to be achieved) provides better opportunities to constrain learners' search for emergent task solutions during discovery learning. It appears that an external focus of attention may not interfere with self-organisation processes of the movement dynamics as athletes explore the tasks. These, and many other issues, could form the basis of a theoretico-practical programme of work on a constraints-led approach to skill acquisition in different codes of football for many years to come.

REFERENCES

Anderson, D.I. and Sidaway, B., 1994, Coordination changes associated with practice of a soccer kick. *Research Quarterly for Exercise and Sport,* **65**, 93–100.

Araújo, D., Davids, K., Sainhas, J. and Fernandes, O., 2002, Emergent decision-making in sport: a constraints-led approach. *Communication to the International Congress on Movement, Attention and Perception,* Poitiers, France.

Araújo, D., Davids, K., Bennett, S.J., Button, C. and Chapman, G., 2003, Emergence of sport skills under constraints. *In Skill Acquisition in Sport: Research, Theory and Practice,* edited by Hodges, N.J. and Williams, A.M. (London: Routledge, Taylor & Francis).

Bain, B., Hayes, D. and Quance, A., 1978, *Coaching Certification Manual - Level two.* (Canada: J. Seaman, Basketball Canada).

Bernstein, N.A., 1967, The Control and Regulation of Movements. (London: Pergamon Press).

Button, C., Bennett, S., Davids, K. and Stephenson, J., 1999, The effects of practicing with a small, heavy soccer ball on the development of soccer related skills. *Communication to British Association of Sports and Exercise Sciences Annual Conference,* Leeds Metropolitan University, UK.

Chapman, G., Bennett, S.J. and Davids, K., 2001, The effects of equipment constraints on the acquisition of juggling and dribbling in soccer. *Communication to 6th Annual Congress of European College of Sport Science (Perspectives and Profiles),* Cologne, Germany.

Davids, K., Lees, A. and Burwitz, L., 2000, Understanding and measuring coordination and control in soccer skills: Implications for talent identification and skill acquisition. *Journal of Sports Sciences,* **18**, 703–714.

Davids, K., Button, C. and Bennett, S.J. 2004, Coordination and Control of Movement in Sport: An Ecological Approach. (Champaign, Ill: Human Kinetics).

Davids, K., Savelsbergh, G.J.P., Bennett, S.J. and Van der Kamp, J., 2002, Interceptive Actions in Sport: Information and Movement. (London: Routledge, Taylor & Francis).

Gréhaigne, J.F., Bouthier, D. and David, B., 1997, Dynamic-system analysis of opponent relationships in collective actions in soccer. *Journal of Sports Sciences,* **15**, 137–149.

Handford, C., Davids, K., Bennett, S. and Button, C., 1997, Skill acquisition in sport: Some applications of an evolving practice ecology. *Journal of Sports Sciences* **15**, 621–640.

McGarry, T., Anderson, D., Wallace, S., Hughes, M. and Franks, I., 2002, Sport competition as a dynamical self-organizing system. *Journal of Sports Sciences,* **20**, 171–181.

Newell, K.M., 1985, Co-ordination, control and skill. In *Differing Perspectives in Motor Learning, Memory and Control,* edited by Goodman, D., Wilberg, R.B. and Franks, I..M. (Elsevier Science Publishers: North Holland), pp. 295–317.

Newell, K.M., 1986, Constraints on the development of coordination. In *Motor Development in Children: Aspects of Coordination and Control,* edited by Wade, M. and Whiting, H.T.A. (Dordrecht, Netherlands: Martinus Nijhoff), pp. 341–360.

Newell, K.M. and McDonald, P.V. 1991, Practice: A search for task solutions. In *American Academy of Physical Education papers: Enhancing Human Performance in Sport: New Concepts and Developments,* edited by Christina, R. and Eckert, H.M. (Champaign, IL: Human Kinetics), pp. 51–60.

Schmidt, R.C., Carello, C., and Turvey, M.T., 1990, Phase transitions and critical fluctuations in the visual coordination of rhythmic movements between people. *Journal of Experimental Psychology: Human Perception and Performance,* **16**, 227–247.

Schmidt, R.C., O'Brien, B. and Sysko, R., 1999, Self-organization of between-persons cooperative tasks and possible applications to sport. *International Journal of Sport Psychology,* **30**, 558–579.

Shea, C.H. and Wulf, G., 1999, Enhancing motor learning through external-focus instructions and feedback. *Human Movement Science,* **18**, 553–571.

Turvey, M.T., 1990, Coordination. *American Psychologist,* **45**, 938–953.

Wulf, G., Lauterbach, B. and Toole, T., 1999, The learning advantages of an external focus of attention in golf. *Research Quarterly for Exercise and Sport,* **70**, 120–126.

Wulf, G., McConnel, N., Gartner, M. and Schwarz, A., 2002, Enhancing the learning of sport skills through external-focus feedback. *Journal of Motor Behaviour,* **34**, 171–182.

83 Soccer as a Dynamical System: Some Theoretical Considerations

Tim McGarry

University of New Brunswick, Canada

1. INTRODUCTION

1.1. The dynamical systems change

Space and time are key variables for identifying patterns in sports contests. In this article, the spatial-temporal interactions between players are considered in terms of a dynamical system. In this view, the dynamical interactions among players are hypothesized to give rise to the behavioural patterns that appear to characterize various types of sports contests. While these patterns often seem open to visual detection, a formal description of these patterns remains equivocal. This article will serve as a platform upon which such a lawful description might be based. With this in mind, the language of dynamical systems was suggested as offering a suitable basis upon which to investigate sports behaviours (McGarry et al., 2002). (See McGarry and Franks, 1996, and McGarry et al., 1999, for earlier work that led to forwarding this consideration.) The general absence of research studies in this area of sports inquiry reflects the newness of this type of approach for sports analysis. For this reason, this article first presents some examples on the dynamical features of sports behaviours from extant data recorded on squash contests. The view of sports contests as a dynamical system is later extended from one-vs-one interactions to many-vs-many interactions, with specific references to soccer. The ideas presented in this article expand upon those reported in McGarry et al. (2002).

1.2. Principles of dynamical systems for rhythmic human coordination tasks

One feature that characterizes a dynamical system is the non-prescribed transition in some order parameter (or collective variable) as a result of changes in some control parameter. The order parameter is a measure of some relationship between the rhythmic components within a dynamical system. The control parameter is some property that constrains the behaviour of the dynamical system. For example, in studies of rhythmic human coordination tasks, the phase relation (a spatial-temporal measure of where one unit—finger, wrist, elbw, foot etc.—is in relation to the other unit in a given cycle) is often used as the order parameter, and cycling frequency as the control parameter (see Kelso et al., 1981, Kelso, 1984, for further details). The system dynamics are not specified in the control parameter, instead new patterns are brought about as a result of self-organizing tendencies from within the system as the system becomes unsettled. In short, the system seeks to "live" within the constraints that surround the system, and changes in the control parameter may serve to destabilise the system as the constraints are changed. Such conditions thus make future transitions more likely as the system seeks a new pattern of stable behaviour to satisfy the new constraints.

There are usually two identified stable phase relations in rhythmic human coordination tasks—in-phase and anti-phase. For the in-phase relation, as one oscillating unit flexes and extends throughout a given cycle, so the other unit likewise flexes and extends in symmetric fashion. In the anti-phase relation, however, as one unit flexes and extends throughout a given cycle, the other unit alternately extends and flexes in asymmetric fashion. In rhythmic coordination tasks, where the cycling frequency is increased in graded fashion from low values to high values, a transition from anti-phase (the starting phase relation) to in-phase is often observed as the cycling frequency passes through some critical region. If the cycling frequency is subsequently decreased in graded fashion from high values to low values, however, then a reverse transition from in-phase to anti-phase does not occur. The susceptibility of a dynamical system to transition as a function of the direction of change in a control parameter is known as hysteresis. Furthermore, if the coordination task begins in the in-phase condition then no transition to anti-phase occurs, regardless of whether the cycling frequency is increased from low values to high values, or vice versa. Further information on the dynamical features of these types of rhythmic human coordination tasks is provided by Haken *et al.* (1985).

The trademark loss of stability in dynamical systems as a result of changes in the control parameter gives rise to some, or all, of the following signature features: (1) increased variability in the order parameter before a phase transition (known as critical fluctuations); (2) increased local relaxation times—the times that the system takes to settle back to the stable state from whence it was perturbed (known as critical slowing down); (3) non-linear changes in the order parameter (known as phase transitions) with linear changes in the control parameter; and (4) hysteresis—the dependency of the phase transition on the pre-existing phase relation, as well as on the direction of change in the control parameter.

The dynamical features of human coordination identified above have been reported for both within-limb (e.g., Kelso, *et al.*, 1991) and between-limb (e.g., Kelso and Jeka, 1992) coordination tasks. These same dynamical traits have likewise been found among individuals who cooperate in the shared pursuit of a coordinated task (e.g., Schmidt *et al.*, 1990). On these latter reports of dynamical tendencies among individuals, we undertook a preliminary analysis of the spatial-temporal relations among players in squash contests as a dynamical system (McGarry *et al.*, 1999). Further considerations of sports contests—squash, tennis, badminton, and soccer—as a dynamical system were presented in McGarry *et al.* (2002). The aim of this article is to continue this line of inquiry for sports analysis.

1.3. Implications of dynamical systems for sports contests

The coupling relations among rhythmic (oscillating) units gives rise to the dynamical features that characterize dynamical systems. In squash contests, as with other sports contests, the players seek to take charge of the game through control of space and time. In squash, this aim is attained through command of the T-position (centre court), a strategy that is shared by both players. Thus, as one player leaves the T to make a shot, the other player moves to the T, and vice versa.

The result of this type of behaviour is for each player to oscillate in reciprocal fashion about the T in an anti-phase relation. The next section presents some data in this regard.

2. SQUASH

2.1. Data collection

Twelve rallies were selected at random from each of four quarter-finals recorded earlier on videotape from the 1988 Canadian Open Men's Squash Championship.

The same videotapes from which data were recorded in the preparation of this article were used in our earlier searches for patterned behaviours, or playing signatures, in squash contests using probability analysis (see McGarry and Franks, 1996). The same videotapes were retained for this article in order to provide future comparisons between previous findings and present findings. This approach means that differences in our abilities to detect patterned features in the data are a function of the type of analysis used, instead of possible changes in the sports contests that were analysed. Errors found after data collection uncovered one rally from each of the second, third and fourth quarter-finals as incomplete.

The kinematics of each player were obtained separately by the real-time tracking from videotape of the movements of each player using a pen and graphics tablet (see McGarry *et al.*, 1999, for further details on the equipment and protocol used to record these data). The kinematic data for each player within a rally were later synchronised to the onset of data collection, as determined from the instant that the server first struck the ball. The x-y coordinates of the graphics tablet, sampled at 10 Hz, were then used to determine the radial distance that each player was from the T at any instant.

The kinematic data of each player from the rallies of the first two quarter-finals were recorded twice to determine intra-rater reliability. Pearson correlation coefficients (r) on the radial data indicated good reliability, N = 46, r_{mean} = 0.947, r_{max} = 0.985, r_{min} = 0.849 (where N is the number of data sets, and N/2 is the number of rallies subjected to reliability analysis).

2.2. The kinematic relations between squash players tends to demonstrate an anti-phase pattern

The radial data of each player in a rally were inspected for an anti-phase relation, as hypothesised, using Pearson correlation coefficients (see Table 1). The results yielded a reasonably strong negative correlation (r_{mean} = −0.454), a finding that is consistent with the tendency towards an anti-phase relation (i.e., as one player approaches the T, the other player leaves the T, and vice versa). On giving prior consideration to using correlation coefficients in this manner, it was found that a lock-step anti-phase relation would yield a correlation of −1.000 between two sinusoids only under conditions of constant amplitude and constant frequency (i.e., any changes in the amplitude and/or frequency of one sinusoid must be likewise matched by equal changes in the other sinusoid). Varying amplitudes and/or frequencies between the sinusoids yielded negative correlations of less than −1.000. The r-values reported in this article should therefore be interpreted in light of this finding. (Similar results were found for measures of point estimate relative phase. Values of π, or values approximate to π, were found for constant and varying conditions of amplitude and/or frequency, respectively.)

Table 1. Pearson correlations (r) of the radial distances from the T in squash of the server and the receiver. See text for further details.

Q-F	N	r Mean	r Maximum	r Minimum
1	12	−0.519	−0.770	−0.317
2	11	−0.406	−0.689	−0.217
3	11	−0.485	−0.750	−0.227
4	11	−0.400	−0.649	−0.212
Σ	45	−0.454	−0.770	−0.210

Figure 1 contains four panels of time series data. In each panel, the radial distance of the server (bold line) and receiver (normal line) from the T is plotted on the y-axis against time on the x-axis. Figure 2 presents the same data as Figure 1 in the form of Lissajous plots. The left panel in Figure 2 corresponds to the first panel in Figure 1, the next panel in Figure 2 to the second panel in Figure 1, and so on. The plots were obtained by recording the radial displacements of the server and the receiver on the x-axis and y-axis, respectively. Pearson correlation coefficients (r) for each panel in Figures 1.1 and 1.2 (from left to right) were −0.770, −0.459, −0.210, and −0.307, respectively. Thus, the first panel is from the rally that contains the highest r-value, the second panel approximates the mean r-value, and the third panel consists of the lowest r-value (see Table 1). The last panel contains data selected on the basis of interest.

Each player in a squash contest tends to oscillate around the T in an anti-phase relation (see Figure 1). The first panel indicates an anti-phase relation throughout the short rally (~14 seconds), from the start to the end. Similarly, this anti-phase relation is documented in the Lissajous plot as witnessed in the negative gradient(s) that characterise this type of phase relation (see left panel, Figure 2). The second panel of Figure 1 also details an anti-phase relation for the squash rally (~28 seconds), albeit with a minor disturbance from this phase relation in the second quarter (~8–14 seconds) of the rally. Once again, the tendency towards an anti-phase relation is witnessed in the relevant Lissajous plot. The third panel of data yielded weaker support for an anti-phase relation (see Figure 1), with a few disturbances from this phase relation witnessed at various junctures throughout the long rally (~46 seconds). Further inspection of the data indicated the appearance and disappearance of a lead-lag relation within the rally on a few separate instances, where one player tended to lead and the other player tended to lag in the phase relation. Variations in the phase relations are further indicated in the inconsistent Lissajous pattern for this rally (see Figure 2). The last rally provided further support for a stable lead-lag relation within a rally, where one player led the other player by a quarter-phase. The quarter-phase relation is a phase relation that is half-way between an in-phase and anti-phase pattern, and is characterised in the Lissajous plot by a circular trace (see Figure 2). These findings yielded support for a stable quarter-phase relation in this instance. In sum, the data from selected rallies indicated the existence within a rally of stable phase relations between the server and receiver for both the anti-phase (first panel, Figure 1) and the quarter-phase (last panel, Figure 1) pattern, together with the possibility of phase transitions

Radial distance from T (m)

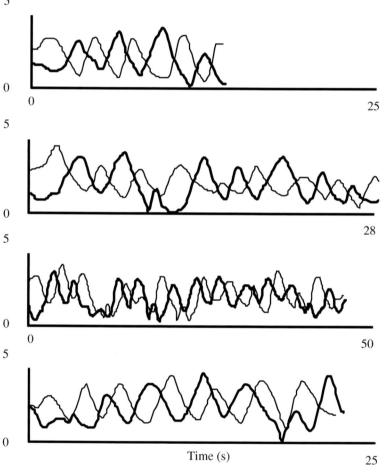

Time (s)

Figure 1. Time series data showing the radial distances from the T of the server and receiver.

Receiver

Server

Figure 2. Lissajous plots of the radius of the server vs radius of the receiver.

between these two stable relations (third panel, Figure 1). This suggestion of phase transitions within a squash rally awaits additional data for further investigation of this issue.

3. ONE-VS-ONE AND MANY-VS-MANY TYPES OF INTERACTIONS

Squash contests may be considered as a dynamical system in which players share information and couple in an anti-phase relation. If sports contests are to be considered as dynamical systems then the signature features of dynamical systems reported earlier should be identified within sports contests. The reader is referred to Araujo *et al.* (2003) for recent undertakings in this regard. For some suggestions on this issue for sports contests, see Schmidt *et al.* (1999) and McGarry *et al.* (2002).

In this view, each player is considered to oscillate around a common locus (i.e., the T), (see upper left panel, Figure 3). The oscillations of the player (solid lines) and opponent (dotted lines) are depicted in a flower-like arrangement around a common locus, with other like excursions remaining possible. In this section, this consideration of couplings within the dyad from sports consisting of one-vs-one type interactions is extended to sports of many-vs-many interactions. This line of reasoning is predicated on the view that many-vs-many interactions are in essence comprised of various one-vs-one interactions.

In squash, each player competes for ownership of shared space, indicating a common (or public) locus of oscillation for interaction within the dyad. The spatial constraints imposed on the players in tennis, however, differ from squash by virtue of the game rules. In tennis each player is awarded exclusive ownership of one half of the court, thus indicating a private locus of oscillation for each player. In this type of sports contest, the players defend their half of the court, and attack their opponent's half of the court. The centre baseline in tennis would seem to suggest itself as a private locus of oscillation for tennis, with the patterned behaviours in tennis being the hypothesised result of coupled interactions amongst the two players (see upper right panel, Figure 3). The same type of thinking applies for the sport of badminton, with the centre of each defending half offering itself as a candidate for a private locus on which each player might oscillate (see middle left panel, Figure 3). The suggestion, then, is that various sports that trade shots within the dyad might subscribe to common principles that underpin the spatial-temporal patterns that describe their interactions.

The idea that dynamical interactions within a dyad might extend to sports contests that contain many-vs-many interactions is exemplified in a consideration of doubles-play in badminton, or tennis. In badminton doubles, the couplings among dyads will be formed both within and between the badminton pairs. For example, each doubles pair in badminton (or tennis) will couple so as to attain a common aim, to defend their own half of the court and/or to attack their opponent's half. Since the shared aims for each doubles pair will bifurcate as the shuttlecock (or ball) is traded, so will the phase relations within each pair change accordingly. Thus, the doubles pair in badminton will tend to transit between a "front-back" relation when attacking and a "side-to-side" relation when defending (see McGarry *et al.*, 2002). Furthermore, not only will couplings be formed within the doubles pairs, but also between the doubles pair, that is to say between individual players within each pair as well as between the pairs themselves (see middle right panel, Figure 3). These types of couplings should be considered as flexible and transient, they are created and destroyed to serve the cooperative and/or competitive aims of the players at the time (McGarry *et al.*, 2002).

The layered couplings hypothesised for doubles-play in badminton (or tennis) were extended to consider the spatial-temporal relations in soccer contests (McGarry *et al.*, 2002). Once again, these couplings are of temporary association in that they are forged and broken in continuous fashion as the game unfolds. These couplings are furthermore suggested to take place on various levels of analysis and timescales (as per dynamical systems), from one-vs-one interactions to many-vs-many. In terms of a one-vs-one interaction in soccer, the attacking player will try to free-up space from the defending player, while the defending player will at the same time try to tie-up the space within which the attacking player may work. These interactions will occur at the same time within many separate dyads, sometimes with and sometimes without ball contact. Similar type relations might take place within multi-dyads, forming units, or sub-units, in which to attack or defend (see bottom panels, Figure 3). The two-vs-one type of interaction, where two attackers work in tandem to create space by stretching the lone defender, provides an example of this type of multi-layered, multi-coupled, multi-dyad type of relation. Interestingly, the interactions among multi-couplings produce patterns of varying and irregular periodicities (cf. von Holst, 1939), a finding that might go some way to explaining the ebb-and-flow game rhythms that seemingly characterise these types of sports contests.

Whatever the level of analysis, from one-vs-one to many-vs-many, the interactions in sports contests might in general terms be thought of in the sense of attacker-defender symmetry. In this view, the attacker seeks to break symmetry with the defender, while the defender tries to maintain symmetry with the attacker. In this way, sports contests might be considered as dynamical systems that live on the boundaries of stability and instability. The facility with which an attacker or defender may destabilize or re-stabilize the dynamical system, respectively, would thus be regarded as a key indicator in our continued search for a lawful description of the spatial-temporal patterns that characterise sports behaviours. There is much work to do in this regard.

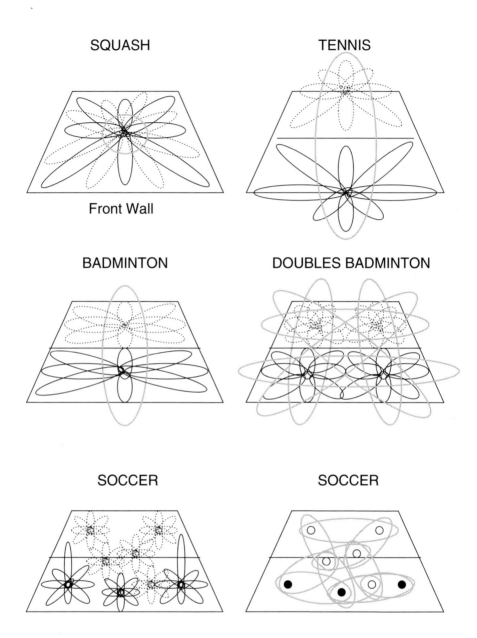

Figure 3. Some possible oscillations of players (solid lines) and opponents (dotted lines) around a central point, or locus, together with some possible couplings (grey solid lines) for one-vs-one and many-vs-many types of interactions in various sports. The suggested couplings are considered to be of temporary association in that they are created and destroyed as the context of the game unfolds.

4. CONCLUSION

In this article, a consideration of sports contests is presented within the framework of dynamical systems. Some data on the kinematic relations within the squash dyad were reported, from which stable anti-phase and quarter-phase relations were interpreted. The idea that the spatial-temporal data that describe the interactions within the squash dyad are the result of a coupling relation between players oscillating on a common locus was extended to badminton (and tennis), including doubles-play. The suggestion that the spatial-temporal relations in doubles-play in badminton may furthermore be the consequence of layers of couplings within and between the badminton pairs provided a bridge to considering soccer (and other team sports) as subscribing to similar underlying principles of space and time. The immediate task is to begin to identify such common principles of space and time that are hypothesised to underpin the unique game rhythms that characterise sports of varying structure and complexity. This article would serve as a basis for this type of undertaking.

REFERENCES

Araujo, D., Davids, K. and Serpa, S., 2003, Decision dynamics and intentional behaviour in one-on-one situations. *In Book of Abstracts, Science and Football V.* Lisbon: Editorial Gymnos, pp. 234–235.

Haken, H., Kelso, J.A.S. and Bunz, H.A., 1985, Theoretical model of phase transitions in human hand movements. *Biological Cybernetics*, **51**, 347–356.

Kelso, J.A.S., 1984, Phase transitions and critical behavior in human bimanual coordination. *American Journal of Physiology: Regulatory, Integrative and Comparative Physiology*, **15**, R1000–R1004.

Kelso, J.A.S. and Jeka, J.J., 1992, Symmetry breaking dynamics of human multilimb coordination. *Journal of Experimental Psychology: Human Perception and Performance*, **18**, 645–668.

Kelso, J.A.S., Holt, K.G., Rubin, P. and Kugler, P.N., 1981, Patterns of human interlimb coordination emerge from the properties of non-linear, limit cycle oscillatory processes: theory and data. *Journal of Motor Behavior*, **13**, 226–261.

Kelso, J.A.S., Buchanan, J.J. and Wallace, S.A., 1991, Order parameters for the neural organization of single, multijoint limb movement patterns. *Experimental Brain Research*, **85**, 432–444.

McGarry, T. and Franks, I.M., 1996, In search of invariant athletic behaviour in competitive sport systems: An example from championship squash match-play. *Journal of Sports Sciences*, **14**, 445–456.

McGarry, T., Khan, M.A. and Franks, I.M., 1999, On the presence and absence of behavioural traits in sport: An example from championship squash match-play. *Journal of Sports Sciences*, **17**, 297–311.

McGarry, T., Anderson, D.I., Wallace, S.A., Hughes, M. and Franks, I.M., 2002, Sport competition as a dynamical self-organizing system. *Journal of Sports Sciences*, **20**, 771–781.

Schmidt, R.C., Carello, C. and Turvey, M.T., 1990, Phase transitions and critical fluctuations in the visual coordination of rhythmic movements between people. *Journal of Experimental Psychology: Human Performance and Perception*, **16**, 227–247.

Schmidt, R.C., O'Brien, B. and Sysko, R., 1999, Self-organization of between person cooperative trials and possible applications to sport. *International Journal of Sport Psychology,* **30**, 558–579.

von Holst, E., 1939, On the nature of order in the central nervous system. In *The Collected Papers of Erich von Holst. The Behavioural Physiology of Man and Animals*, edited by Martin, R., 1973. (Coral Gables, FL: University of Miami Press), pp. 3–32.

84   In Pursuit of an Ecological and Fractal Approach to Soccer Coaching

João Mateus
University of Madeira, Portugal

1. INTRODUCTION

There has been no really effective conceptual breakthrough in team ball games, particularly in soccer, since the publications of Mahlo (1969), Teodorescu (1965, 1977), and Bayer (1979). Nevertheless there have been some very interesting contributions from Menaut (1983), Gréhaigne et al. (1989), Konzag (1990, 1991), Moreno (1994), Garganta (1994, 1997), Gréhaigne and Godbout (1995), Gréhaigne, Bouthier and David (1997), and others.

In the present report, most supportive of the "ecological approach to perception and action" and "complex systems theory", an attempt is made to contribute to a new understanding of soccer, starting by proposing an Attack «» Counter-Attack systematization, instead of the traditional and current Attack » Defence systematization, followed by an ecological, 'glocal' and 'fractal' vision of the game and finishing with some implications of this theory for coaching. In this sense coaching embraces teaching, learning and training as well as practical coaching.

2. CONTEXTUALIZATION

Since Bernstein (1967) it is known that the human body is a complex system because of its coordination of many "biomechanical" degrees of freedom. Knowing that, it will not be difficult to accept that much more complexity will be present when various "human beings" interact and coordinate their actions (not only "movements"), cooperating and competing in a very unstable environment as happens in a soccer game, a 'self-adaptive multi-agent' system. There are irreproducible multi-interactions of team and individual actions - a "coordination dynamics", according to Kelso (1995) - deeply intent on scoring more goals than the adversary.

Soccer is a very complex and dynamic system, sometimes tremendously unstable, particularly in those critically decisive, deeply interactive and fast situations (McGarry et al., 2002). At the same time, it is contained by very precise behavioural limits or environmental constraints. Time and space limits invite us to look at soccer in a non-linear way, like any complex system demands, a "fractal" way (Mandelbrot, 1977).

A fractal is a geometric figure "with a finite area (game court) and an infinite perimeter (with the sum of all movements/actions of the player during the game)," "with the same pattern repeated in different sizes and orientations" (Receive/Pass/Set/Hit). It contains only two dimensions that look the same at any scale (see Chris Lucas, on http://www.calresco.org/fractal.htm)

There is an inseparable relation «organism-task-environment» that "constrains" any perception-action behaviour (Newell, 1986). Newell's Perception and Action "model" is directly related with some other contributions, mainly from Gibson (1966) and Reed (1982, 1996), who considered any organism strictly connected with the environment, an always unstable/dynamic environment. The organism builds the environment and it is built by that environment, more or less, in a very superficial and fast approach. This is the main idea in the "ecological approach to perception and action".

The present intention is to bring this ecologically complex theory to team ball games and to soccer in particular. Other approaches can be included in this multidisciplinary and cross-disciplinary domain of the so-called "sciences of complexity".

There is first a need to look non-linearly at non-linear behaviours. It becomes not so difficult to conclude that there are more and more multi-disciplinary research and theoretical references to study and correlate – from "micro" coordination like the well known "finger wiggling" experiments (Haken et al., 1985) to "meta" coordination like the known hurricane "born" by a "butterfly effect", passing through many others, like the "inter–personal coordination research" (Schmidt et al., 1990). In this particular context it can be realised immediately that:-

– Each player makes the game (each competition that he or she participates in) and is made by that game, in a straight and direct (Michaels and Carello, 1981) perception-action relationship.

– That a game – a particular «ecosystem» living in a particular «habitat», with many different «ecological niches»– is absolutely unique. None of its micro- or macro-coordination features is reproducible.

These conclusions, together, present us the following question:- should the process of coaching soccer integrate a complex, ecological and fractal approach? A positive response would be expected from those referred to above and others who, in different scientific areas try to re-create a "dynamic perspective" of life (van Gelder, 1997), and from those who have an "ecological perspective" too.

It is about time to look at a soccer game as a "concentration of fractals" as Silva (1995) suggested. Two "global" fractals exist in competition, each one represented by one of the teams in play, each one also the resultant of many "local" fractals.

3. SOCCER SYSTEMATIZATIONS

3.1. Conceptualizations

Current conceptualizations and systematizations in soccer persist in describing it as being structured around the quasi-paradigmatic concepts of attack and defence. These are directly related to the omnipresent "ball possession" concept, some kind of linear reactive model, something like - "If the team is in possession of the ball, that team attacks; if the team is not in possession, that team defends". It is already time to question these kinds of old but still current approaches.

If attention is confined to "competitive" soccer games - 11-a-side inside a limited space/"habitat", with very particular rules for interactions - then, perhaps, a soccer game may be considered as an absolutely irreproducible ecological macro-happening expressed in all of its macro and micro competitive situations. There are 22 players on the field of play, 11 in each team, competing to score goals, more goals than the opposing team. Goals are obtained in accordance with the rules, especially one rule that indicates the ball has to be touched not possessed except by the goal-keeper. Also, when the ball is "dead" for free kicks, throw-ins, corner kicks and penalty kicks one player has to move the ball, a team mate has to control the ball, touching it in a discontinuous way.

It is very important to look again at soccer and the nature of ball contact. In a real competitive game, a team cannot really assume any stable ball control over the opposition, be it individual or collective. In this case, perhaps nobody should refer to ball possession, at least as the most important game factor, as it is usual to do. Team or individual discontinuous ball «control» in the majority of soccer games is mostly ephemeral, short, circumstantial and always unstable in the game situation.

The ball is always touched, never really possessed. Each time a player in play touches the ball, there are 21 other players who do not, and that unquestionable truth indicates that, at least, as important as the player who circumstantially (many times, instantaneously) touches the ball, are all the other 21 players.

The static and structural/spatial features of the game (like the often used paradigmatic expressions such as "ball possession", "time of ball possession"», «numerical superiority", "players' positions", "movements of the ball, or of the players" and some other global "sums" and local game "flashes" like these) should be discarded. More attention should be paid to those more functional and dynamic features of the game, those "fluxes or flows" built into the diverse interactions between cooperative and opposition players, with and without the ball. What are really decisive in such a complex game are those cooperative versus opposition "affordances" (Gibson, 1966, 1986) that co-create instantaneous critical emergent conditions to produce goals (McGarry et al., 2002).

In this context, more attention can be paid to some particular soccer game "phase transitions" (Kelso, 1995), maybe the first and last detonator of goals, those pre-goal dynamic situations, and others, wherever and whenever they happen. They can yield more information about soccer than those currently "static" concepts referred to before ("ball possession", "time of ball possession", "numerical superiority", "players positions", "ball movements", "players' movements" and so on).

With regards to the ball-contact nature of soccer (very different to Rugby or American Football), it should be compared with games like tennis (even though it is an individual game) or volleyball. It is very useful to compare soccer with volleyball, paying much attention to the "ball contact/interceptive" nature and everything that constrains the players' decisive interactions and team coordination.

The "fractal" of the game (Reception/Pass – Set – Hit …opponents) becomes more evident.

Soccer is somewhere between a Chess game and a hurricane. Chess - an absolute cognitive, individual game - has no significant action involved, no indispensable muscular activity. Chess pieces can even be "moved" by another person; it is an absolute "perceptive - motor" behaviour with an evident central mental control, even if there is minimal interaction with the adversary, mostly cognitive and emotional. A hurricane, on the contrary, constitutes an absolute non-cognitive behaviour, a tremendous complex and dynamic self-organizing system, a deeply ecological phenomenon, without any kind of central control. A real-time very competitive game of soccer has probably more to do with a hurricane than to any chess game.

A soccer game therefore can be considered as being a global complex, ecological, dynamic and fractal self-adaptive system, with very critical local, emergent, interactive, cooperative and opposition behaviours, particularly those related to "goals". Each local unit – each player – may be viewed as a complex micro self-adaptive system. The outcome is close to the macro-micro and "glocal" (= local + global) complex system of Silva (1995).

3.2. Traditional and current <u>Attack » Defence</u> soccer systematization

"Ball possession" is the major concept in too many analyses of soccer. It is its main "paradigm". The strangest fact is that it is also used in games like volleyball or even tennis, when, particularly, in those games, it has no value at all! There, "ball possession" only applies when there is no game, in pre-service situations. There, literally, any defensive action is always an offensive action, and vice-versa. The concept of "ball possession" is obviously important in games like Rugby, but its generalization, namely to soccer, is a tremendous mistake.

In soccer "ball possession" indicates absolutely nothing about the team's or player's offence or defence. At most, it means that, at a particular moment, one player of one team touches the ball.

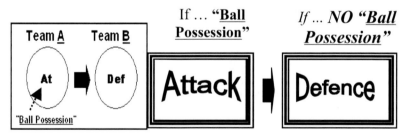

Figure 1. The current (<u>Attack</u> »» <u>Defence</u>) soccer systematisation.

3.3. Present <u>Attack «» Counter-Attack</u> soccer alternative systematization

To clarify the present alternative concept, what is really important in soccer is not ball "possession", it is what may be called ball "des-possession". Ball "des-possession" means:- Pass or Auto-Pass (Dribling); Set (another special Pass, the Pass to the Hitter/Shooter); Hit/Shoot (an even more special Pass, a Pass against the goal-keeper). Without ball "des-possession", there are no goals! So, much more attention must be paid to those very decisive "phase transition" instances (real ball critical "des-possessions") than to any kind of "ball possessions".

In those "des-possessions", especially the very quick ones (some of them quicker than the so-called "reaction speed") we probably have one of the most important questions about soccer. Bootsma (1988), Bootsma and van Wieringen (1990), Bootsma et al. (1991), Sardinha (1992), McGarry et al. (2002), Davids et al. (1994), and others, realised how definitely decisive the on-line self-organization of perception-action can be in a complex system like soccer.

Game complexity in soccer depends not only on the quantity of elements in interaction (one of the fundamental characteristics of complex systems) but also on the quality of those interactions/coordination. In this context, the importance of "ball possession" can be disregarded.

"Ball des-possession" is:

(a) At the individual plan (See Figures 2 and 3):

a.1 – All of those players who are not in contact with the ball. At the same instant, each of those players who are not in contact with the ball do "things", as important as the one usually said to be in "ball possession". They "afford" possibilities of interaction (cooperative "affordances" or opposition "affordances"). Without them, the absolute majority, there is no game at all.

a.2 – The player who is in contact with the ball (that discontinuous contact can assume one and only one of the following expressions: - Reception ... and ... pass, set, hit. Here, the goal-keeper is not considered, nor are "dead-ball" situations. Those are the only situations where "ball possession" in soccer can be asserted.

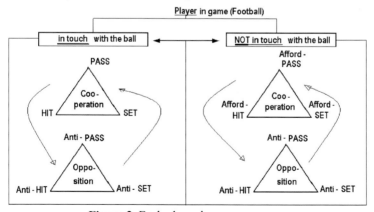

Figure 2. Each player in a soccer game.

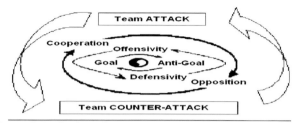

Figure 3. Each player in a soccer game (complement of Fig. 2).

(b) At the collective (team) plan:

A good ball "des-possession" is the key factor to guarantee what is usually called team "ball possession". So, the really decisive notion is ball "des-possession". In that case:

b.1 - The players of that team interact with the ball in a very precise way, and that means passing and/or auto-passing (which is, in any case, a ball "despossession"). Even so, this depends on the pressure from the opposition too.

b.2 - The players of that same team interact with the ball to create potential passing, setting or hitting "affordances" (and that means, again, ball "des-possession").

The conclusion is that:- "ball possession" is a concept only possible with inter-individual precise ball "des-possessions". It is a dynamic concept, not a static concept, inscribed in a "dynamic perspective" as van Gelder (1997) proposed.

Figure 3 shows that any individual player, as any of the two teams in a soccer game, is always "positive" and "negative" at the same time and space (like "Yin" and "Yang"!), simultaneously "offensive" and "defensive", "cooperative" and "opposing", in every game situation. So, attack and counter-attack are two sides of the same "coin". The difference is to be found in the "initial conditions" of each phase:- more stable initial conditions in attack; more unstable initial conditions in counter-attack. Remember, complex systems have great "sensibility to initial conditions".

Figure 4. Present (Attack «» Counter-Attack) soccer game
alternative systematization.

3.4. Global, local and "glocal" references of a soccer game, ecological niche and player fractal structure of behaviour

Two teams competing in an 11-a-side soccer game are in permanent offensive/defensive "coordination dynamics", whether in contact with the ball or not. Any play starts with one team moving a "dead ball". This team is said to be in attack; the opposition team is, at the same time, in counter-attack, and so on.

It is essential to distinguish between individual (defensive/offensive) behaviour and collective/team (attack or counter-attack) behaviour. Within this systematization/approach, defence (defensive attitudes and behaviours) exists in both team phases, in attack and in counter-attack. The same happens to offence (= offensive attitudes and behaviours); it also is always present at any moment and place of the field, in each of the team phases. Any team, in any situation, more or less offensive or defensive, has complementary individual defensive and offensive behaviours. The same happens within each player, who is never 100% offensive and never 100% defensive.

Within this approach, the bigger and important difference between attack and counter-attack is related to the respective "initial conditions", as already referred to:- less unstable in attack team phase; more unstable in counter-attack (which can go with an adversary attack or with an adversary counter-attack). For more details about complex systems, sensibility to "initial conditions", "phase transitions" and "attractors", see Juarrero (1999, p. 151–165).

So, in this proposed "soccer systematization", it is considered that:

- The team in attack is the one that moves a "dead ball". This is the most strategic and cognitive phase, because the team in attack has more time and organizational stability to anticipate and plan eventual future interactions.

- The team in counter-attack is the one that adapts to a current evolving game situation, sometimes in an emergent way, with the ball circulating, and not just after a "dead ball". In this case, both teams can be in counter-attack at the same time (it does not depend only on which player or team is in contact with the ball), or one is in attack and the other one is in counter-attack. This means that a team in counter-attack develops its play in very "unstable" initial conditions, as much unstable as the number, variability and emergent interactions present. The team in counter-attack is, mostly, in self-organized coordination. So, counter-attack is less cognitive, more emergent and ecological tactical than attack, so much more ecological and so much less cognitive as it is faster, variable and surprising.

The term "adapts" is used because the concept of "adaptation" is the more often used "response" concept, usually utilized in training and sport science literature. "Response" would probably be understood as "reaction" to (this is what the usual attack » defence "model" suggests is contained in its main idea or principle). What is intended is that major or minor individual or team active behaviours do not depend only on being in contact with the ball, or not.

This is not a kind of review that demands many "practical" examples. Nevertheless, an example may help to differentiate these two approaches. The following is a "practical" reference:- the soccer goal-keeper is not only a "defender". In many game situations, he must be the first "counter-attacker". In some of those game situations, the goal-keeper can be the first and decisive individual responsible for a goal for his/her team by initiating a very fast counter-attack. In a practice or training context it will be very different (for teaching/coaching/training conception) to consider the "goal-keeper" simply as a defender or, alternatively, as a permanent attacker and counter-attacker.

If it is sufficiently vindicated, the global soccer game "ecosystem" has its local dimension. There, inevitably, is found each different and unique player, a situated player, with himself (or herself), the task and environmental constraints (Newell, 1986). The same can be said about his team game system. The minimum situated action dimension to be considered about any player in a team game is related with the main game references. These are the "attractors": – the goals (goal«»anti-goal), the cooperation «» opposition (See Fig. 4) and, inevitably, the ball. So, what is the real ecological local dimension of the game? It does not exist at all, as it is usually considered. The minimum local dimension of a player in action is not really local, it is "glocal", a micro-macro and "glocal" dimension, according to Silva (1995). Figure 4 illustrates this conviction of the "eternal" glocal dimension of any team game player action. Each player in a game is always in permanent simultaneously "dialogical" offence «» defence attitude and behaviour, independently of being (or not) in contact with the ball, being in attack or in counter-attack, because he is always "connected" with the most distant and macro/global "attractors" of the game (the goals) and, at the same time, with the nearest interactive micro cooperation/opposition coordination dynamics. The player is always "glocally" situated and is in his/her ecological niche (Fig. 5 and Fig. 6).

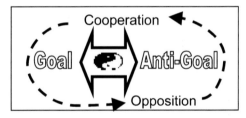

Figure 5. Each player's action "glocally" (micro-macro) situated.

This proposed new way of looking at the soccer player as being inscribed in a particular and irreproducible «game ecosystem», should invite a look at other literature that can help in re-evaluating each player's behaviour in a real game. Such works describe the «fractal structure» of every player's (and team's) movements and actions in a game, the already determined «glocal dimension» of the player's perception-action and each player's «ecological niche» (Odum, 1959; Gibson, 1986). According to Gibson (1986), a niche is a set of affordances, a setting of environmental features that are suitable for the animal, and into which it fits.

These references can complement Newel`s (1986) vision as proposed in Fig. 5.

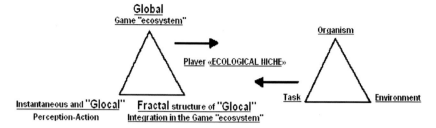

Figure 6. Essay of complementing Newel's 'Perception-Action' «model» (1986), here applied to football.

3.5. Soccer players' «glocalization», «fractalization» and «ecological niche» in a game situation

Each player's perception-action may be "glocalizing" in a soccer game. That "situating" a player's perception-action may be connected with his movement "fractality" structure, then, it will make much more sense to view the concept of "repetition without repetition" (Bernstein, 1967; Vereijken and Whiting, 1990), in a "multi-agent" behaviour. It seems appropriate there is a confluence of those two factors, glocality and fractality (the "self-similar but never equal repetition of any movement, of any action, of any interaction, of any coordination).

That player's behaviour, however, cannot only be explained by his/her "glocalization" and "fractalization". The player's eco-systemic integration demands another factor – "ecological niche". Those three factors, together, help to understand total integration of a player in the team system and then, afterwards, the player's co-integration (cooperative and opposition, local and global = "glocal") in the real and ecological unique total game. This interpretation is consistent with Silva's (1995) "micro-macro" concept and Rosnay's (1975) "macroscope".

According to them, it becomes easier to re-conceptualize a player in a particular team ball-game ecosystem. Here, in a first approach to this concept in ball games, each «player ecological niche» is something like "the essential structural/functional glocal ecosystem interactions that a player needs to be involved in. The essential global features of the game (permanent, general) and local (variable and specialized) behaviours that the player has to accomplish in the team system are preserved, in a way to be the most efficient possible". Figure 7 helps to clarify this definition.

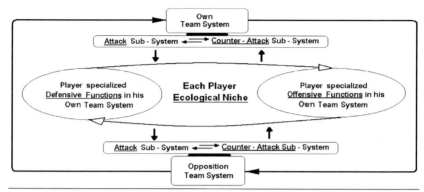

Figure 7. The Player «Ecological niche» in a soccer game.

3.6. «Fractal» representation of a soccer game

As suggested by Silva (1995), a "fractal condition establishes the equilibrium between global permanence and local variability". It "formalizes the function and functionalizes the form". So, the fractal representation of each player in a soccer game can be represented as Figure 8 shows.

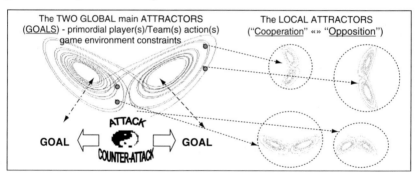

Figure 8. The "glocal" fractal representation of a player/ team action in a game – an interface between the global (represented/designed by an attractor similar to the "Lorenz Strange Attractor" Juarrero, 1999, p.155, at left) and the local (represented/designed by diverse small "Lorenz Strange Attractors", at right).

Here, also is the "Repetition without repetition" idea of Bernstein (1967), and Vereijken and Whiting (1990). The notion is that there are no equal movement repetitions, even less equal action repetitions, but always some "self-similarity" persists (the fractal structure of any behaviour).

3.7. The two exposed soccer systematizations briefly compared

It makes sense to compare very briefly the two systematization approaches outlined before.

The attack » defence systematization revolves around the following not very complex characteristics: - flashes, structural, spatial, mainly static features: players' positions, players movements, ball "possessions", quantities, "numerical superiorities"; predominance of technique and/or cognitive tactics (cognitive complexity); global or local dimensions of analysis and practice; "top-down" and retrospective "model" referential to teach/coach and control; dualistic logics: attack or defence, perceptive or motor (indirect perception).

The attack «» counter-attack systematization is concerned with the following very complex/dynamic characteristics: - "fluxes"/"flows"; structural-functional/temporal-spatial features: players' actions, interactions, coordination, ball "des-possessions", qualities, quality advantages; absolute predominance of ecological tactics (ecological complexity); global + local (= "glocal") and "fractal" approaches in any analysis and practice; "top-down and bottom-up" on-line prospective discovery learning and self-organizing control; non-dualistic logics: attack and counter-attack, perception - action (direct perception).

4. IMPLICATIONS FOR SOCCER COACHING

The soccer coach should never be a "modeller", someone who wants "models" to be strictly followed, copied, reproduced and consumed. Any activity "model", even the very best of the present, has a short and individualized existence. On the contrary, the teacher or coach must be a detonator and co-manager of auto-eco-self-organizing co-individualized proactive and prospective ecological learning.

There are a few more essential coaching considerations and suggestions. First, it is not indifferent to systematize the soccer game in the traditional way, attack » defence or attack «» counter-attack. That must have a concrete "dynamic" expression in coaching soccer.

It is not indifferent to realize that such a multi-interactive complex system (the soccer game) is also a very particular and irreproducible ecological system, created by ecological perception-actions, not "perceptive" (first) and "motor" (after) movements.

There is still much to do in the sense of creating a new theory and methodology of teaching/coaching team ball games, sustained in the most recent "science of complexity" and in an "ecological psychology/ecological approach to perception and action", between other diverse and trans-disciplinary contributions.

The priority in coaching soccer must be what may be called "ecological tactics", not "cognitive tactics".

It is essential to promote a "glocal" attitude and behaviour in that "ecological tactics" - and that means "repeating without repetition" each player's "ecological niche" (the essential network of each player in attack and in counter-attack, his/her proper and unique ecosystem cooperation and opposition "affordances") – are in agreement with the player's own "glocal/fractal" structure of perception-action/coordination. In this way "repeating without repetition" the «ecological niches» in training will help to realize a "specialized essentially ecological tactical training", where the player-team system functions.

"Complexity" in training must not be considered just as one more training "factor" (like volume, intensity and so on), a "mental-informational" factor, a "cognitive complexity" factor. It has to be a transversal factor, the unification factor of training, an "ecological complexity".

The organization of practice that follows the very well known pre-defined "progressions" central sports teaching/learning paradigm does not respect the real ecological complexity of the game, its non-linear nature. Thus, much attention must be paid to what is usually called "simplification". It should not decouple perception from action, and it must maintain its "glocal" (global + local) essential complex, fractal and ecological nature, as it occurs in competition.

Organization of practice must focus on "prospective and proactive ecological «discovery learning» production", not on any kind of "model reproduction" teaching/coaching methodology.

"Variability in practice" should be promoted, especially "ecological niche variability".

The role of the coach may be less to do with instruction and drilling the athlete and more to do with constraining the «ecological niches» sought by the learners in a self-organized and, many times, absolutely emergent way. In this way, the promotion of an "emergent tactics" is employed.

REFERENCES

Bayer, C., 1979, L' enseignement des Jeux Sportifs Collectifs. (Paris: Vigot).

Bernstein, N.A., 1967, The Co-ordination and Regulation of Movements. (Oxford: Pergamon Press).

Bootsma. R.J., 1988, The Timing of Rapid Interceptive Actions: Perception-action Coupling in the Control and Acquisition of Skill. (Amsterdam: Free University Press).

Bootsma, R. J. and van Wieringen, P.W.C., 1990, Timing an attacking forehand drive in table tennis. *Journal of Experimental Psychology*, Human Perception and Performance, **16**, 21–29.

Bootsma, R.J., Houbiers, M.H., Whiting, H.T.A. and van Wieringen, P.C.W., 1991, Acquiring an attacking forehand drive: the effects of static and dynamic environmental conditions. *Research Quarterly for Exercise and Sport*, **62**, 276–284.

Davids, K., Handford, C. and Williams, M., 1994, The natural physical alternative to cognitive theories of motor behavior: an invitation for interdisciplinary research in sports science? Journal of Sports Sciences, **12**, 495–528.

Garganta, J., 1994, Para uma teoria dos jogos desportivos colectivos. In O ensino dos jogos desportivos, edited by Graça, A. and Oliveira, J., (Centro de Estudos dos Jogos Desportivos: FCDE-UP), pp. 11–25.

Garganta, J., 1997, Modelação táctica no futebol - Estudo da organização da fase ofensiva em equipas de alto rendimento. Dissertação de Doutoramento. (Porto: Faculdade de Ciências do Desporto e de Educação Física, Universidade do Porto).

Gibson, J.J., 1966, The Senses Considered as Perceptual Systems. (Boston: Houghton Mifflin).

Gibson, J.J., 1986, The ecological approach to visual perception. (Hillsdale: Lawrence Erlbaum).

Gréhaigne, J.F. and Godbout, P., 1995, Tactical knowledge in team sports from a constructivist and cognitivist perspective. *Quest*, **47**, 490–505.

Gréhaigne, J.F., Bouthier, D. and David, B., 1997, Dynamic-system analysis of opponent relationships in collective actions in soccer. *Journal of Sports Sciences*, **15**, 137–149.

Gréhaigne, J.F., Billard, M., Guillon, R., and Roche, J., 1989, Vers une autre conception de l'enseignement des sports collectifs. In Méthodologie et Didactique de l'EPS, edited by Bui-Xuan, G. (Clermond-Ferrand : Editions AFRAPS (revue STAPS)), pp. 201–216.

Haken, H., Kelso, J.A.S. and Bunz, H., 1985, A theoretical model of phase transitions in human hand movements. *Biological Cybernetics*, **51**, 347–356.

Juarrero, A., 1999, Dynamics in Action – Intentional Behavior as a Complex System. (Cambridge, MA: MIT Press).

Kelso, J.A.S., 1995, Dynamic Patterns - the Self-organization of Brain and Behavior. (Cambridge: MA, MIT Press).

Konzag, I., 1990, Attività cognitiva e formazione del giocatore. Rivista di Cultura Sportiva, IX (20), 14–20.

Konzag, I., 1991, La formazione tecnico-tattica nei giochi sportivi. Rivista di Cultura Sportiva, Numero Monografico, Suppl. **22**, 27–34.

Mahlo, F., 1969, Acte Tactique en Jeu. (Paris: Vigot).

Mandelbrot, K., 1977, The Fractal Geometry of Nature. (NY: Freeman).

McGarry, T., Anderson, D., Wallace, S., Hughes, M. and Franks, I., 2002, Sport competition as a dynamical self-organizing system. *Journal of Sports Sciences*, **20**, 771–781.

Menaut, A., 1983, Jeux sportiffs collectives - niveux de jeu et modèle opératoire. Motricité Humaine, **2**, 15–21.

Michaels, C.F. and Carello, C., 1981, Direct Perception. (New Jersey: Prentice-Hall).

Moreno, J.H., 1994, Analisis de las Estructuras del Juego Deportivo. Publ. (Barcelona: INDE).

Newell, K.M., 1986, Constraints on the development of coordination. In Motor Development in Children - Aspects of Coordination and Control, edited by Wade, M.G. and Whiting, H.T.A. (Dordrecht: Nijhoff), pp. 341–360.

Odum, E.P., 1959, Fundamentals of Ecology. (Philadelphia: W. B. Saunders Co).

Reed, E.S. 1982, An outline of a theory of action systems. *Journal of Motor Behavior*, 14, 98–134.

Reed, E.S., 1996, Encountering the World - Toward an Ecological Psychology. (New York: Oxford, Oxford University Press).

Rosnay, J., 1975, Le Macroscope - vers une vision globale. (Paris: Seuil).

Sardinha, L., 1992, A Coordenação visuo-motora na sincronização de acções rápidas/aplicação ao estudo do remate de Voleibol. Dissertação de Doutoramento, (Lisboa: FMH).

Schmidt, R.C., Carello, C. and Turvey, M.T., 1990, Phase transitions and critical fluctuations in the visual coordination of rhythmic movements between people. *Journal of Experimental Psychology*: Human Perception and Performance, **16**, 227–247.

Silva, P.C., 1995, O lugar do corpo - elementos para uma cartografia fractal. Dissertação de doutoramento. Faculdade de Ciências do Desporto e de Educação Física. Universidade do Porto.

Teodorescu, L., 1965, Principes pour l' étude de la tactique commune aux jeux sportifs collectifs. Revue S.I.E.P.E.P.S., **3**, 29–40.

Teodorescu, L., 1977, Théorie et Méthodologie des Jeux Sportifs. (Paris : Les Editeurs Français Réunis).

van Gelder, T., 1997, The Dynamical Hypothesis in Cognitive Science http//ariel.its.unimelb.edu.au/~tgelder

Vereijken, B. and Whiting, H.T.A., 1990, In defence of discovery learning. *Canadian Journal of Sport Psychology*, **15**, 99–106.

85   Cohesion in Women's Soccer Teams

Z. Papanikolaou, A. Patsiaouras, P. Fourkioti and G. Douka
University of Thessaly/TEFAA, 42100 Trikala, Greece

1. INTRODUCTION

Guidance and communication are undoubtedly the most important parts for the successful route of a soccer team and the completion of its goals. The cohesion among the team members, and also the cohesion among the team members and their coach are very important. Generally speaking, we can find in a team a homogenous construct in the team players' abilities, in their psychological or personal characteristics and in their social origin. In sports, cohesion is defined as a) the attraction among the players, similarity in performance (Biondo and Pirritano, 1985); b) the feelings of satisfaction from the social (Grand and Carron, 1982; Carron, 1990) and the work-related perspective (Martens and Peterson, 1971); c) the acceptance of the team's goals (Grand and Carron, 1982) and the friendly competition among the players (Myers, 1962; Papanikolaou, 1988; Papanikolaou *et al.* in press); d) the understanding, acceptance, and output of the role (Grand and Carron, 1982; Carron, 1984). According to Shaw (1971), cohesion consists of three different sub-meanings:-

- attraction to the team, in the sense that the player does not want to leave the team;
- the team's ethical motivation;
- coordination of the team players' efforts.

Usually the significance of cohesion is faced under two dimensions (Mikalachki, 1969):-

- cohesion as attraction of members between them, collaboration of players of team in independent activities, as also cohesion as a developed system of rights and obligations of the team members;
- cohesion as mechanistic solidarity, collaboration of players within a team in a limited spectrum of activities, and also cohesion as a well developed system of punishment. The system of punishment is used, on one hand to limit the activities of the players and on the other hand to discourages the appearance of independent behaviours.

Also, researchers (Yukelson *et al.*, 1984) examined cohesion as the multi-dimensional psycho-social phenomenon and used methods which analysed factors, so as to determine the factors in the attraction of the team, the valuable roles, the work unity and the team quality, as characteristics of cohesion. In the literature, we found cohesion is related in a positive sense to the good performance of a team. Other studies have shown the exact opposite, although the existence of a positive relationship between the cohesion of the members in a team and the team's performance was not observed (Gill, 1986). There are many reasons for these contradictory results, from the lack of adequate questionnaires for the satisfactory measurement of cohesion to the methodological problems which come from inconsistent ways of measuring cohesion (interviews, questionnaires, videotaping, etc.). Also, the selection of the subjects (participants) in the studies has proved to be a problem because cohesion is a term which can be used and is a part of team sports (soccer, volleyball, basketball, etc.) where cooperative behaviour and dependent activities are observed among the players. It is not entirely clear, however, whether successful performance enhances group "togetherness" or whether cohesion produces performance increments. Investigators have frequently found that cohesiveness is influenced by the relative level of success achieved by a work group (Scott and Cotter, 1984; Papanikolaou, 1988). In contrast, cohesion does not seem to be a part of, or used in sports such as shooting targets, bowling, etc., from which most of the negative results come, since the performance of each player in the team is independent and simply is added to that of the rest of the team.

The objectives of the study were to examine the level of cohesion not only among the players, but also among the players and the coach of women's soccer teams, and to examine the differences in comparison with the Greek national women's soccer team.

2. MATERIALS AND DATA COLLECTION

2.1. Participants

The sample was made up of N = 73 female soccer players. In this sample, 15 were players in the women's national team (M age = 23.93, SD = 3.41). The rest N = 58 competed in the national soccer league (category A) (age M = 22.22, SD = 4.31). The players participated in the particular sport from 1 to 10 years with M = 6.00, SD = 2.24 for the national team and M = 4.33 SD = 2.60 for the rest of the players. Their participation in the study was voluntary.

2.2. Instruments – Procedure

The data were collected using the questionnaire GEQ (Group Environment Questionnaire), (Carron, Widmeyer and Brawley, 1985) in its Greek version. To avoid situation-specific response bias, the questionnaire was administrated to players at times not immediately preceding or subsequent to competition. Administration occurred at weekday practices within the regular season.

3. RESULTS

One-way ANOVA was used in order to evaluate the results and to compare the cohesion of the players of other teams to the players in the national team. Significant statistical differences were found for the factor of cohesion among

Greek national teams in comparison to that of the national women's team ($F_{1,71}$ = 8.931; P < 0.004) (Figure 1).

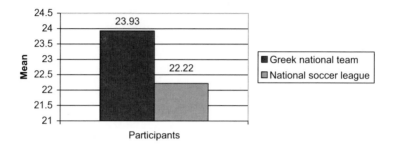

Figure 1. Players' mean cohesion.

4. DISCUSSION

Statistically important differences were observed between the national team players and the remaining players in the cohesion of players with the coach. Research supports the view that the coach's behaviour constitutes a basic mechanism for the creation of a good climate in the team, for the facilitation of its performance and the achievement of objectives (Martens and Peterson, 1971; Papanikolaou, 1988; Papanikolaou *et al.*, in press). According to the above, the leading behaviour of the coach, his personality and his technical knowledge can improve, or destroy the cohesion between the female players of the soccer team. Future studies should be focused on the contribution of the coach in the cohesiveness of soccer teams. Team cohesion is a psychological characteristic (Mikalachki, 1969; VanBergen and Koekebakker, 1959) and the coach must be aware of the psychological well-being of the players as well as their physical well-being. The coach must be sensitive to the need of the players and apply any procedures that would help in the development of cohesiveness within the team. In attempting to develop team cohesion the following ideas and strategies could be used by the coaches (Papanikolaou, 1988):

- develop a team identity;
- enhance individual and group motivation;
- develop social cohesion;
- promote communication;
- develop player satisfaction;
- develop team leadership;
- emphasize the value of discipline;
- stress team concept (emphasis of team work);
- cultivate optimistic attitudes;
- players should help each other;
- discuss positive and negative themes.

REFERENCES

Biondo, R. and Pirritano, M., 1985, The effects of sports practice upon the psycho-social integration of the team. *International Journal of Sport Psychology,* **1,** 28–36.

Carron, A., 1984, Cohesion in sport teams. In *Psychological Foundations of Sport,* edited by Silva, J. and Weinberg, R. (Champaign, IL: Human Kinetics), pp. 340–351.

Carron, A., 1990, Group size in sport and physical activity: Social psychological and performance consequences. *International Journal of Sport Psychology,* **1,** 286–304.

Carron, A., Widmeyer, W. and Brawley, L., 1987, The development of an instrument to assess cohesion in sport teams: The group environment questionnaire. *Journal of Sport Psychology,* **7,** 224–266.

Gill, D.L., 1986, *Psychological Dynamics of Sport.* (Champaign, IL: Human Kinetics).

Grand, R.R. and Carron, A., 1982, Development of a team climate questionnaire. In *Psychology of Sport and Motor Behavior: Research and Practice,* edited by Wankel, L. and Wilberg, R. (Edmonton: Department of Recreation and Leisure Studies, University of Alberta).

Martens, R. and Peterson, J., 1971, Group cohesiveness as a determinant of success and member satisfaction in team performance. *International Review of Sport Psychology,* **6,** 49–71.

Mikalachki, A., 1969, *Group Cohesion Reconsidered.* (London: School of Business Administration).

Myers, A., 1962, Team competition, success, and the adjustment of group members. *Journal of Abnormal and Social Psychology,* **65,** 325–332.

Papanikolaou, K.Z., 1988, The effects of a psychological skills training program on the cohesion of a men's soccer team. Unpublished Master's Thesis, Temple University, Philadelphia.

Papanikolaou, Z., Patsiaouras, A. and Keramidas, P., (in press). Family systems approach in building soccer team. *Inquiries in Sport & Physical Education.*

Scott, K.D. and Cotter, T., 1984, The team that works together earns together. *Personal Journal,* **63,** 58–60.

Shaw, J.I., 1971, Situational factors contributing to a psychological advantage competitive negotiations. *Journal of Personality and Social Psychology,* **19,** 251–260.

VanBergen, A. and Koekebakker, J., 1959, Group cohesiveness in laboratory experiments. *Acta Psychologica,* **16,** 81–98.

Yukelson, D., Weinberg, R. and Jackson, A., 1984, A multidimensional group cohesion instrument for intercollegiate basketball teams. *Journal of Sport Psychology,* **6,** 103–117.

86 Coaching Strategies in a Spanish 1st Division Club's Football School

R. Martinez De Santos[1], J. Castellano[1] and A. Los Arcos[1]
[1]Basque Institute of Physical Education, Vitoria-Gasteiz, Spain

1. INTRODUCTION

The research presented here is the initial results of the *Tajonar-2004* quality project, a sort of melting pot where academic interests and professional needs blend together. The description of coaching strategies employed in the Tajonar School was considered the starting point for a revision of methodological aspects and future training of coaches themselves. In that sense, results shown below are a brief but significant selection of the many aspects taken into account, all of them pertinent features of the strategies that configure what coaching means with respect to C.A. Osasuna minor teams.

2. COACHING

One of us (Martínez de Santos, 2001) has proposed a distinction between two different aspects of coaching: on the one hand is planning; on the other hand is putting this into practice. Assuming that strategic thinking is a demand of the context more than a personal option (Morin, 2003), *coaching strategies* refer to the process of planning, that is, the distribution of resting and practice time into split periods with different contents; in contrast to strategies, *coaching styles* would include those specific aspects of the relationship that coaches establish with players during the sessions. Differences between coaches, methods or programmes can be better explained according to this simple but basic division.

Coaching style is closely bound to what is called *instructional behaviour*. Every coach shows a particular way of conducting practice sessions. Instructors' performance has been analyzed focusing on different aspects (Hughes and Franks, 1997) of their "verbal coaching strategies.

In contrast, planning is the most relevant aspect of training. Playing is what teaches and not the coach. This assumption does not detract from us as coaches; it is quite the reverse, as being aware of this is the first step towards successful instruction.

Teaching is possible when positive transfer processes between motor situations are activated. Parlebas and Dugas (1998) showed that the internal logic of practice situations was at the centre of learning transfer: there is no transfer at all between athletics and team sports; there is positive transfer between traditional games and team sports, and *vice versa*.

It is a truism that one activity cannot generate all effects and that all activities cannot generate one same effect. The selection of motor action logics is the coaches' responsibility and their main task, which is why the term *strategy* is not a synonym of philosophy or general principles of coaching (Hargreaves, 1990).

3. METHODS

3.1. Subjects and material

Six experienced and qualified coaches took part voluntarily in the research. They were informed about the general objectives and conditions of privacy of data.

These coaches were responsible for A and B teams in U-14, U-16 and U-19 age categories. These categories were considered to be the most interesting for both researchers and the Club.

Data collection was based on a *pen and paper* procedure: assistant coaches were asked to register the session on the sheets provided by the Club, with special attention given to time. Every week coaches handed out the reports of the sessions.

A database in Windows Access 2002 was designed for recording the questionnaire for each activity reported, and SPSS 10.0 software was used for statistical analysis.

3.2. Questionnaire

We designed a questionnaire inspired by that used by Parlebas (1998) containing two types of items:-

- *Identification data* inform about the following aspects: identification number of the activity; order number within the session; part of the session; type of activity; name, description.

- Registered elements of the *internal logic* were the relations that the players established with *space, time, materials* and *the other players.*

4. RESULTS AND DISCUSSION

4.1. Time distribution

Time management has already been highlighted as an important aspect of coaching (Kozoll, 1985) from a general point of view. We consider it more productive to look into the temporal structure of sessions and activities. Table 1 shows how long each part of the session lasted. Around 75% of the time was dedicated to specific training contents out of almost 90 min per session, the differences between age groups being non-significant (Univariate Analysis of Variance, UNIANOVA).

Table 1. Mean durations of each part of the session (minutes).

	N	Total time h:min	Mean h:min	Warm-up	Practice	Cool-down	Total
U-14	48	41: 18'	82'05"	16	77	7	100
U-16	49	40 :15'	85'43"	15	72	13	100
U-19	71	55: 38'	84'30"	18	73	9	100

[a] $F = 0.53$ ($P = 0.714$).

It is interesting to note how much time was employed in practice and how much in organization. In Table 2 we can see that task-time was always over 80% of total time, minimum value corresponding to U-19 teams. A t-test for the equality of means showed significant differences between U-14 and U-19 categories ($P<0.05$). Intervention of coaches during U-19 sessions gained importance and suggests a future research topic about styles. The relation between task and break times was evaluated by defining the Task-Time/Break-Time ratio indicator; the absence of significant differences in itself proved to be striking, apart from any strong tendency shown.

Table 2. Mean ± SD durations of task and break periods in central part of the session (minutes).

	% in the session	Task-Time $\overline{X}$	SD	Breaks $\overline{X}$	SD	TT/B Ratio $\overline{X}$	SD
U-14	77	54'59"	8'16"	8'48"	4'10"	7.53	3.54
U-16	73	54'24"	9'24"	8'35"	3'36"	7.58	4.39
U-19	72	49'58"	14'58"	13'37"	6'26"	5.40[a]	7.34

[a] t-test values for comparison of means are 1.790 ($P = 0.076$) for U-14 and 1.749 ($P = 0.083$) for U-16.

4.2. Motor relationships between players

According to Parlebas (1999), uncertainty caused by the relationship between the player and spatial and social milieu is the main trait to grasp under what conditions the player must act. Soccer is characterized by a neutralized playing space and a maximum demand on the part of the relationship with other players. The simultaneous presence of partners and adversaries places the agent in a complex motor situation where *semiotricity* is a main factor of motor competence.

Semiotor demand refers to the deciphering effort a player must make while fulfilling a motor task, depending on the informational traits of the activity. Table 3 illustrates differences found between age groups: a chi-squared test permitted the identification of three different coaching strategies as far as this aspect was concerned (duration was used as a weighting variable for frequency analysis).

Table 3. Semiotor demand per age category.

| | Low | | Medium | High | |
	Psychomotor	Collaboration	Opposition	Collaboration & Opposition	Total
U-14	19.8	11.8	7.4	60.9	100
U-16	23.2	15.3	4.0	57.6	100
U-19	21.4	6.2	3.7	68.6	100
Total	21.5	10.6	4.9	63.1	100

The columns above fall under the heading Semiotor demand[a].

[a] Pearson Chi-Square value = 127.44 ($P = 0.001$).

4.3. Sociomotor space

Space is a major aspect of a game and a primary reference for action. In that sense, we took into consideration several spatial traits. Table 4 displays, a) what kind of space was proposed (free-for-use at the player's convenience; split up into sub-spaces with specific regulations that must be integrated in decision making, or a very constrained use as in corner or free-kicks); b) whether space was *orientated* or not, if there was any goal of any kind that orientated action on one or more axis. Once again, different conceptions appeared enabling us to identify dissimilar strategies: the U-16 teams had a more frequent practice with sub-spaces; non-regulation goals (smaller ones, i.e.) were common in U-14, and use of official goals was *typically* U-19.

Table 4. Type of space and spatial orientation in Collaboration-Opposition activities.

| | Type of space[a] | | | Spatial orientation[b] | | | |
	Free use	Sub-spaces	Set-play	Regular goal	Non-regular	Other aims	No goal
U-14	85.2	11.7	3.1	55.6	18.1	8.6	17.7
U-16	68.2	26.3	5.5	58.3	10.5	12	19.2
U-19	75.6	18.3	6.1	70.6	5.3	8.6	15.5

[a] Pearson Chi-Squared value = 126.392 ($P < 0.001$).
[b] Pearson Chi-Squared value = 200.277 ($P < 0.001$).

One last aspect should be mentioned to illustrate particular uses of common elements: the *IIS-Interaction Individual Space* (Parlebas, 1998). This indicator is calculated by dividing the total play surface among all players. Results can be commented upon in two ways: firstly, figures must be compared to the IIS of soccer (about 320 m^2), which allows one to see how space tended to be reduced in training although not equally in every category; secondly, the behaviour of the standard deviation in relation to the number of players suggests that coaches paid greater attention to this value the more players they put into action to balance offense and defence as they estimated to be appropriate, although UNIANOVA testing showed that there was not a shared logic across categories as far as this trait was concerned. We should not forget either that this quantitative aspect of space is inversely proportional to the difficulty of the task.

Table 5. Mean ± SD Interaction Individual Space in relation to number of players (m^2).

	Number of participants (quartiles) in CO situations[a]							
	3-5		6-11		12-15		16-22	
	$\overline{X}$	SD	$\overline{X}$	SD	$\overline{X}$	SD	$\overline{X}$	SD
U-14	150.09	119.76	56.52	54.84	105.44	72.72	170.89	54.86
U-16	117.58	81.08	81.75	78.25	97.27	70.29	139.18	49.82
U-19	268.93	140.34	132.14	117.15	125.02	61.08	136.66	48.01

[a] $F = 64.399$ ($P < 0.001$).

5. CONCLUSIONS

Coaching strategies found in Tajonar were all *mixed strategies* (Binmore, 1994). At different levels of statistical significance, coaches never used pure strategies (betting always on the same number when playing dice for example) by choosing always the same type of action logic.

Figure 1 is a compilation of *coaching performance indicators* representing a synchronic description of Tajonar's reality at a given moment. Namely: *TT/B ratio:* task-time/break-time ratio; *%-PO/10:* percentage of Collaboration-Opposition practice divided by 10; *IIS-CO/10:* Interaction Individual Space when CO divided by ten; *%-OS/10=* percentage of practice with Orientated Space divided by ten.

Members of Tajonar's staff now have the opportunity to ask themselves if the necessary progression in players' development is sustained by coaching strategies such as the ones represented in Figure 1, and question the *opportunity cost* (Samuelson and Nordhaus, 1992) of their strategy. Has practice time been profitable or would another strategy have been better?

Soccer's internal logic is of a complexity that demands a profound reflection on the coach's part as regards how to act, and of a richness that offers itself as the main instruction tool and most powerful conceptual and practical device. Coaching and strategy only match up if planning is thought to be responsible for the learning process instead of luck and destiny.

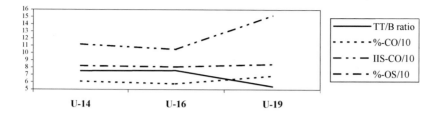

Figure 1. Diachronic relation between several aspects of coaching strategies.

Acknowledgements

We would like to give special thanks to Caja Navarra (Savings Bank of Navarra) for their support, and participant coaches for their collaboration.

REFERENCES

Binmore, K., 1994, *Teoría de Juegos.* (Madrid: McGraw-Hill).

Hargreaves, A., 1990, *Skills and Strategies for Coaching Soccer.* (Champaign, IL: Leisure Press).

Hughes, M. and Franks, I., 1997, *Notational Analysis of Sport.* (London: E & FN Spon).

Kozoll, C.E., 1985, *Coaches Guide to Time Management.* (Champaign, IL: Human Kinetics).

Martínez de Santos, R., 2001, La planificación del entrenamiento como estrategia mixta. In *Aportaciones al Proceso de Enseñanza y Entrenamiento del Baloncesto*, edited by Ibáñez, S.J., y Macías, M.M. (Copegra: Cáceres), pp. 119–127.

Morin, E., 2003, *Introducción al Pensamiento Complejo.* (Barcelona: Gedisa).

Parlebas, P., 1998, Jeux d'enfants s'après Jacques Stella et culture ludique au XVIIe siècle. In *A quoi joue-t-on ? Festival d'histoire de Montbrison.*

Parlebas, P., 1999, *Jeux, sports et sociétés. Lexique de praxéologie motrice* (Paris : INSEP).

Parlebas, P. and Dugas, E., 1998, Transfert d'apprentissage et domaines d'action motrice. *Education Physique et Sportive*, **270**, 41–47.

Samuelson, P.A. and Nordhaus, W.D., 1992, *Economía.* (México: McGraw-Hill).

87 Leadership Behaviour of the Coach in Amateur Soccer Teams

Z. Papanikolaou, A. Patsiaouras and P. Keramidas
University of Thessaly/TEFAA, 42100 Trikala, Greece

1. INTRODUCTION

Guidance and communication are undoubtedly the most important part of leadership in sports and in particular the leadership of the coach in amateur soccer teams. When we refer to leadership, we mean: 1) the behaviour of a leader with the purpose of directing and synchronising the energies of a team (Fiedler, 1967); 2) the two-way oral communication that the people involved have among themselves behaviour-wise (Patsiaouras, 1999); 3) a behaviour process which influences directly people and teams to set goals and to strive for their success (Barron *et. al* 1977); 4) the practice of power and decision-making (Phillips, 1966; Chelladurai and Arnott, 1985).

From the above we conclude that the role of a leader is very important because he/she who must play it, influences the behaviour of the team. In soccer teams, the role of the leader is usually played by the coach. He/she is mainly responsible for the good performance of the athletes, the act of helping players to acquire and improve motor skills, and the consistency and good climate in the team. Despite all the above, it is difficult to determine which leadership style is the most appropriate for soccer teams. In sports, the theoretical realm differs from the bipolar (Fiedler, 1967; Martens, 1987; Patsiaouras, 1999) to the multidimensional leadership model (Chelladurai and Arnott, 1985; Chelladurai, 1990).

The objective of the study was to examine the leadership behaviour of the coaches in amateur soccer teams.

2. MATERIALS AND DATA COLLECTION

2.1. Participants

The sample consisted of twenty coaches of amateur soccer teams. The ages of the participants were between 21 and 45 years of age with $M = 34.25$, $SD = 7.05$. The coaches coached the particular sport for 2 to 14 years with M years of coaching = 6.70, $SD = 3.75$. The coaching diploma which they possessed was for categories A', B', C'. Their participation in the study was voluntary.

2.2. Instruments – Procedure

The data were collected by means of the questionnaire Leadership Scale for Sports (LSS) (Chelladurai and Saleh, 1980) in its Greek version. The data were collected by the researchers in the fields where the coaches trained, after the practice session.

3. RESULTS

The one sample t-test was used for the evaluation of the results. Results indicated that the coaches did apply the motivational factors (social support and positive feedback) more than the two decision-style factors (democratic and autocratic behaviour).

Table 1. One-sample t-test of the factors of the LSS test (P<0.05).

Factors of LSS-test	N	Mean	SD	t-value
Coaching – teaching	20	21.90	1.86	52.62
Democratic behaviour	20	11.85	3.45	15.34
Autocratic behaviour	20	14.15	2.94	21.50
Social support	20	20.55	1.93	47.55
Positive feedback	20	22.15	2.37	41.83

Finally coaches were in favour of the coaching and teaching leadership style.

4. DISCUSSION

From the statistical analysis of the results, it was concluded that the coaches of amateur soccer teams influence their teams positively, care very much for practice and their learning, and have a large sense of social responsibility as far as their weak players, in particular, are concerned. This way they were trying to reward, support, and increase their players' performance, but also improve the relationships among the players. Also, it was observed that there was a slightly higher preference for the autocratic leadership behaviour over the democratic leadership behaviour. Coaching behaviour aimed at improving players' performance by emphasizing and facilitating hard and strenuous training; instructing players in the techniques, skills, and tactics of soccer; clarifying the relationship among the players; and structuring and coordinating the players' activities (Papadogiannis and Mann, 2001). It has been found that experienced male athletes prefer more autocratic behaviour and, at the same time, more social support than less experienced athletes (Chelladurai and Carron, 1982). There is a common tendency to view the autocratic style as something evil, indulged in only by despots and dictators as a device for furthering their own interests. The democratic style is viewed as a humanistic approach aimed at the welfare of the members. Coaches and athletes must understand that these leadership styles are not value laden and that the autocratic style can be associated with humanism and goodness. Finally, research in the area of leadership styles, although rather limited, clearly shows that the autocratic leadership style is quite acceptable to athletes in certain circumstances and motivates them (Patsiaouras, 1999). Coaches need to select a leadership style appropriate to the particular situation rather than being guided by a belief that one style is always superior to the other.

REFERENCES

Barron, R.A., Byme, D. and Kantonitz, B.H., 1977, *Psychology: Understanding Behaviour*. (Philadelphia: W. B. Saunders).

Chelladurai, P., 1990, Leadership in sports: A review. *International Journal of Sport Psychology,* **21**, 328–354.

Chelladurai, P. and Arnott, M., 1985, Decision styles in coaching: Preferences of basketball players. *Research Quarterly for Exercise and Sport,* **56**, 15–24.

Chelladurai, P. and Carron, A.V., 1982, *Task characteristics and individual differences, and their relationship to preferred leadership in sports.* Paper presented at the annual meeting of the North American Society for the Psychology of Sport and Physical Activity, College Park, Maryland.

Chelladurai, P. and Saleh, S.D. 1980, Dimensions of leader behaviour in sports. Development of a leadership scale. *Journal of Sport Psychology*, **2** (1), 34–45.

Fiedler, F.E., 1967, *A Theory of Leadership Effectiveness*. (New York: McGraw-Hill).

Martens, R. 1987, *Coaches Guide to Sport Psychology*. (Champaign IL: Human Kinetics).

Papadogiannis, P. and Mann, D., 2001, Perceived coaching styles and sport cohesion. In International Society of Sport Psychology, 10th World Congress of Sport Psychology. *In the Dawn of the New Millennium, vol. 2, Programme & Proceedings,* edited by Papaioannou, A., Goudas, M. and Theodorakis, Y. (Skiathos: Christodoulidi Publications), pp. 224–226.

Patsiaouras, A., 1999, *Motivation ''die nicht - direktive Methode'' im Hochleistungssport (Volleyball)*. Unveröffentliches Diss., Universität Wien.

Phillips, G.M., 1966, *Communication and the Small Group*. (NY: the Bobbs-Merrill Company).

88 Perceptions Towards the Causes of Success and Failure among Youth Footballers

Mohd. Sofian Bin Omar Fauzee[1] and Shamsharizal Bin Abd. Aziz[2]
[1]University Putra Malaysia, Malaysia
[2]Malacca Matriculation College, Malaysia

1. INTRODUCTION

The theory of attribution had been studied in detail in the sport domain (Rejeski and Brawley, 1983). Sports orientated researchers have usually focused on explanations forwarded by athletes on the experience of success or failure they went through. In general, this theory focused on the process whereby individuals interpret their daily happenings, later try to explain why they happened (Jones et al., 1971). The achievement motivation of the Attribution Theory model specifically reflects the individual's interest in the search for explanations of the achievements he/she had acquired (Weiner, 1985). To simplify, Weiner (1972) combined four main factors, which were ability (stable internal factor), effort (always a changing and unstable internal factor), task difficulty (always stable and unchangeable external factor) and luck (unstable and changeable external factors). These factors were classified as the cause of successes and failures, which were transformed into two dimensions of main causes. These two dimensions were labelled stability and locus of control. The stability dimension consists of stable and unstable while the locus of control dimension consists of internal and external factors. Locus of control means that the individual believes that whatever had happened was caused by him/her or caused by other people. Athletes who are fond of internal control believe that whatever had happened was caused by their own actions. On the other hand, athletes who were inclined towards external control stated that their achievements were mainly influenced by factors such as luck, opportunities and other people.

The purpose of this study was to determine the fondness of young soccer players in explaining the cause of success and failure in football. The causes of success and failure were based on Weiner's Attribution Theory (1972), which consists of ability, effort, task difficulty and luck. There has been no such study on the Attribution Theory being carried out in Malaysia. According to Khoo (2002), more in-depth studies are necessary for the development of sports in Malaysia.

2. METHODS

The subjects for this study consisted of 16 footballers from Malacca Matriculation College, Malaysia. They were the main players often chosen to represent the college in friendly matches. The subjects were also chosen from different positions and the average age was 18.3 (SD 3.4) years. They had experience of playing football for between three to nine years.

The instrument for this study was interview. Questionnaires were used to enable the researcher to gain information on the subjects' perceptions of the causes of their success and failure in football matches according to Weiner's Attribution Theory (1972).

Firstly, the researcher identified the subjects for this study. Secondly, the researcher contacted the subjects to have their agreement to undergo the recorded interview by sending formal letters to them. The interviews took place after the subjects had given their agreements to be interviewed. The interviews were carried out face to face at a suitable and favourable place chosen by the respondents. Each interview lasted 15 min and was recorded on tape. Every word was transcribed and analysed by the researcher assisted by a Masters student in Sport Science. The answers given were classified as 'raw theme'and then categorised into the four dimensions of Weiner's Attribution Theory (1972) namely ability, effort task difficulty and luck.

3. RESULTS

Based on the interview, the researcher managed to identify the attributes of each respondent. The raw themes were divided into the higher order themes before including them into the general dimensions (ability, effort, task difficulty and luck) as outlined in Weiner's Attribution Theory (1972). On the whole there were 83 (53 win/success; 30 lose/failure) raw themes. Altogether 60.2 percent were categorized as ability dimension, 21.8 percent as effort dimension, 8.4 percent as task difficulty dimension and 9.6 percent as luck dimension (Table 1).

4. DISCUSSION

This study observed 16 youth footballers on their perceptions with respect to their success and failure. Their perceptions were tabled according the Weiner's Attribution Theory (1972), which consists of ability, effort, task difficulty and luck. The respondents tended to explain ability as the cause of their success or failure in soccer matches rather than the other aspects.

According to Cox (2002), some young athletes felt that their failures were caused by their lack of ability. This statement supported the findings in this study. There were 18 causes (60%) of failures mentioned by the respondents, which can be categorized into the ability dimension. For instance, among the causes were – low skilled players, blunders, fatigue and lack of understanding among the players. This finding was disappointing because ability is permanent and unchangeable according to Weiner (1972). The players felt that their failures were caused by their own inability, which cannot be changed and therefore they will likely withdraw from the game. McAuley and Gross's (1983) research indicated that the respondents tended to explain their success and failure as due to unstable external factors. Luck was an unstable external factor according to Weiner's attribution model (1972). This was inconsistent with this study's findings as only 6 percent of the themes were found to be relevant to luck. This showed that the respondents in this research had insufficient belief in luck determining the match results. Instead, they were more likely to relate their performance with other factors.

According to Bar-Tal and Frieze (1977) and Feather (1969), male athletes tend to explain that their success and failure were caused by internal factors, namely ability and effort. This finding was quite reasonable because the respondents were more likely to explain that their performance was due to self-achievement. White's (1993) research also supported this finding that male respondents were more likely to relate their success to the internal factors compared to females. At the same time, this present research was found to be less supportive of previous work by Bird and William (1980). They found that male youth players explained that their performances were influenced by effort while in this research only 21.8 percent of the statements about the causes of performance were based on the effort factor.

In conclusion, there was a difference in the finding between earlier studies (especially in the West) and this present study. Therefore, more studies need to be carried out locally. Further cross-cultural studies, especially in Asia, are also suggested in the near future. It is hoped that this study's findings would be beneficial in upgrading the quality of sport in Asia.

REFERENCES

Bar-Tal, D. and Frieze, I., 1977, Achievement motivation for males and females as a determinant of attributions for success and failure. *Sex Roles,* **2**, 301–310.

Bird, A.M. and Williams, J.M., 1980, A developmental-attribution analysis of sex-role stereotypes for sport. *Developmental Psychology,* **16**, 319–322.

Cox, R.H., 2002, *Sport Psychology: Concepts and Application (5ᵗʰ ed.),* (New York: McGraw-Hill).

Feather, N.T., 1969, Attribution of responsibility and valence of success and failure in relation to initial confidence and perceived locus of control. Journal of *Personalty and Social Psychology,* **13**, 129–144.

Jones, E.E., Kanouse, D.E., Kelley, H.H., Nisbett, R.E., Valins, S. and Weiner, B., 1971, *Attributions: Perceiving the Causes of Behaviour.* (Morristown, NJ: General Learning Press).

Khoo, K.K., 2002, Jurulatih perlu kajian mendalam: Mengharap era Baru [Coaches needs research in coaching: Towards the new era]. *Arena Boleepak [Football Arena February].* pp. 56–57.

McAuley, E. and Gross, J.B., 1983, Perceptions of causality in sport: An application of the casual dimension scale. *Journal of Sport Psychology,* **5,** 278–287.

Rejeski, W.J. and Brawley, L.R., 1983, Attribution theory in sport: Current status and new perspectives. *Journal of Sport Psychology,* **5,** 77–99.

Weiner, B., 1972, *Theories of Motivation: From Mechanism to Cognition.* (Chicago: Rand McNally).

Weiner, B., 1985, An attributional theory of achievement motivation and emotion. *Psychological Review,* **92**, 548–573.

White, S.A., 1993, The effects of gender and age on casual attribution in softball players. *International Journal of Sport Psychology,* **24**, 49–58.

89 Psychological Relationship between Trainers and Young Players: Leadership Aspects

R. Vanfraechem-Raway
Laboratory of Motricity Sciences – ISEPK,
Université Libre de Bruxelles

1. INTRODUCTION

Interaction processes between athletes and coaches always have been considered to be determinants of sport performance (Serpa, 1995). It is well recognised that the leadership mode influences group participation as well as group work and group performance. On the other hand we know that at the beginning of the critical adolescence period, the young individual is particularly vulnerable as he or she tries to become independent and to get an adult identity with self-affirmation. The young fails and become adapted to the environment and to self and rejects every restraint. The relation with adults becomes difficult.

The human characteristics thought to be indispensable for an "ideal trainer" are the following:- a non-directive leader responsible with self-consciousness and consciousness of the repercussion of his/her behaviour, good emotional adaptation, comprehensive listening to athletes, and adequate knowledge in socio-psychology (Vanfraechem-Raway, 2002).

The aim of this study was to analyse young players' evaluations of their own trainers and to compare responses with their views about the "ideal trainer". Expectations were that in top level teams there was a concordance between the evaluations the trainer by the players and the trainer's self-evaluation; the best trainers were aware of their own behaviour; and there were a concordance between the evaluations of the trainer by the players and their opinion about "an ideal trainer behaviour".

2. METHODS

2.1. Participants

The participants of this study were 106 football players (age 12.6 years) from 8 national cadet teams, and their coaches (Table 1).

Table 1. Number of players' responses, trainer age and years of practice in top teams and other teams.

	Top teams			Other teams				
	1	2	3	4	5	6	7	8
Players' Responses (n)	13	14	14	14	14	12	13	12
Trainer age	34	28	32	27	33	32	44	38
Years of practice	3	5	3	2	3	2	3	3

2.2. Instruments and procedures

The instruments were:

1) Bortoli questionnaire: a socio-emotional approach of the relation between trainers and players with negative and positive items about the feelings of this relation. We also utilized the same test for ideal trainer image (Bortoli, 1995);
2) Chelladurai (1993) leadership sport scale: an organizational approach with 3 interactive behavioural dimensions (training (T), rewarding (R) and social support (SS)), and 2 leadership behaviours (democratic (D) and autocratic (A)).

The questionnaires for trainers as well as for players were given out after a successful match at the end of the championship.

3. RESULTS

3.1. The feelings of the players about the trainers (Bartoli Questionnaire)

Results in scores (maximal score 5) of the top teams are presented in Table 2. Other teams' results are presented in Table 3.

For the three top teams, the trainers' self-evaluations were in the confidence interval of players' evaluation. There were no significant differences between ideal trainer profile and the real trainer evaluations by players. The ideal profile was the same for trainers and for players. Similar results were found for negative and positive items.

Table 2. Top teams results: players and trainers.

	N	Real trainer		Ideal trainer	
		Positive	Negative	Positive	Negative
Players (T1)	13				
M		3.65	1.18	3.9	1.16
SD		0.5	0.18	0.3	0.2
Confidence interval		0.27	0.1	0.16	0.11
Trainer (1)		3.8	1.1	4.1	1.1
Players (T2)	14				
M		3.86	1.46	4	1.16
SD		0.34	0.29	0.26	0.08
Confidence interval		0.18	0.15	0.14	0.04
Trainer		4	1.3	4.4	1
Players (T3)	14				
M		3.82	1.6	3.83	1.3
SD		0.36	0.27	0.35	0.2
Confidence interval		0.19	0.14	0.18	0.10
Trainer		4	1.4	4.1	1.2

Note. Positive and negative refer to the items evaluated.

For the five other teams, the trainer's self-evaluation was outside the confidence interval of the players' evaluation (for negative and positive items). There were significant differences between ideal trainer profile and real profile trainer evaluation by players (for negative and positive items). The ideal trainer profile was the same for trainer and players like in the top teams.

In Bortoli's items, young players did not appreciate trainers who neglect several players or who were only interested in the results. They did not like trainers who did not accept errors and who were unable to control their own emotional status.

Table 3. Other team's results: players and trainers.

	Real trainer		Ideal trainer		Comparisons	
	Positive items	Negative items	Positive items	Negative items	Positive items	Negative items
Players (T4)						
n = 14						
M̄	3.38	1.48	3.96	1.2	S***	S*
SD	0.18	0.23	0.25	0.18		
Confidence int.	0.18	0.15	0.13	0.09		
Trainer T4	4.2	1.14	4.3	1		
Players (T5)						
n = 14						
M̄	3.3	1.58	3.86	1.3	S***	NS
SD	0.22	0.28	0.18	0.21		
Confidence int.	0.19	0.15	0.09	0.11		
Trainer T5	4.14	1.25	4	1		
Players (T6)						
n = 12						
M	3.2	1.68	3.9	1.1	S*	S*
SD	0.5	0.4	0.3	0.28		
Confidence int.	0.28	0.23	0.17	0.14		
Trainer T6	3.9	1.2	4.5	1		
Players (T7)						
n = 13						
M	3.4	1.5	4.1	1	S***	S*
SD	0.4	0.35	0.35	0.28		
Confidence int.	0.24	0.19	0.2	0.15		
Trainer T7	4	1.4	4.3	1.2		
Players (T8)						
n = 12						
M	3.1	1.7	4.2	1	S***	S**
SD	0.53	0.4	0.55	0.4		
Confidence int.	0.30	0.23	0.55	0.23		
Trainer T8	4.2	1.2	4.5	1.2		

3.2. Trainer Leadership behaviours self-perceived, and perceived by the players (Chelladurai Leadership Sport Scale)

The results of the top teams players are presented in Table 4. Those of the other teams are presented in Table 5.

Table 4. Top teams: result in scores (maximum 5).

Behaviours Teams	T	R	SS	A	D
1. Players M	3.9	4	3.8	2.2	3.6
Confidence interval	0.28	0.4	0.28	0.3	0.28
Trainer	3.8	3.9	3.7	1.9	4
2. Players M	3.9	4.2	3.6	2.9	4.1
Confidence interval	0.37	0.3	0.4	0.3	0.4
Trainer	4.3	4.4	3.4	3.1	4.2
3. Players M	3.9	4.3	3.9	2.3	3.5
Confidence interval	0.27	0.3	0.3	0.4	0.28
Trainer	3.8	4.2	3.8	2.5	3.6

Note. F ANOVA is always significant.

R = Rewarding; T = Training; SS = Social support; D = Democratic; A = Autocratic.

In top teams it was interesting to note the coherence between trainer self-perception and players' perception of the trainer (trainers' perception in the confidence interval of players' evaluation). In the other teams, there was a difference between players and trainers particularly in autocratic behaviour. The importance of the feelings of interactive behaviour is underlined.

Table 5. Other teams.

Teams \ Behaviours	T	R	SS	A	D
4. Players M	3.6	3.6	3.4	2.4	2.2
Confidence interval	0.3	0.4	0.3	0.4	0.4
Trainer	4	4	3.6	3.4	3.1
5. Players M	3.8	4	3.3	3.1	1.6
Confidence interval	0.2	0.2	0.2	0.2	0.2
Trainer	4	4.3	2.9	2.6	2.9
6. Players M	3.9	4.4	3.4	3.3	3.5
Confidence interval	0.3	0.4	0.4	0.3	0.3
Trainer	3.4	3.6	3.9	2.4	3.9
7. Players M	3.6	3.5	2.9	3.7	1.8
Confidence interval	0.3	0.3	0.4	0.2	0.4
Trainer	3.9	3.6	3.4	2.3	3
8. Players M	4.1	4.2	3.1	3.6	3.1
Confidence interval	0.3	0.2	0.2	0.5	0.3
Trainer	3.7	3.6	3.7	3.1	3.6

Note. F ANOVA is always significant.
R = Rewarding; T = Training; SS = Social support; D = Democratic; A = Autocratic.

4. DISCUSSION AND CONCLUSION

According to the literature on adults and youth team sports (Chelladurai, 1984, 1993; Bortoli, 1995; Fonseca, 1995 a,b; Serpa, 1995, 2002; Vanfraechem-Raway, 2001, 2002), our results, even if limited to young soccer players, assessed the importance of knowledge in coach/athletes relationship and thus team efficacy. Moreover, we noted that coaches who had in their professional life a high contact with youth (pedagogical courses concerned with motor learning and experiences of motivation processes) appeared to have a better knowledge of their athletes.

In the top teams examined the three trainers were teachers and in the other teams only one of them was. It is particularly interesting to underline that only trainers of top teams presented a bilateral relationship. Indeed, only those trainers were present in the confidence interval around the mean of players' evaluation mean in both tests.

In Bortoli's test (socio-emotional approach) the good bilateral relationship also appeared in the coherence between the player ideal profile and the real perception of the trainer profile but only in top teams. In the other teams, through Bortoli items analysis, the trainers who had a lack of emotional control, who neglected some players, and who were restrained were rejected. The same aspects appeared in the data from Chelladurai's scale results. In top teams, the social support behaviour was at the same level as the other interactive behaviours in the players' feelings. Autocratic leadership behaviour was at the lowest level. There was a concordance between trainer and players' perceptions.

According to the studies of Chelladurai (1993) and Serpa (1995, 2002), the athletes' satisfaction depended on the players' expectations, and the trainers' real behaviour. In sub-elite team a real bilateral relationship was not evident as the trainers were not aware of the impact of their autocratic behaviour. The lack of satisfaction of those teams could not only be explained by the discordance in bilateral relation but also by the intensive autocratic feelings; this attitude restrained behaviour with adolescents. Present findings are in agreement with Serpa (1995) in his model of coach's ansiogenic behaviour in young soccer teams; it can be even more important because soccer is a highly popular and spectacular sport.

According to Deci and Ryan (1985), feelings of self-competence and self-realisation are essential to get real pleasure from (intrinsic motivation) and thus a deep and regular participation in sport. In order to obtain from young players a committed participation in sports, trainers have to be able to change and to adapt their behaviour to the players, giving an adequate response towards the young players' expectations. Therefore a trainer has to present a good awareness of his own behaviour, and its effect upon the success of the team.

For those reasons, the socio-psychological process has to be a part of the trainer's formation. This is especially important if he or she is concerned with the need of young soccer players to overcome their adolescent disturbances.

REFERENCES

Bortoli, L., 1995, Young athletes' perception of their coach's actual and ideal behavior. In *IXth European Congress on Sport Psychology,* Brussels, edited by Vanfraechem-Raway R. and Auweele, Y.V. (Brussels: FEPSAC).

Chelladurai, P., 1984, Discrepancy between preferences and perceptions of leadership behavior and satisfaction of athletes in various sport. *Journal of Sport Psychology*, 6, 27–41.

Chelladurai, P., 1993, Leadership. In *Handbook of Research on Sport Psychology,* edited by Singer, R., Murphey, M. and Tennant, L. (New York: MacMillan), pp. 647–671.

Deci, E.L. and Ryan, R.M., 1985, *Intrinsic Motivation and Self-determination in Human Behavior.* (New York: Plenum Press).

Fonseca, A.M., 1995a, Coaches' perception of athlete participation motive. In *IXth FEPSAC Congress*, Brussels, edited by Vanfraechem-Raway, R. and Auweele, Y.V. (Brussels: FEPSAC).

Fonseca, A.M., 1995b, Coaches' perception of athlete preferred leadership styles. In *IXth FEPSAC Congress*, Brussels, edited by Vanfraechem-Raway, R. and Auweele, Y.V. (Brussels: FEPSAC).

Serpa, S., 1995, Relationship coach athlete : outstanding trends in Europe research. In *IXth European Congress on Sport Psychology*, Brussels, 305–313, edited by Vanfraechem-Raway, R. and Auweele, Y.V. (Brussels: FEPSAC).

Serpa, S., 2002, Treinador e atleta. A relaçao sagrada. In *Psicologia Aplicada ao Treinador Esportivo*, edited by Becker, B. Jr. (P.A: Brazil), pp. 17–67.

Vanfraechem-Raway, R., 2001, Perception coaching in football studies. In *10th World Congress on Sport Psychology*, Skiathos, edited by Papaioannou, A., Goudas, M. and Theodorakis, Y. Vol. 3, pp. 1170–1173.

Vanfraechem-Raway, R. 2002, O treinador esportivo, motivador e educator. In *Psicologia Aplicada ao Treinador Esportivo*, edited by Becker, Jr. B. (P.A: Brazil), pp. 68–91.

90   Coping Strategies in French high-level Soccer Players during the 2001–2002 Season

Benoît Louvet and Jacques Genty
Centre d'Etudes des Transformations des Activités Physiques et
Sportives UPRES JE 2318 Faculté des Sciences du Sport, Rouen
(France)

1. INTRODUCTION

Few studies in soccer deal with the psychological dimension (Morris, 2000). Nevertheless, this area is now recognized to play an important role in the preparation for performance (Park, 2000). Thus, soccer represents an interesting domain of investigation for sport psychology research.

The tremendous popularity of this sport breeds competitions that are more and more hard-fought. Soccer players are put constantly under pressure and have to face up to various situations in order to manage their own emotions. This management of emotion is called "coping".

Lazarus and Folkman (1984) defined coping as "constantly changing cognitive and behavioural efforts to manage specific external and/or internal demands that are appraised as taxing or exceeding the resources of the person" (p. 141). How people cope has been the subject of a considerable amount of research in sport and health psychology over the past decade (Carver and Scheier, 1994). Indeed, understanding the nature of the coping strategies and the way they are used, forms a real interest in the elaboration of training programmes concerning mental preparation and competition management.

The coping process can be divided into three components. Problem-focused coping refers to cognitive and behavioural efforts designed to identify and solve problems (Lazarus and Folkman, 1984). Emotion-focused coping refers to efforts meant to lessen emotional distress or regulate emotional arousal that are not intended to change the nature of the situation (Lazarus and Folkman, 1984). Avoidance-focused coping represents the actions that are employed in order to disengage oneself from the task and to redirect one's attention on task-irrelevant cues (Gaudreau and Blondin, 2002).

Sports-related research on coping has demonstrated that individuals cope differently across a number of situations employing a variety of problem-focused, emotion-focused and avoidance coping strategies (e.g., Giacobbi and Weinberg, 2000). A consistent finding across studies is that sport performers have a stronger preference for problem-focused coping (e.g., effort, planning, task focus), rather than emotion-focused or avoidance-focused strategies (e.g., distancing, venting of emotions, behavioural or mental disengagement).

Above the nature of coping strategies, the temporal consistency of coping constitutes a major debate and provides information on how these strategies are employed by performers. The issue around this concept lies in the degree to which coping is stable as opposed to variable from situation to situation. On the one hand, the most accepted position is a transactional model. It suggests coping is constantly changing as the nature of the person-environment relationship changes. Consequently, coping is considered as a series of contextual responses that change from situation to situation (Lazarus and Folkman, 1984; Anshel et al., 2001). On the other hand, Carver, Scheier and Weintraub (1989) and Giacobbi and Weinberg (2000) proposed a dispositional analysis of coping that would be stable and consistent across time, meaning that individuals would have strong preferences in the utilization of coping. This area in embedded in what researchers call "coping styles".

There seems to be a lack of research dealing with coping strategies in soccer players. Given that every sport has its own internal logic, individuals would probably react differently according to the type of activities. The examination of inter- and intra-individual differences in soccer could provide a new source of information for soccer specialists.

The aim of this study was to examine, first, if all soccer players use the same coping strategies when faced with stressful encounters (nature of the responses). A second goal was to verify whether soccer players employ the same coping strategies at the same level over time (evolutions of the responses).

1. MATERIAL AND METHODS

2.1. Subjects

The subjects comprised 48 French soccer players with a mean age of 24.46 years ($SD = 4.04$) belonging to three different teams (team 1, N = 17; team 2, N = 17; team 3, N = 14). The three teams participated in the same championship at the highest amateur level. At the end of the season, team 1 was promoted, team 2 stayed in the top five and team 3 fought throughout the season to avoid relegation (Table 1).

Table 1. Ranking of teams over the three periods studied.

	First period		Second period		Third period	
	15th match/30		22nd match/30		29th match/30	
	Points	Rank	Points	Rank	Points	Rank
Team 1	43	3	64	2	85	2
Team 2	46	2	63	4	80	4
Team 3	29	13	40	15	56	13

2.2. Instruments

Coping was assessed using the Coping Strategies in Sport Competition Inventory, (CSSCI, Gaudreau and Blondin, 2002). The CSSCI is a 39-item self-report inventory that yields scores for two general dimensions of coping:- task-focused coping (thought control, mental imagery, relaxation, effort expenditure, logical analysis and seeking support), and emotion-focused coping (venting of unpleasant emotion, mental distraction, disengagement/resignation and social withdrawal). All these sub-scales had four items (except for effort expenditure which has three) and were measured on a 5-point Likert scale ranging from 1 ("not at all") to 5 ("very strongly").

2.3. Procedure

During the second part of the season 2001–2002, these players completed this inventory three times. They were asked to indicate the extent to which each item corresponded to what they did or thought just before and during their last game.

3. RESULTS

3.1. Inter-individual analysis

A Kruskall Wallis test was performed to examine the different levels at which the coping strategies were employed by the three teams during the different periods. For the first period, results revealed no significant differences between the teams. The same phenomenon was observed during the second period except for effort expenditure ($H = 6.5$; $P< 0.05$). However, results showed significant differences between the teams for the third period with four task-focused coping strategies used: thought control ($H = 12.2$; $P< 0.01$), mental imagery ($H = 7.1$; $P< 0.05$), effort expenditure ($H = 8.2$; $P< 0.05$) and logical analysis ($H = 15.2$; $P< 0.01$).

In addition, a Mann-Whitney test was conducted to verify where significant differences occurred. Table 2 indicates all the significant differences and highlights that these differences always appeared with team 1: between team 1 and team 2, and/or between team 1 and team 3.

Table 2. Coping strategies used by the three teams (mean ±SD).

	Team 1	Team 2	Team 3	z
Second period				
Effort expenditure	10.9 ± 2.3	13.0 ± 1.8	11.7 ± 1.4	A -2.5*
Third period				
Thought control	11.1 ± 2.7	13.2 ± 3.7	15.4 ± 3.2	A -2.3* B -3.3**
Mental imagery	10.7 ± 1.9	11.7 ± 3.1	14.0 ± 3.5	B -2.6**
Effort expenditure	10.2 ± 1.3	10.8 ± 2.9	12.5 ± 1.8	B -3.0**
Logical analysis	10.2 ± 2.2	12.9 ± 3.0	14.7 ± 3.3	A -2.5* B -3.6**

Note. Only coping strategies that were significantly different are shown.

A means a significant difference between team 1 and team 2.

B means a significant difference between team 1 and team 3.

*P<0. 05. **P<0. 01.

3.2. Intra-individual analysis

A Friedman test was also conducted to examine the evolution of the coping strategies, for each club, during the three periods of the study. Players in team 1 significantly used four task-focused coping strategies over the time:- mental imagery ($\chi^2 = 8.3$; P < 0.05), effort expenditure ($\chi^2 = 8.0$; P < 0.05), logical analysis ($\chi^2 = 11.7$; P <0.01) and seeking support ($\chi^2 = 9.5$; P < 0.01). Players in team 2 significantly used two task-focused strategies: effort expenditure ($\chi^2 = 6.2$; P <0.05) and logical analysis ($\chi^2 = 6.9$; P< 0.05), whereas the players in team 3, significantly used "thought control" during the three periods ($\chi^2 = 6.1$; P< 0.05).

Furthermore, a Wilcoxon test was conducted on all strategies to find when the significant differences occurred. Results indicated in Table 3 showed when the significant differences appeared for each club. Generally, the significant differences were noticed between the first and the third period of this research. Concerning all the significant differences, team 1 used less thought control, mental imagery, effort expenditure, logical analysis, and more seeking support. Concerning team 2, the utilization of effort expenditure and logical analysis was significantly less important during the half-season examined, whereas the employment of disengagement improved significantly. Results for team 3 showed that thought control and mental imagery were employed significantly more between certain periods.

Table 3. Evolution of coping strategies for the three teams (mean ±SD).

	First period n = 17	Second period n = 17	Third period n = 14	z
Team 1				
Thought control	13.2 ± 2.6	12.8 ± 3.0	11.1 ± 2.7	B -2.0*; C -2.3*
Mental imagery	13.8 ± 2.7	11.1 ± 3.1	10.7 ± 1.9	A -2.3*; B -2.8**
Effort expenditure	12.0 ± 1.7	10.9 ± 2.3	10.2 ± 1.3	B -2.9**
Logical analysis	14.0 ± 1.6	12.5 ± 3.2	10.2 ± 2.2	B -3.5**
Seeking support	8.4 ± 3.0	10.0 ± 2.4	7.2 ± 2.3	A -2.1*
Team 2				
Effort expenditure	12.2 ± 1.6	13.0 ± 1.8	10.8 ± 2.9	B -1.9*; C -2.8**
Logical analysis	14.3 ± 2.1	14.8 ± 2.0	12.9 ± 3.0	B -2.2* ; C -2.2*
Disengagement	5.7 ± 1.5	7.0 ± 2.2	7.8 ± 3.3	A -2.2* ; B -2.3*
Team 3				
Thought control	13.4 ± 2.5	13.4 ± 3.1	15.4 ± 3.2	C -2.1*
Mental imagery	12.1 ± 2.3	12.7 ± 2.7	14.0 ± 3.5	B -2.0*

Note. Only coping strategies that were significantly different are shown.
A means a significant difference between the first and the second period.
B means a significant difference between the first and the third period.
C means a significant difference between the second and the third period.
*P < 0.05. **P < 0.01.

4. DISCUSSION

The purpose of this study was to examine the coping fluctuations of high-level soccer players. Firstly, these performers did not use the same coping strategies at the same level. According to the period of testing, only task-oriented strategies were significantly varied between the teams whereas emotion-oriented strategies were employed at the same level. Consequently, these soccer players preferred focusing on the problem in order to compete. They tried to solve the problems in a cognitive way. This provides consistency with the empirical findings and theoretical beliefs of Crocker and Graham (1995). Furthermore, results emphasized the fact that the significant differences between the teams concerning these task-oriented strategies always appeared in the presence of the team that was promoted at the end of the season. They certainly coped in an appropriate way with precise appraisals and a better control of the stressful encounters due to the competition and its demands.

Secondly, an intra-team analysis underlined that coping has to be understood as a process (Folkman and Lazarus, 1985). Indeed, coping variations were observed for each club over the time. Each team changed several coping strategies especially task-oriented strategies. The results support the transactional approach explained in the literature (Lazarus and Folkman, 1984; Jones and Tebbenham, 2000; Anshel *et al.*, 2001). Another interesting conclusion confirms that the team acceding to the upper level at the end of the championship was the one that changed its coping strategies most frequently. This could explain on the one hand that problem-focused coping seems to be more efficient than emotion or avoidance-focused strategies. On the other hand, the evidence of a transactional way of coping also seems to be more appropriate.

This study highlights the need for other investigations in order to gain more knowledge of the coping process. In fact, further research should focus on the relation between the level of expertise and the performance. Effectively, we have noticed that one of the best teams of this championship did not use the same coping strategies in the same way and at the same level over time compared to the other teams. In addition, research should take into account the real importance of the context in the transactional model, and its effects on the nature of the coping strategies utilized and on the manner they are employed. Indeed, in this study, coping variations seem to be linked to teams' performances. Thus, some explanations could be provided for the important role played by the contextual aspects. This study also presents some interests concerning the different coping strategies employed and their effectiveness with respect to performance. It would also be useful to study some temporal patterns during the different phases of a competition (before, during and after) for each individual.

5. CONCLUSION

This study provides new psychological information on soccer players. Coping, examined as a dynamic and as a transactional process, presents researchers with ways to acquire knowledge for soccer specialists. Coping seems to play an important role in establishing good performance. There is evidence for coaches that it is important to know how players react and face up to the competition, to the opponents' actions, to the pressure, and to the different stressful encounters and variables. Taking this dimension into account can improve the means of managing the group. This underlines the considerable role played by the coach. It can help in constructing new training programmes including mental preparation and stress management techniques. This psychological knowledge can constitute, for coaches, some precious elements and means to accomplish different and difficult missions.

REFERENCES

Anshel, M.H., Kim, K.W., Kim, B.H., Chang, K.J. and Eom, H.J., 2001, A model for coping with stressful events in sport: Theory, applications and future directions. *International Journal of Sport Psychology*, **32**, 43–75.

Carver, C.S. and Scheier, M.F., 1994, Situational coping and coping dispositions in a stressful transaction. *Journal of Personality and Social Psychology*, **66**, 184–195.

Carver, C.S., Scheier, M.F. and Weintraub, J.K., 1989, Assessing coping strategies: A theoretically based approach. *Journal of Personality and Social Psychology*, **56**, 267–283.

Crocker, P.R.E. and Graham, T.R., 1995, Coping by competitive athletes with performance stress: Gender differences and relationships with affect. *The Sport Psychologist*, **9**, 325–338.

Folkman, S. and Lazarus, R.S., 1985, If it changes it must be a process: A study of emotion and coping during three stages of a college examination. *Journal of Personality and Social Psychology*, **48**, 150–170.

Gaudreau, P. and Blondin, J.P., 2002, Development of a questionnaire for the assessment of coping strategies employed by athletes in competitive sport settings. *Psychology of Sport and Exercise*, **3**, 1–34.

Giacobbi, P.R. and Weinberg, R.S., 2000, An examination of coping in sport: Individual trait anxiety differences and situational consistency. *The Sport Psychologist*, **14**, 42–62.

Jones, K.A. and Tebbenham, D., 2000, Causes, consequences and coping with stress in elite performance: A case of study. *Journal of Sports Sciences*, **18**, 50–51.

Lazarus, R.S. and Folkman, S., 1984, *Stress, Appraisal and Coping*. (New York: Springer).

Morris, T., 2000, Psychological characteristics and talent identification in soccer. *Journal of Sports Sciences*, **18**, 715–726.

Park, J.K., 2000, Coping strategies used by Korean national athletes. *The Sport Psychologist*, **14**, 63–80.

91   Judging Offside in Football: Can Attention of Assistant Referees be Educated?

Raôul R.D. Oudejans
Institute for Fundamental and Clinical Human Movement Sciences
Vrije Universiteit, Amsterdam, The Netherlands

1. INTRODUCTION

Following the definition of perception as pick-up or detection of information (Gibson, 1986; Jacobs and Michaels, 2002), in the ecological approach attention is viewed as the control of detection of information (Michaels and Carello, 1981). The information in the perceptual arrays surrounding observers moving around in their natural environment is taken to be inexhaustibly rich. Because observers cannot pick up all the available information at once they have to be selective. Gibson (1966) called this procedure by which inputs are selected *attention* (Michaels and Carello, 1981). This is not to say that attention, or the control of detection of information, is always optimal from the start. Findings with respect to perceptual learning (e.g., Jacobs, 2001; Jacobs and Michaels, 2002) indicate that novices often initially rely on non-specifying variables, as they still have to learn to attend to the more useful (i.e., specifying) sources of information. Specifying information sources are specific to the to-be-perceived properties of the environment. This means that detecting a certain information source that specifies a property of interest in the environment allows the observer to make reliable judgments about this property (Beek *et al.*, 2003). A non-specifying information source might be related to the to-be-perceived property, but it is not specific to this property as its value does not under all circumstances reliably predict the value of this to-be-perceived environmental property (ibid.). The present review is concerned with an exploration of information sources and the education of attention in judging offside in football. Furthermore, ways are considered to improve offside judgments that follow from this discussion on information use by assistant referees.

2. EDUCATION OF ATTENTION

In sports, experts have learned what to attend to those information sources that are relevant for their actions, while leaving unattended those sources that are irrelevant (e.g., Williams and Grant, 1999). In the ecological approach to perception, the learning process to perceptual expertise is called "the education of attention" (Michaels and Carello, 1981; Gibson, 1966; Jacobs, 2001; Jacobs and Michaels, 2002). The education of attention is the process by which one learns which variables to attend to in which situation, that is, the process by which one learns to control the detection of information. Jacobs and Michaels (2002) described this process as follows: "... after a limited amount of practice with feedback, perceivers converge on more useful nonspecifying variables or even on variables that specify to-be-perceived properties" (p. 131). Savelsbergh and Van der Kamp (2000) and Savelsbergh *et al.* (2003) referred to the changes in perceptual learning in terms of different phases of freezing, freeing and exploiting perceptual degrees of freedom, thereby drawing parallels with the different phases of freezing, freeing and exploiting degrees of freedom in motor learning (Bernstein, 1967).

One obvious example of education of attention in sports is reflected in the literature on anticipation in interceptive actions. A common finding in several tasks varying from racket sports (Abernethy and Russell, 1987a, b; Abernethy, 1990) and ice-hockey (Salmela and Fiorito, 1979) to penalty stopping (Savelsbergh *et al.*, 2002) is that compared to novices experts have learned to also to use information available earlier in time to predict the future direction of the shuttle, puck, or ball. This information comes from the movements of the opponent preparing his or her hitting action and is available earlier than information from the flight of the projectile in question. In other words experts have educated their attention to more useful variables to guide their action. In this specific case more useful refers to the fact that being able to use this early information gives the athlete more time to respond properly (return the ball, or making the save by deflecting the ball).

Recent overviews (e.g. Williams and Grant, 1999) make clear that there is still be much to be gained perceptually in sports using specifically designed perceptual training methods aimed at educating the attention of athletes so that they converge on more useful variables for their performance. Successful examples are provided by, for instance, Farrow and Abernethy (2002) and Adolphe *et al.* (1997) who showed improvements in anticipation in tennis and gaze behaviour in volleyball serve reception, respectively, after a perceptual training intervention.

If it is the case that perceptual expertise may increase with experience and that experts have converged on more useful or even specifying variables then why do even the finest experts in judging offside in football, assistant referees (ARs) at European and World Championships, still make relatively many and sometimes decisive errors in judging offside? Why have they not converged onto variables that always specify veridically whether or not a player is offside? To answer these questions, research of Oudejans *et al.* (2000) and its implications will be discussed.

3. VARIABLE USE IN JUDGING OFFSIDE

Sanabria *et al.* (1998) hypothesized that the errors in judging offside are the result of saccadic eye movements from the passer to the last defender (apart from the goal keeper, thus, the last defending field player). In order to determine the moment of passing, Sanabria *et al.* expected that the Assistant Referee (AR) would be watching the passer until the pass was made. As soon as the pass was made the assistant referee would shift gaze from passer to last defender using saccadic eye moments. As it takes about 250–300 ms before the defender is foveated after the pass is made, it is possible that relative player positions have changed substantially (up to 4 m, Sanabria *et al.*, 1998), especially if receiving attacker and last defender are running at full speed in opposite directions. Thus at the moment the AR judges the situation, he may come to a wrong conclusion due to the time delay involved with the saccade from passer to last defender (Sanabria *et al.*, 1998).

The results of the field experiment by Oudejans *et al.* (2000) in which three ARs wearing a miniature head-mounted camera judged 200 played offside situations made clear that the solution offered by Sanabria *et al.* (1998) could not explain the 40 errors that were made. The ARs did not shift their gaze from passer to last defender after the pass was made. Instead ARs appeared to make this gaze shift just prior to the pass so that they already foveated the defender at the moment the pass was made. These data suggest that ARs determined the moment of passing by anticipating the pass in combination with peripheral vision. Informal interviews afterwards with the participating ARs revealed that they also often determine the moment of passing on the basis of the sound of foot-ball contact.

In search for an alternative explanation for errors in judging offside, Oudejans *et al.* (2000) demonstrated that they appear to be the result of ARs using information that does not specify who is closer to the goal (attacker or defender): i.e. the relative positions of the relevant attackers and defenders on the AR's retina. Assistant Referees seem to respond, as they should, to what they see from their position, that is, to the information optically available to them. They judge offside on the basis of the optical angle between defender and attacker which would specify who is closer to the defender's goal line only if the AR were always on the offside line. Oudejans *et al.* (2000) showed, however, that the ARs were frequently off that line when they judged offside in the field experiment, giving them a point of observation from which errors are optically inevitable.

Thus, central idea in the explanation by Oudejans *et al.* (2000) is that ARs are not properly positioned when they make their decisions. This idea arose from the observation in the field experiment that in these simulated offside plays ARs were positioned about 1 m further to the goal line than the offside line. However, it has not been tested where exactly ARs are positioned in real matches when they judge potential offside situations. Therefore, in a follow-up study (Oudejans *et al.*, in preparation) we investigated in four premier league matches in the Dutch League competition where ARs were positioned relative to the last defender when they judged offside. We could confirm that in the majority of the cases ARs were not positioned at the offside line when they judged offside. Instead, ARs were found to lead or trail the last defender by about a metre on average. In addition, 22% of the more difficult cases were judged erroneously. In most cases the fact that the AR viewed the relevant players from an angle provided a plausible explanation for the errors made in judging offside in football.

4. EDUCATION OF ATTENTION OF ASSISTANT REFEREES

The results of Oudejans *et al.* (2000) raise the question as to how it would be possible to improve judgments of offside in football. There are several possibilities that will be discussed in this section.

4.1. Improving the positioning of assistant referees

Perhaps the first suggestion that comes to mind, but that is not directly related to education of attention, is to train ARs in such a way that they position themselves better relative to the offside line hereby minimizing optical distortions. There are three reasons why that will not lead to much improvement in the judgments of offside.

First, when it comes to judging offside, ARs from the outset intend to position themselves in line with the last defender as good as possible. They are not positioned off that line on purpose. In fact, the ARs that were tested by Oudejans *et al.* (2000) indicated in interviews afterwards that they had not been aware at all of the fact that they were not in line with the last defender when they judged offside. So it is questionable whether extra training urging them to be better in line will improve their positioning.

Second, soccer is a very dynamic game with many quick changes in direction of play. Especially the accelerations and directional changes of strikers, and hence, the players defending them, make sure that whole-body tracking of the offside line, in principle, over a distance of about 50 m, is a tough job. One could consider an 'error' of about 1 m in whole-body positioning quite good.

Third, Baldo *et al.* (2002) argued that even when ARs are in line with the last defender the so-called 'flash-lag effect' may lead to the perception of attackers being positioned further than they really are. In the flash-lag effect (see e.g., Baldo and Klein, 1995; Nijhawan, 2001) "a moving object is perceived as spatially leading its real position at an instant defined by a time marker (usually a briefly flashed stimulus)" (Baldo *et al.*, 2002, p. 1205). Taking these three points together it is questionable whether extra training to improve the positioning of ARs would actually lead to improving offside judgments in soccer.

4.2. Educate attention to more useful variables in the current setting

Another possibility for improving judgements that is advocated in the ecological approach is to 'foster reliance on more useful or even specifying variables' as is suggested by Jacobs (2001) and Beek *et al.* (2003). As the ARs appear to use a variable for judging offside that does not specify (i.e., does not veridically present) actual relative player positions, Beek et al. (2003) suggested that given appropriate feedback and practice conditions it would be possible for ARs to "learn not to use the commonly used nonspecifying variable and, perhaps, come to rely on variables that lead to fewer errors" (p. 329). The feasibility of this possibility does, of course, depend on the availability of alternative variables. What are the options for ARs in their natural surroundings?

One of the implications of the results of Oudejans *et al.* (2000) is that ARs seem to have trouble taking into account differences in depth between players. In discussing the problem of perceiving distance Gibson (1950, 1986) noted that distance should be thought of as "extending along the ground instead of through the air" (1979/1986, p. 117). Considered as such distance "is projected as a *gradient* of decreasing optical size and increasing optical density of the features of the ground" (1979/1986, p. 117, see also Gibson, 1950). Gibson (1950) formulated it as follows:

> the basis of the so-called perception of space is the projection of its objects and elements as an image, and the consequent gradual change of size and density in the image as the objects and elements recede from the observer. (p. 78)

Thus, in the gradient theory space perception as advocated by Gibson (1986, 1950) accounts for the distance of all objects in the array, rather than single objects on which attention is focused. If we take, as an example, the apparent size of familiar objects as a cue to their distance, it is clear that in empty space a football player can be seen as Edgar Davids (from the Netherlands; 1.68 m tall) standing nearby or Jan Koller (from the Czech Republic; 2.02 m tall) standing further away. Additional knowledge and interpretation (e.g., team colours) are needed to determine which player of the two one perceives. Although Gibson argued that this is not how distance is perceived in our usual cluttered environment, he admitted that this might be the only solution in certain circumstances, one example being airplane spotting against a clear blue sky. Another example might be judging offside in football. Given the homogenous surface of a football field there is hardly any information provided by texture gradients of relative size and density. When two players, say Davids and Koller, are standing at about 50 m in the distance, their relative size will not be very informative with regard to who is standing the farther away, let alone when they would not differ that much in height.

Cutting and Vishton (1995) discussed the relative efficacy of the various sources of information that can be used to perceive the layout of the environment and especially distances of and differences in depth between the various objects and obstacles in it. The most important examples are convergence and accommodation, binocular disparity, occlusion, relative size and density, motion perspective, aerial perspective, and height in the visual field (see also Gibson, 1950). For an extensive description of these sources, see Gibson (1950) and Cutting and Vishton (1995). It is important to note that beyond about 10 m the quality of perception of depth differences between two objects is already diminishing, with binocular disparity perhaps as only remaining information source that may provide quantitative depth information (e.g., how much further away from the AR is one player compared to another player) on top of the qualitative information (which player is further away), such as occlusion (the [partly] occluded player is obviously further away than the occluding player; Cutting and Vishton, 1995). Beyond about 30 m only qualitative depth information (e.g., occlusion) is available, making it impossible to disambiguate the retinal image of the relative player positions. Thus, from about 10 m onwards the utility of information sources for perceiving (differences in) depth quickly declines (Cutting and Vishton, 1995). Therefore, combined with the fact that ARs are probably often unaware of their mispositioning, it is questionable in many potential offside situations, especially the more difficult cases, whether enough information sources will be available for ARs to judge offside correctly. Beyond about 10 m the perception of differences in depth by ARs is expected to be poor on the basis of the information sources available (Gibson, 1950; Cutting and Vishton, 1995).

In short, with respect to depth perception, a football pitch may not be an optimal environment. In fact, a football pitch may be an exception to the rule advocated in ecological psychology (Gibson, 1986; Michaels and Carello, 1981) that we usually move around in an environment in which the information is inexhaustibly rich. A football pitch is an information-poor environment, at least from the perspective of the AR. Thus, in judging offside convergence onto more useful variables, as suggested by Beek *et al.* (2003) and Jacobs (2001), may not be possible simply because no other variables are available. Therefore, it remains to be seen whether it is possible to educate the attention of ARs to the use of more helpful variables in judging offside in their natural surroundings of a 64–75 m wide football pitch, although it would be too much to conclude at this moment that it is absolutely impossible. Cutting and Vishton (1995) made clear that the utility of certain information sources diminishes with distance. Perhaps ARs can be taught to take advantage of these sources more often and with regard to further distances by actually educating their attention to these variables. Although this might be difficult to achieve next to the pitch, there may be possibilities to train ARs perceptually, not next to the pitch, but in a virtual environment in which one can manipulate variables and what they specify. In a CAVE (Computer Aided Virtual Environment) it should be possible to create conditions that will help ARs to converge onto more useful variables for judging offside in this environment. Once ARs have learned to pick up particular variables in a virtual environment their perceptual skills could perhaps be transferred to the real situation.

4.3. Providing additional useful variables

Although more useful variables may not be available to ARs in their natural surroundings, it may be possible to make additional variables available. Given that height in the visual field can provide depth information (Gibson, 1950; Cutting and Vishton, 1995) one option for providing ARs with additional information is to have them run along the field on a platform with a height of, for instance, 1 or 1.5 m. Although this might provide useful extra information for judging offside, there are also some obvious disadvantages related to the height of the platform. There is the danger for the ARs of falling off and injuring themselves. In addition, it would mean that 50 × 1 × 1 m obstacles would have to be placed on both sides next to the pitch, close enough to the pitch so that the ARs can also perform their other duties. Needless to state such obstacles may also be dangerous for the players.

Following Gibson's gradient theory of distance perception, helping ARs in their perception of depth differences between players might also be accomplished by providing more texture on the field. Although setting up all kinds of obstacles on the field is, of course, not an option, some additional information might be made available by the adding texture to the grass either by mowing it in a certain pattern as is often seen or by adding more lines to the field as is also done in, for instance, American football. Informal interviews with the participating ARs in the study by Oudejans *et al.* (2000) made clear that whenever available they sometimes use information from the lines created by the different mowing lanes in the grass. Additional white lines on the field could also provide this information.

Another example with which additional information can be provided is with the Reference Point System (RPS, see *www.rps.as*) that was developed in Norway. The RPS is a system of lights that helps ARs maintain an accurate angle with play, making the judgement of offside easier. An aluminium profile, containing lights 1.2 m apart, is mounted along the opposite side of the field. The light-beams produced are only visible when the AR is directly opposite. Therefore, seeing a light (or not seeing a light, for that matter) gives the AR constant reference points and a guaranteed perpendicular angle to the developing play. The RPS seems to hold promise when it comes to reducing the number of errors made in judging offside, as it provides ARs with additional information that they can use (a virtual line between themselves and the opposite side of the field) and to which they can relate the offside line and the relevant player positions. The system was tested in Norway and is currently tested in the United Kingdom. Assistant Referees are reported to be extremely positive about it and a reduction of error rate of 50% is claimed (see *www.rps.as*). As it provides new information ARs should be perceptually trained, that is, their attention should be educated, to use the extra information. Given the debate about alternative ways of judging offside (see below), a major advantage of such a system is that, apart from ARs having to learn to use the information provided by the system, it does not interfere with the game of football as it leaves it entirely unaffected.

Next to these three possibilities, there might also be other ways to make additional information available to ARs without interfering with the game itself. In all cases the basic assumption is still that the information is picked up with the human perceptual system with all its qualities but also with its shortcomings. These alternatives will never entirely remove all errors, although significant reductions may be possible.

4.4. Alternative ways to determine offside

Next to the possibilities discussed so far one could, of course, also resort to alternative ways of judging offside, that is, methods with which there is at least some interference with the game of football as it is currently played. As this review is about the education of attention of ARs, these alternative ways to judge offside are not considered in detail, but a few options are mentioned.

First, perhaps the option suggested most often is the use of video replay, which can be used in all televised games. An official next to the pitch has the possibility to view, within seconds, replays of a debatable situation to determine whether a violation of the offside rule has occurred. He or she should decide on the basis of the images and communicate this decision to the referee (and assistant referees). A disadvantage is that play has to be brought to a standstill in anticipation of the decision of the video official. Whether such interruptions are really a problem depends on their length and frequency. If they are only used in crucial situations then perhaps play is only interrupted two to five times per game.

Second, another way of improving offside judgements is to monitor positions of players and ball using modern technology involving sensors and receivers. Sensors should be attached to the players and the receivers somewhere high in the stadium. An example of a system that is already developed is that by Cairos Technologies in Germany (see *www.cairosag.de/english/index.htm*). Information from microchips hidden in the shin-pads of players is transmitted to a computer that can be used to alert the referee, via a wristwatch, when there is a violation of the offside rule. It is yet unclear how robust and accurate such a system would be and what the use of such a system would mean to real match play.

Third, returning to the idea that a heightened point of view provides more useful information for judging offside, another less sophisticated solution would be to have one or more additional officials positioned higher up in the stands to judge offside. Communication with the referee would be necessary and, of course, one or more extra officials are needed. Then again, taking a look at other sports it is clear that the use of more officials is possible. For example, in tennis ten line judges are used, in American football there are seven officials on the field, and in ice-hockey there are two goal judges and a video goal judge next to the three officials on the ice.

Only the future can tell whether any of the above suggestions will ever be actually implemented in football.

5. CONCLUDING REMARKS

Offside judgments are often disputed. This is hardly a surprise if one considers what is often at stake. It is even less surprising if one realizes in what an awkward position the AR is in, both figuratively speaking, with everyone watching and the pressure to perform well, and literally, next to the pitch, just offline, and often with only little information to make proper judgments of offside. Our earlier study (Oudejans *et al.*, 2000) demonstrated that ARs often err in judging offside because they use a so-called 'nonspecifying variable' (Beek *et al.*, 2003) that suffices in many occasions but not in all. Whether ARs' attention can be educated to converge on more useful or even specifying variables as suggested by Beek *et al.* (2003) remains to be seen and will certainly be difficult to achieve in the natural setting of a football match. Providing additional information that can help the ARs in judging offside, for instance, with the RPS system, seems to hold some promise and certainly deserves further testing.

In all cases one should not forget that judging offside is an ensemble of whole-body positioning, gaze behaviour, and anticipation (of foot-ball contact and player positions). It involves a snapshot decision in a very dynamic situation in which the relation between positioning and decision-making appears to be crucial, yet the information available is limited. If the football pitch is such an information-poor environment for assistant referees, this is probably also the case for the referee and the players. There is not much research on perception and decision-making of referees or players that tests behaviour in a field setting in which the available information is similar to the information available in an actual match, and in which the relation between positioning and decision-making is taken into account. Such research is needed to find out whether there are similar perceptual shortcomings, in referees and players. With insight into these shortcomings it is perhaps possible to design training strategies to improve perception and decision-making in football, both for referees and for (youth) players.

REFERENCES

Abernethy, B., 1990, Anticipation in squash: differences in advance cue utilization between expert and novice players. *Journal of Sports Sciences*, **8**, 17–34.

Abernethy, B. and Russell, D.G., 1987a, Expert-novice differences in an applied selective attention task. *Journal of Sport Psychology*, **9**, 326–345.

Abernethy, B. and Russell, D.G., 1987b, The relationship between expertise and visual search strategies in a racquet sport. *Human Movement Science*, **6**, 283–319.

Adolphe, R.M., Vickers, J.N. and Laplante, G., 1997, The effects of training visual attention on gaze behaviour and accuracy: a pilot study. *International Journal of Sports Vision*, **4**, 28–33.

Baldo, M.V.C. and Klein, S.A., 1995, Extrapolation of attention shift? *Nature*, **378**, 565–566.

Baldo, M.V.C., Ranvaud, R.D. and Moyra, E., 2002, Flag errors in soccer games: the flash-lag effect brought to real life. *Perception*, **31**, 1205–1210.

Beek, P.J., Jacobs. D. M., Daffertshofer, A. and Huys, R., 2003, Expert performance in sport: Views from the joint perspectives of ecological psychology and dynamical systems theory. In *Expert Performance in Sport*, edited by Starkes, J. and Ericsson, A. (Champaign, Ill.: Human Kinetics), pp. 321–344.

Bernstein, N.A., 1967, *The Co-ordination and Regulation of Movements.* (Oxford: Pergamon Press).

Cutting, J.E. and Vishton, P.M., 1995, Perceiving the layout and knowing distances: The integration, relative potency, and contextual use of different information about depth. In *Perception of Space and Motion*, edited by Epstein, W. and Rogers, S. (San Diego: Academic Press), pp. 69–117.

Farrow, D. and Abernethy, B., 2002, Can anticipatory skills be learned through implicit video-based perceptual training? *Journal of Sports Sciences*, **20**, 471–485.

Gibson, J.J., 1950, *The Perception of the Visual World.* (Cambridge, MA: The Riverside Press).

Gibson, J.J., 1966, *The Senses Considered as Perceptual Systems.* (Boston: Houghton Mifflin).

Gibson, J.J., 1986, *The Ecological Approach to Visual Perception.* (Hillsdale, NJ: Lawrence Erlbaum Associates).

Jacobs, D.M., 2001, *On Perceiving, Acting, and Learning* (doctoral disseration), (Utrecht: Digital Printing Partners Utrecht).

Jacobs, D.M. and Michaels, C.F., 2002, On the apparent paradox of learning and realism. *Ecological Psychology*, **14**, 127–139.

Michaels, C.F. and Carello, C., 1981, *Direct Perception*. (Englewood Cliffs, NJ: Prentice-Hall).

Nijhawan, R., 2001, The flash-lag phenomenon: object motion and eye movements. *Perception*, **30**, 263–282.

Oudejans, R.R.D., Verheijen, R., Bakker, F.C., Gerrits, J.C., Steinbrückner, M. and Beek, P.J., 2000, Errors in judging 'offside' in football. *Nature*, **404 (6773)**, 33.

Oudejans, R.R.D., Bakker, F.C., Verheijen, R., Steinbrückner, M. and Gerrits, J.C., in preparation, *Positioning of assistant referees in football and its relation to decision-making*.

Salmela, J.H. and Fiorito, P., 1979, Visual cues in ice hockey goaltending. *Canadian Journal of Applied Sport Sciences*, **4**, 56–59.

Sanabria, J., Cenjor, C., Marquez, F., Gutierrez, R., Martinez, D. and Prados-Garcia, J. L., 1998. Oculomotor movement and football's Law 11. The Lancet, **351**, 268.

Savelsbergh, G.J.P. and Van der Kamp, J., 2000, Information in learning to co-ordinate and control movements: Is there a need for specificity of practice? *International Journal of Sport Psychology*, **31**, 467–484.

Savelsbergh, G.J.P., Williams, A.M., Van der Kamp, J. and Ward, P., 2002, Visual search, anticipation and expertise in soccer goalkeepers. *Journal of Sports Sciences*, **20**, 279–287.

Savelsbergh, G.J.P., Van der Kamp, J., Oudejans, R.R.D. and Scott, M.A., 2003 (in press), Perceptual learning is mastering perceptual degrees of freedom. In *Skill Acquisition in Sport: Research, Theory and Practice*, edited by Williams, A.M., Hodges, N.J. and Scott, M.A. (London: Routledge).

Williams, A.M. and Grant, A., 1999, Training perceptual skill in sport. *International Journal of Sport Psychology*, **30**, 194–220.

92 The Effect of Configuration and Content of Pre-Shooting Ball-Possessions Sequences upon Scoring

Marc Verlinden[1], Andy Eeckhout[1], Jelle Van Camp[1], Peter Somers[2], Steve De Decker[1] and Rene Goossens[1]
[1]Vrije Universiteit Brussel, Brussels, Faculty of Physical Education and Physiotherapy, Training and Coaching Department, Belgium
[2]Industriële Hogeschool Antwerpen Mechelen, Belgium

1. INTRODUCTION

As a ball possession phase might create a momentary lapse of dominance during a match, its properties with respect to duration, timing, pace, (geometrical) configuration, complexity, number and type of players involved, the type of actions giving that sequence its content - and probably a number of other parameters - are worthwhile studying for the purpose of knowing why only very few attacks result in a score. It would be better still to know how to exploit the characteristics of those sequences in future games. Many authors have expressed their own point of views to tackle there problems (Grehaigne, 1991; Theis, 1992; Jonsson et al., 2000; Hook and Hughes, 2001; Hughes et al., 2001). Different kinds of methodologies have been applied to reveal the secrets of a score.

It seems that the differences between opponents are so small that a subtle (and perhaps a unique) action may determine the difference between success and failure (Hughes et al., 2001).

It is known from previous research that set plays play a major role in scoring (Bate, 1988; Harris and Reilly, 1988; Zempel and Rudolph, 1990). The purpose of this study to examine the properties of dynamic ball-possession-phases leading towards a score or a score attempt. It is hypothesised that the sequence preceding a score can be distinguished from a sequence that only leads to a scoring-attempt based upon (geometrical) configuration/pattern and content (techno-tactical profile) properties.

2. METHODS

A protocol of systematic observation and registration of ball-possession phases was implemented using CASMAS methodology as described by Dufour (1993). The method is based upon two observers using PC-extended hardware such as a MM1201II-4 Summasketch Graphics Tablet II® and a BBC Concept keyboard™, with the purpose to register continuously x,y co-ordinates of the ball in play and label every player's action on the ball by a well pre-defined and identified type of action. Games were fully notated and tested for reliability. All observed actions were based upon a set of 25 operational definitions (counted without combination options and extension indexes) describing soccer specific motor behaviour (Table 1).

The validity-reliability of the definitions used in this study was over 80% (action identification reliability, player identification reliability and x-y identification reliability).

Table 1. Classification of technical profile (motor behaviour).

Motor Behaviour	Classification into type of action	
Ball driving	Dynamic	Transfer type action
Ball control	Dynamic	Transfer type action
Pass Head/Foot/Blind/Centre	Dynamic	Pass type action
Shot Head/Foot	Dynamic	Shot type action
Interception	Dynamic	Interception type action
Keeper shot high	Dynamic	Pass type action
Keeper ground shot	Static	Pass type action
Keeper Throw	Dynamic	Pass type action
Keeper save	Dynamic	Interception type action
Indirect Free Kicks	Static	Pass type and shot type actions
Direct Free Kick	Static	Shot type action
Corner	Static	Pass type action
Throw In	Static	Pass type action
Offensive 1/1 Foot/Head	Dynamic	1/1 type action
Defensive 1/1 Foot/Head	Dynamic	1/1 type action
Dribble	Dynamic	Transfer type action
Sliding Tackle	Dynamic	1/1 type action
Offside, Foul play	-	Foul type action

The study is based upon 26 matches of the World Championships 1998 (France), from the final down to knock-out stage (last 16).

CASMAS-software - controlling this system as well as analysing the data gathered - is based upon the concept of matching input with output algorithms. In five steps data are processed as follows:-

1. An algorithm is used to select only those ball-possession-sequences that led to a score or scoring-attempt. Penalties were excluded from further analysis. This procedure resulted in 134 ball-possession-sequences of which 67 led to a score and 67 to an attempt to score. These data were split in order to determine differences as the analyses took place.
2. Each ball-possession-sequence produced a list of involved actions (motor behaviour) and their localisation on the field (xy).
3. Based upon the assumption that a sequence has three reliable moments of existence, the following components were considered to compare sequences preceding a score with sequences preceding a scoring attempt:
   a. The initialisation of the sequence
   b. The evolution of the sequence
   c. The finishing of the sequence

4. A calculation-procedure purely based upon the xy co-ordinates of each subdivision is engaged, producing a classification of those patterns in terms of their geometrical aspects.

5. The two data sets were statistically processed by two-tailed and matched t-tests in order to determine significant discrepancies at the 5% level of probability.

3. RESULTS

3.1. The initialisation of ball-possession sequences

3.1.1. Technical profile

Table 2 reveals the initiated actions of the sequences producing comparable profiles for both types of ball-possession sequences. The initiating actions of both types of sequences leading to score and score-attempts did not differ from each other. Only corners and defensive 1/1 situations (foot) showed a non-significant discrepancy. When the classifications were based upon static and dynamic aspects of the initiating action, both types of sequences could not be distinguished from each other.

Table 2. Action profile at the moment of initialisation of a sequence.

Initiating action	Freq. towards scoring attempts	Static/Dynamic Ratio	Freq. towards scores	Static/Dynamic Ratio
Free Kick (static)	11		9	
Corner (static)	3	31%	7	30%
Throw In (static)	7		4	
Interception (dynamic)	33		31	
Defensive 1/1 Foot (dynamic)	6		11	
Defensive 1/1 Head (dynamic)	5	69%	5	70%
Sliding Tackle (dynamic)	2		0	
TOTAL sequences	67	100%	67	100%

3.1.2. Spatial profile

Another property is the localisation of the observed action at the moment of the initiation. Considering three zones, a central part of the pitch and a lateral corridor (Figure 1) and the own/opponents half field, we can determine whether there is a difference in relation to the scoring aspects. Table 3 shows the distribution of the initiation actions from the different zones of the pitch. It is clear that the sequences that led to a score had their initiation more often (but not significantly) occurring on the lateral corridor of the pitch.

Time: 00:22:15
Gain: 34.0m
X Gain: 30m
y Gain: -16m
Actions:12
Players: 1

37/145

Figure 1. Different zones of the soccer pitch.

Table 3. Distribution of localisation of initiating actions of ball-possession sequences

Localisation of initialisation of a ball possession sequence	Number of actions in sequence leading to score	Number of actions in sequence leading to score attempt
Own Field	28	27
Opponent Field	39	40
Central Part	39	46
Lateral part	28	21

3.1.3. Conclusion

Conclusively, the data did not show any significant differences on the level of the technical profile initiating the ball-possession sequence of both types, nor on their commencing co-ordinates.

3.2. The evolution of ball-possession sequences

3.2.1. Technical profile

Analysis of the technical content during a ball-possession sequence revealed comparable trends for both types of sequences. Significant differences were found for two factors. These were the amount of ball controls and the last action, the shot. Ball control is a label (describing a typical soccer motor behaviour) that was given to a player on the ball when the situation demanded a skilful response of that player in order to keep the ball in control. This event is considered not to be a 1/1 situation. Such moments when skilful ball control was needed occurred more often ($P<0.1$) in a sequence leading to a score as opposed to the attempt-sequence.

The outcome of a sequence resulting in a score was more often a shot header ($P<0.1$). Furthermore the amount of passes preceding the score had a mean of 2.5, which is similar to the results obtained by Grehaigne (1991).

Although not significant, the mean number of actions preceding a score (7.05 ± 4.42, max: 18, min: 2) was more than the mean number of actions preceding a score attempt (6.3 ± 4.1, max 19, min: 2).

3.2.2. Spatial profile

Table 4 describes the non-significant but remarkable elements of the spatial properties of the evolution of ball-possession sequences.

Sequences commencing on the observed team's own field contained about double the mean number of actions as opposed to those that commence on the opponent's field.

Both types of sequences, commencing with either dynamic or static actions in the lateral corridor of the pitch, contained more actions when they commenced in the central part of the pitch.

Table 4. Spatial properties of the evolution of ball-possession sequences.

	Own Field	Opponents' Field	Central	Lateral corridor
Sequences leading to score				
Mean total no. of actions	10.29	4.72	6.79	7.39
Mean total static actions	9.33	4.47	5.50	5.13
Mean total dynamic actions	10.40	4.90	6.94	10.42
Sequences leading to score-attempt				
Mean total no. of actions	9.19	4.35	5.80	7.38
Mean total static actions	7.25	4.67	3.67	6.15
Mean total dynamic actions	9.52	4.19	6.32	9.38

Intuitively, one might appreciate that the shortest path (vector-wise) of the possession phase to the goal is a positive element with the advantage of speed, timing, complexity and energy expenditure. If a vector fits the trajectory describing the commencement of the ball-possession sequence to the goal, we can determine the number of times it is crossed during its evolution (Fig. 2). Table 5 shows non-significant differences of crosses between the two types of ball-possession sequences. Three spatial properties were examined, namely the number of crosses of this "shortest route" on the team's own field, on the opponents' field and the number of crossings at the moment of the last action (the assist) before an attempt/score was made. It is clear that the number of crosses preceding a score is higher than the attempt-sequence, with the greatest difference at the opponents' field.

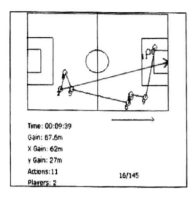

Time: 00:09:39
Gain: 67.6m
X Gain: 62m
y Gain: 27m
Actions:11
Players: 2

16/145

Figure 2. Example of two crosses of the shortest way (vector) to the goal.

Table 5. Number and location of crosses of the shortest way to the goal.

	No. of crosses in seq. leading towards a score-attempt	No. of crosses in seq. leading to a score
Total	32	38
Mean	0.48	0.57
SD	0.68	0.96
Own field	11	10
Opponents' field	14	24
During an assists	7	5

The deviation of the resultant vector describing field-coverage of the ball-possession sequence from the longitudinal axis of the pitch (Fig. 3), could be calculated by the software based upon xy co-ordinates. The following table compares the angles of attack of the overall phase and shows that only a very small and non-significant difference can be observed for the two types of sequences.

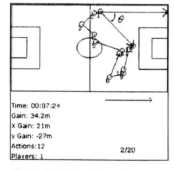

Time: 00:07:24
Gain: 34.2m
X Gain: 21m
y Gain: -27m
Actions:12
Players: 1

2/20

Figure 3. Angle of attack of a sequence.

Table 6. Comparison of the angles of attack of a sequence.

	Seq. leading to score attempt	Seq. leading to score
Mean angle	34.6	33.9
SD	32.0	29.4
Min	0	0
Max	90	90

3.2.3. Conclusion

The data showed a significant difference only on the level of the technical profile during the evolution of the ball-possession sequence, namely that a technical skill (ball control) occurred more often preceding a score and that heading attempts have an efficiency that can lead to scoring. No significant differences could be found when spatial properties (angle of attack, field coverage and crossing of the "shortest route" to the goal) were considered.

3.3. The finishing properties of ball-possession sequences

3.3.1. Field coverage

When the attempt to score is made, some field coverage has been made throughout the whole sequence. This field coverage can be calculated as being the vector describing the distance between the initiation of the ball-possession sequence and the point (xy) at which shooting occurred. It is not the distance covered by the ball! The following table shows distances. It is clear, that for the three factors (total field coverage, field coverage in the x-direction and y-direction) the mean distances preceding a score were higher than for the attempts only.

Furthermore a fairly high degree of correlation (r=0.868) has been found between the total field covered and the x component of it. This means that the higher the field coverage along the longitudinal axis of the pitch the higher the total field coverage of the ball-possession sequence. The correlation between this element and the number of actions included in that sequence is fairly low (r=0.627).

Table 7. Field coverage for both types of sequences (distances in metres).

	Scoring attempts			Scores		
	Field coverage	x-gain	y-gain	Field coverage	x-gain	y-gain
Average	32.7	24.5	13.5	39.3	28.9	16.3
SD	24.2	27.7	12.8	24.9	29.7	13.7
Min	0	−21	0	0	−27	0
Max	83.7	82	42	82.2	81	43

3.3.2. Distance to the goal at the moment of scoring (attempt)

At the moment of an attempt to score, the xy co-ordinates are known. They could provide information on their impact upon scoring.

3.3.3. Conclusions

For both sequences leading to a scoring attempt and towards scores, approximately the same distances are covered containing a longitudinal aspect, but the distance to the goal at the moment of shooting is in both x and y factors significantly smaller ($P<0.01$) when a score is made with a mean distance of 11.3 ($\pm$ 5.9). This figure is comparable to results in the literature.

4. GENERAL CONCLUSIONS

Initiation of the ball possession phase mainly shows similarities instead of differences when a score is compared with an attempt to score.

The evolution of a ball possession phase shows significant differences (P<0.01) at the level of technical performance, namely a necessary ball control occurs more often before a score. Also, heading creates significantly more scores (P<0.01).

Finishing of the sequence reveals that scores are made from a significantly closer distance (x) to the goal (P<0.01) and from a significantly (P<0.05) closer lateral distance (y) of the goal.

REFERENCES

Bate, R., 1988, Football chance: tactics and strategy. In *Science and Football* edited by Reilly, T., Lees, A., Davids, K. and Murphy, W. J. (London: E and Spon, F. N), pp. 293–301.

Dufour, W., 1993, Computer assisted scouting in soccer. In Science and Football 11, edited by Reilly, T., Clarys, J. and Stibbe, A. (London: E. and F.N. Spon), pp. 160–166.

Grehaigne, J-F., 1991, A new method of goal analysis. *Science and Football*, 5, 10–15.

Harris, S. and Reilly, T., 1988, Space, teamwork and attacking success in soccer. In *Science and Football,* edited by Reilly, T, Lees, A, Davids, K. and Murphy, W. J. (London: E and F.N Spon), pp. 322–328.

Hook, C. and Hughes, M., 2001, Patterns of play leading to shots in EURO 2000. *In Book of Proceedings World Congress of Performance Analysis, Cardiff,* pp. 295–302.

Hughes, M., Langridge, C. and Dawkin, N., 2001, Perturbations leading to shooting in soccer. *Notation Analysis of Sport IV*, 2–32.

Jonsson, G., Borrie, A., Bjarkadottir, S. and Gislason, B., 2001, Detecting hidden time patterns in football. In *Book of Abstracts 6th Annual Congress of the European College of Sports Science, Köln*, 656.

Theis, R., 1992, Tor ist tor, *Fussballtraining,* **10**, 35–38.

Zempel, U. and Rudolph, H., 1990, Bei standardsituationen mehr phantasie entwickeln. In *Fussballtraining*, **12**, 27–31.

93   The Relative Effects of Demonstrations and Outcome Information in the Teaching of Novel Motor Skills

Spencer J. Hayes[1], Robert R. Horn[2], Nicola J. Hodges[1],
Mark A. Scott[1] and A. Mark Williams[1]
[1]Research Institute for Sport and Exercise Sciences, Liverpool John
Moores University, UK
[2] Department of Kinesiology, University of Maryland, USA

1. INTRODUCTION

Coaches often provide learners with prospective information outlining what to do (e.g., demonstration or verbal instruction), followed by retrospective information to relay what was done (e.g., outcome information such as knowledge of results or performance). In tasks where there are both outcome goals (e.g., kick a ball a certain distance) and movement goals (i.e., copying a specific technique), demonstrations and feedback interact such that it is important to determine their differential effect on task success. Carroll and Bandura (1982) suggested that the acquisition of a novel skill relayed through a demonstration can be accelerated by the provision of visual feedback. However, the task examined by Carroll and Bandura (1982) only required the reproduction of movement goals. In tasks that require multiple goals (i.e., movement and outcome) outcome information may become the priority at the expense of movement information.

In this report we first compare the results of two studies previously conducted in our laboratory where movement form demonstrations were examined in the presence and absence of outcome feedback. Both studies investigated the acquisition of a football chip shot, which required the participants to chip a football over a height barrier to land on a target. Participants were required to land the ball on the target using the same type of movement pattern as the skilled model. Visual feedback was available in Study 1 (Horn et al., 2002), but not in Study 2, where visual feedback was controlled by liquid crystal occlusion goggles (Horn et al., 2003). Participants in Study 1 failed to adopt the same movement pattern as the model (see Figure 1a), whereas in Study 2 the movement patterns were similar (see Figure 1b). To determine whether these differences were related to feedback, the outcome data were statistically compared from both these studies (see Figure 2). As expected, without visual feedback (Study 2), error was significantly higher throughout practice and retention in comparison to the mean error scores of Study 1. In fact, only in the presence (Study 1) of outcome feedback was there a significant decrease in error from pre-test to retention. The findings indicate that the removal of outcome information encouraged participants to adopt a movement pattern that was similar to the criterion model, but without visual feedback outcome accuracy was poor in comparison to participants in Study 2.

Although it is not surprising that participants failed to reduce outcome error without the aid of error information, what is noteworthy is that participants only adopted the specified movement pattern when the model was the only source of constraining information.

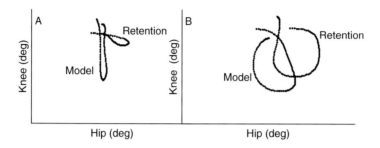

Figure 1. Changes in hip-knee relative motion in comparison to the model for a typical participant in Horn et al. (2002; Study 1, Fig A) and Horn et al. (2003; Study 2, Fig B).

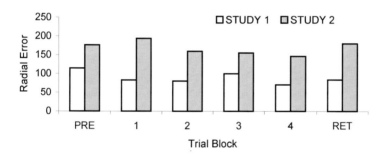

Figure 2. Mean radial error scores during pre-test, acquisition, and retention trial blocks for Horn et al. (2002; Study 1) and Horn et al. (2003; Study 2).

As a result of these differences in performance as a function of augmented information sources, we directly manipulated outcome information to determine the accuracy of movement reproduction. It was predicted that participants who receive additional outcome goals would fail too adopt a movement pattern demonstrated by the model in comparison to those who only received this information.

2. METHODS

Sixteen, primary-age school boys participated; 8 in Group 1 (DEMO+OUTCOME) and 8 in Group 2 (DEMO), $\underline{M}$ age = 6.7 years, $\underline{SD}$ = 0.5

years. Participants were instructed that their primary aim was to copy the movements of the model when performing a goalkeeper's underarm throw. Group 1 members had an additional outcome component that required them to roll a ball to stop on a target line. Movement form was recorded using a VHS video camera. Participants performed 10 acquisition trials, followed by 3 retention trials (24 hours afterwards). Movement form scores were computed based on similarity to the model. Various components of the movement were scored and an aggregate movement form score was calculated (maximum score of 16 for an accurate reproduction). The scores during acquisition were analysed using a 2 (Group) x 2 (Block _ 3 trials) ANOVA, whereas a one-way ANOVA was used to compare scores on the retention test.

3. RESULTS

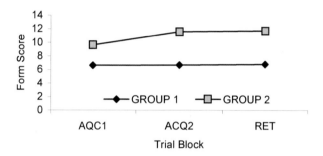

Figure 3. Form scores for Group 1 and Group 2 across Acquisition and Retention.

The form scores for Group 1 (DEMO+OUTCOME) and Group 2 (DEMO) are shown in Figure 3. In acquisition, participants reproduced movements more like the model when they were not provided with a ball and outcome goal (i.e., Group 2, $F_{1, 14} = 16.55$, $P < 0.01$). Group differences remained in retention ($F_{1, 15} = 14.91$, $P < 0.01$).

4. DISCUSSION

These findings support conclusions based on two previous studies conducted in our laboratory (Horn et al., 2002; 2003). When tasks have multiple goals, participants focus on outcome information in their search for a successful outcome, even when the primary aim is to copy the model's movement. Although others have shown that combining demonstrations with feedback is beneficial for skill acquisition, these findings caution against this combination when a desired technique is the primary aim.

The fact that these results have been found with children lead to the conclusion that this preference to focus on outcome information at the expense of movement form is a general learning phenomenon. However, without further studies comparing adults and children directly, it is not possible to determine whether these effects are more pronounced in children. Indeed, Bekkering, Wohlschläger and Gattis (1996) found that young children failed to imitate a simple arm-to-ear action correctly, in terms of choosing the correct arm, but rather imitated the end effect of that action (i.e., the correct ear).

5. GENERAL CONCLUSIONS

When the goal is to imitate a model's movement form, the informational role of a demonstration is decreased when outcome information is present. Only when the primary constraining source of information is the visual demonstration (i.e., the task has no outcome component) are participants likely to adopt the demonstrated movement form. If the task objective is the acquisition of a specific technique or movement form, manipulations to either the saliency of a demonstration (e.g., highlighting information cues or verbally directing attention to critical information) or to practice conditions (i.e., environment) should be considered.

REFERENCES

Bekkering, H., Wohlschläger, A. and Gattis, M., 1996, Motor imitation: What is imitated? Corpus, Psyche et Societas, **3**, 68–74.

Carroll, W. R. and Bandura, A., 1982, The role of visual monitoring in observational learning of action patterns: making the unobservable observable. *Journal of Motor Behavior*, **20**, 153–167.

Horn, R., Williams, A. M. and Scott, M. A., 2002, Learning from demonstration: the role of visual search from video and point-light displays. *Journal of Sports Sciences*, **20**, 253–269.

Horn, R., Williams, A. M., Scott, M. A. and Hodges, N. J., 2003, Visual search and coordination changes in response to video and point-light demonstrations in the absence of intrinsic knowledge of results. *Journal of Motor Behavior*, (in press).

94   The Distribution of Season of Birth among the Players of the 2002 FIFA World Cup

Susan Edgar and Peter O'Donoghue

School of Applied Medical Science and Sports Studies, University of Ulster, Jordanstown, County Antrim, BT37 0QB, UK

1. INTRODUCTION

Season of birth has been shown to have an influence on many aspects of life including lifespan (Doblhammer and Vaupel, 2001), academic attainment (Sharp *et al.*, 1994) as well as practical and written elements of physical education (Bell *et al.*, 1997). Within sport, there is evidence that season of birth affects the chances of success in tennis (Dudink, 1994), ice hockey (Boucher and Mutimer, 1994), baseball (Thompson *et al.*, 1991), swimming (Baxter-Jones, 1995) and some types of cricket play (Edwards, 1994). Musch and Hay (1999) have identified some of the theoretical explanations for season of birth effects on sporting performance. These include:

1. Biological and maturation factors associated with chronological age. These produce a relative age effect when combined with cut-off dates for junior age group competition in sport.
2. Environmental factors during early life such as climate.
3. Socio-cultural influences such as different patterns of birth between different socio-economic groups.
4. Psychological factors with some personality traits being associated with particular seasons of birth.

Season of birth has been shown to have an influence on the chance of playing professional football in European soccer leagues (Brewer *et al.*, 1995). In particular, those players born early in the junior competition year have a greater chance of becoming a professional soccer player than those born late in the competition year (Musch and Hay, 1999; Simmons and Paull, 2001). Musch and Hay (1999) analysed the season of birth profile of four countries with distinct cultures and climates:- Australia, Brazil, Germany and Japan. Results provided strong evidence that the cut-off date for competition age groups produced a strong relative age effect. Furthermore, they found that when the cut-off date in Australia was changed from January to August, there was a corresponding shift in birth date distribution to maintain a relative age effect. Simmons and Paull (2001) produced further evidence of a relative age effect. They found that in England, the UEFA cut-off date of January used by the national youth teams and the cut-off date of September used by the national schools youth teams both produced relative age effects. The relative age effect has been viewed as discriminating against players born late in the junior competition year (Musch and Hay, 1999; Simmons and Paull, 2001). If talented soccer players born late in the competition year fail to become professional players as a result of being disadvantaged by the relative age effect in their county, there is a possibility that the national team will also be disadvantaged.

While there has been considerable research into season of birth bias on the chances of becoming a professional soccer player, there are still important questions to be answered in relation to international soccer. The distribution of birth dates of professional soccer players in a country may be reflected by the subset of players who become internationals and play in major tournaments. Alternatively, talented junior players with the potential to become a senior international player may succeed despite being born late in the junior competition year. Therefore, the purpose of the current investigation was to analyse the season of birth distribution of the players of the 2002 FIFA World Cup finals in Japan and Korea. A further objective of the study was to determine whether or not a season of birth bias on World Cup squad membership affected the performance of the team in the World Cup. The performance of teams would be considered in terms of progression from the group stage of the tournament as well as improvement in FIFA world ranking as a result of performance in the World Cup.

2. METHODS
The dates of birth of all 736 players who were members of the 32 World Cup squads were collected from an internet site provided by an official partner of the tournament (www.fifaworldcup.yahoo.com).   Countries were categorised into regions with Turkey being included within Europe but South Africa being considered separately from African nations in the Northern Hemisphere. The FIFA world rankings for each month since August 1993 are provided by FIFA's official internet site (www.fifa.com). The FIFA ranking points in May 2002 and July 2002 for each of the 32 nations participating in the 2002 World Cup were collected from this internet site.

There are many ways of analysing season of birth effects. Because a relative age effect would theoretically cause a negative relationship between number of professional players and month of birth within junior competition year, some studies have used rank correlations to explore such relationships (Boucher and Mutimer, 1994). Other studies have compared the season of birth distribution of professional soccer players using a chi-squared goodness of fit test with an expected distribution derived from birth distribution for the wider population accessed from National statistics agencies (Musch and Hay, 1994). Baxter-Jones (1995) used a Kolmogorov-Smirnov One Sample test of uniformity to analyse birth date distribution. Dudink (1994) also assumed a uniform season of birth between four three-month seasons of the year. This is a valid assumption as sexual and reproductive life in the human is not generally subject to seasonal variation although there may be minor effects due to urbanisation, industrialisation and religious or cultural traditions (Cowgill, 1966). Using a uniform season of birth distribution also overcomes the issue of variations in season of birth distributions between the calendar years when subjects were born. However, the different numbers of days within different months should also be taken into account (Doblhammer and Vaupel, 2001). The players within the current study were classified as being born in one of four three-month seasons using a start date of August. August was chosen because it is a cut-off date proposed by FIFA in 1988 (Musch and Hay, 1999). A series of chi-squared goodness of fit tests were applied to each region using an expected fraction of 89.25 / 365.25 for the season FMA (February, March and April) and an expected fraction of 92.00 / 365.25 for the other 3 seasons.

A further series of 32 chi-squared goodness of fit tests were applied to the individual World Cup squads to produce chi-squared values that could be used as indicators of a season of birth bias on squad membership. An independent t-test was used to compare the chi-squared values between the 16 teams that qualified for the second round with the 16 teams eliminated at the end of the group stage. Pearson's coefficient of correlation was used to explore the relationship between the teams' chi-squared values and increase in FIFA world ranking points between May 2002 and July 2002.

3. RESULTS

Table 1. Season of birth of players who competed in the FIFA World Cup 2002.

Region	Season of date of birth of players					χ^2_3	P
	Aug–Oct	Nov–Jan	Feb–Apr	May–Jul	All		
Europe	104 (30.1%)	75 (21.7%)	92 (26.7%)	74 (21.4%)	345	7.6	0.055
Asia	25 (27.2%)	20 (21.7%)	25 (27.2%)	22 (23.9%)	92	0.6	0.892
N&C America	23 (33.0%)	14 (20.3%)	13 (18.8%)	19 (27.5%)	69	3.5	0.320
N. Africa	18 (19.6%)	26 (28.3%)	27 (29.3%)	21 (22.8%)	92	2.6	0.455
N. Hemisphere	170 (28.4%)	135 (22.6%)	157 (26.3%)	136 (22.7%)	598	6.3	0.096
S. America	32 (27.8%)	14 (12.2%)	38 (33.0%)	31 (27.0%)	115	11.7	0.009
S. Africa	1 (4.3%)	7 (30.4%)	7 (30.4%)	8 (34.8%)	23	5.4	0.148
S. Hemisphere	33 (23.9%)	21 (15.2%)	45 (32.6%)	39 (28.3%)	138	9.8	0.020
All Players	203 (27.6%)	156 (21.2%)	202 (27.4%)	175 (23.8%)	736	9.6	0.022

The season of birth distribution of the players from each region is summarised in Table 1. In Europe, the highest proportion of players were born between August and October, but season of birth did not have a significant effect. However, when Europe was divided into those 9 countries that qualified for the second round and those 6 that exited at the end of the group stages, there was a contrast in distribution of season of birth. As Table 1 shows, there was a significant seasonal effect for the non-qualifying teams but not for the qualifiers. There was also a significant seasonal effect on South American participants in the World Cup with the highest number of players being born between February and April.

When using the chi-squared value for individual World Cup squads to represent season of birth bias, Germany was found to have the best fit with the expected distribution (χ^2_3 = 0.4). Poland, on the other hand, was found to have the greatest season of birth bias (χ^2_3 = 14.3). The season of birth bias (χ^2_3) for those teams that qualified for the second round (χ^2_3 = 3.1±1.6) was lower than that of those that were eliminated at the end of the group stage (χ^2_3 = 4.9±3.7). While the difference was not statistically significant (t_{30} = 1.8, P = 0.089), there was an observable difference. Figure 1 shows that there was no relationship between season of birth bias (χ^2_3) and increase in FIFA world ranking points between May 2002 and July 2002 (r = –0.030). There were teams with a high season of birth bias, such as Korea, who drastically increased their FIFA world ranking points while other teams with a low season of birth bias, such as China and Slovenia, lost FIFA world ranking points. The three teams with the highest season of birth biases (Poland, Costa Rica and Cameroon) all gained FIFA world ranking points.

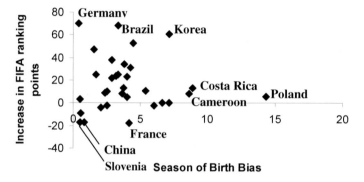

Figure 1. Relationship between season of birth bias (χ^2_3) and improvement in FIFA world ranking points between May 2002 and July 2002.

4. DISCUSSION

The current investigation did not find a significant season of birth bias on the membership of World Cup squads from Europe. However, a similar percentage of European World Cup players were born between August and November as the 30.5% of professional players in Germany (Musch and Hay, 1999) and the 31.1% of professional players in the Netherlands (Dudink, 1994). There were 10 (43.4%) of England's World Cup squad born between September and December which is similar to the 45.6% of the 1722 senior players analysed by Brewer *et al.* (1995). This suggests that the distribution of birth dates of World Cup players does reflect that of professional players in the country. In Japan, where the cut-off date is April, 17 of the 23-man squad were born in the 6 months starting in April. This is actually a greater proportion than the 67% of Japanese professional soccer players born in the same 6-month period (Musch and Hay, 1999). However, there were 9 of the 23-man Swedish World Cup squad born between January and April which is a much lower proportion than the 10 out of 16 senior players or 37 out of 59 junior players from Sweden analysed by Brewer *et al.* (1995). Furthermore, the Brazilian squad contained a distribution of ASO (7), NDJ (2), FMA (7) and MJJ (7) despite their cut-off date of August and a relative age effect for Brazilian soccer players existing (Musch and Hay, 1999).

The current investigation failed to find the hypothesised negative relationship between season of birth bias and improvement in FIFA world ranking points. There are some methodological considerations that may explain this. Firstly, the lowest ranked team participating in the World Cup (China) started the World Cup with a ranking that had steadily risen during the qualifying period to a high of 50th in May 2002. The current investigation only looked at the improvement within the World Cup where China would have played stronger opposition than during the qualifying tournament. The current method did not control for home advantage during the tournament, the difficulty of certain groups within the World Cup or other factors which would have influenced performance.

There was a greater season of birth bias within those squads eliminated after the group stage than within the squads that progressed to round 2. The close to significant difference (P = 0.089) suggests that those countries that qualified for the second round may have developed soccer ability in a way that reduces season of birth bias. If this is the case, then those countries will enjoy a greater selection of quality players born throughout the calendar year than other countries. However, this finding must be viewed with caution for the following reasons:

1. The 23-man squads were those that were selected and not those that the squad management teams would have wished to select. The absence of key players made a difference to the season of birth profile of some squads.
2. The difference between qualifying from the group and not qualifying might have resulted directly or indirectly from a key incident in a single game.
3. Some groups may have been more difficult to qualify from than others.

5. CONCLUSIONS

More players who participated in the 2002 World Cup were born in August (n = 86) than any other month. August was proposed as a cut-off date by FIFA in 1988 which may have advantaged players born in that month as many countries including World Cup finalists Brazil and Germany use the August cut-off date. Within the European representatives at the 2002 World Cup, there was a significant season of birth bias among the 138 players who competed for teams eliminated at the end of the group stage but not within the 207 players who competed for teams that qualified for round 2. This has provided some evidence that a season of birth bias within a squad may be to the detriment of the squad's performance.

REFERENCES

Baxter-Jones, A.D.G., 1995, Growth and development of young athletes: should competition be age related? *Sports Medicine*, **20**, 59–64.
Bell, J.F., Massey, A. and Dexter, T., 1997, Birthdate and ratings of sporting achievement. *European Journal of Physical Education*, **2**, 160–166.

Boucher, J.L. and Mutimer, B.T.P., 1994, The relative age phenomenon in sport; replication and extension with ice-hockey players. *Research Quarterly for Exercise and Sport*, **65**, 377–381.

Brewer, J., Balsom, P.D. and Davis J.A., 1995, Season of birth distribution amongst European soccer players. *Sports, Exercise and Injury*, **1**, 154–157.

Cowgill, U.M., 1966, Season of birth in man: contemporary situation with special reference to Europe and the Southern Hemisphere. *Ecology*, **47**, 614–623.

Doblhammer, G. and Vaupel, J.W., 2001, Lifespan depends on month of birth. *Proceedings of the National Academy of Science*, **98**, 2934–2939.

Dudink, A., 1994, Birth date and sporting success. *Nature*, **368**, 592.

Edwards, S., 1994, Born too late to win? [letter]. *Nature*, **370**, 186.

Musch, J. and Hay, R., 1999, The relative age effect in soccer: cross-cultural evidence for a systematic discrimination against children born late in the competition year. *Sociology of Sport Journal*, **16**, 54–64.

Sharp, C., Hutchison, D. and Whetton, C., 1994, How do season of birth and length of schooling affect children's attainment at key stage 1? *Educational Research*, **36**, 107–121.

Simmons, C. and Paull, G.C., 2001, Season-of-birth bias in association football. *Journal of Sports Sciences*, **19**, 677–686.

Thompson, A., Barnsley, R. and Stebelsky, G., 1991, Born to play ball: the relative age effect and major league baseball. *Sociology of Sport Journal*, **8**, 146–151.

Index